A HISTORY OF ASIA

A HISTORY OF ASIA

VOLUME I *Formation of Civilizations, from Antiquity to 1600*

Woodbridge Bingham UNIVERSITY OF CALIFORNIA

Hilary Conroy UNIVERSITY OF PENNSYLVANIA

Frank W. Iklé UNIVERSITY OF NEW MEXICO

ALLYN AND BACON, INC.   Boston, 1964

To Ursala, Charlotte, and Maurine

ACKNOWLEDGMENTS

FRONTISPIECE: Misty landscape: rounded mountain peaks and trees. Chinese, Sung dynasty, attributed to Mi Fei. Courtesy of Freer Gallery of Art, Washington, D.C.

CHAPTER II. 2.1. From Carleton S. Coon, *The Seven Caves* (New York: Alfred A. Knopf, Inc.). Copyright, 1956 by Carleton S. Coon. 2.2. From Hallam L. Movius, Jr., "The Lower Palaeolithic Cultures of Southern and Eastern Asia," *Transactions, the American Philosophical Society,* New Series—V. 38, Pt. 4 (March, 1949). 2.3. From Chêng Tê-K'un, *Archaeology in China,* Volume I: Prehistoric China (Cambridge: W. Heffer and Sons, Ltd., 1959). 2.4. The Louvre. 2.5. Chêng, *Archaeology in China.* 2.6. From J. E. Kidder, *Japan Before Buddhism,* courtesy of Frederick A. Praeger, Inc.

CHAPTER III. 3.1. The Metropolitan Museum of Art, gift of Matilda W. Bruce, 1907. 3.2. The Metropolitan Museum of Art, Dick Fund, 1959. 3.3., 3.4 The Metropolitan Museum of Art, gift of John D. Rockefeller, Jr., 1932. 3.5. The Iranian Oil Operating Companies.

CHAPTER IV. 4.1. Iraq Petroleum Company. 4.2. Tehran Museum. 4.3. Iraq Petroleum Company. 4.4. Mr. Eric Schroeder and University Prints. 4.5. Freer Gallery of Art.

CHAPTER V. 5.1. The British Museum. 5.2., 5.3. Freer Gallery of Art. 5.4. The Metropolitan Museum of Art, Rogers Fund, 1913. 5.5. Turkish Information Office.

CHAPTER VI. 6.1. The Metropolitan Museum of Art, bequest of Isaac D. Fletcher, 1917. 6.2. The Metropolitan Museum of Art, gift of Alexander Smith Cochran, 1913. 6.3. The Metropolitan Museum of Art, bequest of Cora Timken Burnett, 1957. 6.4. The Metropolitan Museum of Art, Rogers Fund, 1904. 6.5. Courtesy of the Trustees, the National Gallery, London.

CHAPTER VII. 7.1., 7.2. Department of Archaeology, Government of India. 7.3. Museum of Fine Arts, Boston. 7.4. Department of Archaeology, Government of India.

CHAPTER VIII. 8.1. Professor Benjamin Rowland and University Prints, Cambridge, Mass. 8.2. Department of Archaeology, Government of India. 8.3. Press Information Bureau, Government of India.

CHAPTER IX. 9.1. Cincinnati Art Museum. 9.2. Professor Benjamin Rowland and University Prints, Cambridge, Mass. 9.3 City Art Museum of St. Louis. 9.4. Musée Guimet, Paris.

CHAPTER X. 10.1, 10.2. Press Information Bureau, Government of India. 10.3. Museum and Art Gallery, Birmingham, England. 10.4. Department of Archaeology, Government of India. 10.5. Musée Guimet, Paris.

CHAPTER XI. 11.1. Press Information Bureau, Government of India. 11.2. Musée Guimet, Paris. 11.3. The Metropolitan Museum of Art, Eggleston Fund, 1927. 11.4. Nelson Gallery of Art, Kansas City, Mo.

CHAPTER XII. 12.1. Department of Archaeology, Government of India. 12.2. India Office Library, London. 12.3. Press Information Bureau, Government of India. 12.4. Department of Archaeology, Government of India.

CHAPTER XIII. 13.1, 13.2, 13.3. Victoria and Albert Museum, London. 13.4. Press Information Bureau, Government of India.

CHAPTER XIV. 14.1, 14.2, 14.3, 14.4. National Museum of Ethnology, Leiden. 14.5. The Metropolitan Museum of Art, Fletcher Fund, 1935. 14.6. Ministry of Information, Phnom-Penh, Cambodia.

CHAPTER XV. 15.1. Royal Ontario Museum, Toronto. 15.2. British Museum. 15.3, 15.4, 15.5. National Museum of Ethnology, Leiden.

CHAPTER XVI. 16.1. Art Institute of Chicago. 16.2. Nelson Gallery of Art, Kansas City, Mo. 16.3. The Metropolitan Museum of Art, Munsey Bequest, 1931. 16.4. The Minneapolis Institute of Arts, Alfred E. Pillsbury Collection of Chinese Bronzes.

CHAPTER XVII. 17.1. Art Institute of Chicago. 17.2. Nelson Gallery of Art, Kansas City, Mo. 17.3. Victoria and Albert Museum, London. 17.4. Royal Ontario Museum, Toronto. 17.5. Fogg Art Museum, Cambridge, Mass.

CHAPTER XVIII. 18.1. Royal Ontario Museum, Toronto. 18.2. The Metropolitan Museum of Art, Rogers Fund, 1938. 18.3. Nelson Gallery of Art, Kansas City, Mo. 18.4. The University Museum, Philadelphia. 18.5. The Metropolitan Museum of Art, Kennedy Fund, 1926.

CHAPTER XIX. 19.1. The University Museum, Philadelphia. 19.2. Woodbridge Bingham. 19.3. The Metropolitan Museum of Art, Fletcher Fund, 1947, the A. W. Bahr Collection. 19.4. The Metropolitan Museum of Art, Rogers Fund, 1925.

CHAPTER XX. 20.1. The Metropolitan Museum of Art, Fletcher Fund, 1928. 20.2. Honolulu Academy of Arts. 20.3. Freer Gallery of Art. 20.4. Cincinnati Art Museum.

CHAPTER XXI. 21.1. H. D. Martin. 21.2. The Metropolitan Museum of Art, Fletcher Fund, 1947, the A. W. Bahr Collection. 21.3. Bibliothèque Nationale, Paris.

CHAPTER XXII. 22.1. Cincinnati Art Museum. 22.2. H. D. Martin. 22.3. Freer Gallery of Art. 22.4. The Bettmann Archive.

CHAPTER XXIII. 23.1. From M. Hürlimann, *Asia;* courtesy of Thames and Hudson, London. 23.2, 23.3. Freer Gallery of Art. 23.4. The British Museum. 23.5. Woodbridge Bingham.

CHAPTER XXIV. 24.1. Consulate General of Japan, New York. 24.2, 24.3, 24.4. Japan Tourist Association.

CHAPTER XXV. 25.1. The Metropolitan Museum of Art, Rogers Fund, 1917. 25.2. National Museum, Tokyo, and Charles Tuttle. 25.3. Consulate General of Japan, New York.

CHAPTER XXVI. 26.1. National Museum, Tokyo, and Charles Tuttle. 26.2. Okura Museum, Tokyo. 26.3, 26.4. National Museum, Tokyo, and Charles Tuttle.

CHAPTER XXVII. 27.1. Consulate General of Japan, New York. 27.2, 27.3. Japan Tourist Association. 27.4. National Museum, Tokyo. 27.5. Consulate General of Japan, New York.

PREFACE

THIS BOOK HAS BEEN WRITTEN to meet the need for an integrated history of the whole of Asia from antiquity to the present. Experience gained during the last eighteen years in teaching courses on the history of Asia at the University of California, the University of Pennsylvania, Miami University, and the University of New Mexico has convinced the authors of the desirability of such a work. The subject cannot be adequately presented in a unified fashion by relying on the many fine existing works which deal only with parts of the whole history. We have felt the need for a coverage of the subject comparable to the treatment of Europe and the Mediterranean found in the numerous excellent histories of Western civilization.

It is hoped that our work will meet the needs of all teachers of college survey courses in Asia history within the liberal arts curriculum. Also we trust that it may be found useful by anyone wishing to gain a general knowledge of the peoples and cultures of Asia.

In regard to the spelling and pronunciation of certain names and phrases the following cases should be noted. In pronouncing Chinese words certain consonants are read differently when aspirated (with an apostrophe) or unaspirated. Thus *ch, k, p, t,* and *ts* are pronounced like *j, g, b, d,* and *dz* respectively. When aspirated, *ch', k', p', t',* and *ts'* are pronounced like *ch, k, p, t,* and *ts* respectively, as in usual English pronunciation. Among the many Japanese terms containing a long *o* only certain brief words concerning which there may be some confusion of identity have been written with a long mark, for example *nō* and *shō.* Compromises have also been made in rendering Arabic and Indian words, e.g., Moslem yet Umayyad, where English usage competes with "proper" transliteration.

To supplement the narrative treatment of the history in the main text each chapter is followed by a brief list of key dates for that topic. For those who desire to read further, two bibliographical lists of additional readings are provided at the end of each chapter. The first list, of "Supplementary Reading," is intended to suggest useful additional reading for the beginning student. The books listed are limited to those which are both especially useful and relatively easily obtained. Thus the lists can be used to build up a college library in an institution where the history of Asia is being taught for the first time.

In each case the second list, designated "Advanced Reading," offers a selection suitable for those students and teachers who wish to gain access to monographs and other special works primarily in English dealing with the subject and who seek some indiction of what the available materials may be.

From these lists the reader will become aware of the great number of authorities whose works have been referred to in the writing of this history. It has not been feasible to give footnote references to most of the works which have been used by the authors. However, we are deeply aware of how much we owe to the many scholars whose books and articles we have consulted. We take this opportunity to acknowledge our indebtedness.

The authors have received special aid and comment from many sources. At Berkeley, the Institute of Social Sciences and the Institute of International Studies have provided invaluable financial support; with funds provided by the University of California research assistance has been made available. Among the persons who have been helpful in the compilation of material the following deserve special notice: Newton Steward for bibliographical assistance during the early stages; David E. Allen Jr. for bibliographical assistance and research on special problems in the early history of Iran; Mrs. Nikki R. Keddie for research assistance on special topics in the early history of Iran, Central Asia, and the Seljuks; Mrs. Wanda R. Koskinen for research assistance on many aspects of the history and bibliography of Southwest and Southeast Asia; Larry M. Lane for bibliographical assistance; Dr. Jung-pang Lo for advice concerning factual detail and bibliography of early China. To these and to many unnamed individuals we are most grateful.

To the library staffs at Berkeley, at the University of Pennsylvania, and at Miami University we are especially indebted. Also we wish to acknowledge assistance from the staff at the Metropolitan Museum of Art, Widener Library at Harvard, Cleveland Museum of Art, Freer Gallery in Washington, Cincinnati Art Museum, Nelson Gallery in Kansas City, University Museum in Philadelphia, Royal Ontario Museum of Toronto, British Museum in London, Victoria and Albert Museum, Bibliothèque Nationale in Paris, National Museum of Ethnology in Leiden, the Department of Archaeology of India, the National Museum in Tokyo, and many others.

In addition, we wish to thank Professor W. Norman Brown and Professor Ephraim A. Speiser, of the University of Pennsylvania, for advice on outlines of the history of India and Southwest Asia, respectively. For helpful criticism on the chapter concerned with prehistory we are indebted to Professor Theodore D. McCown of the University of California at Berkeley, Professor Wilhelm G. Solheim II of the University of Hawaii, and Dr. Edwin M. Loeb of Berkeley.

The matter of writing and rewriting our material has involved many persons. Among them we wish especially to mention the following: Mrs. Muriel

Sundell and Mrs. Margaret E. Ginner for cheerful and careful secretarial assistance in the preparation of manuscript and in countless minor details. To Mr. Bryce G. Decker and others who have helped in preparing our maps we owe a special debt of gratitude. Mrs. Miriam Ash prepared the index.

The authors join in a particular word of appreciation for the editors of Allyn and Bacon, Mr. John J. DeRemigis and Miss Christine Gonis. With patience and expert criticism they have assisted us in bringing our work into final form.

No one can be more keenly aware of the shortcomings of the present work than are the authors themselves. This is the type of history which could take several lifetimes to perfect. We have felt it was better to produce a work now which would be helpful to our students and to others who wish a general history in this field, rather than to delay this undertaking any longer. While acknowledging the ideas and suggestions of others, we wish to make it clear that all responsibility in the matter of facts and interpretation is our own.

W. B., H. C., F. W. I.

March 1964

CONTENTS

A HISTORY OF ASIA

I ❀❀

INTRODUCTION

THE STUDY OF ASIAN HISTORY is of vital importance for everyone today. Only by taking a world view of man and his development can we understand our own past and the peoples with whom we have to deal. This is necessary not only for the European, the American, or the Australian, but equally for a person from Africa, from Latin America, or, for that matter, from Asia itself.

Such a world view is especially important for Americans because of the extent of the commitments and responsibilities of our nation at the present time. We have missions in foreign lands, we trade with all the world, we exercise political and military leadership in the affairs of remote nations, we provide technical assistance, and we join with the peoples of all countries in membership in various world organizations. To deal effectively with the peoples of all the world we can no longer turn only to Europe and America as the main centers of culture and civilization on which to base our understanding. Today we must think in terms of the non-European parts of the world in their relationships with us as well as our relationships with them. The urgent need for our better understanding is borne in upon us by the questions and issues which are faced by Americans in connection with other areas of the world every day. We have been involved in such problems as the economy of India, the neutrality of states in Southeast Asia, and the recognition of Red China. These are some of the many questions which confront us all the time and which we as citizens need to ponder. Intelligent thinking requires a knowledge of those who live in other countries. We must consider remote parts of the world, such as Iran or Korea, not as mere names on the map or headlines in a newspaper but as made up of human beings with lives and traditions comparable with our own and whom we can understand.

In order to gain this understanding the facts concerning Asia and its history require serious study. The chief reason for this is that in Asia today the influences based on past experience are still so strong that its peoples' ideas and actions can only be appreciated through a knowledge of their background in its many aspects from antiquity down to the present time. It is not enough to understand what the peoples of Asia are thinking and doing today. Their thought and conduct are based largely on past events. Forces from the remote past have much more importance among the peoples of Asia than comparable influences in our own tradition. Hence in philosophy and religion the traditions of the Hindus, of the Buddhists, and of the Moslems, as well as others, need to be carefully studied if we are to appreciate the forces that operate within Asian countries today. Also by studying Asian religions, and philosophy, and artistic ideals, we Westerners may achieve greater insight into our own religious and cultural traditions.

In addition, social and political ideals and ideas of the past persist today. Caste, the importance of family, the codes of those whose forebears were "wearers of swords," ideals of scholarship, and concepts of empire and of kingship are ideas and attitudes which derive from great antiquity. The commerce which now we see in terms of world interdependence also has its roots deep in the past. The silk trade across Asia and the spice trade along the sea routes from the Indies to continental Asia and to Europe are only two examples of this age-old trade. Not only in our own time have the nations and races had close contacts with one another. If we would understand the peoples of Asia, we must note the effect of migrations, such as that of the Turks in the past, and the historic background of frontiers such as that of Tibet today.

In the international relations among Asian states from early times there have been diverse traditions concerning war, and the making of peace, and the formation of alliances. In China and India, for example, these matters have not always had the same significance as in Europe and America, and hence we need to know what concepts have been important in Asia and what traditions are the bases for their thinking.

In its time-span the scope of Asian history as covered in this work is the period from prehistory, when man first made crude stone tools in caves in some part of Asia, to the events of our own day. All the various parts of the continent are thought of as being of one fabric, including many elements which have continued from remote antiquity to the present time. If this should seem to be an introduction of impossibly vast proportions, the authors' only answer is that it is time it were attempted. They feel that the history of Asia, like the history of Western civilization, should be given in broad scope at the introductory level. Too often it has been represented by one of its segments, particularly the Far East in the nineteenth and twentieth centuries or the Near East as a question in European politics, where it is treated as a troublesome adjunct to the history of Western civilization.

The physical setting is that shown on a comprehensive map of the continent of Asia and is interpreted in this book to include all the countries and the bordering islands and archipelagoes of Asia, from Turkey, Syria, and Arabia in the west to Japan in the east, from Siberia to Ceylon, the Russian part of Asia and all the regions between the two extremities. The physical setting in its diversity extends from the arctic to the tropics and the human settlements range from towns on the borders of the sea to camp-sites on remote interior plateaus. The varied geographical features are mentioned in connection with the different parts of the continent as they are covered in this history. With a comprehensive time-span and a broad physical setting the history of Asia is here regarded as including the principal political, social and cultural activities of men in these places during this vast period.

In the interrelationships among various main elements in the history of Asia geographical factors played important parts. Especially noteworthy are the borderlands, the routes of travel, and the centers of exchange, in all of which cultures and peoples came into contact with one another, where religion passed from one region to another, and where trade was carried on.

The aim is to cover the main cultural centers and their traditions, with an emphasis on the differentiation among the older peoples of Asia. There is no such thing as one "Orient," and the use of that word will be avoided in the following pages. There are three principal cultural centers: Southwest Asia, with the focus at first in Mesopotamia and with the main thread of continuity being the great tradition of Iran which includes Islam since the seventh century; secondly, Hindu India; and thirdly, China. These three centers constitute the key elements in the history as here presented. Attention is also given to important marginal regions with unique cultural developments: the great steppe area extending from Manchuria into southern European Russia, the large complex area known as Southeast Asia, and finally Japan, part of the Chinese world and yet the possessor of an important cultural history of its own. Into these great centers of tradition there came external influences—traditions of European origin—whose importance cannot be minimized as a factor in this history. These European influences and their effect, especially since the sixteenth century, are an intrinsic and important part of this study.

Before commencing the history itself it may be well to note some of the special problems and points that may be emphasized in this study and which affect more than one area or one period in time. In the first place, there is the important effect of geography, tending toward the separateness of many regions of Asia, especially in South and East Asia during the early centuries. On the other hand, the proximity of the countries of Southwest Asia to the Mediterranean world and the greater ease of communications into that part of Asia from all directions kept its peoples in closer touch with others both east and west than were many of the inhabitants of countries further east.

Geography has also played its part in a special political and social aspect of Asian history—the conflict between the nomad tribes of steppe areas and mountain regions with the peoples living in permanent agricultural settlements.

The strength of tradition in Asian countries has already been referred to in discussing the need for study of their history. Stress needs to be laid, for example, on the fact that the basic unity of culture in China or in India revolves around certain traditions, ideas, ways of living, which give each of these very large areas a unity within itself which is comparable to the unity of Europe. In connection with these cultural traditions a special feature which provides an integrating factor for the study of Asian history is the spread of religions. A clear understanding of the expansion of religious ideas from one part of Asia to another is a key to the interrelationships, the parallel cultural developments, and the chronological framework of this history. The strength of tradition in Asian countries, as in other parts of the world, is also bound up with the lives of universal or national heroes. Such men as Alexander, Muhammad, Buddha, Chingis Khan, Confucius, and Prince Shotoku have played significant roles both in the actual events of their own times and in the traditions which gathered about their names and their careers. Thus it is important in each case to know the facts and to understand the legends and the continuing influence associated with their names after they died.

In Asian history after the sixteenth century the most important element was the expansion of Europe, a factor connected with many special problems in more than one country. For example, it is significant that the land communications of an earlier time gave way to sea communications as the main lines of commerce and travel. Also with European expansion the scene of Asian history has broadened to include new horizons. In the modern periods, areas previously of little consequence, such as Russia, Australasia, and the Pacific islands became important factors. Some countries and peoples which had little connection with the general history of Asia prior to 1600 played important parts in modern times. The new Western influences in Asia must be thought of not only as ideas, or as institutions, or as names of countries, but as forces associated with the actual people (including immigrants, traders, missionaries, diplomats and military men) who brought them from the Atlantic world of Europe and America to various parts of Asia. Another related line of emphasis in the history of the various Asian countries is the fact that a combination of forces from the West ended the isolation in which many peoples had existed for centuries. An important feature among the changes which have been caused by the Westerners and their ideas is the industrialization which has become prevalent especially in the twentieth century and is today a significant element of the economy in many parts of Asia.

The forces just mentioned and the acceleration of the industrialization process in our own time has resulted in Asia's becoming part of a close-knit international community. Its peoples now share in what has become a world culture; all parts of Asia are affected by such happenings as the Cold War, the activities of the United Nations, and the progress of science. Whatever is of importance to men anywhere is now also of importance to the peoples of Asia. The fact of their participation in world events and world culture marks a new phase in their history to be integrated with that history as a whole.

Asian history as here presented is divided roughly in half at the year 1600. Starting with a chapter on Asian prehistory, the growth of cultures during the centuries before 1600 is considered in five geographical divisions. This arrangement has been made in Volume I because the development of the various Asian peoples before 1600 was much more in isolation from one another than it was in the later periods.

On the other hand, the events and trends of the times since the seventeenth century have been so interrelated in various parts of Asia that they cannot be studied completely in isolation from one another or even in geographical groupings. Hence the material for the period since 1600 has been arranged in three main phases: first, the empires of the old traditions as they existed in the seventeenth and eighteenth centuries; next, the impact of the European-American cultures in Asia, including the development of colonial empires, expansion of Western powers, and the Westernization and growth of various Asian states, bringing the history of all areas down to the Chinese revolution and the outbreak of World War I; finally, the period since 1914 is considered as a time in which revolution and a new vitality among both old and new peoples was a common feature. Asia also in the period commencing with World War I has been part of an interdependent world.

II ❁❁

THE PREHISTORIC

BACKGROUND

To COMMENCE THE STORY OF MAN'S EXISTENCE IN ASIA PROPERLY and in order to gain a real understanding of later developments, we must go back to the beginnings of history itself. Without written materials our sources of information are, of course, very limited. What knowledge we have concerning early man is based on a few artifacts, such as tools of stone and other durable materials, bones, remains of fires, objects of art and decoration, together with geological evidences.

The date for the first emergence of man is known only within a wide range of years; the termination of the "prehistoric" is even less susceptible of exact definition.

The study of available records reveals that the time-span of man's prehistory is about a hundred times longer than the subsequent ages for which written evidences are available. While writing commenced only about 3000 years before Christ, we have actual skeletons as well as primitive tools whose approximate chronology can be identified and from which we know that a type of human being lived in Asia about 500,000 years ago.

In situations where writing is known to have existed, we may consider history to have begun; but only when such writing can be read today and the subject matter thus understood, can we correctly speak of a historical period. This is true for example, in Mesopotamia commencing about 3000 B.C., an age for which we have decipherable written materials. But from the Indus valley of a comparable time the written materials are, as yet, undeciphered and that civilization still remains in a sense prehistoric.

It must also be noted that the use of writing has developed at different times among different peoples, and our knowledge of such development is dependent upon whether or not the materials used have endured with the evidence of the writing upon them. In China we must date history from the time of the earliest "oracle" writings on bone and tortoise shell, even though the sophisticated forms of the language indicate a long previous development.

In many parts of Asia prehistoric cultures persisted side by side with advanced civilizations whose peoples had long been producing written records. Primitive ways of life at the prehistoric level have even survived down to our own time. Thus, when prehistoric times in Asia are here referred to, the reader should have in mind first of all the long span of time before writing was in use anywhere; he should then remember that there were extended periods of overlapping of prehistoric and historic development between different parts of Asia and even within regions of certain specific cultures.

The Periods of Prehistory

Most of prehistory took place during what is known to geologists as the Pleistocene epoch, also referred to as the Glacial epoch, because of the successive stages of glaciation over a large portion of the earth.

It was in Pleistocene times that man first emerged as a distinct form among the animals classed as "primates." The earliest "hominids," or man-like creatures, probably developed in areas of a warm tropical or subtropical climate. It is likely that they limited "their ranges to warm well-watered areas similar to the habitat in which they had originated, where game and plant foods were plentiful and where protection from the elements offered no serious problems." [1] These regions of origin and early habitation probably were in either Africa or Asia, but the precise area is still a matter of conjecture.

Evidences of the earliest men are few and scattered. Some facts are known through the discovery of material remains at certain sites. From these remains definite conclusions can be drawn for these sites. However, lack of materials in a given area does not mean that the area was not inhabited nor that its inhabitants did not pass through a particular stage of development. With this in mind let us note the main periods and cultural stages of prehistory.

Based on systematic study of the limited remains of prehistoric times, certain large divisions have become accepted as indications of the most important

[1] J. E. Weckler, "The Relationship between Neanderthal Man and Homo Sapiens," *American Anthropologist*, LVI, No. 6, Part I (December, 1954), p. 1007.

changes. Although the principal finds for the study of prehistory have been made in Europe and our terminology therefore is based upon knowledge of prehistoric man in Europe rather than in Asia, there are certain basic changes which seem to have a parallel sequence in places far removed from each other. Whatever the reason, the rich discoveries in Europe are near enough alike to those from Asia that a similar terminology can be used to advantage. At the same time the student must remember that great divergences exist and one cannot assume exactly the same cultural changes on both continents.

The general development, which followed the same sequence in both Europe and Asia, is best known from a study of the types of stone tools. "The old stone age" or the "Paleolithic" is the period when men used chipped or flaked stones for their tools in contrast to the later "new stone age," or "Neolithic" period, when stone tools were highly polished, and the later overlapping "Chalcolithic" stage, when copper was first used. When the use of copper gave way to bronze and men began to make written records, prehistory comes to an end. The term "Mesolithic" is used for a period intermediate between Paleolithic and Neolithic.

THE PALEOLITHIC STAGE.   In general the Paleolithic stage was characterized by man's first use of chipped stone tools. Although artifacts of other materials have been discovered which increase our knowledge of Paleolithic man, the stone implements are among those which are best preserved in their original condition and which are available in the greatest quantity.

The evidence of the stone tools alone shows that this period of time— that part of the Pleistocene epoch when men existed and when they were limited to a Paleolithic culture (before the Neolithic stage had appeared anywhere)—was immensely longer than all subsequent periods of human life put together. The earliest tools of chipped stone may have been made a million years ago. The oldest skeletal remains may go back to about 500,000 or 600,000 years (about the time of the first "Ice Age" in Europe), while the beginnings of Neolithic culture are estimated to have taken place at a relatively recent date, after about 8000 B.C.

The Pleistocene epoch is entirely Paleolithic in culture. In nearly all parts of Asia evidence has been found that men went through the Paleolithic stage. The fact that some peoples continued at the Paleolithic level while others had already progressed beyond it and that hence the transition took place at different times in different places does not nullify its significance as a crucial stage of human development.

In the Paleolithic stage man shaped and used various objects for his own benefit. He sustained himself by hunting and by food collecting. He also learned the use of fire. In the earliest known human home, the cave at Chou-k'ou-tien, near Peking, charred bones indicate that Pleistocene man from about 500,000 B.C. was controlling and using fire.[2]

---

[2] Chêng Tê-k'un. *Archaeology in China*. Vol. I, *Prehistoric China* (Cambridge, Mass., 1959), p. 162.

Evidence of the kind found at Chou-k'ou-tien indicates the existence of Paleolithic man at the time of the middle Pleistocene. With this knowledge as a beginning modern scholarship has been able to construct a probable timetable for the prehistory of Asia and to correlate this with the well worked out chronological sequences of European prehistory. While the sequences based on European archaeological finds are useful as a scheme of reference and for comparison, the stages of European Paleolithic developments do not correspond entirely with those in most of Asia.

In general there are two main divisions of Paleolithic culture traditions in Asia. One of these, found in Western Asia and India, has been called the "hand-ax tradition" and is essentially the same as that of Europe and Africa. India is the eastern limit of the hand-ax tradition in Pleistocene times and in India it overlaps the area of the other great stone tool culture, the "chopping-tool tradition." Chopping tools have been found in northwest India and in all the areas east of India, including China and Java.[3]

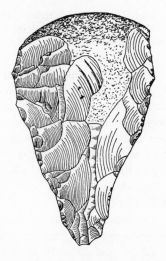

FIGURE 2.1.   A hand-ax, the tool par excellence of the Lower Paleolithic, found in Europe, Africa and India. A pointed tool flaked on both sides, it served as a fine all-purpose cutter.

Sequences of Paleolithic stone tools corresponding to the types found in Europe have been found in Southwest Asia from Palestine to the Caucasus. These range from the most primitive to the most advanced types of hand-axes for over a period of nearly 100,000 years. After the last period of glaciation in Europe, that is at the end of a rainy (or "pluvial") period in Southwest Asia, we come to the dawn of Neolithic culture.

[3] In this chapter the words "chopper" and "chopping tool" are used interchangeably. This simplified usage will need further elaboration for those who go on to read the more technical writings on the subject.

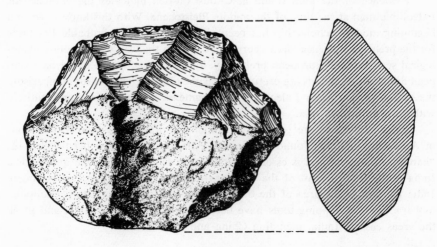

FIGURE 2.2   A chopping tool, Lower Paleolithic. This kind of tool has been found in India and in all the areas east of India, including China and Java. It represents a direct contrast to the hand-ax tradition.

A parallel series of developments may be noted in India. For the early or Lower Pleistocene no implements or other evidences of man have been found. Only for a time corresponding to the second Ice Age in Europe have stone flake tools of a very primitive sort been discovered. For the succeeding second "interglacial" period in northwest India there are evidences of both a chopping-tool culture and hand-ax culture similar to that of Europe. The hand-axes of the next period (corresponding to the third Ice Age) also show similarity to those of peoples farther west. Meanwhile chopping tools are the only type known in the Pleistocene cultures farther east.

From the beginning of middle Pleistocene times, and continuing until Neolithic tools were made, chopping tools were the principal implements which have survived in Burma, China, and Java. In the last two countries skeletal remains older than those found anywhere else on earth have been discovered. Among the more important were "Java Man," *Pithecanthropus erectus,* found in Central Java, and "Peking Man," *Pithecanthropus* (or *Sinanthropus*) *pekinensis,* found in the cave at Chou-k'ou-tien in North China, both of whom manufactured chopping tools some 500,000 or more years ago. These men appear to have lived for thousands of years in a world entirely cut off from the lands and cultures west of India.

Thus a study of the locations of the two types of Paleolithic implements, hand axes and flaked chopping tools, reveals a cultural separation between western and eastern Asia dating back to the earliest period in human development and which continued as a basic feature in the later history. Even though important influences spread from India to eastern Asia and thus served to bridge the gap between the two sections, certain cultural characteristics common to the peoples of India and Southwest Asia have differentiated them from the peoples and cultures of the Far East and Southeast Asia.

For Pleistocene times in Asia the cultural finds lack the richness and variety of those found in Europe. Without cave paintings and sculptured bone objects we cannot reconstruct the life of these Asian peoples in the manner that has succeeded so well for Europe.

We do know that men with modern types of skeletons appeared about the same time in Palestine and in China as they did in the countries north and south of the Mediterranean during the late Paleolithic or Mesolithic (intermediate stone age). At this time of receding glaciers in Europe, distinct varieties or races of men and separate cultures in various areas are known to have existed. Men in parts of Asia, as in Europe, were engaging in advanced types of hunting, fishing and food collecting. This is the period when men in Europe, and presumably in Asia also, developed the use of a bow in hunting. In China and elsewhere Mesolithic culture was characterized by the use of microliths instead of chopping tools.

In late Pleistocene times men began to domesticate plants and animals. This rise of agriculture was a change of utmost importance, but its dating can only be guessed at. Perhaps the oldest cultivation of plants took place along the streams of coastal areas in Southeast Asia among peoples who fished, hunted and collected fibers and fruits which they found useful. It is even more probable that in the hilly woodlands of Southwest Asia men began to select and to cultivate other plants and animals for their own use. We do not know precisely where these agricultural processes began nor in what order, but it is clear that in Asia two diverse systems originated. In India and Southeast Asia many plants, whether used for food or for other purposes, were reproduced by taking a root or other piece of a plant and setting it into the ground to start a new one. In contrast, the early farmers of Southwest Asia, India and China also practiced seed planting.

In either case it seems likely that the long processes of selection and development occurred where men could remain for a length of time and where climatic conditions were fairly comfortable. Unfortunately, the beginnings of agriculture cannot be tied in with the definite sequence of cultural changes found in archeological remains. We do know, however, that after the end of the Pleistocene, about 10,000 to 8,000 B.C., the new revolutionary improvements affected men's lives across all of Asia.

The plants and animals used by the early agriculturists may go back to late Paleolithic or Mesolithic times. Some of the large variety originating in Southeast Asia or eastern India were bananas, pandanus, breadfruits, bamboo and sugar cane—all reproduced by planting pieces of stem or root (vegetative reproduction) and not through seeds. Rice and coconuts also probably originated in South Asia in those very early times. In southern Asia, at the time when this "Old Planting" culture began, men also first domesticated dogs, pigs, chickens, ducks and geese. In contrast, in Asia west of the Indus much of the seed planting had its origins in the cultivation of wheat, peas and beans. Also in Southwest

Asia by about 7000 B.C. were domesticated most of our common herd animals such as sheep, cattle, horses and camels. The Chinese also developed seed planting in their use of millet and soy beans.

These early times also witnessed the spread of plants and animals from one area to another. The domesticated pigs, dogs and chickens which originated in South and Southeast Asia were taken, by Neolithic times, from this area North to China and northwest to the Mediterranean and Western Europe. The use of rice and other plants spread north and south also from Southeast Asia. Herd animals were taken in all directions from the centers of their domestication in Southwest Asia. Similarly, knowledge of the growing of wheat, peas, etc., went east and west from that same area. Since the use of both crops and animals may have spread as early as late Paleolithic or Mesolithic times and since we do not have positively dated physical evidence of this dispersal, it is impossible to set forth any accurate designation of the routes over which they traveled. That cultural ideas were diffused over vast distances is certain, and in the following pages more will be said about developments in various areas and their probable interconnections.

THE NEOLITHIC STAGE.   The period following the Pleistocene, with its Paleolithic culture, and after the intermediate Mesolithic is called Neolithic because this was a "new" stone age, when men were no longer content to use only the chipped stone implements of their ancestors. Neolithic men, in addition to making fine flaked stones such as arrowheads and for the cutting edges of sickles, developed and used polished stone implements. The change in stone tools is given prominence in the names we use, but it was only one aspect of the sweeping changes and improvements which took place in Mesolithic and Neolithic times,

FIGURE 2.3.   Neolithic polished stone adze from northwest China.

from about 8,000 to 5,500 B.C. These dates are only approximate and are applicable mainly to the relatively well-known chronology of Southwest Asia. Microliths appeared in Central and South India only after 2000 B.C. indicating a slower cultural development in that area.

Among the most important aspects of the so-called "Neolithic Revolution" were new methods of obtaining food. While hunting, fishing and the gathering of wild plant foods still continued, with development of the new agriculture (whose origins, as we have seen, may go back long before this time), men now were able to produce their own food. The raising of crops and the use of domesticated animals are important features of the Neolithic economy in both Europe and Asia.

From the early beginnings of agriculture to the practices of late Neolithic times there were many and elaborate developments. The ideas, skills and new tools used in the new activities were the result of long periods of effort. For example, preparation of land for planting in many areas necessitated controlled irrigation. In some areas the natural drying up of marsh lands may have facilitated the agriculture of Neolithic man, while in other situations he had to reclaim swampy areas or bring in extra water through ditches in order to provide the right conditions for farming.

Neolithic men also first developed the production of pottery for their household utensils probably independently both in Southwest Asia and in China. From these centers ideas concerning the making and decoration of earthenware spread from one part of Eurasia to another. A notable feature of this development was the making of painted pottery with similarities between the wares of such far separated places as Mesopotamia, Iran and Baluchistan on the one hand and China on the other. The art of pottery-making reached Japan early during that country's Neolithic stage of development. But in India and Indonesia, further from the centers of origin, there is no evidence of pottery being used until late Neolithic times.

Another great invention of the Neolithic period was the manufacture of cloth. Evidence, such as the stone and clay spindle whorls found in Iran and China, comes from some of the oldest known Neolithic communities.

With these revolutionary improvements in their ways of living, especially in animal domestication and agriculture, the people of Neolithic times found it necessary to live in more or less permanent settlements. Thus the evidences of their activities are found in association with the earliest buildings, such as the ruins in the hills of debris in Southwest Asia (about 4500 B.C.) and the remains of pounded earth village walls in China. With work which required continuous residence in one place, men were now tied to the land as they had not been before.

Interest in the land and its use for farming led to the development of irrigation for the production of better crops. With irrigation came the need for social organization and cooperation in order that a group might work together for the common good. In Southwest Asia those who could then control production through cooperative effort gained power in their communities. Thus social organization marked the beginning of states and warfare (with battle axes and flint daggers) carried on for purposes of control through conquest.

In addition there seem to have existed ideas of religion and magic, as shown from the figurines and amulets in the Neolithic remains in Southwest Asia and Japan. From paintings on rock walls, as in Indonesia and Malaya, we see evidences also of artistic expression.

As arts and crafts developed there arose the desire to exchange products with peoples of other areas. In both Asia and Europe luxury articles, including fine flints, stone weapons, semiprecious stones, copper, shells and pottery were transported over long distances in early trading activity. From Ireland to China, material objects are known to have been dispersed. During this time also (and perhaps much earlier) men from Asia found their way around the North Pacific to the continent of North America. Navigation was developed along the southern coasts of Asia by means of dugout canoes and migrations brought new ideas and practices to the islands of Southeast Asia. The advent of early Neolithic culture to the Philippines is estimated at 5000 B.C.

While there are enough similarities so that we can speak of one Neolithic way of life from the Mediterranean to Japan, it is to be noted that there were many different forms of Neolithic culture. As has been shown above, there was a great variety of plants cultivated and of animals domesticated. Conditions of living, the homes of the people, the objects used in their daily lives and the results of their artistic development differed widely.

During late Neolithic times discoveries and inventions occurred which were as revolutionary in their effects as those which had previously brought about the change from Paleolithic to Neolithic. One of the first was the use of a metal, copper, for making tools and weapons as a supplement to, and gradually as replacement for, the earlier use of less durable substances, such as stone, bone and wood. This started in Southwest Asia between 5000 and 4000 B.C. and gradually spread to other parts of Asia. The effects of the manufacture and use of copper articles were so important that a special term, "Chalcolithic," is often used to designate this beginning stage in men's use of metals, which is still a significant part of our economy today. This Chalcolithic stage is intermediate between the purely Neolithic and the subsequent Bronze Age. However, the fact that stone tools continued to be used along with implements of copper and other metals and that the change from the use of copper to the manufacture of bronze began at different times in different places means that we cannot use the term "the Chalcolithic stage" with any precision. Even though development came gradually and varied from area to area, this beginning of the use of copper is an event of the greatest importance.

The evolution of metallurgy in Southwest Asia was one phase of an era of greater specialization in human activities which included new economic organization, the beginnings of writing and the "urban revolution," thus marking the end of Neolithic times.

Forerunners of Historic Cultures

In the various parts of Asia distinctive cultural variations and interconnections during the long ages of prehistory remained as characteristic features in historic times. Several such characteristics have already been mentioned in the preceding sections of this chapter. The following additional features of the prehistory are especially worth noting.

SOUTHWEST ASIA. As far back as Paleolithic times there existed tastes and customs which are still prevalent in Southwest Asia. For example, these early peoples valued semiprecious stones, such as carnelian, turquoise and lapis lazuli, which are prized today.

Starting with the taming of such herd animals as goats and sheep in Mesolithic times, the peoples of Southwest Asia have been noted for their livestock. By the end of the Neolithic stage or early Chalcolithic period in the region just north of the Caucasus or in the steppe region beyond, horses were tamed by sedentary farmers. Horses became a part of the culture of Southwest Asia and by the end of Chalcolithic times they were used for display, for religious purposes, warfare and trade.

Neolithic ideas of religion and magic in Southwest Asia may be inferred from the remains of female figurines. By late Chalcolithic times clay figures can be identified as depicting a Mother Goddess, deity of procreation and abundance. By this time also the myths and cult practices which were to be characteristic of early historic times were being formulated and passed on by word of mouth.

FIGURE 2.4. Neolithic painted ware from Iran. The wild goat with the enormous horns shows a remarkable sense of decorative effect. This is pottery made on the wheel and combines purely geometric design with animal forms.

The interest of the Iranians in art forms featuring animals and birds may be traced back to the motifs found on pottery of about 4000 B.C. From this period also comes evidence of early metallurgy in Southwest Asia. Specialists appeared who were skilled in the smelting and manufacturing of copper, silver and gold. The idea of working with metals spread by trade and by warfare to Central Asia, to the Aegean among the Trojans and other peoples, and to India before 3000 B.C. About a thousand years later places as remote as Britain and China were sharing in the inventions of Southwest Asia.

The canals, temple architecture, clay seals (used to designate ownership of merchandise) and cuneiform writing of Mesopotamia had their beginnings in the Chalcolithic period and foreshadowed the complex civilization of early historic times. Remains of canals show the importance of irrigation while the contents of graves at places such as Siyalk in Iran indicate a belief in life after death.

Contemporary with the Chalcolithic period in Southwest Asia (that is, prior to the use of bronze in about 2000 B.C.) in Central Asia there was developing a steppe civilization among tribal groups known today as Indo-Europeans. At approximately the time of the invention of bronze, groups of these Indo-Europeans migrated to the south. One part of the first wave went via the Balkans into Asia Minor. There they formed the Hittite confederation whose history is described in the next chapter. Other tribes crossed the Caucasus to move into the upper Euphrates valley where later as the Mitanni they were to oppose the Hittites. Some also moved into the central Zagros mountains of Iran and merged with earlier hill people in that region. The main body of the tribes who migrated at this time went from the steppes into Bactria and through the passes into India in whose history they are known as Indo-Aryans (see Chapter 7). Another wave of migrants from Central Asia came south some centuries later. These were the early Iranians, whose coming into Iran will be described in Chapter 3.

INDIA.   Prior to the coming of Indo-Aryans little is known of India. Neolithic remains are few and scattered. In Chalcolithic times arose the great culture of the Indus valley, the Harappa culture, which will be described in Chapter 7.

SOUTHEAST ASIA.   Although Southeast Asia is remote geographically from the early centers of human culture in Southwest Asia and in China, connections did exist from very ancient times. There are remains of cultural development in Indonesia, mainland Southeast Asia and the Philippines which was parallel to changes in the major centers further north. Significant evidences of this development are the Paleolithic chopping tools of Patjitan and the Solo valley in Java, of the Irrawaddy valley in Burma, Malaya and Thailand, as well as Luzon and Mindanao in the Philippines.

Mesolithic cave men at Hoa-binh in Tongking, in eastern Sumatra and other places in Southeast Asia established patterns of life which are still significant today. Women were the cultivators of gardens and domesticators of animals while the men hunted, built boats and fished.

By Neolithic times in Southeast Asia a racial mixture existed comparable to that found in the area today. Earlier Melanesian or Australian types were joined by proto-Malays or Indonesians, as well as Mongoloid tribes from the north. Associated with the coming of the proto-Malays was a Neolithic culture of skilled craftmanship in polished stone knives, axes and other artifacts. Craftmanship has been a feature of Southeast Asian life ever since.

An important element of East Asian civilization which may have had its beginnings in Southeast Asia is the cultivation of rice with irrigation and terraced fields. This irrigated rice culture spread in Neolithic times among the peoples of South China, Formosa, Korea and Japan.

Other features of Southeast Asian life have persisted from Neolithic to modern times. Examples are the isolated village communities usually found near coasts, along river banks and on gentle slopes favorable for rice culture, and also the placating of local spirits, through animistic worship.

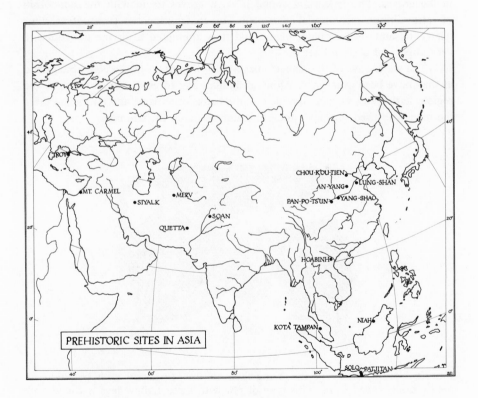

PREHISTORIC SITES IN ASIA

CHINA. A significant feature of early Chinese history had its counterpart in the Paleolithic stage of prehistory. This was the importance of north China. Most of the known Paleolithic remains are in north China and here also was the cradle of Chinese civilization from the Neolithic period into historic Shang times.

On the other hand the skills of the Chinese in the highly sophisticated garden culture for which they have been noted may be traced to early developments in south China. In that region, perhaps as early as 25,000 B.C., men in the Mesolithic stage of development began to cultivate rice and citrus fruits and various other plants, some of which were introduced from Southeast Asia.

By the late Neolithic period (about 3000–1750 B.C.) in north China the Yellow river valley was the scene of cultural developments which were the immediate forerunners of the advanced civilization found later in that region. The remains of hundreds of settled communities have been found. Farming of the rich loess soil supplemented the hunting and fishing practiced in earlier times. The raising of silkworms originated at this time. The "proto-Chinese" of this region made many types of fine pottery including a type uniquely Chinese —the three-legged cooking pot, or tripod with hollow legs. For the use of their dead they placed pots and cups and sometimes polished stone and jade artifacts in the graves. The jade rings found in such graves tie in with the symbolism of later Chinese ceremonial ornaments. In confronting the supernatural they heated ox and deer shoulder blades and thus attempted to divine the future, a very important custom later on.

The waterways of the Yangtze basin were important in the Neolithic period as they have been ever since. Although jungles and forests covered much of the region, settlements were maintained on the banks of streams and rivers and there the men who used polished stone implements made their homes.

FIGURE 2.5.   Pottery of the Yang-shao culture. *Li* tripod with painted geometric designs, red ware. This type of pot with three hollow legs is found only in China. Its manufacture continued into Shang and early Chou times.

JAPAN.   Significant for the future of Japan were the Paleolithic and Neolithic settlers who came from two directions: some from South China and Vietnam and others from mainland Northeast Asia. The earliest known skeletons show that the Japanese people were a mixed race with connections both north and south.

A key feature of Japanese development has been the flow of ideas and practices which came to the island from the continent of Asia. Paleolithic chopping tools, Mesolithic microliths and Neolithic cord-pattern pottery denote successive phases of Japanese prehistoric culture which showed influences from the mainland. The Neolithic culture ended about the third century B.C. with the coming of new immigrants from China and Korea, Mongoloid peoples possessing weapons of metal.

Thus already in prehistoric times events on the continent had their repercussions in Japan and this factor in the development of Japanese culture was to recur many times.

FIGURE 2.6   Jomon period pottery vessel from Japan, Neolithic period. Pottery shows "cord-pattern" decoration, unusual teapot shape.

LAND AND SEA RELATIONS.   The transport of luxury items, semiprecious stones and various ornaments was an element in the development of the distinctive regions of Asia. Both overland and sea routes figured in the communications pioneered by prehistoric peoples. Following in their footsteps the peoples of historic times developed interconnections between groups in interior regions and along the coasts by routes which had been travelled for thousands of years before. Stone artifacts, shells and valuable plants paved the way for textiles, metal goods and the results of skilled craftmanship.

Thus in similar forms during a period of thousands of years, over the length and breadth of Asia prehistoric men laid the foundations of the civilizations which were to come.

BASIC DATES
All dates approximate

600,000–125,000 B.C.	Middle Pleistocene
125,000–25,000 B.C.	Late Pleistocene
600,000–500,000 B.C.	Start of Paleolithic cultures
500,000 B.C.	Peking man; Java man
25,000 B.C.	Start of Mesolithic in China
15,000 B.C.	Start of Mesolithic in Southwest Asia
After 10,000 B.C.	Start of Mesolithic in India, Southeast Asia
8,000–5,000 B.C.	Start of Neolithic in China, Southwest Asia and elsewhere
5,000–4,000 B.C.	Metallurgy (Chalcolithic period) begins in Southwest Asia
5,000–4,000 B.C.	Neolithic culture in Southeast Asia and Philippines
3,100 B.C.	Neolithic in India
3,000 B.C.	Writing used in Mesopotamia
2,000 B.C.	Bronze in China and Southwest Asia
500–200 B.C.	Metallurgy to Philippines and Indonesia
250 B.C.	Bronze to Japan

SUPPLEMENTARY READING

CHILDE, V. GORDON. *What Happened in History.* Rev. ed. Baltimore, 1954. Useful for general concepts as applied to Southwest Asia and Europe, through Roman times.

CLARK, GRAHAME. *World Prehistory, an Outline.* Cambridge, England, 1961. Useful for understanding Asian prehistory in world-wide perspective.

FAIRSERVIS, WALTER A. JR. *The Origins of Oriental Civilization.* New York, 1959. Chiefly on China and Japan, through early historic times.

GHIRSHMAN, R. *Iran: From the Earliest Times to the Islamic Conquest.* Baltimore, 1954. Chapter 1 gives excellent coverage for this one country.

GORDON, D. H. *The Pre-historic Background of Indian Culture.* Bombay, 1958. Excellent coverage of archaeological finds, including Indus culture and after.

GROUSSET, R. *The Civilizations of the East. Vol. I: The Near and Middle East.* New York, 1931. One chapter on prehistory of all Asia.

KIDDER, J. E. JR. *Japan Before Buddhism.* New York, 1959. Excellent for prehistoric and early historic periods.

LINTON, RALPH. *The Tree of Culture.* New York, 1955. Standard anthropology textbook; covers world-wide prehistory and early history.

PIGGOTT, STUART. *Prehistoric India to 1000 B.C.* London, 1952. Includes both Indian and Southwest Asian archaeological background. Covers Indian history through early Aryan times.

TWEEDIE, M. W. F. *Prehistoric Malaya.* Singapore, 1955. A model of clear brief coverage for one country.

ADVANCED READING

CHENG, TE-K'UN. *Archaeology in China. Vol. I: Prehistoric China.* Cambridge, England, 1959. Comprehensive and scholarly survey, includes much material not available elsewhere.

FRANKFORT, HENRI. *The Birth of Civilization in the Near East.* Bloomington, Ind., 1951. Thirty-three pages of scholarly detail and interpretation, limited to Mesopotamia and Egypt.

HEEKEREN, H. R. VAN. "The Stone Age of Indonesia," *Verhandelingen van het Koninklijk Instituut voor Taal-, Land- en Volkenkunde,* Vol. XXI. The Hague, 1957. Comprehensive and scholarly coverage.

MOVIUS, H. L. JR. "The Lower Palaeolithic Cultures of Southern and Eastern Asia," *Transactions, American Philosophical Society, New Series,* XXXVIII, Part 4 (March, 1949). Scholarly monograph of wide scope by an expert.

——— "Palaeolithic Archaeology in Southern and Eastern Asia, exclusive of India," *Journal of World History,* II. Paris, 1954.

RANKE, H., E. A. SPEISER, W. N. BROWN, AND C. W. BISHOP. "The Beginnings of Civilization in the Orient," Supplement to the *Journal of the American Oriental Society* (December, 1939). Baltimore, 1939. Brief scholarly survey of archaeological knowledge up to 1939; covering Mesopotamia, India, and East Asia.

SAUER, CARL O. *Agricultural Origins and Dispersals.* Bowman Memorial Lectures, Series 2 (New York: The American Geographical Society), 1952. Sweeping new theories convincingly presented.

SOLHEIM, WILHELM G. II, ED., AND H. L. MOVIUS JR., GUEST ED. *Asian Perspectives,* II, No. 2 (Winter, 1958), "Special Palaeolithic Issue" (Hongkong, 1960). Details of recent research in East and Southeast Asia.

TERRA, HELMUT DE, AND T. T. PATERSON. *Studies on the Ice Age in India and Associated Human Cultures.* Washington, D.C., 1939. Scholarly monograph.

III

EARLY EMPIRES OF WESTERN ASIA

IN STUDYING THE HISTORY OF ASIA it is logical for those of us who are part of Western civilization to be concerned with the area which is geographically and culturally nearest to Europe. Another reason why students of Asian history must include Western Asia is that here is one of the most important and the earliest known of the cradles of mankind. Equally important as the other great cultural centers of Asia, India and China, and probably older in its civilization than either of these, Southwest Asia was the scene of the origin of many basic characteristics of today's world.

In comparison with other areas, Southwest Asia lacked the focal region which the Yellow river provided in China and the Indus-Ganges regions in India. Within this area, in its long history from antiquity to the present, the center of importance has shifted through the ages. Mesopotamia, Iran, Arabia and Asia Minor each has been at one time or another the central region of power and influence. This fact is due partly to the cultural complexity of the area. Southwest Asia resembled the Indian subcontinent in this regard in including a number of unique regions of separate and original development. Regions such as Palestine, Phoenicia and Armenia do not fit into one unified pattern. Cultural complexity was due to the proximity of powerful cultures in adjoining areas.

These were particularly Egypt, and Greece as a part of the Mediterranean world.

This chapter begins with the invention of writing at the end of the prehistoric period. The main theme is the succession of great empires in Southwest Asia and the development in them and among their neighbors of a highly refined civilization. This civilization will be followed from its early manifestations in Mesopotamia and Iran, in its relationship with the peoples of regions bordering on Mesopotamia, and through the period when the Greeks controlled the whole of Southwest Asia and left their mark in the period of Hellenistic culture.

Geography

The area covered in this section of history extends from what the Romans of a later period called "Asia" (today referred to as Asia Minor), directly to the east as far as the Central Asian parts of the present Soviet Union, south to include modern Afghanistan, Baluchistan, and all of the Asiatic continent south and west of these boundaries. It seems more practical to refer to this general area as "Southwest Asia" than to confuse the student with such terms as Near East, Levant or Middle East. The usages of these terms are so loose today as to afford no real significance for a particular geographical area.

Although varying considerably in altitude and in average temperature from one part to another, the area as a whole has a semidesert climate similar to conditions found in southern and central California. Rainfall comes mostly in winter, the summers are dry and in many parts availability of water and possibilities of irrigation are of utmost importance. To aid in understanding the component parts of Southwest Asia it is helpful to think in terms of six principal regions.

1. The "Fertile Crescent" is a valuable concept, well known to students of western civilization. Within the sweep of Mesopotamia (the Tigris and Euphrates Valleys), Syria, Palestine and the Nile Valley of Egypt on the adjoining African continent, it includes lands of great fertility in which high development of agriculture was possible.

2. South of the region just described extends the great peninsula of Arabia, largely desert, sparsely inhabited at any time and characterized by oasis agriculture and nomadic tribes.

3. Northwest of Syria the peninsula of Asia Minor is in many ways closer geographically and historically to Europe than it is to areas farther east. This is especially true of the Aegean coast. The low coastal fringe of the peninsula is to be differentiated from the semiarid interior tableland, which is made inaccessible by precipitous mountain ranges. Asia Minor is also frequently referred to as Anatolia.

4. East of Anatolia and merging into it is the region of the Armenian highlands. This inland region is today divided among Turkey, Iran and the Soviet Union.

5. A larger region than any of these except Arabia, is the key region of Iran (or Persia). High mountain ranges to the west and in the north cut off from the rest of Asia a highland region, much of which is desert. Iran includes some parts very different from the main plateau area. Among them is the region directly south of the Caspian Sea, humid, tropical and below sea level. Another special area is Khuzistan (or Susiana) at the head of the Persian Gulf and west of the great range of Zagros mountains. Khuzistan is geographically more a part of Mesopotamia than Iran although historically from ancient times down to today it must be considered part of the latter. To the northeast along the border of Central Asia is Khorasan, known in very ancient times as Parthia, and important as a cultural center throughout much of Iranian history. This is a sort of rim area which forms a natural dividing line between the main Iranian plateau and the regions farther north.

6. For the purposes of the early history most of Central Asia must be included in this general area of Southwest Asia. Central Asia is cut off entirely from the sea and the principal subdivisions are to be differentiated through the locations of rivers and mountain ranges. Two important rivers flow from southeast to northwest into the Aral Sea. The Amu Darya (or ancient Oxus) flows from the northern part of modern Afghanistan to the south end of the Aral Sea. South of this river in northern Afghanistan was Bactria. To the north, between the Amu Darya and the more northerly Syr Darya, lies ancient Sogdia, characterized by trading cities recurrently of great importance in the commerce between nations of Asia. Bactria and Sogdia are bordered to the north by steppes and deserts. One small region which does not fall within this category is the agricultural area of Kharism located where the Amu Darya flows into the Aral Sea. To the east these Central Asian regions are sharply divided from Chinese Central Asia and the Indus valley by the massive mountains of the Pamirs and Hindu Kush.

The Early Civilizations of Mesopotamia

What is the present significance of the early civilization in Mesopotamia? One answer is that here were the origins of the cultural stream which came directly to Western Europe and of which we are a part. Here were the city-states and autocratic empires whose forms were like those which developed later in Europe. The political and philosophic concepts of Mesopotamia are in many cases basic principles of our society today. This area is often studied merely as a part of the history of Western civilization; it is also a starting point for much of the history of Asia.

The area of which Mesopotamia was a main center included several peoples of great historical importance. Together they contributed to a little world of cultural development unmatched elsewhere for centuries to come. In this world Sumerians, Babylonians, Assyrians and Chaldeans were particularly important. Their region, Mesopotamia, was the chief center of Western Asia and here man developed a society which included writing, law, the worship of distinctive gods, and a government of kings subordinate to the gods and law. This development was based on the heritage of prehistoric times.

From preliterate man the peoples of Mesopotamia had inherited an advanced material culture: an agricultural system based on irrigation through a network of canals, metal work which meant an extensive commerce with areas where the metals might be obtained and an architecture which expressed itself in buildings of vast proportions.

In his thinking prehistoric man bequeathed to his successors ideas and values which were already highly developed when he first wrote them down. His temples and his art show the supremacy he gave to his great gods, the spirits of the sky, the storm, the earth and the waters of the earth. Their worship was tied to a belief in the authority of human rulers. Yet at the same time decisions were arrived at by a primitive democracy in assemblies of adult freemen.

In Mesopotamia, the leading culture of Western Asia, men found a way to communicate their ideas first by pictographs and then by wedge-shaped marks on clay tablets which developed into one of the great systems of writing of ancient times. This cuneiform writing, developed in Mesopotamia before 3000 B.C., became an international written script and continued to be used by generations of scribes and merchants and officials down to the time of the Achaemenian Persians and until their civilization succumbed to that of the Greeks.

FIGURE 3.1.   Tablets of baked clay with cuneiform inscriptions recording business transactions. Babylonian, sixth-fifth century B.C.

SUMER AND AKKAD.   The story recorded on the clay tablets, and in other remains, opens with the period of Sumer and Akkad, two political and cultural centers of the lower Mesopotamian Valley. In the region between the Tigris

and Euphrates rivers, Sumer was the name of the section near the coast of the
Persian Gulf, at that time further north than it is today. At the ancient town-site
of Ur have been found remains of the "First Dynasty" of what is now known
as the "Early Dynastic period," the first historical period in contrast to the
previous periods known only from archaeological remains. The people of Ur,
and other towns of Sumer spoke Sumerian. Upstream in Akkad were a Semitic
speaking people. This section of the land between the rivers included the site
of the future Babylon and the two sections together, constituting the present
southern part of Iraq, came to be known as Babylonia.

The history of Sumer and Akkad in southern Mesopotamia (or Babylonia) consists of four main parts or subperiods: the time of the First Dynasty
at Ur, from about 2800 to about 2300 B.C.; unification of both regions under
the ruler of Akkad, about 2400 to 2200; a second dynasty at Ur ruling all of
Mesopotamia from about 2200 to 2123; and a third dynasty at Ur which
controlled an empire from Susa in the mountains of western Iran to the Mediterranean Sea, about 2123 to 2015.

In a period centuries before the advanced Harappa culture of the Indus
valley and over a thousand years earlier than the first historical period in
China, the peoples of Sumer and Akkad developed the use of writing and left
to us detailed accounts of a complex and highly advanced civilization. Only
in Egypt, just outside the Asiatic continent, was there a comparable and
contemporary development. For the peoples of Western Asia generally and
during the centuries until the coming of Greek influences, Mesopotamian
civilization is of paramount importance.

While highly developed irrigation agriculture continued to be the basic
occupation, skilled craftsmen used imported materials to produce textiles,
furniture and ornaments of great refinement. In our museums are preserved
examples of brilliant colored fabrics and ornaments of gold. Exchange of
commodities and the need for written contracts had led to the development of
writing. Now bookkeeping, banking and the standardization of weights and
measures were used in the commerce which flourished in Sumer and Akkad
and which spread to neighboring regions. Prices were fixed and trade was regulated by laws whose definition and elaboration are one of the great achievements of this time.

Underlying the written laws in early Mesopotamia were concepts of
religion and society fundamental not only in the history of Western Asia in
this period, but basic for later ideas and actions of men throughout the world.

As do the oracle bones of Shang China so do the cuneiform inscriptions
of Babylonia bring us suddenly face to face with a pantheon and a religious
ideology whose roots are forever lost in the preceding centuries of preliteracy.
We find that the Sumerians and Akkadians thought in terms of a "cosmic state"
in which human society was only a part. Their world order has been termed
"an order of wills" in which everything we conceive of as animate and inanimate
has a will and character of its own. As in other places and times, the main

features of the universe around them were treated by the early Mesopotamians as manifestations of their great gods.

The supreme deity was the god of the sky, who was also the source and active principle in all authority. Decisions, however, were made and confirmed by an assembly of gods, of which the other more prominent were the god of the storm, the element of force in the world; mother earth, the spirit of fertility; and the god of the waters of the earth whose attributes also were creativity, knowledge and skill.

In their speculations about these gods, the early Mesopotamians sought to explain one main theme: "a way of life, the plan of the individual in the order of things." Hence, gods and men were related in myths such as those which told of creation and life after death. Study of "the order of things" gave rise also to the beginnings of astronomy, astrology and mathematics. Worship of the gods led to the building of numerous temples, varying in size from small shrines to great three-stepped pyramids.

Since the cosmic state of the gods was the only true state, the government or society of men was secondary and subordinate. The leaders of communities in Sumer and Akkad held their positions by virtue of the fact that they represented local gods. By the third millenium, from which time come our earliest records, the typical organization is a city-state which was considered to be the manor or estate of a great god. His temple was at the center, he was the landowner. The highest among his staff of human overseers was simultaneously prince and high priest. Within the city-state there might also be other temples and lands belonging to other deities. In the conflict over border lines, water rights and leadership in a larger area the national state developed and this was thought of as an extension of the executive organs of the cosmic or world state. The human ruler, or king, acted for the king among the gods who had been chosen by an assembly of the gods.

The king then in the Mesopotamian city-state did not have the position of divine absolutism held by the pharaohs in Egypt. He had definite responsibilities. In acting for the gods he must maintain internal order, lead the armed forces and protect the land from foreign invaders.

Gradually during the third millenium the power of the king increased and through a more efficient organization he was able to secure a regular application of the accepted rules of justice. His subjects knew what to expect. What in earlier times had been justice granted as a favor gave way to justice as a right. Although representing the gods the king's power was limited. He held office in a social order whose laws were divinely established and which afforded rights to the individual. Ruler and ruled alike must conform to the supreme authority of the law.

The Mesopotamian king was checked not only by the law but also because he shared his authority with an assembly. The underlying belief that all men were equal before the powers of nature found its expression in "a form of government which has to be regarded as a democracy." For the individual

FIGURE 3.2.   Seated figure of a Sumerian king, c. 2100 B.C.

there was the possibility of happiness through the application of justice according to law. The law has been referred to as a body of "divinely sanctioned
norms." Through these rules the gods championed the weak against the rich
and powerful. Kings governed in order to carry out ideals embodied in the
laws and "when the laws of the gods were obeyed oppression would be at
an end."

Expressions of this relationship are found in literature and art. Shamash,
the sun god, is worshipped in a Babylonian hymn as a "Merciful God, who
lifts the lowly and protects the weak." Seals, bas-reliefs and statues in the
round depict the gods and kings referred to on the cuneiform tablets.

These same cuneiform tablets also give us a wealth of detail about the
every day life of the Sumerians. We know that they had regular schools for
the training of scribes, most of whom came from the wealthier portions of
their society, since the poor could hardly afford the time or cost which such
a prolonged education would require. Discipline was strict, with a man "in
charge of the whip" whose ominous title clearly indicated the kind of pedagogy
practised. Students attended school from sunrise to sunset. Teachers were
poorly paid, but sometimes, when the student feared parental displeasure over
his school record, the family might wine and dine them at the young man's
suggestion. Again, the decipherment of these clay tablets has given us much
information about the practice of the earliest physicians. There exists an old
medical "handbook," listing various remedies for various ills, such as salves,
liquids, and drugs, compounded from a great variety of things, such as milk,
snake skin, turtle shell, fir, figs and dates. Unpalatable liquids, to be taken
internally, were put into beer to make prescriptions more attractive. On ag-

riculture, too, the clay tablets are a never failing source of information. How to plow, seed, water, cut, thresh and store—all this is stated in detail.

FIRST BABYLONIAN EMPIRE.   The national state ruled from Ur came to an end in the early part of the second millenium B.C. It was attacked from Elam (modern Khuzistan) in the east and from Syria across the desert to the west. The former kingdom of Sumer and Akkad gave way to Semitic Amorites from Syria who, about 1800 B.C., established a new capital at Babylon within the old Akkad. Most prominent among the rulers of this First Babylonian empire was Hammurabi, who reigned about 1700. Under his centralized administration over all of Mesopotamia and Elam, Babylon became the commercial and cultural focus of Western Asia. Here with further development and refinement were continued the artistic tradition, the literature, the legal system and the religion of Sumer and Akkad.

By the time of Hammurabi a unified code of laws had been established and moral standards developed which became models for many peoples during succeeding centuries in Western Asia and the Mediterranean. It is in this period that the clay documents reveal myths and legends originating in an earlier day. The great epic of *Gilgamesh,* which includes a story of the deluge similar to that of Noah, centers around a new theme: the problem of death.

The rule of the First Babylonian Dynasty was ended by a raid of Hittites from the north and superseded by a line of invading tribesmen, the Kassites, who took over the state organization and civilization in Babylonia.

ASSYRIA.   The territory controlled by the Kassites was smaller than that of their predecessors. During the Kassite period in Mesopotamia there occurred an infiltration of Aramean tribesmen from Arabia, and the ruling power also faced the growing military and political power of new rival states: Elam, Syria, Mitanni in northwest Mesopotamia (about 1475–1275 B.C.) and especially Assyria. The Assyrians, equipped with better means of warfare, including horses and light chariots, emerged from a series of conflicts with other peoples as a military monarchy with its capital at Nineveh. Under the king Tiglath-Pileser I (about 1115–1100) Assyrian forces seized Babylon itself. This was only a beginning. The Assyrians endured centuries of further struggle before they obtained security and finally a great empire. Arameans controlled the crossroads region of Syria. Not until Ashur-nasir-pal II (884–859 B.C.) and his successor was Assyrian rule extended over all of Mesopotamia and over Syria as well. The former ruler was depicted in stone bas-relief armed with a sword whose hilt bore intertwined snarling lions and with his hands grasping a bow and a winecup of victory.

Hunting and combat were the occupations of the Assyrian military despots. Royal audiences, battles and realistic powerful animals characterize their art. Their religion emphasized the importance of the monarchy, war, fertility. The temple, in their architecture, "dominated the palace." With intolerance and terroristic methods they ruled over the first extensive empire of Western Asia.

FIGURE 3.3.   King Ashur-nasir-pal II and his cup bearer. A splendid alabaster
slab from the palace of the Assyrian ruler (885–860 B.C.).

War was the "national industry." Neighboring peoples might revolt as they
did in the early eighth century. Reconquest followed when Tiglath-Pileser III
(746–727 B.C.) took Damascus (732) and Babylon (728). The founder of a
new line, Sargon II (722–705), started a series of further conquests. He destroyed the kingdoms of Israel (722) and Urardhu in Armenia (714). Sennacherib (705–681) annexed all of Babylonia (689); Essar-haddon (681–668) took
Egypt (670); and Ashur-banipal (668–626) destroyed the independence of Elam
(646).

The civilization of preceding dynasties was continued and surpassed by
these Assyrians. In particular Ashur-banipal was known not only as a warrior
but also as a patron of arts and letters. From Egyptians, Hittites and Iranians,
as well as from the heritage of Babylon, the Assyrians developed their own
culture tradition. They organized a strong military empire ruling over subject
peoples beyond their own land. This concept of empire they passed on to the
Medes who seized Nineveh in 612 and who, together with the Chaldeans, put
an end to the Assyrian empire.

FIGURE 3.4. King Sennacherib's cavalry in the mountains. The formidable Assyrian war machine on the march (eighth-seventh century B.C.).

CHALDEAN EMPIRE OR SECOND BABYLONIAN EMPIRE. Power in Mesopotamia centered once more at Babylon. The new Babylonian empire of the Chaldean dynasty, which lasted from 625 to 538 B.C. was founded by Nabopolassar and is particularly noted for the reign of his son, Nebuchadrezzar (Nebuchadnezzar, 605–561), (not to be confused with the twelfth century ruler of that name). Nebuchadrezzar, as we know from the Old Testament, became the most important political and military ruler of Southwest Asia in his day. Conflict with Egypt over control of Palestine resulted in Chaldean success. Four years after the pharaoh Necho of the seventeenth dynasty had gained a victory in Judah, Nebuchadrezzar decisively defeated him at Carchemish on the upper Euphrates, 605. Although Babylon thus dominated the Fertile Crescent, the peoples of Palestine and Phoenicia did not readily submit. Twice Nebuchadrezzar besieged and took Jerusalem, in 597 and 586. He assured his control by destruction of the city and the deportation of almost all the Jewish people from Palestine to Babylon. Tyre held out against the Chaldeans in a siege which lasted for thirteen years.

In Babylon the return of power to that city was celebrated by the new construction of city walls, royal palace and temples. National pride found expression in the worship of Marduk (or Bel) and the suppression of the worship of the gods of other peoples. At the same time there was less real faith and more philosophical skepticism in Mesopotamia than there had been before.

When the Chaldeans were overthrown by the forces of Iran in 538 B.C., the Mesopotamian civilization gave way to a more vigorous culture. On the other hand, the basic way of life, the achievements in art and science have endured through the ages. In this connection we may note particularly the

continuity of legal tradition which had its share in Biblical-Talmudic law
and in the law of Islam; and the religious influences handed down in Judaism,
Christianity and Islam.

Peoples Surrounding Mesopotamia

The traditions of Mesopotamia affected the lives of other peoples and were in
turn affected by them. Unlike the early cultures in the Yellow river and Indus
river valleys, the civilization of the Tigris-Euphrates valley did not have the
relative isolation of China or India. Only for purposes of clarity are we justified
in treating the history of Mesopotamia separately from that of its neighbors.
Actually there was constant contact, including invasion and counterinvasion
from the earliest times.

In noting the peoples surrounding ancient Mesopotamia we may list seven
different groups whose presence in Western Asia is important in the pre-Achae-
menian period. These were Egyptians; Hebrews; Arameans; Phoenicians; peoples of Asia Minor, especially Hittites; Armenians; and peoples of Iran.

EGYPTIANS. The great rival civilization which competed with ancient Mesopotamia in Western Asia was that of Egypt. The civilization of the Nile valley,
even though outside the boundaries of Asia, was more important than any
other as a powerful influence in the regions near the Tigris and Euphrates. The
influence was that of an absolute monarchy. Through the centuries the king
was treated as a god unrestricted by any traditional law. Thus Egypt attained
the greatness of its culture with political and social concepts very different
from those of the Sumerians and Babylonians.

HEBREWS. Of unique significance in the history of Southwest Asia and of
Europe, towards which it faced, is the narrow coastal region of Palestine, and
particularly the Hebrews who inhabited it. These people were a separate political entity for only a relatively short period in ancient times. In spite of its
briefness, however, the early history of the Hebrews, of their ideas, and of
Palestine is an important factor in the story of the lands and peoples surrounding Mesopotamia.

The Hebrews were a Semitic-speaking people who appear to have origi-
nated in the Arabian desert and to have migrated in very early times into
Babylonia, central Syria and Canaan. The Biblical stories of the migrations of
the Hebrews under the patriarchal leader Abraham are substantially correct.
The Hebrews entered Canaan in small pastoral nomadic groups, occupying first
the open country and then gradually migrating into the towns. About 1700
B.C. a mixed group of people known in general as the Hyksos and including
Hittites, Mitanni and others from Central Asia, swept south into Egypt in a
wave of destruction to that kingdom. Since the invaders passed through Pales-

tine some historians believe that a small group of Hebrews may have entered Egypt during these migrations. Other nomadic Hebrews remained in Asia. Some of the latter crossed the Jordan into Palestine in the period beginning about 1400.

It is reasonably certain that from 1500 to 1200 there were many foreigners in Egypt, including small groups of Hebrews. These Hebrew tribes seem to have prospered under the Eighteenth Dynasty, but the increasingly oppressive forced labor policy of the Nineteenth Dynasty brought about the famous Exodus of the Hebrews under the leadership of Moses and the years of camping in the wilderness before they reached the "promised land" of Canaan.

Rivals to the Hebrews appeared. One group of the "Peoples of the Sea," the later "Philistines," settled in the coastal areas of Palestine at about the same time that the Hebrews were settling in the back country. In order to resist the aggression of the Philistines the Hebrew tribes agreed to submit to the leadership of a king. Although Saul, the first man chosen, lacked the complete support of Israel, he laid the foundation for effective resistance to the Philistines and brought about some unity among the various tribes. His successor, the popular David, in addition to unifying the nation, set up a centralized government with an administrative system under the king's authority. This authority was not personal but, as in the ancient Mesopotamian states, was limited by a higher divinely-established law.

David was followed by his son, the great builder, King Solomon, who perfected the system devised by his father. Wealth and prosperity depended partly upon forced labor and high taxes. Concentrated in the hands of corrupt officials, these two policies resulted in unrest among the lower classes. The brief period of a national Hebrew kingdom under Saul, David and Solomon (1028–933) was made possible by the weakness of the other great powers at this time.

With the passing of the strong Hebrew rulers, in 933 the kingdom split south and north into two parts: Judah and Israel. The importance of the pastoral nomadism of Judah to the south and the commercial wealth combined with social discord within Israel to the north tended toward separatism. Neither Israel nor Judah were able to withstand Assyria. Sargon II conquered northern Palestine in 722–705 and forced the Israelites into exile from their native land. Judah was forced to pay tribute and preserved its independence.

The Assyrians, as we have seen, were themselves defeated by the forces of a new Babylonian monarchy which under Nebuchadrezzar took Jerusalem in 597 B.C. Ten years later Judah revolted. To secure control in this region and in revenge against the Hebrews the Babylonians destroyed Jerusalem and took into captivity the peoples of Judah.

The great historic contribution of the Hebrew people lies in their concepts of human life and their religious tradition rather than in their political organization. The democratic ideal of living found in Hebrew thinking goes back to the nomadic times in which social solidarity was present but not as important as freedom of individual action. In the desert each individual was important, and along with this went an elementary sense of justice which outweighed all other virtues. In the early Hebrew nomadic society land was regarded as "ultimately inalienable"; thus tribal rather than private rights were emphasized and served as a check on patriarchal authority. In the development of their laws, the Hebrews borrowed from the peoples around them and adapted these laws to suit their own specific needs. Their own lawmakers were mainly religious leaders of high moral purpose. These priests and prophets developed a moral and religious code whose purpose was one of social and moral improvement for all. This is emphasized in the Hebrew concept of one universal law. The ruler himself was thereby denied the absolute powers usually found in early monarchies. The traditions of freedom inherent in a nomadic life are not only very apparent in Hebrew law, but also appear in the development of the idea of a personal or tribal god.

In the early society of the Hebrews the tribal group, rather than the ruler of a state, had its own relationship with a particular god. The tribe entered into an agreement, or covenant, with their god whereby the deity in return for their obedience, would devote himself to them. From the early practice of tribal covenants grew a fundamental factor of importance regarding the development of Israel as a nation. This was the replacement of the individual tribal covenant with "a national pact between God and His people." In the time of David the god of the Hebrews, Yahweh, came to be considered a national god. This change did not alter the Hebrew concept of God as a very personal deity who was always near at hand, and who could be questioned by his covenanters.

In spite of some resemblances to the Babylonian god Marduk it is to be noted that Yahweh, the god of the Hebrews, was the center of a religion whose moral and spiritual aspects were more important than Mesopotamian values from very early times. The moral tradition of the Hebrews which is found in the Ten Commandments was later supplemented by the religious concepts preached by the prophets, men of high purpose and keen imagination who found a hearing in times of stress. They were intensely nationalistic and protested against idolatry and alien cults as well as against the luxuries and vices of city life. The prophets preached spiritual obedience to the law; the equality of all before the Covenant and in God's sight; and put emphasis on just and righteous behavior. With these as universals, the worship of Yahweh was thought of as a religion for all mankind instead of as merely a tribal religion.

On the other hand during the Babylonian Exile a feeling of separateness and superiority arose among the Hebrews. Special laws regulating their daily lives became more elaborate. This development represented a strenuous effort on the part of the Hebrew religious leaders to preserve the identity of their people while in exile. This intense exclusiveness on the part of the Hebrews was later to clash violently with the spread of Greek influences following Alexander the Great's conquest of Syria and the subsequent attempts to Hellenize the area. Attempts to overcome the social and religious nonconformity of the Jews were not successful and served only to unite the discordant elements among the

Hebrews against the Greeks. As a protest against Hellenism the Hebrews moved further toward racial isolation. This exclusiveness was in contrast to the cosmopolitanism of other religions and peoples during this same period.

ARAMEANS. A people who have been noted for their cosmopolitanism and who, in their origins, were not much different from the Hebrews were the Arameans. They appeared in the fourteenth century B.C. as a Semitic group of nomads whose migrations probably started from the highland region of inner Arabia. They undoubtedly had many tribal names during this period, and it was probably not until 1100 that the name "Aramean" was used. In the thirteenth century Arameans entered the regions of Mesopotamia and Syria and by the eleventh century they had established important trading centers in Syria and the upper Euphrates. In the tenth century, during a period of Assyrian weakness, strong Aramean principalities in Syria, of which the most powerful was Damascus, dominated the caravan route across the desert between Egypt and Babylon which gave them control over the inland trade. Upon the revival of Assyrian power in the ninth century a coalition of Aramean cities successfully defended Syria for many years. But the Assyrian policy of defeating the cities piecemeal finally ended Aramean domination in Syria. Damascus, the most powerful city, fell in 732 B.C.

As in the case of their racial kinsmen, the Hebrews, the greatness of the Arameans is not found in political or military power. They are famous for their language, which spread throughout Western Asia. Aramaic was a more flexible medium of communication than either Hebrew or Arabic, and its simplicity of construction and easier script gave it a decided advantage over Assyrian. This language was introduced into north Syria along with Assyrian political domination, and from the eighth century on it may be referred to as the "official Aramaic" of the Assyrian Empire. The destruction of the Aramean states furthered its spread as an international language because it was then separated from any exclusive connection with one people or religion.

From the tenth to the fourth century B.C. the Arameans enjoyed the position in land trade that the Phoenicians had on the sea. Their control of the cities along the Euphrates trade route, as well as a great talent for commerce gave them a commercial pre-eminence which lasted well beyond their political span of life. Their trading activities also served to spread the Aramaic language which maintained its supremacy against Hellenism, and was not displaced as a common tongue until the Moslem conquest.

PHOENICIANS. Another famous trading people were the Phoenicians. At the eastern end of the Mediterranean, hemmed in between the mountains and the sea, Tyre, Sidon and some other coastal towns constituted the tiny country of Phoenicia. The people were of Semitic origin and their language differed little from Canaanite and later Hebrew. Connections with Egypt were important and during several periods in early historic times the Phoenician cities were subject to Egyptian rule.

Men of initiative and practical ability, the Phoenicians were quick to adopt the inventions of other nations for their own use. Among the greatest of their adoptions was the idea of phonetic writing. The Phoenicians used what had been developed by their neighbors to evolve a short series of symbols or a limited number of letters. The use of this alphabet by the Phoenician traders caused it to be widely accepted and from this were derived the principal ancient and modern alphabets of the western world.

The Phoenicians at an early date demonstrated their ability to engage in commerce. Their opportunities were greatly enlarged after the fall of Crete in 1200 B.C. to the "Peoples of the Sea." Then the Phoenicians traded throughout the Mediterranean and beyond. Their colonies in Cyprus, Rhodes, Crete and later as far away as Spain, served to relieve the population pressure of the Phoenician mainland and were important trading centers. Land trade flourished also and the Phoenicians became middlemen for that part of the world.

The Phoenician city-states meanwhile carried on a series of struggles to maintain their independence against the great land empires which from the ninth century onward succeeded one another as the dominant powers of Southwest Asia. The Assyrians and Babylonians gained the submission of Tyre and Sidon only after long and bitter sieges. When the Achaemenian Persians built up their empire the Phoenician cities prospered as vassal states. The Macedonian Alexander the Great repeated the earlier process, however, and insisted upon complete control, which was obtained only after Tyre had withstood a ten months' siege. The inability of the Phoenicians to maintain their status as independent trading cities in the face of the overwhelming forces of imperial armies is a phenomenon to be noted in both the commercial and political development of Asia.

ARMENIANS. In Armenia a high degree of culture commenced with the "Kingdom of Van." Later Armenians who had come from Thrace and had long been living in Asia Minor came into the region. The Armenians are mentioned for the first time on the great rock inscription of the Persian emperor Darius at Behistun in the Zagros mountains. Hence it is believed that by this time the Armenians had supplanted the Khaldians of Van.

During the time when the Iranian empires of the Medes and Persians dominated this part of the world the Armenians served as allies and vassals. The Achaemenian emperors depended upon them both for troops and for horses. Alexander and the Greeks never completely conquered the Armenians although the local princes were forced to pay tribute, and commerce with the Greeks brought new cultural influences into the country. Not until much later, after the Seleucid forces had been defeated at Magnesia in Asia Minor by the Romans in 190 B.C., did the Armenians establish strong independent kingdoms of their own.

HITTITES. In the rugged plateau peninsula of Asia Minor in ancient times the leading people were the Hittites. Their capital city, Hattusas, was in an easily defensible highland stronghold about 100 miles east of modern Ankara. From there in the time of the first Babylonian empire they dominated an area including most of Asia Minor and extending to the upper Euphrates Valley.

The king of the Hittites seems in earliest times to have been limited by the power of the nobles. Later his power was more nearly absolute and included military, judicial and religious supremacy among his people. The king personally officiated as general and priest, but he was not considered a god as were the pharaohs of Egypt.

The state depended for support upon a privileged court nobility and vassal princes in outlying area. Although agriculture predominated among the people, the Hittites' exploitation of metals found in Asia Minor was the basis for much of their power and wealth. These metals included silver, copper and particularly iron. The technique of iron-working was first mastered by the Hittites but its use did not become general until later.

Strong political organization and skill in fighting led to survival of the Hittite kingdom for a period of centuries. Much of their culture came from their association with Mesopotamia. An event of importance in their relations with the states to the south was the Hittite invasion of Mesopotamia in about 1600 which resulted in the end of the First Babylonian Dynasty.

For a time the power of the Hittites was challenged by the emergence of an Indo-European dynasty, the Mitanni, in the area of modern Aleppo. The leadership of a Hittite king Suppiluliumas (1375–1335 B.C.), marked the beginning of a period known as the "New Kingdom." Suppiluliumas consolidated his own position and then set about settling accounts with the Mitanni. From them he conquered Carchemish and Syria from the Euphrates to the sea became a Hittite dependency. After a long period of peace, during which the Hittites strengthened their hold on Syria, Ramses II of Egypt attempted to revive the colonial empire of the Eighteenth Dynasty, but in this he was unsuccessful, and was defeated by the Hittites in 1289 B.C. at the battle of Kadesh. This was followed by a period of Egyptian-Hittite rapprochement probably brought about by the rising power of Assyria. Within a hundred years, however, the Hittite kingdom ceased to exist. This collapse was part of the sweeping changes in the eastern Mediterranean caused by migrations of the "Peoples of the Sea." To judge from the legend of Homer, Phrygians soon took the place of the Hittites in Asia Minor.

In art the Hittites borrowed many subjects from Syria. Egyptian influence can be seen in the human-headed sphinxes found at Hattusas and in the winged sun-disc over the head of every Hittite king. The Hittites produced animal figures in bronze and gold, cylinder seals of great skill and under the New Kingdom, monumental bas-reliefs in stone. The traditional winged monsters of the Hittites seem to have influenced Assyrian and Persian art.

The strength of their army lay in the Hittites' intensive development of a new weapon, the light horse-drawn chariot which appeared in Western Asia after 1600 B.C. This invention created a revolution in the nature of warfare, and from this time on speed and space to maneuver became determining factors in battle.

IRANIANS.   From very early prehistoric times men have been living on the Iranian plateau. The ancestry of these early inhabitants is not definitely known, but by the fifth millenium B.C. they had, in addition to hunting, extended their activities to agriculture and stock breeding. Further advances in civilization were made throughout the fourth millenium when tools and modes of living underwent changes involving inventiveness and a greater degree of skill. These changes were due in part to the fact that ideas and peoples circulated in and through Iran from very early times because of that region's intermediary position between East and West.

From the beginning of the third millenium B.C., there emerged in Khuzistan, the southwest part of Iran, the state of Elam, which because of its geographical position showed signs of strong Mesopotamian influence. Elam, with its capital of Susa, enjoyed a brief span of independence and power before it was overcome by the Akkadians.

The early "Iranians" were an Indo-European speaking group of people who appear in Western Asia during the second millenium B.C. Racially there may have been a connection between the early peoples of Mesopotamia, already mentioned, and the Iranians, who came later into Southwest Asia. The latter probably came to the Iranian plateau from the Eurasian plains of southern Russia and brought with them horses, hitherto unknown in the Mesopotamian area. The penetration of these people into Western Asia became more pronounced at the beginning of the first millennium B.C., when new waves of invaders absorbed the local population and finally, after several centuries became masters of the Iranian plateau. Here many cultural changes took place. These nomadic horsemen, hitherto only concerned with flocks and herds, also became interested in agriculture and developed an irrigation system of underground canals called *qanats*. Wooden houses and tents were used for living quarters. The Iranians made pottery decorated with horse and sum designs for domestic and ritual uses. About 1500 B.C. Iran's rich deposits of iron ore began to be developed.

The earliest Iranians appear to have been nature worshippers who regarded the heavens, fire, wind and rain as divine; darkness and drought were evil. For a long period they had shared a common religion and culture with the Aryans of India, who had similar legends and terms used for the gods. In Iran *ahura* represented the gods, *deva*, the demons; however, in India the deva were superior beings and the ahura were demoniac. Evil spirits in Iran had to be overcome by the good spirits who depended on man's sacrifices and prayers for their success. At the head of the Iranian pantheon stood *Ahura* ("Lord") or *Mazda* ("Wise") and in time both these manifestations of the supreme being were combined to form *Ahura-Mazda*, the "Wise Lord."

Second only to Ahura-Mazda was Mithra, a god of the open air, who was connected with the sun, pastures and justice in some of his manifestations. Mithra also appears as the god of war, and sacrifices were made to him to appease the evil side of his nature. Fire played an important part in the ritual practices of the Iranians, who worshipped their gods without temples or altars, and who made their sacrifices and lit their sacred fires on bare mountains.

Not much is known about the history of the Iranians prior to the Assyrian empire. But in the annals of the Assyrian ruler Shalmaneser III we learn of tribute being received from the local rulers residing near Lake Urmia. The Assyrian campaigns from 1100–674 within the western half of the Iranian plateau prove that there was no organized power to oppose them effectively and that the entire area must have paid tribute when Assyria was strong. It may be assumed that Assyrian influence permeated Iran and that it was less strong in the more remote parts of the country. Some of the Medes were subject to Assyria, while other tribes' resistance or acquiescence to Assyrian domination depended upon the momentary strength of that power. The expansion of the Assyrian Empire led to conflict with Elam over the control of Babylonia and constant intervention in the neighboring Iranian plateau. Under Sargon II (722–705) Media became the battle area. The Assyrian king captured thousands of prisoners and horses. The latter were important for the Assyrians as cavalry remounts and when in the seventh century B.C. new invaders, the Scythians, appeared, they proved to be particularly troublesome to the Assyrians because they interfered with the supply of horses in Media.

The Scythian and Cimmerian invasions caused serious disturbances in northwest Iran. The invaders came as plundering hordes of mounted warriors sweeping in from the steppe. The people of the Iranian plateau, being closest to Central Asia, were perpetually aware of the struggle between the nomad and the tiller of the soil. The *Turan* or enemy from the north became a symbol of all that was barbaric.

The Iranian Empire

Early in his reign the Median ruler Cyaxares (625–593) attempted to take the Assyrian city of Nineveh. Just at the moment when his efforts appeared to be successful, a horde of Scythians descended upon Media, forcing Cyaxares to abandon his siege of Nineveh and return to defend his own territory. He was defeated and the Scythians quickly overran Media. Encouraged by their success, they attacked Assyria and also devastated Asia Minor. The years of Scythian domination were not wasted by Cyaxares. He reorganized his army and incorporated many Scythian methods of warfare, such as the use of bows and arrows and the tactics of the Scythian horsemen. Cyaxares developed three classes of mobile troops: spearmen, bowmen and cavalrymen. After defeating the Scythians with their own weapons, and having made himself master of the western portion of the Iranian plateau, Cyaxares, allied with the Babylonians, turned on Assyria and put an end to the power of that country. During the next few years Cyaxares fought the armies of Lydia without decisive result until an eclipse of the sun during a battle brought the war to an end, and the boundary between Media and Lydia was fixed at the Halys River. With the exception of Lydia, all of Western Asia was now divided between the Median and Chaldean empires.

CYRUS.   Foreseeing the Median threat to his kingdom, the Chaldean king entered into an alliance with Cyrus the Great (550–530) ruler of a powerful new kingdom which had appeared in Parsa (or Persia), now known as Fars. The alliance between Cyrus and the Chaldeans soon led to a hard-fought struggle with the Medes, who were overcome in 550. Cyrus was aided in his conquest of Media by the unpopularity of the Median ruler, who, when attacked by the Persians, was surrendered by his own people. Cyrus united Persia and Media under his rule to form the nucleus of a new and powerful empire, that of the Achaemenid (or Achaemenian) Persians.

After the defeat of Media, Cyrus embarked upon a campaign to subdue Lydia and the wealthy Greek cities on the coast of Asia Minor. He completed this conquest in 546, and then turned to the east, where he conquered an area that extended to the Indus River. Returning from this campaign, Cyrus turned upon his former Babylonian allies. Their capital fell without resistance, and Cyrus, presenting himself to the Babylonians as a liberator rather than a conqueror, took the title "King of Babylon."

Upon the death of Cyrus, his son and heir Cambyses (530–522) was left to carry out an expedition against Egypt which had been planned by the former. In this he was successful, but he failed in his plans to extend Persian hegemony still further in Africa, over Carthage, Ammon and Ethiopia. On his way back to Persia from Egypt, Cambyses learned of a revolt led by a pretender to the throne and either committed suicide or fatally wounded himself during the course of an epileptic fit.

DARIUS.   The army remained loyal to his successor, Darius I (521–485). After executing the pretender to the throne and putting down a series of revolts in all parts of the empire, Darius was able to unify the empire consolidated by Cyrus and thus to bring about a peace which lasted for two centuries. He showed a great genius for organization in addition to being a skillful warrior. Even his enemies had respect for him and it is a tribute to his organizing ability that the empire lasted unbroken through many generations until the conquest of Alexander.

The Achaemenian administrative organization was a benevolent despotism, uniform and orderly, and so well established that it continued to function even under weak rulers. The country was divided into twenty satrapies with civil and

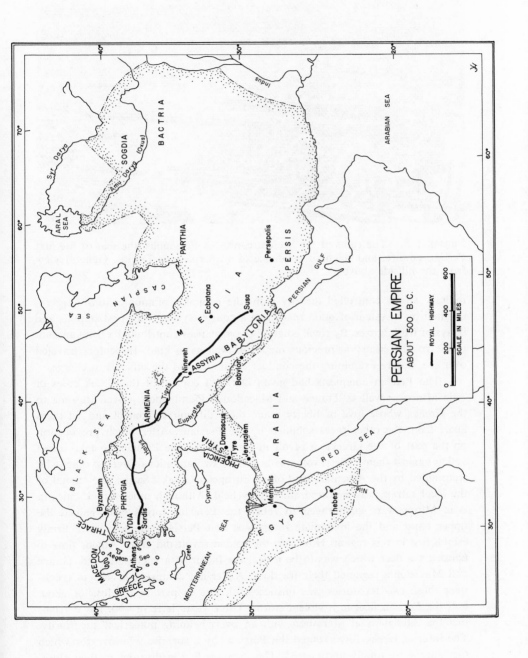

PERSIAN EMPIRE
ABOUT 500 B.C.

— ROYAL HIGHWAY

SCALE IN MILES
0   200   400   600

FIGURE 3.5.   The ruins of the ancient capital at Persepolis, the seat of the first
Persian empire, and splendid residence of such rulers as Darius. General view
from the hillside above.

military affairs controlled directly from the capital. Communications were facilitated by a system of good roads and a courier system with post-stations and
relays of fresh horses. By royal edict all the provinces contributed a fixed amount
to the royal treasury in precious metals as well as in kind. Inspectors traveled
over the empire examining the conduct of affairs and the officials in charge.

The Persian conquests had given Darius I control of the Greek cities of
Asia Minor as well as Thrace and Macedonia. Domination proved irksome to
the Greeks whose love of liberty made them difficult to control and set them
apart from the other races subdued by the Persians. After much provocation
on the part of the Greeks, a revolt in Ionia forced the Persians to take direct
action against them. The revolt was begun by two ambitious Greek tyrants who
were aided by the Athenians and other European Greeks. Sardis, the capital of
the local satrap, was captured and briefly held. Although other Greek cities in
Asia Minor were encouraged to rebel, the Persians forces soon gained the
upper hand and the immediate result was that Persian rule was more firmly
established in this region. However, the Ionian revolt did allow Athens time to
construct a fleet which was to be a decisive factor at a later date, and Thrace
and Macedonia regained their freedom. A Persian campaign in 493 to recon-
quer these two territories was unsuccessful, due in part to the loss of about
half the Persian fleet in a violent storm. Three years later in 490, the Persians
met the Athenians at Marathon with an overwhelming numerical superiority.
The inferior Greek force routed the Persians by a surprise offensive for which
the latter were totally unprepared. The Persians fled in disorder to their ships.
Few battles in history have had greater moral significance by instilling self-
confidence into the Greek mind. Until then the might of Persia had been
irresistible.

Under Xerxes, one of the greatest expeditions of ancient times was gathered together for the purpose of defeating Hellas. At first the Persians were successful, defeating the Greeks at Thermopylae and capturing Athens; but beginning in 480 the Persians suffered a series of defeats at Salamis, Plataea, Mycale and Sestos. The size of the Persian force, its remoteness from its source of supplies, the bitter hostility the Persians had aroused in the Greeks, the use of heavier weapons and armor by the Greeks and the inability of the Persians to use their cavalry to its maximum effectiveness due to the terrain all contributed to the Greek victory. Another factor was the feeble character of Xerxes, who fled to Asia, and during the remainder of his reign refused to face the problem of Hellas, other than to supplement Persian diplomacy with gold. Thanks to the weakness of Xerxes, most of the Greek settlements in Asia Minor gained a greater degree of liberty.

During this period some Greek influence penetrated the western portions of the Persian Empire with the spread of the Greek language, art, sculpture, literature and coins. At the same time the culture of Persia was built firmly upon Iranian tradition and the civilization of Mesopotamia and Egypt. This is evidenced by the great palace of Persepolis, from the bas-reliefs and inscriptions of which we obtain a first hand account of the Persian ideas of government.

ZOROASTRIANISM.   The religion of the Achaemenid Persians developed from that of the early Iranians. It was polytheistic but developed a strong trend in the direction of the worship of one god, Ahura-Mazda. The great religious prophet of Iranian religion was Zoroaster, a contemporary of Cyrus the Great. Zoroaster converted a local ruler in northern Iran (Parthia) about 550 B.C. This ruler became a satrap under Darius and by the time of the last Achaemenid ruler Zoroastrianism, as the worship of Ahura-Mazda came to be known, was the leading religion of the Iranian aristocracy. Zoroaster was considered divine. In the Zoroastrian view this world is very real and man is set in its center to serve as redeemer and perfecter. Zoroaster saw life as a ceaseless struggle between the forces of good personified in Ahura-Mazda, and the forces of evil personified in Ahriman. This concept of dualism, the constant battle between good and evil in all spheres of life, remained the salient feature of religious thought in Iran. The worship of Mithra also constituted a part of the Zoroastrian religion. Despite its dualistic character Zoroastrianism has been called an imperfect monotheism which in its ethical precepts was at that time almost as advanced as Judaism. Zoroastrianism did not manifest itself in the building of great temples. The use of simple open air altars, the lighting of fires and animal sacrifices formed the principal rituals.

The Greeks

Until the fourth century B.C. Southwest Asia had developed from centers within itself. Religion, politics and social custom originated mainly in Mesopo-

tamia, Iran and adjoining regions of Asia. The peoples within the great Achaemenian Empire were only slightly influenced by their European neighbors in
Hellas (Greece). Suddenly they found themselves under Greek domination and
this period, though short, was to be of vast significance in the centuries to
come because it interjected a new influence into the life of Asia.

The creation of a new strong state which might rival the Persian empire
was begun by Philip of Macedonia. Philip combined military force with political
genius and made himself master of Greece. His son Alexander, who was brought
up in the Greek cultural tradition, carried on his father's work and in a period
of 13 years (336–323 B.C.) conquered the Achaemenid Persian empire.

ALEXANDER.   Although Persia had revealed military weakness during the preceding period, the great Achaemenian empire was still intact and controlled vast
resources. Alexander's conquest was by no means an easy one. His army was a
relatively small group for the magnitude of his undertaking and probably consisted of about 30,000 infantry and 5,000 cavalry. It was a well trained army,
however, whose morale was high from a succession of victories and its training
and equipment were in advance of anything yet seen in that part of the world.

In his Asiatic campaigns Alexander first gained control of Asia Minor and
Syria. Later he moved south against the cities of Phoenicia. Most of these surrendered. Tyre's resistance ended only after a long siege and in retaliation
Alexander acted more severely than usual. Destruction of the city was complete;
the entire population was put to the sword or sold into slavery. Alexander next
advanced on Egypt in 331. He encountered little resistance and was acclaimed
by the people who resented the oppressive policies of the Persian satrap. While
in Egypt he visited the oasis of Ammon and there was hailed as divine. With
this occasion began the association of divinity and kingship which gradually
permeated the Greek world.

From Egypt Alexander went east to conquer Mesopotamia and Iran. He
was welcomed in Babylon. In Iran the king, Darius III, engaged in battle but
fled before he was really defeated. At Susa Alexander sat on the royal throne
and was proclaimed "King of Asia." By his personality and by his conduct,
Alexander rallied many Persians to his support.

During the next few years Alexander continued his conquest of eastern
Iran and in the spring of 327 he crossed the Hindu Kush and entered India
where he extended his frontiers to an Eastern tributary of the Indus river (see
Chapter 9). A refusal to march further on the part of his troops forced him to
return to Susa. Alexander's empire, now larger than the conquered Persian
Empire, extended from the Balkans to the Indus river and from the Caucasus
Mountains to the cataracts of the Nile. Greek garrisons were established across
the land from Alexandria in Egypt to the trading centers of central Asia.

With Alexander fusion of Greek and Persian culture was a definite policy
for the maintenance of the peace upon which he depended. Considering himself
a successor of the Achaemenians, Alexander paid honor to the epitaph of

Cyrus, he married the daughter of Darius III, held spectacles and lavish entertainment, bestowed noble Persian women upon his friends and in general adopted the ideas of monarchy then prevalent in Iran. He introduced the custom of prostration before the king which was not popular with his Greek followers. Also unpopular with the Macedonians was his adoption of many Persian court ceremonies. At the same time Alexander saw the dangers inherent in a luxurious mode of life and insisted that his generals go on long marches and hunting expeditions to counteract this tendency.

During the last few months of his life, Alexander spent much time on the organization of his empire. He infused broader and more humane principles and ideas into the methods of the Achaemenian kings. He continued the division of the empire into satrapies, utilizing Persian as well as Macedonian satraps. He adopted the policy of relying on the conquered people to help him govern this vast area and in doing so won a certain amount of loyalty from them because of his desire to govern in their interest as well as in that of the Greeks. Alexander's ambition was to link the east and the west. Unfortunately his lifetime was too short to achieve this aim and upon his death in 323 B.C. his vast empire at once began to crumble.

SUCCESSOR STATES OF ALEXANDER.   At the death of Alexander his generals, the Diadochi, fought and divided his empire. During the next 40 years his former companions engaged in murderous struggles. Alexander's concept of one political unit was abandoned, but we must note that many parts of the empire remained Greek. By 301 B.C. the situation was stabilized with the formation of three kingdoms: the Ptolemaic monarchy in Egypt, the Macedonian monarchy in Europe and the Seleucid monarchy in Asia. The latter was the most important since it included most of the Fertile Crescent, Persia and the eastern satrapies.

The kingdom of the Seleucids was founded by Seleucus I Nicator in 305 B.C. He attempted to maintain Greek authority as far east as the Indus valley but was there checked in battle by the founder of another Asian dynasty of prime importance, the Maurya emperor Chandragupta, who had just unified northern India for the first time in its history. Seleucus I and his successors waged continual warfare against the Ptolemies of Egypt for control of Syria and access to the Mediterranean.

In the second century B.C. Rome, a new Mediterranean power, threatened their position. Antiochus III, the Great (223–187 B.C.) was able to extend Seleucid authority both east and west. But in the year 190 a Roman army under Lucius Scipio and his brother Africanus crossed the Hellespont to enter Asia Minor and there defeated Antiochus in the battle of Magnesia. This was the beginning of Roman power on the continent of Asia. During the following years and until the rise of Parthia the Seleucid kingdom was the chief obstacle to the growing eastern influence of Rome.

Within their own territory the Seleucids were confronted with separatist tendencies. Among the regions which broke away to form independent states were Armenia and three in Asia Minor: Pergamum in the extreme west, Pontus in the old center of Hittite power, and Bithynia.

In northeastern Iran and beyond, in Central Asia, Seleucid authority was difficult to maintain. The satrapy of Bactria included territory extending north of the Amu Darya (Oxus) and south into modern Afghanistan. Its geographical position was important because of the transit trade which linked Iran, India, Siberia and China through this region. Alexander had left a garrison of 20,000 men to guard Bactria. By the time of the Seleucids the satrap became independent in all but name and from about 250 B.C. we may date the formation of an independent Greek kingdom in this region. In this, the most advanced Hellenic post toward the east, the Greeks of Bactria and the Iranians over whom they ruled continued Greek cultural traditions and transmitted Greek influences to the world of Buddhism in India, Central Asia and beyond.

The satrapy of Parthia (modern Khorasan) was invaded by horsemen from the steppes to the north and the region was lost to Seleucid control at about the same time as Bactria. But, as we shall see in the next chapter, Greek as well as Iranian influences continued strong even among the newcomers.

HELLENISM. The greatest of Alexander's accomplishments was the diffusion of Hellenism throughout Western Asia. Greek culture had penetrated Asia Minor before Alexander's conquests but under Alexander the Greeks became the dominant element as far east as India. Under the Seleucids Hellenism became firmly established.

In Alexander's attempt to unite the cultures of East and West one of his principal means was the foundation of cities on the Hellenistic model. He established them everywhere he went, from Alexandria, Egypt, to the interior of Bactria. These towns were garrisoned by Alexander's soldiers and settlers were brought from Greece itself. In Iran the way of life demonstrated in the towns by Greeks and Macedonians served to attract and influence many Iranians. Those who entered into the life of these centers of Greek culture were from the upper and middle classes of Persians; lower class and country people were little affected. As a result of the Persian element in the political and administrative setup of the empire, there developed a mixed society.

Commerce and a revival of prosperity came as a result of Alexander's building of towns and of roads and canals to connect them. As trade increased merchants and their wares penetrated to the more distant corners of the empire. Troops and traders spread the Greek language. Greek replaced Aramaic as the language of government and business. Many of the people who inhabited the Iranian plateau became bi-lingual and the urban population kept the use of Greek long after the fall of the Seleucid empire. The Greek tradition in Iran was to be an important element in the Parthian empire.

The effects of Hellenism differed greatly from one region to another. In Asia Minor commercial, artistic and political opportunities drew many immigrants from Greece. Greek forms of art and literature flourished and deeply affected the region for centuries to come.

In many regions the majority of the population continued in long accustomed ways, with the worship of their own gods, and speaking in their own tongues. In Iran, as noted above, there was much Greek influence, yet Zoroastrian Mazdaism had its adherents especially among the princes of Fars. In Palestine the Hebrews resisted vigorously. Seleucid attempts to enforce Jewish worship of Greek gods were unsuccessful and served only to strengthen anti-Greek feeling and the Jews' religious and racial isolation. The cosmopolitan character of Hellenistic civilization remained foreign to the greater part of the populations of Western Asia.

A fusion of culture did take place, however. Hellenism was important in all the regions of Southwest Asia and on the other hand the Hellenic world from this time on had incorporated within it political and religious concepts which had originated in Asia.

BASIC DATES

C. 2800–2200 B.C.	Sumer and Akkad
C. 1800–1600 B.C.	First Babylonian empire
C. 1200–606 B.C.	Assyrian empire
625–538 B.C.	Chaldean empire
C. 1750–1200 B.C.	Hittite kingdoms
C. 1200–933 B.C.	Hebrews in Palestine
933 B.C.	Split into Israel and Judea
722 B.C.	Israel conquered by Assyria
586 B.C.	Judea conquered by Chaldeans
12th century and after	Phoenicians
C. 600–330 B.C.	Achaemenid Persians
550–530 B.C.	Cyrus the Great
530–522 B.C.	Cambyses
521–486 B.C.	Darius I
486–465 B.C.	Xerxes I
336–323 B.C.	Alexander the Great
330 B.C.	Macedonian conquest of Iran
327–325 B.C.	Macedonian invasion of Punjab
305–129 B.C.	Seleucids

SUPPLEMENTARY READING

CHILDE, V. G., *What Happened in History*. London, 1952. An excellent paperback raising important questions about the earliest activities of man.

————*New Light on the Most Ancient East*. New York, 1934. Deals specifically with Mesopotamia.

FINEGAN, F. *Light From the Ancient Past*. Princeton, N. J., 1959.

GROUSSET, R. *Civilizations of the East, Vol. I: The Near and Middle East*. New York, 1934. A general cultural survey.

HITTI, P. *The Near East in History*. Princeton, N. J., 1961. A recent, solid text.

LAISTNER, M. L. W. *A Survey of Ancient History*. Boston, 1929.

MOSCATI, S. *The Face of the Ancient Orient*. London, 1961. A fascinating analysis of the early empires of the Near East.

SANFORD, E. M. *The Mediterranean World in Ancient Times*. New York, 1938. A standard, thorough text.

ADVANCED READING

BEVAN, E. R. *The House of Seleucus*. London, 1902. The standard work.

BUDGE, E. *Babylonian Life and History*. London, 1886.

FRANKFORT, H. *The Birth of Civilization in the Near East*. Bloomington, 1951. A series of essays, posing some fundamental questions; by a famous French scholar.

GHIRSHMAN, R. *Iran*. London, 1954. A paperback which includes the archaeology of early Persia.

GOODSPEED, G. S. *History of the Babylonians and Assyrians*. New York, 1902.

GURNEY, O. R. *The Hittites*. London, 1952.

HUART, C. *Ancient Persia and Iranian Civilization*. New York, 1927. Especially interesting for the study of religious developments.

JOHNS, C. H. W. *Ancient Babylonia*. New York, 1913.

KRAMER, S. *History Begins at Sumer*. Garden City, N. Y., 1959. A paperback dealing with the daily activities of the people of Sumer; by a leading authority.

MC COWN, C. C. *The Genesis of the Social Gospel*. New York, 1929.

OLMSTEAD, A. T. *History of Assyria*. New York, 1923.

————*History of the Persian Empire*. Chicago, 1948.

————*History of Palestine and Syria to the Macedonian Conquest*. New York, 1931. Three good studies, especially the first two, by an American historian.

ORLINSKY, H. M. *Ancient Israel*. Ithaca, N.Y., 1954. History of the Hebrews to 400 B.C.

ROGERS, R. W. *A History of Babylonia and Assyria*. New York, 1915.

SMITH, S. *Early History of Assyria to 1000 B.C.* London, 1928.

SPEISER, E. A. "The Ancient Near East and Modern Philosophies of History," *Proceedings of the American Philosophical Society*, XCV, No. 6 (December 1951), pp. 583–588.

SYKES, P. *A History of Persia*. Oxford, 1915.

————*Persia*. Oxford, 1922. An abbreviated version of the former.

IV ❈

PARTHIANS, ROMANS,

AND SASSANIANS

During the period following Alexander and the various Greek successor states Iran is the focus of importance in Southwest Asia. Neither Mesopotamia, Arabia nor Turkey figured so prominently and hence, for a period of some 800 years, the history of the area may be simplified by following events in Iran and the relationship of other happenings to them. The period from the third century B.C. up to the seventh century of our era may be conveniently divided into two dynasties: the Parthians, or Arsacids, and the Sassanians. While the main emphasis is on these two Iranian empires, it should also be noted that three other factors were present in Western Asia at this time, factors which are important in themselves as well as in relation to Iran: the Roman empire which throughout this period was an Asiatic power; the steppe peoples of Central Asia; the rise and spread of Christianity.

Among the factors which brought Iran into contact with neighboring peoples and more remote countries during this time were the processes of trade. As we shall see in studying the details of the dynastic periods covered in this chapter, Iran's role in international trade was a central one inasmuch as this country was in a key position among the states of Europe and Asia.

A dominant note throughout this pre-Moslem history of southwest Asia is the Iranian religion. Zoroastrianism took shape during this time and later, after the Moslem conquest, it was to provide a link with the past.

49

The Parthian Empire

The Parthians were Iranians who came originally from the steppes of Central Asia. Recent excavations have shown that their patriarchal nomadic or semi-settled society centered around a noble class which owned slaves and cattle. The dynasty takes its name, Arsacid, from Arsaces I who made himself independent of the Seleucids in about 250 B.C. In the area which already in Greek times had been known as Parthia, Arsaces founded an independent kingdom.

The successors of Arsaces revived the Achaemenian title of "the Great King" or "King of Kings." Meanwhile the Seleucids were still powerful and the Parthians were forced to fight for their existence both against the Greek power in the west and against nomadic tribes in the north. One of the more important Parthian kings was Mithridates I (171–138) who expanded Parthian territory and made it a genuine empire. He extended the frontiers westward into Mesopotamia and to the east of Persia into the Punjab of India. To the northeast his frontiers extended to Merv. Phraates II (138–124) expanded the state all the way to the Euphrates. In his time he had to meet the invasion of Scythians (Sakas) from the northeast. His successor Mithridates II "the Great" (124–88) definitely checked the Scythian threat, defeated Armenians and came into contact with the new growing power of Rome.

Wars against the Romans were an important element in the Parthian period. The two empires competed for control in Mesopotamia and Armenia. Famous in the annals of the Parthians was the Emperor Orodes (57–37) whose forces defeated those of the Roman Triumvir, Crassus, at Carrhae in the Mesopotamian desert (53 B.C.). The strength of the Parthian kingdom in Iran is notable in a time when Rome was attaining supremacy in the Mediterranean world. The Romans were defeated on more than one occasion and, during periods of uneasy truce, they were forced to recognize some degree of equality of the Parthian state with themselves.

Arsacid power, however, did not remain unified during the latter centuries of the dynasty. The empire, with its capital at Ctesiphon on the Tigris, was faced with a political cleavage when a group of Parthians (or Pahlavas) made themselves independent in eastern Iran about 30 B.C. Dependence upon the local nobility for men to resist the nomadic invasions from the steppes promoted a system of feudal satraps governing in a semi-independent manner and whose position tended to become hereditary, thus weakening the central authority of the state.

In the first 150 years of the Christian era the Parthian government was not only harassed by nomadic attacks from the north, but also torn by wars between rival candidates for the throne. Both of these factors facilitated the expansion of the Roman empire in Asia.

A period of unification came with the reign of Vologases III (A.D. 147–191). Although the Parthian state was strengthened it was not the equal of imperial Rome. The armies of Marcus Aurelius sacked and burned the Parthian

FIGURE 4.1. The great arch of Ctesiphon, south of Baghdad, is all that remains of the Parthian empire.

capital and for a time controlled both Armenia and Mesopotamia. The Arsacid dynasty finally ended when an Iranian revolt succeeded in the area of Persis and when Ardashir seized and killed the last Arsacid, Artabanus V, at Hormuz, 226.

In their culture the Parthians continued both the traditions of Achaemenian Iran and of the Greeks. The term "Philhellene" (Friend of the Greeks) was used on their coins. Greek manners were fashionable at the court. The Emperor Orodes was actually listening to a play written by the famous Greek dramatist Euripides when the news came of the victory over the Romans at Carrhae and when he received the head of Crassus.

Hellenism continued but Iranian cultural traditions gradually became predominant. Old Aryan cults persisted, including the widespread worship of the goddess Anahita. Mazdaism continued, especially in Persis. According to tradition a first century Parthian king collected Zoroastrian texts and from these the oldest section of the *Avesta*, the "Gathas," may have taken definite written form. There is some reason to believe that ideas which were definitely derived from the Greeks were incorporated into Zoroastrian writings at this time. There is also strong evidence that all the Zoroastrian writings may have been written down later, during the Sassanian period.

It was through the Parthians that the later Sassanians acquired and adopted some of the main features of Persian Achaemenian art. Parthian sculpture shows definite Greek influence plus a tendency to present their Hellenic themes in peculiarly Parthian form. They stressed elongation of figures, stylization of garments and all bas-relief figures were shown in the front view. There was a deterioration of technique in the attempt to revive the older tradition.

FIGURE 4.2. Bronze statue of a Parthian warrior. The stylization of garments and frontal view indicate deterioration of techniques.

The influence of Parthian art forms spread widely, both east and west. Evidences of this have been found in the art of Asia Minor, southern Russia, Central Asia, China and India. In Indian art the Parthian influence is particularly noteworthy. Where Hellenistic ideas were present, the cultural contribution was further effected in Parthian times. The famous Graeco-Buddhist art of Gandhara is a combination of Greek, Iranian and older Indian art forms. Even at Sanchi and at Jaggayyepeta in south India, Iranian motifs are to be found. Meanwhile, through the spread of Gandhara art, Parthian as well as other art forms went to Central Asia and the Far East. This transmission of cultural influences was an important aspect of the extensive trade relationship of Iran in Parthian times.

The Roman Empire in Asia

Before we can adequately understand the important trade relations of the Parthians and the spread of Iranian influence during this period, we must turn to the large section of Asia which during this time was under Roman domination. Rome at the height of her power governed not only a large part of Europe together with the north coast of Africa, but was also an important power in Asia.

During the Greek wars of the end of the third century B.C., the Romans secured the support of the Kingdom of Pergamum in western Asia Minor as an ally. This drew Rome into conflict with the imperial forces of the Seleucids, who as successors of Alexander were also concerned with the politics of Greece and Macedonia. After the Romans had successfully defeated the Macedonians (200–196 B.C.) they turned against the Seleucid emperor, Antiochus III, whose forces had been victorious from Syria to the Indus valley, and drove his troops out of Greece (191).

The next step was the landing of Roman forces on the continent of Asia. Under the leadership of the Scipios in 190 B.C. a Roman army first entered Asia Minor and at Magnesia defeated the Emperor Antiochus again. In the succeeding year, the Romans exercised control through a number of small states protected by and subservient to them. Pergamum was at first enlarged and later (129 B.C.) absorbed into the empire as the "Province of Asia."

PONTUS. The only strong opposition to the Roman advance in Asia Minor came from the Kingdom of Pontus, originally a small kingdom on the Black Sea. Under the able leadership of their king, Mithridates IV, the state had expanded in all directions. Three wars against the Romans in the 80's and 70's of the first century B.C. resulted in the destruction of Pontus and the further extension of Roman rule over a large part of Asia Minor. The noted general Pompey extended the authority of Rome into Syria and, as a basis of government, created three new "provinces": Bithynia, Cilicia and Syria. Other regions became "client" principalities. Among these was Judea in Palestine.

During the third Mithridatic War the king of Pontus enlisted the support of his son-in-law, the ruler of Armenia. This brought about Roman invasion of Armenia and the establishment of a protectorate.

ARMENIA. In that country a flourishing state known as Greater Armenia had been founded in 166 B.C. by Artaxes I whose reign was the highest point in Armenia's political history. It was also a time when overland trade routes to India and China were developed from this region. The Armenian kingdom was not a strongly unified state but rather a heterogeneous group of tribes and peoples. When Lucullus and Pompey attacked it, it fell apart (69–66) and Armenia was subject to Rome for nearly a century.

After the expansion under Pompey Roman power was in contact with the Parthian empire in Iran. The Romans, however, met their match when they attempted to subdue the Parthians, and were only able to hold their own in a long series of wars. The two empires competed for control in certain strategic border areas, especially Armenia, whose status was that of a buffer state in which Roman rule was not consistently maintained. Roman interest continued, however, largely because of the demand for silk from Han China and because one of the branches of the main caravan lines across Asia led through Armenia. The political status of Armenia was important to Rome, but during most of the Republic and the empire this country remained under the political and cultural influence of Iran.

PARTHIAN WARS. In the struggle for control in Armenia and the other border regions Romans and Parthians faced each other in several prolonged conflicts. Roman forces were decisively defeated when Crassus was captured at Carrhae in the Mesopotamian desert in 53 B.C. The superiority of Parthian military tactics enabled the Iranians to maintain their position on the Euphrates frontier.

Several leaders famous in Roman history were involved in the wars against the Parthians. Mark Antony was defeated by them in 36 B.C. Caesar Augustus developed the resources of Asia Minor as an integral part of the Empire but preferred peace with Parthia to the uncertainties of attempting to gain complete control in Armenia. After inconclusive campaigns in the time of Nero there followed a period of peace between Romans and Parthians for about fifty years.

Particularly important for the history of the Near East were the Parthian wars carried on by the Emperor Trajan. Conflict came when the Parthian king Chosroes attempted to control Armenia. Trajan advanced into central Mesopotamia and as a result of the Parthian war of 114–116 temporarily created Roman provinces in "Assyria," "Babylonia" and "Armenia." The succeeding period was one of fluctuating boundaries when the Armenians found themselves first under Roman rule and later under Parthian.

In Mesopotamia during a large part of this period of the early Caesars the boundary between the two empires was on the upper Euphrates River at a point where a trans-Asiatic trade route left that river and crossed the desert to Palmyra. Here in a frontier fort at Dura-Europos have been found the remains of a chapel where Roman soldiers once worshipped.

JUDEA. The Roman sphere in Asia, from the beginning, included the land of Judea. It was during the time of Roman control in Palestine that Jesus of Nazareth lived and preached in that area. A Jewish revolt broke out in Judea (A.D. 66–70). The governor of Syria failed to suppress it and a Roman army under the emperor Vespasian and later under his son, Titus, subdued the country, taking Jerusalem after a siege in A.D. 70. This was the time of the destruction of the temple and the abolition of the Jewish National Council. Following these events special Roman forces were quartered in Jerusalem.

ROMAN IMPERIALISM. Behind the Armenian and Mesopotamian frontiers, the Romans established an empire. It in great part consisted of an enlargement of what Rome started with, a league of cities. Hence during most of their period of control in Asia the urban life coming down from Hellenic times and earlier was continued. Later, in the face of economic crisis in the third century A.D., the Roman central government took over administration and the old urban life of the Graeco-Roman world came to an end.

Meanwhile Asian ideas permeated the Mediterranean world. An important instance in the political sphere was the deification of the Emperor. This idea originated in Asia Minor and was transmitted to the Romans through the example of Alexander and the later Greek tradition.

Influences from the Mediterranean also spread eastward under Roman rule. In the realm of philosophy Platonic ideas became mixed with Oriental mysticism. "Neo-Platonism" started in Alexandria in Egypt with Plotinus (204–270) and others, and in later times came to have an important effect on the thinking of the peoples of Southwest Asia.

In religion Iranian influence made itself felt among the Romans. The art and architectural remains at Dura-Europos show evidence of important cross-cultural trends. These remains indicate that Roman soldiers worshipped an Iranian deity, Mithra. Recent archaeological findings as far away as London have shown that the Romans maintained a Mithraic temple even in England. The art work is Parthian, some of the subject matter is Hellenistic and together they indicate a real joining of two cultures at the frontier and beyond. Some description of Mithraism and its importance in the mingling of ideas is presented in connection with the development of Christianity.

Bactria and the Steppe

Beyond the Parthian frontiers to the northeast the Iranians confronted a succession of political groups who came into Central Asia from outside. Their neighbors at the start of the Arsacid dynasty in Iran were Bactrian Greeks who were the heirs to Seleucid power in the valley of the Amu Darya.

GREEKS. In about 250 B.C. the Greek satrap appointed by the Seleucid emperor to rule in Bactria made himself an independent king and no longer recognized Seleucid overlordship. This was unlike the situation in Persia where not Greeks, but Iranian Parthians assumed control as Seleucid power waned. In Bactria Greek rulers kept power in their own hands and for a time followed an expansionist policy. They gained control of Afghanistan and pushed into northern India about 200 B.C. The enlarging of the kingdom, however, had the effect of splitting it into two parts, one north of the Hindu Kush passes where a rebel, Eucratides, seized control in 175 B.C. while his master, Demetrius, was in India. Eucratides, however, was not long secure in Bactria. Within a few years he and his followers were themselves dislodged from their holdings north of the passes by pressures from the Parthians on the west and even more important from the nomadic Scythians (or Sakas) who were pushing in upon them from the north and northeast. They moved south to Kabul and from there descendants of Eucratides ruled a part of the Punjab for nearly a century, while descendants of Demetrius headed a rival kingdom farther south and east. These Indo-Greek kings and their kingdoms gradually became submerged in Indian civilization and left behind little influence of Greek culture except in Buddhist sculpture and in coinage, developments which are further discussed in Chapter 9.

SAKAS AND YÜEH-CHI. Meanwhile the Sakas, who established themselves in the valley of the Amu Darya (c. 150–140 B.C.), were in turn subjected to powerful pressure from outside, this time from the east. The pressure came from one of the great migrations of history, a migration which brought a populous and powerful tribe known as the Yüeh-chi from northwest China (present day Kansu) past the deserts of the Tarim Basin, through the Pamirs, and into the hospitable Amu Darya valley — there to challenge the Sakas. This migration had been set in motion by wars on the Chinese northern frontier which had involved the Yüeh-chi only indirectly, for they were friendly to the Chinese. These wars were between China and a nomadic confederation known as the Hsiung-nu, which controlled Mongolia and threatened the northern frontiers of China itself. During the half century after 210 B.C. when the first Han rulers were consolidating their power in China, the Hsiung-nu menace necessitated the Chinese court buying them off with silks, wine, grain, chariots and Chinese princesses. Unfortunately for them the Yüeh-chi were in a strategic position along the trade routes to the west over which Han and Hsiung-nu competed for control. After suffering several Hsiung-nu invasions in about 174 to 160 B.C. they began a great exodus to the west. The migration took many years and some of those Yüeh-chi who had remained behind were still being battered by their northern enemies some twenty-five years later. But by the middle of the second century B.C. the majority of the Yüeh-chi people were making their way across the Pamirs into the Syr Darya valley and beyond. There they pushed into the Sakas who in turn moved into Bactria and forced the Greeks to move southward into India, as already related. But the Yüeh-chi did not stop. They followed the Sakas into Bactria, and the latter, finding it impossible to move farther west because of Parthian control in that direction, made their way south in the wake of the Greeks, moved through Afghanistan and on across the passes into northern India where they may have contributed to the disappearance of the Greek kingdoms. Eventually the Sakas moved as far south as Ujjain. Again the Yüeh-chi followed them, though retaining Bactria as their base of activity. Moving into Afghanistan in the first century A.D. they were, by the end of that century, in control of a vast area extending from Bactria to the lower Indus valley, including the Punjab. From this time on, one tribe among them, the Kushan (or Kushana) gained the ascendancy and the kingdom they organized came to be known by that name.

The Kushan domain extended from Han China's outposts in the Takla Makan desert (Khotan, Kashgar) on the east to Parthian borders on the west, and south across the passes as far as Sind and Gujarat in India. Here the Kushan were near the Arabian Sea. Their empire also included parts of the upper Gangetic plain. To the north, beyond Bactria, Kushan influence, through alliances, extended along the lower Amu Darya to the Aral Sea and even to the shores of the Caspian. Thus the Kushan controlled part of the direct trade route between Rome and China.

Eastward Trade and Cultural Exchange in Parthian Times

The Kushan power in Central Asia was only one of several factors in an international trade of vital concern to the powers of Southwest Asia. Control of Armenia, as has been noted, was important to Rome as a route to the Far East and a means by which Parthia as middleman might be avoided. The Parthians, and the Sassanians after them, were determined to maintain this middleman's position and to see to it that goods moving from the Far East to the West (whether to Roman or Byzantine territory) would pass through Persian hands and pay Persian tolls. The state wealth of Parthia was in no small measure dependent on the profits of this trade; in fact, it was only with Mithridates II's stabilization of Parthian control over the whole middle route which lay between the areas of Chinese and Roman control that Parthia achieved the wealth and the strength to challenge Rome.

Parthian determination to prevent direct contact between emissaries of China and Rome is well illustrated in the adventure of Kan Ying, an envoy of the Chinese general Pan Ch'ao, whose forces penetrated far into Central Asia toward the end of the first century A.D. Pan dispatched his envoy into Parthian territory with orders to proceed on to the land of Ta Ch'in (Roman controlled western Asia) and establish contacts. Kan got as far as the Persian Gulf where, however, the Parthians dissuaded him from going farther by telling him exaggerated tales of the perils of the journey ahead. Kan returned to China with his mission not accomplished.

Rome on her part made continuous efforts to avoid Parthia. This became a real possibility when the Roman conquest of Egypt early in the first century A.D. gave her control of Red Sea routes leading by sea to the Persian Gulf, northern India and China. The all-sea route at this early stage was long and dangerous, and although Roman empire merchants did succeed in completing the arduous voyage to China as early as 166 A.D., the bulk of the trade con-

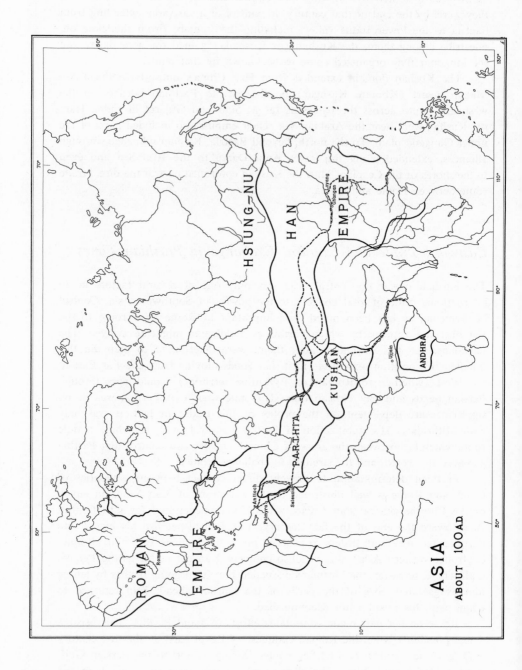

ASIA

ABOUT 100 A.D.

tinued to pass over land routes. Avoiding Parthia on land brought the Roman traders into contact with the Kushans.

Since Kushan influence extended from the Caspian in the north to Sind and Gujarat in the south, if the Romans could get in contact with them at either point the Kushans could serve as middlemen. Hence such an arrangement also would be disadvantageous to the Parthians.

Although the Kushans conducted successful warfare against the Parthians they could not displace the latter entirely. The roads across Iran still remained the most direct routes between Rome on the one hand and the Kushan and the countries beyond on the other.

FIGURE 4.3. The magnificent ruins of Palmyra, the great trading center in the desert. Built in the third century, these buildings illustrate the influence of Roman styles.

The times when the trade flourished were periods of prosperity in Western Asia. The cities of the Roman Orient were busy with the reweaving of Chinese silks so as to make them more transparent and thus to meet the demand of Roman ladies. This was the period when Palmyra and Petra developed as centers of the Roman commerce to the east. The cities and their trade suffered in time of wars and political disruption. When these disturbances interfered with the flow of goods they also became important reasons for attempts to develop alternate routes.

On land by caravan, and on the sea by ship traveled ideas as well as goods. The spread of Iranian religion to the West has already been noted. To Central Asia also in Parthian times came Persian concepts which had their influence in Buddhism and in the art which from Central Asia went on to China.

Early Christianity in Asia

Among the powerful ideological forces which spread out from Southwest Asia in the times of Parthia and Rome was the Christian religion. Although this is primarily a matter for the historians of the Mediterranean and the West, the factor of Christianity is, of course, an important one in any history which deals with Asia. In this chapter the presentation is limited to Christianity in its Asiatic aspects, those which had a particular significance for Asia and were to have a continuing influence there. Attention is directed to the Asian (Syrian or Nestorian, and Armenian) types.

Christianity owed much to Southwest Asian religions which had preceded it. This is clear as regards Judaism which provided the Old Testament tradition and from which Christianity emerged seemingly as a new Jewish sect. The birth of such a sect need not be considered strange. What was unusual was that its followers should break away from Judaism and become more inclusive and widely spread than the parent religion. In this, Christianity's appeal to the Gentiles was all important. "Great as was Paul's work in winning release for Christians from the bondage of the Jewish law, greater still was his trans- formation of the simple faith of the Apostles into a religion acceptable to the gentile, i.e. Hellenized-oriental mentality." [1]

In part this was due to the fact that these Hellenized-oriental Gentiles who populated the great cities of Southwest Asia were already much attracted to the mystery religions or cults which were characteristic of the age. Though these cults were many and varied, the main outlines of their beliefs displayed a remarkable similarity, whether they were of the Eleusinian, Dionysian, or Orphic variety from Greece, worshipers of Isis and Osiris from Egypt, believers in Aphrodite and Adonis from Syria, followers of the Great Mother of the Gods from Anatolia, or adherents of Mithraism from Iran. They served as semisecret brotherhoods bringing mutual solace and mystic hope to poor, degraded, uprooted people for whom the spread of Roman power had meant disruption of national life and of traditional values. Whatever their origins such people were alike in their misery and their receptivity to mysteries which promised escape from earthly suffering. Though Christianity, as its subsequent history revealed, was much richer both in ethical and religious content than any of these, nevertheless its early spread was enhanced by the disposition toward mystery cults among the non-Roman peoples of the Roman Orient.

[1] Ralph Turner, *The Great Cultural Traditions*, II (New York, 1941), p. 1045.

MITHRAISM.   Christianity was also influenced by ideas and practices in other religions. A striking example is Mithraism which was a very serious competitor for Christianity through the first four centuries of the Christian era. As mentioned previously, Mithra was primarily one of the gods of the Zoroastrian pantheon whose standing was slightly below that of the supreme god Ahura Mazda and around whom as early as the fourth century B.C. a special cult had developed. Mithra was conceived of as playing a leading role in the Zoroastrian struggle of Good against Evil and as having repeatedly thwarted the efforts of Ahriman (Evil) to ruin humankind by drought, flood and the like. The ceremonial of Mithraism was elaborate and its observance was limited to men. It consisted of seven stages through which members of the sect might pass. They were baptized in the blood of a bull slaughtered for the purpose, and thus they began a "new life." By following lives of abstinence and asceticism and practicing the virtues of honesty, loyalty and brotherhood they might be eligible to communion with Mithra and eventually receive from him the blessing of immortality. For all the many differences between Mithraism and Christianity there were also interesting resemblances: baptism, a sacramental meal, burning of candles before an altar, belief in immortality, resurrection, last judgment, blissful heaven, miserable hell, the observation of a Sun-day (in contrast to the Jewish Sabbath), and the special observation of December 25 as a great feast day. Mithraism began to spread westward from the time of Pompey's campaigns in Western Asia (74–63 B.C.), and it shortly achieved wide popularity in the Roman empire, especially among slaves and soldiers.

NESTORIANISM.   Two variants of Christianity developed in Western Asia. Until the Europeans came in numbers after the fifteenth century, the Syrian (Nestorian) and Armenian churches occupied a far more important place in Asian history than the churches of the Roman and Greek world. It is noteworthy that before Emperor Constantine's adoption of Christianity in 312 that faith had a greater success in Western Asia where it began than in Europe. Radiating from great Christian centers in Antioch and Edessa the Syrian branch of Christianity spread far and wide. After the destruction of Jerusalem by the Romans in A.D. 70 Antioch became the first capital of Christianity and maintained a position of leadership for several centuries. This religious center lay in the Greek-speaking part of Syria and the incorporation of Hellenic influences into Christian doctrine began there. At Antioch also was organized the first school of Christian learning, and for a time this city exercised a real authority over surrounding sees.

The greatest figure of the Syrian church was Nestorius, who died about 451. He became prominent when many doctrinal arguments were besetting the church. Constantine a century before had tried to fix the basic doctrines of Christianity and for this purpose had called a church council at Nicaea in 325, but the points at issue were not resolved. The theological argument crystallized about the question of the nature of Christ: was he human or divine or both? This question, became involved in the competition between important political interests of the fourth century. Antioch opposed Alexandria for leadership in the church and the Roman emperor was anxious to settle the affair in such a way as to reinforce his own power and prestige.

Nestorius was a presbyter and monk of Antioch and a principal advocate of the thesis held by the Antioch school that Christ was not a divine figure, but rather that he was possessed of a human nature and that, as a corollary, Mary could not possibly be called the "Mother of God." Jesus was man, not God, and his mother was a human being, Mary. In addition the Antioch school opposed the idea of purgatory, the use of images and held that lower orders of the clergy might marry. In 428 Nestorius became Bishop of Constantinople and it seemed that the Antioch school was in the ascendancy. His appointment stirred a bitter controversy, however. Some monks at Constantinople were disaffected and they were reinforced by outcries and plots from Alexandria, where Bishop Cyril became Nestorius' chief antagonist, and also from Rome.

The Emperor called another council at Ephesus in 431 to settle the dispute and to again attempt to "fix" the dogma. Instead a bitter controversy developed. But in the end the opponents of Nestorius carried the day. Deposed from his bishopric at Constantinople and ordered to retire to a monastery to ponder his sins, he chose to break with the church and depart into exile.

Before his death Nestorius elaborated his faith in speech and in writing. His ideas became the basic doctrines of an independent Nestorian (Syrian) branch of Christianity, which though regarded as heresy by the Western church nevertheless continued to have a wide popularity in Asia. Actually the break with Western Christianity improved rather than impaired the fortunes of the Syrian church in Asia inasmuch as the Sassanian government in Iran, convinced that the Nestorians were no longer allied with their enemies of the Roman world, began to tolerate their faith in Persia.

Syrian Christianity spread rapidly along the trade routes to the East. In 635 it was introduced into China, where Nestorian monks are reported to have been received by the emperor T'ang T'ai-tsung. Nestorianism never obtained a large following among the Chinese, but it did enjoy some success among Central Asian peoples, including the Mongols. Such places as Herat, Samarkand and Balkh became centers of Nestorian Christianity and European travelers to the court of the Mongol Khans in the thirteenth century were surprised and horrified to meet there a number of "heretic" Christians. Nestorianism also found many followers in India, particularly on the Malabar coast.

ARMENIAN CHRISTIANITY. Armenian Christianity had a similarly stormy career, but its position was buttressed by the fact that it had a national home. Armenia was the first organized state to adopt Christianity as its official religion. This occurred in the late third century, after a long period which saw the gradual spread of Christianity among the Armenians from the Syrian centers at Antioch and Edessa. Gregory the Illuminator is reputed to have accomplished the conversion of the king and persuaded him to destroy the temples of other religions. Hatred of the Persians, who under the Sassanian emperors repeatedly invaded Armenia and who on several occasions brought it temporarily under Persian control, served to strengthen the popular devotion to Christianity. When in the fifth century the Persians made a great effort to force Zoroastrianism on the country, the Armenians reacted violently to preserve their national faith.

Meanwhile, however, Armenian Christianity, like Syrian, ran afoul of the Western Christian effort to standardize the doctrine. The Armenians were monophysite, by which they held that Christ had a "single nature" which was divine. But the Armenian church survived all persecutions and controversies, whether from East or West, and remained the symbol of Armenian national identity.

While Christianity was expanding in the Mediterranean area and becoming established as a national faith in Armenia the people of Iran were little influenced. A strong indigenous Persian tradition dating back to the Achaemenians continued in Parthian times and resulted in a new imperial dynasty whose religion and politics were distinctively Iranian and apart from the Mediterranean world.

The Sassanian Empire

In Persis, Iran's most strongly Zoroastrian Mazdaist region, a successful revolt against Parthian supremacy resulted in the establishing of a new imperial line. Ardashir I (226–240) was the first king of the Sassanian, or Sassanid, dynasty (226–651).

After Ardashir had defeated the last Parthian ruler, Artabanus V, he subjugated the rest of Iran, took the Parthian capital at Ctesiphon and gained control of Mesopotamia as far as the Euphrates, where Roman legions stood on the other side. In the east his borders touched Kushan-controlled central Asia. Ardashir was soon at war with the forces of Rome, and he was, in fact, so successful against them along the Mesopotamian frontier that they had no strength to throw against him when suddenly he moved to invade Armenia. This had probably been his main objective all the time, for the Armenian king was an Arsacid relative of the former Parthian rulers of Iran and was giving refuge to many Parthian nobles who had fled into Armenia to escape Ardashir's vengeance. Ardashir conquered the country and annexed it, and though the Romans were determined that Armenia should not permanently be assigned to Sassanian overlordship, they could do nothing to prevent it at the time.

Ardashir was succeeded by his son Shapur I (240–271) who was equally successful in his military operations. He crushed a revolt in Armenia, pushed across the Euphrates to wrest most of Syria from Roman control and in 260 captured the Roman emperor, Valerian. In addition Shapur forced the Kushans to the east to accept a ruler who recognized Sassanian overlordship. After the death of Shapur I the Romans regained power in Syria and even placed a Roman candidate on the throne of Armenia.

SHAPUR II.   Shapur II came to the Persian throne in 309 and ruled for seventy years. In his reign Sassanian Persia reached the zenith of its power. Shapur

FIGURE 4.4   The investiture of Ardashir I from Naqsh-i-Rustam.

did not win every battle against the Romans, but he won the campaigns. A climax was reached when the emperor Julian advanced his forces to the Tigris in 363 and was waylaid by Shapur and forced to retreat. Julian himself was slain in battle, and afterwards the Romans agreed to a peace treaty which, in addition to recognizing Persian supremacy in Mesopotamia, renounced any Roman claims to Armenia.

Meanwhile the Sassanians organized their governmental structure on new lines. Ardashir I began emphasizing the close cooperation of the throne and the Zoroastrian priesthood. Under Achaemenians and Parthians this priesthood had been important but not as much so as under the Sassanians. Ardashir founded his power upon a combination of church and state. He used the clergy to legitimize his own accession and in turn granted them special privileges. To a national church whose hierarchy was led by a chief priest, Ardashir assigned lands and he allowed the priests to collect tithes from the faithful. Adherence to the national church was compulsory and an inquisition was organized with the objective of converting all dissidents within a year. Although this proved to be impossible, fierce persecutions of unbelievers were repeatedly conducted and religious orthodoxy was generally enforced.

The determination of an orthodox theology was begun by Ardashir. He ordered the gathering together of previous versions of the *Avesta* that they might be edited and formed into an authorized canon. The process was completed in the reign of Shapur I.

MANICHAEISM.   During the time of Shapur I a divergent form of Zoroastrianism had its beginnings. Mani, a Persian living in Mesopotamia, announced in the year A.D. 242 that he was the prophet of a new religion. While Mani in his teaching sharpened the unrelenting dualism of Zoroastrianism, of Good-Light versus Evil-Darkness he was responsive also to non-Zoroastrian ideas, Indian and, especially, Christian, for he considered himself an apostle of Jesus. He regarded all things of the flesh as the work of the devil, and he demanded that the "elect" of the faith lead a severely ascetic life, foregoing marriage, the use of wine or meat, the ownership of property, and even bathing. "Listeners," who constituted the majority of the followers of the faith, might marry, eat flesh, and drink wine but they were enjoined to frequent prayer and fasting and to the contribution of one-tenth of their income to the "elect." In return, after death and after a period of purification, they would be permitted entry into paradise. Also present were certain ideas and practices which were shared with Christianity, not only in the acceptance of Jesus as a central figure (though not *the* central figure) of the faith but in the assigning of a monklike role to the "elect," the concept of struggle between God and the devil, and the attribution of bodily and material desires to Satan. In fact some Manichaeists considered themselves Christians and it has been suggested that Manichaeism might best be classified as an aberrant form of Christianity. Mani, himself, was executed and his skin stuffed with straw by the Sassanian authorities in Persia (273) for preaching heresy against Zoroastrian Mazdaism, which by that time had become the official religion of an intolerant state.

MAZDAISM.   Orthodox Zoroastrianism as it emerged in the Sassanian period emphasized the role of Ahura Mazda, the god of light and righteousness, and hence is generally known as Mazdaism. In its theology Sassanian Mazdaism emphasized the struggle between good and evil, the veneration of earth and water and especially of fire. In its ethics, truthfulness, brotherly love, moderation and respect for property were to be enforced by well-defined punishments. Most of this teaching was not new in Iran. But the codifying and the ecclesiastical organization had not been accomplished before. The Mazdaist church was really a part of the Sassanian state machinery.

The position of the King of Kings in Sassanid Persia was made far stronger than it had ever been in Parthian times because of the close working alliance between king and priesthood fashioned by Ardashir I. But after his reign the priests were able to wield a considerable power over the king. Ardashir through consecration by the great council of priests was made vicar of the Mazdaist church and the representative of Ahura Mazda on earth. In this process he set a precedent by which succession to the throne became dependent on securing such sanction and consecration. Theoretically the king could choose his own successor, not only from among his own sons but also from among the various members of the ruling house in general. But when this selection had to have the approval of the priests, in the last analysis of the chief priest, they could, in fact, block the election of a king. The investiture itself involved religious cere-monies, specifically a visit on foot to the Royal Temple of Fire to offer gifts at the fire altar and to take the vows of kingship.

In addition to the crucial influence they could exert on the selection of a candidate for the throne the Mazdaist priesthood, as spiritual advisors and mentors of the king, exercised a continuing influence on him through most of his reign. They claimed the ability to make predictions, and these predictions had to be taken into account if state affairs were to be managed successfully. In addition, priestly representatives were often to be found on royal commissions charged with the conduct of inquisitions and of even purely secular affairs.

Mazdaism became so strong that in the fourth century several Sassanian monarchs tried to break or reduce its power. One of these kings was deposed, two were assassinated and one was exiled. Its authority remained unchecked and throughout the dynasty a political-religious management of the state prevailed.

On the more purely secular side, the Sassanian government ruled over a society with a definite stratification. Uppermost were priests and officials, then warriors, then "intellectuals" of various kinds, such as scribes, and lastly "workers," who comprised the great mass of the population. Although these classes were neither as elaborate nor as rigid as the caste system of India, movement from one category to another was very difficult. In theory a change could be made only with the express permission of the king. There were various injunctions on the evils of class intermingling, and there were institutionalized differentiations in dress and possessions to emphasize distinctions.

SASSANIAN ADMINISTRATION.   The principal organ of the central administra-tion was the bureau (*diwan*). Exactly how many of these bureaus there were or what precise area of administration each encompassed is not known, but from seals possessed by the king we learn of the existence of bureaus of finance, criminal justice, secretariat, secret chancellory and a bureau for the distribution of awards and commissions. That there were also bureaus for the control of military affairs, postal service and such other state functions would seem a reasonable assumption even though their seals are lacking.

For purposes of local administration the empire was divided into four *toparchies,* each of which was headed by a shah (king) who, though subordinate to the Sassanid King of Kings, was of royal rank. In fact, frequently those who were possibly in line to succeed the Great King were prepared (and tested) by being assigned to rule a *toparchy.* We see the workings of the system most clearly and at its best in the time of Anushirwan "the Just" (also known as Chosroes), who ruled from 531–539. The four governors of east, west, north, and south respectively were all powerful monarchs, but Anushirwan kept them in line with close personal supervision. He was well served in this by a veritable army of intelligence agents. Roads were kept in scrupulous repair and this made possible fairly rapid communication throughout the empire. The tax system, at least under Anushirwan, is reputed to have been efficient and fair, with frequent land and production surveys being made. A fixed money tax was levied on the land itself and a percentage of the produce was also due the government, not so much, however, as to discourage maximum productive effort. There were also taxes on fruit and other special possessions, and there was a poll tax on Christians and Jews, which no doubt was assiduously collected since Mazdaist priests frequently served as tax inspectors.

THE SASSANIAN ARMY.   The Sassanian army was a powerful instrument. Elephant troops were supported by a heavily armored horse cavalry. These, when well organized, gave the army a tremendous striking force. An infantry made up of lightly armed but well trained bowmen and spearmen constituted the other branch of the army. Unlike the sometimes irregular levies of soldiers upon which the Parthians had relied, these troops were fully able to match the Romans, even in pitched battles and in such "scientific warfare" as that involved in the besieging of cities. They used trenches, wattled shields, battering rams and stone-throwing engines of destruction. With these, during the later campaigns of the dynasty, practically every fortified city which they seriously challenged was taken. The soldiers in the Great King's army were well looked after; their pay was small, but for men in standard units it was regular. Withholding the pay of substandard contingents seems to have been the principal technique by which the king insured maximum devotion to duty and efficiency among his fighting men.

In international politics the main concern of the Sassanian empire continued to be the competition with Rome, although the ultimate disasters which befell the state were not to be effected by the Romans. Shapur I had eliminated the Kushan threat in the third century and with the gradual disappearance of that power Persia's eastern borders were relatively secure until the Hephthalites (White Huns) in the fifth century. Meanwhile relations with Rome continued on an uncertain basis. Though Shapur II, the "Great," had won control of Mesopotamia and Armenia from the Romans, his successors were unable to hold this advantage. For a time a pro-Roman faction gained ascendancy in Armenia; they were overturned by a Persian-aided coup d'état. Rome and Persia were again on the brink of war over Armenia in 383, but the following year a truce and treaty was arranged and Armenia was partitioned. In each sector reigned an Arsacid, but in the eastern part the Persians dominated and in the west the Romans. This arrangement, though most unfortunate for Armenia, allowed an uneasy but peaceful coexistence for several decades between the empires of the Romans and the Sassanians.

During this period the Roman empire was no longer the strong state of the early Caesars. Political control was divided between Rome and Constantinople (founded in 330), the Western empire was subjected to a series of invasions by various Germanic tribes and after 395 the "Roman" power which opposed the Sassanians was that of the Eastern, or Byzantine, empire.

THE HEPHTHALITE (WHITE HUN) MENACE.   While their western frontiers were a constant source of anxiety to the Sassanians, this dynasty, as the Parthians before them, found it necessary also to watch their borders in Central Asia. King Shapur I exercised control over the later Kushan princes, and Shapur II (309-379) settled groups of newly arrived nomads, the Hephthalites in Kushan territory as "confederates" of the Sassanians.

By the early fifth century these same Hephthalites were the dominant tribe in central Asia, including Bactria (425). They fought a series of wars against the Sassanians (428-484). During the latter part of the fifth century the Hephthalite pressure on Iran's northeastern frontier required even more attention on the part of Persian monarchs than the Roman power to the west. Numerous campaigns were conducted against the Huns with varying success. These operations culminated in a disastrous Sassanian invasion of Hephthalite territory (483). King Firoz (Peroz) led an army which included some 500 elephants into Bactria; he was trapped and defeated near Balkh. The Sassanian king himself was killed, and his successor staved off a Hephthalite invasion for two years only by payment of tribute.

At the turn of the sixth century the threat of the Hephthalites was still a matter of concern to the Sassanians. After years of fighting (503–513) between the Sassanians and the Hephthalites under their famous leader Mihiragula, the latter were chiefly involved in campaigns in India and were no longer a serious threat to the eastern border of Iran.

Byzantine forces invaded Persian Armenia in 526; in spite of some victories in Armenia and in Mesopotamia and in spite of the leadership of a great general, Belisarius, they did not gain any decisive military success.

ANUSHIRWAN.   Anushirwan, Chosroes I, was concerned with internal political and religious problems and made peace with the Byzantine emperor, Justinian. The latter was primarily interested in the reconquest of Italy and North Africa and a treaty was signed between Justinian and Anushirwan (533) in which all outstanding issues were temporarily settled.

Anushirwan, alarmed at the success of Belisarius in reconquering the Roman West, commenced in 540 a great war against Justinian. Throwing his forces across the Euphrates, he surprised the Romans, moved rapidly through Mesopotamia into Syria, seized and sacked the city of Antioch, and levied tribute on city after city. The war thus inaugurated was fought sporadically until 577, with the Persians advancing to the Black Sea and generally holding the advantage. Another treaty of peace was finally agreed upon in 562. The Persians retreated from their most advanced holdings on the Black Sea and the Romans paid them to withdraw.

After conclusion of peace with Constantinople, Anushirwan, in alliance with the rising Turkish power in central Asia, defeated the Hephthalites and secured added territory in Bactria. A sign of the strength of the Iranian empire under Anushirwan was the fact that military assistance was sent all the way to Yemen (570) where the Arabs of that region were freed from Abyssinian Christians and brought under Persian suzerainty.

Still another war against the Romans of Constantinople broke out in the 570's. Persian Armenia was overrun by Byzantine troops who, however, were unable to make much headway elsewhere. Anushirwan, now past seventy but still leading his troops, was forced in the last year of his life to retreat to Ctesiphon, the old Parthian capital on the Tigris.

When Anushirwan died in 579 the Iranian state was resisting enemies from both east and west as it had throughout the centuries. The Byzantine empire in the west was now in alliance with the Turks, successors to the Hephthalites in Central Asia. In the succeeding decade a rebellious general temporarily gained control within Iran. Sassanian authority was re-established only after Maurice, the emperor at Constantinople, had intervened on behalf of Chosroes II, the grandson of Anushirwan.

Chosroes II (589–628) is known also as Parviz, "the conqueror." When Maurice was assassinated he undertook a war of revenge during which the Sassanians conquered most of the Roman Orient. They attacked through Armenia, seized Edessa, and reached the Bosphorus near Scutari in 610. Then they undertook to subdue the principal cities in Western Asia. Chosroes II captured Antioch, Damascus and Jerusalem in succession, and moved into Egypt. These campaigns lasted for years (603–620) and threatened the center of Byzantine power, the city of Constantinople itself.

Meanwhile after years of preparation the Byzantine emperor Heraclius was able to command military strength sufficient to repulse the Iranians. During the years 622 to 627 the Byzantine armies everywhere defeated the Persians. Northwest Iran and Mesopotamia were invaded.

DECLINE OF THE SASSANIAN STATE. The Sassanian state showed itself to be weak in the face of serious attack. The army had become too big, taxation requirements to support it too heavy and the kings were too much devoted to luxurious living. After Chosroes II for fourteen years (628–641) rivalries, assassinations and various movements against the Sassanian government brought about a disintegration into feudalistic relationships. In place of the powerful Sassanian empire there emerged numerous petty states. Meanwhile Byzantine forces withdrew behind their former boundaries and the central authority in Iran attempted to rally the forces of the old empire in the face of a new threat from outside.

This fatal threat appeared when Moslem Arab forces first entered Persian territory in 633. The story of Islam and the sensational advance of the Moslems east and west will be told in the following chapter. Here are noted simply the stages in the defeat of the Sassanians.

Muhammad, the founder of Islam, had died in 632. But under his successors, the Caliphs, the religious and political state he established was rapidly expanded. Syria was overrun by the Arabs in 635–636. Shortly afterwards the fate of the Sassanian empire was decided with a defeat at Kadisya on one of the Euphrates canals (637).

The Sassanian king, Yezdegerd III, abandoned the old capital Ctesiphon with its treasures and attempted a stand at Nehawand in Media, 641. In spite of his numerical superiority and excellent fortifications the zeal of the Arabs won the day. This was the end of any effective Sassanian resistance and marks the termination of a period in Iranian history. Moslem forces gained control of the whole of Iran within the next few years. By 650 the Arabs were engaging the Turks in Bactria and the last Sassanian prince was finding a refuge in T'ang China.

TRADE.   Many of the political changes and international rivalries of Sassanian times were due, as in Parthian times, to the trade between the empires which was a factor of continuing concern to the states involved. The Parthian position, astride the long silk route which led from Ch'ang-an to Rome, and the part the Parthians played so shrewdly, keeping the principals apart and yet letting their goods through, has already been mentioned. The Sassanians were perhaps not so interested in trade as the Parthians, for their empire was better organized and they were not so completely dependent upon the revenues derived from it as were the Parthians; but they fostered it nevertheless. The Sassanians also managed the commerce better for their own interests than had the Arsacids. Whereas the earlier dynasty could only partially control the routes, even through Iran, and had no control whatsoever over the sea route to the east, the Sassanians were strong enough to control them all. They set up a strict state administration of external commerce, organized and licensed stations where trade might be carried out, and established various monopolies. Traders from the Mediterranean tried to evade the Sassanian monopoly but they had less success than in Parthian times. Justinian made the most vigorous effort to break through Sassanian control of the trade routes. He tried to develop a sea route via Ethiopia, and when this met with little success he tried a land route skirting Sassanian domains to the north. This was used for a time but by the seventh century Byzantium was no longer able to handle such difficult enterprises.

With the spread of Arab control over most of Southwest Asia a new expanded market developed. The Iranians, who had been experts in international trade for centuries, continued to play an important role. They knew the routes. Through their country passed the main transcontinental roads, and the Iranians had extensive business experience. In times of military operations and political change or in times of peace they could not be dispensed with.

As the Arabs took over control politically in Iran, so in occupying Mesopotamia and Persia they inherited the great national culture of the Sassanians which the latter had based on Achaemenian and Parthian foundations.

ART.   In their art the Sassanians, as in the case of religion and political organization, tended to diverge from the tradition of Hellenism which had been important in Parthian times. Iranian aspects were emphasized more and more.

FIGURE 4.5. Sassanian silver memorial plate showing Shapur II in a boar hunt. A splendid example of Sassanian craftsmanship.

For example, in their weapons, men's costumes and armor, and in horse trappings characteristically Iranian styles were evolved. These subjects in turn were depicted on gilt and silver dishes whose designs indicate a spirit of nationalistic pride.

For their body armor chain mail was developed by the Sassanians. For their ladies, dress fashions, fabrics and cosmetics were created. All these were to be copied throughout the length of Asia.

Religion and religious art forms spread to the east. The Turks of Central Asia were influenced by Sassanian Mazdaism and Manichaeism. Manichaean paintings and religious figurines have been found in parts of Turkistan occupied by Uighur Turks in the period following the Sassanian.

Sassanian articles traveled west to the Byzantine Empire and beyond. For example, the imperial costume of Constantinople was introduced from Iran by Diocletian. In architecture a strong Iranian strain runs through the decorative motifs of Byzantine buildings. Further north the Scythian art of southern Russia shows both Greek and Iranian influences, and it is known that Sassanian metalwork was imported into that area.

Probably the greatest cultural influence of Sassanian Persia was exerted on the conquerors of Iran, the Arabs, and on those other peoples who after

being converted to the Moslem faith were to make up the vast Islamic world.
The Arabs had little culture of their own, and consequently the rich Iranian
culture which they won by conquest had a profound effect on them. From
western Asia the Arabs carried Iranian cultural influence across North Africa
and as far west as the Iberian peninsula.

BASIC DATES

329–c. 139 B.C.	Greeks in Bactria
249 B.C.– A.D. 226	Arsacid dynasty of Parthia
249 B.C.– 247 B.C.	Arsaces I
C. 297 B.C.	Armenia becomes Christian
C. 200–175 B.C.	Greeks conquer Punjab
C. 200–40 B.C.	Greeks rule Kabul
190 B.C.	Romans defeat Seleucids at Magnesia
C. 174–160 B.C.	Yüeh- chi invade Central Asia
C. 150 B.C.	Sakas occupy Sogdia
C. 139 B.C.	Sakas occupy Bactria
129 B.C.	Province of "Asia"
C. 75 B.C.	Sakas invade India
C. 75 B.C.	Yüeh-chi in Bactria
65–62 B.C.	Four Eastern Roman provinces formed
1st cent. B.C. to C. A.D. 225	Kushan rulers of Yüeh-chi
C. A.D. 78–96	Kanishka
A.D. 113–117	Trajan's Parthian war
A.D. 226–651	Sassanian empire
215–273	Mani
226–240	Ardashir I
2nd and 3rd centuries A.D.	Syrian type of Christianity
309–379	Shapur II
A.D. 312	Conversion of Constantine
A.D. 325	Council of Nicaea
3rd to 7th centuries	Wars with Sassanian empire
A.D. 425	White Huns (Hephthalites) occupy Bactria
C. A.D. 451	Nestorius dies
5th and 6th centuries A.D.	Monophysite doctrine in Greek church
502–C. A.D. 528	Mihiragula invades India
531–579	Anushirwan the Just (Chosroes)
552–A.D. 650	Turks predominant in Central Asia
589–628	Khusru Parviz (Chosroes II)
A.D. 635	Syrian church in China
A.D. 635–639	Moslem Arabs take Syria and Mesopotamia
641	Battle of Nehawand

SUPPLEMENTARY READING

GROUSSET, R. *The Civilizations of the East, Vol. I: The Near and Middle East.* New York, 1934.

HITTI, P. *The Near East in History.* Princeton, N. J., 1961.

HUART, C. *Ancient Persia and Iranian Civilization.* New York, 1927.

SANFORD, E. M. *The Mediterranean World in Ancient Times.* New York, 1938.

ADVANCED READING

ARBERRY, A. J., ET AL. *The Legacy of Persia.* Oxford, 1953.

BROWNE, E. G. *Literary History of Persia.* London, 1906.

BURY, J. B. *History of the Later Roman Empire.* A classic by a famous nineteenth-century historian.

DEBEVOISE, N. C. *A Political History of Parthia.* Chicago, 1938. A good book on a little-known subject.

GHIRSHMAN, R. *Iran.* London, 1954. Covers the Parthian and Sassanian periods.

GIBBON, E. *The Decline and Fall of the Roman Empire.* This multi-volume classic first appeared in 1776-1788 and is still available in many editions.

HITTI, P. *A History of the Arabs.* Princeton, N. J., 1943.

HUDSON, G. F. *Europe and China.* London, 1931.

SYKES, P. *A History of Persia.* Oxford, 1922.

TARN, W. W. *The Greeks in Bactria and India.* Cambridge, 1938. This fascinating book, based primarily on numismatic evidence, reconstructs history almost in the vein of a detective story.

VASILIEV, A. A. *History of the Byzantine Empire,* Madison, Wis., 1928. A standard work.

V

THE EXPANSION

OF ISLAM, 622 - 1220

THE RISE OF ISLAM and its development as the dominant force in Southwest Asia is the main theme in a six hundred year period beginning in the seventh century. As we have already noted, the achievement of the Arabs was accomplished partly at the expense of the Persian Sassanian empire, and that state ceased to exist after it was overthrown by the successors of Muhammad. On the other hand the Graeco-Roman Byzantine empire resisted the Arab advance and continued to be a factor of political and cultural importance in Asia until the fifteenth century. The detailed history of Byzantium (Constantinople), its court, its Orthodox Christian organization, and its key economic position between East and West is a prominent feature of the European Middle Ages. As such it is not within the scope of this volume. References to Asian historical events connected with the Byzantine empire and Europe in general are here presented with only passing mention of the Europe of that time and will require fuller study from other sources for an understanding of the European aspects of this history.

Sassanian-Byzantine rivalry was in its final phase at the beginning of the seventh century. These two empires, although strong, wealthy, and impressively organized in their rule of subject populations, were to go down before the impact of a new religious impulse,

Islam, an impulse carried principally by two population groups which as yet had had no influence whatever on the main course of events in Western Asia. These were the Arabs, who had lived heretofore as poor, disunited quarreling tribes in the inhospitable Arabian peninsula, and the Turks, who first came into prominence about 550 as a nomadic power on the western borders of China.

Islam, which means literally "submission to God's will," began with one man Muhammad, who under extraordinary circumstances declared himself to be the messenger of God, convinced a large number of his fellow Arabs of the truth of his assertion, and started a campaign which was to carry his teachings halfway around the world, as far west as the Iberian peninsula and east to the Philippine Islands. Of course, many elements other than the personality and the teachings of the man Muhammad played a role in the shaping of this new religion, but in its origins it is very much the work of one man and strongly reflects his own personal experiences and attitudes.

Muhammad

Muhammad was born in about 570 in Mecca, a city located midway down the Arabian peninsula near the Red Sea coast, a trading center which attracted caravans from all over Arabia and which, because of the presence there of a much venerated black meteor stone, was a place of pilgrimage also. This does not mean, however, that Mecca exercised any political, commercial, or religious authority over all of Arabia. The peninsula was divided up among numerous tribes, each of which was fiercely independent of the others and recognized no law superior to its own tribal customs and regulations. Warfare between various tribes was nearly constant. The strong bonds of tribal loyalty tended to bring entire groups into conflict even when the quarrel had its origins in a blood feud between individuals.

In Mecca conditions were more peaceful, partly because commerce required a certain stability and safety of persons involved, and the presence there of a sacred stone helped establish a tradition that blood should not be spilled in Mecca, though anything might happen just outside its gates. But Mecca was merely a part of the holdings of one tribe, the wealthy Quraysh (Quraish), among whom the Umayyah clan constituted a leading element. The clan of Muhammad was another less prominent subdivision of the Quraysh. As a group this tribe was noted for skill in business and this enabled them to make Mecca a commercial rendezvous for all Arabia. Even the growth in religious significance of the black meteor, called Ka'bah, was probably cultivated by the Quraysh in the interest of trade.

LIFE OF MUHAMMAD. There seem to be no claims of divine portents surrounding the birth of Muhammad, no virgin mother or other such miraculous happenings as have been ascribed to Jesus. Muhammad was the son of a small merchant. Orphaned as a small child, Muhammad was raised by his grandfather

FIGURE 5.1.   Muhammad on a mythical beast ascending the heavens.

and when old enough he went into business, eventually becoming the caravan agent for a wealthy merchant's widow. This lady had had two previous husbands, and she seems to have been shrewd and astute enough in the caravan trade to have prospered despite their premature departure. Sometime after he came into her employ she suggested marriage to Muhammad who accepted, although a full fifteen years younger than she. This woman, Khadijah, the first wife of Muhammad, is of some interest for she was apparently the first to be convinced of the truth of his "message from God."

Muhammad married at about twenty-five years of age, and for a number of years thereafter he gave no outward indication of the role he was to play. He fathered six children, including two sons, both of whom died very young, and four daughters, and he continued to be active in his wife's business. He seems to have been a handsome man, rather shy and reserved.

In his business contacts through the years Muhammad met a variety of people. He became acquainted with Jews and Christians, both of whom were active in Arabian trade, had settlements in Arabian towns such as Mecca and Medina, and maintained connections with the trading cities of Palestine and Syria. Muhammad probably made at least one trip north himself, to Bostra, near Jerusalem. That Muhammad was interested in their religious ideas is attested by his many allusions to biblical figures and happenings in his later religious teaching, but there is no evidence that he received any precise religious instruction from them; on the contrary his biblical knowledge was rather vague.

One Judeo-Christian idea must have stood out boldly and clearly amidst the heterogenous religious ideas of the Arabian tribes, that of one god, a central godhead. It may be presumed that an inquiring and sensitive person who had felt the impact of the death of his two sons would ponder on this, and perhaps argue the question with some of his business acquaintances. But Muhammad was not easily persuaded to accept monotheism; indeed, one of his sons seems to have been named for a Meccan tribal god.

Muhammad's religious speculations were climaxed by lonely wandering into the desert wherein he sought divine guidance, and at last, according to his account, he found it. A mysterious figure appeared to him on Mount Hira who, he was convinced, brought him a message direct from God. Exactly what this message was, or what Muhammad thought it was, is not known in its original form for he did not personally write it down.

MUHAMMAD'S RELIGIOUS IDEAS. The experience on Mount Hira, when reduced to its fundamental meaning, simply convinced Muhammad of the existence of one god and of the fact that he, Muhammad, was God's messenger on earth. With this central conviction, Muhammad then turned to his rather haphazard knowledge of the Judeo-Christian tradition and sought to fit together their teachings and his experiences. He came to the conclusion that the mysterious figure he had seen was the angel Gabriel, and that the message of God had been delivered earlier to other prophets, biblical figures like Moses, Noah, Abraham and Jesus, whose efforts to spread the word resulted in the production of "the Book," the Bible. This was indeed a "Book of God," but incomplete and insufficient without his own message, which was the most perfect and the last. His mission, as he saw it, was to bring all people to faith in and submission to the will of God and to an acceptance of his corrected version of "the Book." The one God he called Allah, which may have been an Arabic rendition of an Aramaic word meaning universal god or it may have been the name of a principal god of the Black Meteor cult, thus raised to a universal application.

Muhammad's wife and daughters and a few friends were quickly convinced of the truth of his experience, but for a number of years his teaching had no effect beyond this small circle. Muhammad's conversion to the one god, Allah, occurred when he was about forty years old, around the year 610. However, his teachings did not excite much interest in Mecca until approximately 615, at which time he sent some of his followers out of Mecca to the protection of the Christian ruler of Abyssinia lest they be persecuted. Muhammad himself remained, secure in the protection of his clan, who refused to allow him to be persecuted even though some of its members did not like his teaching. In 619 Muhammad lost his first and most faithful follower through the death of his wife Khadijah. By this time he was gaining converts in larger numbers. Some were people of considerable importance in Mecca and this tended to crystallize the opposition and make it more determined.

When a man who was extremely antagonistic to the new faith became head of Muhammad's own clan, the Prophet's position in Mecca became impossible.

He therefore began, about 620, to think in terms of leaving the city, and after some indecision he finally decided to accept an invitation to go to Mecca's neighboring and rival city of Yathrib, which later he renamed Medina. The choice of Medina was an intelligent one for Muhammad's purpose. The city was ridden with factional strife, amidst which Muhammad could and did become a mediator. Furthermore, the people there were by no means unacquainted with the idea of one god, for there was a large Jewish community with which Muhammad seems to have expected to forge a common bond. It is interesting in view of the later Moslem antagonism to unbelievers, including Jews and Christians, that in these early days Muhammad regarded these "people of the Book" as kindred spirits, who knew the truth of one god and who only lacked the knowledge of the finally delineated "message from God" which he was bringing to them.

THE HEGIRA.   In 622 Muhammad and his followers left Mecca for Medina. This event is the *Hegira* (or *Hijrah*) from which the Moslem calendar is dated. In Medina Muhammad was successful in mediating the disputes and assuming the leadership of the whole Arab community. Thus, beginning with his followers in Medina at this time, Muhammad established his rule over a religio-political community whose separate existence under his direction constituted the earliest phase of the great Islamic empire of later times. But the Jews in Medina did not accept Muhammad. This resulted in long arguments with their leaders, and Muhammad went to great lengths to emphasize that his teaching was compatible with theirs. He adopted some of their fast days and added a third daily prayer, Jewish fashion, to the two which he had earlier prescribed for his followers. With the Jews' refusal to acknowledge his teaching and leadership, Muhammad became increasingly irritated and ended by attacking, driving them from the city and seizing their property.

During his sojourn at Medina, as his power and confidence grew, Muhammad seems to have reached the conclusion that his mission was so great and his judgment so infallible that any means might be used to bring unbelievers to submission to his true faith. If conversion was not forthcoming after invitation or persuasion, then force might be used, and any booty taken in the process was the reward of the faithful. He began to organize raids against caravans bound to and from Mecca. Though there was some opposition to this as dishonorable even among Medinese, they were generally persuaded by the sight of the booty collected on some of the successful expeditions. Meccans, of course, became furious with both Medina and Muhammad and began preparations to subdue them. These preparations came to a climax in 627 when an army of 10,000 moved against Medina and laid siege to the city. To meet the threat Muhammad roused his followers to a high point of zeal and energy, and they, staving off the Meccan attack by means of trenches, eventually forced the lifting of the siege.

After this fiasco the Meccans began to negotiate with Muhammad. A treaty resulted in which it was agreed that Mecca would once again become the religious (and commercial) center of Arabia, Muhammad would be welcomed into the city as its religious leader. The negotiations, handled through members of Muhammad's clan who had remained in Mecca, were somewhat tedious but the result was never in doubt. Even before the final settlement many of the leading men of Mecca professed themselves adherents of the new Islamic faith. Muhammad meanwhile had ceased to talk of his original idea that the one god of the Jews and Christians was indeed Allah; rather he emphasized more and more the Arabian character of his teachings and reintroduced the Ka'bah as a truly sacred stone now presided over by Allah.

In 630 Muhammad returned to Mecca in triumph, his way so well prepared that only a small group within the city thought seriously of offering resistance. These were speedily dispersed. After this one by one the tribes of Arabia submitted to the authority of Muhammad. He sent religious teachers and tax collectors among them; if the tribes refused to honor such agents as these, then he sent his Bedouin warriors against them. There was some resistance but by 632, when Muhammad died in the midst of plans to send armies north against Byzantine territory, Arabia was within his grasp. Significantly, the old tribal cults offered no competition to Islam; only the Jews and Christians held steadfast against the demand for submission to the new faith, and unable to change their views, Muhammad developed a policy of levying on them a special tribute in return for which they were allowed freedom of worship.

THE KORAN.   It was not until some years after Muhammad's death that his sayings and teachings were transcribed in their standard form. This book, the Koran (Qur'an), has become the holy book of the Islamic faith. Those who compiled the Koran sought to reproduce as accurately as possible the words of the Prophet; hence even though it is a later version of what Muhammad said, it should not be underestimated as a historical source. In many ways the Koran is easier to appraise critically than the Bible, because it is fundamentally the teaching of one man, rather than, as with the Bible, of many, and it was set down in at least semidefinitive form shortly after the author's death. Furthermore Muhammad, unlike Jesus, was anxious that his teachings be set down in writing since he thought they comprised a final rendering of "God's Book," whose truth Jews and Christians had caught in part through their prophets and which he now had in final form. Muhammad had a secretary, Zayd ibn-Thābit, who could write, and there is evidence that some of the early stalwarts of Islam, Umar, Ali, and Uthman, were listed as being among some seventeen men from the Quraysh tribe who knew how to write. The early pronouncements of Muhammad were set forth publicly as decrees at Medina, and therefore would likely have been preserved in a fixed form. Specialist "Koran reciters" preserved the teachings orally. There were nevertheless several versions of the Koran which had to be considered when the overall compilation was undertaken in 651, and all but one of these were burned in order that there be no question as to the official text. The Koran shows a rather clear progression of style from the early terse, compact, intense pronouncements of one who had newly come to consider himself a prophet to the more wordy and polished arguments of a preacher-politician,

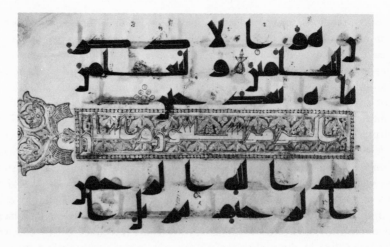

FIGURE 5.2.   A page of the Koran, eighth century.

who is at pains to show his personal attitudes and activities in consonance with
the great truth he is revealing.

Tenets of Islam

The non-Moslem who views the Koran is perhaps first of all struck by the way
in which Muhammad identifies his private inclinations with the will of Allah. For
example, after the death of Khadijah, he took a number of other wives and several concubines. Later, after some years of living with a harem of several wives,
Muhammad finally settled down with one. In the Koran, however, it was set
forth as the will of Allah that all believers may have a maximum of four wives,
except the Prophet who might have as many as he pleased. On another occasion
a scandal arose when one of the Prophet's wives, the daughter of his close friend
Abu Bakr, apparently stayed out all night with another man. Some of his followers urged Muhammad to divorce her. Since she was his favorite he refused to
do so and instead set forth as the will of Allah the dictum that there must be
four eyewitnesses to sustain a case of adultery, for which, in this case, there were
not. Allah's will concerning wine was first reported as indicating that wine is
desirable. Later, after Muhammad's soldiers of the faith were found to be
drinking too much, wine was interdicted, but they might count on having plenty
in heaven. In heaven the Koran also states that there are to be ever youthful
and beautiful virgins "with large dark eyes like pearls hidden in their shells" for
the gratification of the masculine faithful. In another case of inconsistency the
Prophet first denounced idolatry, and then when it became expedient for his re-
entry into Mecca, he embraced the Ka'bah. In spite of such anomalies the faithful have not been deterred from confidence in the Prophet or the "Book of Allah."

There are also great truths and noble ideas in the Koranic teachings. These
ideas were much in contrast to the poor Arabian heritage out of which they came.

The message of Muhammad has a dignity and universality which is comparable with the best in other great religions of the world. There are few other religious teachings in which the concept of the essential equality and brotherhood of men without regard to race or class is so vigorously set forth. Slave and ruler alike are enjoined to kneel together in submission to Allah's will.

The Islamic brotherhood was defined as including only Moslems, those who acknowledged Allah in accordance with Muhammad's prescription. Thus while the idea of brotherhood among the faithful was a great advance over the blood feud tribalism of pre-Islamic Arabia, Islam has not proved conducive to brotherhood in the world-wide sense. Muhammad's use of force against Jews and others, when he found persuasion to no avail, found koranic expression in the exhortation to holy war *(jihad)* against infidels. Even in the holy month, when Moslems were enjoined against eating or drinking from dawn to sunset, it was decreed that they should proceed with jihad. Brotherhood yet jihad; here would seem to lie the fundamental contradiction in Islam.

Other basic tenets of the Islamic faith include almsgiving, prayer, fasting, and pilgrimage. The giving of alms to poor and unfortunate members of society is a never ceasing obligation to the Moslem. Perhaps Muhammad's memories of his own orphaned childhood contributed to his concern for widows and orphans; however that may be, the insistence on charity as Allah's will constitutes one of the noblest features of Islam.

Prayer, frequently and humbly performed, is another pillar of the faith. Muhammad at first prescribed two prayers a day, then at Medina, in deference to Jewish tradition, three per day, but later the number was fixed at five, early morning, noon, mid-afternoon, sunset and dark. The prayers are partly a purification process, partly a profession of faith toward Allah and partly a symbol of the brotherhood of Islam. The Moslem turns toward Mecca when he prays; on Friday noon the prayer is done in public at a mosque, led by a special prayer leader *(imam)*, who may also deliver an address. Muhammad himself led public prayers during his lifetime.

Muhammad first demanded fast days of his followers during the period in which he was seeking rapprochement with the Jews at Medina; certain Jewish fast days were to be observed. This ripened into koranic injunction to fasting "a certain number of days that you may fear Allah." If sick or on a journey one may forego fasting if he will make it up by fasting on other than the designated days, or he may redeem his neglect of fasting by supporting a "poor man," presumably for an equivalent number of days. In addition to special individual fast days, one entire month called Ramadan was set aside especially for fasting. During this time no food should be eaten between dawn and sunset, though after dark a feast may be prepared. This fast was enjoined because, according to the Koran, it was during this month that the Koran itself was sent down from heaven.

Pilgrimage refers to pilgrimage to Mecca, specifically to the holy stone, Ka'bah, which each Moslem from whatever part of the world should undertake at least once in his lifetime. In the Koran, he who would profane the Ka'bah shall receive "grievous torment." This point is interpreted to imply a justification for the banning of unbelievers from the holy precincts. Wearing of special garments, a shaven head, and special ceremonies are associated with the pilgrimage.

Stressed again and again through the whole koramic teaching is the fundamental insistence on acceptance of the one god, Allah, and Muhammad as his messenger, and the promise of doom for those who do not adopt these precepts. Allah is represented as merciful and patient. There is, however, a "last day," a judgment day on which the earth will be shaken, the mountains crumbled, and each man judged in accordance with his deeds. Those people of the right hand (e.g., those whose book of deeds is placed in their right hand) will be allowed entry into paradise, but the people of the left hand shall suffer damnation amidst burning winds and scalding water. The day of judgment will come suddenly, without warning, its time known only to Allah.

The Early Caliphs, 632–661

The death of Muhammad in 632 posed a crisis for Islam. Who would assume the leadership of the new religion? Muhammad's sons had preceded him in death, and though his single surviving daughter, Fatima, or one of her sons might have been considered his heir, none of these was entrusted with the leadership. Muhammad left no will, indeed was prevented by his followers from making one at the last moment lest his feverish condition make it unintelligible or misleading. Ali, the husband of Fatima and son-in-law of the Prophet, was a strong candidate but there were various groups anxious to assert their prior claim. The choice fell on the aged and venerable Abu Bakr, the father of Muhammad's favorite second wife and one of the earliest converts to the faith. He became *caliph,* or successor, to Muhammad but not to the extent of assuming the "messenger of Allah" role. The caliph was not presumed to have supernatural powers but he was accepted as religious and political leader by the inner circle of Islam. He received oaths of allegiance from the chieftains of various tribes and was known as "defender of the faith."

ABU BAKR.   Abu Bakr's principal objective was the expansion of Islam northward into Byzantine territory, following out the plan envisaged by Muhammad at the time of death. The new caliph sent troops north against the Byzantines, but he was soon forced to recall them to combat the numerous rebellions against his authority in Arabia. Many groups, even though they had accepted Islam, indicated unwillingness to pay taxes into the coffers of the new leadership. It required intensive military activity over many months before all Arabia accepted the leadership of the new caliph. When this was accomplished, once again Abu Bakr turned his small, but compact and zealous armies outward from Arabia. On this occasion they moved into Mesopotamia against Sassanian Persians whom they easily defeated. Then Abu Bakr renewed the Byzantine campaign, sending troops into Syria, with the objective of taking Damascus. The caliph himself did not live to see this accomplished for he died in 634, but Damascus fell to the Arabs in the autumn of 635.

UMAR. After Abu Bakr's death Umar, also one of the early followers of Muhammad, and one who had been high in Moslem councils during the exile in Medina, became caliph. His immediate problem was a military one resulting from the expansion into Byzantine territories. The Byzantine emperor Heraclius, alarmed by the Moslem advance, sent a large army commanded by his brother against the Arabs. This Byzantine army outnumbered the Arabs, but it contained discontented elements, particularly the Armenians, which failed to withstand the Arab onslaught. The Byzantine rout was complete and the Arabs moved northward with ease, annexing the whole of Syria, including the great city of Antioch.

In many cases the Syrian towns welcomed the Arab forces, possibly to align themselves with the winning side and perhaps because the Moslem demands upon occupying a town were not harsh. The caliph demanded a poll tax, levied on every non-Moslem inhabitant, but otherwise did not interfere with the activities or the faith of the nonbelievers.

Meanwhile to the east Sassanian troops were being raised to drive the Moslems out of Mesopotamia. The Iranian forces were large but poorly disciplined compared to the Arabs. The Arabs won a major victory over the Persians in 637 which advanced their area of control from the Euphrates to the Tigris with Ctesiphon, the Sassanian capital, just beyond. Shortly thereafter, as the Arabs crossed the Tigris, the King of Kings, his court, and the army of defence of Ctesiphon abandoned the city and fled eastward. From this rich Persian capital city the Moslems obtained enough treasure to finance a dozen further campaigns. The final stand and decisive defeat of the Sassanians occurred at Nehawand in 641. By that time other Moslem troops moving northeastward from Syria were in northern Mesopotamia receiving the surrender of Edessa and other important cities in that area; and simultaneously a front was opened in Egypt where the Moslems in September 642 moved into the great port city of Alexandria, following evacuation by the Byzantines. In 644, when the caliph Umar was assassinated by a Persian slave, a great part of Southwest Asia, as well as Egypt, was subject to Moslem rule.

This expansion was truly phenomenal. To explain it one must point to a variety of reasons. The most striking was the religious zeal which gave a sense of conviction to each soldier that he fought in Allah's cause, and that if slain in battle, immediate entry into paradise would be his reward.

Religion is not the only explanation. There was clearly an economic motivation. As the Arabs moved out of their inhospitable home land into richer areas beyond its borders, their dissatisfaction with a life barren of most luxuries must have been increased by the sight of great cities and their rich and varied treasure of material comforts. Once Arabia had been subdued, an iron hand would have been required to suppress the energy which religious zeal and economic needs had set in motion; to contain this energy would have invited disaster to those who attempted it. Religious zeal and economic motivation together with the drive engendered by military success appear to have been basic elements in the Arabian impulse to expansion.

Why were the conquests so rapid and apparently so easy? Although we know that the unwieldy armies of Byzantium and Persia were outmatched by the smaller but more mobile and hard-hitting Moslem forces, this does not explain how the followers of Muhammad could fasten their rule on millions of people without enduring long and bitter guerrilla warfare. The fact was that Syrians, Mesopotamians, and Egyptians hoped to find in Moslem rule some relief from the tyranny of Byzantine and Persian overlords. The caliphate, in the early phases of the expansion, held out some promise of this. Conversion or the sword (the jihad principle) was not applicable to "people of the Book," the Jews and Christians, who, in conformance with the practice Muhammad had developed in Arabia, upon payment of a poll tax were left free to worship as they pleased. This practice was also applied to Zoroastrians. In general, local regulations and governmental apparatus were not drastically changed; Arab officials took over the top posts and the treasuries which had been no concern of the local population anyway.

These Arab officials stabilized the situation quickly, regularized tax collections, opened the way to advantageous treatment to those who would accept Islam, and required military service of none but Moslems. In a short time the Arabs as a ruling caste became as luxury-minded and avaricious as had been Byzantine and Persian overlords, but at first their austere background and tastes probably created an illusion of improvement to the subject peoples.

UTHMAN.   The next two caliphs were Uthman, an Umayyah clansman (644–656), and Ali, the son-in-law of Muhammad (656–661). The years of their respective leadership were a period of intense rivalry, plot and counterplot within the inner circles of Islam between the Umayyah on the one hand and the "family of the Prophet" as represented by Ali on the other. Ali at the same time was detested by Muhammad's surviving wife Aishah, the daughter of Abu Bakr.

When Uthman was assassinated in 656 Ali became caliph in spite of the Umayyah. However, Uthman proved to be worth more to the Umayyah dead than alive. The most powerful member of the clan, Mu'awiyah, governor of Syria, proclaimed himself the avenger of the murdered Uthman and entered upon open revolt against Ali. The latter, already troubled by intrigues and revolts in Arabia which had been abetted by Aishah, found himself unable to meet the challenge of the wily Umayyah leader. He attempted to compromise but, as in the case of his two predecessors, Ali's end came with assassination (661).

The Umayyad Caliphate

Mu'awiyah threw aside any pretense of following an electoral procedure; he had already proclaimed himself caliph even before Ali's death. He now proceeded to establish his capital at Damascus. Next the protagonists of Ali in Arabia were isolated and Ali's son Husain (Hussein) with a band of followers were killed at Kerbela in 680. Not only was Mu'awiyah able to convince almost all the chiefs of Islam to accept his authority but also to swear allegiance to his son, thereby eliminating the question of succession after his death. He thus transformed the religious caliphate into a family dynasty, that of the Umayyads, which was to rule one of the largest empires the world has ever seen.

Although the Umayyad caliphs at the height of their power ruled an empire which stretched from the Indus and Syr rivers across western Asia and North Africa to the Spanish Pyrenees, the history of their era is a dreary story of wars, plots and massacres. During this period the acts done in the name of Allah made a mockery of those noble sentiments set forth in the Koran; the main political characteristic is the continuation of the Umayyad-Alid rivalry which had poisoned the regimes of the last two orthodox caliphs.

It may be said that the "ghosts" of Ali and his son Husain plagued the whole Umayyad dynasty. Under their rule the custom was begun of cursing Ali in the mosques of Syria. Supporters of the Umayyads put his followers to flight, and the caliph himself received the head of Husain after Kerbela. In spite of persecution the pro-Ali sentiment remained alive and eventually found strong support in Iran, which was naturally antagonistic to Arab rule conducted from the Damascus court.

SHI'A.   The pro-Ali movement was religious as well as political. It developed a special separatist creed (Shi'a) which has ever since then opposed the orthodox (Sunni) interpretation of the faith. Under Shi'a doctrine the true succession of Muhammad ran through the family of Ali to a series of imams found only among his descendants. The imam, in contrast to the caliph, was more than a temporal "defender of the faith." In addition he possessed "secret knowledge" not written in the Koran but passed down orally from Muhammad through Ali. The imam, though not a direct messenger of Allah like Muhammad, nevertheless had a certain divine connection which rendered him infallible in interpreting the faith. Thus the leader of Shi'a was a much holier figure than the secularized caliph. The conviction that the Shi'ites were superior in religious sensitivity to the orthodox Moslems doubtless gave much spiritual sustenance to the organizers of the revolt against the Umayyad power, even though later on Abbasid leadership paid little respect to the Shi'ite beliefs.

MOSLEM EXPANSION.   Thus the Umayyad government faced a constant undercurrent of revolt in the pro-Ali movement. It was also weakened by fierce disputes among the Umayyad leadership itself on almost every occasion when a new caliph came into power. In spite of these factors the caliphate had adequate energy and a sufficient measure of internal control of the empire to engage in large scale expansionist military campaigns. They warred against the Byzantines in the north, invading Asia Minor several times, annexing the island of Cyprus, and besieged the great city of Byzantium itself in 668, almost continuously from

674–679, and again in 716–717. In addition, Moslem arms swept across North Africa and in 711 Tarik, after whom Gibraltar is named (from Gebel Tarik, the "mountain of Tarik"), led 7000 Arabs into Spain. Thus began the conquest of the Iberian peninsula. When completed the Moslem forces crossed the Pyrenees in an attempt to conquer France but were stopped at Tours by Charles Martel in 732.

Simultaneously with the Spanish campaign at the western extremity of the Moslem empire, another, half across the world, was launched into northwest India (711). Sind was conquered and the lower Indus river brought under Umayyad control in the following year. Successful campaigns were also fought in eastern Iran and Central Asia.

These campaigns were launched by the greatest and fiercest of Umayyad viceroys, al-Hajjaj, who during the decade after his appointment as governor of Arabia in 692 crushed the anti-Umayyad opposition movement in Arabia and in Mesopotamia and then launched the Persian campaigns. Western Persia was easily brought under control but the Khorasan district was traditionally independent in its relationships even with Persia, and it took the Moslems some years to subdue eastern Iran. That area and areas farther east, including the cities of Balkh, Bukhara and Samarkand, were at last brought entirely under Moslem rule by Kotaiba (Qutayba), governor of Khorasan under al-Hajjaj. In his campaigns between 705–715, Kotaiba recovered Balkh, conquered Bukhara and Samarkand, and established nominal Moslem rule in the area between the Amu Darya and the Syr Darya.

CHANGES IN ISLAM.   Such far flung and diverse campaigning required larger numbers of men for the armies of the caliph than the original strictly Arab components could supply. More and more "neo-Moslems" were used in the army. These were non-Arabian Moslems, at first chiefly Syrians, men who had accepted conversion to Islam and thus were relieved of the discriminatory poll tax, but who still were not given the fullest privileges of Islamic brotherhood. The latter could be had only if they entered the army of the faithful and hence many of them did so. Syrian troops based at the Moslem Mesopotamian headquarters at Kufah on the Euphrates played a large role in the subjugation of eastern Persia. When eastern Persia had been secured Kotaiba demanded military service of Persian subjects.

Thus a degree of cosmopolitanism entered Islam. Inclusion of foreigners in the army of the faithful was only one indication of the breakdown of the distinctively Arabian character of Islam in its earlier years. Each caliph, of course, had his own ideas about how far neo-Moslems and non-Moslems were to be allowed to participate in the government of the empire. Mu'awiyah had a Christian financial advisor and a Jewish convert as teacher-counselor and "historian" at his court. Among the retainers of Umayyad caliphs and governors many leading literary figures, poets and "historians" alike, were non-Moslem or neo-Moslem. Court physicians too were generally non-Arab and often non-

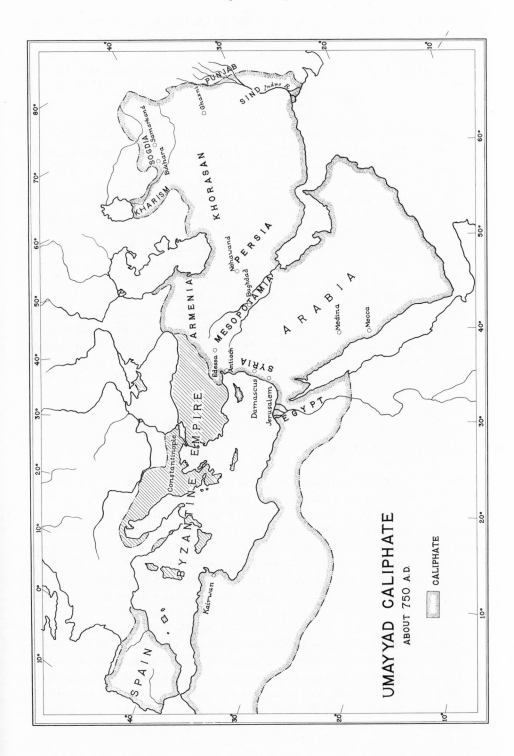

UMAYYAD CALIPHATE

ABOUT 750 A.D.

CALIPHATE

Moslem. The physician of Mu'awiyah was a Christian, that of Marwan I a Jew of Persian origin and that of al-Hajjaj a Greek. The special skills of writers and doctors made them particularly useful.

The greatest factor in making Islam cosmopolitan was intermarriage, or rather concubinage, between Arab conqueror and non-Arab subject. In the course of the Moslem campaigns thousands of slaves were taken, and women in great numbers were added to influential Arab households throughout the Moslem world. When a child was born to such a slave woman he became a free Moslem; and the sons of non-Arab slave women were soon playing leading roles in the administration of every part of the Umayyad empire.

The caliphs varied in allowing these tendencies to develop. Umar II (717–720), who was noted for his piety, tried to prevent Christians and Jews from holding public office. He required them to wear special costumes and he forbade them the use of the turban. But his restrictions did not stem the tide.

A most important determinant in the broadening of Islam was the fact that the culture of the conquered areas was far richer than that of the Arabs who conquered. Beyond the religious tenets of Islam, the Arabic language itself, first used as a stabilized written vehicle of expression in the Koran, was the only major Arab contribution to the newly conquered lands. The language of administration was Arabic, and thus the tendency was for Arabic to become dominant throughout the caliphate. The cultural heritage which was translated into Arabic terminology, on the other hand, was not Arabian; it was made up of Syrian, Persian, Greek, Armenian, Egyptian and other elements. The flowering of this new combined civilization came later in Abbasid times.

The Abbasid Caliphate

The revolutionary movement which was to overthrow the Umayyad dynasty had its first successes in Khorasan. There an "Abbasid party" (named after Abbas, uncle of Muhammad) comprised of Iranians who opposed Arab rule as foreign domination and Shi'ite supporters of "the Family of the Prophet" began to propagandize openly from about 745. Evidently the movement had great strength even before that time for the Umayyad governors of the province were utterly unable to suppress them. The people of Khorasan had no primary connection with the Abbasid-Shi'ite coalition. The group originated in Iraq where recognition that Abbas and Ali, the objects of veneration of the respective elements of the coalition, were both members of the "Family of the Prophet" made possible the joining of forces. In Khorasan the people were simply anti-Umayyad, as indeed were most Persians; but, being less integrated into the Umayyad system of control and with many sons in administrative posts, they were in a better position to nourish a revolutionary movement. Abbasid agents became fully aware of this in the course of their efforts to secure support, and therefore they concentrated first attention on Khorasan.

Open revolt commenced in Khorasan in June 747 with the unfurling of the previously secret Abbasid black banner of "legitimacy." The Umayyad governor appealed for help to his caliph, Marwan II, but the relief forces were disastrously defeated by the rebels the following year (748). When Merv, the capital of Khorasan, was taken by the insurgents, events moved with a swiftness which must be taken as proof not only of the superior organization of the revolutionaries but of widespread dissatisfaction with Umayyad rule throughout Western Asia.

After the great success in Khorasan, Abbasid leaders together with the chiefs of Khorasan repaired to Kufah; in November 749 Abu-al-Abbas was publicly enthroned as the first Abbasid caliph. Marwan tried to rally Syrian support behind him, but it was halfhearted, and soon Umayyad forces everywhere were in retreat. Marwan himself was caught and killed in August 750, Damascus was taken, and scions of the Umayyad house were relentlessly pursued to near extermination. One of the very few who evaded the Abbasids' murderous hands was Abd-al-Rahman, a grandson of the tenth caliph of Damascus. His escape from the Abbasids, flight across North Africa and establishment of the Umayyad caliphate at Cordova, Spain in 756 form one of the most dramatic episodes in Arabic history. In following up their attack the Abbasids desecrated the tombs of the Umayyads, and only the one belonging to the pious Umar II was not violated.

At its end the Umayyad dynasty could command no substantial support. It was as if the whole Moslem world had indeed accepted the Abbasid dictum that they had violated the heritage of the Prophet. The Abbasids proclaimed a new era wherein presumably the true religious aspect of the state would be emphasized and never, in Umayyad fashion, be profaned. However, this was not to be the case.

BAGHDAD AS NEW CAPITAL. The Abbasid caliphs soon found themselves embarrassed by the religiosity of their Shi'ite supporters. Undertaking to break away from that influence, the Abbasids began by moving the seat of government out of Shi'ite-dominated Kufah. They first went to various nearby places and finally settled on Baghdad. This city, founded by al-Mansur, the second Abbasid caliph, in 762, served as the permanent capital of the Abbasid empire until it fell to the Mongols in 1258. For several centuries Baghdad was one of the greatest cities in the world, rich and elegant, a center of cultural and political activity with which only Constantinople could be compared. The Abbasid capital, which was constructed in four years, required the energies of a hundred thousand workmen and the expenditure of 4,883,000 dirhams, but when it was finished it stood as an almost impregnable fortress, surrounded by three walls and moats, and in a controlling position on the great Tigris-Euphrates waterway.

Al-Mansur, caliph from 754–775, ruled the empire with the same ruthless energy which went into the building of Baghdad. He sought out and executed the disgruntled leaders of Shi'a, forcing that movement into quiescence. He put down several insurrections against his authority in Iran, including one in Khorasan where the governor showed too much independence to suit the caliph.

Khorasan, the frontier But of Islam, continued to give rise to dissident movements and strange sects which again and again troubled the caliphs at Baghdad. Al-Mansur was never able to recapture the frontiers which the Umayyads had held in North Africa and Spain. Egypt, Tripoli and Tunis at one time submitted to his authority but this control was tenuous at best and during most of the Abbasid period these areas were actually independent of Baghdad. However, the Asian portion of al-Mansur's domain was even larger than the comparable territory of the Umayyads, for he made conquests in the Caspian area, including Baku, he invaded Afghanistan and seized part of northwest India. As in Umayyad times, Sind and Baluchistan were provinces of the caliphate. Wars against Byzantium were continued but without noticeable territorial gain.

ABBASID ADMINISTRATION. The Abbasid government, situated on the Tigris at Baghdad not far from the old Sassanian capital of Ctesiphon, was much more susceptible to Iranian influence and orientation than Damascus had been. This was reflected in the governmental structure itself, as established by al-Mansur and continued by his successors. The first officer of the realm, beneath the caliph, was the vizir, a Persian office which al-Mansur seems to have incorporated into his government in order to obtain necessary advice from Persian sources. The first vizir under the Abbasids was the son of a Buddhist priest (called a *barmak*) from Balkh. This man was an exceedingly loyal, helpful, and influential counselor to al-Mansur. Thereafter Barmakids, i.e. descendants of this barmak, occupied the office by hereditary right until the early tenth century. They were extremely powerful, being given the responsibility even of selecting and deposing governors of provinces and of presiding over cabinet meetings of the highest officials of the realm. When a caliph was weak or inattentive to matters of state it was the vizir who actually ruled. However, none of them challenged the right to succession to the office of caliph as resident in the family of Abbas. All succeeding Abbasid caliphs were in fact lineal descendants of al-Mansur.

The empire was divided into provinces, some 24 at its height. They varied in size; Egypt, for example, constituted one province. But Mesopotamia was broken into four, wherein the southernmost province, governed from Basra, included Bahrein and Uma on the Arabian coast; the eastern (Persian Iraq) extended as far east as Isfahan; the northern extended to Armenia and the Caspian, including Tabriz; and the western, with its capital at Mosul, extended to the border of Asia Minor. Thus a very considerable part of Western Asia was linked directly to the headquarters of Abbasid power, Mesopotamia. Some governors were of higher rank than others and presumably had broader powers, but in practice much depended on the personal qualities of the man himself. Communications within the empire were never sufficient to prevent a considerable degree of decentralization, although a postal service which included the use of carrier pigeons, was maintained. The postal authorities also compiled maps, made surveys and operated the caliph's spy system.

The Abbasid treasury seems to have been amply supplied from tax collections. Moslems paid a property tax and non-Moslems paid this plus the poll tax. There were also various merchandising and business taxes levied on non-Moslems. Booty and tribute from frontier military campaigns continued to add to revenues, and when a rich man fell from the favor of the caliph or vizir his wealth was confiscated. With the monies thus collected Baghdad was lavishly furnished and came to support a high consuming population. But in al-Mansur's time there was also considerable attention to public works, roadbuilding, and to the construction of mosques throughout the empire. The bases of justice and law were religious, the Koran being the basic text, and judges were without exception Moslem theologians who decided cases and imposed punishments in accordance with their interpretation of Koranic precepts.

Al-Mansur was the real founder of the Abbasid dynasty. However, the caliphs of that line whose names have been most famous were Harun al-Rashid (785–809) and al-Mamun (813–833), neither of whom compared with al-Mansur in administrative capacity or political sagacity and certainly not in frugality. These later caliphs reaped and expended the rewards of the system he established. Much of their vast expenditure went to support a luxurious and indolent court, which required thousands of slaves to answer its every whim and which by its elaborate harem system became the model of debauchery pictured in the *Arabian Nights* of Harun's time. Certainly Harun and al-Mamun cannot be credited with a sense of duty or even compassion for their subjects whose tax monies they so cheerfully spent. Nor were they pious or intelligent. Much of their greatness is due to their anxiety to increase the glory of their capital. They invited to Baghdad and sponsored many able men of letters and arts, men of diverse cultural background, Persian, Indian, Syrian, Armenian, Greek, who brought with them their books and collected others. For the sake of inter-communication between the scholars of foreign background as well as for transmission to their Arabic-speaking patrons, the caliphs, it was necessary that these works first of all be translated into Arabic. This was accomplished on a magnificent scale, especially after Mamun established an academy, called the House of Science, at Baghdad, which undertook translations as a major share of its activity.

ABBASID CULTURE. By the eleventh century academies had been established in practically every important city in the empire, and the intellectual quickening had ripened into a veritable renaissance. Important work was done in almost every field of learning known to ancient or medieval man. Law and theology were peculiarly favorite fields for Moslem Arab intellectuals, but medicine, astronomy, mathematics, alchemy, geography, philology, linguistics, history and pure literature, especially poetry, attracted scholars of every sort. Not only were old materials collected, translated and preserved but important advances were made in all these fields. In medicine, for example, though there was little knowledge of anatomy, there was a considerable knowledge and use of drugs; apothecary shops were established, physicians and druggists were required to pass tests and the first hospital in the Islamic world was established

FIGURE 5.3.   An illustration from an Arabic translation of the *Materia Medica* of Dioscorides made in Baghdad in Abbasid times.

in Baghdad in the ninth century. Al-Razi, probably the greatest and most original of the Moslem physicians was also a prolific writer on medical subjects. His works were later translated into Latin and passed into Europe as standard medical texts. This was characteristic of other areas of learning as well. The Arabs translated, preserved, and added to the work the ancients had done in all fields, and from the Arabs this learning eventually found its way into Europe in the late medieval era of the Crusaders' contacts.

Astronomy made great strides under Abbasid sponsorship. An observatory was among the many buildings erected for the advancement of learning in Baghdad. Under al-Mamun, astronomers, assuming a hypothesis that the earth was round, calculated its circumference with remarkably accurate results. They improved on the Gregorian calendar, introduced the Hindu zero into mathematics and compiled the first textbook on algebra. Translation of this work and others of the author, al-Kharizmi, introduced Arabic numerals to Europe. Ptolemy's geography was translated into Arabic and improved on, for the Moslems, with their koranic injunctions concerning pilgrimages, had a great interest in and need for practical geography. Histories were compiled. Islam was an "historical religion" and the place of Muhammad in history was of

FIGURE 5.4. A star map showing the constellation of the Gemini, or Twins. A fine example of Arab astronomical work. From the manuscript of the *Book of the Fixed Stars* of 'Abd ar-Rahman as-Sufi (905–986), Persian.

great importance. This had to be "accurately" established, and the events which flowed from it explained in logical, albeit religio-historical terms. Moslem historians developed a sophisticated methodology which utilized eyewitness reports, oral transmission and written documents as three types of historical evidence. Unfortunately they also developed the practice of simply omitting mention of a great man's bad deeds and of happenings which contravened Islamic regulations. The general tenet was that history should be instructive and therefore should not record evil things. In spite of this basic flaw important historical work was done, including al-Tabari's monumental universal history in the ninth century.

DECLINE OF ABBASID POWER. The breakup of the Abbasid empire must be attributed to several diverse causes: revolts within the empire which kept it in turmoil and split off large territorial segments; the intrusion of Turks into the armies of the caliph with the result that, as his bodyguards, they became more powerful than the caliph himself; a deterioration in Abbasid fortunes in the wars against the Byzantines, a situation climaxed by the coming of the Crusaders; and lastly, a series of Mongol invasions which culminated in 1258 with the capture of Baghdad itself.

After al-Mamun there were continuous internal troubles, of which only a few examples will be given. A rebellious kingdom of Negro slaves controlled southern Mesopotamia from Basra (869–883) in defiance of Abbasid authority. No sooner was that put down than a group known as the Qarmatians rose in

Iraq, expanded into Arabia and even seized Mecca and the Black Stone in 928. After that event Abbasid authority was unable to re-establish itself in Arabia. From 868 Egypt was generally beyond the control of the Baghdad caliph, and in the tenth century the Fatimids, claiming descent from Muhammad's daughter and hence legitimacy as caliphs, established a dynasty there in competition with the Abbasids. They expanded into Syria and helped to undermine Abbasid authority. After 969 when an Armenian general named John Tzimisces seized the Byzantine throne and began an aggressive war in northern Mesopotamia and Syria, Abbasid fortunes waned steadily in those regions. Then the Crusaders came, took Jerusalem in 1099 and proceeded to inaugurate western Christian rule in Palestine and Syria, opening a long struggle with the Egyptian caliphate over their control. To this the Abbasids were mere bystanders. The "Latin States" established by the Crusaders were almost entirely eliminated by Saladin, who ruled in Egypt from 1171 until his death in 1193. The region of his conquests extended as far as Mosul in Mesopotamia. For another hundred years, until long after the arrival of the Mongols, the struggle continued and western Christians competed with Moslems for control of Lebanon and Palestine.

Meanwhile the Abbasids were also losing control of the eastern portion of their empire. Already in the time of al-Mamun, Khorasan under a line of Persian rulers became independent. They were followed by two other Persian groups in eastern Iran, the second of which was the Samanids (872–999). These Moslem Iranians ruled from Bukhara and during their time they fostered a revival of Persian culture under which many Arabic works were translated back into Persian. The Samanids were largely responsible for the conversion of Turkish tribes to Islam and, by giving them a taste of Persian culture, arousing their interest in the Abbasid controlled lands of southwestern Asia.

The Turks

Throughout the period we have been studying in this chapter and on into the thirteenth century a second force from the outside greatly affected the area of Persian culture. This force, that of the nomads from the steppe, was in fact the same that Zoroaster spoke about in describing the tribesmen from the north as a force of evil threatening the life of the settled agriculturalists of the Iranian plateau. Enemies from the steppe had been a constant threat to the Sassanians. By the middle of the sixth century, as we have seen, the ruling tribes were Turks. They had overcome the White Huns and made themselves masters of the steppe from modern Mongolia over to the Amu Darya. In the centuries from Muhammad until Chingis Khan Turkish "barbarians" had their effect on Persia and the whole of Southwest Asia.

Who were these Turks who were predominant in Central Asia from the middle of the sixth century to the middle of the seventh? They were a nomadic steppe people, perhaps part Hsiung-nu or Hun, who came from the region near Issyk-kol north of the Heavenly Mountains (T'ien-shan). Their name was "T'u-chüeh" or "Kök Turks" and they considered themselves distinct from the Huns. It is to be noted that the word "Turks," probably first used by the Moslems, is not used for persons of one race or tribe but has been employed since the sixth century to designate a group of peoples all of whom used one form or another of a Turkish family of languages. Until modern times the name Turk has been used with a linguistic rather than a racial meaning.

The Turks then did not suddenly originate in Central Asia. Nomadic groups speaking Turkish seem to have existed from an early period. Tribal people such as the Hsiung-nu in Mongolia or the Hephthalites, who were the dominant power in Central Asia up to the middle of the sixth century, were probably Turks in the linguistic sense. When one of these nomadic groups formed a strong political unit, engaged in extensive military operations or, needing such goods as textiles, moved in to dominate a settled agricultural area this group became a significant factor in the history of Asia. The Kök Turks did all of these things in the sixth to eighth centuries. In the process their political unity which existed during the middle of the sixth century ended. By the end of the century they were divided into two major tribal groups, the Eastern and the Western Turks. The latter in ruling agricultural regions gave up to some extent their nomadic life. At the same time the people among whom they and other Turks lived adopted the Turkish language and thus also became Turks.

When the Kök Turks created their great steppe empire, including the ancient trading centers of Sogdia and the Tarim basin, they found a civilization that was largely Iranian. The cultural focus of their world in the beginning of the period was Sassanian Iran.

KARLUK TURKS. Among the Western Turks were the Karluk. The Chinese aided them to become the ruling tribe and they continued as the dominant group of Western Turks from the 740's to 1130. At first they were only a loose organization of tribes. Later their authority competed with that of T'ang China and they were a major factor in the struggle for power in Central Asia. T'ang forces under the Korean general Kao Hsien-chih defeated them in 747–749 and they in turn joined with the Arabs to inflict an important defeat upon Kao and his T'ang forces at the Battle of Athlach in 751. The center of Karluk power was at Issyk-kol north of the T'ien-shan (after 776) and for a long time they controlled the western oases of Chinese Turkistan.

The Turks of Central Asia in the sixth, seventh and eighth centuries occupied a strategic situation. Economically they were important because of their control of the land routes from East to West. Politically they held a key position in a power struggle involving T'ang China, Turks in Mongolia, Tibetans and (after the time of Kotaiba) the caliphate. Their intermediate position between these various political forces was reflected in the cultural influences among these early Turks.

The Karluk were in particularly close contact with the Iranians both before and after the coming of Islam. The Arab invasion of Iran in the seventh century brought about a new emigration from Persia into the lands controlled by the Turks. Thus an interest in Mazdaism and Manichaeism among the Turks and peoples to the east was reinforced. At this same time the Turkish tribes were on the borders of the great T'ang empire and were constantly influenced from that direction also.

With the Islamic conquests reaching up to include the Sogdian cities of Bukhara and Samarkand a new cultural wave from Iran made itself felt in Turkish society. From the beginning of the eighth century the influence of Islam was important. The Moslems, whether Arabs or Persians, came into Central Asia with a higher material culture than the Turks. Merchandise from the south, including textiles and sweet foods, played its part along with spiritual factors in the spread of the new religion. Thus the religion of Muhammad was adopted by nomad tribes to the north and by the tenth century it had spread peacefully to the peoples of the oases in Chinese Turkistan.

In the ninth and tenth centuries the principal dynasty among the Karluk Turks was the Qarakhanid dynasty or line of Ilek Khans. They were the first important Turkish ruling group to be converted to Islam. Their capital was Kashgar in the Tarim basin. This Turkish line competed with the Iranian Samanids for power in Central Asia; they checked the authority of that Iranian dynasty, some Turks were employed by the Samanids as frontier guards, and finally the Qarakhanid (Karluk) empire eliminated the Samanid power in the years 999–1000. Meanwhile, as a result of close association with the Samanids, the Qarakhanids adopted Islam as their religion.

Adoption of the religion of Muhammad did not mean peace for the Karluk Turks. In one direction they faced attackers from whom they defended their religion in the east. And within Central Asia they faced the opposition of another Moslem Turkish tribe.

GHAZNI TURKS.   In the time of the Karluks and Samanids another line of Moslem Turks became prominent. These Turks started as mercenaries in the pay of the Samanids. The founder, Sabuktegin, was originally a slave of the Samanid ruler in northeast Persia. His center of power after 962 was at Ghazni in Afghanistan. Later with Ghazni as a base they gained control in Khorasan (994), and held that region until the coming of the Seljuks in the middle of the eleventh century.

The Ghazni Turks kept their capital in Afghanistan and turned their military power to the southeast across the passes into the plains of India. Under Sabuktegin and his son Mahmud (997–1030) they raided the wealthy cities of the Punjab. During the time of Mahmud's extensive raids into India he developed a center of Moslem-Persian culture at Ghazni and enriched it by wealth looted from the temples and palaces of Hindustan.

Mahmud encouraged the work of authors and learned men. At Ghazni the scholar al-Beruni (973–1048) wrote about Indian civilization and poets were encouraged to practice their craft. The most famous among the latter was Firdausi who wrote his epic poem, *Shah-nama*, under Mahmud's patronage and even dedicated it to him (1010). Thus the Persian cultural tradition was carried on by a Turkish dynasty amid the mountains of Afghanistan.

In one of his last campaigns Mahmud temporarily extended his authority as far west as Isfahan. But after Mahmud's death his successors lost control in Khorasan and other parts of Iran and centered their attention on their domains in Afghanistan and the Punjab.

The splendor of Ghazni was ended when the town was sacked by a rival Turkish Prince from Ghor in 1150. The rulers of Ghor, of whom the most notable was Muhammad Ghori, again led Turkish forces into India, this time to conquer and remain as rulers.

SELJUK TURKS. In addition to their expansion into India, the Turks spread still further westward to become, for a time, the dominant power in Iran and to give their name as a lasting designation to the Anatolian peninsula. As in the case of Ghazni and Ghor, the new leaders were Moslems. Coming from the steppes of Turkistan the nomadic Seljuks settled in the area of Bukhara where they adopted the Sunnite form of Islam. Slowly but surely the Seljuks expanded and consolidated their power in Iran at the expense of the Ghazni Turks and others. In 1055 the Seljuk leader, Tughril Beg, made his entry into Baghdad where the caliph, as the spiritual leader, proclaimed him "sultan" or "he who has authority," (a political title) and hailed him as "King of the East and of the West." After overcoming opposition, Tughril and his successors ruled one Moslem empire extending from Palestine to Sogdia.

Following Tughril as sultans in Iran and Mesopotamia were two rulers, his nephew Alp Arslan (1063–1072) and the latter's son Malik Shah (1072–1092). The period under these two outstanding men was one which saw the development of the Seljuk empire and Turkish power, and in addition was a brilliant intellectual and artistic era in the Moslem world. Under Alp Arslan hostilities against Byzantium were resumed. Since the later years of Tughril Beg's reign, rivalries among frontier chieftains, lack of discipline and a weakening of the Byzantine army had made it possible for groups of Turkish nomads to carry their raids deeper and deeper into Byzantine territory. At last Byzantium reacted, and under the emperor Romanus Diogenes a campaign into Syria was undertaken. The culmination occurred in mid-summer 1071 when Alp Arslan defeated the Byzantine emperor at Manzikert and took him prisoner. This battle completed the ruin of the Byzantine army and marked the beginning of a new period in Turkish expansion into the territory of the empire. Unhindered by Byzantine forces, the nomadic raiders came into Asia Minor and remained, thus laying the basis for permanent Turkish suzerainty in that region.

Under Malik Shah, Seljuk power reached its height. The Seljuk domain included Asia Minor, Syria, Mesopotamia and Iran. In the religious sphere orthodoxy triumphed, the Sunni form of Islam replacing that of the Shi'a. Malik Shah was a builder as well as a ruler, and under his guidance and patronage, existing roads and canals were repaired and new ones built. Mosques and schools as well as royal residences were erected.

FIGURE 5.5.   The Slender Minaret at Konya, Turkey from the Seljuk period.
The magnificent decorations on the doorway show Persian artistic influence.

Culturally, the Seljuk period brought a "renaissance" of the Persian language and literature as well as the carrying of Persian cultural traditions into
Asia Minor. This flowering of Persian culture under the Seljuks was brought
into being by the lack of anything comparable among these Turks before they
entered Iran and by their rapid adoption of the Arab-Persian civilization which
they inherited. Seljuk patronage made possible the revision of the Persian
calendar, the erection of an academy for higher learning, the Nizamiyah, in
Baghdad, the endowment of hospitals, the production of works of art in silver
and an era noteworthy for literature. From the pen of Nizam-al-mulk, vizir to
both Alp Arslan and Malik Shah, came a remarkable treatise on the art of
government, the *Siyasat-nama*. The great astronomer-poet, Umar al-Khayyam
(Omar Khayyam), who took part in the revision of the calendar, is best known
to readers of today as the author of the *Rubaiyat*, rather than as one of the
most brilliant scientific men of his era.

The brief period of political unity and cultural brilliance under the reigns
of the first three Seljuk sultans was brought to an abrupt close upon the death
of Malik Shah. The danger to the Seljuk empire was in the nature of the dynasty
itself since the Seljuks had never completely abandoned the tribal concepts of
organization and power. This situation was aggravated by the granting of military fiefs which became hereditary and which led to the establishment of semi-

independent states. It required a dominant personality to hold all these segments together. Rivalry between the heirs of Malik Shah, the lack of a strong vizir, along with administrative and economic disorder, led to the partitioning of the empire and to a chaotic situation which became worse with every change of ruler. The Seljuk heirs of the Iranian portion of the empire maintained their rule against new invasions of Turks but were ultimately overthrown by another Turkish dynasty headed by the shahs of Kharism.

One branch of the Seljuks established themselves in the area around Konya in Asia Minor. Mindful of the governmental and cultural traditions of the region from which they had come, the Seljuks concentrated their efforts on turning the portion of Asia Minor occupied by them into a Moslem principality resembling the emirates of Syria and Mesopotamia. The transplanted culture of Persia replaced the remaining traces of Hellenism which had existed under Byzantine rule, and Iranian influence ultimately came to be supreme in Asia Minor. The Seljuk rulers of Rum, as their emirate was called, successfully resisted all encroachments on their territory until 1302 when they were superseded by the Ottoman Turks.

Kharism

Since ancient times a great trading center known as Kharism (Kwarism) had existed on the lower reaches of the Amu Darya. Archaeological finds show remains of cities and a varied commerce. Local rulers in the tenth century had relations with Turks to the east and Russians on the Volga. Kharism, during the period of expansion of the Seljuk Turks, was part of their empire. The princes of Kharism were Moslems and served as cup-bearers at the court of the Seljuk Sultans Malik and Sanjar. They also were forced to pay tribute to the Kara-khitai who had superseded the Karluk to the east. Later, in the troubled years of Sultan Sanjar's rule, Atsiz of Kharism instigated the Kara-khitai to invade Iran. The Seljuks were decisively defeated (1141) and Atsiz of Kharism was able to assert his independence.

Although opposed and sometimes defeated by the Kara-khitai and faced with the growing strength of Ghor in Afghanistan, the shahs of Kharism gradually extended their power in Central Asia during the latter part of the twelfth century. When in 1194 Tughril III, the last Seljuk ruler in Iran, was overthrown by Takash, shah of Kharism (1173–1200), the way was clear for Kharismian expansion. No strong power existed in Persia and the next shah of Kharism, Ala-u-Din Muhammad (1200–1220), was able to gain control of most of the country from Balkh and Samarkand in the east to Fars in the west.

In the east the forces of Muhammad Shah invaded the territory held by the princes of Ghor and conquered the famous strongholds of Ghor and Ghazni. Thus the beginning of the thirteenth century showed an empire of considerable extent based on its capital south of the Aral Sea.

The shahs of Kharism, as has been noted, were forced in the twelfth century to acknowledge the overlordship of the Kara-khitai who controlled a large part of Turkistan. This ruling tribe had come from southern Manchuria and eastern Inner Mongolia and were a remnant of the Khitan or Liao Dynasty whose control in northeast Asia lasted from about 947 to 1125. The first of the Kara-khitai had overthrown Karluk power in 1130. Their capital was at the ancient Turkish center near Issyk-kol and from there they dominated the oases of the Tarim basin including the Uighur Turks at Turfan.

The Kara-khitai competed with Kharism for control in Fergana and Sogdia (1141–1208). This competition was sharpened by the fact that while both ruling tribes controlled what were largely Turkish states, the people of Kharism were Moslem while the people of Kara-khitai were not.

During this period of violent political change and Turkish domination in Iran some of the most famous Persian poets lived and wrote. Their environment was the world of Islam but it showed a new characteristically Persian aspect of Islam. Nizami (1140–1202) revealed a Neo-Platonic influence in his narrative writing, based some of his work on Greek sources and produced such purely Persian novels as the *Story of Chosroes and Shirin*. The metaphysical Sufi poets who imbued their descriptions of wine and human love with mystical meaning have as one of their most famous representatives Sa'di, who lived from about 1184 to 1292 and hence probably grew up in the period before the coming of the Mongols.

From Moslem cities in Central Asia all the way to the highlands of Anatolia and controlling the centers where Arabian Islam had superseded more ancient cultures, various Turkish lines held sway. The Turks who came into these areas brought much of Central Asian nomadic custom with them, but for the most part they took over the traditions of Islamic culture of the preceding 500 years.

In Iran Seljuks gave way to the shahs of Kharism and under their control essentially Persian traditions now overlaid with Arabian Islam added Turkish characteristics. These traditions in their modified form were spread by conquests and trade and exerted a strong influence throughout Southwest Asia.

The Islamic-Persian-Turkish world was developing certain definite characteristics which were to withstand the Mongol hordes of the immediate future and the more persistent European-Christian expansion of later centuries.

BASIC DATES

C. 571–632	Muhammad
622	Hegira
632–634	Abu Bakr
634–644	Umar
641	Nehawand
644–656	Uthman

661–750	Umayyad caliphate
705–715	Kotaiba conquers Sogdia
712	Conquest of Sind
711–715	Conquest of Spain
732	Poitiers
C. 745–1130	Karluks, leading Turks
750–1258	Abbasid caliphate
751	Battle of Athlach
754–775	Al-Mansur
775–785	Al-Mahdi
785–809	Harun al-Rashid
813–833	Mamun the Great
C. 870	Egypt and Persia independent
872–999	Samanids
920–942	Byzantine empire extends into Mesopotamia
929–1096	Syria and Mesopotamia under separate dynasties
969–1025	Byzantine empire extends into Syria
977–1150	Ghazni Turks
977–997	Sabuktegin
C. 985	Seljuk Turks enter Sogdia
997–1030	Mahmud of Ghazni
1055–1194	Seljuk sultanate in Baghdad
1063–1073	Alp Arslan
1064–1092	Expansion of Seljuks
1071	Battle of Manzikert
1073–1092	Malik Shah
1090	Rise of Assassins
1096–1099	First Crusade
1157	Rise of Kharism Shah
1175–1206	Muhammad Ghori conquers Punjab
1219–1221	Mongols conquer Kharism
1243	Mongols defeat Seljuks
1243	Battle of Kosedagh

SUPPLEMENTARY READING

ARNOLD, T. *The Preaching of Islam*. London, 1913. Old, but still a good survey.

BROCKELMAN, C. *A History of the Islamic Peoples*. New York, 1947. A translation from the German; definitive but formidable.

FISHER, S. *The Middle East*. New York, 1959.

GIBB, H. A. R. *Mohammedanism*. New York, 1955. An excellent study.

GROUSSET, R. *The Civilizations of the East, Vol. I: The Near and Middle East*. New York, 1934.

GUILLAUME, A. *Islam*. London, 1962. An excellent French study.

HITTI, P. *The Arabs*. Princeton, N. J., 1943.

——— *The Near East in History*. Princeton, N. J., 1961.

HURGRONJE, C. S. *Mohammedanism*. New York, 1937. An old, but classic work.

LEWIS, B. *The Arabs in History*. New York, 1950.

SYKES, P. *A History of Persia*. Oxford, 1922.

TRITTON, A. *Islam*. New York, 1958.

ADVANCED READING

ARBERRY, A., ED. *The Legacy of Persia*. Oxford, 1953. A collection of essays by various authorities.

GIBB, H. A. R. *The Arab Conquests in Central Asia*. London, 1923. The definitive study.

HODGSON, M. *The Order of Assassins*. Gravenhage, 1955.

LANE-POOLE, S. *The Speeches and Table-talk of the Prophet Mohammed*. London, 1882. Selections from the Koran.

────── *Saladin and the Fall of the Kingdom of Jerusalem*. New York, 1898.

LEVY, R. *Persian Literature*. Oxford, 1923.

────── *The Sociology of Islam*. Cambridge, 1957.

MARGOLIOUTH, D. S. *Mohammed and the Rise of Islam*. New York, 1905.

MASSE, H. *Islam*. New York, 1938.

O'LEARY, DE LACEY. *Arabic Thought*. New York, 1939.

POPE, A. *An Introduction to Persian Art*. New York, 1931.

VASILIEV, A. *History of the Byzantine Empire*. Madison, Wis., 1928.

VON GRUNEBAUM, G. *Medieval Islam*. Chicago, 1953.

WILBER, D. *Iran*. Princeton, N. J., 1948.

VI ✻✻✻

MONGOLS AND TURKS IN

WESTERN ASIA, 1200-1600

FOLLOWING THE PERIOD OF BYZANTINE, Seljuk Turk and Kharism greatness, the history of Southwest Asia from the thirteenth to the sixteenth century is essentially the story of three great ruling dynasties, the Mongols, the Ottoman Turks and the Iranian Safavids. The first of these powers affected the whole history of Asia from east to west. The second carried on Islamic traditions and put an end to Christian political power at Constantinople and the third was another manifestation of strong Iranian tradition reasserting itself in spite of cultural and military invasion.

In this same period in Europe a period of many relatively weak states gave way to the development of a group of strong national kingdoms. This was at least partly due to the growth of international trade in which both west and east shared during that time. Previously Seljuk domination in Southwest Asia had meant a closing of commercial routes while the Crusades had led to increased demand for luxury goods. With the opening of land communications by the Mongols and the connections via Arab-controlled sea routes in southern Asia to the spice islands, trade within and through Southwest Asia developed as never before. Commercial centers, the exchange of ideas, and a widespread encouragement and diffusion of culture (especially from Iran) were among the results. In this general setting the three great dynasties each developed its own special form of political and cultural greatness.

The Mongols

One of the most famous dynasties in all history was that of the Mongols. Under the leadership of Chingis Khan (Genghis Khan) and his successors they created an imperial domain larger than any that had previously existed in Europe or Asia. Most of the events concerning this family and their rule form part of the history of China and hence will not here be presented in detail. At the same time, the role that Chingis and his descendants played in Central and Southwest Asia throughout the period under consideration is an important part of its history.

CHINGIS KHAN. Chingis Khan, as will be more fully described in Chapter 21, arose to power in the region which has ever since taken the name of his tribe, Mongolia. The Mongols were one of several groups of clans living a pastoral existence in steppe country and bound together by common traditions and blood ties. There was a constant state of warfare and raids between them and other tribes. In this environment Chingis led his people to victory over the neighboring tribes and unified them under his banner as Khan. Army and civil administration were more highly organized than under any previous leaders of nomadic groups. This was due to the personal genius of Chingis Khan who was for his people the ideal steppe warrior.

While Chingis Khan campaigned on the borders of China in 1209–1215 and faced the strongly established empire of Chin, which was to resist the impact of his forces for another 20 years, he was at the same time making ready to suppress those who would oppose him in Turkistan, particularly the Shah of Kharism.

At first Chingis Khan interested himself in free trade relations between the two empires and an envoy from the shah was well received at the Mongol capital. When, however, a large trade caravan from Mongolia reached the borders of Kharism territory at Otrar and was there seized and plundered, Chingis decided on a full-scale invasion.

After careful preparations, 100,000 Mongol and vassal forces crossed the Altai. The ensuing campaign against the centers of Kharismian power to the west was a complete success for Chingis Khan. Bukhara (1219) and Samarkand (1220) were captured, looted, burned and the people enslaved. The Kharismian leaders were forced to flee. Balkh, in ancient Bactria, was completely destroyed and its population slaughtered. Thus were three centers of Moslem Turkish-Persian culture obliterated.

The same pattern of conquest was followed in the campaigns beyond the Amu-darya in Khorasan. Fortified cities such as Merv might resist Mongol siege engines for a short time and the leaders might hope for clemency when they surrendered, but in town after town the submissive inhabitants were treacherously slaughtered *en masse*. Artisans useful to the Mongols were exempted and were deported from their homes.

The Shah of Kharism had fled and died on the shores of the Caspian. His son Jalal-ud-din for a time successfully resisted Mongol forces in Afghanistan and then fled into India. This prompted Chingis to follow him across the passes and into the Indus valley (1221). Jalal-ud-din's forces were defeated but he escaped. The Mongols plundered the Punjab and the northwest but did not establish any government within the borders of India. The court of the Moslem "Slave Dynasty" at Delhi became a center of refuge for the adherents of Islam who were able to escape Mongol domination in Central Asia.

The operations in India were undertaken by only part of the Mongol forces. Other leaders with their armies meanwhile had moved north and west. Juchi took his forces north of the Aral Sea and founded a separate Mongol domain later known as the Kipchak empire or Khanate of the Golden Horde. Other forces followed up the pursuit of the Shah of Kharism into north central Iran by looting, destruction and massacre of the populace in one town after another in the northwest. Beyond the Caucasus, as treated in Chapter 21 in greater detail, Georgia was raided by the armies of the Mongol generals, Jebe and Subotai. They campaigned in southern Russia and defeated a strong force of Russians and Cumans in 1223, then turned east to overcome an army of Bulgars on the upper Volga. Other Mongols continued the destruction in northern Iran in 1224. From the terror of the Mongols it is said that "not one-thousandth of the population escaped."

In spite of the elimination of resistance, Iran was not made part of the Mongol empire until later. The Kharismian Jalal-ud-din returned from India, regained control in Kharism and some degree of power in Iran at the time of the death of Chingis (1227). He continued to oppose the Mongols until their next campaign into Iran in 1231.

Chingis made the long journey back to Mongolia in 1223–1225, returning to handle the problems of his expanding Far Eastern empire, including those of his Chinese frontiers. Successful campaigns had been waged by his generals in China, Manchuria and Korea during his absence. But the Tangut state of Hsi Hsia in northwest China continued to resist Mongol overlordship. Several campaigns had already been undertaken against Hsi Hsia. Now Chingis engaged in carefully planned operations to subdue once and for all the centers of Hsi Hsia power. It was during these hostilities that Chingis died of a sudden illness (1227).

SUCCESSORS OF CHINGIS KHAN. In Southwest Asia the destructive aspects of Chingis Khan's invasions were especially apparent. The Mongols did not stay to rule in Iran until later. But the administrative genius of the conqueror brought about the incorporation, within one great empire, of territories all the way from the Volga and Kharism in the west to Korea in the east. Members of Chingis's family were assigned various portions but all were responsible to the Grand Khan at Karakorum. His eldest son Juchi, as noted above, ruled in the steppes north of the Caspian and Aral Seas, also in Kharism. This came to be known as the Khanate of the Kipchak or of the Golden Horde. Chagatai governed the areas of modern Turkistan (Russian and Chinese) and Afghanistan from Bukhara and Ghazni to the Altai mountains. Tului, Chingis's youngest son, acted as regent for the whole empire until in 1229 a general assembly of chiefs elected another son Ogodai as Grand Khan.

The opening of continuous trade routes from east to west across Asia has often been stressed as an accomplishment of the Mongols. This is true, but at the beginning it should be noted that the great trading cities of Central Asia had been utterly destroyed. Artisans by the thousands had been deported to the Far East. Hence, for a time the highways of Central Asia were deserted.

The Mongols had not attempted to garrison or control Iran. Soon after Chingis returned to Mongolia the Kharismian prince Jalal-ud-din returned from India to Iran. For a time he campaigned successfully in the northwest in spite of uncertain support from local leaders and determined opposition from the Christian Georgians. But Iran remained disorganized up to the time of a renewed Mongol invasion in 1227. In that year a battle disastrous for Jalal-ud-din and very costly for the Mongols was fought near Isfahan. The Mongols temporarily retreated to Khorasan. As Sultan of the Kharismian dynasty, Jalal-ud-din had strong support, but warfare within Iran continued to such a degree that the Mongols were able to invade and plunder at will. An army of some 30,000 men was sent into the country by the government of Ogodai. After defections from among the feudal warriors of Iran and a defeat by the Mongols in 1231, Jalal-ud-din was captured and killed by Kurdish tribesmen.

The Mongol forces which had beaten Jalal-ud-din repeated the raiding and slaughter carried out earlier by Chingis's armies as far west as Mesopotamia, Aleppo and Armenia (1233–1236). Not until some years later with the establishment of the Il-Khanate in the middle of the thirteenth century, did any strong or unified government exist in Iran or southwest Asia.

After the death of Ogodai in 1241 there was no strong central authority in the Mongol domains. Disorganization prevailed until Kuyuk, son of Ogodai, became Grand Khan (1246–1248). Another period of divided leadership followed until the accession of Tului's son Mangu in 1251.

During the time of Ogodai and after his death, such Mongol administration as existed in Southwest Asia was located mainly on the northeastern borders of Iran in ancient Sogdia. Orderly government alternated with harsh repression depending on which group of officials was in control. Management of local officials in Iran was made difficult by the need to refer decisions to the court in Mongolia at a time when the center of power at that court was uncertain.

From Central Asia and Iran Mongol forces were sent in 1243 into Asia Minor. In that region Seljuk Turks, who had previously acknowledged the suzerainty of Kharism, maintained an independent Moslem state between the Christian Byzantines further west and the areas which had already suffered from Mongol invasion. The state, weakened by luxurious living and rebellion, was in no condition to resist a Mongol army and the Seljuks were badly defeated at Kösedagh in 1243. The Mongols exacted tribute and became the suzerain power in eastern Asia Minor.

Mongol armies expanded the area of their power still further in this time of divided leadership. The region north of Lake Van was invaded (1245), the princes of Mosul and Damascus paid tribute to the Mongols (1245) and the King of Lesser Armenia in the area of Tarsus became their vassal (1246).

Mongol authority had made itself felt on the borders of the Black Sea and of the Mediterranean (see Chapter 21). Conquering hordes had swept into Central Europe, going as far as the shores of the Adriatic Sea in 1241. Hence even the peoples of Western Europe were very much aware of their importance.

In the tradition of the Crusades and with the new religious zeal of the thirteenth century, Western Europeans directed their attention towards Asia. It was known that the Mongols had attacked the Moslems and that the invaders on the other hand were tolerant toward all religions. It was hoped that the Mongols might be used as allies and possibly become converts to Christianity in the common fight against Islam. To secure information and to act as missionaries Franciscan friars were sent to the Mongol empire by Pope Innocent IV in 1245. The mission headed by an Italian, John of Plano Carpini, made the difficult journey overland and reached Karakorum in the summer of 1246. Carpini brought back to Europe information concerning the Mongols and the election of Kuyuk as Grand Khan, but he accomplished no definite result in the way of better relations.

Another Franciscan, William of Rubruck, reached the Mongol capital in 1253. Sent by King Louis IX of France as diplomat and missionary, Rubruck visited the leaders of the Golden Horde on the Volga and then crossed the eastern steppes to Mongolia. He was well received by the new Grand Khan, Mangu, and returned to write a detailed account of his experiences. Thus Europeans learned much about the vast Mongol empire but this seems to have had little effect on the international relations of the time.

THE IL-KHANATE. Mangu, grandson of Chingis and son of Tului, became the titular head of the Mongol world in 1251. In the history of Asia his reign (1251–1259) is important because of the conquests of China and Iran. In the former, the Grand Khan and his brother Kublai collaborated; in the latter, he employed another brother Hulagu. It was only from his time that permanent Mongol rule was established in Southwest Asia. The empire of the "Il-Khans" (The Khans), who ruled Iran 1256–1349, was then established. Their authority was secure when they captured Baghdad in 1258 and put an end to the ancient Abbasid Caliphate which had been the either actual or nominal power in Mesopotamia since 750.

By this time, notwithstanding the nominal overlordship of the Grand Khans ruling the Far East, the empire of the Mongols was actually split into four parts. Chagatai and his successors ruled in Central Asia; to the northwest from

Kharism to Moscow and down to the Black Sea the Kipchak Empire or Golden Horde was the dominant power. These other great Mongol states disputed power with the Il-Khanate. Hence the Il-Khans had to resist attacks both from Russia and from Central Asia. Meanwhile they continued war against the Moslems. From Baghdad they had gone on into Syria and there for the first time were faced with a strong Moslem army, that of the Mamluks of Egypt. The latter defeated the Mongols at Ain Jalut in 1260. This marks the first point at which a real check came to the further sweep in the spread of the empire. The Mamluks repeated the performance at the Battle of Abulistin in 1277.

EUROPEAN TRAVELERS.   Meanwhile this great empire spreading from Syria to the Sea of Japan offered an invitation to merchants, who quickly took advantage of the "Pax Tartarica," to travel from one end of Asia to another with their wares. For the first time in several centuries it was possible to cross the Asian continent with a degree of safety. For a hundred years, from about 1240 until about 1340, foreign merchants, missionaries and other travelers were protected and encouraged to use the transcontinental routes between Russia and China.

Among the travelers were the brothers Polo who on their second trip took with them the man who was to become one of the most famous authors as well as travelers of Europe, Marco Polo. He came with his father and uncle from Venice to the eastern Mediterranean and traveled from Armenia down through Mesopotamia to the Persian Gulf, thence by water to Hormuz and across Iran into Bactria and beyond. This journey and his return trip, which he made 1292–1293, is the basis for one of the best first-hand accounts of Southwest Asia during this period. Marco Polo tells us of the lawlessness among the people and princes of Iran and how they were kept in order only through fear of the government of the Grand Khan, "the Tartar of the Sunrising." He appreciated the system of escorts provided by the Mongols.

DECLINE OF IL-KHANATE.   Ghazan Khan (1295–1304) was the first of the Il-Khans to proclaim himself a Moslem. In spite of adhering to Islam, Ghazan engaged in inconclusive warfare with the Mamluks. He was faced with rebellion within Iran and invasion from the Chagatai Khanate to the northeast. Ghazan was able to defend the Il-Khanate and to earn the title of the "Great Il-Khan" because of reforms in the government for which his reign is famous.

The reformed administration of Ghazan Khan did not long endure. Less competent Il-Khans followed after his reign and the line of rulers ended completely in 1349. These Iranian monarchs were all Moslems; Ghazan was Sunni, but from the time of his successor the Il-Khans supported the Shi'a sect, which from this period until today has generally been the Persian national faith.

During the dynasty of the Il-Khans in Iran, changes among the Turks of Southwest Asia foreshadowed the development of a new power in part of Asia. The fragment of the old Seljuk empire which continued as the state of Rum with its capital at Konia was subject to Mongol domination and ended in about 1300. Meanwhile a migration of tribes was taking place which brought some two million additional Turks into Asia Minor during the time of the Il-Khans. A diminishing Byzantine empire exercised little authority in the peninsula, and in the rugged plateau country of western Asia Minor a new Turkish tribe began to be a factor of importance.

Osman, traditional founder of the Turkish Ottoman dynasty, was organizing a new tribal leadership during the years 1290 to 1326. Although the Mongols during this period were putting an end to Seljuk authority further east, Osman's activity was a long way from Tabriz, the capital of the Il-Khans, and was not in any way hindered by them.

The Il-Khanate was followed by five minor dynasties in Iran from 1335 to 1395. In the fourteenth century they shared control of Southwest Asia not only with Turks, but also with a small Black Sea state known as the Empire of Trebizond, with the state of Lesser Armenia on the Mediterranean and with Mamluks of Egypt.

The political fragmentation in the middle of the fourteenth century was accompanied by a lack of security for travelers and an end of the commercial operations across Asia that had been possible in the time of Marco Polo. The northern route to China could not be used and there was no longer easy communication across Iran. This cessation of trade along the transcontinental route occurred before the Ottoman Turks became an important influence in Southwest Asia.

Culture of Iran, 1200–c.1400

In spite of a series of foreign rulers from the steppe, Iranian culture continued as in previous periods to be something stronger and more lasting than that of the foreign intruders. In fact, as we have seen before in the time of the Seljuks, this continuity of the great cultural traditions is a strong factor in the history of Persia.

On the religious side, within the world of Islam there continued the development of tendencies quite different from the original teaching of the Prophet. The influence of ascetics and mystics in the twelfth century led to formation of various sects of Sufism, popular orders in which hundreds of thousands took part. In the thirteenth century the Sufi orders continued and new brotherhoods of mystics developed.

The founder of one of the great orders of Sufis was Rumi (died 1273), probably the greatest mystical poet of Persia. His writing deals with such topics as supernatural music and the understanding of the infinite. His followers later became important in Ottoman Turkey as the "Whirling Dervishes."

Among the poets who wrote in the Sufi tradition, others especially worthy of note and famous ever since in Iranian literary history were the moralist Sa'di (Saadi; 1184–c. 1282) and the philosopher Hafiz (died 1393).

This same time is one of the great periods in Persian art. The Mongols encouraged the development of painting which, because of their interest, shows influences from China. Much of the painting was done as book illustrations. The interest in pictorial representation is shown also in the marvelous pottery of the thirteenth and fourteenth centuries. The principal locality where this was produced was Rayy (Rhages). The bowls and other vessels were decorated with pictures in blue, green and some red, including mounted figures all of which show themselves to be predecessors of the later famous Persian miniatures. Chinese influence in the pictorial art of Iran continues as an important element in the culture of the following period.

FIGURE 6.1.   Persian Rayy ceramics. A jug decorated with mounted figures, a predecessor of later Persian miniature painting.

Timur and his Successors in Central Asia

TIMUR.   Both politically and culturally the rule of Timur and his successors continues the preceding period of Moslem Mongols. No new element entered into Iranian or Southwest Asian history. From this time on the forces that competed with one another were almost all of them Moslem. Islam had spread even into the border areas of the north and northeast. The Golden Horde adopted Islam some time after 1340. The religion of Muhammad spread also among other Mongols and Turks of the Central Asiatic steppes, including the Chagatai Mongols in about 1340. Thus when Timur led Mongols and Turks into Iran and Asia Minor he led Moslem tribesmen against other Moslems.

At the end of the fourteenth century there were no strong empires in Western or Central Asia, nor in northern India. Only fragments of the former Chagatai Empire remained. This gave opportunity for Timur, a Turkish tribal leader who claimed descent from Chingis Khan, to make himself master in northern Afghanistan and at Balkh and Samarkand. Timur, who is usually

known in the West as Tamerlane, lived from 1336 to 1405. He became famous
not only as a ruthless conqueror but also as a great builder and patron of art
and literature.

Timur's conquests began when he usurped the power of the Chagatai
Khan and established himself at Samarkand (1369); with that city as his
capital he became the ruler of Central Asia. By 1380 he was directing his forces
against the successors of the Il-Khanate in Persia. Years of campaigning made
Timur master of all of Persia. Resistance was followed by terrible massacres
of tens of thousands, comparable to the slaughter by the earlier Mongols in the
days of Chingis and Ogodai.

Thus Timur became ruler of an expanding empire and the most powerful
figure in the Iranian cultural area. He had completely conquered Persia and
established his control even over Mesopotamia by 1393. His power extended
to the northwest as far as Armenia. In 1395, after a new ruler of the Kipchak
Mongols, Toktamish, had undertaken an offensive against Timur, the latter
counter-attacked. He invaded the Kipchak domain and went on into Russia
as far as Moscow, which was held by his forces for over a year. Toktamish was
decisively defeated and the Golden Horde made subservient to Timur.

To the southeast of Iran Timur moved, as previous strong rulers over
Central Asia had done before him, across the Hindu Kush mountains and into
the Punjab (1398). There he found the Sultanate of Delhi split up into independent provinces, and when he marched south across the Indus with a force
of 9,000 horsemen he had no difficulty in reaching Delhi and occupying the
capital. Massacres, especially of Hindus, and looting marked this gigantic raid.
Many of the people of Delhi, especially artisans, were taken back to Central
Asia as slaves. Quantities of precious stones, gold and silver were among the
valuables with which Timur and his troops returned to enrich Samarkand.

On hearing that a Persian prince, who was a refugee in Egypt, had returned
to Mesopotamia and had raised a revolt against him in Baghdad, Timur led
his armies in a victorious campaign which included the capture of Sivas in
Asia Minor and the taking of Aleppo, Damascus and Baghdad (1400–1401).

The political and military prestige of Timur was heightened by his success
in fighting against the newly powerful Ottoman Turks. Under Bayazid I their
authority had been extended over most of Asia Minor. When Timur seized
Sivas Bayazid raised a large army to combat him. Timur invaded the heart of
Anatolia in 1402 and captured Bayazid in person. Timur's forces overran Asia
Minor and controlled the area until his death three years later.

Timur's ambitions went beyond such deeds as defeat of the Ottoman Turks
and capture of the capital of northern India and extended to the possibility of
invading the Far East. He was in the process of planning an attack on Ming
China when he died in 1405. Most of his empire fell apart after his death.

Since the conquests of Timur extended from the Persian Gulf in the south
to the subjugation of tribes on the Volga in the north, the result was the disruption of trade from east to west, especially via the northern routes along the
steppes to the Black Sea. Timur was interested in commerce but only as a means

of enriching his capital, Samarkand. Through his efforts that city became a thriving center of exchange between China and India on the one hand and Southwest Asia and the Mediterranean world on the other. Among the commodities which were transmitted through Samarkand were silk, rhubarb, musk and precious stones from China, spices and fine fabrics from India and furs from the north. Products of Asia reached Europe by two main caravan routes: through Kharism, across Russia to Nizhni Novgorod and Moscow and thence to the merchants of the Hanseatic League; through Herat, Tabriz and across Armenia to Trebizond, and so to the merchants of Genoa, Venice and Pisa. The line of traffic from Baghdad to Beirut was no longer a favored route.

Travelers of Timur's time noted the facilities given to trade across his empire and especially they emphasized the volume of business at Samarkand. One writer, Clavijo, mentions a single caravan from China in which there were 800 camels. Samarkand was also a center of productivity in many lines. Agriculture was encouraged with irrigation development, sericulture was promoted, and the artisans brought into the capital included skilled workers from many parts of Southwest Asia. Weavers from Damascus, cotton manufacturers from Aleppo, goldsmiths from Georgia were among those who had been compelled to migrate to Samarkand. Numerous fine buildings, including a library filled with looted manuscript volumes, were erected by the Emperor Timur and his successors.

SHAH RUKH.   Timur's son Shah Rukh was appointed governor of Khorasan by his father. During his reign as emperor (1404–1447), Shah Rukh continued to exercise political control over a vast area. Within Iran opposition was suppressed. In the northwestern province of Azerbaijan, Turkoman leaders known as the dynasty of "Black Sheep," and who exercised some power in the region from 1390 to 1467, were defeated in a series of battles fought against Shah Rukh and were forced to acknowledge the supremacy of the emperor's government in Samarkand.

That capital under Timur and Shah Rukh and their successors was the cultural center of a unified Persia. Poets and scholars were attracted to the court of Shah Rukh. At Samarkand may still be seen today some of the finest examples of Moslem-Iranian architecture. Mosques, palaces and other edifices were embellished with colored tiles in a style combining the best of Persian tradition with the great developments of Sung and Ming China. The skilled workers mentioned above made Samarkand the metropolis of artistic production in many lines. Armor and carpets, books and paintings all became works of art in their hands. Traditions from Mongol times and the new trade with Ming China coming to this Islamic-Iranian center brought about a fusion of Chinese and Persian styles. This showed itself not only in building architecture but also in the details of gardens and especially in painting.

Both painting and poetry were of such quality in the time of Timur and his successors as to merit the term of an "Iranian Renaissance." The painters of Herat and Samarkand, under the patronage of the dynasty of Timur and

FIGURE 6.2. Persian miniature of the fifteenth century. The king issues orders to his officers of state.

of the Uzbek Shaybani and his line in the sixteenth century, developed a beauty of form and color which found its expression in the world-famous Persian miniatures. In these one can see clearly a combination of Chinese and old Iranian influences.

Turkomans and Uzbeks

The patrons of artists and poets, the later princes of Timur's line, held only part of the former empire of their great ancestor. From the end of the fourteenth century two important groups of Turkomans were a factor of political importance in the mountainous regions of northwestern Iran and Armenia. Both tribes had close personal connections with the family of Timur. The founder of the White Sheep Turkomans (Ak-Koyunlu) had been given a grant of land in Armenia and Mesopotamia by the emperor Timur; their capital was at Diyarbakir, near the headwaters of the Tigris. For a time the White Sheep were overshadowed in importance by the Black Sheep Turkomans (Kara-Koyunlu) whose base was in Azerbaijan and eastern Armenia. As noted above, these Black Sheep Turkomans were defeated and made subject to Shah Rukh. To cement the relationship the latter took the sister of the tribal chief as his wife. This tribe continued as the ruling group in western Persia until 1467, and for a time in the middle of the century the reigning chief extended his conquests to include the whole of Iran.

The White Sheep Turkomans rose to pre-eminence in Iran under one strong leader, Uzun Hasan. This tribal chief held his own in wars in three directions. He raided Ottoman territory in eastern Asia Minor in the 1460's and 1470's but was checked on both occasions by Muhammad II, the conqueror of Constantinople. Uzun Hasan's position in Azerbaijan was attacked by one of the successors of Timur from Samarkand; the latter was completely defeated by the White Sheep Turkomans. In the same year, 1467, Uzun Hasan attacked the chief of the Black Sheep Turkomans at Diyarbakir and succeeded in putting an end to their power. Thus he established himself not only in the northwest but made himself master of the whole of Iran.

The greatness of Uzun Hasan's leadership was acknowledged beyond the borders of Iran. In his wars against the Ottomans he was in alliance with the Venetians who were unsuccessfully resisting the Ottoman progress as a Mediterranean power. Uzun Hasan was married to a daughter of one of the last emperors of Trebizond. Europeans who came to his court in his old age were impressed by his majestic bearing and his skill as a horseman. When Uzun Hasan died in 1478 there followed a struggle for power in Iran which continued until the end of the century.

Figure 6.3.　A contemporary portrait of Shaybani Khan Uzbek, attributed to Bihzad; fifteenth century.

Taking advantage of the political confusion an Uzbek (Uzbeg) tribal leader, Shaybani Khan, conquered much of Central Asia in the latter part of the fifteenth century. The Uzbek line were to rule in Sogdia until the Russian conquest in the nineteenth century. Meanwhile, in 1500 the Uzbeks faced the competition of two great leaders, the Mogul Babur in Central Asia and the Safavi Ismail in Iran.

The Safavids in the Sixteenth Century

From the struggle for power in Iran at the end of the fifteenth century there arose a line of rulers who were to be one of the most famous dynasties in that country's history. These were the Safavids (1501–1736). They claimed descent from Sheik Safi-ud-din, a Sufi saint and preacher, who had been a leader of a Dervish order in Ardebil in Azerbaijan.

SHAH ISMAIL.   The founder of the new dynasty, Shah Ismail, was a Shi'a Turk whose success was largely based on his appeal to the Shi'ites, both Turks and Persians, against the rising power of the Sunni Ottomans.

In the years to come, especially from the time of Shah Abbas at the end of the century, the Safavid dynasty was to emerge as a strong Iranian nation, self-contained, powerful and respected. The rise of a truly native dynasty after a lapse of centuries resulted in the revival of a Persian national spirit which is comparable to the Persian spirit of the Sassanian period after it had shaken off the long period of Graeco-Parthian domination. However, in contrast to the Sassanian period, Persia under the Safavids remained a state limited to the Iranian plateau. There were no attempts at far reaching conquests or at the establishment of a world empire and Persian armies were never dispatched against Constantinople, Samarkand or Delhi.

To speak of Persian nationalism during this period is to introduce a misleading notion, since the word nationalism describes in its developed modern form a nineteenth-century phenomenon. Rather one might call this a period in which neither language nor race, but religion, in the form of Shi'a, welded Persia into a strong state approaching in its nature a theocracy. The Safavid shah was believed to possess supernatural qualities which may be compared with the qualities of the Dalai Lama at Lhasa; indeed, he was almost the emanation of the godhead itself, and in theory ruled a theocracy far more true to the definition than the one Calvin had set up at Geneva. The parallel with the Reformation is striking. Shah Ismail, the man responsible for this religious-national revival, believed strictly, as did Calvin, in the necessity of holding political power in order to establish the true faith. It was as priest-king that he gained the throne after years spent in hiding, and his conscious policy as ruler was to create a strong central power based squarely on religion. It was after his defeat of the White Sheep Turkomans that he took the title of Shah of Iran (1502).

Because the strength of the new Persian state was founded on religion, Shi'ite Islam became identified with Iran, and a new and vigorous contest soon broke out against the Sunni Turk. But the Shah's religious followers, the mainly

Turkish "Redheads" or Qizilbash (the name was taken from their red cap with twelve tassels worn in honor of the twelve Shi'ite imams), remained undaunted even in the face of their great military reverses. Ismail, after crushing Uzbek opposition in the northeast (1510), was attacked by the Ottoman, Selim the Grim. The latter first massacred all Shi'a believers within the Turkish empire and then with the aid of Ottoman artillery inflicted a terrible defeat upon Ismail at Chaldiran, in 1514. The Persian shah in spite of this, still managed to maintain the state as an expression of Persian Shi'a religious and national resistance to the Sunni-Ottoman threat. A foundation for Persia as a national state had been laid by Ismail.

Shah Ismail's reign is significant in the international relations of the time not only for the wars against his rivals, but because during this period the Portuguese forces reached the Persian coast after having gone around Africa at the end of the fifteenth century. The Portuguese established themselves at Hormuz in the year 1507 and were in control of the trade of that port for the next fifteen years.

SHAH TAHMASP.   Shah Ismail was succeeded at his death in 1524 by his son Tahmasp. In the 52 years of his reign Persia was subject to continuous Turkish attacks by Suleiman the Magnificent, and the religious and national spirit of resistance consequently was kept alive.

The reign of Shah Tahmasp was one of the great periods in the history of Iranian art. Following in the tradition of Khorasan and Samarkand of an earlier time, the Shah encouraged painters who are known today as the "celebrated masters" of miniature painting. Among these should be noted especially Agha Mirak and others of his school who depicted scenes of court life, hunting, famous battles and religious inspiration.

The succeeding reign of Ismail II was a short unpleasant interlude. After poisoning his father and killing off all relatives and rivals, he died one year later (1577). This interlude, and the short period of civil strife which followed, were soon to be eclipsed by the reign of the greatest of the Safavids, the man who again raised Persia to a position of international importance, Shah Abbas I, the Great (1587–1629). The splendor of his empire is described in Volume II. In connection with the painting of his time, it is to be noted that the reign of Shah Abbas is the high point in the cultural development mentioned above.

Afghans and Moguls

The greatness of Iranian culture in the fifteenth and sixteenth centuries was to have a strong influence both towards the east in the Moslem dominions of India and towards the west in the Ottoman empire. By the end of the fifteenth century at Delhi many hardy warriors from the rugged mountainous region of old Gandhara, including the former Turkish strongholds of Ghazni and Ghor (the area now known as Afghanistan), had been employed as mercenary troops by the princes of northern India. The name Afghan began to be applied to these mountain people in the days of the Ghazni Turks. Both Turks and Afghans were from that time involved in the politics and warfare of, northern India.

An Afghan family of the name of Lodi attained a position of power in northwest India during the fifteenth century. It continued as the Lodi Dynasty until 1526. In that year a new ruler in Central Asia, the Mogul Babur, won control at the Battle of Panipat, as will be discussed in Chapter 13.

The coming of Afghans, Moguls and other Moslem Central Asians into India is important in the history of Southwest Asia because this was the beginning of a long period of Persian influence on the culture of India in painting, architecture and literature. Moslem Persian ideas coming by way of Samarkand and Afghanistan contributed a whole new stream of artistic growth in the country to which they were transplanted. The combined cultural heritage of the steppe and of Persian-Arabic Islam was also the background of the Ottoman Turks in their rise to power in the west.

Ottoman Empire in Asia

The Ottomans were important in the history of Asia as a new powerful dynasty which promoted Islamic tradition in opposition to the Christian world of the Europeans. Their development from the origins of Ottoman power in the thirteenth century to the climax of growth in the sixteenth may be covered briefly in four main phases: the beginnings of the empire under the first three rulers, the establishment of Ottoman pre-eminence in the Balkans and in Asia Minor, the growth of empire to include important parts of three continents, and the height of Ottoman power under Suleiman the Magnificent.

The several Turkish tribes of Asia Minor in the thirteenth century, as previously mentioned, constituted separate principalities. Beyond the range of the authority of the Il-Khans in Iran and with only a weak Byzantine government in nearby Constantinople there was ample opportunity for a capable tribal leader to develop a new center of power in this region. The last remnant of Seljuk authority at Konia was all but ended and Osman in the northwestern part of Asia Minor was able to establish his rule as a completely independent prince. From his name Osman (or Othman) the western designation Ottoman is derived.

Many of the Turkish tribes had previously been converted to Islam but Osman and his tribe did not become Moslems until about 1290. This date is generally given as the beginning of his reign and from this time on the newly converted tribesmen were active in simultaneously spreading the faith at the expense of the Greek Orthodox Christians and building a small but powerful principality among both the Christians and Moslems of Asia Minor. Warfare against the Greeks of Constantinople commenced in 1301. By the time of Osman's death in 1326 fortresses, coastal ports and finally the important city of Brusa had fallen into his hands.

Osman's able son, Orkhan I (1326–1359) and the latter's vizir Ala-ud-din, created a well-organized state and a well-disciplined army directly loyal to the sovereign. The remaining Byzantine portion of Asia Minor (all of the northwest part of the peninsula) was conquered, 1326 to 1337. Soon thereafter, in the 1340's, the Ottomans crossed the Bosphorus to assist the Byzantine emperor, Cantacuzene, against his enemies. With the taking of a fortress in Thrace the Turks obtained a position on the European continent. Their first definite settlement outside of Asia occurred in 1354. The participation of the Ottomans in events beyond the Straits is a matter of European history and will be touched on only lightly in this survey.

Both in their European possessions and their Anatolian homeland the Ottoman Turks maintained and extended control by the quality of their admin- istration. Not only were these Moslem Turks tolerant of the faith of their Christian subjects but they also took Christian children into the Sultan's house- hold and trained them as a body of civil and military officials.

The Ottoman military system was further developed in the reign of Mu- rad I (1359–1389) by the creation of a corps of "Janissaries," Christian slaves organized as a special part of the Sultan's army. Within this corps were included Greeks, Bulgars, and Serbs captured in battle. The most significant conquest in the Turkish advance into Europe at this time was the taking of Adrianople, 1365. In the next year this city was made the Ottoman capital.

Thus a dynasty originating as nomadic tribesmen whose ancestors came from the steppes of Central Asia became a factor of political importance in the affairs of Europe. When in the latter part of Murad's reign the King of Bulgaria and the Republic of Ragusa on the Adriatic paid tribute to these Moslem Turks even the Pope was alarmed and encouraged the formation of an army to resist them. The attackers were defeated and the Turks proceeded to conquer most of Bulgaria as well as Macedonia.

In Asia Minor Ottoman territory was extended eastward at the expense of emirates which had previously been independent. Much of Kermian came to the Sultan as the dowry of the princess who married his son, Bayazid. Other regions were purchased or conquered.

Under the leadership of Murad the Ottomans expanded still further into Europe. The Serbs were forced to pay tribute and at the battle of Kossovo in 1389 Murad and Bayazid won a decisive victory over larger Slavic forces. Mean- while Genoa and Venice had acknowledged the position of the Turks by making treaties with the Sultan.

Bayazid I continued his father's policies by gaining control of Asia Minor as far east as Sivas, raiding Hungary and invading Greece. Constantinople was attacked but resisted a siege of seven years (1391–1398). In the east the Otto- man armies finally met their match. As mentioned before, the great conqueror Timur extended his empire as far as Sivas. Bayazid arrogantly refused to come to terms and in 1402 Timur defeated the Sultan at Ankara and took him prisoner, thus temporarily ending Ottoman control in Asia Minor. After a decade of civil war between the sons of Bayazid, during which time no European forces

FIGURE 6.4. A Turkish coat of mail and helmet of the fifteenth century.

took advantage of the weakening of the sultanate, sole power was secure again in the hands of one man.

In the next two centuries the Ottoman sultanate became an empire embracing significant portions of Europe, Asia, and Africa. At the start attention was directed towards consolidation of authority and the establishing of friendly relations with the Byzantine emperor and the Venetians. However, the period generally is characterized by a series of wars against European states. The reign of Muhammad II (1451–1481) was marked by the taking of Constantinople in 1453 and the Turkish advance into Serbia and Albania. A great war against Venice resulted in control of the Aegean and of Greece by the Ottomans and a peace treaty signed in 1479. Muhammad failed in his attempts to take Belgrade or Rhodes. In Asia Ottoman territory was threatened by the invasion of the White Sheep Turkoman, Uzun Hasan. The well-disciplined Janissaries and their use of field artillery ended the warfare of 1472–1473 successfully for the Ottoman Turks.

By the beginning of the sixteenth century Iran, as has been noted, was the scene of a religio-political revival under the Safavid Shah Ismail. The Shi'a sect was being promoted even among the Turks of neighboring Ottoman territory. The Ottomans who were Sunni, or orthodox, Moslems suppressed and persecuted the Shi'ites. Selim the Grim (1512–1520) even proceeded to invade Iran, where he defeated the Safavid forces at Chaldiran in 1514. He entered Tabriz

FIGURE 6.5. Portrait of Muhammad II, the victor over Constantinople, by Gentile Bellini, a Venetian Renaissance master.

in triumph and sent back to Constantinople thousands of artisans and other workmen.

In the following years Selim's armies invaded Syria, defeated the Mamluks, and occupied Egypt. The Sherif of Mecca acknowledged Ottoman supremacy in the Islamic world; from this time on the Sultan took also the spiritual title of *caliph*. In less than nine years Selim's forces had nearly doubled the territory of the Ottoman empire.

Under Suleiman the Magnificent (1520–1566) the Ottoman forces reached a climax of success. Advances in Europe and the Mediterranean went as far as the gates of Vienna to the north and to include Algeria in the west. The Ottoman state was thoroughly involved in the wars and politics of Europe and the Mediterranean. In addition, Suleiman twice invaded Persia (1534, 1548). Mesopotamia was seized and held until the twentieth century. After another war against the Safavid Shah Tahmasp peace was concluded between Ottomans and Safavids in 1555.

The Sultan who ruled this enormous empire, Suleiman, was noted for the justice and the benevolence of his rule. His ability, his character, and his intellectual qualities made him one of the great figures of Turkish history and help to explain the successes of his reign.

The cultural development of Ottoman Turkey reached a climax in the sixteenth century built upon a combination of the Byzantine heritage and the great culture of Islamic Iran, especially the latter. In poetry, gardens, and mosque architecture the main tradition was Persian. A high point, and one which displays Turkish originality in faience and mosaic, is the mosque of Suleiman in Constantinople. The administrative system which was started by the early Ottomans and was an important factor in the great extension of power in the sixteenth century is described in Volume II.

BASIC DATES

1206–1227	Chingis Khan
1219–1223	Mongol campaigns in Central Asia, Iran, India and Russia
1229–1241	Ogodai Grand Khan
1243	Mongols defeat Seljuks
1251–1259	Mangu Grand Khan
1256–1349	Empire of Il-Khans
1258	Hulagu captures Baghdad
1260	Mongols defeated by Mamluks at Ain Jalut
1290–1326	Osman I founder of Ottoman dynasty
1295–1304	Ghazan Khan in Iran
1326–1359	Orkhan I
1335–1395	Five minor dynasties in Iran
1365	Turks capture Adrianople
1369–1405	Timur (Tamerlane)
1387–1502	Turkoman dynasty of the White Sheep in Iran
1389–1402	Bayazid I
1402	Bayazid defeated by Timur at Ankara
1404–1447	Shah Rukh
1451–1481	Muhammad II
1453	Ottoman capture of Constantinople
1499–1524	Shah Ismail, founder of Safavids
1512–1520	Selim I
1520–1566	Suleiman I the Magnificent
1524–1576	Shah Tahmasp
1587–1629	Shah Abbas I, the Great

SUPPLEMENTARY READING

BROCKELMAN, C. *A History of the Islamic Peoples.* New York, 1947.

GROUSSET, R. *The Civilizations of the East, Vol. I: The Near and Middle East.* New York, 1934.

HITTI, P. *The Near East in History*. Princeton, N. J., 1961.
FISHER, S. *The Middle East*. New York, 1959.

ADVANCED READING

ALDERSON, A. D. *The Structure of the Ottoman Dynasty*. Oxford, 1956.

ARBERRY, A. J. *Persian Poems*. London, 1954.

BARTHOLD, W. *Turkestan Down to the Mongol Invasion*. London, 1928. A classic study by a Russian historian.

CREASY, E. S. *History of the Ottoman Turks*. New York, 1878. Although very old, it remains an important standard work.

HUDSON, G. F. *Europe and China*. London, 1931.

IBN BATTUTA (H. A. R. GIBB, ED.). *Travels of Ibn Battuta*. London, 1929.

LANE-POOLE, S. *The Story of Turkey*. New York, 1888.

LYBYER, A. *The Government of the Ottoman Empire in the Time of Suleiman the Magnificent*. Cambridge, Mass., 1913. An excellent work by the foremost American historian of the Ottoman Turks.

MOULE, A AND P. PELLIOT, EDS. *Marco Polo: The Description of the World*. London, 1938. An excellent edition of the great traveler.

PRAWDIN, M. *The Mongol Empire*. London, 1952. The best book on the subject.

SYKES, P. *A History of Persia*. Oxford, 1922.

TOYNBEE, A. AND K. KIRKWOOD. *Turkey*. New York, 1927.

WITTEK, P. *The Rise of the Ottoman Empire*. London, 1938.

VII ✳✳✳

EARLY INDIA TO 600 B.C.

THIS CHAPTER, after outlining the basic elements of the geography of India, is concerned with the two chief roots of its history: the creation of the Indus river civilization and the Aryan invasions. Out of a fusion of the two arose the distinct and particular culture called Hinduism.

Geography

In the history of India, a name derived from that of the country of the river Indus, geography plays the important part in the shaping of her culture as it does for all areas of human settlement, but in this case it does so in a most immediate and striking fashion. To mention but her land frontier, her monsoon, and the problem of seapower in the Indian Ocean is to indicate essentials of Indian history.

India is a vast subcontinent in the form of a great triangle, its base being the Himalayas, its apex projecting far out into the sea, bounded on the east by the Bay of Bengal and on the west by the Indian Ocean. This land, of vast extent and of many types and areas of population, is inhabited by 400 million people, roughly one fifth of the world's population, and thus is one of the most densely populated areas of the world. Four principal natural regions form this subcontinent: the Himalayas, the northern river plains, the Deccan plateau and the Tamil peninsula.

The Himalaya mountains are a series of stupendous ranges, the loftiest in the world, with an average elevation of 19,000 feet, which shut off India from the rest of Asia for a distance of 1,600 miles between Assam in the east and Baluchistan in the west. Flanking the Himalayas both east and west are north-south ranges, which separate India from Burma in the east, and from the Iranian plateau in the west. The Burmese ranges, high and inaccessible, and protected by jungle-clad and most unhealthy foothills present some of the most difficult terrain which may be imagined. The Hindu Kush mountains, with an average crestline of 15,000 feet also present great natural obstacles to land communication. Yet this tremendous Himalayan mountain barrier, together with its eastern and western flanks is not absolutely impenetrable. There are passes to the north, such as the Mustagh and the Karakoram, but their elevation is above 18,000 feet, and thus they have never furnished practicable routes into India. It is only in the northwest that this great natural frontier is pierced by usable passes, notably the Khyber and Bolan, which from time immemorial have served the invader as gateways to India.

The northern river plains form the second of the great natural regions of India. They are composed of vast, open, level, alluvial tracts and they are the richest and most densely populated areas of India. It is here that the main life of India took place, here that the seats of the principal empires were founded and that the most interesting scenes in Indian history were enacted. These great alluvial plains are formed by three distinct river systems, that of the Indus, the Ganges and the Brahmaputra.

To the south of the Gangetic river plain lies the third of the major natural regions of India: the Deccan plateau. Its northern escarpment is formed by the jungle-clad Vindhya mountains which form an effective barrier, broken only by a few difficult passes, between the Deccan and the northern plains. On its eastern and western side the Deccan plateau terminates with the Ghat hill ranges. At the foot of both the Western and Eastern Ghats are narrow alluvial plains with few good natural harbors.

Beyond the Deccan plateau to the south lies the fourth natural region of India: the Tamil peninsula. This consists chiefly of a broad plain, more tropical and less forbidding than the Deccan, and well isolated from the rest of India.

The influence of topography on Indian history is paralleled by the importance of its climate, since India's economic well-being depends largely on the monsoon. The seasonal rhythm of rainfall, the chief characteristic of a monsoon climate, determines for a large part of the country the success or failure of the planted crops. The monsoon, moist winds from the Arabian Sea and the Gulf of Bengal, begins in May and lasts usually until September. As this influx of warm sea air meets landmasses, and is forced to rise over such barriers as the Western and Eastern Ghats, and then the enormous Himalaya mountains, it cools and thus loses the capacity to retain moisture. This moisture is released; the rainy season is the result. Rainfall varies from over 100 inches in the southern Himalayas to about 25 inches in the Delhi area, whereas further west between the Punjab and the Ganges plain, the dry Rajputana, rainfall does not exceed 5 inches.

During the winter months the opposite regime prevails, but in much less marked form. The winter monsoon is, of course, of far less importance in the crop cycle than is the southwest monsoon from the sea. In particular the Deccan and the Tamil peninsula are entirely dependent on its occurrence; if the monsoon stays out, or is much reduced, the rivers go dry, crops wither, and famine stalks the land. In contrast to this the fertile low-lying northern river plains are much less dependent on the monsoon rains, since their great rivers carry always enough water from the melted snows of Tibet and the Himalayas to allow some agriculture even during seasons when the monsoon has failed to come. This goes far to explain the predominance of the river plains in Indian history. Thus, geographical conditions and environment play a very large role in the development of Indian civilization, comparable to that exercised by geography on the civilizations of Egypt and ancient Greece.

Incredibly high mountains, vast tracts of fertile river lands, densely forested plateau areas difficult of access, tropical rain forests and deserts, the wettest and some of the driest spots on the globe, all may be found on this subcontinent. Yet geographical diversity, and even isolation of natural regions, did not prevent the development of an Indian unity, a unity which did not depend on political suzerainty, but rather was the result of the growth of Hinduism, the culture of India. It is this cultural unity which permits of the speaking of Indian civilization.

Indus Civilization

Man has lived in India from very remote times. Numerous races, with a great variety of languages, have made of the country a veritable ethnological museum. One of the earliest areas of neolithic culture is found in Upper Sind, the lower Indus and Baluchistan, and technically known as the Amri-Nal culture. Here the painted pottery, the copper tools and clay figurines, and above all the carvings of the great humped Indian bull on cups indicating bull worship, point to a direct connection with the great Indus civilization of the Indus river valley. Neolithic Amri-Nal most likely was the predecessor of the latter, and it is with that civilization that we now must concern ourselves at length, since it is the Indus civilization which gave India characteristic, independent, and individual traits which in some forms have endured to the present.

The Indus civilization, also sometimes referred to as the Harappa culture from one of its chief sites, was one of the world's great civilizations. It arose on the vast, alluvial plain of the Indus river among climatic conditions requiring irrigation works for large-scale agriculture due to deficient rainfall. Thus, the Indus civilization required organized cooperative efforts to control and direct flood waters; consequently those civilizing processes which began and were developed here bear close analogies with those of the great river valley civilizations of Egypt, Mesopotamia and the Yellow river in China. The Indus civilization is then a major representative of a basic form of ancient Asiatic societies.

It was brought to light rather excitingly in the twenties and thirties of our century. After Indian archeologists had begun individual and isolated digging, and when finds indicated the great importance of its nature, the British Indian government under Sir John Marshall began intensive excavations on a large scale, with great scientific thoroughness. In 1922 its two chief sites were excavated at Mohenjo-Daro ("the place of the dead") in southern Sind, and Harappa, 400 miles north in the Punjab. In addition over 45 other settlements were discovered, all presenting uniform products of a homogeneous culture down to the detail of town-planning, house size, pottery patterns and uniform script. By the thirties it had become clear that here was found one of the world's great independent civilizations, to be dated about 2300–1600 B.C. It was a great urban civilization on a scale vaster even than that of either Egypt or Mesopotamia, since it comprised an area of unified culture of over 700 miles linked by an easily navigable river.

Its two large cities, Mohenjo-Daro and Harappa, were laid out in streets running north-south, and east-west, intersecting at right angles. Their main streets, of constant width, extended for half a mile. Each site is dominated

FIGURE 7.1.   Mohenjo-Daro: drain and street.

by an impressive citadel, with defensive walls of 30 feet, containing ceremonial terraces and monumental gateways, as well as other large buildings, some provided with drains and used for baths, others possibly given to religious use.

Below the citadel are the remains of the city, its streets, shops and dwelling houses—flat-roofed buildings consisting of burned brick with neither ornamentation nor stone work. Residential architecture indicates a clear distinction as to class and wealth; spacious two-storey houses, with private courtyards, bathrooms and separate wells, superior to the ordinary dwelling of the Mesopotamian civilizations, alternated with rows of two-room detached cottages for the use of artisans and workmen. In addition there were shops, granaries and flour-mills, probably operated by slave labor. A distinctive feature of the Indus civilization was the excellence of its sanitary engineering. Most houses possessed their own wells and bathrooms, the brickstones of which are polished by generations of bare feet. From the bathroom sewage was carried by means of brick-lined drains into the street, and thence by covered drainage canals into cesspools. In addition some houses were equipped with rubbish chutes, leading to a refuse bin outside.

FIGURE 7.2.   Mohenjo-Daro: Great Bath.

One gains the unmistakable impression that here was a complex urban civilization, consisting of highly organized communities under a strong system of centralized government. This impression of centralized power, probably by priest-kings ruling exaltedly from the citadel over an autocratic and absolute state is reinforced not only by the uniformity of the culture, but also by its conservatism. No changes in structure, style, or decoration took place. Rebuilding after disastrous floods followed the established patterns and life continued unchanged.

The base of the Indus civilization economy was agriculture, although commerce probably played no small part in the form of cotton exports to Mesopotamia. Trade contacts with Southwest Asia certainly existed, as proven by the discovery of Indus civilization seals in Sumer, and this trade in all likelihood was carried on by sea. But it was agriculture which supported a large population able to produce surplus crops for local consumption and for export. It could do this because the climate was wetter than at present, supporting a fauna which included the tiger, the rhinoceros and the elephant. The major crops were barley and wheat among the cereals, and dates, sesame, peas, and melons, seeds of which were found in excavation. Cotton was extensively grown, spun and woven, furnishing cloth and a valuable export item. Remains show that the domesticated animals included the Indian humped bull or zebu, the short-horned bull, water buffalo, goat, sheep, pig, dog, cat, camel, ass, elephant, horse, and fowl. Wheeled vehicles and boats provided means of transport.

The Indus civilization had entered the Bronze age in technology, both copper and bronze being widely used in tools and weapons, gold and silver in jewelry. A great variety of tools, some produced with considerable skill, were found, such as saws, knives, beakers, hatchets, and fishhooks. On the other hand, weapons were rare and of inferior quality, probably indicating the unwarlike nature of the people of Harappa and Mohenjo-Daro. Both the sword and defensive armor were absent; the sling instead seems to have been the most common weapon used, together with the bow, spear, axe, and dagger. Some fine jewelry was produced, such as gold and silver earrings, necklaces, bangles, combs, and mirrors, as well as beads of semiprecious stones. Although advanced in technique, the pottery is uniform in design and execution, strictly utilitarian and gives a rather uncomfortable feeling of a civilization lacking in imagination. But the pottery toys are both delightful and enlightening. One encounters clay

Figure 7.3.   Group of clay figurines and toys from the Indus valley civilization.

carts and oxen figurines, bulls with heads which could be made to nod by means of a string, whistles, dice, and other items which still show that they were molded by the hands of children since little fingerprints are indelibly impressed on their crude forms. The cart, here appearing as a child's plaything, is exactly the same cart used today in the same locality, a definte proof of the continuity of the Indus civilization to the present.

One of the greater puzzles of the Indus civilization is its writing. Inscriptions found on seals in a pictographic language so far have resisted decipherment. It is very likely that the idea of writing was derived from Mesopotamia. If analogy hold true, which it may not, then one might assume that the inscriptions of the seals refer to names of officials, or property owners. There is no question but that the civilization was conscious of commercial economy since it developed its own uniform system of weights and the seals may very likely have been used to stamp individual owner's property.

In addition to providing a script these distinctive seals give us a foretaste of later Indian art. Animals abound on them—the bull, elephant, rhinoceros, crocodile, tiger and a rather mysterious unicorn. Their artistic treatment is full of animal realism; muscles ripple under the skin of the bull. We shall encounter this close realistic observation again in later art periods.

Ornamented bronze and stone sculpture is another source of much information about the civilization, since it shows details of clothing, hairdressing, and physical types. Here we encounter in some examples, notably a famous bronze nude dancing girl from Mohenjo-Daro, an elegance of movement distinctly foreshadowing the development of Indian art. The subtle modeling of the human figure, and the rare power of expression met with in these statues again point to a continuity in Indian art.

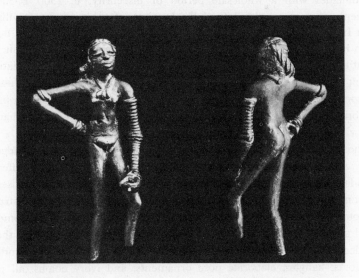

FIGURE 7.4.   Mohenjo-Daro: bronze dancing girl.

From the engraved seals, the clay figurines, and the statuary some aspects of the religion of the Harappa civilization may be postulated. The cult of the Mother goddess, perhaps from Asia Minor, flourished, but in addition the bull was worshipped and the prototype of the later great Indian god Shiva appears on the steatite seals. The religion of the Indus civilization was already typically Indian. The cults of the Mother goddess, animism, and the cult of Shiva are still today the most potent forces in popular worship. Shiva may have the distinction of being the most ancient divinity still worshipped. The religion was distinct from any Semitic cult of Mesopotamia, and is the precursor of modern Hinduism.

Who were the people of the Indus civilization? Apparently they were of mixed groups, since skeletal remains differ as do the physical types encountered on the figurines. A statue of a man shows thick lips, flat nose, narrow eyes, and a beard, but there is no doubt that other racial traits were also found. The Indus civilization preceded the incursion of the Aryans, its people probably had some Dravidian admixtures, and the best that can be said from physical anthropology is that they were made up from a mixture of racial types.

Signs of decline and decadence are unmistakable prior to the final destruction of the Indus civilization. Old bricks were used again in new construction, mean houses were erected on the site of spacious mansions, and building regulations were abandoned so that structures encroached upon the streets. In Harappa huddled skeletons of persons murdered on the street or on staircases are mute evidence of violence, jewels hoarded for safety show fear, and evidence of raids is found by the presence of swords and radically different pottery. A violent end seems the best explanation for its disappearance, since such a peaceful and wealthy town must have been most attractive to a warlike raider. This coincides with a wholesale period of insecurity, c. 1500 B.C., when movements of new peoples caused the breakup of many ancient civilizations both in India and Southwest Asia. The sack of cities at that time was not confined to Harappa in India. Barbarians attacked Mesopotamia and in Asia Minor the Hittites created a new state. All the great ancient river valley civilizations of Asia felt the impact of new blood, new ideas, and new techniques brought by new peoples. In the case of the Indus river civilization it was the Aryan invasion which broke it up, but not before basic elements of that civilization had been mixed with and assimilated by the culture of the invader.

The Indus civilization presents a thoroughly individual and independent culture. Although it stood in contact with Mesopotamia, it was yet different in its standard of living and its emphasis on religious privileges. Its houses were more commodious, and included well-built baths. Magnificent temple structures were notably absent. Overcome by the invader from the northwest, some basic cultural traits of Harappa and Mohenjo-Daro have endured and form the basis of modern Indian culture. Material examples for this are to be found in its carts, boats, bangles, elaborate nose ornaments, and ivory combs, all present today in the villages of the Punjab. More significantly, it is the art and the religion of the Indus civilization, already Indian in its basic elements, which continues, and gives Hinduism threads leading back into prehistory.

Aryan Invasion

The second event of great importance in early Indian history was the coming of the Aryan invader from the north. Between 1500 and 1200 B.C. a series of invasions brought these people to the Punjab, from somewhere in the steppes of South Russia and east of the Caspian via Iran and the passes of the northwest. The Aryans were tall, with fair hair, long heads, and straight noses. They spoke Sanskrit, an Indo-European language which later on became the classical language of India, and which belongs to the same family of languages as Persian, Greek, Latin, Celtic, Teutonic, and Slavic. The Aryan culture resembles that of the Mitanni of northern Syria and the Kassites of Mesopotamia, and both religion and language connect them also with the Hittites of Asia Minor. The Aryans (meaning "kinsmen") at this stage were "people who did not know a city"; theirs was an agricultural and pastoral economy. When the Aryan barbarian arrived in the Indus river valley he encountered there a civilized region, a literate and urban culture, and he destroyed it but not before being greatly influenced by it.

The Aryan invasion was led by warriors, but it was not an invasion of an army. Rather, successive waves of immigrants over hundreds of years took possession of the Indus valley, and then pushed east to the Jumna and the Ganges. A number of tribes, five or perhaps more, participated. Each tribe was a unit, ruled by a hereditary king (*raja*) whose power was limited by the tribal assembly. In turn each tribe consisted of a group of patriarchal families. The wars were fought by the aristocratic warrior, mobile and lightly armed, in his war chariot driven by his charioteer, very much as wars were fought in Homeric Greece. Commoners served on foot, but mattered little, at least in the fine poetry which tells of the Aryan exploits. The warrior's chief weapon was the bow and arrow, but he also fought with sword and axe.

War was constant, and the Aryans delighted in it. Not only did they overwhelm the settled civilization of the Indus, but they also fought the *dasyu*, the dark-skinned, flat-nosed, short Dravidians (earlier inhabitants of central and south India), to whom hostile and contemptuous reference was made, and who were distinguished because of their color from the Aryan. The Aryan described his opponents in these wars as black, unintelligent, indifferent to the gods, wealthy and living in fortified strongholds where they hoarded great stores of gold. It was there they were overwhelmed, their forts wrecked and their stores plundered. Presumably this description fits Harappa. But above all the Aryans fought among each other, another Homeric trait. If they were not fighting, then they hunted with great pleasure such dangerous game as lion or boar. .

Our information about the Aryans is derived, not from archaeology, but from literary sources, the *Vedas*. The Vedic literature, (the term means "knowledge"), gives us a somewhat dim picture of the life of the Aryans, it does not give any chronology, and consequently one can only outline in broad terms conditions as they existed over a very long period of time, at least a thousand years. The Vedas were considered to be inspired and revealed literature, and they were painstakingly preserved. They were composed in elaborate Sanskrit, the wording of which was conceived to be magical and which was not to be altered. They were handed down from father to son, orally and secretly, and they were not written down until much later times.

The *Rigveda* is the oldest, composed probably in the twelfth or eleventh century B.C. in north India; it contains a large collection of hymns and magic spells. Next is the *Samaveda* containing verses from the *Rigveda* arranged in the form of a hymn book for the guidance of chanters; the third Veda is the *Yajurveda*, probably of the tenth or ninth century B.C., consisting of prose prayers and spells; and finally comes the *Atharvaveda* which contains verse incantations full of what appears to be Dravidian influence.

To this Vedic literature in poem form there was later added a body of prose writings. Great collections of theological and ritual treatises, designed as manuals of worship and religious precepts, the *Brahmanas*, made their appearance from the eighth century B.C. on; to them were added in the sixth century the *Upanishads*, philosophical tracts which form the foundation of modern Hindu philosophy. These contained secret teachings of metaphysics, philosophical discourses, and speculative ideas, and, like the Vedas, they were considered inspired. Finally a body of writing known as the *sutras* embodied traditional learning in regard to law, ceremonial, and ritual. All of these were written in Sanskrit, a language which tended to become more and more a language of the learned, since the lower classes spoke a dialect known as Prakrit.

We shall consider the religious and philosophical content of the Vedas and the later works presently; for the moment we can derive from them a picture of the life of the times. Aryan society was organized along patriarchal lines. The father of the family possessed complete power, but women nevertheless held high positions; marriage was considered a fine ideal, and was entered into for life. Child marriages were not known but slavery existed, although apparently not on a very extensive scale.

A group of families made up a village. Houses were rectangular, with thatched roofs and constructed of wood with clay floors. In the center of the house was the hearth where the sacred fire burned, a place of religious importance.

As is the case of most simple pastoral and agricultural societies, the grain crop, herds of cattle, and flocks of sheep were of supreme economic importance, wealth being expressed in terms of head of cattle. The chief crops were barley, wheat, and lentils; the ground was ploughed by an ox-drawn plough, then manured and irrigated. The most important domesticated animal of the Aryans was the horse, the characteristic animal of their society. Not used for riding, since the stirrup was not known, but rather with the chariot, its importance in war was decisive. The dog was another favored animal. The Aryan family dressed with woolen cloth, not cotton, and wore some gold ornaments. Their food at this early stage included, in addition to agricultural products, beef, in striking contrast to later times. Drink was supplied by mead, and by a beer, called *sura*, brewed from grain. Then there was a very special drink, called *soma*, but this was an intoxicant, and was used exclusively in religious ceremonies. The dead were buried or cremated.

The Aryans were skilled craftsmen and artisans. They tanned leather, carpentered wood, and worked as specialized metal smiths in bronze and copper. Iron appeared rather late, in approximately the eighth century B.C.

For amusement there were bards who told stories, music, the somewhat wild sport of chariot racing, and, above all, there seemed to have been gambling. Throwing dice was a passion, and many injunctions in the Vedas preach abstinence from this habit.

Aryan society in many aspects recalls that of Homeric Greece. Its attitude toward life, as seen in its early religion, is also vigorous and objective, quite unlike the pessimism of later India. Its gods are primarily nature gods, benevolent toward man, and if the right sacrifices are performed and the correct words chanted man quite frankly can expect celestial favors. The universe was conceived to be a whole, inhabited by innumerable gods, demons, ghosts, guardians, and lovely nymphs. Mountains and rivers also were deified. But, unlike Greek religion, the major gods were rather vague, their form was nebulous, and they were far less anthropomorphic than those inhabiting Mount Olympus. The Aryans, in further contrast, had no temples or images of their divinities. This early Aryan religion is the religion of a people still half nomadic, and the similarity between it and the early Iranian religion is striking. The Vedas and the *Avesta* have many things in common, and the presence of the fire cult, and the soma sacrifice among both Aryan in India and Iranian in Persia argues powerfully for a common background, probably somewhere in the steppes of Central Asia.

The most human god of the Aryans was Indra, and he reflects quite clearly their ideal. He is the hero-warrior, colossal, strong-armed, potbellied, blessed with an enormous appetite, and a heavy drinker. Fighting from his golden war chariot he raids for cattle and overcomes opposition by the use of his huge thunderbolt. He is the warrior-god to whom the Aryans sacrificed cows and bulls for success in fighting. Most exalted of the gods was Varuna, god of the firmament and the sky. The sun and the stars are his eyes, he controls the universe and sees all things that pass below, even the thoughts of men. One more deity does perhaps deserve some special mention, and that is Rudra, the god of the whirlwind, the dispenser of rain and the embodiment of cosmic forces. Rudra is the god inherited from Harappa, and he eventually came to be known as Shiva.

The coming of the torrential monsoon rains must have made a deep impression upon the Aryan invader from arid lands, just as the heat and the fertility of the rich tropical earth were also novel experiences, and the new environment of India soon modified his religious outlook. Some gods of the Vedas have definitely a pre-Indian background, and one of these is fire. Agni, as it was known, was celebrated as a universal force, and each dwelling contained a sacred altar fire. The fire-cult parallels closely that of the Iranians, and is a sign of their common ancestry, as is also the cult of soma, the divinity of an intoxicating beverage, clear and beautiful and potent, from the now lost soma or "moon plant."

Not more than the mere beginnings of speculations which go beyond polytheism are discernible in the Vedas. The really important thing is to understand the changes which Aryan society underwent after it had settled in India. Both the ancient Indus civilization and Dravidian influences remolded and reshaped the culture of the seminomadic, pastoral, nature-worshipping Aryan. The ancient Harappa civilization, urban, elaborate, authoritarian, and centralized handed down its traditions, some of which were to be reasserted with the coming of the Maurya empire. In religion and in social structure, too, the past traditions survived, and out of the blending of the old and the new, the pre-Aryan and the Aryan, emerged Hinduism.

Hinduism

Hinduism may be described as a complete way of life. It is not merely a religion, but it also embraces philosophy, law, social and economic life. It arose from the fusion of partly Dravidian, partly Harappan elements with those of the Aryan newcomer, and it came to fruition on the upper Ganges, the sacred river, where increasingly powerful Aryan kings had shaped territorial kingdoms.

One of the foremost writers on Hinduism has said that the favorite occupation of the Indian mind can be found in religion.[1] As of Spain, so also of India, one may state with some truth that both were intoxicated by religion, and that their fullest expression is found in it.

The most significant advance in the religion of Hinduism is the emergence of a trinity of gods replacing the vague polytheism of the early Vedas—Vishnu, Shiva, and Brahma are the principal deities emerging from this fusion. Vishnu is the preserver of the world, a mild and benevolent god, with many incarnations such as the boar, the lion, and also Krishna, a god dark in color and most probably of Dravidian origin. Personal devotion to Krishna leads to personal salvation, an early appearance of the doctrine of love and devotion, which later became a prominent feature of Hindu theology. Shiva, the second member of the trinity, is the opposite of Vishnu. He is the evil god, the destroyer, and the symbol of death. He is to be feared and appeased, rather than loved, and his aspects are severe and terrible. Shiva, it will be remembered, was a divinity of the Indus civilization, which had become identified with the Aryan Rudra, and

[1] Sir Charles Eliot, *Hinduism and Buddhism* (London, 1954), p. 13.

emerged as the second most important god of Hinduism. His symbol, as it had been in Mohenjo-Daro, is the bull. Finally, there is the third divinity, the supreme god, Brahma. Originally merely a ritual word, Brahma became a god, but remains rather vague and nebulous. He is the creator of the universe, but is neutral, neither to be loved nor feared. He is part of every man's soul, or better, the essence of every man's soul is part of him. These developments, the replacement of a popular polytheism of benevolent nature gods as seen in the *Rigveda* by the creation of a trinity of personal gods with distinct and often fearful attributes, can be traced in the last of the Vedas, the *Atharvaveda*. When it was written the religious outlook of the Aryan had profoundly changed.

While religion underwent new expression great philosophic advances took place. From the seventh and sixth centuries B.C. stem the *Upanishads* and their commentaries, an immense mass of speculative philosophic literature, concerned with the ultimate questions of the origin, the purpose, and the destiny of man. Here Hindu thought developed a theory of spiritual monism; it insisted on the ultimate unity of the universe and on an absolute reality not directly approachable by human beings. The basic premise of Indian metaphysics is the world soul, or *atma*, which permeates the soul of man like salt does water. In the *Chandogya Upanishad* is the story of the sage who orders a boy to throw a lump of salt into a basin of water. Next morning they return, and the boy is told to take out the salt and taste the water. Even as the salt remains in the water, and (although its presence cannot be seen) its taste is all-pervading, so is the essence of the man's soul with the soul of the universe.

The sage declaims:

> Even so, that Reality is here in this body,
>   though thou dost not perceive it,
> That atom, which forms the essence of the universe,
>   that is the Truth, that is the soul, that art thou.[2]

That phrase, "that art thou" (*tat tvam asi*), is the key to the belief that the subtle essence of the soul of man is in reality identical with the all-compassing world soul, atma, the absolute. From here it is merely a religious step to identify the soul of the universe, atma, with the supreme godhead and divine substance, called Brahma. And what is this atma, this absolute? It is:

> A motion and a spirit that impels all thinking things,
>   all objects of all thought and rolls through all things.[3]

The discovery that man's spirit is not particular and mortal, but is part of the immortal universal is almost parallel to Platonic thought as expressed in some dialogues, such as the *Phaedo*. And similar also to the Greek philosopher's famous myth of Er in the *Republic* is the insistence of Hindu thought on continuity, specifically the continuity of the soul. This introduces the second major

[2] H. G. Rawlinson, *India: A Short Cultural History* (London: The Cresset Press, 1937), p. 41.
[3] *Ibid.,* p. 91.

premise of Indian metaphysics: the doctrine of successive rebirths of the soul, metempsychosis or, to use the Indian term, *samsara*. Nothing is permanent, not even the gods, for they must die; not even death is permanent, for it must turn into new life. Thus the soul wanders from body to body, and is continuously reborn. However, the condition of its rebirth may greatly differ. Just as a man acts, just as he behaves, so he becomes in the next rebirth. The sum total of past actions, *karma*, determines the nature of the present state of the soul. Man in the present phase has some freedom of will, he can act in such a way as to improve his next rebirth, or he can act wickedly and reappear in the soul of outcastes, or even animals, and unpleasant ones at that, such as dogs, swine or reptiles. From these two premises, the individual soul's identification with the absolute soul of the universe and the constant cycle of rebirths which the soul must undergo, arises the ideal of Hindu metaphysics: release from rebirth and union with the absolute reality. This is *moksha*, or liberation.

To the philosophers of the *Upanishads* the greatest good was this termination of the soul's separate existence, its release from all liability to future rebirths, its absorption into the changeless and timeless state, and its identification with Brahma, itself a god. In this fashion unending joy is attained. Moksha means existence without pain, life without end, freedom from rebirth, and man becoming god.

The essential question which remained was how to achieve this ideal. The answer was knowledge—knowledge that the whole world of phenomena is illusory, that although to many ordinary minds the world presents many pleasurable aspects temporal existence is nevertheless painful, and that the undesirable entanglement of spirit in matter must be ended. The soul must strive for goals beyond this world, each spiritual being must earn its release from the grip of matter by individual effort. Only thus can the soul arrive at release, at complete freedom from material contact, at the splendid isolation of union with the world soul.

The necessary corollary to this doctrine is that life is an evil; Hinduism has become a religion of pessimism. If the soul is to know itself, the world must be sacrificed without regret. Closely connected, and made understandable by this pessimistic outlook, is the tendency toward extreme asceticism in Hinduism. Desire can be harshly suppressed and the karma of the soul can be exhausted and relieved by penance. Intense concentration, certain postures of the body and the practice of breath control give superhuman strength to the holy men, the yogis, engaged in overcoming the process of samsara. Meditation and asceticism are thus both used before the mind can apprehend the higher truth.

Paralleling and connected with these great developments in Hindu thought was the rise to prominence of the priesthood, a development of the greatest consequences to India's social structure, since with it came the caste system. As religion and metaphysics became elaborated, so did the ritual of religion. Sacrifices became more involved and magical, every word uttered by the priest was pregnant with meaning, every one of his movements momentous in results. Very soon the priest, or *Brahman*, advanced the idea that he could influence the gods, even to the point of compulsion, if the ritual was conducted correctly.

By using certain acts and formulae, known only to him, he argued that he could coerce the gods. If the Brahman priests could control the gods they were of course indispensable. They must be reverenced, they must be propitiated, and not the least, they must be paid their fees at every turn.

The claim toward omnipotence by the priesthood meant that they soon set themselves apart from the rest of the population as a hereditary and privileged group. With this step, the so-called caste system, an integral part of Hinduism, became fully developed. It was a unique development in Indian civilization, and it did not exist in the age of the early Vedas. The early Aryans did draw a color line, varna, against the Dravidians and against slaves. This may be the origin of caste, but the real responsibility toward an inflexible and rigid division of society into castes rests with the Brahmans.

Caste is derived from a Portuguese word meaning race, and it may be defined as a mutually exclusive social group in which membership is determined by birth. Race, belief, and sometimes even occupation, make no difference. One is born into a caste; membership in it is then confirmed by formal initiation and one can lose caste only by formal expulsion. Caste established a code of rules which govern food, marriage, often but not always a particular form of occupation (there have been low caste princes whose touch of the hand would have defiled a pauper), clothing, and social life. Of these regulations the one limiting marriage has been the most stable one.

Under the caste system Indian society was divided into four major caste groups. First ranking were the *Brahmans*, the priests and scholars, the intellectual aristocracy. Next came the *Kshatriyas*, composed of rulers and warriors. The third group are the *Vaishyas*, the commoners, including farmers, workers and traders. Finally is the lowest caste, the *Sudras*, composed of servants, serfs, and those generally engaged in menial work. Outside these four orders, and inestimably below a person belonging even to the lowest caste, were those who had no caste, the *outcastes*. And here too gradation reigned, the lowest of the low outcastes were the Chandals: offspring of an illicit union between a Brahman woman and a sudra.

It must not be supposed that caste ends with this simple division into four groups and the excluded. Quite otherwise, caste is a bewildering structure since each main caste contains subcastes. There is an elaborate variety of subcastes and mixed castes. Some castes are clearly functional, such as the washermen, the barbers, and the bards; others are tribal and may be composed of the descendants of primitive aboriginal tribes; yet others are sectarian or are produced by fission from an already existing caste. There are castes started by outcastes; again, a new occupation may mean the start of a new subcaste and so forth. It is estimated that India came to have over 2,300 castes.

Each caste has its own set of rules, *dharma*, received by divine sanction, and these rules govern behavior and customs. Violation of these rules, in particular those about marriage and food, involves an unpleasant and costly expiation, and may mean expulsion and loss of caste. Caste determined a man's place in Indian society, from Brahmans to untouchables. How can it be accepted, and why did one resign oneself to a place unalterably fixed in society? The answer is that belief in karma and rebirth point out an escape and induce resignation. As man behaves, so he is reborn.

Caste, the social aspect of Hinduism, is perhaps its most important part. One was not a Hindu unless one was a member of a caste. One's beliefs may be elastic, and varied, but caste membership is rigid. It is possible to have free thought, but not a free life. Although caste occurs everywhere it must be noted that it is least rigid in the north of India, particularly in the Punjab, the classic locus of new peoples and new ideas. Caste is especially strict in south India, which has become the most rigid area. In judging caste not much can be said for it. It is true that under the caste system each separate group gains in homogeneity and solidarity but this is offset by the fundamental fact that caste divides the people, and has been one of the major reasons for India's political weakness when confronted by an alien invader.

The essential tenets of Hinduism are in religion the emergence of a trinity of personal gods, in thought spiritual monism coupled with the doctrine of rebirth and karma, and in society the caste structure. A product of the Indus civilization, the Dravidian inhabitants of the Ganges basin, and the Indo-Aryan invader, Hinduism by 600 B.C. had become a definite and complete way of life.

To illustrate Hinduism as it was lived, to describe its society and its activities, and to gain as much factual information of its life as possible we can turn to the two great Sanskrit epics, the *Ramayana* and the *Mahabharata*. It will be remembered that the Vedic literature is not concerned with history, but contains only religion and philosophy. The epics also are not historical accounts but stories of traditional legends. However, they give us much information of the life of the times, and the way of its society, as it took place in the Ganges basin in the centuries before definite historical dates can be ascertained. The time of origin of the two epics is not at all clear, but probably they were first written down about 200 A.D., that is most parts of them, although other sections were composed at definitely later times.

The first work, the *Ramayana*, tells of the career and adventures of King Rama and his devoted wife Sita. The story deals with the exile, hardships, and final glory of Rama. The *Ramayana* is the picture of the ideal man and the ideal woman triumphing over all difficulties, however great.

Quite different in content is the *Mahabharata*. This, the longest poem in the world with over 100,000 couplets, is a sort of glorified history based at least in its kernel upon some dimly-remembered historical events. It was not this long to begin with, but grew in time to its present very great length, and much of it is of later date than A.D. 200. Its setting is also north India, near present Delhi, and it tells of the struggle between two parties, the Kurus and the Pandus. The greater part of the epic deals with a great battle of eighteen days and the deeds of valor performed by both sides; it is rather like the *Iliad*.

The epics describe a state of society which is very much like that of the Greece of Homer. The Indo-Aryans lived in the Ganges valley, in a number of kingdoms, and became city-dwellers. The cities were surrounded by walls and moats, and were laid out in squares around the heart of the city in which stood the palace of the king. In the palace, spaciously built, were meeting halls, courts for dispensing justice, gambling and music rooms, and even a cockpit and places for contests with wild beasts. The king, or *raja*, ruled the people, not because of might alone, but also by virtue of his morality. A wicked king may be deposed; a king who injures his people instead of protecting them should be killed, "like a mad dog."

The king was surrounded by his councillors, and was guided in his decisions by their advice. He spent his time in hunting and fighting. A code of chivalry governed warfare, the right of sanctuary, and obligations of hospitality were recognized and honored. One was not to fight against those who have yielded, against women, and against low-born fellows. The greatest glory to the warrior is to die in battle; it insured eternal fame. "Sweet it is to die in battle, the path to heaven lies in fighting." Gambling, cockfighting, and wrestling were the amusements preferred in peace. The cow was now regarded as sacred, but meat, except beef, was still eaten.

Women occupied a high place in society. When a princess came of age she could choose her own suitor, and as in the *Ramayana*, she shared the fate of her husband. As Sita says:

> My mother often taught me and my father often spake
> That her home the wedded woman doth beside her husband make,
> As the shadow to the substance, to her lord the faithful wife,
> And she parts not from her consort till she parts with fleeting life.
> Therefore let me seek the jungle where the jungle rangers rove,
> Dearer than the royal palace, where I share my husband's love! [4]

Little interest in the common people is displayed in the two epics. Taxes seemed to have been fairly light, and they were adjusted to varying needs. Many crafts were practiced in the cities; we hear of merchants, gem-cutters, weavers, armourers, carpenters, glass-makers, workers in ivory, cooks, incense sellers, goldsmiths, wood-workers, shampooers, physicians, lamp-makers, wine-sellers, washermen, tailors, and actors. Slaves were on the whole not badly treated.

By the time of the epics Hinduism had been fully formed and had penetrated all of India. Caste dominated, reverence was paid to Brahmans, and the cow was venerated. Sanskrit had become a sacred language and the authority of the Vedas and the later prose works was undisputed. In religion a trinity of gods had been established, and in philosophy an admirable idealistic system had been worked out, involving the most subtle questions of metaphysics. The fundamental civilization of India had come into being.

BASIC DATES

2300–1600 B.C.	Indus civilization
1500–1200 B.C.	Indo-Aryan invasions
1200–1000 B.C.	*Rigveda*
800–600 B.C.	*Upanishads*

[4] Rawlinson, *op. cit.*, pp. 36–37.

SUPPLEMENTARY READING

BASHAM, A. L. *The Wonder That Was India.* London, 1954. An excellent, brief topical introduction.

DE BARY, W. T., ED. *Sources of Indian Tradition.* New York, 1958. An invaluable source collection containing major excerpts of documents for all of Indian history.

MORELAND, W. H. AND A. C. CHATTERJEE. *A Short History of India.* London, 1920.

PIGGOTT, S. *Prehistoric India.* Baltimore, 1952. Excellent account; in paperback.

RAWLINSON, H. G. *India: A Short Cultural History.* London, 1937. The best one-volume interpretive work.

SMITH, V. A. *The Oxford History of India,* 3rd ed. Oxford, 1958. Standard reference.

SPEAR, P. *India, Pakistan and the West.* Oxford, 1958. Well-written, short account.

ADVANCED READING

BROWN, N. W. *The United States and India and Pakistan.* Cambridge, Mass., 1953.

CRESSEY, G. B. *Asia's Lands and Peoples.* New York, 1949. Standard geography.

DUNBAR, G. *History of India.* London, 1943.

HOPKINS, E. W. *The Religions of India.* Boston, 1895.

MARSHALL, J. H. *Mohenjo-daro and the Indus Civilization.* London, 1931.

MAC KAY, E. *Early Indus Civilizations.* London, 1948.

O'MALLEY, L. S. S. *Indian Caste Customs.* Cambridge, 1932.

RAPSON, E. J. *Cambridge History of India, Vol. I.* New York, 1922.

RHYS, E. *The Ramayana and the Mahabharata.* London, 1929.

WHEELER, M. *Early India and Pakistan to Ashoka.* New York, 1959.

VIII ❀❀

INDIA FROM BUDDHA

TO THE MAURYA EMPIRE

Dissent from Hinduism: Jainism and Buddhism

The preceding chapter dealt with the development of Hinduism as a way of life which encompassed philosophy, religion, and social structure. Its thought, as propounded in the *Upanishads,* developed the concepts of the absolute reality of the world soul; of metempsychosis or the transmigration of souls and its determinant, karma; and of the ultimate termination of existence and union with the infinite. Its religion had created the trinity of Vishnu, Shiva, and Brahma, and had been accompanied by the growth of power of the priesthood. Its society had been rigidly stratified by the caste system.

Against all these developments there arose powerful voices of dissent. Backed by royalty, who naturally mistrusted and looked with jaundiced eyes upon the strength of the priesthood, there developed in India in the sixth century B.C. a great number of schools which argued against Brahman teaching and Brahman influence. This was particularly true in the lands of the Ganges basin, where the country had been most recently settled, and new tribes had been civilized by Hinduism. Among the many new schools, only two became important: Jainism and Buddhism. The great historical leaders of both were not original creators, for both had many forerunners and previous prophets. But in the sixth century they forged ahead and became great religions, under the leadership of Mahavira and Gautama Buddha.

Both Jainism and original Buddhism in opposition to traditional Vedic teaching posit the complete independence of the human mind, able to solve all problems by pure reason. No priesthood is needed. Both also deny the existence of a supreme deity, and are intensely practical in their teaching. But both religions do take over from Hinduism the outlook that existence is an evil, and the theory of metempsychosis or reincarnation.

The virtual founder of Jainism was Vardhamana, later called Mahavira. The son of a Kshatriya family which had close ties with the royal family of Magadha in the western Ganges basin, he was born in 599 B.C. Until the age of thirty he lived the ordinary life of a man of his caste, was married, and had children. All this he foresook when he reached middle age, and for twelve years he wandered in the forests, leading a life of extreme asceticism. After subjecting himself to this regime, Mahavira obtained enlightenment at the age of 42, while sitting in deep meditation:

> Omniscient and comprehending all objects, he knew all conditions of the world, of gods, men and demons; whence all come, where they go, whether they are born as men or animals, or become gods or hell-beings: their food, drink, doings, desires, and the thoughts of their minds; he saw and knew all conditions in the whole world of all living beings.[1]

Mahavira then wandered and preached throughout India for thirty years. Using Prakrit, the language of the common people, instead of Sanskrit, he preached against the tyranny of the Brahman priesthood, and ignored the Vedas and the caste system. Jainism, as taught by Mahavira, is essentially atheistic, since it denies a divine creative spirit. Instead it might perhaps be called a philosophic animism. It views the universe as filled with infinite numbers of eternal, indestructible, and individual souls. These are incarnated not merely in organic substances, such as men, animals, or plants, but even the earth, wind, fire, or minerals possess souls and are conscious. The aim of all these souls is to escape their material bonds, and to be free forever. Thus Jainism, like Hinduism, is also a religion of pessimism and looks upon life as an evil, perpetuated by transmigration. How to escape rebirth? Mahavira answered this query by postulating intensive contemplation by the individual which will produce right knowledge, which in turn will eliminate all earthly passions from the body. When this state has been attained, the soul leaves the body to be eternally free, karma and samsara are no more.

Mahavira formulated five vows, which if kept, lead to the attainment of right knowledge and aid in the process of intense contemplation. These are poverty, chastity, honesty, truth and, particularly, respect for the life of all beings. This last commandment, not to injure and to respect life in any form, and to practice nonviolence, *ahimsa,* against all beings, is especially characteristic

---

[1] H. G. Rawlinson, *op. cit.*, p. 44.

of Jainism and is pushed to an extreme extent. Since all natural objects possess souls, it is possible to inflict pain on a stone. The Jain walks veiled, lest he inhale any living organism; he sweeps the ground before him so that no animate thing may be destroyed by his foot; and he strains his drinking water in order to avoid swallowing any living thing. Even his food is not prepared over fire, since the flame also is animate.

As befitting the austere views of Mahavira, the external practices of the Jains are most severe. Jainism espouses extreme asceticism. Fasting, yoga practices, meditation in certain difficult postures, and other austerities are prescribed for the purpose of contemplation. Religious suicide, by starvation, is permitted. One important feature of Jainism, which also occurs in Buddhism, is the formation of a religious order of monks, practicing charity, poverty, and chastity alongside a congregation of laymen.

When Mahavira began his preaching and wandering career he soon collected a body of followers, and when he died in 527 Jainism had become an established religion. As is the case with most religions, after the death of its founder dissensions and schisms set in. The major sectarian split was between those of his adherents who abandoned all clothing and wandered around India stark naked, "sky-clad," and those who kept clothes. Jainism, although it never extended beyond the confines of India and never became a great world religion as did its major rival, Buddhism, continued in India throughout all historical vicissitudes. Today it is found primarily in western India, in Gujarat and Rajputana and is estimated to have about one and one-half million followers. The Jains think of themselves as a reformed Hindu sect, and the powerful influence of the caste system has tended to overshadow the basic differences between it and Hinduism. Jains are apt to be wealthy and many merchants and bankers belong to the religion, as agricultural occupations are forbidden to a member of the Jain religion since they involve the tearing up of the ground and the death of insects. Thus Jainism presents an interesting eastern correlation between religion and the rise of capitalism. One of the curious institutions practiced by Jains is the establishment and endowment of animal hospitals for the care of aged and sick beasts and birds of all kinds, including vermin.

It is perhaps easy to be repelled by the extreme practices of Jainism, its asceticism and the degree to which respect toward living beings, such as rats and fleas, is carried; but one does well to remember that Mahavira's creed embodied high ideals. Its "reverence toward life" and its doctrine of nonviolence are very much present in the twentieth century, espoused in India by Gandhi. Furthermore Jainism emphasized the ability of the individual human mind by means of reason to free itself from all material bonds, and it is this aspect of Jainism which gives it a claim toward a new view of life, distinct from Hinduism.

There are many parallels between Jainism and its great contemporary religion, Buddhism. Buddhism also sounds a voice of protest against the priesthood, caste, and the Vedas; it too looks upon existence as an evil and is concerned with the search toward the means to accomplish freedom from it; and even in its practical aspects it has many similarities with the teachings of

Mahavira. Although far less extreme in its asceticism, Buddhism also contains monasticism and provides for lay congregations.

Similar also, up to a point, are the lives of the two great founders, Mahavira and the Buddha; both came from the same kind of background, both renounced worldly life, and both found enlightenment. Only in the means towards achievement of liberation, and in their final ideal do they differ profoundly.

The *Buddha* (the name means the one who has attained to the supreme knowledge of things spiritual) was born in 563 B.C. at Kapilavastu in the foothill country of the Himalayas near Nepal. His personal name was Siddhartha, his family name Gautama, and since he was the son of a minor raja in a small tribal republic of the Sakya clan, he often is also referred to as *Sakyamuni,* the sage of the Sakyas, or as *Gautama.* The name Buddha is really only proper for his career after his enlightenment, but it is the most famous, and we shall use it consistently for the sake of convenience. Until the age of twenty-nine Buddha led the conventional Kshatriya life of a man of his class and position. Hunting, pleasure, and family life occupied his time. When nineteen years old he married a beautiful cousin and had a son by her. Yet among all these delights a feeling of discontent stole over him. One day, so legend has it, as he was riding he met three men—the first broken by age, poor, bent, enfeebled, the second suffering horribly from some loathsome disease, and the third a corpse, unburied, swollen, eyeless, mauled by passing birds and beasts. Overcome by the miseries of humanity, and the superficiality and emptiness of pleasure, Buddha decided to abandon the world and to meditate upon a way toward salvation. This is the "great renunciation":

In this, the Buddha did no more than other countless yogis had done before him, and he embarked upon a traditional life of rigid asceticism. For six years in the forest he practiced fasting, trance without breathing, and mental concentration. A sense of futility overcame him, and he decided to abandon this regime to the shock and disappointment of a handful of followers who had been attracted by his career of self-denial and penances. Shortly after this, the Buddha, while sitting under the sacred pipal tree at a place called Buddh Gaya, concentrated his thought on the world's universal grief and the means of abolishing it. Suddenly, according to the legend, he was assailed by Mara, the prince of darkness, who attempted by terror and temptation to shake him of his purpose to effect salvation for all mankind. Rising above all assault, the Buddha then received illumination; he had become the Enlightened One.

In clear and simple language, the Buddha defined his teaching. Using numbers as mnemonic devices, he outlined the middle way, the eight-fold path, and the ten commandments. In this fashion does man reach salvation: by practicing the middle way of both avoiding the excesses of self-indulgence and shunning self-torturing asceticism; by following the eight-fold path of seeking what was right in eight categories of thought, word, and deed—kindness to all living things, purity of heart, truthfulness, charity, abstention from fault-finding, covetousness, hatred, and violence; and finally by practicing the ten negative commandments of not to kill, not to steal, not to commit adultery, not to lie, not to speak evil, not to be trouble-tongued, not to use fine, flattering speech, not to covet, not to be angry, and not to take heretical views.

This indicated the practical way toward salvation, but the Buddha had yet to tell of the reason for salvation, and of the ultimate goal which salvation implied. This he did in a series of sermons, the first and perhaps most famous of which was delivered at the deer park at Benares. There he preached, or "set the wheel of the law rolling," of the four great truths: sorrow, the cause of sorrow, removal of sorrow, the way leading toward removal of sorrow. These are the four great truths:

1. All existence is sorrow, human existence is pain.
2. The cause of this sorrow is desire, the thirst for existence.
3. Sorrow and the thirst for existence which leads from rebirth to rebirth must be removed.
4. The removal of sorrow and the thirst for existence is achieved by the eightfold path.

Here we have the basic view of the Buddha on the nature of existence, and its cause. That existence is an evil from which an escape must be found implies the same pessimism already encountered in Hinduism, but deliverance is now possible by a practical way of life, attainable by all, not just by a privileged few. Salvation is open to all irrespective of caste.

And what is the ultimate goal of salvation? Salvation is the extinction of karma, which determines man's present condition in life on the basis of past merits and the attainment of a blessed state, *nirvana*. The concept of nirvana is a difficult one indeed, and made purposely so by the Buddha. It is release from decay, disease, death, sorrow, and impurity; it is extinction of lust, anger, ignorance, and the craving for existence; and it confers consummate peace and spiritual freedom. Nirvana is not a union with the world soul or with God, as in Hinduism, Islam, or Christianity; it is cessation of being, but not necessarily extinction of being. On this all-important point, the difference between these two states, the Buddha refused an answer. When pressed by his disciples to explain the state of a saint after death, he declared that such a discussion was unprofitable. Neither calm, insight, comprehension, or enlightenment would be gained thereby.

In other words, nirvana is not nothingness, it does not imply nonexistence, but it does imply cessation of being. Beyond this the Buddha remained silent. The foremost goal is to lead a religious life at the end of which death is met fearlessly as an incident of little moment. Discussions of nirvana, the soul, and the infinity of the universe are unprofitable. The main characteristic of the Buddha's teachings was their moral nature. The Buddha was occupied with the ideals of righteousness and ethical problems, like many of the other great founders of religions; but unlike Christ or Muhammad, he was not concerned with the kingdom of heaven. Buddhism, as taught by its founder, is a practical rule for a moral life, no more, no less. The Buddha was only indirectly a social reformer. He ignored, but did not preach against, the caste system and he never specifically rejected the general beliefs in Hindu gods. He took over the concept of karma and rebirth, but stayed silent on the question of the existence of the soul, or atma, or of a supreme deity. Buddha preached not a heresy in active revolt against the past. He pointed toward a new way, by which he quietly abandoned old traditions and instituted a fresh religion.

As a practical teacher the Buddha understood, as had the Jains, the importance of providing a way of life for his religious followers who donned the yellow robe, took tonsure, and led a monastic life of poverty, chastity, and obedience. He also organized an order for laymen and women from all walks of life. The monastic corporation and the lay orders gave permanence to Buddhism. The wandering monk or nun, clad in yellow, begging for food, and retiring for meditation, soon was to become a characteristic feature of Indian life. The monk and the Buddhist layman together transmitted the word of Buddha abroad.

After his first great sermon in the deer park in Benares the Buddha preached and wandered for 46 years, attracting, if we are to believe the sacred scriptures, a few disciples wherever he went. The theme of his sermons was constant: the condition of craving was bad, it produced sorrow and misery. Release could be found in following an ethical code. But to the essentials of Buddhism he added many other ideals, such as the principle of impersonal and universal love toward all beings, even toward enemies. He died, at the age of eighty, near Kushinagara in 483 B.C. His last words were to his despairing disciples: "work out your own salvation with diligence, only you can do it."

These words re-emphasize the individual salvation open to all men by their own efforts. Salvation is achieved by works and knowledge combined. Works include self-training, right thinking, and constantly living up to the highest ideal; knowledge means constant appeal to reason, so that reason can distinguish between real and false values, and mind can understand the deceptive nature of desire and its insatiableness. With these two concepts, virtue and knowledge, Buddha is close to Platonic thought. The resultant state of salvation, vague perhaps, is one of spiritual equilibrium and calmness.

After his death his body was cremated, and his ashes divided. Mounds or stupas were built containing them and form the first great Buddhist architectural structures.

The Buddha's personal teachings are preserved in a collection known as the *Tripitaka,* or the three baskets. Written in Nepal in Sanskrit, and in Ceylon in Pali, they are the original source for early Buddhism. They are formed of three books, as the title indicates. The first deals with the discipline of the monastic order, the second contains stories and sayings, and the third contains the higher philosophy of Buddhism. Together with the Tripitaka there soon arose a literature of Buddhism, known as birth-stories, or *jatakas,* full of moral tales of the life of the Buddha, and earlier events.

The Tripitaka and the jatakas are sources for the early form of Buddhism, the original teachings. This original teaching is called *Theravada* or *Hinayana* Buddhism of the lesser vehicle, which from the first century A.D. on must be distinguished from *Mahayana* or the greater vehicle. Theravada is the Buddhism wherein lofty ethics prepare each individual for salvation. As we shall see, it was rivaled by Mahayana Buddhism. In Mahayana the Buddha himself becomes a divine being to be worshipped. Supernatural power and miraculous feats are claimed for him. In addition to the Buddha, a host of other deities were then also introduced.

It must be understood that neither Jainism nor Buddhism ever really superseded Hinduism in any way. One can not really speak of a Buddhist period in Indian history. But as soon as these dissenting religions emerged they modified Hinduism. Each religious system borrowed ideas from the other, and the mutual exchange of ideas proved fruitful. For Hinduism it meant a gradual trend away from bloody sacrifices, the tyranny of the priesthood, and the introduction of new ethical concepts. Jainism remained a small, but nevertheless vital segment of Indian religious life. Buddhism finally was to become a great world religion, to be exported to the greater part of Asia.

Northern India and Invasion from the West

In the sixth century B.C. it becomes possible to discern political developments in India. First from a few Jain and Buddhist sources, then from writings of the Persians and the Greeks, the Indian scene is suddenly illuminated.

From the seventh century a number of small kingdoms, under strong royal control, grew in the Gangetic plain. These kingdoms frequently engaged in war, either against Dravidians or among themselves. Gradually some rival kingdoms grew in size and absorbed their competitors. Among these rival states Magadha took the lead. Located in the east central Ganges basin, it was ruled by the Saisunaga dynasty, a ruling Kshatriya class which may have been of Mongolian type, akin to the Tibetans. Religious literature mentions a King Bimbisara of Magadha, himself a Jain who at the same time was a patron of the Buddha. Despite his religious inclinations this ruler of Magadha kept a strong army and prohibited his soldiers from joining Buddhist monastic congregations. King Bimbisara traditionally is said to have been murdered by his son, Ajatasatru. The parricide may have been morally reprehensible, but he strengthened his kingdom. Making excellent use of the army, which possessed siege engines and armored cars, he extended his domains to the west. He also built a new capital at Pataliputra, the present Patna.

The Saisunaga dynasty was overthrown by a low caste dynasty, the Nandas, whose first king, a sudra, had begun life as a barber. Under the Nandas too, Jainism and Buddhism made headway in the Ganges basin, and we are indebted to their religious writings for the little historical information outlined so far. But suddenly a brief foreign interlude follows and furnishes a comparatively detailed and complete historical picture of India. This resulted from the fascinating, but ephemeral coming of the Persians and the Greeks to India.

During the reign of the Achaemenids, the founders of the first great world empire, Persians entered India. As described in Chapter 3, under Cyrus Persian influence had extended into Afghanistan and Baluchistan, and under his successor, Darius I, Persian armies conquered part of India. In 516 B.C. Darius annexed Gandhara and the lower Indus valley, and made that territory his twentieth satrapy. It seems to have been an extremely valuable territory since the Persians were enriched by its alluvial gold.

Darius explored the Indus valley, made it a regular division of his empire with Persian officials, and introduced the Karoshti alphabet, derived from the Aramean, which later on became one of the two major Indian alphabets. In addition to gold the new province also provided soldiers for the Persian army. Xerxes in his invasion of Greece of 480 B.C. used contingents of Indian cavalry and infantry. Herodotus knew India; it was "the furthest part of the inhabited world toward the east."

With Persian control of the Indus valley close touch between India and the west was firmly established. Indian merchants made voyages into Persian waters, the peacock was introduced into Greece from India, and Indian thought influenced Greek thinkers. How much, and to what degree is far from clear. Parallels between Orphism and Buddhism are certainly very close. Plato, as previously remarked, shows many similarities to Indian philosophy. The myth of Er in the closing pages of the *Republic* states the Hindu doctrines of karma and reincarnation: "each soul returning to a second life, and receiving the one agreeable to his desire." Also, the myth of the cave points out the illusory character of sense objects, a point of view shared by the Buddhists with their concept of illusion or *maya*.

The sudden and complete collapse of the Persian world by the conquests of the young Alexander of Macedon introduced the Greeks to India. Alexander the Great meant not to conquer merely Persia, but literally the world. In 330 B.C. Alexander crushed the last of the Achaemenians. The next year the young hero pushed on into Afghanistan, and established a city at the site of Kandahar. After four years of campaigning, Alexander finally crossed the Indus in 326 B.C.

His army, composed of only 30,000 infantry, 4,000 cavalry, and 300 chariots, marched into the Punjab and advanced to Taxila, a wealthy and cultured city, where he and his small force were given a friendly welcome. From Taxila Alexander advanced into the Punjab and at the crossing of the Jhelum was forced to fight an Indian king, whom the Greeks knew as Porus. It was a complete rout for the Indian king; cavalry had proven superior against the traditional Hindu order of battle, a fact which recurs time and time again. But the victory was only possible because of the consummate leadership of Alexander. Indian losses were terrible. Porus himself was captured but was generously treated by the young conqueror. Alexander appointed him as his viceroy to rule the newly conquered land.

After the battle of the Jhelum, Alexander was determined to advance further into the Ganges basin. However, when the Greek troops reached the river Beas they refused to cross. Despite a fervent speech of their leader, who promised them the riches of all Asia, the troops could not be swayed. Alexander's speech was received in ominous silence, and he retired to sulk for three days in his tent. Then he gave in; the Greeks had reached the furthest limit of their willingness to follow. Alexander, after erecting twelve altars on the banks of the Beas to mark the spot of his furthest advance, returned to the Punjab. In October of 326, the army of 30,000 men embarked and sailed down the Indus to the sea. After occasional flurries of fighting, the delta was reached and the Greeks had their first experience with the tide, a strange and puzzling phenomenon.

Since Alexander regarded his conquests in the Punjab as lasting, he divided his possessions into satrapies. Greek walled cities with a nucleus of Greek citizens were established, and were intended to be permanent colonies. Docks were built in the port at the mouth of the Indus for the sake of the commerce which Alexander anticipated. India, just as Persia, was to be Hellenized. This task completed, Alexander returned west. In 323 the conqueror of the world, aged thirty-two, died in Babylon, and with him died Greek authority in India. The export of Hellenism was purely ephemeral; Alexander was only an episode in Indian history. Incomparable as a soldier, his feats were marvelous, but they did not include the Westernization of the subcontinent.

On the death of Alexander began the great struggle for division of the empire. In this contest Seleucus Nicator I, the founder of the house of the Seleucids, obtained the satrapies left in India. After firmly establishing his power in Mesopotamia, Seleucus advanced into India to re-establish Greek power, but he was checked and forced to withdraw. In 305 Seleucus gave up all of Alexander's conquests in the Indus plain. This check to the power of the Seleucids was inflicted by a newly united, strong Indian power, that of the Mauryas.

The Maurya Empire

The Maurya empire was founded by Chandragupta Maurya, the commander-in-chief of the Nanda king of Magadha. He, together with a shrewd Brahman minister Kautilya, plotted against the ruler. The conspiracy was discovered and both Chandragupta and Kautilya had to flee Magadha. They went to the Punjab where tradition attributes to them a meeting with Alexander the Great. After the Macedonian's return to Babylon Chandragupta managed to collect some troops and to inflict a defeat upon the few Greeks still left in the Indus basin. After seizing power in the west, he moved to Magadha in the Gangetic plain, and there killed the Nanda king establishing in 322 B.C. the Maurya empire. Later, in 305, Chandragupta confronted the Seleucid forces with a huge army and forced them to give up all claims to the lands which Alexander had conquered in India. Chandragupta then possessed a powerful army estimated at 9,000 elephants and 600,000 infantry. A treaty was signed between the two monarchs in which Afghanistan was handed over to the Maurya, and the

Hindu Kush became the frontier between the two states. In addition, Chandragupta added Malwa and Gujarat in the west, and Bengal in the east, to his
dominion, creating the first Indian empire in history, extending from the
waters of the Bay of Bengal to the snowy Hindu Kush mountains.

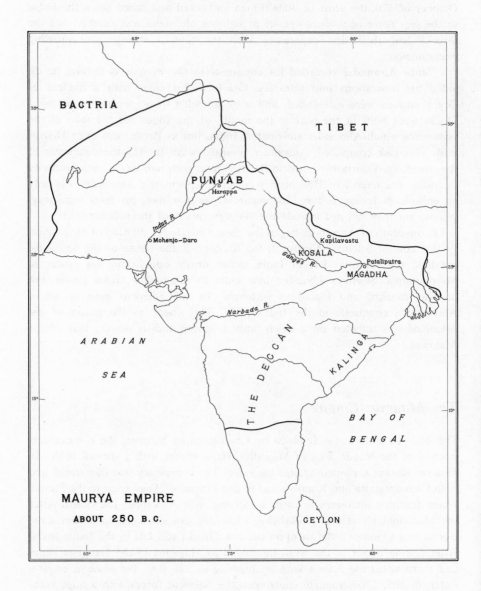

The Maurya ruler, as part of his treaty with Seleucus Nicator I, had entered into a marriage alliance, and in consequence of the good diplomatic
relations thereby established between the two powers, a Greek envoy, Megasthenes, was dispatched to reside at Pataliputra, the capital of the Maurya empire.

Megasthenes, an acute observer, wrote down his impressions and his excellent and detailed descriptions of the Maurya empire are the chief source of information for the rule of Chandragupta Maurya.

Megasthenes furnished a vivid picture of the daily life of the monarch. Chandragupta lived a closely guarded and carefully protected existence, in great fear of assassination. His palace was a maze of secret underground passages and staircases, hollow pillars and collapsible floors, all designed to cope with any attempt upon the life of the ruler. The fear is understandable in view of the fact that Chandragupta ruled harshly and very oppressively, and remained a most unpopular king. All food and drink was carefully tasted before he ate, and no one was allowed into his presence without a permit. A bodyguard of armed women kept watch day and night, and except on festival occasions, or for rare hunts beyond the confines of his residence, Chandragupta seldom left his palace. There he was surrounded by a host of slave girls who cooked and served his food on gold plates six feet in diameter, made music, danced and entertained him.

Despite seclusion and fear, Chandragupta devoted almost all of his life to the state. Over thirteen hours a day were spent in public business. During this period he heard reports, received the three or four ministers of his small cabinet in utmost secrecy ("even the birds did not know where they met"), and conducted audiences. His few hours of recreation were spent in hunting, chariot racing, and the inspection of troops.

This rigorous regime by Chandragupta served the needs of an elaborate and highly centralized administration. In essence the Maurya empire was an autocratic state founded upon a centralized bureaucracy. This first Indian empire does not appear to have been so very different from what we can determine of the structure of the state in Harappa.

Autocracy and centralization were the key words. An elaborate bureaucracy ruled. The empire was divided into three provinces, ruled by viceroys strictly dependent on the king. Beneath the viceroys served commissioners and district officers. The chief officials occupied hereditary positions, but it was possible for a low-born person to rise to some eminence in the service of the state.

Another characteristic of the Maurya empire was its huge army. A war office was in charge of a military force consisting of 600,000 infantry, 9,000 war elephants, four-horsed chariots and cavalry, war engines, archers, and auxiliary forest tribes. The soldiers were well paid and supplied by the war office with weapons and horses which were returned after use. The art of war was carefully studied and the troops served in organized formations. Reserves and guard regiments were maintained.

The main structure of the autocratic Maurya government was its centralized nature and its huge army, yet there was also a recognition of a social system which ultimately depended on the self-governing village community. Some freedom on the local level of government was unavoidable in such a huge structure. The picture of the Maurya empire which then emerges is very much the picture of later Indian political units. These features of autocracy, centralization, a large army, and a degree of local self-government, shall be encountered again, not only in India, but in China as well.

The size of the bureaucracy and of the army required much revenue, which was derived primarily from agriculture. All land belonged to the king, and one-fourth of its products were handed over to the treasury. The state, of course, had an interest in increased productivity and supported irrigation and drainage works. Rice was the chief crop, and two harvests a year seemed to be normal practice. Just as agriculture was under an elaborate bureaucracy, so were all other activities. Forestry, mining, commerce—all had their own officials. There were superintendents of temples, of public works, and of customs. The cities too had their own municipal boards which kept a register of population and property. Special attention was paid to foreigners. They had to travel about with passports and were strictly controlled. When they fell sick the city put them in a hospital, when they died, they were buried at the city's expense. Everybody was registered and everybody needed identification papers; the Maurya empire bore a strong resmblance to today's police state.

An excellent espionage service insured effective control by the government over all individuals and kept them under constant supervision. Spies were everywhere, among the high and the low, ministers or beggars, actors and dancers; even the blind, deaf and dumb were utilized. Ascetics and wandering orphans were particularly useful secret sources of information. The spies were trained in special schools, where they learned the use of ciphers, the care of courier pigeons, and other essentials of their craft. A central collecting agency served as the clearing house of all reports; if the news brought by some spy proved false he was promptly punished. Counterspies were employed to spy upon spies, and the cardinal principle was that no spy should know the identity of other spies. Another device of the Maurya police state was to tempt and bribe government officials. If they accepted they were of course promptly cashiered. It was rule by mutual suspicion and general treachery. In addition to the system of spies there were also traveling inspectors throughout the empire, who made confidential reports on the state of affairs. Nevertheless, or perhaps because of this atmosphere of intense distrust, corruption was only too rife. The *Arthasastra*, a handbook of politics, mentions forty methods of embezzlement. Suspicion and spying proved no incentive to honesty.

Justice in the Maurya empire was harsh, as one might expect in such an autocratic state. Punishments were severe, although they were graded according to the status of the offender in society. Sometimes punishment was inflicted secretly—the offender simply disappeared from amidst his fellows, a method intended to inculcate terror.

The state controlled and supervised all aspects of economic life. Craftsmen were organized into guilds and strictly regulated. An attempt was made by the government to control and fix prices, and to regulate sales. The Maurya empire was based, of course, primarily on an agricultural economy, but the state supported trade and it seems to have flourished. Merchants benefited from an excellent system of roads which were provided with inns and rest houses at intervals. Some coastal shipping supplemented land transportation. A courier service on the roads provided an efficient and rapid system of communication. The state did not interfere in religion and Hinduism, Buddhism, and Jainism all existed side by side. The most popular deities seem to have been Vishnu and Shiva.

The foreign policy of Chandragupta Maurya is closely associated with the famous treatise on politics, the *Arthasastra,* attributed to Kautilya. Although it is not clear exactly when this book was written, it does present a definite statement of Hindu theory of government and diplomacy as practiced by the Maurya Empire. Its influence on later statecraft was enormous. Kautilya advocated a diplomacy of extreme expedience; everything was permitted for the sake of conquest. Treachery and dissension were authorized means of foreign policy and for this reason the *Arthasastra* has often been compared to Machiavelli's *The Prince.* The text is written lucidly and with great detail. The qualifications of an ambassador, his rank, the advantage of his possessing wit, the dangers besetting him such as women, liquor, and untrustworthy informers are all delineated, and seem applicable to the foreign service of any modern nation. The ambassador's main task is to furnish information and to advance his king's power by all means, including espionage and subversion. Seduction, poison, and arson are excellent weapons, if judiciously used. Beggars and intoxicated persons are fine sources of information, if carefully cultivated. Yet the *Arthasastra* is more than a handbook of diplomacy and espionage; it is also an analysis of political power. A careful study of relationships among foreign powers leads Kautilya to formulate certain maxims regarding the respective advantages of belligerency and neutrality. As a whole, he concludes, it is wise to make war when you are the superior power, and to maintain peace when you are inferior. It is always of the greatest importance to cultivate the enemy of your enemy. In this sense the *Arthasastra* is an amoral book, but it aleo proclaims the ideal of a united India, ruled by a supreme ruler, the *chakravartin,* just as Machiavelli exalted a united Italy in his concluding chapter.

Chandragupta died in 297 after firmly establishing his power and handing it on to his son Bindusara. Bindusara had a long reign and followed the policy of expansion inherited from his father. Conquests to the south of the Vindhya mountains added the Deccan clear to the Penner river to the Maurya dominions and rounded out the empire. The policy of friendship with his western neighbor, the Seleucid king, was also continued along traditional lines. A letter is extant from Bindusara to Antiochus I, requesting that sweet wine, figs, and a philosopher be sent to the court in India. In reply the first two items arrived, but philosophers, Antiochus regretfully stated, were not just then on the market. Little else is known of Chandragupta's son. But his grandson, Asoka, the third of the Maurya line, who ruled from 274 B.C. to 236 B.C. is one of the world's great figures.

Asoka

For the events of Asoka's career we possess unique sources; a series of his own inscriptions in granite rock and sandstone pillars. Asoka had been one of many sons of Bindusara. He first served as viceroy in the west, and after he ascended the throne continued to further expand his empire. When not at war, he enjoyed hunting, drinking, and dancing. In 262, in order to round out his dominions, he conquered the region known as Kalinga. This area in southeast India on the shores of the Gulf of Bengal, corresponding to present day Orissa, was inhabited by a Dravidian population. They stoutly resisted Maurya arms and the war became one of extermination in which over 100,000 people were slain. With Asoka's conquest of Kalinga, the Maurya empire reached its greatest territorial extent stretching from Mysore to the Himalayas, and from Assam to the Hindu Kush. Not all of it was under the direct control of the Maurya government, since many autonomous states and wild tribes were also included, but as a whole the excellent bureaucratic organization fashioned by Chandragupta provided for efficient rule. Under the king were four viceroys appointed to the largest subdivisions of the realm, and they were provided with commissioners and district officers.

If the Kalinga war had given Asoka's empire the greatest extent, it also proved to have a more wide-reaching effect than mere territorial acquisition. It deeply influenced the king's mind and converted him to Buddhism. He had been under the influence of Buddhist teachers before, but the horror of the war and the accompanying butchery instilled in him great remorse for his deeds:

> The Kalingas were conquered by His Sacred and Gracious Majesty the king when he had been consecrated eight years. 150,000 persons were thence carried away captive, 100,000 more were slain and many times that number perished . . . Thus arose His Majesty's remorse for having conquered the Kalingas because the conquest of a country previously unconquered involves the slaughter, death and carrying away captive of the people . . . if a hundredth, nay a thousandth part of the persons who were then slain, carried away captive, or done to death were now to suffer the same fate, it would be a matter of remorse to his majesty.[3]

As this rock inscription indicates, deep remorse overtook Asoka and in 261 B.C. he became a convert to the teaching of the Buddha, resolved to lead the righteous life. At the end of his life he donned the yellow robe, became a Buddhist monk and recluse, and died in a monastery.

Asoka's embracing of Buddhism did not mean that he no longer reigned; it did mean that henceforth his rule was governed by Buddhist ethical considerations. His aim was to follow the law of piety, *dhamma*. Dhamma as Asoka understood it included the Buddhist principles of compassion, alms giving, truth, purity, gentleness, and saintliness; that is, a code of practical ethics for everyday life was emphasized and not a metaphysical system. The emperor foreswore war and taught nonviolence (ahimsa) and peace ruled the Maurya

---

[3] Vincent A. Smith, *Asoka* (London, 1909), p. 24.

empire. Even against the unruly and wild hill tribes a policy of friendliness was adopted by the state which seems to have been most effective.

Asoka was constantly concerned for the welfare of his subjects and wanted to be regarded as the father of his people:

> Just as a man, having made over his child to a skillful nurse feels confident and says to himself: the skillful nurse is eager to care for the happiness of my child, even so my governors have been created for the welfare and happiness of my country.[4]

The state provided for shade trees on the roads, dug wells for water, established hospitals. Officials of the state, in addition to their duties, were ordered to teach the people morality, to inculcate in them reverence for parents and elders, truthfulness, friendliness, and respect for all living things. All over the Maurya possessions, the emperor caused inscriptions to be carved in rocks or on stone pillars, recording the edicts praising the law of piety. "Let small and great exert themselves" was his constant exhortation.

Other measures included the abolition of hunting, and the royal kitchens served meat no more. Even prisoners condemned to die were given a reprieve of three days in which to prepare an appeal or prepare themselves for death. Asoka stood for complete religious toleration; men must not disparage the religion of others: "By thus acting, a man exalts his own sect and at the same time does service to the sects of other people." Dhamma consisted of practical and simple duties, and what Asoka did was to accomplish a great moral reform in India. He was neither a theologian nor a philosopher, but a benefactor to mankind by introducing ethics into government and society.

Above all, Asoka's greatest achievement was the spread of Buddhism as a world religion. His was a conquest, not by force, but by the spread of the Buddhist law of piety. He wanted unity in Buddhist religion, and called a council at Patna in 253 B.C. which began the development of the Buddhist canon, while at the same time, on his orders, missionaries were sent out abroad. His aim was world peace and his missionaries went in all directions. These missionaries went to Gandhara and Kashmir in the northwest, into the Deccan and to Ceylon in the south and across the Gulf of Bengal to Burma; they were also sent to Egypt, Syria, Macedonia, and Greece in the west. Some of these missionaries left no trace and had no visible success; others, particularly those in Ceylon and Burma, were highly effective.

Asoka is a figure of the stature of Marcus Aurelius and Constantine in the Western world, and he is perhaps even greater than either. He was a great moral reformer with high ideals of righteousness, and he renounced war as policy and put a stop to cruelty, and he was responsible for the spread to most of Asia of a great religion. Unlike the Stoic, Marcus Aurelius, whose *Meditations* were of a private nature, Asoka put ethical principles into public life; unlike Constantine who accepted Christianity in the face of necessity and made a virtue out of something which could no longer be avoided, Asoka espoused Buddhism voluntarily and sincerely, and nourished its growth so that eventually

[4] *Ibid.*, p. 185.

it civilized vast parts of the Asiatic continent. He put his immense autocratic power and his diplomatic influence into the service of the Buddhist religion.

Wherever Buddhism later went from India, to Ceylon, Burma, Siam, Cambodia, China, Korea, Mongolia, Tibet, and Japan, it exercised tremendous civilizing influence. The law of cause and effect, karma, supplanted the caprice of demons and tribal gods, and in the place of tribal customs and taboo Buddhism brought a developed system of morals. Even to areas which had already developed their own great culture, such as China, Buddhism brought new values and wrought great changes.

Ceylon is the most direct example of Asoka's labors. He sent his brother Mahendra, helped by his sister, as missionaries to Tissa, king of Ceylon. With their arrival Buddhism was actively and energetically propagated and brought a high culture to Ceylon.

The remaining years of the Maurya empire are inevitably something of an anticlimax. Little is known about Asoka's successors, the empire soon disintegrated and the dynasty ended in 185 B.C. The last Maurya ruler was murdered by a Brahman, Pushyamitra, who established a new dynasty, that of the Sungas. The Sungas represented a Brahman reaction against Buddhism; Buddhist followers were persecuted and the old Hindu horse sacrifice was reinstituted. But the Sungas ruled but a shadow of the former empire, Kalinga had long since revolted, and in the northwest a whole series of new and dangerous invaders had established themselves.

Maurya Culture

Asoka's inscriptions on rocks and pillars are the earliest extant examples of Indian writing, but they show evidence in the perfection of their calligraphy that writing must have been in practice a long time before. Two alphabets are used: one is Brahmi from which most present-day Indian scripts are derived; the other is Kharoshti. Both record the edicts in vernacular Prakrit, and not in sacred Sanskrit. Kharoshti occurred in the northwest and was derived from Aramean; the origin of Brahmi remains a problem.

The Maurya period was one of great advances in architecture and sculpture. Few existing secular monuments can convey an impression of the grandeur of public buildings, such as the palace at Pataliputra. Stone and burnt bricks were used instead of wood. The workmanship in the sculpture of the stone columns on which Asoka's edicts were recorded is of very high quality. These columns posed real engineering problems in their erection on famous Buddhist sites, since these monolithic highly polished sandstone pillars were forty to fifty feet high and weighed at least fifty tons. In the sculpture of these columns, their crowning glory, distinct Persian and perhaps even Hellenic influences are visible. One of the finest of these, and a masterpiece, is the column at Sarnath of the four lions upholding the Buddhist wheel of law. The lions rest on a bell capital of re-

FIGURE 8.1.   The lion capital of Sarnath.

versed lotus flowers and point to the four cardinal directions. The lions are
sculptured in round, with swelling veins and tense muscles, full of life and realism;
at the same time they convey an expression of idealistic dignity. The idealism of
the lions clearly shows Persian influence. Similar animals are encountered at Persepolis, yet Achaemenid technique had been assimilated with an indigenous
Indian element producing faithful animal realism. It is not too much to say that
except for Athenian sculpture in the Periclean age, such Maurya sculpture
embodies standards of art as high as any encountered in the ancient world.
Excellent workmanship and care is also revealed in the lustre of the tapered
monoliths themselves. They shone so that later travelers were deceived in thinking that they were made of metals, rather than stone. This same high skill and
craftsmanship is also encountered in Maurya jewelry.

Apart from the few scanty remains of Pataliputra and Asoka's pillars,
Maurya art has mainly survived in religious monuments. Two major forms exist;
the monastic cave dwelling and the Buddhist stupa. Cave dwellings were used
in the annual rainy season by monastic communities. They were excavated out
of the living rock of hillsides involving great skill and considerable craftsmanship
for cutting into hard gneiss. The stupa originally was a mound erected over a
grave to harbor Buddhist relics such as the ashes of Gautama. Gradually it
evolved into a massive hemispherical mound surrounded by railings with gateways at the four cardinal points. Within the railing a processional pathway en-
circled the stupa and the procession by pilgrims around the stupa was considered
an act of devotion. The summit of the mound was crowned by a mast and tiers of
circular stone umbrellas.

FIGURE 8.2.   The great stupa of Sanchi.

With the stupa was connected an elaborate religious symbolism; it was an architectural diagram of the cosmos. The mound, a solid hemispheric dome, indicated the dome of heaven enclosing the world. The mast put on top of the mound represented the world axis, and the tiers of umbrellas above the heaven of the gods. Although belonging to the post-Maurya period, strictly speaking, and built around 50 B.C., the great stupa of Sanchi is the finest example of the early Buddhist stupas, many of which were built during Asoka's reign. It is a mound fifty-six feet high, surrounded by a railed platform with four richly decorated gateways. Hidden in the jungle of central India, it escaped desecration and destruction. The sculpture in relief is justly famous. Its principal object is to illustrate scenes from the life of the Buddha as told in the jatakas. Modelled upon earlier wood carvings, these stone relief scenes on the gateways represent a truly Indian indigenous art, with the same love of naturalism already encountered in the steatite seals of animals at Harappa. Many facts regarding everyday life and customs are represented and scenes of actual Indian village life alternate with animal scenes from the jungle. It must be noted that the Buddha is here never represented; only his symbols are portrayed in this early Buddhist art. His presence in form is indicated by an empty throne and a pair of his footprints showing the wheel of the law imprinted on his soles. The sculpture at Sanchi is full of interest in and love of life, in a spirit unlike that of the first great sermon at Benares. The jungle seems to have become a terrestrial paradise, where sympathy has been extended toward all living beings. Rather than of renunciation, Sanchi speaks of spontaneous joy of life. The whole

FIGURE 8.3.   North gate of the stupa at Sanchi; subjects taken from the Buddhist jatakas.

creation seems to worship the Buddha. With its naturalism, and in its observation of life, Sanchi sculpture is great Indian art, the principles of which, inherited from the Indus civilization, found expression in Buddhist religious architecture.

BASIC DATES

C. 560–480 B.C.	Gautama Buddha
C. 540–468 B.C.	Vardhamana Mahavira
C. 540–490 B.C.	Magadha, King Bimbisara
521–519 B.C.	Achaemenid Darius I annexes Indus valley
C. 490–460 B.C.	Magadha, King Ajatasatru
327–325 B.C.	Alexander the Great in India
C. 321–297 B.C.	Chandragupta Maurya and the founding of the Maurya Empire
C. 274–236 B.C.	Asoka
185 B.C.	Maurya dynasty ends, start of Sunga dynasty

SUPPLEMENTARY READING

BASHAM, A. L. *The Wonder That Was India*. London, 1954.

DE BARY, W., ED. *Sources of Indian Tradition*. New York, 1958.

DUNBAR, G. *History of India*. London, 1943.

MORELAND, W. H. AND A. C. CHATTERJEE. *A Short History of India*. London, 1920.

RAWLINSON, H. G. *India: A Short Cultural History*. London, 1937.

SMITH, V. A. *The Oxford History of India*, 3rd ed. Oxford, 1958.

———— *Asoka*. Oxford, 1909.

ADVANCED READING

CONZE, E. *Buddhism*. New York, 1951. A good modern survey.

ELIOT, C. *Hinduism and Buddhism*. London, 1954.

GROUSSET, R. *The Civilizations of the East, Vol. II: India*. London, 1931.

MORGAN, K. *The Path of the Buddha*. New York, 1956.

ROWLAND, B. *The Art and Architecture of India*. Baltimore, 1956.

SHAMASASTRY, R. *Kautilya's Arthasastra*. Mysore, 1956.

THAPAR, R. *Asoka and the Decline of the Mauryas*. Oxford, 1961.

THOMAS, E. J. *Life of Buddha*. New York, 1927.

IX

INDIA AFTER THE MAURYAS, 185 B.C. - A.D. 320

THE REIGN OF THE LAST GREAT MAURYA EMPEROR, ASOKA, had seen an attempt to make India a great world power. His achievement had been tremendous: he had ruled over a strong central government, he had renounced war and introduced the principle of piety into government, and he had made of Buddhism a world religion. Yet very soon after his death the Maurya empire broke up, and by 185 B.C. had ceased to exist. One can only speculate upon the reasons for this rapid disintegration; what is certain is only that India entered a period of great turmoil after the collapse of the Maurya state. Foreign invasions on the northwest frontier followed one upon the other, and for centuries alien conquerors ruled parts of India. The Ganges basin, the original homeland of the Mauryas, lost its significance, and new powers arose in the Deccan and in the Tamil peninsula of the extreme south. For the historian this is a most difficult period since little in the way of materials is available and one can only trace in broad outlines its major developments.

Northern and Central India

In the old region of Magadha on the banks of the Ganges, the Sunga dynasty inherited the ruins of the Maurya empire. It was founded by Pushyamitra, who is said to have murdered the last of the Maurya rulers, and for some time the Sungas were dominant in central and northern India. With the Sungas came a reaction against Buddhism; Brahmanism was restored to high honor and the old Aryan horse sacrifice was reinstituted. Pushyamitra is depicted in Buddhist literature as a relentless persecutor of that religion, and although no doubt this role was exaggerated, there is little question that Buddhism suffered from lack of state support, and that Brahmans again occupied positions of great power. The Sunga period lasted from 185 B.C. to 72 B.C., but even during this short span large areas which formerly had been part of the Maurya empire regained their independence. This was the case with Kalinga in the southeast whose conquest had so profoundly changed Asoka, and also with Taxila in the northwest where the Sungas encountered the new power of Greek invaders. But even apart from the loss of the outlying territories the Sungas controlled only a shadow of the former glory of the Maurya state; we have evidence from coins that a number of independent states existed in the very Ganges basin, which were ruled by military clans of the Kshatriya caste organized in tribal oligarchies.

Very soon the role of the leading state in central India fell to the new power of Andhra, and for two centuries this kingdom located on the east coast of India between the Godavari and the Kistna rivers, to the south of Kalinga, became the paramount state. Very little is known of its origin (c. 225 B.C.), but it appears that its inhabitants belonged to the Dravidian races characterized by dark skin, long heads, curly hair, broad noses, and dark eyes. After 110 B.C. Andhra expanded rapidly and fought, frequently with success, against the Sungas of Magadha. The Andhra kings assumed the appellation "lords of the Deccan" and, not satisfied with conquests in central India, extended their power to the north into Malwa and to the west clear across the peninsula to the sea. The Andhras at their height of power, extending from coast to coast, were prosperous orthodox Hindu rulers, yet tolerant and at times even patrons of Buddhism. The state was divided into three provinces, each ruled by a hereditary chieftain, and from the dark obscurity of the period little can be gleaned except that internal conflicts seem to have been frequent. Commerce was carried on extensively and merchants were organized into guilds. Punched coins were used already for money in the time before Asoka. Prakrit was the spoken language. On the local level there was some village self-government. The history of Andhra offers a very good example of the importance of coins for historical reconstruction; coin inscriptions and their dates are the main source for the political history of Andhra. The great importance of numismatics as an auxiliary science in Indian history begins with Andhra, but by no means ends there; we shall see time and time again that information gleaned from coins is the chief evidence for historical events.

Since the kings of Andhra were tolerant, Buddhist art flourished in the state continuing the tradition of both the rock-hewn monastery and the stupa. Andhra created some magnificent Buddhist masterpieces. A very fine example of the cave monastery is the sanctuary at Karli near Bombay. It was cut into the hillside as a place of retirement and meditation for Buddhist monks and consists of a great central hall in the form of a basilica, ending in an apse where stood a stone stupa with an umbrella on top. In addition there were small, flat-roofed cells for the monks themselves, also cut out from the rock. Karli is an enormously impressive cave temple where a sense of mystery is created by the permanent twilight of the interior and the whole central hall with its gigantic pillars and its shadowy depths gives a feeling of a world of unreality.

But above all, Andhra Buddhist art is famous for the sculpture of Amaravati. Here, at the mouth of the Kistna river, a stupa was decorated with innumerable carvings of low relief, depicting scenes from the life of the Buddha. Palaces, walled towns, houses, temples, all are here, and as one critic wrote: "it would hardly be possible to exaggerate the luxurious beauty or the technical proficiency of the Amaravati reliefs. This is the most voluptuous and the most delicate flower of India's sculpture." [1] Completed between the first and

FIGURE 9.1. Sculpture from Amaravati, Andhra period (second-third century A.D.). The throne of the Buddha is shown but he is not represented in human form.

[1] Rawlinson, *op. cit.*, p. 165.

third century A.D., the art of Amaravati was developed definitely out of the traditions of Sanchi and represents indigenous Indian art. It is a splendid exhibition of artistic skill. The sculpture along a 600-foot railing is of extraordinary richness. The design and the lavishness of decoration over a vast expanse of stone as well as the drawing of an infinite variety of patterns produce a scene of unequalled splendor. Two types of sculpture are found, one in which the Buddha, true to the early Buddhist artistic canons, is not yet represented, and one of later date in which he is. Supple dancing nudes of almost incredible lightness and airiness convey a feeling of sensuality, while vigorous realism and love of life in scenes from town life illustrate the flexibility of this Indian art. Amaravati is a monument to perfect composition and a work of art of exceeding beauty.

Gandhara and the Northwest

An India where peace and security had disappeared with the downfall of the Maurya empire was a disunited India, incapable of resisting attacks from the outside, and indeed the decline of the Mauryas is the prelude to successive waves of foreign conquests. All these alien invaders came by the same route, the northwest border, and consequently the Punjab was again the chief center of activity. Here in the northwest and the district of Gandhara waves of invaders from Bactria came to establish kingdoms and to rule part of the subcontinent.

The first of these were the Greeks, who entered India between 200 and 175 B.C. from Bactria, the independent Greek state which had been set up in the rich land between the Amu-darya river and the Hindu Kush mountains. There in 250 B.C. Diodotus had successfully revolted against the rule of the Seleucids, and had formed his own kingdom (see Chapter 4). His successor was Demetrius who, after conquering Afghanistan, crossed the Hindu Kush c. 184 B.C. into India. He may have been propelled to do so because of the pressure of Scythian nomads, the Sakas, who encroached upon the Bactrian borders. Demetrius consciously copied Alexander; his coins proclaimed him "the Invincible King." It may perfectly well be that his actions were modelled upon those of the Macedonian, thinking of creating a new Greek empire in India. The Greeks under his leadership rapidly took Gandhara in the northwest, Taxila, and then Sind in the south of the Indus valley. Demetrius' lieutenant, Menander, a most able military commander, made a powerful raid deep into the Ganges basin and clashed with the Sungas of Magadha. Menander, by skillful use of cavalry, almost managed to get possession of Pataliputra. While Menander was thus fruitfully engaged in advancing deep into India, the Greeks, true to their devotion to fratricidal struggles, revolted in Bactria in 167 against the rule of Demetrius. Demetrius lost and, with his death, the Bactrian kingdom passed into the hands of a new Greek king, Eucratides. But Menander in India did not acknowledge the new ruler, and since Eucratides also expanded into India, there came to exist by 167 B.C. two rival Greek dynasties in India. Menander, now proclaimed king, controlled the territory from Gandhara to Mathura, while the house of Eucratides effectively controlled the lands to the west of the Jhelum and Afghanistan.

Menander and his successors, as well as the line of Greek kings of the rival dynasty of Eucratides, ruled what essentially amounted to an Indian empire, rather than a Greek one. A small nucleus of Greek officials and a few troops settled in military colonies, ran a collection of vassal states and free peoples, more or less on a partnership basis. Menander did control much territory, (although his limits to the south are not clearly defined), he did rule in Kathiawar and in Gujarat, and there were probably a number of Greek cities in the Sind as well; still, in order for such a small minority to rule over parts of India more than military force was needed.

Menander found his solution to the problem in the espousal of Buddhism. He championed that religion as a political factor against the Brahman rule of the Sungas, and thus occupied not only the position of a second Alexander, but also that of a second Asoka. He himself may have become a convert to the teachings of the Buddha; if he did not, he certainly supported it and he appears in Buddhist literature as King Milinda. In the *Milindapanha,* the "questions of Milinda," Menander is described:

> as in wisdom, so in strength of body, swiftness and valour there was found none equal to Milinda in all India. He was rich too, mighty in wealth and prosperity, and the number of his armed hosts knew no end.[2]

In this book, almost a Platonic dialogue in form, a Buddhist monk, Nagasena, solves the king's puzzles and cures him of his heretical tendencies. Finally, after many questions and answers, Milinda is said to become a convert.

Whatever Menander's personal relations with Buddhism may have been, it is clear that these Greeks, at the extreme periphery of the Hellenistic world, in a strange and even fantastic environment, had to have recourse to an alien religion if they wanted to continue to rule with success. Hellenism, and its culture, no longer were the civilizing factors; a boundary had been reached here in the Punjab where Greeks became assimilated to India, and where Greek civilizing influences had reached their furthest limits.

Most of the information for this strange episode in Indian history, Greek rule, comes to us from coins. These coins are among the finest in the ancient world, and their lifelike portraits of these kings and kinglets are not rivaled until the art of the Renaissance. Technically, too, they excel, since in some of them the minters used nickel, a metal not known in modern coins until the eighteenth century. But quite apart from their great artistic beauty, the intrinsic value of their psychological portrayals, and their technical quality, these coins of the late Hellenistic world show clearly the process of assimilation of the Greeks into

---

[2] Rawlinson, *India: A Short Cultural History* (London, 1937), p. 91.

India. At first strictly Hellenistic, the coins soon became Indianized, square-shaped and bilingual. Their Greek and Indian legends, written on the obverse in Greek letters and on the reverse in Brahmi or Kharoshti, furnished the clue to, and made possible, the decipherment of Asoka's inscriptions. Even the influence of Buddhism may be traced on them since some of the later coins portray the Buddhist wheel of the law.

The Greek element in India became rapidy assimilated, as seen not only in numismatic evidence, but also in art styles. Greek techniques and methods of sculpture came to express Indian content, and foreign forms became transmuted and synthesized. Possibly India did benefit from some Greek influence in astronomy, astrology, and medicine. The influence of Greek drama on Indian theatre is a more doubtful proposition. As for philosophy, it seems more likely that independent, parallel development took place.

In the Punjab Hellenism ceased to conquer when it met with an Indian civilization strong enough to conquer it. Greek rule did not merely come to an end because the Greeks were assimilated into an Indian environment, but the Greeks were also eventually overwhelmed by new invading tribes.

The next of these invaders were the Scythian nomads known as the Sakas who had for centuries more or less paid allegiance to the Persian empire, and regularly associated and even intermixed with the Parthians. Due to pressures which originated in Central Asia, a process discussed more fully in the section on Bactria and the steppe of Chapter 4, the Sakas and some Parthians conquered Bactria against the divided Greeks who ruled there. Then, after 135 B.C. the Sakas entered India by way of Baluchistan. Some of the Parthians associated with them, known in Indian history as Pahlavas, also went along. The Saka conquest of India began in the southern Punjab and moved upstream along the Indus river. By about 75 B.C. Gandhara fell to their king Maues, and they controlled most of the Punjab as far as the Jumna. About 50 B.C. another of their kings, Azes I, took the city of Sialkot from the Greeks, and by 25 B.C. the Sakas had ended all Greek resistance and had conquered all of northwestern India to the western edge of the Ganges plain. They also extended their power to the south, where they reached the sea coast in Gujarat, and where they remained an important power for centuries. Their most powerful kingdom was in the region of Malwa, just to the west of the Ganges valley, where a dynasty of western Saka satraps ruled successfully from A.D. 120 to A.D. 395. Here their capital was Ujjain, a center of Sanskrit learning. In Malwa they came in conflict with the great power of central India, the Andhras, and engaged in a long struggle. It is most likely that the Sakas are the ancestors of some of the later Rajput principalities which became a most significant military class in later Indian history.

The political power of the Sakas, with the exception of the Ujjain satraps, just as that of the Greeks, lasted only a very short time. After a century they were soon swallowed up and assimilated into Hindu society, and left few marks on Indian culture. And as the Sakas had conquered the Greeks, so it became now their turn to be ruled by yet another nomad conqueror, the Kushans.[3]

The Kushan invasion which replaced Saka rule in India was the last one of a series which had begun far to the east, on the borders of China. There, in Kansu, a people known as the Yüeh-chi had become displaced by nomads of Mongolia (see Chapter 4). In 174 B.C. the Yüeh-chi were forced out of their original home and about a half-million of them migrated to the west across the Tarim basin, entering the area between the Syr-darya and the Amu-darya rivers. In turn, they drove the Sakas before them, so that by 125 B.C. the Saka pressured Bactria and conquered the remaining Greeks. The Yüeh-chi again followed the Sakas to the west and in turn occupied Bactria, thus causing the Saka invasion of India. After having pushed the Sakas out of Bactria, the Yüeh-chi settled in that country, and so once more Bactria was destined to become the nursery of a great power.

The Yüeh-chi were composed of five tribes, and one of them, the Kushans, assumed the leadership so that the Yüeh-chi power is more conveniently called the Kushan empire after c. A.D. 25 when King Kadphises won complete supremacy over the rest of the Yüeh-chi tribesmen and built a Kushan empire extending into India. The chronology of the Kushan period is still not settled in all detail and all dates must be considered approximate, but it is safe to say that by A.D. 50 the Kushian empire encompassed an area from the Ganges to the Tarim, reaching the sea in Sind. Southern Afghanistan, Taxila, the lower Indus and Sind, the Punjab, and parts of central India had all become subject to Kushan rule, although the center of the empire remained in Bactria and Central Asia. The Kushans thus occupied an intermediate and connecting position between India and China.

Under Kadphises II the Kushans were clearly supreme in the Punjab and reduced the Sakas to tributary vassals, while their boundaries in the south were pushed down the Ganges valley. At the same time Kadphises II expanded in Central Asia to the east, reaching the limits of his empire in Kashgar, and even beyond, in present Chinese Turkistan. However, here the Kushans were checked in a conflict with the Han dynasty, and in A.D. 90 the Kushans were defeated by the great Han general, Pan Ch'ao. From this date on the Kushans paid "tribute" to the Han empire. Contact and trade with China, which this tribute implied, on one frontier were correlated with extensive trade on the other end, and the Kushan empire soon began a most flourishing trade between China and the West, as described in the Chapter 4. Parthia was the great obstacle to the Romans, eager for Chinese silk, and the Kushans profited as middlemen, bypassing the Parthians in Persia and channeling Far Eastern luxury goods to the Indian seaboard and thence by sea to Alexandria. We possess good descrip-

---

[3] One effect related to the Saka invasion was the creation of a strong state in Parthia by the Parthians who were closely connected with the Sakas. The fact that to the west of India arose a strong new empire, that of Parthia, hostile to Rome, soon meant that earlier Indian contacts with the West ceased and that India's intercourse henceforth swung eastward toward China. With the rise of Parthia Western sources end for India, and instead our knowledge of Indian history is derived from Chinese records.

tions of the trade by a sea captain of that city and can gauge the importance of it by the fact that in A.D. 99 a Kushan embassy arrived in Rome where it was splendidly welcomed by Trajan whose interest in trade and in overcoming Parthia found in the Kushan empire a most welcome ally.

The height of the Kushan empire was reached with the reign of Kanishka, who ruled probably between A.D. 78 and 96. A grandson of Kadphises II, Kanishka maintained his capital at Peshawar and later at Mathura and was famous not only in India, but also across Central Asia and in China. Kanishka consolidated Kushan control in the basins of the Indus and the Ganges, ruled over the Sakas in Ujjain, and made his power felt as far as Benares and the

FIGURE 9.2.   Statue of Kanishka, the Kushan ruler. The long padded coat, the riding boots and spurs are more characteristic of Turkistan than India.

Vindhya mountains in the south. Kanishka also added Kashmir to the Indian possessions of the Kushans. In the West he carried on a fairly successful war against the power of the Parthians, and in Central Asia, the real home of Kushan power, he saw to it that his power was firmly established in Turkistan and beyond to Kashgar and Khotan.

Kanishka also became a convert to Buddhism as had apparently Menander before him. This fact is of the greatest significance since it illustrates the opposition of Hinduism toward the foreign invader wherein a closed caste system with its logical rigidity had no place for the foreign conqueror unwilling to assimilate. On the other hand, Kanishka's espousal of Buddhism gave that religion a great impetus in its movement from India into Central Asia and thence to China, while its adoption by a foreign ruler fatally weakened its importance in its Indian homeland. Kanishka had been converted by a Buddhist scholar, and the Kushan king gave enthusiastic support to his new faith. At Peshawar, his first capital, he founded a great Buddhist monastery which became one of the most famous seats of learning, and under his patronage the fourth great Buddhist council was held in Kashmir where five hundred Buddhist scholars attended. Meeting for six months, they laid down canons of the religion and formulated new commentaries in the form of a Buddhist encyclopedia. The need to hold such a council and to agree on accepted standards from greatly varying interpretations makes clear the fact that Buddhism by the first century of the Christian era had begun to change significantly. Already here the rise of Mahayana, to be presently discussed, is in evidence.

His advocacy of Buddhism, of course, insured Kanishka a place in Buddhist legend, but on his coins appear also Greek (Helios, Heracles), Indian (Vishnu), and Persian (Mithra) deities. And indeed it is the fact that the Kushan empire was an empire astride some of the great cultural centers of Asia, that gives it its great importance in history. Located on both sides of the mountains separating India from China, it became the most significant intermediary between the two great cultures. Along its trade routes Mahayana Buddhism found its way from its homeland, India, to Central Asia, China, Korea, and Japan. Other facets of Indian culture were also exported, notably Indian writing which was encountered in Central Asia. In addition, the Kushans also represented an intermediary power between the West, i.e., Rome and the Hellenistic world, and Asia. Kushan relations with Rome were excellent, since both powers warred against their common enemy, the Parthians. We have already indicated the treatment Trajan gave a Kushan embassy in A.D. 99 when their ambassadors were given the extraordinary compliment of being given senatorial seats in the arena, and a brisk trade flourished between the two powers. Rome was, above all, most anxious for Chinese silks, and these, together with spices and condiments from India, made their way via the Persian Gulf and the Euphrates to the Roman colonies in Asia Minor such as Antioch. In return the Kushans received Roman gold, Greek wines, and "choice girls for the royal harem." In imitation of the Roman empire the Kushan mint at Peshawar struck gold coins of the same weight and design. In addition to these articles of commerce, Hellenistic art also made its way into India and into Central Asia and China.

It must be clear from the foregoing that the Kushan geographical position gave the empire enormous importance. Quite apart from material considerations, such as trade and artistic techniques which flowed from the West to India and China, it also made possible the great spiritual link of India with most of the rest of Asia, the common faith of Buddhism.

Mahayana Buddhism

The Buddhism exported from India by way of the Kushan empire was Mahayana Buddhism. Mahayana, or the "Greater Vehicle," was a gradual de-

velopment from the original form of Theravada Buddhism (also known as
Hinayana or the "Lesser Vehicle"), which today persists only in Ceylon and
Southeast Asia. The original form of Buddhism had been essentially a moral
code demanding individual contemplation and postulating salvation in the form
of escape from the pain of being. It had been monastic and rather conservative,
the notion of divine and supernatural powers, miracles, gods and images all
being absent from what amounted to a practical system of ethics. By the time
of the Kushan empire, fundamental changes in this Buddhism had taken place,
and what had been originally a moral philosophy for the few had become a
religion for all, promising happiness to all living creatures. The reason for such
basic changes may be found in two main developments, the attempts to reconcile
Hinduism with Buddhism, and the number of new influences which had penetrated northwest India in the wake of many invaders. Greek, Christian, Zoroastrian, and Central Asian religious concepts all contributed to this development, their spread being facilitated by the excellent communications existing
at the time of the Kushans between the Roman empire and Persia, Central
Asia and Chinese Turkistan.

Four major differences characterize Mahayana Buddhism. First is the
doctrine that the Buddha himself is a supernatural being and that there are
not only one but innumerable Buddhas distributed through infinite space and
time. The second point is the belief in *Bodhisattvas*. Third is the emphasis on a
special doctrine of salvation by faith in a particular Buddha. Finally, Mahayana
Buddhism is characterized by a worship of images and by an elaboration of
the religious ritual.

In Mahayana Buddhism Gautama is deified, the Buddha himself has become
a God. From veneration of a dead teacher a shift has taken place to the worship
of a living Saviour. His words are divine and promise divine healing power:

> I am the Father of the world, the self-born, the healer, the protector of
> all creatures. Knowing them to be perverted, infatuated and ignorant, I
> teach final rest, myself not being at rest.[4]

In addition, the historical Buddha recedes, and spiritual reincarnations of the
Buddha, repeatedly born, occupy the forefront together with other Buddhist
deities, the *Bodhisattvas*. These are persons who have stayed their entrance
into nirvana in order to help mankind and to bring it within the reach of all.
The idea of Bodhisattvas, "radiant deities," seems to have been taken over
from Zoroastrianism. The Bodhisattvas may be described as splendid angels
of mercy, not yet Buddhas themselves, who because of compassion and love
for all beings, have postponed their own deliverance. Moved by the sufferings
of the world they work for the deliverance of others. Among the most important
of these Bodhisattvas, one may mention Avalokitesvara, Maitreya (the future
Buddha), and Manjusri.

Mahayana also contains a much more personal, more emotional approach
to religion, and that is salvation by pure faith. Faith in certain spiritual Buddhas,

particularly in the "Buddha of measureless light," Amida or Amitabha, replaced for some belief in the traditional and historical Buddha. In some countries, notably China and Japan, Amida became the most important Buddha. In Amidism too, as among the Bodhisattvas, compassion replaced wisdom, and altruistic ethics and love for all beings promise deliverance into a "Western paradise." This is a real heaven, full of pleasure, and quite a different goal from nirvana.

Finally, accompanying the cult of spiritual Buddhas and Bodhisattvas, Mahayana Buddhism developed a most elaborate ritual with many scriptures or sutras, images, and flourishing temples to house them. Emphasis on metaphysics replaced the early stress on simple works and simple living. Deities, heaven, and temples are the hallmark of the new, as contrasted with the old. An apt comparison is the contrast between the Gospel Christianity as taught by Jesus and the great scholastic structure of the Catholic Church of the twelfth century.

A development of particular importance within Mahayana Buddhism was the use of images of the Buddha. They make their first appearance in the celebrated Gandhara school of Graeco-Buddhist art which extended from c. 100 B.C. to the fifth century A.D., although its most flourishing period was A.D. 50–200. This Graeco-Buddhist art employed Greek methods of composition and techniques in depicting Indian subjects. The central idea of this art was the representation of the Buddha as a man.

The rise of this particular art style is, of course, the result of its connection with the Kushan empire. A wealthy, prosperous state, open to influences from all directions along the great trading routes, it naturally was a place of intense artistic activity. Royal patronage by Kushan princes, especially Kanishka, stimulated production. He built a tower which marked the transition from the Buddhist mound, the stupa, to the later pagoda form exported to China and Japan. He also employed many Greek sculptors and architects at his court. Here late provincial Hellenistic art styles, particularly those of the schools of Pergamum and Ephesus in Asia Minor, were used to depict Hindu and Buddhist deities in human form.

The basic idea, that of representing the Buddha as a man, is Greek. The Buddha in this cosmopolitan Gandharan art becomes Hellenic: his features are Greek rather than Indian, his monastic robe is draped in classical folds, and he approaches the ideal of the classical statue of Apollo. In some examples of the many clay, slate, or stucco sculptures extant from Gandhara the Buddha appears sitting in European fashion, sometimes with a mustache. His head now is that of a Greek philosopher or that of the god Apollo.

Although the Buddha image predominates in Gandhara sculpture, Greek gods are introduced as well; Zeus, Heracles, Poseidon, and Pallas Athene all make their appearance in this strange world where Greek models are used to tell stories based on Indian jatakas of the life and times of the Buddha. The Greek orders in Ionic columns and Corinthian capitals are used to frame

FIGURE 9.3. Head of the Buddha; an example of Graeco-Buddhist art of Gandhara, third-fifth centuries A.D. The Buddha is represented as a man, a Greek concept. His face is that of a Greek god embodying classical concepts of beauty.

Buddhist and Hindu deities, clad in Hellenistic dress, in scenes which had their origin in the basin of the Ganges.

The net result of this Gaeco-Buddhist art is a distinct charm, a feeling of an exotic and foreign world, yet it is perhaps not really great art. At its best it is characterized by calm dignity, grace and a kind of sweet beauty, but as a result of a synthesis only half-understood Gandharan art does suffer from the lack of spontaneous inspiration. By itself, it is an art of little sincerity and emotion, at times soft in execution, and mostly deficient in character. But its main importance has not yet been touched upon, and it is this: Gandharan art is the parent of all Buddhist art in Asia, with the exception of India and areas in Southeast Asia under India's cultural influence.

Gandharan productivity was great; between A.D. 100 and 300 it had a very large output, and both in its idea (the Greek idea of an anthropomorphic God) and its style (late Hellenistic) Gandharan concepts and examples found their way, again thanks to Kushan control, into Central Asia and then all the way to the Pacific. The Graeco-Buddhist prototype appears in the Buddhist art not only of Chinese Turkistan, but also in Chinese, Korean, Mongolian, and even Japanese art. Wherever Buddhism went there went this art style, and although it was greatly modified by the indigenous influences of the great artistic

FIGURE 9.4. Gandharan art; statue of the Bodhisattva, Maitreya. Typical of Hellenistic influence are the classical treatment of the folds of drapery and the mustache.

canons of China and Japan, a Greek concept is present, however faint; the very representation of the Buddha as a human being is derived from the Aegean.

In India itself the art of Gandhara soon became Indianized. Greek influence died out rapidly and Gandhara exerted but small influence. There is at least the possibility that an indigenous development of the Buddha image in India also took place. In any case, it is clear that Mahayana Buddhist art in India did for the most part develop independently of Greek influence. Both the art of Amaravati in the south in the Andhra kingdom, already mentioned, and the art of Mathura, the sacred city on the Jumna in the north, are Mahayana Buddhist art of distinctly indigenous origin, having direct links with the great art of Sanchi. The same subjects as at Sanchi again appear in Mathura except that in its red sandstone sculpture the Buddha now also is represented in a seat of honor. The iconography of the Buddhist image becomes highly developed: the Buddha now shows distinctive marks, all signs of physical perfection and supernatural powers. His ears have elongated earlobes, his hair is curly and cut short, between the eyebrows a tuft of hair, and on top of his head a cranial prominence are evidence of his divine nature. The nimbus, too, makes its appearance, and is a distinguishing mark of the Buddha in this sculpture. Particular emphasis is paid to the symbolic position of the hands, the mudras, and each hand gesture acquires now a special meaning.

Mahayana Buddhism owed its rise to the Kushan empire, and it now remains only to outline briefly the decline of the Kushan power, after the death of its greatest ruler, Kanishka, who was smothered by his officers. He was succeeded by his son, Huvishka, whose coins show him to be a burly, middle-aged man with a large nose. He managed to retain most of his empire in India and also held firmly to the oasis cities Kashgar, Yarkand, and Khotan in Chinese Turkistan. Huvishka, like his father, was a Buddhist, and he founded a magnificent monastery at Mathura. Yet with his reign decay began to set in and soon the Kushan power in India was restricted to the Punjab. Huvishka's successor was Vasudeva, whose Indian name alone illustrates the progress of Indianization which the Kushans underwent, just as had been the case with the Greeks and the Sakas before them. His coins show Shiva, and the Indian bull; others from his mint also show Persian influence. Kushan culture was not strong enough to resist the civilizing influences of powerful neighboring empires. Vasudeva may have lost most of Afghanistan to the Sassanian kings of Persia. The process of assimilation and disintegration proceeded rapidly; by about A.D. 200 the once mighty Kushan empire had broken up into a number of small and insignificant states in northwest India, while other unimportant Kushan kings managed to rule in Kabul until the fifth century. Each wave of foreign conquest, Greek, Saka, and Kushan, had for a while ruled north India, but proved unable to withstand the groundswell of Indian civilization and was absorbed into it after performing exceedingly valuable services as cultural intermediary between India, the Far East, and the West.

The Deccan

The Deccan and the Tamil peninsula were the last part of India invaded by the Indo-Aryans. These were areas inhabited by dark-skinned Dravidians and primitive hill and jungle tribes. The Telugu-speaking Andhras, still wild at the time of Asoka, were the first to create a strong kingdom which extended into the Deccan. It was this power which clashed for many years with the Saka satraps of Malwa at the time of the great Andhra expansion from coast to coast. By about A.D. 225 the Andhra kingdom declined and in its turn there arose a new power in the Deccan, that of the Pallava dynasty. The origin of the name remains obscure; it seems to indicate the name of the dynasty, but not that of the people, and has nothing to do with the Parthian Pahlavas, associates of the Sakas. Rebel Pallava governors set up their independent state after crushing the original Andhra dynasty at a time when Andhra had withdrawn from western India, and had been reduced to the east coast. For five hundred years from A.D. 300 on the power of the Pallava kingdom was the dominant power in the Deccan, as will be further discussed in Chapter 11.

Pallava's role as a point of departure for the export of Hinduism to Southeast Asia will be discussed after briefly glancing first at the Tamil states and their sea trade.

Pallava seems to have been founded around a nucleus of predatory tribes, who under the leadership of the Pallava kings (the name is synonymous in Tamil with robber or rascal) were formed into a strong and certainly aggressive power, which lasted until A.D. 888. Its culture was primarily Hindu, but Dravidian influences were very strong. Possibly the Pallava kingdom represented an outpost of Hinduism on its gradual advance towards the south. Its capital was located at the city of Kanchi, where Sanskrit rather than Tamil was the language, and it soon became famous as a great seat of learning in southern India. Religious toleration was the order of the day, Hindus, Jains, and Mahayana Buddhists flourished side by side. From Pallava went traders across the Bay of Bengal to Southeast Asia and Buddhist missionaries to Burma and Siam.

Tamil States and Sea Trade

Since prehistoric times the extreme south of India, the Tamil peninsula, was inhabited by Dravidian speaking Tamils. Early in its history the land was divided into three kingdoms, the Chola state on the east or Coromandel coast, the Chera Kingdom on the west or Malabar coast, and the land of the Pandyas in the extreme south. The northern influence of the Indo-Aryan civilization produced merely a superficial veneer, and the area as a whole possessed a quite distinct Tamil culture, independent of Brahmanism. The Dravidian language was already too well developed for Sanskrit to do more than merely enrich its vocabulary, and the real index of Hinduism, the caste system, was adopted only in much modified form. Thus, although the priests, or Brahmans, did assert their own prerogatives, the castes of the Kshatriyas and Vaisyas were absent, society being made up only of Brahmans, sudras, and outcastes. In religion the common people still continued ancient ancestral cults of gods, goddesses or "mothers," and demons. During the Maurya period Jain and Buddhist missionaries dispatched by Asoka reached the Tamil kingdoms, and the capital of Pandya, Madura, soon became an important literary center. Moral maxims in the Tamil language still in common use today are characteristic of its output. This Dravidian culture welcomed all religious newcomers and religious toleration was the common practice.

Each kingdom was governed by an ornate royal court and the kings as a rule patronized literature, music, and the drama. On the local level there was some self-government. The unit was the village, and a group of villages chose representatives to an assembly which appointed officials to administer justice and to supervise roads and irrigation.

The Tamil peasants were skilled workers of the land and the soil was tilled and irrigated. Pearl and conch fisheries, going back to prehistoric times, supplemented agriculture. But most important, at least from an historical point of view, was the overseas trade carried on by the Tamil kingdoms both to the west and to the east.

The great pear-shaped island at the southeast of the Indian peninsula is Ceylon. All three kingdoms, Chola, Chera, and Pandya made it a practice to fight on occasion against each other and to contest control over Ceylon. The original inhabitants of Ceylon were the Veddas, a primitive tribe which still survives. At an early date Indian immigrants from Orissa and Gujarat found their way to the island, and Ceylon had achieved a considerable state of civilization when in 246 B.C. the Buddhist mission sent out by Asoka and headed by his son and daughter, arrived. A branch of the sacred Bodhi tree was planted at Anuradhapura in the center of the island, and a flourishing Buddhist culture was established there with many monasteries and pagodas. Soon after this Ceylon became the object of an often fierce struggle between the three rival Tamil states, and the island suffered from frequent invasions until the Tamils, after much fluctuating fortune, were finally driven out in the second century A.D. Anuradhapura was reoccupied, and imposing pagodas of dazzling white plaster honored the Buddha. There was a nine-story palace, with sixteen hundred pillars and bronze roofs, a Buddha made of jasper holding in his hand a pearl of priceless quality, and above all, there was the tooth of the Buddha himself, which had been smuggled to Ceylon from India in the hair of a princess and which was the center of great public religious festivals. The state was prosperous and large-scale irrigation provided a sound base for its economy until the ninth century.

There had been trade between India and the regions to its west and its east since prehistoric times. As far as trade with the west was concerned, this had begun already with the age of Harappa and the Indus civilization when cotton made its way into Mesopotamia. By the seventh and sixth centuries B.C. three great trade routes had developed: the easiest and oldest leading from the mouth of the Indus via the Persian Gulf to the mouth of the Euphrates and Babylonia; the overland route leading via the passes of the northwest frontier to the Iranian plateau and thence to the Caspian or the Levant; and finally the very old sea route from Indian ports to Yemen, the Red Sea, Egypt and Phoenicia and thence to Greece, where as early as 450 B.C. rice and the peacock had arrived. There is no question that trade contacts increased greatly with the coming of Alexander and his Seleucid successors, but the really great expansion of trade was the result of the extension of the Roman empire into the Near East, with its demands for a variety of imported goods. It has already been mentioned that the establishment of a hostile empire in Parthia led to close connection between Rome and the Kushans, and in consequence to trade being diverted away from the overland route and into maritime channels. This commerce was greatly facilitated by the utilization of the monsoon winds for sailing from the African shores direct to the coast of India. The Arabs had discovered the southwest monsoon before its traditional discoverer, Hippalus, who in A.D. 45 sailed directly to the mouth of the Indus and thereby eliminated the perilous and time-consuming coasting voyages. But after Hippalus, direct monsoon voyages became the established pattern and they speeded trade enormously. These voyages now became a routine trip of about two months, the record being held by a vessel which made the trip from Arabia to Ceylon in only 15 days.

Trade boomed with the demands of the luxury-consuming Roman empire and benefited greatly from the facilitated navigation. A large volume of commerce flowed between India and the Mediterranean, and to the old items of cotton, teak, ebony, and sandalwood which had been exported from India even before the Mauryas, there was now added a long list of specialized and costly goods. These included spices, precious stones, rice, rare animals and other sundry luxury goods. The list is long and makes for wishful reading: pepper, ginger, cinnamon, diamonds, agates, aquamarine, sapphires, crystal, beryl, amethyst, onyx, pearls, ivory, tortoise shell; monkeys, tigers and rhinoceros, peaches, apricots and indigo, silk, muslins, parrots, and slave girls all went west and were exchanged primarily for Roman gold. The Roman demand for luxury goods, which had to be paid for in precious metal, reached its height during the reign of Nero. Enough evidence for this flow of gold to India has been unearthed in the Tamil peninsula in huge hoards of coins to give an idea of the size of the trade involved. Large numbers of Roman gold coins, some even commemorating Claudius's conquest of Britain, were found in southern India, and it seems that the Romans conducted trade by means of permanent agencies on Indian soil, much like the later factories of the Portuguese, Dutch, and English.

The Tamil kingdoms in the south of India could and did supply some of these items of the luxury trade, and this accounts partially for their importance in the flow of goods, but the source of many other items was to be found beyond the Bay of Bengal in Southeast Asia, as even Pliny knew when he wrote that the best quality of tortoise shell derived from there. So trade from southern India to the east was an equally important development and gave added stature to the kingdoms of Chera, Chola, and Pandya as great commercial exchange entrepôts where goods coming from the east were reshipped to go west.

This trade from India to the east, just as trade to the west, dates from very early times, when ships coasted along the Bay of Bengal from the mouth of the Ganges to Ceylon, then crossed the ocean to Burma, Sumatra, and the Malay peninsula. The jatakas, or Buddhist birth stories, contain abundant references to early voyages across the Bay of Bengal, and so even has the *Rigveda* where may be found some accounts of sea travel. With the great increase of luxury-goods trade with Rome, trade with Southeast Asia from India naturally spurted, since many of the goods in demand such as spices, scented woods and perfumed resins, had their origin in Southeast Asia. Improved navigation went hand in hand with increased commerce, and the ships which now sailed east were often large enough for eight hundred passengers, with high stem and stern, and three masts with sails and oars. Sometimes vessels carried aboard land birds which could be released at sea and whose flight might guide toward the nearest land, perhaps a not too satisfactory means of ascertaining one's intended course. In exchange these large sea-going vessels exported primarily cotton from India to the regions of the Malay peninsula and Indonesia, a trade which was mainly in the hands of merchants from Gujarat on the Indian west coast. The significant thing in the trade of India to the east was that it was carried on by Indian ships, with Indian crews and carrying Indian merchandise, in total contrast with the Arab and Egyptian ships which handled the trade between India and the west. Thus, the need for reshipment in southern India gave commercial greatness to Tamil ports.

Hindu Colonization

Relations between India and Southeast Asia go back to prehistoric times. Both Indians and Malays were seafaring people, sailing the Indian Ocean for purposes of trade. Intensification of trade meant even greater intercourse, and bearers of Indian culture followed in the wake of Indian merchants. Indian learned Brahmans, Buddhist monks, Malay pilgrims visiting India, and "returned students," all were carriers of Hindu civilization. This is not a question of mass immigrations, or a sudden process resulting in displacement or eviction of peoples; rather one must think of this Hindu colonization as a slow, long drawn-out movement which along commercial paths brought to Southeast Asia Indian religions, arts, and customs. In the ancient states of mainland Southeast Asia and Indonesia as brought out in Chapter 14 the bearers of this Hindu culture found already organized societies with their own definite form of civilization, to which they added Indian concepts of royalty in political thought, Sanskrit as a sacred language and its literature as a new cultural heritage, and the great religions of Brahmanism and Buddhism. Hindu colonization in this form began as early as the fourth and third centuries B.C., early migrations taking place mostly from the Indian east coast states of Kalinga, Andhra, and then Pallava. Later, the sources of much of this peaceful and progressive migration were the Tamil kingdoms, mainly Chola. These Indian colonists and their later descendants soon became the governing class of various states and were the leaders in the process of Indianization. As early as the fifth century A.D. almost everywhere in Southeast Asia Sanskrit, Brahmanism, and Buddhism were firmly superimposed upon the region.

In Burma, geographically the closest to India, Hindu colonists arrived by sea from India perhaps from the first century B.C. on, and greatly influenced the Mon, Tibeto-Burman, and Tai tribes they encountered. By the third century A.D. a number of Indian trading centers had been established along the Burmese coast, the most important of which were located at the mouths of rivers, such as Prome near the mouth of the Irrawaddy, Pegu in the central delta area, and Thaton near the delta of the Salween. From these beginnings they grew into commercial kingdoms.

Hindu civilization came to Siam during the first century A.D. and to Cambodia a century later. Two Hinduized kingdoms arose here, Funan in the south, which was ruled by a Brahman dynasty, and Chenla in the north. In both of these Hinduized kingdoms the dominant religion was Brahmanism, although Mahayana Buddhism and Shivaism and Vishnuism also flourished.

In Champa, on the east coast of Indo-China, colonists from the Andhra kingdom established a Hindu merchant colony, and in A.D. 192 an organized kingdom was formed. Shivaism was the predominant religion here although Buddhism was also honored. Champa was a completely Hinduized kingdom; its capital took the name of Indrapura. Due to poor soils Champa's wealth derived largely from seaborne commerce and piracy, two occupations not necessarily sharply differentiated. In the islands of Indonesia Indian civilization came by about the beginning of the first century A.D. and its impact was to be profound.

In this fashion the world of Southeast Asia became to a degree an extension of the world of India, and one can speak of a Greater India in this region.

BASIC DATES

C. 200–175 B.C.	Bactrian Greek invasions
C. 185–72 B.C.	Sunga dynasty
C. 180–160 B.C.	Menander
C. 100 B.C.– A.D. 225	Andhra dynasty
C. 75 B.C.	Saka invasions
C. A.D. 78–96	Kanishka
C. A.D. 120–395	Saka satraps in Malwa
1st century A.D.	Kushan supremacy established in Punjab
C. 1st–3rd centuries A.D.	Early Tamil kingdoms
C. A.D. 325	Rise of the Pallavas

SUPPLEMENTARY READING

BASHAM, A. L. *The Wonder That Was India*. London, 1954.

DE BARY, W. T., ED. *Sources of Indian Tradition*. New York, 1958.

DUNBAR, G. *History of India*. London, 1943.

ELIOT, C. *Hinduism and Buddhism*. London, 1954.

MORELAND, W. H. AND A. C. CHATTERJEE. *A Short History of India*. London, 1920.

RAWLINSON, H. G. *India: A Short Cultural History*. London, 1937.

SMITH, V. A. *The Oxford History of India*, 3rd ed. Oxford, 1958.

ADVANCED READING

CONZE, E. *Buddhism: Its Essence and Development.* New York, 1951.

GROUSSET, R. *The Civilizations of the East, Vol. II: India.* London, 1931.

MORGAN, K. *The Path of the Buddha.* New York, 1956.

RAWLINSON, H. G. *Intercourse Between India and the Western World from the Earliest Times to the Fall of Rome.* Very good on early Indian maritime trade.

ROWLAND, B. *The Art and Architecture of India.* Baltimore, 1956.

TARN, W. W. *The Greeks in Bactria and India.* Cambridge, 1951.

X

INDIA: GUPTA EMPIRE

TO THE NINTH CENTURY

The Gupta Empire

The Gupta empire, coming after a dark and obscure period in Indian history, and preceding the Moslem conquest, was the golden age of Hindu culture. The empire was founded by a new dynasty, the Gupta, which reigned from 320 to about 535, but for convenience's sake the reign of Harsha, who ruled from 607 to 647, is included as part of that great period of Hindu culture.

The founder of the Gupta empire, Chandragupta I, began life as an adventurer of low origin, and seems to have come from Mongoloid foothill people. He managed to become the petty ruler of Bihar, and then, by a successful marriage, obtained control of the old Maurya center of Magadha, with its ancient capital of Patna. Establishing his dynasty in 320, he began to extend his domains to the west along the Ganges, but the real building of an empire was left to his son, Samudragupta, who reigned from 330 to 375. His father had chosen him as his successor, and this choice was well justified, for indeed Samudragupta proved to be the most powerful king of the dynasty. Warlike, he began at once a series of successful campaigns to "conquer the four quarters". In these wars he gained control of all of the Ganges basin, and most of northern India, and then extended his power to the south by many raids. The limits of his empire were the Brahmaputra in the east, with Assam paying tribute, and the Jumna in the west, with tribute flowing in from the Punjab and Rajputana, although the independent Saka satraps in the west managed to hold out against him. In the north his power was recognized in Nepal, and to the south the Narbada river was the limit of his territory. In 340 he marched 3,000 miles with his army to reach the Kistna river. But this southern campaign, during which he defeated a king of the Pallava kingdom at Kanchi, the inhabitants of the Kalinga area, and many jungle tribes, remained merely a raid, producing only a great amount of booty, which permitted him to use gold for his coins, and the temporary submission of the people which the Gupta forces encountered.

Samudragupta then built the first Indian empire since the days of the Mauryas, and with reason could he call himself the "exterminator of all other kings". Beyond the frontiers of his state he maintained friendly relations with the Kushan kings at Kabul, and with Ceylon to the south. Himself an orthodox Brahman, he made a point of reviving Brahmanism and reinstituted the old Aryan horse sacrifice rite, but he remained religiously tolerant and employed Buddhists in his service. Personally talented and versatile, Samudragupta played music, especially the lyre, collected books for his library and showed great interest in literature, to the degree that he became known as the "poet king," and the golden age of Hindu literature begins during his reign. Many splendid buildings gave lustre to his court.

His son succeeded him in 375 and, taking the title of Chandragupta II Vikramaditya, or "sun of valour," proved himself a worthy successor to his father during his long rule which extended to 413. Also of a warlike disposition, and personally most courageous, as some of his coins illustrate by depicting him in single combat with fierce lions, he continued the work of extending the Gupta empire. His main achievement was the conquest of the prosperous Saka states in the west, and he annexed both Malwa and Gujarat, as well as the peninsula of Kathiawar, thus gaining access to the sea not only in the east in Bengal, but in the west as well. The Gupta empire's access to the sea brought immediate fruit in the commercial contacts which he was able to establish with Egypt. Treading in the footsteps of his father, the second Chandragupta also continued the policy of raids into the south. His successes are recorded in the famous iron pillar at Delhi, which shows the advanced state of metallurgy of Hindu India. A large mass of iron, which never rusted, the pillar was far ahead of European technology. Chandragupta II chose a new capital, Ayodhya in Oudh, and this became the center of the Gupta empire which reached the height of its glory and its prosperity during his rule, and that of his successor, Kumaragupta, who reigned from 413 to 455. The Gupta empire now reached its greatest extent, and was ruled by an orderly bureaucracy in charge of provincial and district administration. Government was, of course, autocratic; the king ruled absolutely, with the aid of his council of ministers and a large staff of record keepers, in the traditions of the absolutist Maurya monarchy.

FIGURE 10.1. The Iron Pillar at Delhi. The pillar, which has never rusted, is an example of the technological accomplishments of the Gupta period.

Our knowledge of the Gupta empire is derived not so much from Indian sources as from those of the outside. The records of Chinese Buddhist pilgrims who came to India in search of authentic Buddhist scriptures are the unique source of the most valuable information concerning the Gupta epoch. The first of these Chinese wanderers in the homeland of the Enlightened One was Fa Hsien. In 405 he left China and visited the Punjab, the Ganges valley, and Bengal; then went by ship to Ceylon and finally returned to China in 411 via Java. Although his chief interest was the search for full and better texts on Buddhist monastic discipline, and his account is mainly that of a pilgrim primarily interested in religious matters, Fa Hsien nevertheless gives a good picture of India during the Gupta era. India appeared to be a prosperous and peaceful country, ruled by an efficient government, with a very high standard of justice.

Fa Hsien apparently failed to realize how much ground Buddhism seemed to be already losing in India, but he did express dismay at how deserted some of the holy places of Buddhism had become. The country around the birthplace of the Buddha had become desolate and barren, with few inhabitants, and attacks by elephants and lions had to be feared by pious pilgrims to this holy region.

The Gupta emperors were all Hindu rulers, but there was no religious fanaticism; both religions respected each other and did not meet in conflict. Hinduism predominated in the Ganges basin, where Buddhism seemed to lose ground, but in Bengal in the east, and along the western portions of the empire Buddhism remained a major faith.

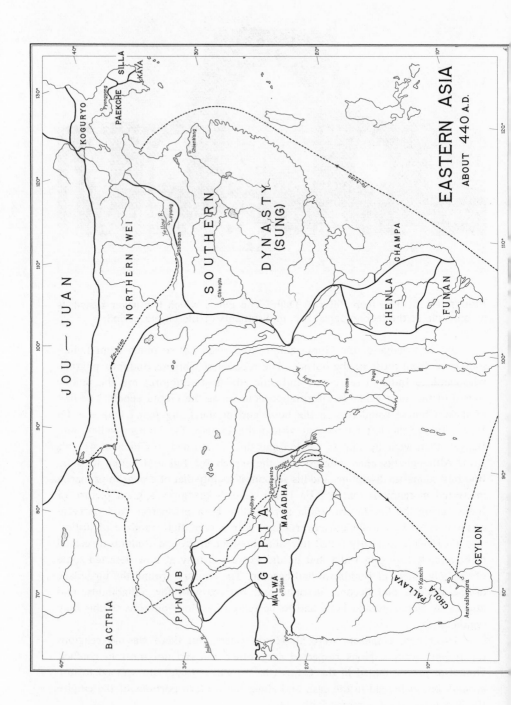

EASTERN ASIA
ABOUT 440 A.D.

After 455 the Gupta power declined, and the empire broke up. Primarily responsible for this political disintegration were the activities of nomads in the northwest. These newcomers were the White Huns or Hepthalites, probably related to the feared Huns of Attila, the "scourge of God" of Western Europe. They came from Central Asia and appeared about 425 on the banks of the Amu-darya. Settling in Bactria, they extended their power into Afghanistan, and then began to penetrate India via the strategic passes of the northwest frontier, the gateway of all previous invaders of India. In 455 they were met by the Gupta forces under Skandagupta, and defeated, but this proved to be merely a postponement of disaster. In 464 they occupied Gandhara, and from 470 on they became a permanent danger to India. For a short while their attention was drawn to the west, when they invaded Persia in 484, defeated and slew a Sassanid king (see Chapter 4), but from then on their major interest was India. Their ruler Toramana, who controlled the Punjab from his capital at Sialkot, raided the Indus basin as far as Malwa. His successor was Mihiragula, who seemed to have been singularly ruthless and oppressive, and who certainly contributed a major share to the decline of Buddhism by systematically slaughtering all monks, and destroying all monasteries and stupas wherever encountered. Under him, the kingdom of the White Huns reached all the way from Persia to Khotan in Central Asia, with its center of power in the Punjab region. The Guptas were forced to pay tribute to him, a sign of their rapidly declining fortunes. Although Mihiragula himself was checked in his Indian exploits by a Hindu confederacy under the king of Ujjain in 528, and was forced to find refuge in Kashmir, the basic damage to the Gupta empire was irremediable, and the dynasty ended in 535.

The fate of the White Huns themselves may briefly be sketched; in Central Asia their empire was broken by the Turks, and they disappeared; in India they settled down, intermarried, and soon became absorbed into Hindu society.

With the overthrow of the Gupta empire, the history of India becomes enshrouded in obscurity until the seventh century. For almost a century there is nothing but a blank.

Harsha

In the eastern Punjab in the frontier state of Thaneswar on the upper Jumna there came to power in 606 a youth barely 16 years old. This boy, Harsha, had inherited from his father this small kingdom, and now set about by deliberate and systematic planning to conquer all of northern India after the pattern of the Guptas. The details of his campaigns are far from certain, but we do know that he had a large army, the creation it seems of his father, and within six years he had built an empire. Harsha's state was not as extensive as the domain of the imperial Guptas, and its boundaries to the south were also more limited. Harsha could not penetrate the Deccan beyond its natural frontiers, the Vindhya mountains, where he was defeated and checked in 640 at the Narbada river by the Chalukya monarch Pulakesin II, who used elephants crazed with dope to great success against his powerful northern rival.

As his new state emerged Harsha built a capital at Kanauj, and made it into a magnificent, wealthy, and well-fortified city, four miles in length and one mile wide. From all accounts, both his own and those of foreign observers, Harsha proved to be an exceptionally able and just ruler, incessantly devoted to the administration of his empire. If not giving audience at his royal capital of Kanauj, Harsha made royal progresses through his dominion, constantly checking the conditions of his rule. Harsha protected religion, and was given to great charitable deeds, but he was not a religious zealot, since he eclectically favored both Buddhism and the cult of Shiva. He also was a great patron of literature, composed poetry, and wrote plays.

Hsuan-tsang, the Chinese Buddhist pilgrim, was in India from 630 to 643, and his eyewitness account of the country under Harsha's rule is a most important document, both reliable and perceptive. Hsuan-tsang had left China and come to India via the land route, travelling by way of the Tarim basin, Tashkent, Samarkand, Hindu Kush, Kabul, and Gandhara, for the primary purpose of finding Buddhist manuscripts and to visit the sacred places of Buddhism in India. But, compared with Fa Hsien, he had keener vision. He clearly understood that Buddhism had become a declining religion within India, observed the advances of Hinduism at Buddhism's expense, and noted how much Buddhism had suffered by the ravages of the White Huns. While stopping in Buddhist monasteries in the Gandhara region he observed how that region had become desolate, with few inhabitants in the villages, and the remaining monasteries in a most dilapidated condition. When later visiting the birthplace of the Buddha, the area of Kapilavastu, he found it already deserted and abandoned.

Judging from the accounts of Hsuan-tsang, the administrative system of Harsha was quite similar to that of the Mauryas and the Guptas, with the significant difference that all officials were paid in grants of land, rather than in money. The kingdom appeared well-organized, with an elaborate bureaucracy attending to its affairs and a large army for the king's protection. It is possible that Harsha's control was not quite as strong as that of his Gupta predecessors; one obtains the impression that his state was more in the nature of a collection of subordinate kingdoms rather than a closely controlled empire. Taxation seems to have been relatively light, since revenue consisted of only one-sixth of the total agricultural production. Harsha's India enjoyed great prosperity, and this is reflected in its coins which were minted from gold and silver. The penal code also was most lenient, the punishment for treason being merely life imprisonment.

Learning was highly esteemed, and the monasteries provided free education, together with room and board, for students from all parts of the kingdom. The curriculum customarily included grammar, mechanics, medicine, logic, and metaphysics. Discipline was severe, and discussion and debate were the principal methods of teaching.

Hsuan-tsang himself devoted much time to learning at the Buddhist monastery at Nalanda, where he pursued his studies of the idealist tendencies of Mahayana Buddhism. He soon became the champion of Mahayana doctrines in disputes with adherents of the original Theravada or Hinayana beliefs, and attracted the attention of Harsha. His contact with the king ripened into a firm friendship, so much so that Harsha was persuaded into calling a great public assembly to be held in Kanauj in 643, where the merits of Hinayana and Mahayana thought were to be debated. This Buddhist council was attended by 3,000 monks, as well as over 2,000 Brahmans and Jains, and was held in a vast debating hall of the royal capital. During the ensuing debates Hsuan-tsang argued most successfully in favor of Mayahana doctrines, and earned a great triumph, the king himself being impressed by Mayahana beliefs. This success of Mahayana Buddhism so infuriated the Brahmans that they plotted against Harsha. They set fire to a thatched pavilion and in the ensuing confusion a hired assassin attempted to stab the king, but Harsha personally disarmed him and punished the ringleaders.

One of the things which impressed Hsuan-tsang very much was the custom of the king to dispose of all the wealth of his treasury periodically every five years to the needy. In a great charity festival which lasted 75 days, the king gave all his possessions to half a million monks, priests, orphans, and the poor. Harsha handed over his jewels and ornaments, and even his clothes, and dressed himself in old second-hand garments while he worshipped the Buddha on the "plain of almsgiving". Everything in the treasury, except horses, elephants and military accoutrements, were so disposed by Harsha.

This was perhaps really not more than a hidden tax on Harsha's vassal kings who immediately had to repurchase his jewelry and garments, and return them to the royal treasury. Nevertheless there is no question about Harsha's devotion to Buddhism, and his close friendship with Hsuan-tsang. When the latter finally turned to his way home, laden with Buddhist manuscripts, relics, and images, the parting was a sorrowful one. The pilgrim's estimate of the king makes Harsha appear a truly remarkable man, a great ruler, soldier, administrator, a patron of literature, poet, dramatist, and a pious and merciful human being:

> His skill in literature was profound. He cherished and protected the four kinds of creatures and deeply respected the three Treasures. From the time of his birth to his last hour, his face never crimsoned with anger, nor did his hands ever injure a living thing. During the fifty years and more of his reign, the wild beasts became familiar with men and the people did not injure or slay them. Such were his love and humanity.[1]

Harsha also maintained friendly relations with as distant a power as China. He sent an embassy to the great T'ang court at Ch'angan, and emperor T'ai-tsung returned this mission, with rather strange consequences. It happened that just before the arrival of the Chinese ambassador Harsha had been murdered, and

---

[1] Rawlinson, *op. cit.*, p. 121.

his throne usurped by his minister Arjuna. Arjuna promptly attacked the Chinese embassy when it arrived, and the envoy had to flee for his life to Nepal, where he got in touch with the strong Tibetan king Srong-tsan Gam-po (about 630–650) and complained about his treatment. A joint Tibeto-Nepalese army was organized in response, and descended into India through the Himalayas, where it defeated an Indian army with great slaughter. The usurping minister, Arjuna, was captured, and sent as prisoner to China. It was only the rule of Harsha as absolute autocrat which cemented a strong kingdom, for once his hand had been withdrawn the structure promptly collapsed, and with it the last great Hindu kingdom of the north.

Small States in North India

After the death of Harsha India lapsed more or less into political anarchy, the Ganges basin and western India going their separate ways. In the Ganges basin confusion reigned until the eighth century, when a relatively strong dynasty of the Pala kings established itself in Bengal and Magadha. These rulers patronized Buddhism once more, and it is during their period that Indian Buddhism developed trends toward Tantrism with faith in magic and supernatural intervention. After 1125 the Pala kings were succeeded by the Sena dynasty, an orthodox Brahman line, which flourished until the arrival of the Moslems. They stood in very close relations with Tibet, and Tantric Buddhism made its way during this period from Bengal to Tibet.

The history of the Punjab during these centuries remains obscure. Kashmir in the far northwest developed into a fairly strong kingdom during the seventh and eighth centuries, but more important and more interesting were developments in Rajputana. Here a number of Hindu principalities arose, governed by princes of Gurjara background. The claims of these Rajput princes were that they had descended straight from the old Kshatriya caste of the original Aryan invaders of India, but it is far more likely that the Gurjara princes descended from a great variety of racial stocks, the residue of all the invaders arriving in India from the northwest, such as the Sakas and the White Huns, who established themselves in small principalities and ruled despotically. These Rajputs, or "sons of kings," as they called themselves, formed an exclusive and haughty military aristocracy, with high standards of chivalry, comparable with the best of European medieval knighthood. One encounters here the same passion for war and hunting and with it the same demands for unconditional loyalty of one's followers. Women enjoyed an extraordinarily high position, and were chivalrously protected and their heroic deeds acclaimed. In war, a foul blow was never struck. Learning was patronized, and the petty Rajput courts were centers, not merely of trade and commerce, but also of scholarship. In particular the bards played a very prominent role in this society. Their importance was established by the fact they they alone were able to establish the genealogy of the ruler, and trace its descent in song from the Aryan ancestors of the dim past, and in consequence their persons as historians of the clan were sacrosanct. In the splendid palaces of the fortified Rajput cities there arose then a quite distinct Rajput culture, with its own special values of chivalry and loyalty extending into death, which may perhaps be best exemplified by a short poem of a Rajput lady whose husband has fallen in battle and who addresses the son who brings her the news of his death:

> "Boy, tell me, ere I go, how bore himself my Lord?"
> "As a reaper of the harvest of battle! I followed his steps as the humble gleaner of his sword. On the bed of honour he spread a carpet of the slain, whereon, a barbarian his pillow, he sleeps ringed by his foes."
> "Yet once again, oh boy, tell me how my lord bore himself?"
> "Oh mother, who can tell his deeds? He left no foe to dread or to admire him."
> She smiled farewell to the boy, and adding "My lord will chide my delay," sprang into the flames.[2]

Indian Civilization During the Gupta Period

The most remarkable developments in religion are those concerned with the changes in Buddhism and Hinduism. Buddhism showed obvious signs of decline. Its decreasing vigor is not so much to be explained by antagonism directed against it, rather its differences with Hinduism tended to become obliterated, and popular Buddhism steadily approached popular Hinduism. Buddhist shrines and monasteries were now used by Hindus as well, and except for short, though striking, instances of Buddhism's assertion, such as the assembly at Kanauj when Hsuan Tsang won victories for his Mahayana beliefs, the general tendency was toward assimilation. The signs of decline were obvious; so famous a place as Sanchi was now in ruins, and there were few Buddhists to be encountered in places outside Kanauj, the Punjab, and Bengal. At the end of this period Buddhism disappeared completely in India, to continue only in Ceylon, Southeast Asia, and the Far East.

The decay of Buddhism, and the influence of Hinduism upon it, are also illustrated by the growth of a new school of Buddhist religious expression, that of Tantrism (although, reciprocally, Tantrism also influenced Hinduism). Developed in Bengal, and patronized there by the Pala kings, Tantric Buddhism owes its existence to the influence of many Hindu ideas, particularly those connected with Shivaism. Tantrism is a strange mixture of faith in the supernatural intervention of Buddhas and Bodhisattvas with belief in magic and sorcery. It may be said to be a mixture of terror and sensuality, at once mystical and gross. A host of new, strange, and terrible divinities were introduced, together with violent rituals involving animal sacrifices, and faith in the miraculous powers of certain diagrams. From Bengal this form of Buddhism made its way across the Himalayas to Tibet, where it gained a permanent and solid foothold.

[2] Rawlinson, *op. cit.,* p. 202.

Fundamental changes were made in Hinduism, as well. The Brahman priests once more asserted their power and, in answer to the Jains and Buddhists, developed Hinduism as a practical way of life, offering salvation to all irrespective of caste. This they did by stressing moral and religious ideas, and above all, by developing the theory that salvation could be gained by devotion to the Hindu deities. In a series of long Sanskrit poems and treatises, known as the *puranas,* the priests glorified two Hindu gods, Shiva and Vishnu, and emphasized man's devotion to them. The puranas are legendary accounts of the creation of the world, and the actions therein of the gods, saints, and heroes. They have been extremely popular in Hinduism to this day, their nearest parallel in the West being perhaps Milton's *Paradise Lost.*

During this period Brahma, the creator and the world soul, began to recede in the Hindu trinity, and the embodiment of the forces of preservation and those of destruction, Vishnu and Shiva, became exalted as great gods, giant cosmic forces in whom centered the philosophy, poetry, and passion of the devotees of this popular religion. Vishnu is the mild and benevolent deity, the god of preservation who saves and loves. Shiva is the opposite, the god of terror and destruction, the manslayer and sender of disease who must be feared. In the new Hinduism, which had become definitely anthropomorphic, both of these gods were treated as royal personages, living in temples, and being offered flowers, fruit, and incense. They were represented by an idol, many-headed and many-armed, to whom worship and sacrifice is due. Incidentally, the cow by now had become also definitely sacred. Accompanying this anthropomorphism was an exuberant mythology, in which the gods were often given monstrous forms and lived in celestial residences with their wives. This popular Hinduism, with its exaltation of Shiva and Vishnu became the leading form of Hindu religion and is still today the religion of the masses of India.

One special feature of popular Hinduism was the emergence of the doctrine of the incarnations of gods (*avatars*) in other forms. Vishnu, for instance, appears often in the guise of Rama, Krishna, and even in that of the Buddha. The incarnation of Vishnu as Krishna became especially popular, and as such as he appears in the epic *Mahabharata* in the section which is known as the "Song of the Adorable," or the *Bhagavad Gita,* composed probably as late as the eighth or ninth century. In the *Bhagavad Gita* the love of the soul for God, the power of faith, and the efficacy of grace are fully established. Loving faith, and the individual's personal devotion to God are its main tenets, and the *Bhagavad Gita* soon assumed, and maintained, such respect in Indian eyes that even today it may be used for an oath in a court of law, as is the Bible in the West or the Koran among the Moslems.

In the *Bhagavad Gita* Krishna is the charioteer of a king, about to engage in decisive battle against his enemies who had deprived him of his kingdom. The king hesitates, awed by the fearful loss of life which the struggle surely will entail, but Krishna reassures him and tells him that what is important is to act; in this case to engage in battle. Action in honor of God, regardless of what that action may be, is always good. All service is of equal value, if it is performed in honor of God, and although renunciation and action both may lead to the supreme good, of the two, action is preferable. With its stress on action rather like modern existentialism, the *Bhagavad Gita* in moving words formulates what love of God and action in his honor accomplish for the individual.

This doctrine of love of the soul for God knows no caste distinction. By trust and devotion to God those who renounce the world and also those who work in it, both high caste priests and rulers, and low caste people, women and even evil doers may win certain salvation.

In literature the Gupta period and the reign of Harsha saw the creation of a large body of works in Sanskrit. It was dominated by Kalidasa, India's greatest lyric poet and dramatist. A native of Ujjain, the capital of Malwa, Kalidasa wrote from about 400 to 455, and enjoyed the patronage of the Gupta court. His most famous poem, the "Cloud Messenger," a love lyric, was admired in Europe by no less a person than Goethe, particularly for its sensitive appreciation of the beauties of nature. The poem deals with an official who is banished to the hills of central India, and who sends a cloud as his messenger to his wife living in the foothills of the Himalayas, and it contains a description of the country over which the cloud passes with splendid passages full of deep understanding of the Indian countryside.

Works in many other literary genres were produced during this period, such as epics, beast stories, and fables, some of which eventually made their way via Baghdad to Europe, where they provided subject matter to such poets as Chaucer and Shakespeare. Prayer books, composed to furnish the orthodox Brahmans with a definitive collection of prayers, as well as law books, are other works indicative of the wide range of this golden age of Hindu literature. In the "Code of Manu" are compiled laws setting down the rules of all castes as regards food and marriage, and contrasting the upper castes against the untouchables and outcastes. With this law book the caste system received its final codification.

Indian drama, at its zenith during this time, seems to have originated from dancing, and its connection and debt, if any, to Greek drama, remains still a problematical and debated question. Unlike Greek drama, the plays were performed in the courtyards of private houses, not in public amphitheatres, and the main interest and most prominent theme was love rather than tragedy. The stage was plain; all actors were male; the parts of women were played by boys. Since most, although not all, plots deal with romantic love, there is relatively little action. The plays, unlike poetry, epics and fables, were written in a mixture of Sanskrit and Prakrit, the popular language.

Perhaps the most famous of all Indian plays is the *Little Clay Cart*, a sort of detective story in which the hero is saved at the very last moment before his execution. *Sakuntala,* by the great Kalidasa, is probably the finest play of the Indian theatre, with a wide range of emotions, and powerful descriptions of nature. When the heroine, Sakuntala, leaves her home and her parents, to seek

her king-husband who has forgotten her existence, voices in the air bid her
farewell:

> Thy journey be auspicious; may the breeze,
> Gentle and soothing, fan thy cheek: may lakes
> All bright with lily-cups, delight thine eyes;
> The sunbeam's heat be cooled by shady trees;
> The dust beneath thy feet the pollen be of lotuses.[3]

In contrast to this rather gentle and melancholy tone, Indian drama is fully
able to depict other emotions as well, such as the vivid horror powerfully described in a later play, when the spirits in the temple of the demon-goddess
are invoked:

> Now wake the terrors of the place, beset
> With crowding and malignant fiends; the flames
> From funeral pyres scarce lend their sullen light,
> Clogged with their fleshy prey, to dissipate
> The fearful gloom that hems them in. Pale ghosts
> Sport with foul goblins, and their dissonant mirth,
> In shrill respondent shrieks is echoed round.[4]

The Gupta period was also remarkable in the development of science. The
great university of Nalanda has already been described, and here, as in other
institutions, science was an integral part of the curriculum. In medicine, dissec-
tion was practiced, and Indian medical students were taught how to hold the
lancet, how to cut and pierce with it, how to extract darts and cleanse wounds,
how to apply ointments, and to administer emetics. Indian medicine later had
great influence among the Arab doctors of the Abbasid caliphate at Baghdad.
In mathematics Indian scholars calculated the value of pi, worked with tables
of sines, and operated with simple equations. India was deeply indebted to the
work of the Alexandrian Greeks in astronomy: "The Greeks are barbarians, but
the science of astronomy originated with them, and for this they must be
reverenced like gods." The Indians added to Greek knowledge and developed
some striking theories such as the one concerning gravitation, which in a sense
anticipated Newton by proclaiming that by a law of nature all things fall to the
earth. Indian astronomers were well aware of the daily rotation of the earth
around its axis, and were able to explain accurately the causes of eclipses of
the sun.

In applied science the Gupta period did excellent work in metallurgy. The
solid 23-foot iron pillar of Delhi, which never rusted, has already been mentioned,
and metal work for arms and armour was far superior to anything in the
West. This skill appears to have been exported to the Sassanian empire in
Persia, where its heavy armed cavalry profited by it, and thence finally found
its way into Europe.

The art of the Gupta period in Indian history is of the greatest importance.
It was during this era that the definite canon of Indian aesthetics was formulated.
Indian artistic tendencies, which had begun in the far distant past of Mohenjo-

[3] Rawlinson, *op. cit.*, p. 138.
[4] *Ibid.*

Daro, and had been fully developed in the art of Sanchi and Amaravati, now found perfection.

Hindu shrines which had begun as simple buildings with flat roofs, without spires, and had employed short pillars with square capitals were developed into large temples. These shrines were elaborated into great towering structures, with bulging steeples and a cap on top. In northern India temples employed primarily

FIGURE 10.2.   Khajuraho temple, northern India. A good example of the northern style which uses the curvilinear tower.

the curvilinear tower, whereas in the south the pyramidal tower was favored. The towers gradually increased in size, the decorations became richer and temples on the grand scale such as Khajuraho (tenth century) or Mount Abu in Gujarat were structures full of richness, delicacy, and great beauty. Inside, the temples contained a sanctuary, with the image of a god, and the interiors were often magnificently decorated in ornate and floral styles.

Work in sculpture was consummate. Mastery over the material was complete, as the creation of free standing colossal copper or sandstone Buddha statues demonstrates. In some of the famous Gupta statues of the Buddha of the fifth century this mastery of technique is coupled with great spiritual quality of expression, and in the words of one art historian all Gupta sculpture is marked: "by a finished mastery in execution and a majestic serenity in expression that

FIGURE 10.3.   Colossal copper Buddha; remarkable both for mastery of technique, as well as calmness of expression.

FIGURE 10.4.   Buddha from Mathura. An excellent example of India's "classical" style; the image conveys great beauty and a sense of spiritual repose.

have seldom been equalled in any other school of art." [5] The Buddha appears often with an enormous nimbus around his head, and his body is clearly visible through the folds of diaphonous garments. Through the waves of these transparent draperies the body is revealed and modelled with close attention to anatomical detail. The faces are tranquil, the limbs harmonious, and the pose of the body of great suppleness, imitating in three bends the natural curve of a

[5] B. Rowland, *The Art and Architecture of India* (Baltimore, 1958), p. 138.

flower. The final result is the feeling of great terrestrial beauty devoted to a spiritual experience.

In painting, too, the Gupta period is the culmination of Indian art. In the rock temple of Ajanta, a series of frescoes, dating mostly from the seventh century, tell the story of the life of the Buddha. The Ajanta frescoes take their subject mostly from the jatakas.

FIGURE 10.5. Detail from the Ajanta frescoes. The female figures combine grace, tenderness and voluptuousness.

Such a painting as the "beautiful Bodhisattva," clad in transparent gauze, mitred, and with a blue lotus in his hand, is one of the great masterpieces of all art. His noble simplicity, dignity and harmony invite comparison with the works of Botticelli. In his long peaceful body, his oval face with long eyes, and his reserved and melancholy expression one finds the embodiment of compassion and tenderness. At the same time, the art of Ajanta is full of love of life and nature. The animal realism, already familiar from Sanchi, gives vigor and life to jungle scenes and fighting buffaloes; in the female nude body grace, free lines and gentleness of expression combine to produce an impression at once of voluptuousness and of tenderness.

Gupta painting is a great synthesis, in which the gentleness and sweetness of Buddhist mysticism are fused with the old Indian naturalism of Sanchi. Its bold drawing, its decorative designs, its infinite variety and its boundless imagination devoted to spiritual experience are its outstanding characteristics.

Gupta art, the "classical" art of India, was of tremendous importance for all Buddhist art of Southeast Asia, Central Asia, China and Japan. It gave that art its norm, and the sculpture and painting of the Gupta period occupy a position parallel to that of Greek and Roman art in the West, in which European artistic canons found their standards of perfection. The final solution of the problems of form and content provided a firm basis for original artistic expression, and whether in Cambodia, Java or Japan, the powerful yet subtle influence of Gupta art may always be detected. The process of exporting Indian culture abroad which had begun much earlier than the Gupta, now became greatly intensified as the result of constant and lively exchange of ideas, and it extended to the east, to the north and to the west.

To the east, across the Bay of Bengal, intercourse with Burma, which was already ancient, increased greatly. Early voyages to Burma, which are evidenced in some of the jatakas, now multiplied, and together with brisk trade, Buddhism made its way into that kingdom where it soon became the state religion. Beyond Burma, to Malaya, Cambodia, Java and the whole great insular world of Southeast Asia, Indian passenger ships accommodating up to 200 persons plied regularly carrying traders, colonists and ideas. Hindu merchants and settlers colonized Java, and other areas of Southeast Asia, and took along with them both Hinduism and Buddhism. In Southeast Asia new mixed cultures were the consequence, as will be discussed in Chapter 14, consisting of both indigenous and newly imported Indian cultural facets. Buddhism was perhaps the main vehicle of Indian influence during this period, and it created for itself its greatest monument, Borobudur in Java.

Gupta cultural expansion to the north was primarily important in the spread of Buddhism. Indian merchants and priests crossed the high mountain passes of the Hindu Kush and Pamir ranges, and penetrated the Tarim basin of Central Asia. At Khotan, one of the oases of this huge arid depression, archaeological discoveries by Sir Marc Aurel Stein during the first years of this century brought to light a mixed culture, in which sand-buried sites and rubbish heaps yielded Buddhist shrines and Buddhist texts written in Indian alphabets in Sanskrit and Prakrit. Indian Buddhist influence in Central Asia was of particular significance because it was from here that it went on to China, Japan and Korea. Gupta Buddhist art together with the Graeco-Buddhist art of Gandhara and Iranian art, was also exported to the Far East via Central Asia, and the routes across the Tarim basin became the most important channel

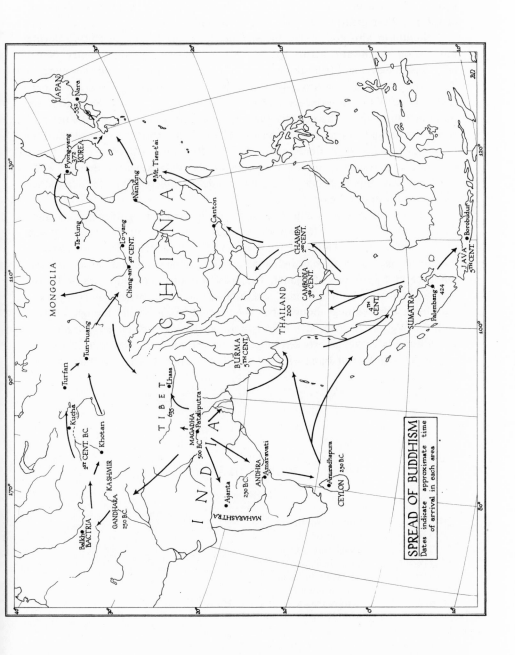

SPREAD OF BUDDHISM

Dates indicate approximate time
of arrival in each area

of communications between India and China. Indian missionaries with Buddhist texts now reached China, and Indian intercourse with the great civilizations of the Far East greatly increased during the Gupta period.

Buddhism also constituted the significant export of Indian culture during this period northward across the Himalayas. In the foothill country Nepal embraced it early, and from there it found its way into the high Tibetan plateau. The strong Tibetan king Srong-tsan Gam-po, who founded Lhasa in 639, married both a Chinese princess and a Nepalese princess, and he vigorously promoted throughout the country the religion of his two consorts. Politics and religion were judiciously fused, and the Tibetan king shortly assumed the role of an incarnation of a Bodhisattva. Tibetan Buddhism stayed in close touch with India, particularly during the reign of the Pala kings in Bengal, when Tantrism was imported into Tibet, and made of Tibetan Buddhism a rather unique and lasting religion.

The export of Gupta culture to the West is the least significant, and intercourse with that area of the world gradually dwindled with the fall of Rome and the subsequent creation of Islam as an effective barrier. Even so, contacts continued, as seen in Roman influence on Gupta coins, and the strong Persian influence in the frescoes of Ajanta. The possibility of Greek influence on Indian drama has already been indicated, and the fact that Gupta astronomers appreciated Greek astronomical thought has been stated. As a whole, though, contact with the West seemed to have been largely on the material plane of trade; and the cultural interchange between Gupta India and the West was more limited as compared with that of India with the world of Southeast Asia and the Far East.

BASIC DATES

320–535	Gupta Empire
320–326	Chandragupta
330–375	Samudragupta
375–413	Chandragupta II
401–410	Fa Hsien in India
413–455	Kumaragupta
500–502	Toramana, ruler of White Huns
502–528	Mihiragula
6th to 11th centuries	Rajput principalities
607–647	Harsha
630–643	Hsuan-tsang in India
725–1197	Pala kings
1125–1225	Sena kings

SUPPLEMENTARY READING

BASHAM, A. L. *The Wonder That Was India.* London, 1954.

DE BARY, W. T. ED. *Sources of Indian Tradition.* New York, 1958.

DUNBAR, G. *History of India.* London, 1943.

ELIOT, C. *Hinduism and Buddhism.* London, 1954.

MORELAND, W. H. AND A. C. CHATTERJEE. *A Short History of India.* London, 1920.

MORGAN, K. *The Path of the Buddha.* New York, 1956.

RAWLINSON, H. G. *India: A Short Cultural History.* London, 1937.

SMITH, V. A. *The Oxford History of India,* 3rd ed. Oxford, 1958.

ADVANCED READING

BEAL, S. *Si-yu-ki: Buddhist Records of the Western World.* Calcutta, 1957. Accounts of India by Chinese Buddhist pilgrims.

CONZE, E. *Buddhism: Its Essence and Development.* New York, 1951.

GROUSSET, R. *The Civilizations of the East, Vol. II: India.* London, 1931. Excellent on Gupta art.

———— *In the Footsteps of the Buddha.* London, 1932. An account of the travels of the famous Hsuan-tsang.

ROWLAND, B. *The Art and Architecture of India.* Baltimore, 1956.

STEIN, M. A. *On Ancient Central Asian Tracks.* London, 1933. Interesting record of archaeological finds in the Tarim basin.

XI ❀❀❀

MEDIEVAL HINDU STATES

AND MOSLEM INVADERS

TO 1206

North and Central India at the Coming
of the Moslems

THE RAJPUTS. In the period of transition between the great kingdom of Harsha and the coming of the Moslem invasions the central feature seems to be the revived power of Hindu culture. Despite political disunity and the decline of Buddhism which disappeared entirely except in Bengal and Bihar, the cultural unity of Hinduism in northern and central India remained preserved, while in the south, in the Tamil states, the power of Hinduism expressed itself brilliantly in religious thought and artistic masterpieces.

Politically, northern India split up into a number of separate Hindu principalities, most of them ruled by the military class known as Rajputs. The Rajputs gave their undivided patronage to the Brahmans and to Hinduism; and where Buddhism did not perish it was soon assimilated and absorbed in this strong resurgent wave of the oldest of Indian religions.

The Rajput princes were patrons of culture and of learning, some were great builders of fortresses, reservoirs and works of irrigation and some of their petty states flourished in great prosperity, but their main passion was war. Nothing delighted the Rajput princes more than to go to war against each other. This they could do easily

enough in the absence of a strong central authority and without a threat of
foreign invasion. But indulgence in continuous war among themselves resulted
in the weakening of their power, and, when in the tenth century a real menace
appeared, the Rajputs were neither able nor prepared to resist the Moslems.
The arrival of a most aggressive Moslem power, using new methods of warfare,
soon overthrew Rajput resistance and brought northern India under the sway of
the new invaders.

MAHARASHTRA.   More effective resistance was offered to the Moslems by the
independent kingdoms of central and western India. In the western Deccan, in
the region known as Maharashtra, there arose the Chalukya dynasty which ruled
from about 550 to 753. The Chalukya dynasty, composed originally of foreign
Gurjara princes, made a powerful kingdom of Maharashtra. The Chalukyas
successfully resisted the encroachments of Harsha into the Deccan, and in 620
their king, Pulakesin II, signally defeated his armies. Maharashtra exchanged
embassies with Persia and maintained friendly relations with the Arabs. Its
primary enemy was the Hindu kingdom of Pallava on the east coast of India
on the Bay of Bengal south of the Kistna river, and for years war was waged
between them. The kingdom of Maharashtra, as were the Rajput principalities,
was staunchly Hindu, but Buddhism was at least tolerated.

In 753 the Chalukya dynasty gave way to the Rashtrakuta dynasty, an
indigenous line which had risen from some petty chieftains, and which ruled
Maharashtra until 973. They, too, favored Hinduism, and under their patronage
some of the greatest monuments of all Hindu art were built—the magnificent,
decorated rock-cut shrines of Ellora and Elephanta. The Great Temple to Shiva
at Ellora, carved in its entirety out of the cliff, is an architectural marvel, and
dates from the reign of Krishna I (757–800).

In the rock temple of Elephanta, on an island in Bombay harbor, was
carved the image of the three-faced Shiva, the most majestic representation of
a pantheistic deity. The central head represents Brahma or Shiva as the creator,
with a calm and serene face; to the right is the gentle, smiling image of Parvati,
the female embodiment of Shiva; and to the left appears Shiva as the destroyer,
terrible to behold, with menacing brows, half-open lips and fangs showing at
the corner of the mouth. But all these three countenances of one being are
perfectly balanced, and harmonized without trace of effort. In the image of
Shiva of Elephanta all universal forces, immanent in all things, are superbly
blended.

The Rashtrakuta dynasty of Maharashtra continued the unceasing wars
waged against the kingdom of Pallava. Although the Jains still maintained
themselves, Buddhism now disappeared completely. In 973 the Chalukya dynasty
once more returned to power, and the kingdom of Maharashtra was governed
by it until the time when Hindu rule in the Deccan was finally ended by the
Moslems. In 1318 the Moslems struck the final blow, the last Hindu ruler was
killed, and the Deccan became annexed by the new foreign power.

FIGURE 11.1.   Interior of the rock temple to Shiva at Ellora, Chalukya period
(eighth century). The temple is carved from the solid rock.

Tamil States

In southern India, two Hindu Tamil kingdoms were the dominant powers during
this period. Pallava, the first of these (see Chapter 9), held power from about
600 to 888, and it in turn was succeeded by the kingdom of Chola, which expanded rapidly and became a great power, having influence for a time in Ceylon,
Burma, Sumatra, and even Malacca. Both of these Tamil kingdoms championed
Hinduism.

PALLAVA.   Pallava, with its capital at Kanchi, rapidly came to control the
whole of the Tamil peninsula to the south. From Kanchi Hindu merchants and
colonizers spread Hinduism abroad, and the hinduized kingdom of Champa
and the Khmer states of the mainland of Southeast Asia derived their culture
from this center (see Chapter 14). Jainism and Buddhism were quickly absorbed,
and the cults of Shiva and Vishnu became the leading religion. Pallava profited by
the trade carried on in the Indian ocean, since the chief maritime route between
the Abbasids to the west and the T'ang empire to the east made use of Pallava
and its offspring, Champa, on the east coast of the Indo-Chinese peninsula.
The art of Pallava reached a high degree of excellence in the sculpture of the
great seashore temple complex of Mamallapuram, which shows close affinity
with Hindu monuments of Southeast Asia. The group known as the "Descent
of the Ganges," on a huge granite ledge near the seashore, is a great masterpiece

FIGURE 11.2.   Sculpture from Mammalapuram, Pallava period. The "Descent of the Ganges" is a vast tableau representing groups of goddesses, ascetics and animals around a great cascade.

in its power of composition, and its dramatic effect. Here a vast tableau, over thirty yards long, depicts with freshness and directness a group of goddesses, ascetics and animals around a great cascade. The elongated female nude figures are full of grace and elegance; animal life is observed with keen awareness coupled with a sense of humor as in the groups of monkeys engaged in the entertaining process of searching for fleas. The essential nature of the figures, both human and animal, is comprehended and expressed in the most simple form, with powerful effect.

CHOLA.   The kingdom of Pallava fell to the power of Chola about 1000. Very likely it was weakened by the incessant wars against the Chalukyas in the north. The rise of Chola did not mean, however, any lessening of Indian influence abroad; rather Chola played very much the same role as had Pallava and connections with Ceylon, Burma and Southeast Asia continued and were stronger than ever before. Chola developed a powerful navy, and in the reign of Rajaraja the Great, between 985 and 1018, Chola became a great naval power. It successfully invaded Ceylon, attacked Sumatra and forced Malacca and even Java to pay tribute. Its seapower completely controlled the Bay of Bengal, and the Laccadives, Maldives, Nicobar and Andaman islands all were brought under the sway of its navy. In the Tamil peninsula itself Chola subdued the kingdoms of Pandya, at the tip of India, and Chera on the west coast. It remained the one great power of south India until the thirteenth century.

Chola, just as Pallava before, was a great champion of Hinduism. Shiva was the chief deity worshipped. Great temples in stone, where massive pyramidal towers crowned central shrines in the center of huge courtyards, bore witness to religious devotion. A characteristic feature of Chola's government was the existence of local self-government, by local assemblies, in the villages. The state surveyed the land, and collected about one-sixth of the total production as revenue. Its kings also paid attention to the needs of agriculture, and were builders of vast irrigation schemes. As one might expect from its position as a great naval power, its efforts to stimulate agricultural production and its gold coinage, Chola was a very prosperous kingdom.

For two centuries Chola remained the great power of south India, but from the twelfth century on difficulties increased. It suffered a Ceylonese invasion, and a Moslem raid, and then in the thirteenth century Pandya rebelled with success. This was followed by civil war in Chola itself, and in the fourteenth century it disintegrated completely.

TAMIL CULTURE.   In the culture of the south, Tamil literature stressed an emotional theism in Hinduism which seems to be derived from an early Dravidian background. In the ninth century Sankara, an ascetic whose influence reached all over India, gave this view its best expression. According to the absolute, unqualified monism which Sankara preached nothing exists except Brahman or the world soul. The Hindu triad of Shiva, Vishnu and Brahma are in reality but a manifestation of Brahman, the sole impersonal reality: "Whatever is is in

FIGURE 11.3. Stone statue of seated Brahma, south Indian, tenth-eleventh century.

reality one." All the objects of the senses are illusion (*maya*) for which the human soul thirsts in its ignorance. Man must dispel this ignorance, Sankara taught, and achieve by his own efforts the immediate contact with the great being whom he worships. Liberation for the individual then consists of the soul's effort to look through the veil of illusion, to recognize itself to be Brahman, and to gain in that recognition deliverance from the influence of maya and to assert its true nature as the absolute and eternal Brahman. When Sankara lay on his deathbed in the Himalayas he apologized for having visited any temples, since such visits implied a denial that the deity is everywhere. But Sankara was not only the great exponent of this emotional theism, but also played a major role in Hindu philosophy as an important systematizer. Writing a great number of commentaries, his role in this regard is similar to that of St. Thomas Aquinas in the West as a genius of synthesis.

Sankara found a great successor in another Tamil philosopher and poet, Ramanuja, who lived about 1100. Ramanuja agreed with his predecessor that Brahman is total reality, but he also gave to the world soul the positive qualities of love and grace and emphasized the concept of personal devotion, *bakhti*, to it. Thus he argued that by intensive personal devotion the individual may gain an intuitive perception of God, or the world soul, and might thus arrive at the enjoyment of personal bliss.

In the visual arts Tamil culture is particularly noteworthy for its bronze sculpture. The figure of Shiva, performing the cosmic dance or dance of life,

FIGURE 11.4.   Bronze dancing Shiva; Chola, fourteenth century. Shiva performs the dance of life.

is all rhythm and exaltation, his elegant and delicate gestures enhancing the beauty of religious expression.

Moslem Raids in Northern India

It was the Moslem invasions of India which attacked the tradition and power of Hinduism, more successfully so in the north, less in the south. In them two stages may be distinguished —that of raiding, and that of permanent conquest. The Moslems came as invaders, as had many people before them, but unlike their many predecessors they were not absorbed into Indian society. Islam and Hinduism proved incompatible faiths; Moslem monotheism, hatred of idolatry and doctrine of social equality kept Hindu and Moslem apart.

ARABS IN SIND. As far as India is concerned, its earliest contacts with the Moslems, a kind of unimportant prelude, was with the Arabs of the Umayyad caliphate. Some Arabs entered India via Baluchistan and also by sea along the Makeran coast, and in 711 their leader, Muhammad Qasim, invaded the lower Indus valley and captured Sind. But here the conquest of the Arabs stopped. The Arabs were primarily interested in trade, and so were not motivated by religious or political animosity toward the Hindus. In these Arab colonies of Sind, Hindus were treated in the same category with the Jews and Christians, that is, they were tolerated as long as they paid a poll tax known as the *jizya*. The Umayyad caliphate gave its blessing to this arrangement, and trade, the mainstay of the early Arab policy toward its Indian possessions, remained the governing factor in the relations between Arabs and Hindus, permitting both to flourish side by side. But the Arab control of Sind remained a mere episode of little significance since the major Moslem impact on India came from quite a different direction, Afghanistan, and was carried by quite a different people, the Turks, whose origins and rise to power were discussed in Chapter 5. This people, with the fervor of new converts, soon became predominant in shaping the destiny of Islam. Two factors in particular gave them great strength and flexibility: their chance to rise from slavery to kingship, without any attached stigma, and their religious enthusiasm engendered by recent conversion. Turkish strength and fervor accounted for a great deal in the successful repulse of the Crusaders, and in India too, Turkish fanaticism drastically changed that country's history.

It was these formidable Turks, who during the eleventh and twelfth century raided India from the northwest, and who in the thirteenth century established a permanent Turkish kingdom in India at Delhi.

THE TURKS OF GHAZNI. As already briefly mentioned in Chapter 5, in the small independent state of Ghazni in Afghanistan, a slave became the king. He was Sabuktegin, who ruled Ghazni from 977 to 997. He enlarged his kingdom to the Amu-darya river in the north, and then incorporated Kabul in his domain. The frontier of the Ghazni ruler reached the Indus in India, but did not go beyond; however he made a point of raiding across the river. On these raids Sabuktegin defeated some Hindu forces in 989, and again in 991 he encountered little in the way of united resistance. This apparent weakness of India greatly stimulated Sabuktegin's successor, Mahmud of Ghazni, and it soon became part of his foreign policy not to let much more than a year go by without an invasion of India. Vowing "holy war," Mahmud raided the unhappy country 17 times between 997 and 1030. This brought him in not only millions as booty in treasures and slaves, but also earned for him the name of Mahmud "the image breaker."

Mahmud of Ghazni then annexed the Punjab, but did not go beyond that area in terms of permanent conquest. His main interest continued to be raids for plunder. He sacked Mathura and then in 1018 with 100,000 horses he plundered Kanauj, the ancient capital of Harsha, with the gain of enormous wealth. The loosely organized Hindu hosts which the Rajputs put in his way proved totally ineffective, and all the Rajput warriors could do to retrieve their honor was to commit the fearful rite of *jauhar*, or mass suicide.

In 1024 Mahmud carried out his most famous foray against the great, famed temple of Shiva at Somnath in Kathiawar. An audacious dash to the sea, after crossing the desert, brought him and 30,000 Moslem horsemen to the temple. Somnath was one of the most venerated of Hindu temples; it had 1,000 Brahmans, 300 barbers and 350 temple prostitutes in constant attendance, and its chief idol, a huge *lingam*, the phallic symbol of Shiva, was washed daily in water from the sacred Ganges carried over 750 miles to Somnath. After fierce fighting Mahmud and his men gained entry and they put to death over 50,000 Hindus. The idol of Shiva was destroyed by blows from the mace of Mahmud himself, and fragments were dispatched to Mecca and Medina and to Ghazni to be stepped upon by the faithful. This great act of iconoclasm, with its fearful slaughter, brought enormous booty; it is estimated that Mahmud took back with him over two million dinars in treasure and such great numbers of slaves that their market price in Bactria and Mesopotamia fell to very low levels.

Essentially then, India represented to the early Turks a fine and inexhaustible source of plunder, not a region to be permanently conquered. Massacres, desecration and looting certainly did not augur for a good beginning in the relations between the Moslems and the Hindus, and a great deal of permanent feuding of later ages had its roots in this early relationship.

This is not to say that the Turks were savages—far from it. Mahmud considered himself not a king of India, but a king of Ghazni, and he lavished upon his capital all that his avarice had gained in the valleys of the Indus and the Ganges.

He maintained an elaborate and well-ordered court, built mosques, libraries and aqueducts in his capital, and esteemed the society of learned men. Persian was the language of this Islamic court, and many of the most famous men of Persian literature found a ready patron in Mahmud of Ghazni. Al-Beruni especially was a great literary and scientific figure of Islamic culture who came to Ghazni from Khiva and went to study in the Punjab after the Moslem occupation of that province. An outstanding scientist, whose special fields of interest were astronomy, chemistry, physics and mineralogy, he was greatly interested in Hindu philosophy and learned Sanskrit for the purpose of its study. Al-Beruni wrote a *History of India*, in which, uniquely, a Moslem dealt at length and with great interest with the customs and manners of infidels.

Al-Beruni noted the relatively high position women enjoyed; they were educated, often knew Sanskrit, and took an active part in life; but he also commented on the prevalence of *suttee*, the self-immolation of widows, and on the increasing incidence of child marriages. He commented upon the power of the Brahmans whereas a significant silence enshrouds the Buddhists, and even the Jains. Al-Beruni also comments favorably on the light taxes prevalent in the subcontinent.

How could the Turks, cultivated men, builders, patrons of the arts, lend themselves to acts of such fanatic destructiveness as those which characterized the raids of Mahmud of Ghazni? The answer to this question lies partially at least in their religious outlook as new converts. Imbued with the fierce monotheism of Islam, in which any visible representation of the deity was sin, they came into India with its thousands of idols not only in search of plunder but also to forcibly convert the infidels or to exterminate them. The choice was simple: Islam or death. In addition to the religious factor there was the social one, the impact of a society in which all men were brothers upon the caste system of India, whose basic presupposition rested on inequality. Al-Beruni writes:

> We Muslims, of course, stand entirely on the other side of the question; considering all men as equal, except in piety, and this is the greatest obstacle which prevents any approach or understanding between Hindus and Muslims.

The clash then, between the Turkish religious fanatics and the Hindus was a very great clash, both in religious and in social matters. A permanent legacy of bitterness was created by the wholesale slaughter of Brahmans and of sacred cattle for food and the wholesale desecration of Hindu temples.

This original policy of destruction eventually had to be modified, since the alternative was the difficult job of extirpating all Hindus. In time some methods were developed which permitted coexistence of both groups. The chief device developed in this respect was the poll tax, or jizya, which was imposed upon the Hindus.

As a matter of fact, as the permanent conquest was eventually achieved, conditions in India soon became much less disturbed. Hindus, if they paid the special tax, were more or less left alone; the peasant merely paid a different ruler, and no great economic and social upheaval followed in the wake of the final conquest, which however did not come until the passing of the rulers of Ghazni.

Conquests of North India: The Turks of Ghor

Mahmud of Ghazni, the iconoclast and desecrator, died in 1030, and his dynasty soon shrank in importance, maintaining only a very slender hold on the Punjab. In Afghanistan the Ghaznavids were wracked by rebellion and factional warfare, and they lost their territory to groups of new Turks, of whom the most important was the group of Afghan Turks known as the Ghoris. Ghor was a mountain principality in western Afghanistan, and it was the rulers of Ghor who in the twelfth century were destined to accomplish the conquest of northern India, a different matter altogether from the previous raids of the Ghaznavids. In 1150 Ghazni itself was sacked and annexed by the Ghori Turks, and under the leadership of a very able and energetic sultan, Muhammad Ghori, inroads were now

begun against the Punjab and as far south as Gujarat. In 1187 Muhammad
Ghori occupied and annexed the Punjab, and with it the strategic entrance to
the Ganges basin, but then he was defeated by the troops of a Hindu confederacy
at the first battle of Tarain. Undaunted, Muhammad returned with about 12,000
horsemen in 1192 and fought to victory the second battle of Tarain at the
same spot.

This threw open the whole Ganges basin to the mounted archers of the
Turks; it was the decisive battle which ensured the ultimate success of the
Moslem conquest of India. Muhammad Ghori pushed his advantage at once,
and moved into the Ganges valley. Delhi was taken, and then Kanauj.

Everywhere that the Turks appeared:

> The temples were converted into mosques and abodes of goodness, the
> ejaculations of the beadcounters and the voices of the summoners to
> prayer ascended to the highest heaven and the very name of idolatry was
> annihilated.[1]

Muhammad Ghori appointed a former slave of his, Kutbu-d-din Aibak, as
his general and viceroy in the task of completing the conquest of the Ganges
basin for him. Aibak was an active, energetic man, an accomplished horseman
and archer, whom Muhammad Ghori trusted completely after he had risen
in his service from slave to general. His confidence was not misplaced for
Aibak carried out his task with brilliance. In 1194 he marched down the river,
took Benares, and a few years later, in 1199, he entered the province of Bihar,
a Buddhist stronghold. Here the Turks destroyed all Buddhist monasteries,
slaughtered all Buddhist monks (only a few escaped to Tibet) and utterly
extinguished Buddhism. The great university at Nalanda was sacked, its library
destroyed, its temples desecrated and booty requiring 1,400 camels was collected.
It was the final ruin of Buddhism in India, and the erection of mosques everywhere signaled the arrival of a new faith. From Bihar, Aibak in 1200 marched
further east into Bengal, where he put an end to the Sena dynasty by an audacious feat. In 1202, Aibak in person with only 18 men disguised as horse traders
entered its capital, and suddenly cut down the Sena raja's guard. The king, at
his meal, heard the sudden uproar, and fled precipitately, and Bengal fell to
Aibak. With the conquest of Bengal only a few Rajput principalities in Malwa
and part of Gujarat remained in Hindu hands; for the rest Hindu rule in
northern India had ended.

Muhammad Ghori's ambition was not centered on India alone, he was also
active in Central Asia where he defeated Khiva, while his subordinate was busy
conquering India. A minor rebellion brought Muhammad Ghori back south to
India, and he firmly reestablished his authority there with the help of Aibak.
On his way back to Turkistan Muhammad was murdered and in consequence
Aibak succeeded him in 1206. Aibak became the founder and first sultan of
the Slave dynasty in Delhi. The rise of a slave to the sultanate, however, was in

---

[1] Rawlinson, *op. cit.*, p. 211.

no way unique; it had occured already among the Seljuk Turks and the Mamluks in Egypt. The Turkish sultanate of Delhi, which Aibak founded, was to rule India, often with great vigor, until the coming of the Moguls.

From the Indian point of view the question of why the Moslem conquest of India was achieved with such relative ease needs some comment. There was certainly no lack of valor—Rajput military feats had proven that time and time again. But the fatal flaw must be found in the social organization of Hindu society, its caste system. Fighting was left to only one class, the martial Kshatriyas, while the rest of the population was not merely untrained, but was by and large indifferent. There did not exist a national feeling against the Moslem invaders, nor was it possible to rouse such a feeling effectively due to the many internecine quarrels of the Rajput princes themselves. Another factor which played a role was Hindu pride. Al-Beruni had already perceived the fact that they were too self-centered to recognize the existence of outside nations, and did not prepare accordingly for the defense of the country. In battle, Indian military tactics were the same tactics which had been used unsuccessfully against Alexander. The infantry at times resembled more a rabble of undisciplined men, and elephants were utterly useless against cavalry and a danger also to their own troops once they had been wounded. The issue was not long in doubt when India had to face the hardy and strong Turks—excellent horsemen, motivated by the lure of great booty and by the fighting creed of Islam, which stipulated either the extermination of all infidels, or immediate entry after death for the Moslem into paradise as alternatives in battle.

BASIC DATES

550–753	Chalukya dynasty
C. 600–888	Pallava
711	Muhammad ibn Qasim in Sind
753–973	Rashtrakuta dynasty
From early 10th century	Chola
977–997	Sabuktegin of Ghazni
997–1030	Mahmud of Ghazni
1175–1206	Muhammad Ghori
1192	Battle of Tarain
1193–1199	Conquest of Ganges basin
1206	Kutbu-d-din-Aibak

SUPPLEMENTARY READING

BASHAM, A. L. *The Wonder That Was India.* London, 1954.

DE BARY, W. T., ED. *Sources of Indian Tradition.* New York, 1958.

DUNBAR, G. *History of India.* London, 1943.

MORELAND, W. H. AND A. C. CHATTERJEE. *A Short History of India.* London, 1920.

RAWLINSON, H. G. *India: A Short Cultural History.* London, 1937.

SMITH, V. A. *The Oxford History of India,* 3rd ed. Oxford, 1958.

ADVANCED READING

GROUSSET, R. *The Civilizations of the East, Vol. II: India.* London, 1931.

RAPSON, E. J. *The Cambridge History of India, Vol. III.* New York, 1922. Exhaustive treatment of the early Moslem period.

ROWLAND, B. *The Art and Architecture of India.* Baltimore, 1956.

XII ✺

THE SULTANATE

OF DELHI, 1206 - 1526

Three Strong Dynasties: Slave, Khilji, and Tughlak

The Slave Dynasty was established at Delhi in 1206 by Aibak, the slave of Muhammad Ghori, and from this time on India was strongly governed by Moslem sultans. The Slave dynasty was succeeded in 1290 by the Khilji dynasty which held power to 1318, and it in turn was replaced by the Tughlak dynasty, the last of the strong Delhi sultanates, which ruled from that year to 1388. For all three of these dynasties—the Slave, Khilji, and Tughlak—certain generalizations may validly be drawn as regards the nature of their power, their general organization, their strength and their weaknesses.

The Delhi sultanate under all three dynasties was an autocratic state, with unlimited powers vested in the person of the sultan. In this the Delhi sultanate resembled the Seljuk and Ottoman Turkish states (cf. Chapter 6). The sources of this power were derived from his royal army, and from the armed forces of his military nobility which served him as governors of provinces with troops of their own. Government business was conducted in departments, each of which was headed by a minister. The prime minister, or vizir, administered the all-important collection of revenues and the finance department.

The army of the Delhi sultans had originally been composed entirely of cavalry, the weapon which had proved so effective in the conquest of India. Later, elephants were added, but infantry remained always negligible. The assignment system was tried at first, whereby certain villages were assigned the support of the troops, each detachment living in its assigned villages; but the danger of slow mobilization inherent in this system eventually led towards the creation of a standing army at the capital, paid in cash and available immediately.

The key person in the administration of the provinces was the governor. He maintained his court in a fortress, collected provincial revenues, and had at his disposal armed forces to crush any attempted rebellion. The success of his administration was determined mainly by his personal character. The stability of the regime thus largely depended upon the loyalty of the provincial governors, chiefs of the military nobility. The Delhi sultan chose them for their personal quality, and not because of noble birth. Many slaves, as we have already seen, rose to the highest position in the state, and no stigma was attached to slavery. The sultan's palace was the chief school of administration. Here, from among his favorites, he selected by personal choice those who seemed the best fitted and most loyal subordinates.

The weakness in this sort of administration is clear at once: everything depended on the strictly personal loyalty of the chief officials to the ruler. Succession troubles were a constantly recurring and serious theme, and the ambitions of slaves often proved a great source of danger to the ruling sultans. In short, the individual factor in this personal autocracy played a decisive part.

The attitude of the Delhi sultanate towards Hindus differed radically from the days of Mahmud the image breaker and exterminator of infidels. Once the Turks had come to stay, some modification was essential, and the fierce iconoclasm of the early days gave way to studied toleration. In the cities, Hindus were usually not especially oppressed; the Brahman priests in Delhi for instance were exempt from the poll tax. In trade the value of the Hindu merchants was recognized, and in a measure they enjoyed some protection. In the country districts Moslem officials as a rule treated the Hindu peasants well, and their administration often stood in contrast to those areas where Hindu officials collected the revenue; invariably the Hindu employees of the Delhi sultanate treated the peasants more harshly and exacted more from them. The main principle of the collection of revenue was to get as much as possible. Revenues were farmed out by the governor of each province, and apart from an agreed sum to be handed over to the governor out of which he paid his troops and the share owed the sultan, the rest belonged to the appointed collector of revenue himself. Under this system the rapacity of those Hindu landholders or *zamindars* who kept their position under the Turkish conquest, stood often in marked contrast to the methods of Moslem officials.

The Delhi sultanate's foreign policy essentially consisted of the simple aim of extension by conquest. However, during the first century of its existence, this goal was halted because of the new and terrible Mongol danger on the northwest frontier. Consequently in the thirteenth century the Mongol threat caused consolidation rather than an extension of the sultanate. In 1220 the Mongols entered India with Chingis himself in pursuit of the valorous son of the fugitive sultan of Kharism, and his troops ravaged and plundered the Punjab (see Chapter 6). Delhi itself was threatened by the Mongols, and the Delhi sultanate found itself cut off from contact with the Turks in the west. It was not until the fourteenth century, when the threat of the Mongols had been dispelled, that expansion could begin. But once the defenses of the sultanate had been organized on the frontiers in the northwest, the later sultans of Delhi lost no time. Malwa and Gujarat were annexed, and then a series of spectacular Moslem campaigns into the Deccan followed so that by the end of the period Moslem power had been definitely established as far south as the Kistna river. After this, apart from a few small independent Rajput states, the Delhi sultans were able to control the greater part of northern India with firm hands, and their possessions seemed secure from foreign invasion.

After Aibak founded the Slave dynasty, the first of the three strong Turkish sultanates of Delhi, he did not reign long, dying in 1210 after a polo accident. Disorder and revolt followed his death. Finally Iltutmish, his son-in-law who also had begun life as a slave, managed to obtain the throne, but no sooner was he seated securely upon it than he had to face the first of the terrible Mongol invasions. The Mongols made a horrible impression on the Turks, as this description by Amir Khusru makes quite clear:

Their eyes were so narrow and piercing that they might have bored a hole in a brazen vessel. Their stink was more horrible than their colour. Their faces were set on their bodies as if they had no neck. Their cheeks resembled soft leathern bottles, full of wrinkles and knots. Their noses extended from cheek to cheek, and their mouths from cheek-bone to cheek-bone. Their nostrils resembled rotten graves, and from them the hair descended as far as the lips.[1]

Iltutmish chose as his successor a most able person, who resisted both the raids of the Mongols and internal disorders and turbulence, and that was his own daughter, Raziya. Possessed of excellent virtues, very capable and courageous, she nevertheless could not overcome the fatal flaw of being a woman. Intrigues against her in the capital combined with the rebellion of provincial governors and eventually culminated in the successful assassination of her and her husband in 1240. For the next six years the Delhi sultanate suffered from disorders and misgovernment. In 1246 stability was recovered when Nasir-ud-din Mahmud became the reigning sultan. He was a pious, amiable, scholarly and rather ineffective individual, but he employed in his services a slave by the name of Balban, who practically ruled the kingdom and who later succeeded him on the throne of Delhi. Balban's effective power lasted from 1246 to 1287 and in those forty years he governed India with considerable success. Balban repelled the raids of the Mongols, who never ceased to be a constant source of trouble, and he crushed the rebellions of some Mongols who had entered the

---

[1] Rawlinson, *op. cit.,* p. 224.

service of the Delhi sultanate at the time of Chingis' raid into India. Some fifteen Moslem kings and princes found refuge from the Mongols at the court of Balban. Balban took strong measures against rebellious nobles, and with very severe measures ruled his sultanate with iron will and iron hand. Exercising his authority in distant provinces by garrisons of his troops, he achieved a good measure of actual control. Despite his firm rule and his severe measures, the bulk of the Hindu population prospered under him: many minor posts in the administration were held in Hindu hands, and no general Hindu uprising occurred in his reign. As a whole Balban proved to be a temperate, just and basically tolerant ruler, who gave the Slave dynasty one of its strongest and ablest reigns. In 1285, to his great sorrow Balban lost his son, a promising young man who was killed in an encounter with the Mongols. He himself died two years later. His immediate successor was rather unfortunate in his addiction to excessive debauchery, and the first of the Delhi sultanate dynasties came to an end.

In 1290 the Khilji dynasty, which lasted until 1318, succeeded the Slave dynasty at Delhi. It was founded by Jalal-ud-din, but the significant reign was that of Alau-d-din Khilji, his nephew, who ruled from 1296–1318. A man of fiendish cruelty, ambitious to excess, and treacherous, nevertheless Alau-d-din was one of the strongest of all Turkish sultans in India, whose reign, albeit one of terror in which no one was spared who provoked his displeasure, was at the same time one of great strength. Calling himself a second Alexander, Alau-d-din brought most of southern India under the Moslem domination and his heavy hand gave peace and prosperity to his kingdom. His great unrestrained ambition led him to the murder of his uncle, the founder of the Khilji dynasty. In 1294 Alau-d-din conducted a spectacular raid deep into the Deccan, and he returned with enormous plunder. "Scattering gold and collecting followers," he made use of his riches to win over to him a segment of Turkish nobility, so that when he murdered his unsuspecting relative in 1296 after his return from the Deccan he was able to ascend the throne without opposition.

Once in a position of power, he saw to it that the Moslem nobility was immediately eliminated from any share in his rule. He abolished, with one stroke, all grants and stipends to Moslem nobles, so that they had to depend completely upon him for their livelihood. Next, he forbade all wine parties, being suitable places where plots might be hatched against him, and he saw to it that his decrees were enforced by omnipresent espionage and ferocious penalties. A curtain of dread, and a hush of silence descended upon his Moslem subjects, but his control was firm, and his sway undisputed.

Alau-d-din Khilji's reduction of his Moslem nobles to utter dependence upon him was paralleled by his policy of oppression toward his Hindu subjects. A systematic policy of impoverishment was marked by setting compulsory taxes at half their total income, while decrees prohibiting any Hindu to carry arms or to ride horses further discriminated against them and kept them in strict obedience. As a whole, these measures directed against rebellion worked out well enough; families were held responsible for the conduct of their chiefs, and constant supervision ensured the strong centralized power of the sultan and a minimum of opposition. Control was also extended into the economic sphere, where by means of regulated prices and a ration system and with the help of a large staff of officials the state maintained close watch over supplies and transport, and gave some measure of prosperity to the sultanate and the Moslems, if not to the oppressed Hindus.

In foreign affairs the Mongols were Alau-d-din's first and most pressing concern. Their invasions continued, sometimes on a vast scale as when 120,000 of them invaded India, ravaged the country and besieged the sultan himself. After their withdrawal Alau-d-din energetically attempted to prevent further incursions by organizing an efficient frontier defense, entrusted to the very able Tughlak. The army was enlarged and reorganized, and it now became a large standing army paid in cash. With these forces the Mongols could be kept in check, and the army could be used once more for conquest within India. Gujarat was conquered in 1297, and many of the Rajput fortresses soon shared the same fate. After the west had been subdued, there then followed, between 1306 and 1311, campaigns into south India, and the extension of some control by the Delhi sultanate in that region. Under the leadership of an eunuch and ex-slave, Malik Kafir, Moslem armies spectacularly marched all the way down to the southernmost tip of India. The Deccan and the Tamil peninsula were thoroughly and systematically plundered by the Khilji forces. The spoils were enormous, and Hindu power was extinguished almost everywhere in the south. The high point of Alau-d-din's reign was reached when he could claim at least slight Moslem control over the whole of southern India. The Mongols had been repelled, rebellion of his subjects had been made almost impossible, money was cheap, prices rigidly controlled and his kingdom enjoyed peace. His reign stands out as that of the strongest Turkish sultan.

The last years of Alau-d-din were characterized by his personal excesses, which ruined his health, weakened his will, and caused his judgment to fail. Palace intrigues once more began to flourish, and he was finally murdered by the eunuch Kafir. The Khilji dynasty effectively came to an end, and the Delhi sultanate passed into the hands of Tughlak, the defender of the frontiers against the Mongols.

Tughlak Shah, the founder of the Tughlak dynasty which was the last of the three strong dynasties ruling at Delhi and which lasted until 1388, was a pleasant figure who ruled for four years from 1321 to 1325. During this time he quelled disorders, carried out reforms and reorganized the kingdom extending his powers into the Deccan. However, his career was cut short by the ambition of his son who in 1325 murdered him ingeniously by causing a pavilion to collapse on him. Muhammad Tughlak thus came to the throne of Delhi, and his reign, which lasted from 1325 to 1351, marks a turning point in the history of the Turkish sultanate.

Muhammad Tughlak certainly was an extraordinary person, whose complex personality contained a mixture of opposites rarely met with in any ruler. A man restless, versatile, unstable and ferocious, he was full of contradictions. At once flagrantly arrogant, and deeply devout, full of pride and of humility, rapacious and generous to the point of lavishness, a lover of justice and a ruler of ferocious cruelty, devoted to his people and suddenly hostile toward them, Muhammad Tughlak thoroughly ruined his kingdom. We are fortunate enough to possess a description of his court by the great African traveler Ibn Batuta, who visited Delhi between 1342 and 1347 in the course of his far flung travels.

Ibn Batuta describes Muhammad Tughlak as a learned scholar, with a taste for philosophy and science. He was deeply religious and gave precedence in audience to Moslem preachers, judges and holy men over his own nobles, generals and foreigners. Yet the same man indulged in wild and fantastic schemes, and was possessed by a passion for shedding blood. At his door there could always be found some corpse that had been executed.

Small wonder that his reign was one of almost continuous rebellion, rebellion which was punished in the most atrocious forms possible. One of Muhammad Tughlak's most cruel devices was to flay his opponents alive, then to roast the corpse and to send the cooked flesh to the family of the rebel, while his skin was stuffed and displayed publicly. But cruelty did not deter his subjects and his reign saw the revolt of Bengal, and of all the territory south of the Narbada river. In 1340 the governors of Bengal cut away from the Delhi sultan, and seven years later the Deccan followed suit, where an independent Moslem kingdom, that of the Bahmani, was set up as the result of his misrule.

Muhammad Tughlak's reign was not merely productive of rebellion, it also included serious military failures. In wars against Persia over Khorasan, in his campaigns against south India, which he tried to recover, and against Nepal he was defeated. One of his schemes, utterly mad, was to conquer China by way of Tibet. In 1337 he sent an army of 100,000 cavalry into the Himalayan foothills toward the passes of Tibet, but it was catastrophically destroyed enroute. The sultan had the thirteen survivors decapitated at once to soothe his rage over the failure. Other mad schemes included the celebrated Delhi deportation. Some inhabitants of Delhi wrote scurrilous verses ridiculing the government and the sultan, deeply annoyed at this, lost his temper, and ordered all the people of Delhi to leave the city within three days. They were to wander over 600 miles to the site of a new capital Daulatabad, and Delhi, as great a city as Cairo or Baghdad, was to be completely deserted. Many of the inhabitants died enroute, and the project finally had to be abandoned, but the damage had already been done.

Constant rebellion, fierce civil war, bankruptcy and famine were the companions of his reign at the end, and when he died a general sigh of relief greeted his demise: "the king was freed from his people, and they from their king".

Muhammad Tughlak was succeeded by his cousin, Firoz Shah, who reigned from 1351 to 1388. His rule was intelligent and benevolent. Although Firoz Shah himself was perhaps weak, he enjoyed the services of able ministers, one of them a Brahman who had accepted Islam. Under the last of the Tughlak rulers India entered upon a short golden age, in which excellent administration caused disorder to disappear and vast public works brought prosperity. The wealth of the country was extensively developed by irrigation schemes, such as wells, dams, canals and reservoirs.

Futile wars, undertaken in Bengal and Sind, did not deter Firoz Shah from devoting himself to the welfare of his subjects, and in addition to engaging in a great building program he established employment and marriage bureaus to take care of Moslem widows and orphans, and he abolished torture. The main criticism of him is that he encouraged decentralization of authority by paying government officials once again in land grants rather than in money, and that he thus weakened the power of the sultan, causing his subordinates to act independently.

Firoz Shah Tughlak was a strict Moslem, and displayed signs of religious intolerance. He turned against the Brahman priests and forced them to pay the hated poll tax, and he forbade the erection of Hindu temples; but at the same time he made earnest efforts at conversion of Hindus, and he promised exemption from the jizya to the new converts. Part of the existing Moslem population of India and Pakistan of today originated through his efforts.

But the rule of Firoz Shah was the last of an age of peace and prosperity, and the short golden age was extinguished in utter darkness and misery. His death was followed by civil war and confusion. India again seemed a profitable country to invade, and the open invitation to invasion was accepted by Timur of Samarkand who, in 1398, came through the passes and permitted the sack of Delhi by his 90,000 horsemen who plundered and massacred ruthlessly. Delhi was completely destroyed, and the few remaining survivors who had escaped the fury of Timur died soon enough from famine and pestilence: "for two whole months not a bird moved a wing in the city." When Timur returned to Samarkand there were none of his followers who did not have at least 20 slaves abducted from India. The Turkish sultanate of Delhi lay in ruin, completely devastated, and in state of chaos, and the succeeding rulers at Delhi, until the arrival of the Moguls under Babur in 1526, were insignificant. Two very weak Afghan dynasties succeeded the Tughlak dynasty, the last of which, the Lodi, ruled in Delhi from 1450 to 1526. Their territory consisted of Delhi, and the country immediately surrounding its walls, while the history of the period is little more than a record of raids to collect revenue or tribute.

There were some features of Islamic life in India which did persist, and some adjustments were made between Hindu and Moslem during the centuries of the Delhi sultanate. During this period Urdu was developed, a language mixed from Persian and Hindu roots, which served as lingua franca and facilitated communication between the two alien groups. Some Moslem customs, such as the seclusion of women (*purdah*), Moslem ceremonial, and Moslem dress, were adopted by the Hindus, while a considerable number of Hindus found employment with the Turkish overlord. Mixed marriages occasionally occurred leading to a beginning of breakdown of the barriers between the Hindus and Moslems.

Independent Moslem Kingdoms

The new formation of independent Moslem kingdoms in India was the direct result of the common rebellion against the tyranny and misrule of Muhammad Tughlak. Bengal was proclaimed an independent state by the governor of that rich province. However it was not a completely homogeneous Moslem sultanate, since the great Hindu landholders were still strong, even to the degree of persecuting Moslems. The later sultans of Bengal, however, were devout Moslem Negroes who had risen to that position from humble beginnings as African slaves, and who persecuted Hindus.

In the Deccan, Moslems founded the Bahmani dynasty in 1347 which, until about 1500, ruled an area stretching from sea to sea. The Bahmani sultan made yearly visits, or royal progresses, through his four provinces, but his control over his officials was seriously weakened by the many splits and dissensions at his court. Religious tensions among his subjects were complicated by his employment of great numbers of foreign adventurers, Arabs, Persians and Africans. Most of the Africans and the Deccanis were of Sunni inclination, whereas the Persians were all Shi'a, and their mutual jealousies and constant strife, sometimes erupting in massacres, were a source of serious weakness to the Bahmani state.

As a whole the rule of the Bahmani sultans was not unduly oppressive; it certainly compared favorably in this respect with Delhi. The Bahmani rulers controlled a mixed population of Urdu-speaking Moslems and Hindus. They interfered very little with the Hindu peasants, and encouraged their activities by building irrigation works and stimulating trade. In foreign relations, the Bahmani sultanate was engaged in almost constant war and a seemingly continuous struggle against its Hindu neighbor to the south, the kingdom of Vijayanagar. The wars against Vijayanagar were on a grand scale, and they resulted in great loss of life, particularly at first when there were general massacres of noncombatants on both sides. The Bahmanis employed Turkish mercenaries in their service, and introduced the use of artillery into India. Often the wars, based primarily on religious antagonism, were triggered by the most trivial of reasons. The "war of the goldsmith's daughter" of 1406 began when the Hindu raja of Vijayanagar insisted on obtaining such a girl from Moslem territory. One result of these wars was the construction of tremendous fortresses in the Deccan.

The government of the Bahmani sultanate was an autocracy as was that of Delhi, dependent on the personal character of the king and the loyalty of his governors. Some of the Bahmani sultans were excellent rulers, such as Mahmud II, who was not merely a great builder but also a patron of the arts and literature who welcomed the great Persian poet Hafiz at his court, and who was served by excellent ministers. Another was Firoz Shah Bahmani, an amiable, accomplished, and generous prince, under whom the Bahmani kingdom reached its height. He was a scholar, was interested in religion and created for his kingdom a new capital at Bidar, in a healthful and beautiful location on top of the Deccan highlands.

Other independent Moslem states were also established in Gujarat, Malwa and in Kashmir. The sultanate in Gujarat, with its capital at Ahmadabad, "the

Venice of India," was founded about 1400 and was greatly prosperous because of its trade in silks and cottons which were exported over the Arabian Sea. Ahmadabad was a very rich city, adorned with famous mosques and tall and graceful minarets.

Later on the Bahmani sultanate of the Deccan was split up by the provincial governors, and five Moslem states were formed where once there had been only one. Of these five, Bijapur was the most important. It was well governed by enlightened rulers of whom one even went so far as to marry a Hindu princess and to employ many Hindu ministers. Bijapur was renowned for its famous buildings, such as the great mosque and mausoleum of Gol Gumbaz with its

FIGURE 12.1. Gol Gumbaz in Bijapur. The second largest dome in the world is set on plain but massive walls surrounded by four corner turrets and shows a union of Moslem and Hindu tastes.

gigantic dome, the second largest in the world. It, too, continued the traditional warfare against the southern Hindu kingdom of Vijayanagar. The other four Moslem states were Bidar, Golconda, Berar and Ahmadnagar, all of which were eventually absorbed into the great Mogul empire.

Hindu Empire of Vijayanagar

To the south of these independent Moslem kingdoms there existed the Hindu state of Vijayanagar. Only a few ruins remain today as mute evidence of its past greatness. Vijayanagar controlled all India south of the Kistna river from 1336 to 1555, and served as a bulwark against the Moslem invasions. It began its rise as a refuge for fugitives from the Moslem raids and Vijayanagar, or the "city of victory," soon developed into a large capital on the Tungabadhra river, well-fortified with massive walls, and controlling a densely populated, fertile and prosperous kingdom. The old Tamil traditions were preserved here, and Hindu society with its multiplicity of religions, special traditions and institutions, successfully survived the Moslem menace. Hindu independence and Hindu culture lasted for two centuries, until it was finally destroyed in 1565. In its rich cultural development stress was laid of course on Hindu religion, the Vedas, and the worship of Vishnu. The cow was sacred, and zealously protected.

The chief problem of Vijayanagar was expansion, and it was almost constantly engaged in warfare with the Bahmani dynasty of the Deccan. These wars were long, exhausting, and marked by heavy casualties, both military and civilian. Later, there was some modification of this slaughter by the signing of conventions sparing civilian populations.

The height of Vijayanagar's power came during the reign of King Krishnadeva (1509-1530). His position was strengthened by the dissolution of his chief antagonist, the Bahmani sultans, into five small states. For a time Vijayanagar was easily the strongest single entity in the Indian peninsula, with a dominant position which included the whole of southern India from sea to sea south of the Kistna river. Its wealth was fabulous, and all foreign observers were astonished at its grandeur and luxury.

FIGURE 12.2.   The Lotus Mahal, Vijayanagar. A good example of the ruined splendor of that south Indian state.

Foreign trade was a major source of income. In exchange for horses and European luxury textiles, Vijayanagar supplied the foreign traders with precious stones, chiefly diamonds which were mined in great quantities. Gold, rubies, emeralds, and pearls were also articles of trade, and so common that many common citizens wore quantities of jewels and of gold. Foreigners were much impressed by this splendor, and Domingo Paes, a Portuguese horsetrader, compared Vijayanagar to Rome.

The other source of income, apart from government-supported trade, were the very large revenues which the king enjoyed from the land. Heavy taxes on the total yield of production which was stimulated by careful administration, government irrigation works, and loans produced immense sums, most of which were consumed in the elaborate court ceremonial and the ostentatious luxury of the king and his immediate retinue. Athanasius Nikitin, a Russian merchant, who was in Vijayanagar in 1470 commented upon the discrepancies of society:

> The land is overstocked with people; but those in the country are very miserable, while the nobles are extremely opulent and delight in luxury. They are wont to be carried on their silver beds, preceded by some twenty chargers caparisoned in gold and followed by 300 men on horseback and 500 on foot, and by hornmen, ten torchbearers and ten musicians.[2]

It appears then that the lot of the common people was a hard one; punishments certainly were ferocious. For theft, of however small an amount, a hand or a foot was cut off, or the culprit was hanged by a hook through his chin. Traitors were executed by being impaled alive. The government of Vijayanagar was thoroughly autocratic, and Krishnadeva ruled with powers approaching that of a god.

However, the splendor of Vijayanagar was subject to decay and gradual decline. In the end the Moslems of the Deccan united in a general Moslem league to effect the downfall of the hated Hindu kingdom. Doom overtook the Hindu kingdom when the Moslems finally defeated Vijayanagar in the decisive battle of Talikot in 1565. The Moslems had the advantage of superior artillery, about 600 guns, and also better cavalry. The Hindu raja, who was very old, was carried to the battlefield in a litter, but he was captured suddenly by the Moslems, his head struck off on the spot, and then shown to his Hindu subjects who broke and fled in abject terror. The Moslem armies unexpectedly entered the city of Vijayanagar and wrought tremendous havoc: they slaughtered the people, destroyed all the temples, and literally made Vijayanagar into a place of ruins. Their booty and plunder, as one might expect, were on the grand scale; every Moslem private suddenly was rich beyond dreams in gold, jewels, arms, and slaves. From the defeat of Talikot in 1565 Vijayanagar never recovered; its power was decisively destroyed, and Hindu power in the south of India had come to an end. While the political power of Hinduism ended with the fall of Vijayanagar, it nevertheless managed to exercise considerable influence on Islam in the field of religious thought and in the arts.

[2] G. Dunbar, History of India (London: Ivor Nicolson & Watson Ltd., 1943), p. 147.

Hinduism and Islam: Sikhism and Indo-Moslem Art

A most significant attempt at a synthesis of Hinduism and Islam during this period resulted in the creation of a new religion in India, Sikhism, which today counts about five million adherents. This new religion, which originally arose as a pious sect of peaceable Hindus, had its roots in the pantheism of the Sufis, the Persian mystics, whose doctrines were imported by Moslem divines of the Delhi court.

In the fourteenth century Kabir, a Moslem weaver of Benares, had proclaimed the essential unity of God and the futility of mere forms of worship. He proclaimed that God was everywhere and that religious institutions were valueless. He developed a devotional religion which antedated Sikhism. With a good deal of devotional poetry Kabir wrote:

> God is One, whether we worship Him as Allah or as Rama. The Hindu worships him on the eleventh day; the Muhammedan fasts at Ramazan, but God made all the days and all the months. The Hindu god lives at Benares; the Muhammedan god at Mecca; but He who made the world lives not in a city made by hands. There is one Father of Hindu and Mussulman, One God in all matter: He is the Lord of all the earth, my Guardian, and my Priest.

Kabir was very influential on Guru Nanak, the true founder of Sikhism. Guru Nanak, who worked in the Punjab, made the effort at uniting the two faiths, Hinduism and Islam. He stressed, of course, the essential unity of God, but he also added to this concept the notion of *bhakti*, the old Hindu idea of salvation by grace and love. Sikhism became a pure theistic religion, denying the idolatry and the caste system of the Hindus, and Moslem religious institutions and theology. The story is told of Guru Nanak that he once fell asleep with his feet stretched out in the direction of Mecca. When a devout follower of the prophet kicked him rudely for this insult against God, he answered by requesting him to turn his feet into any direction in which God was not.

The age of the sultanate of Delhi saw not merely the successful attempt to create a religious synthesis, Sikhism, it also illustrates the same kind of synthesis in the field of art, and in architecture in particular. Some of the finest monuments of Indo-Moslem art date from this period, and they demonstrate the fusion of Indian and Central Asian concepts. The Kutb Minar, or tower of victory, at Delhi, which was completed in 1198 is a white marble and red sandstone structure, 238 feet high with five stories, in which the work of Hindu masons was utilized and Indian strength and grace are evident particularly in the decorative ornaments of the exuberant balconies. Hindu influence may also be seen in the fine screens of arches, where geometrical design and lacework patterns predominate, while the Moslems contributed in turn the pointed arch and the dome and they introduced to Indian soil such religious structures as the mosque and the minaret.

One of the finest of the architectural achievements of the Delhi sultanate is the mausoleum of Tughlak Shah, a few miles south of modern Delhi, an

FIGURE 12.3. Kutb Minar, Delhi (1198). A white marble and red sandstone tower of victory. The elaborate decorations on the balconies show Hindu influence.

FIGURE 12.4. The tomb of Tughlak Shah, Delhi. A simple but effective example of Indo-Moslem art.

austere and stately structure, set on a lake, with sloping walls and massive towers. Another structure, already mentioned, is the huge Gol Gumbaz at Bijapur, a mausoleum with a gigantic circular dome, the second largest in the world, which shows Turkish architectural influence. Here, too, full technical mastery of the domed roof is combined with plain and massive walls and four corner turrets, the whole lending austere dignity to this successful example of the joining of Hindu and Islamic tastes.

The Portuguese

During the fifteenth century a new factor entered Indian life. The first Westerners in any number arrived in the persons of the Portuguese. At this time Portugal had established a strong monarchy and had available the necessary capital for expansion. The guiding force for this expansion was provided by Prince Henry the Navigator who patronized the search for a new route eastward to break the Venetian monopoly of the spice trade in the Mediterranean. In 1487 Bartholomeo Diaz rounded the Cape of Good Hope and in 1498 Vasco da Gama reached the great spice port of Calicut on India's Malabar coast.

Calicut was the transhipment port for spices coming from the East Indies and the export point for Indian spices. Here Arab traders enjoyed concessions and were soon hostile to the Portuguese and their threat to Arab commercial interests. Arab-Portuguese rivalry in trade was settled finally by force. In a series of expeditions sent from 1500 to 1509 the Portuguese broke Arab seapower. Portuguese commercial supremacy in the area was then consolidated by Afonso Albuquerque who from 1509 to 1515 founded a maritime empire based entirely on seapower. Albuquerque opposed the acquisition of territory believing that all that was necessary were a few strategic fortified naval bases from which control of trade could be maintained. During these years the Portuguese established such bases as Socotra, Ormuz, and Goa and acquired the port of Malacca.

Once the chain of fortified bases had been established the Portuguese were able to monopolize the lucrative spice trade and reap enormous profits. With the backing of seapower, Portuguese vessels alone became the carriers of certain commodities such as pepper, cloves, nutmeg, mace, and silk. Coastal trade in Indian waters was permitted by Indian ships if they obtained a license from the Portuguese, and even then they were closely policed by Portuguese gunboats. Pepper, cloves, and nutmeg now found their way to Europe exclusively in Portuguese ships.

In their settlement on Goa the Portuguese maintained tolerance of the Hindus, employing them as officials and troops. Mutual hostility to Moslems made the Portuguese cordial to the Hindu kingdom of Vijayanagar and a trade developed with the Portuguese supplying horses to Vijayanagar. The Portuguese rarely interfered with local customs on Goa, except for forbidding *suttee*, the burning of widows. Religion became an issue only in later years when missionary activity in India increased. Franciscans, Dominicans, and Jesuits arrived carrying with them both religious zeal and the intolerance exemplified by the Inquisition, introduced in 1540. Religious influence grew at the expense of considerations of trade. Hindu temples were destroyed and within a century there were twice as many priests as Portuguese laymen on Goa.

Portuguese power in India began to decline soon after it reached its zenith. The fall of Vijayanagar in 1565 was a blow to the rich trade between Goa and the Hindu state. Another factor was the increasing corruption and arrogance of the Portuguese themselves. Manpower was steadily depleted until the Portuguese were forced to bring criminals from the prisons of Lisbon to maintain their diminished ranks. The most serious disaster occurred in 1588. In 1580 Portugal had formed a union with Spain. When the Spanish Armada went down in the waters of the English Channel, Portuguese seapower went down with it. This loss of seapower was irreplaceable and opened the way to other European ships to sail in eastern waters.

Portuguese activity in India had an important effect on Europe by producing an economic transformation in the West and ushering in a new commercial age but to India at the time it was but a passing event, barely noticed and of no seeming consequence. It does, however, mark the first important intrusion of Europeans into India, an intrusion which would be repeated with vast and far-reaching consequences in later centuries.

BASIC DATES

1206–1290	Slave dynasty
1206–1211	Kutbu-d-din Aibak
1221–1222	Chingis Khan invades Punjab
1290–1318	Khilji dynasty
1294–1316	Alau-d-din
1321–1388	Tughlak dynasty
1321–1325	Tughlak Shah
1325–1351	Muhammad Tughlak
1336–1564	Vijayanagar
1340	Bengal independent
1347–1500	Bahmani dynasty in Deccan
1351–1388	Firoz Shah
1398	Sack of Delhi by Timur
1450–1526	Afghan Lodi dynasty
1469–1539	Guru Nanak
1490–1686	Bijapur
1498	Vasco da Gama at Calicut
1509–1530	Krishnadeva
1510	Albuquerque takes Goa
1565	Talikot

SUPPLEMENTARY READING

DE BARY, W. T., ED. *Sources of Indian Tradition.* New York, 1958.

DUNBAR, G. *History of India.* London, 1943.

MORELAND, W. H. AND A. C. CHATTERJEE. *A Short History of India.* London, 1920.

RAWLINSON, H. G. *India: A Short Cultural History.* London, 1937.

SMITH, V. A. *The Oxford History of India,* 3rd ed. Oxford, 1958.

ADVANCED READING

ELIOT, C. E. *Hinduism and Buddhism.* London, 1954.

GROUSSET, R. *The Civilizations of the East, Vol. II: India.* London, 1931.

HUDSON, G. F. *Europe and China.* London, 1931. Contains a fine chapter on the coming of the Portuguese.

PANIKKAR, K. M. *Asia and Western Dominance.* New York, 1954. An interesting, but sometimes overdrawn view of the Portuguese in India by an Indian scholar.

RAPSON, E. J. *The Cambridge History of India,* Vol. III. New York, 1922.

ROWLAND, B. *The Art and Architecture of India.* Baltimore, 1956.

SEWELL, R. *A Forgotten Empire.* London, 1900. A study of Vijayanagar.

XIII ✵✵✵

THE RISE OF THE MOGULS

Founding of the Mogul Empire

The word Mogul used in describing this empire is a corruption of Mongol and is applied to that empire in India which begins with Babur. The empire which he established marks the beginning of a clearly defined period in Indian history. Beginning as a strictly Islamic power it saw also a new attempt at synthesis between Hindu and Moslem during the reign of the great figure, Akbar.

Babur was born in 1483 of mixed Mongol and Turkish parentage. On his mother's side Babur was descended from Timur and on his father's side from Chingis Khan. Babur's father was the ruler of the petty principality of Ferghana on the Syr-darya river in Turkistan. Babur grew to be a man who loved life in all its forms, whether it be drinking, fighting or the quiet pleasures of fragrant gardens. In 1497 he realized his first great ambition, by conquering the magnificent city of Samarkand, formerly Timur's capital. But a revolt soon followed, his troops deserted him and he was cast out. Babur then lost Ferghana too, falling from king to refugee.

Exile was followed by many more adventures, sieges, fights and conquests, and the youth of Babur reminds one of the life of a romantic knight errant. His struggle to preserve at least his sovereignty in his native land was ineffectual, and in 1504 Babur had become tired of wandering about "like a king on a chessboard," but in that year chance enabled him to seize Kabul in Afghanistan with the help of less than 300 ill-clad followers. Once Babur had become

king of Kabul, he began to cast his eyes on India. Babur's real opportunity came
in 1524 with the defection of the government of Lahore to his side from the arrogant, haughty and unpopular Sultan Ibrahim Lodi of the Afghan Lodi dynasty
of Delhi which had exercised rather feeble control of the Delhi sultanate since
1450. The Lodis had transferred their capital to Agra, and some order had been
restored during the vigorous reign of Sikander Shah, but many of these gains
were lost under Ibrahim Lodi. He was parsimonious, distrusted his nobles and
antagonized the Afghan chieftains.

Babur crossed into India with a force of not more than 12,000 men when
called upon by the rebellious governor of the Punjab. His troops defeated those
of Lodi on 12 April 1526 at Panipat. The battle of Panipat on that day decided
the fate of India for two and a half centuries.

The forces of Babur were heavily outnumbered by the Afghan army of
100,000 troops and 1,000 elephants. Babur did possess, however, matchlock
muskets and an artillery serviced by Ottoman Turks. Babur used a wagon fortress
(an Ottoman idea) designed to break any cavalry attack should Ibrahim be so
unwise as to attempt it. Ibrahim Lodi, without plan or experience, did just that,
and ordered his huge army into an attack, which Babur repulsed from his strong
entrenched position. In the ensuing rout and confusion, the Afghan elephants
panicked, as elephants had done many times in Indian history since the fight
of Porus against Alexander. Babur then let loose his own cavalry charges from
both sides, which resulted in the total defeat and destruction of the Lodi army.
The corpse of Ibrahim himself, and of over 20,000 Afghans on the field, illustrated the soundness of the Ottoman tactics of a strong holding position coupled
with flank attacks.

After the battle of Panipat, Babur occupied Delhi and Agra, and by 1529
his empire reached from Bactria to Bengal. The spoils of his conquest were
very great in terms of gold, silver, jewels, precious cloth, but Babur himself
was not favorably impressed with India:

Hindustan is a country that has few pleasures to recommend it. The
people are not handsome. They have no idea of the charms of a friendly
society, of frankly mixing together, or familiar intercourse. They have
no genius nor comprehension of mind, no politeness of manner, no
kindness or fellow feeling, no ingenuity or mechanical invention in planning or executing their handicraft works, no skill or knowledge in design
or architecture; they have no horses, no good flesh, no grapes or musk-
melons, no good fruits, no ice cold water, no good food or bread in their
bazaars, no baths or colleges, no candles, no torches, not a candlestick
. . . . Besides their rivers and standing waters, they have some running
water in their ravines and hollows; they have no aqueducts or canals in
their gardens or palaces. In their buildings they study neither elegance
nor climate, appearance nor regularity . . . . The chief excellency of
Hindustan is that it is a large country and has abundance of gold and
silver.[1]

[1] *Memoirs* as quoted in H. G. Rawlinson, *India: A Short Cultural History* (London, 1937), p. 286.

After a successful appeal to his soldiers, who were hillmen not fond of the Indian climate, to remain in India Babur still had one more enemy before India was all his, and that was a Rajput confederacy led by a formidable warrior, the energetic and vigorous Rana Sangrama of Chitor. In facing the strong Rajput forces Babur once again resorted to the same tactics which had won at Panipat, the construction of a temporary wagon fortress. But his Afghan troops, when they saw what appeared to be overwhelming Hindu numbers, began to desert their leader, and Babur was forced to extreme measures to restore confidence in him: he abjured the use of alcohol of which he had been a free imbiber. All the wine carried in his train was poured out onto the ground, his gold and silver drinking cups were broken up and given to the poor, and Babur then took a solemn vow never to drink again. He addressed his troops in these fine and moving words:

> Noblemen and soldiers! Every man that comes into the world is subject to dissolution. When we are passed away and gone, God only survives, unchangeable. Whoever comes to the feast of life must, before it is over, drink from the cup of death. He who arrives at the inn of mortality must one day inevitably take his departure from that house of sorrow— the world. How much better is it to die with honor than to live with infamy! [2]

His speech made a great impression upon his troops, and they went into desperate action against their enemies. The battle of Kanua was fought on March 16, 1527, with Babur's firearms deciding the day in his favor. With this victory any chance of Hindu rule of north India evaporated, and Babur now firmly established the Mogul dynasty. However Babur was barely able to consolidate his control and to engage in incompleted wars in Bihar and Bengal before his health began to fail. The Indian climate proved fatal, and he died at the early age of 47, in 1530. His body was buried, as he wished, in his favorite city of Kabul.

Babur is certainly one of the most human and appealing of all Indian kings. He was cheerful, courageous, a great warrior and adventurer who led a hard life, but also an accomplished poet who wrote in Persian, and a master of Turkish prose. He was a born leader, a scholar and a statesman, but he never lacked a sense of humor, and above all, a sense of beauty. His admirable memoirs make delightful reading in their feeling for nature.

Babur was succeeded by his son Humayun, who although able, genial and witty, was at the same time indolent, addicted to opium and rarely resolute. When he ascended the Mogul throne in 1530 success at first was his companion, and he extended his Indian possessions into Malwa and Gujarat; but this promising beginning was cut short by the rise of a most dangerous opponent, Sher Shah, in Bihar. Sher Shah was an Afghan noble who had served at the court of the Lodis in Delhi, and he revolted against Babur's son. In 1539 he surprised the Mogul army on the banks of the Ganges, utterly routed it, and the luckless

---

[2] *Ibid.*, p. 289.

FIGURE 13.1.   Babur laying out a garden near Agra.

Humayun was forced to flee for his life, leaving behind him all his baggage, treasure and women. After terrible privations Humayun and a devoted band of forty followers finally found refuge and cordial welcome in Persia, where Shah Tamasp gave friendship and aid on the condition that Humayun embrace the Shi'a sect of Islam with which wish Humayun at least outwardly complied. It seemed as if the Moguls had already run their course, and that Babur's conquest had been nullified by this disaster which had overtaken his favorite son.

While Humayun was forced into exile in Persia, Sher Shah ruled India from 1540 to 1545. The rule of this Afghan noble soon proved to be one of the best India had ever enjoyed. Sher Shah was not only an expert soldier, but also a wise and judicious administrator devoted to public service. When once he was told that his beard was growing white he replied that it was true, that he had obtained the throne only in the evening of his life, a circumstance which he greatly regretted since it left him such a short time to be of use to his country and people. Having gained experience in the management of the estates of his father, Sher Shah devoted a great deal of attention to the building of an excellent administrative system which was to become the foundation upon which the later Mogul administration was based. The chief task of the officials was to assess and collect revenue, which was based on the fixed sum representing one-third of the total produce. Each official was appointed to administer a group of villages, and these in turn were grouped into districts. Village headmen were made responsible for crimes of all sorts which might occur within their jurisdiction.

Sher Shah was also a tireless worker in the interests of justice. He ruthlessly eliminated oppression wherever he found it and he set up courts of justice wherever he went. He was also a great patron of all charities. He provided many roads of India with walled rest houses, and planted with shade-giving trees, while drinking wells were dug alongside to increase the material comfort of travelers. In 1545 Sher Shah was accidentally killed in the explosion of a powder magazine, but the five years of his reign are of critical importance since they saw the laying of the administrative foundations of the entire Mogul empire. After Sher Shah's untimely death Humayun, a refugee in Persia, was able to re-establish his authority in India. After recovering the boundary districts of Kandahar and Kabul he returned to India in 1555 with the aid of Persian cavalry. Humayun reascended the Mogul throne that same year, but he died in 1556 as the result of a fall and the fortunes of the Mogul empire rested with his son Akbar, a boy of 13, who had been born in 1542 in the Indian desert during Humayun's desperate wanderings.

Akbar

Akbar reigned from 1556 to 1605, and he was thus a contemporary of Elizabeth of England and Shah Abbas of Persia, both of whom he eclipsed as a very great man and noble ruler. After Humayun's death, Hemu, a Hindu general, drove the Mogul troops out of Agra and assumed the vacant throne. Hemu had a powerful army, with many elephants, which the Moguls faced at the second battle of Panipat in November, 1556. For a while the outcome was in doubt, but a stray arrow in the eye rendered Hemu unconscious, and the Moguls, under the nominal command of the boy Akbar, won. Hemu was captured and immediately executed, and the victory was decisive in ending all internal danger to the continuance of Mogul rule in India. In 1568 Akbar assumed personal control over India.

The reign of Akbar may first of all be considered as that of a great conqueror who, motivated by ambition, expanded his power in all directions. Akbar's career of warfare began with the conquest of the Rajputs, a feat which was completed by 1569. Those Hindu rulers who submitted to the Moguls were not displaced, but were left in authority, a policy foreshadowing the later attitude of Akbar toward his Hindu subjects.

In 1572 Akbar campaigned against Gujarat, and as a result the Mogul empire gained access to the sea where Akbar encountered the Portuguese. He was impressed by their ships, their artillery, and their merchandise, and he came to a friendly agreement with them.

After these great successes in the west Akbar turned his armies to the east. In 1574 Bihar was annexed, followed by Bengal in 1576. Akbar also made Afghanistan, Baluchistan and Kashmir parts of his empire.

Having brought all of northern India within his empire, Akbar then moved south into the Deccan against the small independent Moslem successor states to the Bahmani dynasty. By 1600 three of these had been taken and he also had definite plans to proceed and conquer the remaining two states, and to expel the Portuguese, but these plans he was unable to complete. At his death the Moguls controlled an empire which extended from Assam to Khorasan, a territory greater than that ruled by any previous Indian state. He might have done even more except that the last years of his career of conquest were disturbed

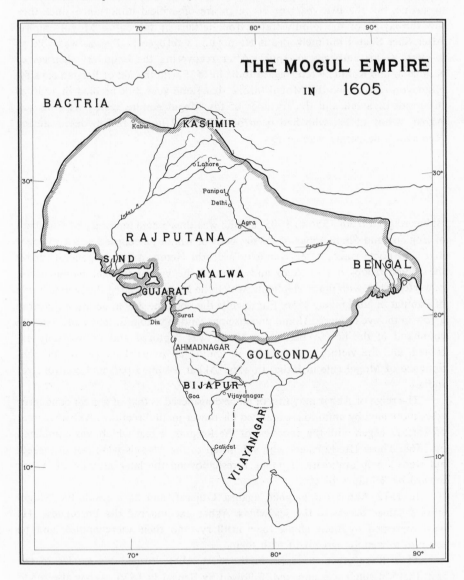

by the rebellion of his son Salim, the future Emperor Jahangir. Military success was his own achievement for it was his personal leadership which had given the impetus to this enormous expansion of the Mogul rule, from the precarious hold on the Punjab which Akbar held as a boy to the establishment of the greatest of all Indian empires.

The personal element in Indian history was rarely more important, and more clearly demonstrated, than by this Mogul ruler who shaped the destinies of India largely by his own character and consequently a study of this personality is most important if one is to understand the events of his reign.

There are a number of sources, of varying merit, which give us a picture of the great Mogul emperor. The most intimate, but also the one given over to uncritical admiration, is the *Akbarnama* or *Deeds of Akbar*, which was written by Abul Fazl, his close friend. Other sources include the excellent descriptions by the Jesuits who frequented the Mogul court. They all describe him as a man whose whole mien was in accord with the ideal of kingly dignity. "His expression is tranquil, serene and open, full also of dignity, and when he is angry awful majesty," declared one observer.

Akbar led an active and healthful life, eating only one meal a day, a meatless one (the result of Jain influence). His strength and endurance were never impaired by his addiction to drink and opium. Akbar had a passion for sports, particularly hunting, where he was fearless in encountering any beast, even going so far as to kill a tiger while he was on foot. He needed but little sleep, and was strong and tireless in all of his exertions. His manners were charming, and he knew the art of being great with the great, and lowly with the low. He was prompt in action, deliberate in policy and he maintained as a rule perfect self-control.

As a boy Akbar had preferred sports to lessons and so the emperor never learned how to read or write, but although illiterate he was a great listener and his fine memory mastered an enormous volume of information which had been read to him from the 24,000 manuscripts in his library.

Akbar possessed an inquiring mind, so complex that even the Jesuits who excelled at the fine art of character study and who knew him well, could not fully understand it. They could never predict his actions nor all the motives behind them.

Akbar was remarkable for his versatility and wide range of interest. He possessed great mechanical aptitude, enjoying working with his hands, whether in the arts, sports or mechanics. He learned to draw, was a first-rate polo player who invented a lighted polo ball so that the game could be played at night and was skilled in metallurgy where he designed an improved gun which could fire seventeen rounds at once. Akbar was interested in music, and played some instruments, the kettledrum being his favorite. Akbar also displayed love of beauty and a passion for theology. His attainments in diverse fields find perhaps their closest counterpart in the restless drive and energy of another great autocrat, Peter the Great of Russia.

AKBAR'S RELIGION.   Akbar was always deeply interested in religion and philosophy, searching ceaselessly for truth. A sincerely religious man, the emperor "never for one moment forgot God," as his son declared. Early in his

FIGURE 13.2.   Akbar hunting.

youth Akbar had been introduced to the mystical doctrines of the Persian
Sufis, and when less than 20 he had his first spiritual crisis when he rode into the
desert for solitary meditation. "I experienced an internal bitterness, and from
lack of spiritual provision for my last journey, my soul was seized with
exceeding sorrow." [3]

Akbar at first was satisfied with Islam, but after 1575 when he was 33 and
had completed his major conquests, the emperor became increasingly absorbed
in religious inquiry. He would pass solitary nights in prayer and meditation,

[3] Rawlinson, op. cit., p. 299.

thanking God for his past successes, and contemplating the nature of religious truth. From solitary meditation Akbar turned to learned formal discussions with various theologians, and in 1575 he built what was called the Hall of Worship, within whose walls he could discuss with freedom the most abstruse problems of theology with learned men from all religions. Akbar was fascinated by the different points raised by the disputants.

In these discussions various Islamic schools first had the ascendancy, but Akbar quickly broadened their scope and invited Hindus, Parsees, Zoroastrians, Jains and Christians to debate the nature of religious truth. The Zoroastrians impressed the emperor with their cult of the sun and fire and the Jains caused him to abstain from eating meat and to prohibit the killing of animals, but most interesting of all perhaps was the influence of the teachings of Christianity which were expounded at his court by Portuguese Jesuits expressly invited from Goa for that purpose. Akbar permitted the Jesuits their own chapel, and he gave them full liberty to preach. The Gospel was translated into Persian, and Akbar attended in person the Christian sacrament of mass. Around his neck he wore a medallion of the Virgin, he devoutly kissed the Bible, and seemed to have had a genuine admiration for the Christian religion. Akbar participated eagerly in the religious disputations of the Jesuits, which often resulted in victories for them over their opponents. The Jesuits had high and genuine hopes that they might achieve the conversion of Akbar to the Christian faith, but they were soon disillusioned, for Christian dogma did not ultimately satisfy Akbar. Akbar could not bring himself to believe in the divine truth of just one religion.

In 1578 the Emperor underwent another spiritual crisis. He called off the hunt on which he was engaged and gave strict orders not to touch even the feather of a finch. He meditated entire nights on God and "reverence for the great giver" filled his heart. In this mood he sought the company of a celebrated Sufi holy man and his sons. One of these was the very learned Abul Fazl, who became Akbar's intimate friend, advisor and secretary and who was the author of the vast encyclopedia *Ain-i-Akbari* or *Institutes of Akbar*, a detailed description of the administration of the Mogul empire. Under the influence of the Sufi mystics Akbar added to the regular Thursday night religious discussions held in the Hall of Worship his own private devotions four times a day, at sunrise, noon, sunset, and midnight.

The mystic inclinations of the emperor produced an increasing hostility against orthodox Islam in his mind, and during this period Akbar began to adopt Parsee and Hindu religious customs, and he proclaimed universal toleration for all creeds. There followed in 1579 the "Infallibility Decree," which prepared the way for the emperor's decision to decide himself questions of religion and to make religious reforms.

The solution of Akbar's religious problems was found in the invention of an entirely new religion, the "Din Ilahi" or "Divine Faith," a creation of Akbar himself. In 1582 he established this pure, although perhaps a trifle vague, theism, of which he was the sole exponent in his role of vice-regent of God on earth. Essentially the new authoritative creed was an eclectic one, which borrowed its essentials from all religions everywhere, since to Akbar truth had never been restricted to one particular faith. The motives for this unprecedented step were both political and religious. On the one hand Akbar found personal fulfillment, while on the other there was the emperor's genuine hope that with the Din Ilahi he could provide a common faith to unify all his subjects. In some ways one might compare the establishment of this new religion to Henry VIII's act of supremacy, but it was even more ambitious. With it Akbar also expected to realize the great dream of uniting the mutually hostile Hindus and Moslems, and so to produce a new India.

The external observances of the new cult were borrowed mostly from the Parsees, the Jains, and the Hindus. There was one God, but the sun, stars, and fire might also be worshipped. Worship was to be private, and no priesthood was needed. Cattle slaughtering was expressly forbidden. In some respects the new faith was a reaction against orthodox Islam, and Akbar took some steps to repress his original faith. The building of new mosques was interdicted, and Moslem prayers, the pilgrimage to Mecca and Ramadan were all prohibited, while the name Muhammad could no longer be used within the empire.

However, Akbar's new synthetic faith, a most remarkable creation, proved soon to be a disappointment. It had no appeal to the masses, and even at court there were few adherents. The new religion did not survive his death; the fine ideal of uniting all elements of India failed of realization. To create this union through a new religion was, however, but one of Akbar's attempts. The emperor followed similar policies in the conduct of the secular administration of the Mogul state.

AKBAR'S NATIONAL POLICIES.   In the national policies which Akbar formulated for India his constant principle was to be a truly national ruler of the country and to unite all of his subjects into one great Indian empire. This concept was realized by Akbar's policy of religious toleration, which was designed to make Hindu chiefs and subjects loyal to the Mogul regime. Rarely has the significant and decisive role of the individual in history been more clearly demonstrated than in Akbar's policies and those of his successors.

The basic step by which Akbar gained wide support for himself was to remove discriminatory practices against Hindus, and to establish their equality with Moslems. The hated poll tax and the tax on Hindu pilgrims were abolished, Hindus were given official positions in the government and were made socially welcome at court. Some of the Rajput nobles indeed were treated on a par with the relatives of the imperial family and were appointed and advanced to highest posts; one of them was made viceroy at Kabul. There was no interference in the territory of Hindu rulers, nor was there any special tribute levied. Akbar himself married a Hindu princess.

Akbar's conciliatory attitude won him the loyalty of the Rajput princes, and Hindu chiefs became the stoutest of defenders of the Mogul empire. The policy of toleration was furthermore reinforced by Akbar's system of justice and his careful observance of Hindu customs. Although he did oppose suttee, the practice of self-immolation by widows, he made the slaughter of cows a capital offense.

Akbar's policy was immensely successful, and his aim to be a truly Indian ruler, and to found an Indian dynasty was realized during his reign. Although he built upon and used the skill of others, since he erected his administrative structure on Sher Shah's foundation and made excellent use of a fine Hindu minister of his own, Raja Todar Mal, still the credit of establishing a united India on a new basis of equality and toleration is due to him. In conformity with his vision of a united India his was a rule of justice and law, and his administrative system is still the basis of much of modern India.

This system owes much to Sher Shah, and to the help of Akbar's Hindu minister Raja Todar Mal, but it was supervised by a mind which was capable of grasping both the broad and original principles of government as well as one that had an extraordinary capacity for laborious attention to detail. Our source for the details of the administration is the *Institutes of Akbar*.

At the head of the government stood of course the emperor, an autocrat who ruled by divine right, bound only by the moral precepts of the Koran. As in the Ottoman or the Persian empires much depended on the personal character of the ruler. He was served by a graded state service of salaried officials, whose rank was expressed in terms of cavalry commands. Each state official was paid a cash salary. He might be assigned to any job, depending upon the personal judgment of the emperor. Excellent pay, and the promise of rapid advance, attracted the best men in India and from abroad into the Mogul service. Upon the death of an official his wealth was inherited by the emperor and his rank became vacant so that the evils of heredity were avoided.

The organization of the state service was centered in the highest official beneath the throne, the prime minister, who was in charge of the three major subdivisions, the court, the army and the empire. Each of these subdivisions was governed by minute and detailed regulations. The court included in addition to the imperial household such varied departments as the mint, which provided an adequate, excellently-minted and reliable currency, the body guard of the emperor, and public works. The army, commanded by Akbar himself as commander-in-chief, was headed by a paymaster general, whose duty it was to see that all contingents were kept up to full strength. The cavalry and artillery were the best paid and the most favored of the branches, with the cavalry serving as the most important branch in an army which was not overly large. The military forces of the Moguls were augmented in case of war by irregular contingents. Organization followed the decimal system, from Commanders of 10,000 down to Commanders of 10. The service which governed the empire was also based on salaried officials whose sole interest it was to strengthen central authority.

Akbar retained the innovation of Sher Shah who had separated the general administration of the empire from the assessment and collection of land revenue. An entirely separate set of revenue officials were in charge of the revenue, and this proved to be a very successful arrangement.

For purposes of general administration the empire was divided into fifteen provinces, each under a governor who was responsible for law and public order, but not for financial affairs. Large cities in the empire had city governors, *kotwals,* with wide powers. An elaborate register of houses and persons was kept, and spies were employed to funnel intelligence to the provincial and city authorities. These authorities were also in charge of such diverse matters as the regulation of prices and the maintenance of correct weights and measures. In turn, each province was subdivided into districts where the subordinates of the governors carried out similar functions of maintaining public peace.

The revenue administration was headed by a revenue minister who had the right of direct access to the emperor. His officials formed a completely separate body of men, independent from the governors of provinces. They were in charge of the assessment and collection of the land revenue; thus the state ensured for itself a direct relation with the individual peasant. In addition, the revenue service was responsible for the collection of customs duties and sales taxes. Except in some areas which were specifically reserved for the imperial treasury, and in Bengal, all land in India was taxed on the principle that it was the actual cultivator of the soil who was responsible for the payment of the revenue. Taxes were regularized, so that each unit of an area cultivated was charged with a sum of money, generally about one-third of the average annual yield, but provisions for different rates for different crops and for the reduction of taxes when needed were also embodied in the revenue regulations. To stimulate agricultural development revenue collectors had the right to reduce taxes in cases where wastelands were newly brought under cultivation. Later in the reign provisions were made for lump payments which were assessed on a whole village instead, in which case the village headman was made responsible for the revenue to be collected.

In the administration of law, no real separate judiciary existed in the Mogul dominions, the emperor himself being the fountain of justice, and theoretically at least, the final arbiter of disputes.

Since salaries of Mogul officials in all branches of the administration were excellent whether in the court service, the army, the general administration or the revenue service, Akbar was assured a steady supply of able men, 70 per cent of whom were foreigners such as Persians and Afghans, the rest being Indian Moslems and Hindus. These officials formed the wealthy upper class of the empire. The middle class in this society was formed by a small but prosperous segment of merchants. The rest of India was constituted by the lower classes with no economic reserve of any kind and living as a whole on a bare subsistence level. There is no question that the masses of India were desperately poor, and that India was a fine example of the extreme disparities of luxury and poverty, yet as a whole it is fair to say that the Mogul empire during the early seventeenth century was not only the best organized, but even the most prosperous empire in the world. If the lower classes were poor, they were so by European standards, and despite low standards general contentment prevailed in the empire.

FIGURE 13.3.   Akbar receiving the Persian ambassador at Agra. This double-page from the *Akbarnama* gives an indication of the splendor of the Mogul court.

The display and luxury of the free-spending and lavish court was fabulous. Ice was brought daily to Akbar from the snowy mountains, as were select fruits from Kashmir and Kabul. Each elephant in the Mogul stables had a quota of four servants. Labor at the court was exceedingly cheap, for it was either poorly paid or it consisted of slaves. Yet the great economic drain of a large nonproductive class did not result in a deterioration of the Mogul economy during the reign of Akbar; his excellent administration maintained the empire economically strong and vigorous. It was only under the economic practices of his successors that the Mogul empire began to decline.

In the areas of trade and industry the Mogul government here too did its best to stimulate increased activity. Akbar abolished tolls and levies on commerce, imposed low customs duties and made his roads as safe as he could. India became economically self-supporting, and required no essential imports. A few metals, raw materials and luxury articles were the chief imports, together with gold and silver. So favorable a balance of trade existed that Sir Thomas Roe, the first English envoy to the Mogul court exclaimed that "Europe bleedeth to enrich Asia," although most of the precious metal was hoarded and not put into circulation.

The most extensive Indian industry was cotton-weaving, followed by the
making of silk and other textile products. Indian exports, although not too
significant in this period, were primarily cotton goods which made their way to
Arabia, Burma and the East Indies, together with the old standbys, pepper, spices
and drugs. Trade, inland, coastal or overseas, was largely in the hands of Moslems, and it was sufficiently flourishing so that the general picture of the Mogul
empire during Akbar's rule is that of a highly prosperous state.

Akbar excelled also as a patron of the arts. His library contained some
24,000 manuscript volumes, and both Persian and Hindu writers found employment at the Mogul court. Persian literature was highly prized, but there were
also many translations from the Hindu epics, such as the *Mahabharata*. Hindu
musicians and painters contributed to the imposing magnificence of Akbar's
court.

Of special importance are the buildings which were constructed during
this period. Akbar took a very great interest in architecture; many buildings
were his own conceptions and were built under his personal supervision: "His
majesty plans splendid edifices, and dresses the work of his mind and heart
in the garment of stone and clay." [4] In Agra the stone fort, of commanding
height and great size, dates from his reign; but the most characteristic and
the principal architectural monuments of Akbar's are to be found in the now
ruined capital of Fathpur Sikri 26 miles outside Agra. In these red sandstone
buildings with battlemented walls Akbar made use of both Hindu and Moslem
features, and developed a distinct style. Fathpur Sikri, rapidly built to accom-
modate his court, was used however only until 1585, when apparently the
bad water supply of the site caused its abandonment. There were in Fathpur
Sikri a great centrally located mosque, palaces, audience halls, baths, gardens
and even a lake six miles long, but the finest structure of them all is the magnificent triumphal entrance arch, the "Bulawand Darwaza," or "Lofty Gateway,"
erected as a memorial to the conquest of Gujarat. A superb structure, it contains
the famous inscription which was composed by the Emperor: "Jesus, son of
Mary (on whom may be peace), said: 'The world is a bridge; pass over it,
but build no house upon it.' Who hopes for an hour, hopes for eternity. The
world is an hour: spend it in prayer, for what follows is unseen." Due to Akbar's
policy of religious toleration the period witnessed also the building of many
Hindu temples in India.

Akbar's last years were difficult. Two of his sons had died in delirium
tremens caused by excessive drinking, and then Prince Salim revolted against
his father. He caused Akbar's friend and minister Abul Fazl to be treacherously
slain. In 1605 Akbar died of dysentery, and his bones were hastily interred.
India had been united, it was well organized and efficiently administered and
there was general contentment. Akbar's conscious policy of religious toleration,
the basis for his unification, was eminently successful, and promised a great

[4] V. A. Smith, *Akbar* (London, 1917), p. 436.

FIGURE 13.4. Bulawand Darwaza at Fathpur Sikri.

future for the Mogul empire. From his vision of a united India Akbar emerges as a noble figure, one of the most oustanding in world history.

If so much attention has been paid to the records of the Mogul emperors and their court, and little time has been devoted to the history of the Indian people themselves, this must find its excuse in the fact that in Indian history social conditions changed little from the times of Megasthenes, when compared with the history of those who had wealth, power and knowledge. The ruler and his character are of critical importance in the understanding of India during the Moslem period as a whole, and Indian history consequently must stress the accounts of king, court and conqueror, rather than concern itself with social and economic evolution.

BASIC DATES

1524	Babur invades Punjab
1526	Battle of Panipat
1530–1556	Humayun
1539–1545	Sher Shah
1556–1605	Akbar

1556	2nd battle of Panipat
1569	Conquest of Rajputana
1573	Conquest of Gujarat
1576	Conquest of Bengal
1582	Din Ilahi
1593–1601	Conquest in Deccan
1601–1604	Revolt of Prince Salim

SUPPLEMENTARY READING

DE BARY, W. T., ED. *Sources of Indian Tradition.* New York, 1958.

DUNBAR, G. *History of India.* London, 1943.

MORELAND, W. H. AND A. C. CHATTERJEE. *A Short History of India.* London, 1920.

RAWLINSON, H. G. *India: A Short Cultural History.* London, 1937.

SMITH, V. A. *The Oxford History of India,* 3rd ed. Oxford, 1958.

ADVANCED READING

EDWARDES, S. M. AND H. GARRETT. *Mughal Rule in India.* Oxford, 1930.

LANE-POOLE, S. *Babar.* Delhi, 1957. A fine biography, drawing heavily on Babur's memoirs.

MORELAND, W. H. *India at the Death of Akbar.* London, 1920. An excellent economic and social study.

RAPSON, E. J. *The Cambridge History of India, Vol. III.* New York, 1922.

SMITH, V. A. *Akbar, the Great Mogul.* Oxford, 1917.

XIV ❈

SOUTHEAST ASIA TO THE

THIRTEENTH CENTURY

THE MAIN FEATURE OF THE HISTORY OF SOUTHEAST ASIA during the period up to the thirteenth century was the coming and establishment of Hindu civilization in that area. The setting was one of great river valleys and archipelagoes near which pass some of the most ancient trading routes in the world. The peoples were diverse, mostly Malays, whose culture showed evidences of ancient contacts with civilizations of continental Asia. Here came influences from India which affected these countries politically and culturally and resulted in the establishment of kingdoms whose ideology was largely derived from Hinduism and Buddhism, civilizations which shared in the greatness of Indian culture. Regional kingdoms on the mainland and island principalities in Indonesia both adopted Indian religions and ways of life. By the thirteenth century, great states had been created which made the names of Singosari, Pagan and Angkor famous over wide areas. Into their domains by the end of this period came a few Moslems from the West, an indication of the very different cultural pattern of the centuries to come. But they were also to be greatly influenced by events connected with the coming of the Mongols.

Beginnings of History

TROPICAL SETTING AND WATER COMMUNICATIONS.   Southeast Asia has
many features quite different from the areas thus far studied. Land communications are relatively unimportant. Most of the peoples from ancient times have
journeyed from other regions of Southeast Asia or within Southeast Asia itself
by water routes. This area lies altogether within the tropics, and thus the climate
is one in which men did not have to struggle for a livelihood as they did in colder
areas, in particular contrast to the steppe areas and regions further north. The
warm humid countries of Southeast Asia may be divided into two groups. First,
there are the valleys whose rivers come down from the frontiers of Burma and
China, each of which constitutes an important region: the Irrawaddy together
with the Sittang and Salween in Burma; the Chao Phraya, sometimes known as
the Menam, in Siam (or Thailand); and the Mekong River, the great artery of
Indo-China. South of these a part of the continent closely related to the islands
is the Malay peninsula. Separate from the mainland regions are the great island
archipelagoes of Indonesia and, off to the northeast, the Philippines. They include some of the largest islands in the world and areas which are comparable
to the great nations of the earth in respect to extent of territory. For example,
the Indonesian islands have a land area about one quarter of that of the continental United States but extend over an area comparable to the whole of the
United States.

Another characteristic common to most of the lands of Southeast Asia
was their remoteness. Interior valleys on the mainland were relatively secluded
from the principal lines of communications and some island regions in the
archipelagoes were very far from the main travel routes, particularly in parts
of Indonesia and all of the Philippines.

This area may not appear to have the integrating influence of a great continental area with its land routes connecting the different parts. It must be
remembered, however, that from ancient times, rivers, seas and straits have
been easier to traverse than mountain ranges and deserts, and hence the peoples
of Southeast Asia who lived on the margins of the mainland countries, in the
peninsula of Malaya and in the islands to the southeast were in close contact
with each other and with peoples from other parts of Asia who ventured to
explore the water routes along the coasts.

EARLY RACES AND SOCIETIES.   The peoples who were in Southeast Asia at
the end of the Neolithic period, as noted in Chapter 2, were proto-Malays. These
peoples were followed by new arrivals coming in waves or slow stages of
migration, mostly entering through the narrow river valleys between China
and Burma enticed by the broader valleys further south, with some going on
from there to the coasts of the peninsula and the islands.

These people, who brought with them the use of metals, were of the same
general racial type as the proto-Malays, and even down to our own time these
Malays or Indonesians remain the basic element of the population of the Indo-

Chinese mainland. In Indonesia today there are some relatively pure Malays, such peoples as the Bataks in the interior of Sumatra and the Dyaks in Borneo. Other Malays along the coasts of Sumatra, in Java and as far east as Bali are more of a mixed type.

Mixtures followed from the fact that along with the Indonesians other peoples also migrated into the Indo-Chinese peninsula and beyond. The principal ethnic groups, who were basically Indonesian and who remain in these regions today, were the Malays of the Malay peninsula, the Chams on the east coast of the Indo-Chinese peninsula and the Khmers and the Mons in the valleys of present Burma and Thailand.

The newcomers, starting with the Malays or Indonesians, who can be traced back long before 500 B.C., brought with them weapons, tools and ornaments of bronze and iron and gradually settled the different regions. Their culture, now known as the Dongson culture, had already reached the Philippines some time between 500 and 200 B.C. and Borneo by about 250 B.C.

The Dongson culture is sometimes termed the "protohistoric" because the most ancient writing known in the area dates from this period. However, for the most part our knowledge of these peoples and their culture comes from archaeological remains rather than from any inscriptions or other written sources.

The coming of these people and their bronze-iron age culture marks what Professor Lauriston Sharp has called "a massive discontinuity with the past." Their religion was constituted of animism, worship of ancestors and the god of the soil, and included the worship of mountains in opposition to the sea, a sort of dualism. They brought a culture well advanced in such aspects as ideas of the state and caste structure. Their highly developed skill in navigation included some knowledge of astronomy, and their merchants are said to have traveled widely. These peoples employed an irrigated rice culture using draft animals, such as the ox and the buffalo. Southeast Asian arts and technology in protohistoric times included the manufacture of huge bronze kettle drums, one of the characteristic remains of Dongson culture. These peoples also left behind them stone monuments which probably had some connection with their religion.

An example of Dongson age changes may be noted as this culture reached the Philippines between 300 to 200 B.C. and continued on there until about the third century A.D. At this time the original inhabitants learned about rice culture and rice terraces, copper and bronze tools and ornaments, large dugout boats, houses with pyramidal roofs, and mining and smelting of metals. During Dongson times this bronze-iron age culture was confined to small communities along the coasts and rivers. It lacked any large political organizations.

All of the early peoples of Southeast Asia did not remain on the Indo-Chinese peninsula and in the archipelagoes off the coasts. Migrations which had already started in prehistoric times continued during this period until about A.D. 500, by which time Southeast Asia had come under the dominance of Indian culture. Peoples, such as the Polynesians, many of them still in a Neolithic stage of culture, passed through the islands and finally made their

way to the various island groups of the Pacific. Some of the long voyages into
Micronesia and Polynesia began only in the fourth century A.D. Hence, peoples
from the mainland and islands of Southeast Asia, perhaps fleeing from others
of a higher culture who entered where they had lived, moved on through Southeast Asia and into the Pacific.

Ancient Mainland Kingdoms

HINDU AND BUDDHIST STATES.   Into the various regions of Southeast Asia
with their ancient culture came migrants by sea from India. Transients and
settlers brought with them a distinctive culture, one which was to have a profound influence both on the mainland and in the islands of Southeast Asia.

These colonists from India started migrating perhaps in the fourth and
third centuries B.C., in any case before written records. Hence we can only
conjecture when and how they came. These Indians probably came slowly and
they may have arrived in separate migrations. The earliest dateable evidence of
their culture in the area is from between the first and third centuries A.D.

There is evidence of possible "waves of influence," starting with traders,
coming in the first centuries, next bringing Buddhism from north India between
the second and fifth centuries, later spreading Hindu influences from south India,
and concluding with Mahayana influences from south India in about the eighth
and ninth centuries. The earliest written information indicates the existence of
Hindu states on the mainland in Burma, Siam (modern Thailand), Cambodia
and Champa.

In Burma the Hindu colonies date from about the first century B.C. In
that region during the next few centuries coastal trading centers developed and
gradually became small commercial kingdoms. Prome at the mouth of the
Irrawaddy, Pegu in the central delta area, and Thaton near the Salween were
among the more important. In Burma, the earliest known inscriptions are
fragments of Buddhist scripture of about A.D. 500 in the writing of the south
Indian kingdom of Pallava. Thus Hindus brought with them writing as part of
their culture and later Buddhism arrived, especially the Theravada Buddhism
of south India.

In Siam, the Mon-Khmer peoples were influenced by Hindu civilization,
probably during the first centuries A.D. Inscriptions date Buddhist kingdoms
in the area to about 200. Inscriptions of the sixth to eighth centuries indicate
the existence of the kingdom of Dvaravati in the lower part of Chao Phraya
river valley, and of Haripunjaya further upstream. The southern kingdom of
Dvaravati was annexed by the Khmers from Cambodia in the eleventh century,
while the northern kingdom lasted until the Tai migrations from the north
in the thirteenth century.

For Cambodia there are also records of the ancient periods. From the
Chinese we learn of the state known to them as Funan, the first great power

in Southeast Asian history, which was founded about the first century A.D. and lasted until the middle of the sixth century. The people of Funan were a seafaring people and traded with the Chinese. Their religious practices included the worship of sacred mountains and cobras. By the time they were known to the Chinese, Indian Brahmanism was the prevailing faith although Buddhism had reached Cambodia by the third century. In the sixth century another Cambodian state, Chen-la, which originated in the region north of Funan, conquered the latter and dominated the area until the great period of Angkor. The Chen-la unified kingdom lasted until 802.

Further east, along the coasts of what is now central Vietnam, was the state of Champa, founded by Hindu colonists probably about the end of the second century. Midway between China and Malaya, Champa was very favorably located either for commerce or for profiting from commerce by piracy.

From Champa writings inscribed on stone in about A.D. 400 we know that the king was supported by a Shivaite tradition and that the Buddhists, whose religion had reached Champa in the second century, used an old Pallava alphabet for writing verses in Sanskrit. From the fifth to the seventh centuries border warfare between the Chams and the Chinese who controlled Tongking alternated with trade missions from Champa to the Chinese court. Champa was an important stopping place for travelers from the Abbasid caliphate to the T'ang empire and it also was an intermediate point for the spice trade coming from the Indies to China.

Chinese Borderlands

Definitely part of Southeast Asia but quite different in their history from the other regions of the mainland and the islands, which became predominantly Hindu, were the regions of northern Indo-China, and the Chinese southwest province of Yunnan (to use their modern names). Here were peoples who were from antiquity closely connected with China. Racially many of them were related to the modern Tai of Thailand (this spelling of Tai in "Thailand" has recently been officially adopted), and according to some records they may originally have come into what is now northern Vietnam (or Annam) from China. In any case, their history is closely related to that of China, although the peoples are separate and different from the Chinese.

In the Red river valley of Tongking and south along the coast bordering on Champa were the Vietnamese, who were subject to invasions from China. As soon as the Chinese under the First Emperor of the Ch'in had unified the whole country, at the end of the third century B.C. (see Chapter 16), they moved south into the area of Tongking. The conquest was temporary, since the Ch'in did not last, but the area was reconquered under the Han in the second century B.C. making Tongking henceforth an integral part of China. The Vietnamese ruling class adopted many features of Chinese civilization and for several centuries the country was part of a unified China or of the Chinese empire of the south. Yet it must be remembered that these were a people distinct from the Chinese with a language and culture of their own.

Inland in highland country difficult of access either from the lowlands of northern Vietnam or from other provinces of west or southwest China was Yunnan, in which a separate state known as Nan-chao existed for many centuries. This region was inhabited by many different tribes, some of whom were forced into the mountains by the expanding Chinese and among whom the Tai were especially important. Especially significant for the history of Southeast Asia was the fact that the people of Nan-chao were very early converted to Buddhism. Nan-chao remained a separate political entity unconquered by the Chinese and sometimes even staging invasions into China itself (as in the mid-ninth century) and was not incorporated into China until the time of the Mongols in the thirteenth century.

Island Peoples and States

INDONESIA BEFORE 700.   Part of the general movement of Indian people into Southeast Asia was the progress of Indian culture through the straits and into the islands further south — from the peninsula of Malaya, to the great island of Sumatra and beyond to Java. Not long after, their influence was felt in Borneo and the Philippines with the beginnings of Brahman settlements. The culture was Brahman in the sense that the prevailing influence was that of a Hindu priest class although it included also strong elements of Buddhism. During the first centuries A.D. the importance of Buddhism increased until in southern Sumatra the kingdom of Srivijaya emerged as a strong Buddhist state and became a great power in the area.

Indian settlers coming from south India and making their homes on the Malay peninsula and in the islands beyond came in sufficient numbers to be influential by about the first century A.D. While the migration of such settlers may have begun centuries before, it is only from the first or second century A.D. that the names of Srivijaya on the Palembang river in southern Sumatra and of Malayu somewhat to the northwest became known. There were also settlements in central Java and on the Malay peninsula.

By the fourth century people who used the south Indian Pallava script left records in Malaya indicating that Mahayana Buddhism was already influential on the peninsula, the region of transit to and from Indonesia. In addition, after 400 there is definite information concerning relations with China and mainland Southeast Asia. Traders had been going up and down the coasts for centuries, but now in the beginning of the fifth century Chinese interested in Indian Buddhism set out as pilgrims by sea to India. One of these, a monk named Fa Hsien, left an account which tells something of the area. Fa Hsien found very little Buddhism in Southeast Asia. He commented on the fact that Brahman cults were to be found on Java and Sumatra and that the worship of Shiva was predominant.

Supplementing Fa Hsien's writings, we know from other sources that Buddhism had reached Indonesia by the fifth century. According to tradition Buddhism first came to Sumatra in the year 424. Buddhist inscriptions of the fifth century also indicate the presence of that religion in the area. On the other hand, important rock inscriptions of the fifth century from west and central Java reveal the importance of Brahmanism and Hindu rites as well as the use of irrigation in agriculture.

By the fifth century Indian influences had also reached Borneo as shown by remaining Buddhist inscriptions as well as Hindu and Buddhist images in Gupta style. A Hindu Indonesian state was established in east Borneo.

To the Philippines after the third century A.D. went people who brought Indian influences from Malaya and Indonesia. Although there is no evidence of direct contact between India and the Philippines, some scattered finds in the southern and central Philippines such as coins, gold beads and other jewelry together with metal images indicate the Indian influences that came via Indonesia to the Philippines. One important indication of Indian culture in the Philippines was the use of a script similar to the Pallava script of south India. This script has actually continued in use into the twentieth century in some remote parts of the Philippines.

By the sixth and seventh centuries various island areas were also in direct contact with China. There is evidence of trade between the Philippines and China sometime after the fifth century.

One of the small states influenced by culture from India and which played an important part in Southeast Asia for centuries was Srivijaya with its capital at Palembang, in southern Sumatra. From the fifth to the seventh centuries Srivijaya, being in a strategic position on the Straits of Malacca, profited from the sea trade which passed from places as far as Arabia in the west and China in the east. Srivijaya established regular communications with both India and China. The rulers at Palembang profited as the ships passed through the islands either north to China or northwest towards India, Persia and Arabia. These contacts and this trade had probably existed for centuries before there were any precise historical records. The first definite information of men from Srivijaya going to China is an account of a trade mission in the year 670.

In the sixth and seventh centuries Srivijaya became the real successor to Funan as the predominating political and commercial power in Southeast Asia. Its supremacy extended over south Sumatra and the island of Banka near the east coast of Sumatra. The Sumatrans from Palembang also invaded west Java.

Meanwhile, starting in the fifth century (perhaps as early as 424), Buddhism of the north Indian Mahayana variety came into Sumatra. Mahayana Buddhism also was to be found at this time in Malaya and Cambodia. This spread of the Mahayana type of Buddhism reflects the influence of the Pala dynasty of Bengal (see Chapter 10).

Palembang became an important Buddhist center and as such served as a stopping-place for Chinese pilgrims going by sea to and from the holy land of Buddhism in the Ganges Valley. This was particularly true in the seventh century. At the end of that century the Chinese Buddhist pilgrim I-tsing noted that there were over a thousand Buddhist monks in Srivijaya.

This marks the beginning of an important kingdom in this area, with its prestige and wealth based partly on trade and partly on religious connections with both India and China. It is to be noted however that in the sixth and seventh centuries, despite the strong Indian connection, whether Buddhist or Brahman, among the upper classes, the mass of the population remained attached to the animistic cults and ancestor worship which had been typical of the general culture of the area before Indian influence.

JAVANESE CULTURAL GREATNESS TO 1100.   In continuing the history of the island peoples and states we should note that the history of Indonesia is not clearly known. The rise and fall of states is only vaguely understood from existing records and hence has been subject to controversy. Various versions of events have appeared in standard books. Here we shall simply point out a few key elements in the history of Java for the period from about 700 to 1100.

Javanese civilization was at this time already a harmonious blend between the earlier local culture and Indian influences. The language was Indonesian in essence but already full of Sanskrit words and phrases.

FIGURE 14.1.   Chandi Puntadeva, a Brahman temple from the earliest period of Hindu-Javanese art (eighth century).

The history of Java during this time falls naturally into two parts: the dominance of the Sailendra dynasty in the central Javanese state of Mataram, a period of great Buddhist monuments, and secondly, the post-Sailendra period in Mataram when Brahman influences were paramount. The state of Mataram may have been the leading state of central Java from as early as 570. Its special importance commenced in the early eighth century with the founding of a line of rulers by King Sanjaya (732 to about 760). The religion and the culture was Brahmanist. King Sanjaya himself was a patron of Shiva and Brahman temples associated with this period survive in central Java.

FIGURE 14.2. Borobudur from the northwest.

The rise of the great Sailendra dynasty in central Java is associated with the introduction of Mahayana Buddhism about 750, and possibly this meant the disestablishment of earlier Brahmanist interests. Under powerful kings who were patrons of Mahayana Buddhism with all its richness of legend and imagery, great temples were built, magnificent statues were carved during a period of Indonesian artistic creativeness. The Sailendra dynasty in Java dates from 760 to 860.

Among the more important surviving Buddhist temples erected in central Java under the Sailendra is the Chandi Mendut, whose small stone shrine includes a gigantic Buddha in the Gupta style flanked by Bodhisattvas seated on each side. The most famous of the monuments is the Borobudur, founded in 772, whose magnificent architecture rises on a hilltop in central Java in six square terraces and three circular platforms above these terraces. On each terrace in the galleries are bas-reliefs in some 1,300 panels, depicting the life of the Buddha and the *jataka* stories and constituting a gallery of some of the finest Indian-influenced works of art in the world. The bas-relief scenes, however, depict Javanese people in a Javanese setting in spite of the Indian origin of

FIGURE 14.3.   Relief from the main wall of the first gallery at Borobudur. The
top relief shows a scene from the life of the Buddha taken from a jataka. The
lower relief shows the arrival of a ship typical of those sailing between India
and Java.

the material. Above, under bell-shaped structures, are some four hundred
images of Buddha. The Buddhist sculpture at Mendut and Borobudur is believed
to combine both Mahayana Buddhism and ancestor worship, by equating in its
symbolism the royal ancestors with Bodhisattvas.

During the Sailendra period in Java there was also, as would be expected,
an interest in Indian literature, and translations were made from Sanskrit into
the old Javanese language. It was a time not only of cultural expansion but also
of growing political influence along the east coast of Malaya and possibly even
into Cambodia.

In Java, by the beginning of the tenth century the Brahmanist rulers of
Mataram were re-established and constructed the beautiful Brahman temples
at Prambanan not far from where Borobudur had been erected over a hundred
years before. Among the buildings, which date from about 910–919, the largest
is dedicated to Shiva, and the less important include temples to Vishnu and
Brahma, decorated with lively sculpture in bas-relief. Hindu Brahmanism continued in central Java where Buddhism was not to flourish again until the
thirteenth century. In this religion ceremonies seem to have been performed according to Indonesian rites by invoking these Indian deities, since animistic
beliefs continued and Shivaism acquired elements of the worship of a native
fertility goddess. In time Indonesian civilization became more Indonesian in
character than Hindu.

FIGURE 14.4.   Relief from the temple of Shiva at Pramabanan, tenth century. The subject matter is taken from the *Ramayana*. A demon having taken the form of a deer is killed by an arrow shot by Rama.

Shortly after the building of the Prambanan temples the capital of Mataram was moved to east Java and the old capital was mostly abandoned. In east Java, Mataram power increased and cultural development continued. Some of the great Hindu-Javanese literature was created in east Java in the tenth century. Here was composed the Javanese *Ramayana* and works such as a treatise on Tantric Buddhism. The use of the Hindu epics in Javanese literature has been particularly important for the drama which has continued as a body of national tradition to the present.

From east Java, Mataram religious and cultural influence extended to other parts of Indonesia and rivalled the authority of Srivijaya in the west. For example, on Bali in about 989–1007 the daughter of a Mataram prince married a prince of Bali and brought with her Hindu and Tantric Buddhist influences that became a part of Balinese culture.

Toward the end of the tenth century a war broke out between the east Javanese of Mataram and Srivijaya (990–1007) resulting in the defeat of the Javanese and the destruction of their capital. Srivijaya became master of the seas near Java and Sumatra, including the important Sunda Straits, and the power of Mataram diminished after this time.

Internal development and cultural greatness continued however in east Java, especially during the reign of King Airlangga (1019–1049). This cultural development included the codification of Javanese law and the translation of Sanskrit texts, such as the *Mahabharata*, into Javanese prose about the year 1000. Great literary and dramatic writings also were produced in Airlangga's time. Most famous is the tale of Arjuna, developed from the story in the

Mahabharata, which has become a popular theme in the Javanese *wayang,* or shadow theatre.

SRIVIJAYA: 800–1200.   Srivijaya greatness extended from the ninth century to the eleventh, when under the Sailendra dynasty the kingdom became a commercial and colonial empire based at Palembang in south Sumatra. Trade monopoly, control of the straits, settlements throughout Indonesia and colonies to the north sustained its power. Later Srivijaya supremacy was challenged and its culture changed. The trade monopoly was attacked first from Chola in south India and then from a new strong state in Java. Finally Moslems coming in greater numbers and making converts in the area began a new period in Sumatran and Indonesian history.

The Sailendra dynasty, previously the ruling line on Java, became also the dominant element at Palembang on Sumatra in the ninth century when a Sailendra prince married a Srivijaya princess in Sumatra, and later became the ruler of Srivijaya. For a short time there were two branches of the Sailendra family ruling simultaneously over two separate independent kingdoms, in central Java and in southern Sumatra. The Sailendra became the controlling influence in Sumatra at the very time that their rule was ending in Java.

The Sailendra on Sumatra became a great economic power through commercial monopoly at the beginning of the period when spices became important in international trade. Sailendra authority was extended by gaining control over Malayu in east Sumatra, Johore, ports on the Sunda Straits, and over parts of Java. A Srivijaya prince even went to Cambodia where he became ruler and extended Hindu-Indonesian influence in that direction. The Sailendra of Srivijaya established colonies on other islands as far away as the Moluccas and the southern Philippines. Commercial settlements were established in Borneo and the Sulu archipelago, where Brahman and Buddhist colonies had probably existed since the eighth or ninth centuries. In the southern Philippines and Borneo traders from Srivijaya were in contact with Chinese merchants, and the remains of ceramics, brass and metal ware of the T'ang and Sung periods in such areas as Borneo give evidence of the Chinese contacts.

Srivijaya commercial settlements spread even northward to Hainan on the southern coast of China and the island of Formosa (Taiwan). Although the height of Srivijaya's political importance was reached early in the eleventh century, many of these colonies and outposts of Sumatran influence doubtless continued even after the political prestige of Palembang had ceased to be important.

During the time of Sailendra predominance in Indonesia a new element was attracted by the commercial possibilities of the area. Following a tradition of commerce that had brought Arab and Persian traders to these countries long before, Moslem traders of the Abbasid caliphate and from India were active in Indonesia from the eighth century onwards. By the middle of the tenth century a small Arab state was established in the northern part of Sumatra. Such activity had little effect on the predominantly Buddhist-Hindu culture of the great commercial power of Srivijaya, but it became very important after the twelfth century.

By the end of the tenth century the rulers of Srivijaya were forced to meet the attacks of competitors for their trade monopoly. We have noted that the war between Mataram and Srivijaya of 990–1007 ended in the destruction of the Javanese capital and an assertion of Sumatran supremacy over Java and the neighboring seas. At that time Srivijaya's success was partly due to friendly relations with other great Asian powers, including the Sung in China and the rulers of south India.

The turning point came through rivalry and naval competition from a new great state in southern India, the empire of Chola. Ships from Chola first began to raid eastward in areas of Srivijaya influence about 1007. Then in a great maritime expedition the forces of Rajendra Choladeva I invaded the heart of the Srivijaya empire in 1025, attacking Palembang and invading the Malay peninsula, the northern parts of Sumatra and the Nicobar islands.

After the great raid from Chola in 1025, Srivijaya power was re-established over Sumatra. Even though the Sumatrans never fully regained their widespread political control, their state remained a great power into the thirteenth century. As long as Srivijaya could dominate the Straits of Malacca and Sunda they had an opportunity to tax the commerce of all of Southeast Asia and the Far East.

Srivijaya suffered from rivalry in other directions, such as the Tai advances down the Malay peninsula. Finally, in the thirteenth century, the Javanese under Kertanagara, established a new power at Singosari and disputed the control of both straits, heralding the beginning of the end of Srivijaya.

Later Hinduized Kingdoms of "Further India"

EAST JAVA: SINGOSARI. During the period of the decline of Srivijaya other powers, chiefly Singosari, became important in the regions of the Malay peninsula and the islands of Indonesia.

In east Java, under a successor of Airlangga, the state Kadiri became a literary center and commercial power in the twelfth century. From their capital at Kadiri the east Javanese controlled the eastern archipelago, including the Spice islands (the Moluccas). Hindu culture was dominant in that area, a politico-religious cult of Vishnu being especially popular.

In a revolution against the ruler of Kadiri in 1222, a new regime was set up with its capital in another town, Singosari, from which the kingdom took its name. During the next seventy years this state became one of the great kingdoms of Southeast Asia. The official faith of Singosari was a synthetic religion combining both Shivaism and Buddhism.

In the latter part of the century Singosari produced a great warrior king, Kertanagara (1268–1292), who established his sovereignty over most of Java and then proceeded to conquer some of the dominions that had formerly been subject to Srivijaya, and generally gained the leadership in the Indies. The suzerainty of Kertanagara was recognized on Sumatra, as well as in other islands, including southeast Borneo and the Moluccas, and also in Pahang in eastern Malaya. The power of this Hindu state lasted until the Mongol invasion (see Chapter 22).

PAGAN.   Another kingdom which endured until the Mongol conquests in Asia was established in Burma in the eleventh century. A leader named Anawrata seized power in 1044 and organized a kingdom which lasted until 1287 in central Burma at Pagan. His success was dependent partly upon his development of an irrigation system for rice production. With better supplies he was able to maintain a strong army and thus to expand his territory, particularly at the expense of Thaton, a small principality near the Salween river. The move against Thaton was made on the pretext of obtaining Buddhist scriptures, since Anawrata was much interested in the encouragement and support of Theravada (Hinayana) Buddhism. He also conquered Pegu, another Theravada state in southern Burma. Anawrata also led his forces to the north, where he conquered the coastal region of Arakan, and invaded the Buddhist kingdom of Nan-chao in southwest China.

After Anawrata there were ten successors to the throne of Pagan. Because of their interest in Theravada Buddhism and the buildings they erected they have been known as the "Dynasty of the Temple Builders." Pagan became the religious, literary and political center of Burma. Through their interest in Theravada Buddhism the people of Pagan entered into cordial relations with Ceylon; hence many influences of art and architecture came to Burma from Ceylon. The state of Pagan was also in contact with Sung China and a mission is known to have gone to the Sung court in 1106. By the thirteenth century weak monarchs reigned at Pagan and the state declined in power. The end of the great period of Pagan came with the invasions of Mongol forces from China (see Chapter 22).

THE KHMER KINGDOMS.   One of the greatest kingdoms of Southeast Asian history arose in Cambodia. We have noted that the kingdom known to the Chinese as Chen-la superseded Funan in Cambodia in the sixth century. In this kingdom the ruling line were of Khmer stock; their power lasted until 802. Among the Khmers of Chen-la Buddhism was prominent but Shivaism entered and gradually became the state religion. Following the Chen-la period there was a time of Sailendra influence from Indonesia. This was succeeded by one of the great periods in the history of the Indo-Chinese peninsula.

At the beginning of the ninth century a prince from Srivijaya known as Jayavarman II united Cambodia and began the great Khmer empire, which flourished from the ninth to the twelfth century. The capital of the Khmer kingdom was at Angkor, founded at the end of the ninth century. The civilization of the Khmers is known chiefly from Angkor, its architecture, its sculpture and its inscriptions. These buildings are Cambodian in style and Indian in

FIGURE 14.5.   Head of the Buddha with halo of Naga (sacred king cobra) heads, eleventh century. Khmer art from Cambodia.

spirit, a unique flowering of the culture which had come from southern India. To one who has seen the Pallava stone buildings at Mamallapuram near Madras in south India there is something familiar about the form of the buildings at Angkor.

The Khmer capital and temples were planned to accord with the cosmological ideas of the Cambodians as affected by influences from India. A cosmic pattern, a model of the world of Brahmanism and Mahayana Buddhism, was integrated in the forms and design of the capital city. Angkor, with its fine temples on mounds, embodied ideas also of a divine kingship, expressed in magical religious symbolism. The cult of the god-king was bound up with the worship of Shiva and other gods, and the belief that a deceased king might become afterwards Shiva or Vishnu or Buddha. These religious ideas were the beliefs of the court and the aristocracy at Angkor. Popular faith did not inspire the erection of these tremendous monuments.

The Khmers expanded their Cambodian empire to include part of the territories of their neighbors. Wars were directed against Champa, and in the eleventh century they moved against the Mon kingdom of Dvaravati in southern Siam and conquered that section of modern Thailand.

The Khmer king, Suryavarman II (1113–1150) seized a part of Champa and campaigned as far north as Tongking in the Red river valley of Indo-China. During the twelfth century the Khmers gradually gained control of all of modern Thailand.

Suryavarman II is remembered particularly because the greatest of all Khmer temples, the Angkor Vat, was commenced during his reign, in about

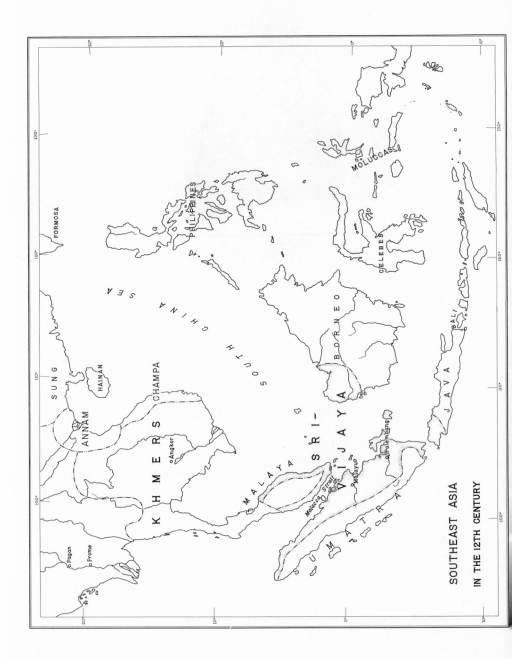

SOUTHEAST ASIA

IN THE 12TH CENTURY

1115. This temple is a funerary temple in Suryavarman's honor; the deity who was worshipped there after his death was the Khmer king identified with Vishnu. The Angkor Vat is one of the most magnificent buildings in the world, with a great rectangular enclosure within which arises a pyramid with terraces of cloisters, arcades and towers. On the walls of the arcades and on every door frame to the topmost shrine is beautiful bas-relief carving.

Due to the greatness of Angkor and the extent of its power over a large part of Indo-China (see map opposite), the Khmers were confronted with the hostility of their neighbors, some of whom they had formerly subdued. Angkor was attacked and devastated by the Chams in 1177.

FIGURE 14.6.   Side view of the temple complex of Angkor Vat, twelfth century. A great pyramid rises in the center of a rectangular enclosure.

Decline was followed by a continuation of Angkor greatness and the creation of a new capital, Angkor Thom, which has survived to this day, in the form of a great square surrounded by walls and moats, the moats themselves being crossed by balustrades of massive cobras upheld by giants. Over the gateways are the four faces of an Indian deity, identified with the god-king, in this case the builder, Jayavarman VII. The symmetrical pattern and the cosmological principles were borne out in the terraces and lofty temples at the center of the royal city. Angkor Thom was created in its present form during the last years of the twelfth century.

The Khmers expanded again in the early thirteenth century and gained complete control over Champa. But in the thirteenth century a new people, the

Tai, in Siam gradually conquered much of the territory previously held by the Khmers. The Tai invasion stimulated by the great Mongol advance discussed in Chapter 22, together with a revolt of the Chams in the fourteenth century brought the end of Khmer power.

In thirteenth-century Southeast Asia, there were then three major kingdoms, Singosari, Pagan and that of the Khmers. All of these offered a unique combination of older, indigenous culture going back to the Dongson period and beyond combined with strong elements of Hinduism and Buddhism. All of these were also more or less affected by the coming of the Mongols. The greatness of this early period may be seen in the culture which has survived the coming of other influences in those countries, such as the shadow plays of Java, the dances at the courts of the kings of Cambodia and Thailand, the music, the art designs, the architectural motifs, as well as literary and moral traditions. These strong traditions persisted even after the entry of new peoples and new ideas.

BASIC DATES

Before 500 B.C.	Beginning of Dongson culture
4th or 3rd century B.C.	Start of migrations from India
C. 1st century B.C.	Hindu colonies in Burma
1st or 2nd century A.D.	Founding of Srivijaya and Malayu on Sumatra
C. 1st to 6th century	Funan in Cambodia
C. 192	Founding of Champa
C. 200	Buddhist kingdoms in Siam
411	Fa Hsien visits Sumatra
424	Buddhism to Sumatra
C. 500	Buddhism in Burma
6th century to 802	Chen-la in Cambodia
About 570	Beginning of importance of Mataram on Java
732 to about 760	King Sanjaya of Mataram
760 to 860	Sailendra Dynasty in Java
772	Founding of Borobudur
8th century	Moslem traders to Indonesia
C. 802 to 850	King Jayavarman II, founder of Khmer Empire
C. 802 to 1431	Angkor Monarchy
990 to 1007	War between Mataram and Srivijaya
1019 to 1049	King Airlangga in East Java
1025	Chola invasion of Srivijaya
1044 to 1077	King Anawrata of Pagan
1044 to 1287	Empire of Pagan
1113 to 1150	King Suryavarman II at Angkor
1117 to 1222	Kadiri in East Java
1222 to 1292	Singosari in East Java
1268 to 1292	King Kertanagara

SUPPLEMENTARY READING

CADY, J. *Southeast Asia: Its Historical Development,* New York, 1963.

GRAHAM, W. A. *Siam,* 2 vols. London, 1924. Comprehensive description of Thailand, including the history.

GROUSSET, R. *The Civilizations of the East, Vol. II: India.* London, 1931. Includes material on Southeast Asia.

———————— *In the Footsteps of the Buddha.* London, 1932. Discusses Chinese Buddhists who visited South and Southeast Asia.

HARRISON. B. *South-east Asia: A Short History,* 2nd ed. London, 1963. Concise, readable outline. The only work of its kind in English.

KEESING, F. M. *The Philippines: A Nation in the Making.* Shanghai, 1937. Introductory historical survey.

VLEKKE, B. H. M. *Nusantara: A History of the East Indian Archipelago.* Cambridge, Mass., 1943. History of Indonesia to 1941 by a Dutch authority includes brief coverage of this early period.

————————*The Story of the Dutch East Indies.* Cambridge, Mass., 1946. An abbreviated version of *Nusantara.*

WALKER, G. B. *Angkor Empire.* Calcutta, 1955. Generally accurate account of Khmer empire and monuments.

WOOD, W. A. R. *History of Siam, from the Earliest Times to the Year 1781,* 2nd ed., rev. Bangkok, 1933. A standard work. Contains a supplement dealing with more recent events.

ADVANCED READING

BRIGGS, L. P. *The Ancient Khmer Empire.* Philadelphia, 1951. Scholarly history of rulers, religion, and architecture.

COEDES, G. *États Hindouisés d'Indochine et d'Indonésie.* Paris, 1948. Comprehensive history of early Southeast Asia.

COOMARASWAMY, A. K. *History of Indian and Indonesian Art.* London, 1927. Basic for understanding Indian influences.

DE KLERCK, E. S. *History of the Netherlands East Indies,* Vol. I. Rotterdam, 1938. Comprehensive and detailed.

HALL, D. G. E. *Burma.* London, 1950. Standard work by an expert.

———————— *A History of Southeast Asia,* New York, 1955.

HARVEY, G. E. *History of Burma.* London, 1925. Standard and comprehensive.

KROM, N. J. *Barabudur, Archaeological Description.* The Hague, 1927. Deals with the great Buddhist monument in central Java.

LE MAY, R. S. *The Culture of South-East Asia: The Heritage of India.* London, 1954. Concerned mainly with architecture and sculpture.

LOEB, E. M. "Sumatra: Its History and People," *Wiener Beiträge zur Kulturgeschichte und Linguistik, III.* Vienna, 1935. Scholarly study by an American ethnologist.

MAJUMDAR, R. C. *Ancient Indian Colonies in the Far East, Vol. I: Champa.* Lahore, 1927; *Vol. II: Scvarnadvipa.* Dacca, 1937–38.

MOOKERJI, R. *A History of Indian Shipping and Maritime Activity from the Earliest Times.* Bombay, 1912.

SCHELTEMA, J. F. *Monumental Java.* London, 1912. Concerning Shivaite and Buddhist art; illustrated.

TWEEDIE, M. W. F. "The Bronze and Iron Ages in Malaya," in *Prehistoric Malaya,* pp. 27–43. Singapore, 1955.

WALES, H. G. Q. *The Making of Greater India: A Study in Southeast Asian Culture Change.* London, 1957. Concerned with early Indian artistic and religious influences.

WHEATLEY, P. *The Golden Khersonese: Studies in the Historical Geography of the Malay Peninsula before A.D. 1500.* Kuala Lumpur, 1961. Malaya as known to the earliest historians of East and West.

XV

NEW FORCES IN

SOUTHEAST ASIA, 1200-1600

A Buddhist-Hindu World

The central fact concerning Southeast Asia, mainland, peninsula and islands, in the thirteenth century was the influence of Hinduism-Buddhism to the extent that states, commerce and organized religious bodies had affiliations with India and Ceylon. During the fourteenth to sixteenth centuries, however, new influences entered this area. Among them were peoples from the West who brought two great religions which had originated in the Middle East-Mediterranean area and which were completely new to the peoples of Southeast Asia, with their strongly indianized cultures.

The mainland countries constituted of Buddhist-Hindu states in the great river valleys, attracted migrants (already Buddhist) from the mountainous area of southwest China. The result of this influx into Siam and Burma was the establishment of the Tai, Shan and Burmese kingdoms. To the south, in Malaya and Indonesia, the last great Hindu empire, Madjapahit, gave way to Islamic expansion, the second of the great outside influences of the period.

To both areas, mainland kingdoms and island principalities, came for the first time numbers of Europeans, primarily Portuguese, who brought with them Christianity and who through their seapower established Portuguese control over parts of Indonesia. Shortly afterwards, also during the sixteenth century, came the Spanish from across the Pacific to extend their rule into the Philippines and increase European influences into Southeast Asia and the Far East.

BUDDHIST AND HINDU KINGDOMS.   In the twelfth century the main cultural influence in Southeast Asia was Buddhism. In Java, Singosari was a center of Buddhist influence under the great king, Kertanagara. In Siam, two Buddhist kingdoms divided the Chao Phraya valley, Haripunjaya in the north and Dvaravati, more or less subordinate to Khmer authority, in the south. To the west in Burma the great temple-building dynasty of Pagan gave evidence of the importance of Theravada (Hinayana) Buddhism and connections with Ceylon. Among the Khmers of Cambodia and beyond them in coastal Champa were states where Brahmanism prevailed and Buddhism played a minor role. The new force which came into this area was the influx of peoples from the north. Nan-chao, the source of many of these migrations, was also Buddhist. These migrants continued to maintain the prevailing faith of Southeast Asia.

Mainland Migrants and New States

TAI MIGRATIONS AND KINGDOMS.   As prehistoric men had done in earlier ages and like the carriers of the Dongson culture centuries ago, peoples seeking more living space migrated from the highlands between Tibet, Burma and China, down through rugged country of giant ridges and deep streams in the borders between Burma, Laos and Siam, into river valleys where they settled among the earlier inhabitants. The infiltration seems to have been mostly a peaceful one until the chiefs among the migrating tribesmen began to overthrow local governments and establish regimes of their own. Then they entered history as contenders for power in the mainland regions of Southeast Asia and in Assam.

NAN-CHAO.   One of the chief sources of such migration in the thirteenth century was the Buddhist kingdom of Nan-chao on the Chinese borderlands. For several centuries tribesmen, unconnected with any official policy of invasion and migrating on their own, had moved gradually from the mountainous country of Nan-chao and the surrounding regions toward the south and southwest into Siam and Burma. After Nan-chao's annexation in 1253 by the Mongols this process of emigration was greatly accelerated.

Migrants coming into Siam called themselves Tai ("the free people"). They were similar racially to others known as the Shan, who moved westward into Burma in about the same period.

When the great Khmer empire was no longer at the height of its power leaders among the Tai in the center of the Chao Phraya basin seized the town of Sukotai which had formerly been part of the old Haripunjaya. This was in 1238. By 1256, the Tai ruler of this region took the title "King of Sukotai." [1]

The warrior king who established the kingdom of Sukotai is known as Rama the Brave, or Rama Khamheng (1283–c.1317). He seized the Sukotai region from the Khmers and also expanded to the south in the Chao Phraya basin and the Malay peninsula, taking land inhabited chiefly by Mons, thereby acquiring the old Dvaravati territory. This enlarged kingdom, not as large as the present Siam, or Thailand, was however a new entity, a new strong state in a region where no power had competed successfully with the Khmers for two hundred years. Siam became a prosperous state, where the influences of Buddhist and north Indian art which the Tai had brought with them from Nan-chao combined with Cambodian influences of the Khmer period to form a distinct Tai culture, some of the aspects of which will be noted further on. Rama the Brave adopted the writing of his subjects; the script used by the Mons and the Khmers became the official language of the Tai in 1283. Rama also realized the importance of maintaining relations with strong powers. He entered into cordial relations with the Chinese, who at that time were ruled by the Mongol (Yuan) dynasty. By sending emissaries to Yuan China, Rama was able to import artisans who began the production of Chinese ceramics in Siam.

Meanwhile north of Sukotai, another purely Tai state was established about 1260 in what had been the northern part of old Haripunjaya. During the last decade of the thirteenth century a new city, Chieng-mai, was founded, and the state took its name from the capital city. The Tai of Chieng-mai, like the others who had come into Siam, were pious Buddhists and thus continued the traditions of Nan-chao and of the older kingdoms of Siam.

AYUTHIA AFTER 1350.   From northern Siam in the beginning of the fourteenth century Tai invaders came south of Sukotai to occupy the site of ancient Lopburi, an important Khmer cultural center in the days of Angkor greatness. South of Lopburi they established a new capital, Ayuthia, under a king (*phra*), called Ramathibodi (or Ramadhipati). His reign (1350–1369) inaugurated the great period of Ayuthia. King Ramathibodi was especially renowned for his legal system and his organization of government which continued down to the nineteenth century and is a partial basis for the royal Thai government of today.

King Ramathibodi had to deal with other principalities competing for power in Siam. He gained control of Sukotai, and shortly after his death his successor added Chieng-mai in the north to the regions controlled by Ayuthia. Thus, starting in the fourteenth century and continuing to the eighteenth, there was one royal government of a united Siamese kingdom.

[1] The state of Sukotai also was called Sien (or Syam), a name used by the Khmers and the Chinese and hence not favored by the modern Tai, who have preferred to revive the use of their own word for themselves in designating their country as "Thailand" instead of Siam. The word Siam is used in this book, however, since it was for centuries the name most commonly used for that country.

FIGURE 15.1.   Bronze head of the Buddha, Ayuthia, sixteenth century.

From the reign of Ramathibodi attacks were made on Cambodia which continued into the fifteenth century. In 1431 the Tai captured Angkor in a great raid which brought them loot and many prisoners, although they did not at that time establish political control over that part of Cambodia. This disaster, however, marked the end of Angkor's importance. The royal city, Angkor Thom, was evacuated in 1432, and the petty kings of Cambodia fled south to establish themselves in 1434 in a new capital at Phnom-Penh, which is still the capital of Cambodia.

In the fifteenth century Siamese forces also invaded the Malay peninsula to attempt to establish hegemony in that region. The Moslem Malays at Malacca, who were extending their influence to the north, faced the expanding power of Siam and were compelled to pay tribute to the Siamese. The Moslem traders at Malacca, in close touch with the Chinese, appealed to one of the first emperors of the Ming dynasty (Yung-lo) in 1414, to come to their aid. This was one of the reasons why the Chinese in subsequent years sent armed ships to enforce their authority along the trade routes of Southeast Asia. By such intervention they preserved the independence of Malacca in the face of Siamese pressure (see Chapter 23).

War with one's neighbors seems to have been the normal condition among the states of Southeast Asia during these centuries. In the sixteenth century marauding bands from Siam crossed into Burma and began hostilities which

FIGURE 15.2. Walking Buddha from Ayuthia.

were to be disastrous for the kingdom of Ayuthia. The Burmese were at this time consolidated under the Toungoo dynasty and they made two extended invasions into Siam during the second of which they sacked the capital, Ayuthia. They retained control of Siam for fifteen years (1569–1584).

By the end of the sixteenth century a strong king, Phra Naret, ruled Siam. Founding a strong monarchy at Ayuthia, he checked Burmese forces in Siam and personally led Siamese armies in two invasions of Burma. The strong line of rulers established by Naret continued for a hundred and seventy-five years.

The founder of the Sukotai kingdom began a great period of cultural development in Siam, characterized by Buddhist influences derived from India as well as the older traditions of the Mons and Khmers of Angkor culture. The Tai upon entering Siam assimilated many aspects of Cambodian culture, including political organization, writing and the art forms. From the Mons and Khmers, and indirectly from India, the Tai drew their system of law and their judicial tradition.

The most important element in Siamese culture during the Ayuthia period, however, was Theravada Buddhism, with its direct contact with the great Buddhist centers in Ceylon. Pali became the sacred language of Siam and the Siamese Buddhist church a part of the Buddhist church of Ceylon. Although the great Buddhist sculpture of the Ayuthia period shows its inheritance from the fine stone carving of the Khmers, the religious influences of the past were completely superseded. Theravada Buddhism became the official and dominant religion throughout Siam and spread also to Cambodia, where it replaced the older Hinduism and Mahayana Buddhist influences of Angkor times.

BURMA, 1200-1486.   In order to understand the events of the sixteenth century and Siam's relations with her neighbor to the west, we must turn to the history of Burma. In Burma from the greatness of Pagan in the twelfth century to the reunification of Burma under the Toungoo dynasty at the end of the fifteenth there were long centuries of division when the country was absorbing new peoples from the interior of Asia and a new vital form of Buddhism from Ceylon. During this period of contention various groups fought within Burma, while outside intervention also contributed to changed political conditions.

At Pagan in the late twelfth and early thirteenth century one of the successors of Anawrata enjoyed a long reign marked by internal peace, irrigation work and the introduction of Buddhism from Ceylon. Many Burmese monks went to Ceylon for long periods of study and for ordination, and fine temples were constructed. Most significant for the future of the country was the beginning of popular Buddhism, a religion extending to more than the court and the aristocracy. In the thirteenth century monastic life was an important element in Burmese society, and more splendid temples were erected, in spite of the fact that the dynasty of Pagan was reaching its end. A weak king ruled from 1254 to 1287, when international relations suddenly became of crucial importance. This was the time of the Mongol conquest and consolidation of power in China, the end of Nan-chao independence, and the arrival of envoys from the court of Kublai Khan who demanded tribute from the ruler of Pagan. The Burmese king refused to receive the envoys in 1271 and had two representatives of Kublai executed in 1273. From that time until 1287 there was intermittent warfare and raids between Pagan and Yuan China. The Mongols, operating from Yunnan province, gradually extended their control over north and central Burma and organized them as Chinese provinces. Pagan was occupied for a number of years but the advance of the Shan peoples prevented the establishment of a stable Mongol administration in northern Burma. The king of Pagan did, however, acknowledge the Mongols as overlords.

During the thirteenth century, Shan tribesmen moved into northern or upper Burma in much the same way that their relatives, the Tai, were coming into Siam. From the northeastern frontiers they invaded the region of Pagan gaining control of a vital irrigated section. They also seized and killed the king who was a Mongol puppet (1299).

The Shan people entered Burma in small groups under various chieftains. Some of these chieftains divided and dominated much of the territory of north Burma, and became strong enough to beat off the Mongols in their last attempt to reassert authority over Burma (1300). The country fell into a state of chaos. The kingdom of Pagan was at an end, and anarchy prevailed in large parts of the country.

While more Shan were still entering the country, those Shan chieftains already ruling in Burma began to attack each other. This was the beginning of some 250 years of contention in Burma, during which diverse peoples were involved in the highly complicated political situation. Together with Burmese, there were the older Mon people who had been there since ancient times, especially in southern Burma. Arakanese on the coast of the Bay of Bengal formed a separate entity. To these must be added various tribes of Shan who had recently come into the fertile regions. Finally, the situation was further complicated during this long period by the fact that both the Tai of Ayuthia in Siam and the Tai of Laos became involved in the political affairs of Burma.

In considering the events of these centuries of rivalries and confusion, we shall limit our discussions to the main elements involved. Three centers were particularly important: the government established at Ava, not far from present Mandalay in north-central Burma; Pegu, further south near the coast; and Toungoo, in between the first two. In addition, the Ming Chinese, after the establishment of that dynasty in 1368 and its assertion of authority over southwest China, also intervened in Burma.

Let us first note the situation in Ava. This kingdom or principality was founded in 1364 or 1365 and was Burmese in its culture. Ava was not a Shan state, as has sometimes been asserted. An important ruler of Ava, King Mingyi Swasawke (1368–1401) stressed his descent from the Pagan dynasty. He found the hostile and disruptive Shan in north Burma one of the chief difficulties in maintaining his power. In this struggle the king sought aid from the Ming viceroy of Yunnan in 1383. King Mingyi Swasawke also desired ports to the south and hence moved against the Mon kingdom of Pegu, near the coast. The king of Ava took the old town of Prome but failed to capture Pegu.

During the fifteenth century the Ava kings had to sustain attacks from the Shan and at the same time they were faced with internal revolts and disorder. The end came when the kingdom was invaded and the capital looted by Shan from north Burma in 1527.

Pegu, the Mon kingdom in southern Burma, was founded originally with its capital from 1281 to 1363 at Martaban on the coast. Throughout its history the kingdom was dependent very largely on trade; control of coastal ports was important. During the latter half of the fourteenth century the Tai attacked Martaban and partly because of this the Mon rulers moved their capital to the town of Pegu, in the delta region. This town was the capital from 1369 to 1539. Among its rulers one man particularly stands out—King Razadarit, who ruled from 1385 to 1423. He withstood attacks from the Siamese in one direction and from Ava in the other, was an able administrator and helped establish Pegu as a kingdom which endured for some 150 years. The fifteenth and early sixteenth centuries were a period of peace and prosperity for Pegu. Controlling most of southern Burma and particularly the ports, the kingdom of Pegu profited from the growing commerce of the time.

Religion was a strong force. The famous Shwe Dagon pagoda at Rangoon, begun much earlier, was raised during the fifteenth century to a height of 302 feet, and the buildings nearby enlarged so that the whole assumed much the same shape that it has today as one of the most famous architectural landmarks of Burma. The interest in religion led people from Pegu to go to Ceylon, the center of Theravada Buddhism. This time, especially the last decades of the fifteenth century, was a period of religious revival and of reform within Buddhism. European visitors came to Pegu and wrote of the splendor of the king and the capital in the fifteenth and sixteenth centuries. When the Portuguese first reached Southeast Asia they established a trading agency at Martaban, in 1519. Pegu's fall came with the rise and conquests of the third important center in Burma, Toungoo.

TOUNGOO AND THE UNIFICATION OF BURMA.   Toungoo is on the Sittang river between the Salween and Irrawaddy rivers in south-central Burma. Only a fortified village existed there at first, a refuge to which Burmese fled from the disorders connected with the influx of Shan tribesmen further north. By the middle of the fourteenth century the chief of the Burmese at Toungoo took the title of king, and founded a dynasty (1347–1752). The state did not enjoy a peaceful existence however, inasmuch as both Ava in the north and Pegu in the south attempted to control the region and end the independence of the new little kingdom.

Toungoo kept its independence during the disturbed years previously described. Three famous kings were able to strengthen and unify Burma. In 1487, an able ruler, King Minkyinyo, took advantage of the chaos in Burma and enlarged the territory of his kingdom. He seized the irrigated region of central Burma just south of Mandalay and was then in a position to offer refuge to other Burmese who fled from the disturbances further north. Burmese chiefs who had left Ava congregated at Toungoo, so that by 1527 Toungoo became the most important political center in the country. During the reign of Minkyinyo, preparations were made at Toungoo for an attack on Pegu further south.

Minkyinyo's successor, Tabin Shweti (1531–1550), conquered most of Burma during his reign. Tabin Shweti imposed Toungoo rule on the Irrawaddy delta, put an end to the independent state of Pegu, and also gained control of the Tenasserim coast of southernmost Burma. To the north he moved against old Pagan and gained control of that area. But Ava and upper Burma still retained its independence during his reign.

The third of these three famous rulers, Bayinnaung, was the brother-in-law of Tabin Shweti and had aided the latter in his campaigns and attempts to establish control. Bayinnaung found it necessary to re-establish by force the rule of Toungoo over all the regions conquered by his brother-in-law. Then in 1554–1555 he attacked Ava ending that kingdom's independence. The following year he began to campaign against the Shan states to the east, and in 1557 he turned south and east to attack and destroy the north Siamese kingdom of Chieng-mai. It was in this period also that he was involved in fighting against the king of Luang Prabang in Laos and also established Burmese suzerainty over the Shan states.

The ambitions of Bayinnaung led him to invade southern Siam as well, and to seize the capital, Ayuthia (in 1564 and again in 1569). A vassal of Bayinnaung ruled at Ayuthia for fifteen years (see p. 269).

Later in his reign, before his death in 1581, Bayinnaung was concerned with promoting Theravada Buddhism and relations with Ceylon, with military operations against the Laotians (who resisted Burmese authority), and with maintaining his control over Arakan.

Although military campaigns impoverished the state, Burma remained united as one kingdom without the internal dissensions and divisions of earlier times. The dynasty of Toungoo which established a unified Burmese kingdom lasted until 1752.

VIETNAM (ANNAM), 1200–1600.   From the thirteenth to the sixteenth centuries the area today known as Indo-China, with the exception of Laos, which was mentioned in the last section as having a history bound up with that of the Tai and the Burmese, was largely separated from the rest of Southeast Asia and more closely associated with China. Hence, most of the elements of Vietnamese history are covered in the chapters dealing with China.

In the thirteenth century the Mongols overran Vietnam but failed to establish their authority. The Mongols were followed by a period of warfare between Annam in the north and Champa further south in the fourteenth century. By 1471 most of Champa had been conquered. On the other hand, the Ming rulers became interested in again controlling the ancient Chinese province of Vietnam (Annam).

The new effort of the Chinese to reoccupy their former southern province came under the great Ming Yung-lo emperor when in 1406 the Chinese supported one of the claimants to the throne in Vietnam. Ming forces occupied the country. In a famous battle in which they gained control of the country in 1411, the Chinese used firearms, a new form of warfare in this part of the world.

Ming intervention led to annexation and a thorough reorganization of the Vietnamese administrative system by the Chinese. But it was only a matter of a few years before the Chinese had to withdraw and to abandon their authority. In the war between Vietnamese and Chinese from 1417 to 1428 a new Vietnamese leader gained the upper hand and recaptured control of the country from the Chinese. Le Loi led the resistance against the Chinese and ruled as king from 1418 to 1433. A few years after the conclusion of the war in 1428 the Chinese recognized Le Loi as king of Annam. During his reign, Le Loi adopted many of the reform measures which the Ming had instituted and retained organization of the government along Chinese lines. In so doing, his action was much the same as what had been done in Korea and which was to be the pattern during the Yi dynasty in that country. Although there was a strong new nationalism among the Vietnamese and the rulers spoke of themselves as "emperors" during the time of the Le dynasty, in their communications with the Chinese court they admitted vassalage to the Chinese rulers and they continued to look to China as a source of culture and ideas. The Le dynasty retained the throne in Vietnam from 1428 to 1788, a period of consolidation and expansion.

Indonesia From Brahmanism to Islam

MADJAPAHIT EMPIRE.   The Javanese state of Singosari was succeeded by Madjapahit, the last great empire with an Indian culture. Madjapahit's ascendancy was in the fourteenth century and ended in the fifteenth when this commercial empire disintegrated as Moslem princes gained power in most of Indonesia.

The most noteworthy ruler of Singosari at the end of the thirteenth century was Kertanagara (1268–1292), who combined the promotion of Buddhism with the formation of a confederacy of Indonesian states. His empire-building may have been carried out partly to meet the threat of Mongol expansion, whose conquest of China took place during Kertanagara's reign. Kublai Khan sent an envoy to Java who was tattooed on the face by order of the king and sent back to China. As a result the Mongols planned an expedition to avenge the insult. But before they could arrive in Java, Kertanagara's plans collapsed and he was killed by his vassal, the king of Kadiri, thus ending the state of Singosari. In 1293 Kertanagara's son-in-law moved his capital some thirty miles northwest of Singosari to the town of Madjapahit.

In the same year a Mongol expedition of some one thousand ships sailed from China to east Java. The new ruler at Madjapahit turned to the Mongols to assist him in attacking his rival, the king of Kadiri, involving them in a local civil war which gained them nothing. After the founder of Madjapahit had used the Mongols to his advantage he then attacked them and they were forced to evacuate (see also Chapter 22).

Madjapahit became the capital of a great commercial empire in the Indies. The rulers of Madjapahit gained control of all except western Java, and extended their authority over southwest Borneo, as well as a little town on an island off the tip of the Malay peninsula, Singapore, which had been founded in 1160.

There followed the age of Hayam Wuruk, the great king of fourteenth-century Java. Java's greatness during this time was largely due to Gaja Mada, who became prime minister in 1330 even before Hayam Wuruk came to the throne. Gaja Mada, whose influence lasted until his death in 1364, built up Madjapahit to pre-eminence among the islands of Indonesia and on the peninsula of Malaya.

Hayam Wuruk reigned from 1350 to 1389. His empire included not only the areas previously mentioned but most of Sumatra, a large part of the Malay peninsula, southern and western Borneo, southern Celebes, the Moluccas, most of the Philippines, and probably part of western New Guinea. He also claimed a protectorate over Siam, Cambodia, Champa and Vietnam. In the islands, however, the authority of Madjapahit extended only along the coasts. The government of Madjapahit depended upon commercial and sea power; as such they dominated the ports, the key points in Indonesia. The great period of Madjapahit was limited to only about forty-five years, from the early years of the authority of Gaja Mada in 1335 until about 1380. Within this time Srivijaya was conquered as Palembang was taken by the forces of Madjapahit in 1377.

Madjapahit controlled a commercial empire through governors and armed forces maintained at forts where they exacted heavy tribute from the trade which circulated among the islands and which went from the islands to China, Indo-China and India. The town of Madjapahit became a great capital city. Other towns also prospered under their rule, particularly Surabaya on the coast and other ports of Java.

Within the Madjapahit empire both Buddhism and Brahmanism were tolerated. The Buddhist and Brahman (Shivaite) organizations were used to extend political and commercial influence. Traditionally the systems of religious worship and ritual of both Hinduism and Buddhism were provided by the rulers and the aristocracy, while the Indonesian people themselves in their own fields and villages retained much of the older and less sophisticated cus-

FIGURE 15.3.   Remains of a brick gateway, Madjapahit, fourteenth century.

FIGURE 15.4.   Terracotta head of a Madjapahit princess.

toms and beliefs. Nevertheless the difference between Buddhism and Hinduism disappeared more and more, as kings bequeathed their ashes to both Hindu and Buddhist mausoleums, as both faiths came to be worshipped in the same building, and as the different deities of Shiva and the Buddha became synthesized into one. The Indian contributions to Indonesian culture came to be more fully assimilated and purely Indonesian elements and attitudes asserted themselves, a development which can be seen clearly in architecture. The easy acceptance of a new faith, Islam, later on can also be explained by the fact that once it was accepted by the rulers it became adopted by the people by virtue of being imposed from above.

After Hayam Wuruk's death in 1389, civil war and strife over disputed dynastic succession wracked the Madjapahit empire. By 1410 the authority of Madjapahit extended only to parts of Java and a few small islands to the east and by 1428, was limited to part of east Java, although the principality continued as a center of Hindu culture until the sixteenth century.

The last stage of Madjapahit came between 1513 and 1528, when a small remnant of the once great empire was attacked by a coalition of Moslem states, marking the end of a period of Hindu cultural dominance which had lasted for many centuries. Members of the court of Madjapahit at the time of its final collapse fled to Bali, immediately to the east of Java, where strong traditions of Brahmanism have continued down to this day.

SUMATRA: 1200-1400.   In Sumatra and Malaya during the thirteenth and fourteenth centuries there existed a complex political and cultural situation reflecting strong outside influences. The remnant of Srivijaya power at Palembang was finally ended by the invasion from Madjapahit in 1377. This old Sumatran principality, relatively small compared to the greatness of Srivijaya at its zenith, had survived through most of these two centuries.

FIGURE 15.5. Relief from east Javanese Hindu temple of the fourteenth century depicting the son of Krishna.

There was also another center of Javanese influence in the state of Malayu on the East coast of Sumatra. Malayu had close ties with Singosari in Java, and gave Singosari support in opposition to the traditional center of Srivijaya at Palembang, as well as against the attempted Mongol conquest of Singosari in 1293. Thus Malayu in a sense was an outpost of Javanese Hindu influence. Its importance is shown by the fact that after a time the word "Malayu" was used for the whole island. Colonists went from there to the Malay peninsula, and the rulers sent embassies to China.

Based on Arab settlements of an earlier period on Sumatra, Moslem principalities along the north coasts of the island constituted a third political element of importance in Sumatra during the thirteenth and fourteenth centuries. These Moslem states, whose beginnings and whose spread of authority we shall note in more detail in the next section, existed during the time of the power of Srivijaya, of Singosari and Malayu, and later during the time of influence of Madjapahit throughout Indonesia. The Moslem princes were forced to recognize these other states as the paramount powers in Indonesia, but differences in religion kept them apart.

When Madjapahit domination spread in the fourteenth century the Javanese controlled all the coastal regions of Sumatra. Consequently, Moslem traders fled across the straits from the region of Madjapahit domination on Sumatra into Malacca. By 1400 Moslems were in control of that port, with its strategic position along the straits separating the Indian Ocean and the South China Sea.

Concerning Sumatra and neighboring regions in the thirteenth and fourteenth centuries, we are fortunate in having descriptions by travelers who came from the West, and through these first-hand accounts we can better understand something of the conditions of politics, religion and life of the people. The two whose travel reports are particularly worth noting are Marco Polo and Ibn Batuta.

Marco Polo's travels have already been mentioned in connection with his description of Persia (see Chapter 6). He continued his overland travels to China and left a remarkable and famous description of that country in the time of Kublai Khan (see Chapter 22). On his long journey, from 1275 to 1292, he also learned about Southeast Asia and saw some regions for himself. When he left China, he sailed from Ch'üan-chou, on the southeast coast before Kublai Khan's fleet left to attempt to punish the Javanese Kertanagara. Polo returned home from China by sea and hence had some first-hand experience in Sumatra and among the countries with which we are presently concerned.

Polo probably did not actually visit Java. Some of his information about the island is inaccurate. However, it seems worthwhile to quote what he believed to have been true about the island, which as will be noted is substantially in accordance with what we have previously learned.

> When you sail from Champa, 1500 miles in a course between south and south-east, you come to a great Island called Java. And the experienced mariners of those Islands who know the matter well, say that it is the greatest Island in the world, and has a compass of more than 3000 miles. It is subject to a great King tributary to no one else in the world. The people are Idolaters. The Island is of surpassing wealth, producing black pepper, nutmegs, spikenard, galingale, cubebs, cloves, and all other kinds of spices. This Island is also frequented by a vast amount of shipping, and by merchants who buy and sell costly goods from which they reap great profit. Indeed the treasure of this Island is so great as to be past telling. And I can assure you the Great Khan never could get possession of this Island, on account of its great distance, and the great expense of an expedition thither. The merchants of Zayton (Ch'üan-chou) and Manzi (South China) draw annually great returns from this country.[2]

Most interesting for our understanding of Indonesia during this period is the fact that Polo stated there were Moslem traders in the ports of Sumatra and that among eight small principalities on the island, two of them, Perlak and Pasai, were Moslem.

---

[2] Adapted from H. Yule and H. Cordier, *The Book of Ser Marco Polo* (London: John Murray, 1903), pp. 272–274.

The great North African Moslem traveler, Ibn Batuta, has already been mentioned for his visits to Moslem lands further west. In passing through Southeast Asia in his journeying of 30 years he was in Indonesia during the time of Madjapahit domination and was on Java about 1346.

In 1345 he stayed in Sumatra two weeks at the court of a Moslem prince at Samudra near Pasai on the northern tip of the island. Among other things Ibn Batuta took an interest in the commerce of Sumatran ports and noted that Malay aloes wood was being sold by Arab traders to the people of Sumatra in exchange for cloth. He also visited the Malay peninsula and went from this region to a port which he refers as to "Tawalisi," perhaps in the kingdom of Sulu off the northeast coast of Boreno.

MOSLEM TRADERS AND RULERS.   The most important development in Malaya and Indonesia in the centuries immediately before the coming of the Europeans was the spread of Islam. Traders from India and Southwest Asia brought their religion to Sumatra, Malaya and Java. Gradually conversions took place, and the port of Malacca became a Moslem trading city and a center for propagation of the faith. The effects were to be seen all the way from the straits to the southern Philippines, and finally even the most conservative of the principalities in Java succumbed to the spreading influence of this new religion.

From the thirteenth to the sixteenth centuries traders arriving from the Moslem regions of India and Southwest Asia came to northern Sumatra, the straits and Java, and at such ports as Grisek on Java, eagerly participated in the spice trade. These merchants were from Bengal, Gujarat and from Persian Gulf ports.

During the thirteenth century in Sumatra their influence extended beyond matters of trade. They began to make conversions to Islam. As far as is known, the first Indonesian Moslem ruler was at Pasai in northwest Sumatra in the thirteenth century. By the fourteenth century Moslems controlled the carrying trade of the Indian Ocean, and their ships (Arab, Persian and Indian) brought the products of the Far East, Southeast Asia, India and Ceylon to the Persian Gulf and to the Red Sea for trans-shipment to Europe. Thus, in the fourteenth century they were active in the area where the power of Madjapahit rose and declined. In eastern Sumatra and northern Java Gujarati and Bengali merchants came to intermediate ports, Grisek and elsewhere, in order to gain the spices of the Moluccas.

A feature of this influx of traders and new ideas in the fifteenth century was the rise of Malacca in southern Malaya as a great commercial center. Moslem traders who came to Malacca combined religion with their business enterprises. The ruler of Malacca in the first quarter of the fifteenth century married a Moslem princess from Pasai, and raised his children in the Islamic faith.

Malacca after about 1445 became a spearhead for Islam, and by the end of the fifteenth century had also become the main trading center and chief commercial power of Southeast Asia. Travelers to Malacca from further east were influenced by what they saw at this focal point. Members of ruling families noted the commercial success of Moslem merchants, and in coastal areas everywhere influential people turned to the new religion. In this process the "Sayyids" were particularly important. The term Sayyids is used for the principal descendants of Muhammad and in this case denotes a class who were leaders in spreading Islam. Their daughters were married to the local rulers and thus their descendants, who were Moslems, gained positions of control.

When the Chinese envoy Cheng Ho visited Sumatra in 1413 he noted the progress of Islam in that region, even though Palembang, the old capital of Srivijaya, was still Buddhist. Between about 1407 and 1480 the faith spread to Borneo, Sulu and parts of Mindanao, the largest island in the southern Philippines. Simultaneously, as mentioned below, Islam also expanded in Java. By the end of the fifteenth century some twenty states located on the islands of Java, Sumatra, Borneo, Celebes, Moluccas, the Philippines and on the Malay peninsula had adopted Islam as a state religion. Moslem traders and religious leaders dominated the important seaports and in the interior cities. Arabic writing, used by the Moslems, came into general use throughout Indonesia. One result of the spread of Islam, with its doctrine of the equality of all men before God, was that the government in these areas became somewhat more liberal and democratic.

Islam also progressed in Java, that ancient stronghold of Hinduism, Buddhism and Indonesian culture. The first of the important coastal towns of Java to become Moslem was Demak in 1477. The town of Cheribon was a Moslem settlement from its founding in 1480 (although there is a tradition that the first Javanese became a Moslem there in the twelfth century). In these ports, the Moslem Javanese rulers asserted their independence of Madjapahit and the little states became centers for the further spread of Islam. They also were centers of commercial prosperity. These Moslem principalities, including Demak and other states in northern Java and Madura, are said to have attacked and overrun Madjapahit in 1478. By the end of the fifteenth century only a very unimportant Hindu "King of Java" continued the Madjapahit tradition and after 1528 Madjapahit disappeared entirely. In the early sixteenth century, Islamic forces from Cheribon spread the faith by conquering other principalities in west Java.

Thus Islam became the official religion of the leading states in Sumatra and Java, the two key islands of Indonesia. The faith spread further east, as we have mentioned, to the Spice islands and north to the southern Philippines in the late fourteenth century. This new religious force, coming from the west, was from that time on the dominant cultural influence in the area. At this same time Arab and other Moslem merchants from India and Southwest Asia completely controlled the spice trade originating in Indonesia.

The Coming of the Europeans

THE PORTUGUESE IN INDONESIA.   The spice trade, which brought the Arabs and other Moslems to Indonesia, also attracted the Portuguese, and the power which they built up along the coasts of Asia in the sixteenth century was principally based on their control of this trade, a control which lasted until they had to face the competition of other Europeans in the seventeenth century.

The Arabs had only recently begun to build up a trade empire based on Malacca at the time that the Portuguese first came. The spices of the Indies had been the Portuguese objective since Vasco da Gama came round the Cape of Good Hope and reached India in the last decade of the fifteenth century. Within a few years the Portuguese had gained mastery of the seas along the coasts of Iran and India and by 1510 Albuquerque had taken the port of Goa from the Moslem state of Bijapur on the west coast of India.

In the year after the seizure of Goa Albuquerque and his naval forces attacked and captured Malacca. We have noted that this port was a key point in the Moslem control of the spice trade coming from Indonesia. Albuquerque's objectives in attacking Malacca have survived in his own words.

The first [aim] is the great service which we shall perform to Our Lord in casting the Moors out of this country, and quenching the fire of the sect of Mahomet so that it may never burst out again hereafter . . . And the other reason is the service we shall render to the King Dom Manoel in taking this city, because it is the source of all the spiceries and drugs which the Moors carry every year hence to the [Straits of Bab-el-Mandeb] without our being able to prevent them . . . for I hold it certain that if we take this trade of Malacca away from them, Cairo and Mecca will be entirely ruined, and Venice will receive no spiceries unless her merchants go and buy them in Portugal.[3]

In view of his aims, it is therefore not surprising that when Albuquerque took Malacca he massacred the Moslems and spared the other inhabitants. Shortly thereafter he revealed his main purpose by sending envoys to Siam and other nearby kingdoms of Southeast Asia to negotiate trade agreements. Within a few years the Portuguese built up a commercial monopoly in Indonesia based on seapower and a line of strategic forts extending from Malacca on the straits to Amboyna among the Spice islands. As the Arabs had done before them the Portuguese used Malacca as a center for control and commerce, as well as a point of departure for transportation to Europe.

Portuguese patrols prevented the merchant ships of other countries from entering the area. There was not yet any rivalry from the northern Europeans, but the Spaniards outfitted ships on the coasts of Mexico and attempted to trade with the Spice islands by sailing west across the Pacific. The Portuguese effectively kept them out, or seized their ships and took the Spaniards prisoner when they encroached on the area of Portuguese control.

With a monopoly of the Indonesian trade in their hands the Portuguese expanded their operations. The sixteenth century was the height of their greatness on the waters of South, Southeast and East Asia. In 1514 the first Portuguese ships reached China and brought back information leading to the establishment of trade with that country. Their conduct in the following years antagonized

---

[3] G. F. Hudson, *Europe and China* (London: Arnold, 1931), p. 201.

the Chinese, however, and it was not until 1557 that they were able to make a regular settlement at Macao on the southern part of the Canton delta and from there secure a monopoly of trade going between China and the Indies (see Volume II). They also controlled Indonesian commerce with Siam, and with Japan, to say nothing of the trade from the Far East to India and Europe.

The decline in Portuguese power in the eastern seas came during the latter part of the century. The great profits attracted men who were unable to make the exertions and suffer the sacrifices of the earlier pioneers in the developing of trade. More importantly, the Portuguese simply did not have the manpower to keep the growing stream of Asia trade in their own hands. They also made enemies among some of the peoples with whom they dealt. But especially important in leading to the Portuguese decline were their European involvements. They had to use foreign sailors on their ships who learned the secrets of the trade. The union of Portugal with Spain in 1580 committed them to war with the Dutch and English and hence they lost their business with northern Europe. Then by the end of the century both the Dutch and English were determined to send their own ships to the Indies and to break the monopoly of the Portuguese. During the first twenty years of the seventeenth century the Dutch drove the Portuguese from Ceylon, and from Amboyna in the Spice islands, and established themselves on Java. The British defeated them on the coast of India and also seized their fort at Hormuz on the coast of Persia. The crowning blow came when the Dutch seized Malacca in 1641 (see Volume II). Thus was concluded the period of Portuguese influence in Southeast Asia and the history of Malacca and the Indies until Dutch expansion.

THE SPANISH IN THE PHILIPPINES.   Shortly after the coming of the Portuguese to Southeast Asia the Spanish also sought to engage in the lucrative trade of the Spice islands. They came from their bases in the western hemisphere across the Pacific and reached the Philippines. In that region they found peoples who were only in partial contact with the rest of Southeast Asia. A minority group were the Moslems who were well established in Mindanao and in Sulu during the fifteenth century. A few were in the northern islands including a Moslem prince at Manila. The first Spanish settlement was made at Cebu in 1565, and within five years they had established their authority over most of the Philippine islands. But they never conquered the people in the south, whom they named "Moros" after the Moslems who had held southern Spain, nor did they conquer the mountain districts. Except for these areas, the Spaniards created a compact empire in the Philippine islands. They, as the Portuguese had done elsewhere, brought with them representatives of the Roman Catholic Church, and in this instance the church became the predominant influence during three centuries of European control in the Philippines. The strong Spanish Catholic influence in the Philippines set a limit to the spread of Islam in that part of the world. A fuller treatment of this phase of Southeast Asian history in the sixteenth century will be found in Volume II.

DIVERGENT INTERESTS IN SIXTEENTH-CENTURY SOUTHEAST ASIA. By the end of the sixteenth century in Southeast Asia there were five main cultural elements in the area. Acknowledging the suzerainty of the Chinese was the Vietnamese Le dynasty along the coast of Indo-China. This was the only part of the area which historically was primarily part of the sphere of Chinese culture. In the other parts of mainland Southeast Asia were two nation-states, unified under the Burmese and the Tai and both of them culturally affiliated to the Theravada Buddhism of Ceylon. Thirdly, to the south of these mainland states, in the Malay peninsula, in most of the islands of Indonesia and in the southern Philippines were Moslems, all more or less independent, in many little principalities, but constituting the controlling element among the Malays, Sumatrans, Javanese, the "Moros" of the southern Philippines and others.

The fourth element was the power of Portugal. Controlling most of the seas between Europe and Japan, including the important Straits of Sunda and of Malacca in Southeast Asia, the Portuguese were in a dominant position at the ports of these other peoples, but their control did not extend to the interior of the great islands and peninsulas of Southeast Asia.

Finally, as we have noted, there were the Spanish in the Philippines, where they had established a Christian colony among peoples related to those of Indonesia but who were thus cut off from Indonesia culturally and destined for some three hundred years to be a part of the Christian European world.

BASIC DATES

1238	Tai seize Sukotai in Siam
1252	Mongols invade Nan-chao
1271-1300	Burmese-Mongol hostilities
1280-1752	Toungoo dynasty in Burma
1293	Founding of Madjapahit. Mongol forces on Java.
1330-1389	Period of Madjapahit greatness
1350-1767	Kingdom of Ayuthia
1364-1555	Kingdom of Ava in Burma
1369-1539	Mon kingdom of Pegu
1377	Madjapahit forces take Palembang
15th century	Spread of Islam in Indonesia
1406, 1411	Ming campaigns in Vietnam
1428-1788	Le dynasty in Vietnam
1431	Tai capture Angkor
1486–1581	Three great kings of Toungoo
1511-1641	Portuguese hold Malacca
1521	Spanish under Magellan reach Philippines
1527	Shan loot Ava
1557	Burmese destroy Chieng-mai
1564	Burmese seize Ayuthia
1565	Start of Spanish rule in Philippines
1569-1584	Burmese control Siam

SUPPLEMENTARY READING

HARRISON, B. *South-East Asia: A Short History,* 2nd ed. London, 1963.
HUDSON, G. F. *Europe and China.* London, 1931. Chapter 6.
STEIGER, G. N. *History of the Far East.* Boston, 1944. Chapters 14 and 16.
VLEKKE, B. H. M. *The Story of the Dutch East Indies.* Cambridge, Mass., 1946.

ADVANCED READING

ARNOLD, T. W. *The Preaching of Islam: A History of the Propagation of the Muslim Faith.* London, 1913. The spread of Islam outside Arabia.
DE KLERCK, E. S. *History of the Netherlands East Indies.* Rotterdam, 1938.
GIBB, H. A. R., TR. *Ibn Battuta, Travels, 1325–54.* London, 1929. Source material on fourteenth-century Asia.
HALL, D. G. E. *Burma.* London, 1950.
————*A History of South-East Asia.* New York, 1955.
PIGAFETTA, A. *Magellan's Voyage Around the World.* Cleveland, 1906. Contemporary source material.
STEPHENS, H. M. *Albuquerque.* Oxford, 1892. A short biography.
VLEKKE, B. H. M. *Nusantara: A History of the East Indian Archipelago.* Cambridge, Mass., 1943.
WHEATLEY, P. *The Golden Khersonese: Studies in the Historical Geography of the Malay Peninsula before A.D. 1500.* Kuala Lumpur, 1961.
WOOD, W. A. R. *A History of Siam.* Bangkok, 1933.
YULE, H. AND H. CORDIER. *The Book of Ser Marco Polo,* 3rd ed. New York, 1929.

XVI 粼粼

CHINA BEFORE CONFUCIUS

IN TURNING FROM INDIA AND SOUTHEAST ASIA TO CHINA we enter a world isolated geographically from regions further west. In the "Far Eastern" part of Asia the Chinese developed in a unique manner and at the same time had a wide influence throughout East Asia. It is important therefore to note the principal geographical features of the East Asian world centering on China. Significant also is the continuity with the prehistoric eras, mentioned in Chapter 2. In order to understand the earliest concepts of Chinese history we must also consider the legends, legends which gradually merge into verifiable history as the story proceeds.

During the Shang period, the first we know much about in Chinese history, there existed a highly developed autocratic society. The Shang was followed by the Chou (pronounced "jo"). The early part of the Chou, covered in this chapter, was marked by the development of a noble class and of separate states within what we think of as China. Our aim here is to stress the concepts, the social relations, the events and developments of early periods which are basic to the understanding of China in all its subsequent history.

The Chinese World

To the early traveler from the West China seemed an isolated world in itself. Whether approached from the seas or overland across the Pamirs, this part of Asia, because of its remoteness, was called the

"Far East" by Europeans. In contrast to this foreign view were the ideas of the Chinese themselves, to whom China was the center of their world and hence referred to as the "Middle Kingdom." The cultural unity of China, characterized by a common language and literature, made the other regions of East Asia seem peripheral to the central kingdom of China. This cultural unity has existed from earliest times and is partly dependent upon geography, since absence of major geographical barriers among the three main divisions of China made the process of unification easy.

The three main divisions of China are the north, the Yangtze valley, and the south coast, all of which are characterized by important river valleys. In the north the Yellow river flows first through the highlands of the Central Yellow river basin, an area of yellowish-brown, wind-blown loess soil. Next the lower Yellow river basin is a broad flood plain, subject to frequent inundation. The river has changed course through the ages, flowing either to the north or south of the Shantung peninsula. The North China Plain has also been the usual location of the Chinese capital, including the present capital of Peking. Another center of historical significance in north China is the valley of the Wei to the west.

North China for a great part of the year is brown and dust-blown. Transportation across the plains and going into the highlands has been by carts. The growing season lasts from four to six months and is devoted mainly to wheat, millet, and beans. Rains are irregular and vary greatly within the region from 20 to 30 inches along the coast to semiarid conditions bordering the deserts to the north. Winters are cold.

In contrast, the south is a land of greenness. From the Yangtze valley to the areas further south there is a growing season of from six to nine months allowing for two to three crops a year, the most important being rice. Often there are heavy rains; in central China the average is 40 inches of rain a year and on the south coast some 60 inches. Throughout this area summers are hot and humid while winters are cold and humid. An important feature of the south has been the reliance on water transportation rather than roads. Smaller rivers and canals connect with larger rivers and lakes providing water courses which have been the main means of communication throughout history. People who live their entire lives on boats may be found from the Yangtze delta to the delta of the West river at Canton.

The lower Yangtze region has been for many centuries the heart of the country, because of its climate and agricultural fertility. It is an agricultural area cut off from water communication with the south by the South Yangtze hills. The upper Yangtze, or Szechuan, is relatively remote from the rest of the country. It is subtropical and fertile but access is difficult through the gorges of the Yangtze and it is still partly inhabited by aborigines.

The south coast is a region of mountains and little valleys, the most important being the West river valley. Its broken coastline is very beautiful with beaches, inlets, and little coves providing opportunities for piracy and irregular trade since antiquity. It was along this southeast coast that the earliest traders came to China and here are located the important ports, such as Canton.

Surrounding China are five major border areas: Chinese Turkistan (Sinkiang), Tibet, Mongolia, Korea, and Vietnam. Among the border areas the high plateau of Tibet is one of the most inaccessible, and one of the great natural barriers of Asia, being bordered by the great Himalayas on the south and the Kunlun mountains to the north. Tibet has been a separate country and developed its own culture. North of Tibet is the area generally referred to as Chinese Turkistan bordered by the Pamir mountains on the west and traversed from west to east by the T'ien-shan range, which lies north of the Tarim basin. The Tarim basin is a desert region marked by oases along its northern rim and to the south. Trade routes along the edges of the desert and north of the T'ien-shan were important in providing Chinese contacts with India and western Asia.

To the northeast of Turkistan are the Altai mountains which divide that region from Mongolia, a land of desert and grass steppe, including vast stretches of uninhabitable land such as the Gobi desert. This is the land of nomads who have swept down frequently in the past from their steppes into the more populous agricultural areas of China. Pressure for such invasions has been strongly influenced by the lack of rain in this area, much of which receives less than ten inches a year.

The Mongolian steppe region extends from northern Turkistan to the east into Manchuria. This region, connected with north China by a narrow corridor of coastal plain, includes fertile, well-watered plains in the south and very fertile plains, little used in historic times, in the north. In addition to plains and steppe, there is also a forested mountain region in the southeast bordering on Korea.

The Yalu river divides Manchuria from the Korean peninsula to the south. Korea resembles somewhat both north China and Japan in having cold winters and hot summers. The peninsula is subdivided into small areas, as is Japan, by mountains and streams. There is no natural division between north and south; any such division has been the result of political and military considerations. During most of its history Korea has been an integral unit, lying both geographically and culturally between China and Japan.

Another marginal country adjoins China's southern borders. The northern part of what is today called Vietnam, usually referred to as Annam by the Chinese, has been a part of China through much of its history. This region of the Red river valley of Tongking is a tropical area extending from a coastal plain to interior mountain valleys cut by the north-south streams of the central Indo-Chinese highlands.

Origins of a Great Civilization

HISTORICAL BEGINNINGS AND LEGENDS. Within China but more particularly within the region of the Yellow river in the north, a continuity of cultural development existed going back to prehistoric times. During the centuries after

2000 B.C. bronze making, which may have come from the West, began to be developed. During the early Bronze age the Chinese also learned to use the threads from the cocoon of the silkworm in making silk and developed the use of the wheel for agricultural and military purposes. More significantly, writing began although this is known only from later evidence.

According to ancient legends, China was formed under the leadership of mythical emperors, men who were culture heroes to the Chinese. To various individual leaders were later attributed the invention of certain basic elements of an agricultural civilization.

Among the little village-states of the lower Yellow river plain there was one community which is known in the later legends as "Hsia." This Hsia was mentioned in later writings as a dynasty, but it probably was only a petty state, yet important enough to be remembered later on. One of these early dynasties definitely existed, for in this case there is a literary tradition which was confirmed by archaeological finds. The state and the dynasty, which is known not only from the stories which have come down concerning it but also from remaining physical evidence, was the Shang.

THE SHANG PERIOD.   The beginnings of the Shang dynasty and cultural period are very obscure. We do have evidence that there was a continuity of the culture going back to the times of prehistoric man in north China. By the start of the historic period the civilization of the people living in the Yellow river valley had already reached a high degree of development and included a political system, religious ideas, an elaborate society, an advanced economy, artistic expression, as well as literary production. In comparison with India we may note that Shang culture was at its height about a thousand years later than the Indus valley civilization.

Shang culture may be said to date back to about 1750 B.C. The actual founding of the dynasty itself is much disputed. It is possible that the dynasty began about 1523 B.C. The great period of Shang culture dates from about 1400, and the dynasty lasted until the Chou conquest in 1028.

Politically the Shang was a union of petty kingdoms limited to the region of the lower Yellow river valley, although at the height of its power Shang influence was probably felt from the Wei valley to the sea and from the northern steppe as far south as the Yangtze basin. The Shang governing group or clan commanded thousands of troops, undertook public works, and supervised the collection and storage of grain and metals which were part of the basis of their power. With this power they developed an authoritarian monarchy, a small state wielding power over similar neighboring but smaller communities. There was within the political framework a sharp cleavage between the rulers and the ruled.

Political power was also maintained by the authority of religion. The Shang ruler also served as high priest and chief calendar-maker. The calendar was important because agriculture was the basis of society and the king must propitiate the gods of grain and of the soil and the heavenly gods on whose influence the economy and the prosperity of the state depended. Thus agriculture was organized in a centralized way by the Shang rulers. The highly developed crafts and industries were also organized under the control of the king, and the products of these industries served the needs of royalty and nobility.

The most profitable enterprise undertaken by the Shang kings was war. Through victory the kings increased their wealth and also obtained servants, slaves, and victims to be sacrificed to the ancestors. Shang power became dangerous to their neighbors, who spoke of the Shang ruling class as "the great terror of the east." The chief enemies of the Shang were to the north and to the west, including the Chou in the valley of the Wei, whose power finally overthrew the Shang.

The great period of Shang culture began in the fourteenth century. In about the year 1300 the city of Anyang was founded. This capital city of the Shang was known to the people of the day as the "Great City Shang." It was probably a walled city, with houses similar to Chinese houses in recent times. There were a number of large buildings, particularly in the palace area, including government buildings such as treasuries as well as temples and tombs.

We have mentioned that the Shang was a union of petty kingdoms or states. Hereditary nobility of various ranks ruled over states of varying size. Their power was centered in one or more towns within their territory. These lords owed allegiance and loyal service to the Shang king. They followed him in his wars and expeditions, helped guard the frontiers, presented regular tribute, and supplied manpower for war and for labor. The king in turn supported and protected the rulers of the subordinate states. He consulted the gods concerning their welfare, controlled their taxes, and gave military assistance if a lord was attacked. It is known that during the reign of the last Shang king one expedition to the south to help a loyal vassal lasted for a period of some 260 days.

The king personally attended to the affairs of state. Under him were various civil and military officials including high-ranking secretarial officials. Among the most important of these were councillors; chroniclers who attended to records, edicts, and archives; diviners, interpreters of the wishes of the gods; and priests who attended to sacrificial rituals. The military establishment included both infantry and men mounted in chariots.

Shang political power, as mentioned above, was closely related to the state religion in which various deities were worshipped and to whom sacrifices were made. These included the spirit ancestors of the kings, the "Ruler Above" or *Shang-ti,* and various nature gods. In their religious conceptions the Shang believed that man was at the center of the universe. The heavenly world, as well as the earthly world with which they were concerned, was connected with man and hence of interest to them. The approach to the gods led to the interpretation of cracks on heated bones and tortoise shells, and this in turn was recorded by writing inscribed on these bones and shells. This divination and this writing we shall mention again further on.

Worship of ancestors was the primary aspect of Shang religion and took shape in the performance of rituals, including the making of both animal and human sacrifices. Sacrifices were made to the ancestors to secure their favors. The help of the ancestors was also sought by making tomb offerings including bronzes, pottery, sculpture, weapons, and helmets.

The oracle bones show that there were more sacrifices made to the ancestors than to all other deities. At the time the gods were consulted the cracks on these heated ox bones or tortoise shells were interpreted. Sometimes the questions that had been asked of the gods and the interpretation of their replies might be carved on the bone. Thus we know something of the subjects about which the Shang rulers and their diviners asked the gods. They were concerned with sacrifices, announcements to spirits, journeys, hunting, war, crops, weather, illness, and miscellaneous matters such as lucky days and diplomatic questions.

Shang society was sharply divided between the warrior nobility who were the upper class and who engaged in ancestral worship, and the common people. Most of our information concerns the ruling family and the nobility. We know that the rulers were all of one family or clan, and succession was often from elder brother to younger brother.

The Shang economy was firmly based on agriculture. Millet was a staple food since Neolithic times, but wheat also was cultivated by the Shang people. Stock included sheep, cattle, and horses. There is only slight evidence of any irrigation being carried out at this time. The farmers also produced silk.

A profitable occupation of the time was hunting. Trade was mostly restricted to the exchanges within small self-contained communities. However the presence of cowrie shell money among the remains of this period indicates interest in remote areas and the possibility of exchange over long distances.

Shang warfare was conducted with the composite bow, with bronze spears and arrowheads, dagger axes, the use of bronze armor, and—an important adjunct—chariots used by the nobility.

SHANG CULTURE. Along with their high level of political and social organization the Shang reached a very advanced stage of material and artistic accomplishment. Pottery-making advanced beyond the production of Neolithic times. Shang artisans began to glaze their pots and to use kaolin, which resulted in a finer quality of pottery. In addition the art of carving used new techniques in working marble and jade.

Of particular importance in the Shang period was the unique development of bronze casting. The technique of bronze casting may have been learned from people further west, but it was raised to an unusually high point by the Shang people. They produced some of the finest bronze casting ever done anywhere, with sharp edges and corners, with good taste and strength of design.

The highly conventionalized designs found on the bronzes, as well as on marble, involved the use of animal forms. Especially notable are those patterns which included the representation of horned animals, and a composite animal style in which many animal forms might be contained in one composition. It is

FIGURE 16.1. Shang carved bone fragment from Anyang representing a horned animal. The horns, eyes, noseridge, nostrils, and mouth are presented in highly conventionalized style.

FIGURE 16.2. Shang beaker of type *ku*, c. 1200 B.C. Marvelously elongated lines, combined with great skill in bronze casting.

FIGURE 16.3. A set of Shang sacrificial vessels.

probable that these designs had religious significance but very little is known about this point.

Most important in its future effect and for our knowledge of the period is the Shang writing. Its beginnings may have been in early Shang if not in Neolithic times. It was a script which developed from pictograms and included both pictograms and ideograms. The writing of Shang times represents an advanced stage in the development of the Chinese written language as we know it today. This language is one of the most complete, complex, and sophisticated systems known. As used on the oracle bones of Shang times it already included every important principle in the formation of modern Chinese. Thus the Shang language was neither crude nor primitive and it specialized in the representation of ideas and vivid pictures. As noted before, there was a religious motive in the need for communication with departed ancestors and hence for inscribing questions and answers in connection with divination.

Shang writing is found not only on the oracle bones but also on the bronzes, on other bone and horn articles as well as on pottery, stone, and jade. Official records were probably kept on silk and bamboo as well as on wooden tablets, but these articles have perished and long since disappeared.

The sphere of influence of Shang culture spread from its original center in the lower Yellow river valley and extended to the northwest, to the east coast and into the Yangtze valley, where traces of the culture have recently been found.

The Early, or Western, Chou

WESTERN CHOU (ABOUT 1050 TO 771 B.C.). In the Wei river valley in the west a new line of kings rose who superseded the Shang as supreme rulers in China and developed a system of states with regular relationships between rulers and nobility. This line is known to history as the dynasty of the Chou.

After gaining undisputed leadership of the tribes in the Wei river basin, Chou princes, asserting their independence of the Shang, sent expeditions to the east. The second ruler in the line of famous *wang,* or kings, defeated the Shang in about 1028 B.C. and destroyed the Shang capital at Anyang. Later campaigns made Chou domination of the Shang region permanent. Although the Chou government differed from that of the Shang, the Chou rulers adopted Shang culture with enthusiasm. One period merged into the other culturally.

Because the first Chou capital was located in the Wei river valley until 771 B.C., this part of the dynastic period is known as the Western Chou. At its height Western Chou territory extended from southern Manchuria to parts of the Yangtze valley and from eastern Kansu to the sea coast.

Chou government was aristocratic, but during the period under consideration there was a time when the kings actually ruled, starting in the time of King Wu, the conqueror of the Shang, and his younger brother, the Duke of Chou.

Later, in order to govern their expanded domain the Chou kings created a number of fiefs which were granted to relatives and those who aided in the conquest. This resulted in a system more like European feudalism than that which had existed in the times of the Shang. Land was given to nobles in return for their contributing to revenue, preventing rebellion, and leading soldiers to fight in the service of the king. Society thus became stratified between hereditary lords, hereditary aristocratic fighting men, and the lower classes, chiefly peasants. While it had many feudal aspects, in some ways the Chou governmental system was simply an extension of a tribal type of organization.

Chou society was also characterized by two important features: the family group and the possession of land by a nobleman or lord. The basic unit of ancient Chinese society was the noble or patrician family. Members of a family possessed a sense of unity in being descended from a common ancestor and they bore his clan name, or *hsing*. From the noble ancestor they inherited the right to own land, a right restricted to patricians alone. On the land of a patrician lord there would be a number of villages. Hence these villages were united politically and socially under his control, and also shared a common religion. The religious element of this society lay in the fact that all the families bearing the same surname formed a religious unit by adhering to the cult of the first ancestor, whom they looked back to as the originator of the family name.

The feudal aristocracy from about 1027 to 771 paid regular tribute to the king and thus acknowledged his authority. But by the ninth century royal power and influence had diminished, threatened both by the great nobles and by border tribes.

By the ninth century many nobles were practically independent. The more powerful accumulated great personal wealth and maintained private armies. Gradually many nobles disregarded the king's commands and ceased contributing revenue to the Chou government.

Despite his weakening military authority, a Chou king, Li, was particularly cruel in suppressing his critics thus inspiring a revolt against his rule in 841 B.C. (the first accurate historical date in Chinese history). The king was forced to flee while members of the nobility assumed the regency for the heir apparent. The heir, enthroned in 827, was able but was harassed by constant warfare with the barbarians on the western frontiers.

A second reason for the end of Western Chou rule was the threat of border tribes. In 771 B.C. rebellious nobles in alliance with non-Chinese barbarians invaded the capital, slew the king, and forced the court to flee. The Chou capital ceased to be located in the Wei valley and the Chou kings never regained actual power. They continued to rule as nominal heads of state, but 771 marks the end of Chou administrative authority.

WESTERN CHOU CULTURE. The principal aspect of Chou culture is continuity with the Shang. The Chou adopted the advanced culture of the previous five hundred years, building upon it and adding certain modifications of their own which make a distinctive change from the previous period.

The principal deity of the state religion, which was the basis of the political power of the ruling line, was "heaven." To this deity the Chou kings referred when speaking of themselves as "Son of Heaven," and so presumed to mediate between men and the supreme deity. They looked to heaven for justification of their actions and conceived of their authority as being based on the "mandate of heaven." Thus they believed it was in accordance with the will of heaven that the Chou line had superseded the divinely-protected Shang of the previous period. The concept of a supreme "ruler above" of Shang times was identified with the Chou deity "heaven."

Ancient Chinese religion was one of social groups, not of individuals. Ceremonies and rites might be carried on by nobles, but they were doing this on behalf of the social group and not as a matter of individual religious experience. In the general Chou politico-religious system there were two important cults, one that of the gods of the soil (or land) and the other, already mentioned, the cult of ancestor worship.

The "god of the soil (or earth)" was worshipped at an earthen mound known as "an altar of the land." This mound in each community became the symbol of territorial authority, implying the protection and favor of the god of the earth, the god of that particular earth. For the worship of ancestral spirits temples were erected in the capitals of the various princes. Each of these was a center for state functions and symbolic of an hereditary family. In the conquest of a given region the altars of the land and the ancestral temples had to be destroyed as symbols of the power of the previous rulers.

Celebrations at shrines served by both nobleman and villager were geared to the seasons, and derived from peasant harvest festivals and other such occasions. The most solemn of all the royal rituals were the offerings to the god on high (heaven) at the spring and autumn sacrifices. On these occasions prayers were made for divine intervention and goodwill. The gods came to be conceived of more or less as persons with superhuman qualities and influence for good and evil in the lives of the people. This concept goes back to Shang times as illustrated in the divination recorded on the oracle bones.

Those who officiated in the ceremonies connected with the worship of these deities in the different states of China during West Chou times were not priests. There was no hereditary sacred caste such as existed in India. Instead the lords themselves and their officials, officials who specialized in religious functions, performed the ceremonies.

Evidence of the magnificence of the ceremonies has come down to us in the bronze vessels and jade ceremonial objects which were used by the Chou aristocracy in their rites. The early Chou bronzes and jades show essential continuity from the arts of Shang times, especially in the stylized animal shapes and designs of the bronzes. In the casting Chou workmanship is not as fine as the highly developed bronze art of the Shang period.

Changes indicating differences in the styles of the Chou ceremonial objects, as compared with the earlier Shang works, were notable after about the year 1000 B.C. and included such innovations as animal sculpture in bronze. The

FIGURE 16.4.   A bronze water buffalo of the Chou period. The shapes and designs are much heavier and bulkier than those of Shang bronzes.

shapes and designs were new. They were unlike the Shang bronzes in that they were heavy, bulky and more formal in appearance and weight.

The ritual jades of Chou times included flat rings or discs with a center hole, perhaps solar emblems, as well as jade knives somewhat like the ancient halberds and axe daggers. Another Chou type was in the shape of a rectangular block with a cylindrical hollow tube through the center, which perhaps may have symbolized the four cardinal points.

The Middle Chou

MIDDLE CHOU POLITICS.   When the Western Chou court fled from the Wei river region they went east to the small valley of the Lo and there established a new Chou "capital" at Lo-yang. Hence, the period from 770 to the third century B.C. is referred to as the Eastern Chou. The first three hundred years of the Eastern Chou (approximately to the time of Confucius) is the Middle Chou, a period of division into numerous autonomous states.

In Middle Chou the king was a puppet while the hereditary aristocracy increased their own power. The Chou kings, who ruled over only a very small domain surrounding Lo-yang, might be consulted on questions such as the legitimacy of claimants to the authority in some state or another. Actually it was often the kings themselves who appealed to one of the strong nobles in one of the nominally subordinate states. China was split up into a number of more or less independent states with varying levels of culture and civilization. Some of these inherited directly the culture of the Shang and the Early Chou, and some, which had been outside the main cultural stream, during this time gradually became more Chinese.

Chou politics was characterized by an internal struggle among the various political and cultural units, the states. The large number of states in Western Chou times were reduced by the eighth century to some ten states which dominated the others, most notably the four great states of Ch'i (pronounced Chee) in the northeast, Chin (Jin) in Shansi to the north, Ch'in (Chin) in the northwest, and Ch'u (Choo) in the Yangtze Valley.

During the Middle Chou interstate relations between these various principalities were characterized by strict rules of conduct, whether in diplomacy or in warfare, and the leadership within the states was based on principles of legitimacy.

Among the ten states there arose a system of hegemony or domination by a series of leaders who came to be known as "First Nobles." Each in turn made his own state the principal power among the Chinese states. Each First Noble depended on his own personal ability. He actually exercised most of the powers and functions of a king, helping to repel invasions, directing punitive expeditions, arbitrating differences between other feudal princes, punishing those who disobeyed his orders, and receiving revenues which formerly would have gone to the Chou king.

These First Nobles depended upon the prestige of the Chou king to enhance their own power. Under the slogan, "revere the king and expel the barbarians!," they brought together the various states of north China with a common aim. While the First Noble exerted authority nominally on behalf of the king, he actually promoted his own interests and those of a block of states which resisted subversion from within and attack from without. Among the First Nobles the most successful was Duke Huan of Ch'i in northeast China. He was the first of the princes to achieve a position of leadership among the states and hence to be called First Noble.

Anarchy prevailed when Duke Huan ascended the throne of Ch'i in 685 B.C. China was disturbed by succession disputes within various small states in north China and also among the members of the ruling Chou family itself. These conflicts were often settled by assassinations and usurpations, and at the same time the country suffered from inroads of barbarian peoples from the north, the west, and the south. In this general atmosphere the father of Duke Huan had previously subjugated two of the small states, Wei on the Yellow river and Lu in western Shantung, and thus had strengthened the power of Ch'i. Duke Huan gained control of his state only after a struggle within Ch'i and a campaign against the state of Lu, which had supported his rival.

Among the leaders who opposed Duke Huan was Kuan Chung, an advisor of his rival, who was taken prisoner in the fighting with Lu. Because of Kuan Chung's ability Duke Huan took him into his employment and made him the chief minister in Ch'i. Much subsequent governmental policy was formulated by Kuan Chung. With Kuan Chung's assistance various reforms were effected in Ch'i. Centralized power was developed through uniform taxes, state monopolies, and an improved bureaucracy. Commerce was encouraged. The armed forces were supported by a regular military conscription.

Duke Huan of Ch'i took the lead as head of a confederation of states in north China. In addition to the four states which rallied to his banner at the beginning, two others were forced to become members of the league. Interstate conferences began in 681, and in the succeeding years military action was taken against those who were reluctant to join. For some years Duke Huan was constantly engaged in the problem of enforcing his leadership over this league of states. It was necessary for him to invade Lu again, to defeat the small state of Cheng, and also to invade Wei in order to maintain his hegemony in the federation.

Until 656 B.C., Duke Huan, while maintaining his leadership among the states, carried on campaigns against the large southern state of Ch'u and also against barbarians on the frontiers. Later the league dominated by Ch'i dealt also with the question of succession in the ruling family of Chou. In 652, the Duke brought the league members together to sign a peace pact. They were to acknowledge the suzerainty of Chou and at the same time to promise to aid each other against their enemies.[1]

Duke Huan of Ch'i's leadership in North China lasted thirty-six years, until his death in 643 B.C. Although his hegemony was only over the lower Yellow river states and did not include Chin and Ch'in, nevertheless it was largely due to him and his allies that the barbarians were kept out of the heart of China during his time. Also because of his leadership the Chinese continued the reverence for the Chou king and loyalty to his central authority, however weak, which was a key factor in maintaining the dynasty for centuries to come. In later years the leadership went first to Chin in the north central part of China and afterwards to other states.

The system of hegemony or leadership through a First Noble in one strong state ended with the rise of peripheral states, particularly in the south. The state of Ch'u had been outside of the old area of Shang and Chou culture and only gradually became more Chinese in its civilization. It was far enough removed from the center of authority whether exercised by the Chou kings or the First Nobles in the north to refer to their rulers as *wang* right from the beginning. Later, in the sixth century, two other states rose to power in the lower Yangtze valley; first the state of Wu and then the state of Yueh. These were definitely "barbarian" states outside the old culture system of the north.

MIDDLE CHOU SOCIETY. The social system of the Chou period was based on land, the main feature being a hereditary landed aristocracy. Trade provided another means of attaining wealth. This was a period of dynamic growth, when, for example, in the sixth century iron came into general use and trade was carried on over long distances by the use of horses and the building of roads. A type of copper money (not yet in the form of coins) also facilitated commercial transactions. Although trade was mainly limited to such things as special foods, furs, and silk, it did lead to the development of a wealthy class and did result in a more luxurious living for some of the nobility.

[1] Manuscript essay by J. P. Lo entitled "Case Studies of Chinese Political Leaders. No. 1: Duke Huan of Ch'i," (Seattle, 1961).

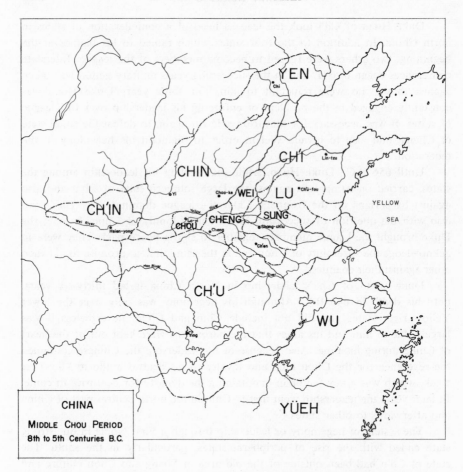

CHINA

MIDDLE CHOU PERIOD
8th to 5th Centuries B.C.

Among the hereditary aristocracy there was a series of gradations of rank. This class and its various strata had some resemblance to the nobility of medieval Europe. In China it should be noted there were neither the sharp distinctions nor the rigid caste system which existed in India. Some men advanced in social standing, and there were families which declined and which became members of the lower classes.

There was a definite distinction, however, between the superior men (the nobility) and those classed as inferior. Most of the peasantry were not really free but were subject to the power of their rulers. No appeal could be made beyond the man's own superior. At the lowest level of society there were also slaves, persons who perhaps had originally been captured as prisoners of war or who might have been brought to this level through being condemned as criminals. Such condemnation was sometimes merely a matter of having offended one of the superior class.

In this aristocracy of Middle Chou times the family was of prime importance. The family might consist of several generations living together in the same household under the authority of members of the eldest generation. They held goods and property more or less in common. Marriage was of great importance of bringing new members into the household. Marriages were arranged by parents and go-betweens, although cases of elopement were not unknown.

In this family system women had a subordinate position. This fact is referred to in a poem of the time in which it is said a man may have sons and in that case they will sleep on couches and play with sceptres, whereas if he has daughters they will be sleeping on the ground and will have only tiles to play with. Although women were definitely subordinate in Chou society, an elder matriarch (i.e., an older woman who was the sole survivor of an early generation) might have authority such as a younger woman could not expect to have.

The system of inheritance was one in which the eldest son of the first wife was the principal beneficiary. However, in a polygamous society there were not unnaturally occasions for plotting by lesser wives on behalf of their own sons.

In this system the individual had definite responsibilities within the family group, a feature of Chinese society which has continued into modern times. The young had certain duties to perform in relation to their parents and elders. In addition, there were the obligations to keep harmony within the family, as illustrated in the following poem.

> Of all the men in the world
> None are equal to brothers . . .
> Brothers may quarrel inside the walls,
> But they will oppose insult from without . . .
> Loving union with wife and children
> Is like the music of lutes;
> But it is the accord of brothers
> Which makes harmony and happiness lasting.[2]

MIDDLE CHOU CULTURE.   We have noted above that the social concepts of the time were embodied in poetry. These poems are contained in the *Classic of Poetry* or *Book of Songs* (or *Odes*) which provides much information about the life of the eighth and seventh centuries B.C. The *Book of Songs* tells of social conditions, courtship and marriage, errant lovers, the misery of soldiers, and contains popular myths and legends.

This poetry was only part of the very extensive Chou literature, some of which has survived. Originally there were also records of various kinds, an indication of high literacy among the aristocracy. Histories were kept in great detail, histories of the royal house and of some of the states. Occasionally writing would be used to put an inscription on a ceremonial bronze, particularly something that had to do with recording the prestige of the person who had the bronze made. Other literary works of the time included texts on omens and divination, rituals, and affairs of the court.

    [2] James Legge, *The Chinese Classics,* Vol. IV (London: Trübner & Co., 1871), pp. 250–252. By permission of Routledge and Kegan Paul Ltd.

During the entire Eastern Chou period, the culture of the central states in the north gradually spread so that people who were formerly referred to as "barbarians" were more and more drawn into the mainstream of Chinese culture and politics. This was important to the north and west, where pastoral peoples became a part of the Chinese community. Other peoples along the east coast who were closely allied in culture and language to the Chinese of the Yellow river valley were now more fully integrated into Chinese society. And finally, peoples using other languages, those residing in the Yangtze valley, were affected by a migration of people from the north into their region. In this last case the result was the creation of the two new states referred to above, Wu in the lower Yangtze valley and Yueh directly to the southeast.

China's Place in Asia

It may be useful at this point to compare the culture of Shang and Chou China in early times with developments in other areas. There are certain important similarities and many striking differences.

In the first place, agriculture was generally of prime importance. In China, north India, and Mesopotamia, civilization developed in the great river valleys. In China, as in India, the ruling classes had hereditary rights. People of the lower classes were much restricted and there was no real concern with the rights of the human individual. In those societies there was no tradition of the individual freedom as existed among the Hebrews and in Mesopotamia.

In most parts of Asia there was no early political unity. This was characteristic of India and a great part of Southwest Asia. In India there was no widespread political unification until the time of the Maurya empire in the fourth century B.C., and in Southwest Asia there was no all-embracing political authority until the founding of the Achaemenian Persian empire in the sixth century B.C. Early unifying empires in Mesopotamia actually extended over only small areas in Southwest Asia.

In China, on the other hand, while there was some diversity north and south, nevertheless in these early times there was one dominant culture—first the Shang and after that the Chou. Although there was political division among many states, there was the strong concept of political unity. The people of Chou times continued to respect the Chou king at Lo-yang, in spite of the real autonomy of most of the princes and of the fact that the king had no effective power.

While the peoples of both India and China were concerned with religion (indeed this is characteristic of the early peoples all across Asia), nevertheless only in India do we have both a great interest in metaphysical speculation and the development of a dominant priestly class. In India the Brahmins were set aside as a hereditary sacred caste who alone might serve as the interpreters of religion. In China there was nothing like this. There was, to be sure, the aristocracy who controlled the land. But it was the aristocracy itself and its subordinates who officiated in their own religion.

The most important distinction between India and China in this early time is the fact that in India there was a caste system, an institution which has lasted down through the centuries. On the other hand, in China, although there was the distinction between the nobility and the common man, there was no concept of a hereditary incapacity transmitted from father to son which would prevent someone of a lower class from rising up by his own efforts. Families might rise and fall in the social scale, and at any one time there was a series of gradations without any abrupt cleavages between particular classes.

BASIC DATES

C. 2000 B.C.	Start of Chinese Early Bronze civilization
C. 1750 B.C.	Start of Shang culture
C. 1523 B.C.	
to 1028 B.C.	Shang dynasty
C. 1300 B.C.	Founding of Anyang
C. 1050 to	
771 B.C.	Western Chou dynasty
About 1028 B.C.	Chou conquest of Shang
841 B.C.	Revolt against King Li of Chou
770 to 256 B.C.	Eastern Chou dynasty
770 to about 500	
B.C.	"Middle Chou"
685 to 643 B.C.	Duke Huan of Ch'i

SUPPLEMENTARY READING

CREEL, H. G. *The Birth of China.* New York, 1954.

CRESSEY, G. B. *China's Geographic Foundations.* New York, 1934.

FAIRBANK, J. K. *The United States and China.* Cambridge, Mass., 1961. Well-written and lucidly presented introduction to Chinese civilization.

FITZGERALD, C. P. *China: A Short Cultural History.* London, 1950.

GOODRICH, L. C. *A Short History of the Chinese People,* 3rd ed. New York, 1959.

GROUSSET, R. *The Civilizations of the East, Vol. III: China.* New York, 1935.

LATOURETTE, K. S. *The Chinese: Their History and Culture.* New York, 1946. A standard text.

REISCHAUER, E. O. AND J. K. FAIRBANK. *East Asia: The Great Tradition.* Boston, 1958. An excellent and recent text by the leading American scholars in the field.

SICKMAN, L. AND A. SOPER. *The Art and Architecture of China.* Baltimore, 1956. Authoritative.

SULLIVAN, M. *An Introduction to Chinese Art.* Berkeley, Cal., 1961.

ADVANCED READING

BODDE, D. "Myths of Ancient China," in S. N. KRAMER, ed., *Mythologies of the Ancient World*. Chicago, 1961.

CHENG, T. K. *Archaeology in China*. Vol. II: *Shang China*. Cambridge, 1960.

CREEL, H. G. *Studies in Early Chinese Culture,* First Series. Baltimore, 1937.

FUNG, Y. L. *A Short History of Chinese Philosophy*. New York, 1945.

LI CHI. *The Beginnings of Chinese Civilization: Three Lectures Illustrated with Finds at Anyang*. Seattle, 1957.

SIREN, O. *A History of Early Chinese Art*. London, 1929.

WALEY, A. *The Book of Songs*. London, 1937.

XVII ❀❀

CHINA FROM CONFUCIUS

TO THE HAN EMPIRE

AFTER CENTURIES OF A HIGH DEGREE of cultural development accompanied by increasing disunity among its various parts in the period between the sixth century B.C. and the third century A.D. China achieved a degree of unification which was to be one of the main characteristics of Chinese civilization in later ages. This unification was effected politically by the state of Ch'in and ideologically by the teacher Confucius and his followers. It was perfected by the rise, development, and endurance of the great Han empire. The Han used the ideology of Confucius, continued the political unification brought about by the Ch'in, and achieved a new territorial greatness as well as commercial development.

Also by Han times there was in China one prevailing literary tradition. The great books of China were the "Classics" of Confucius and his followers. During the Han dynasty comprehensive histories were written and these became part of the tradition. This body of literature in one written classical language was an important unifying force and valued by schoolmasters and politicians of China from Chou times to the twentieth century.

In contrast to Europe, divided after the fall of the Roman empire, China after the Han continued to have a strong feeling of unity in spite of long periods of political division. One dominant culture led the Chinese to think of themselves as "men of Han," members of one country and of the leading race within their world. China was the "Middle Kingdom" and within its embrace were border peoples of lesser importance, such as the peoples of Korea, Annam (Vietnam), Tibet, and the steppe areas to the north and west.

Confucius: His Time and Career

THE LATE CHOU PERIOD.   The last three centuries of the Eastern Chou may be referred to as the Late Chou. This period followed the Middle Chou and began with the time of Confucius. The Late Chou extended from the alignment of new strong feudal states during the fifth century until the third century, when the Chou line was extinguished and the state of Ch'in became supreme. This was a period of violent political change, social disintegration, and rebuilding. At the time when Confucius lived and when several states were contending for supremacy within China, Chinese culture was also spread among the alien races within China proper and to tribes on the borders. The powerful border states such as Ch'in and Chin in the north and also Ch'i in the northeast were conquering tribes which were formerly outside the sphere of Chinese culture. Southern states, namely Ch'u in central China and Wu in the southern Yangtze region, which were beyond the sphere of Chinese culture and outside the Chinese family of states at the beginning of the Eastern Chou, gradually became larger and more Chinese in their culture.

The political feature of the time was the struggle for supremacy among the strong feudal states, particularly the great states of Chin, Ch'in, Ch'i, and Ch'u. We shall note the final stages of this struggle in a succeeding section. In the process of this struggle many smaller states were destroyed and hence old feudal families were ruined, eliminated, or disrupted. Other families came into prominence in the political and social change of the time.

The result of the fall in status of older educated noble families was that aristocrats turned to new occupations. Some of them in the northeast, for example, turned to the manufacture of salt. Some went into other kinds of business. Those who had scholarly training often went into schoolteaching.

In the struggle for supremacy among the Chinese states the rulers and their families realized that they needed advisers, men who were skilled in politics and diplomacy. Thus each ruler was especially eager to find men well-versed in political science who might aid him in strengthening his own organization. In the next section we shall see how Confucius and his ideas came to meet the need of the time.

While some felt the need for a practical social-political philosophy in a time of disturbance, the nobility of this period maintained their interest in ancient religious beliefs and reliance on the gods as described in Chapter 16. This meant observance of ceremonies and the continued manufacture of bronze vessels and jades for use in the rituals. The spreading rivalry for power among states and nobility in the Late Chou period was reflected in a rivalry in display of wealth and pomp and a development of a highly refined "luxury art." The perfection of craftsmanship in the ritual jades culminates in this period. Bronzes once more attained a quality similar to that of Shang and Early Chou times. In addition there was greater detail in the work of this period, such as the use of gold and silver, and inlays of turquoise and semiprecious stones.

The making of artistic objects for display purposes gave rise to new patterns and types. The so-called Scytho-Siberian animal styles from Central Asia were introduced and influenced Late Chou bronze art. Some of the bronze vessels were in the shape of lively animals, sometimes with extravagant forms, including in the end of Late Chou the use of the dragon which became so important in Chinese art in later periods. From the tombs of the feudal princes of this period we have available horses and human figures made of bronze. Also in some instances wooden figures have been recovered from the early tombs.

CONFUCIUS (551-479 B.C.). We have noted that amid the political and social changes of Chou times men looked for new ways in which to govern and order their society. The disturbances and violence of this period resulted in increasing consideration of man and his adjustment to the social environment. One who was particularly concerned with the place of man in society was Confucius.

The latinized form Confucius comes from the Chinese K'ung Fu-tzu, meaning K'ung the Teacher. This man was a son of a minor official in the state of Lu, south of T'aishan in Shantung, during the sixth century B.C. Confucius started his career as a teacher. He was at one time advisor to the princely ruler in his home state, the Duke of Lu. But Confucius himself was not employed in any definite capacity as an official. For many years he had no political influence, but studied and taught, sometimes living in Lu, sometimes in nearby states.

Confucius had definite ideals which he attempted to inculcate among his disciples, his pupils, and among the officials who would listen to him. However, he did not receive the attention which he hoped to have in Lu. For about fourteen years he traveled with a group of followers in various states of north-central China seeking a ruler who might put his principles into effect. The last years of his life were spent in Lu.

Confucius was much interested in morality and has sometimes been termed China's first great moralist. He sought a way of living which may be described as a moderate way, a middle path, or a path of compromise. In so doing Confucius advocated a conservative social philosophy loyal to the old traditions.

In his conservatism he advocated the preservation of the best of the old traditions and was much interested in standards of human conduct. Confucius stressed certain definite virtues and ethics, the conduct and behavior of human beings, particularly in each person's contact with others. He believed that there were certain relationships that should be maintained between members of the feudal aristocracy and those beneath them. And he stressed the patterns of conduct within the family, as for example between elder and younger members of the group. In teaching these things Confucius did not discuss religion, being more concerned with the affairs of men in their mortal lives.

Confucius was a defender of authority in his belief that the subject owed loyalty to the ruler. Confucius advocated a government by regulations, with proper respect for authority, but at the same time he stressed the idea that a father in a family or a ruler in a state must set the correct moral example to those under his authority. Position and status in society, for Confucius, carried with them certain responsibilities. An official must speak and act in accordance with what was expected of a man in his office.

If men in their private lives or in government activities were to behave according to a certain pattern they must be educated in order to fulfill their responsibilities. Confucius said to his disciples, "Learning without thought is useless. Thought without learning is dangerous." On another occasion Confucius said to one of his disciples, "Shall I teach you the meaning of knowledge? When you know a thing to recognize that you know it, and when you do not know to recognize that you do not know—that is knowledge."

Contending States and New Ideas

WARRING STATES PERIOD.   As the name "Warring States" implies, this was a time of struggle for leadership among the several feudal states. The contest finally culminated in the rise to absolute power of the state of Ch'in. During the time of Confucius there occurred an event of key importance in the competition among the states. This was the disintegration of one of the greater states of the preceding period, the state of Chin, in modern Shansi, which broke up into three smaller competing states. New principalities known as Chao, Wei, and Han shared authority in the area of the former Chin state.

While Lu in Shantung and some other small states in north-central China survived, the real struggle for power concerned primarily Ch'i in northern Shantung, Ch'u in the central Yangtze valley, Yen in the northeast, the three successor states of Chin, and most important, the state of Ch'in to the northwest including as its key area the Wei river valley.

To the above powers should be added the newly important state of Yueh in the lower Yangtze valley and along the southeast coast. Yueh in 473 conquered the old Wu in the lower Yangtze valley. Later, by the middle of the fourth century B.C., the old area of Wu was taken from Yueh by Ch'u and the fight to win all of China began to be narrowed to a contest between Ch'u in the south and Ch'in in the northwest.

Rulers of the greater states took for their own use the title of king (wang) which had formerly been reserved for their suzerain, the Chou ruler. Now even the three successor states of the old Chin area took the title of king, thus signifying their practical independence from the Chou. The end of the period came with the extinction of the Chou state in 256 B.C. Warfare continued until the final elimination in 221 B.C. of all the states except Ch'in, as will be noted in more detail later on.

Until the fifth century B.C. there were certain well-recognized ceremonies by which states dealt with each other. The increasingly intense competition between the states meant that strategy and clever diplomacy became more important, and warfare itself became more ruthless. At the same time there came to be felt the need for specialists in philosophy and politics, as will be explained in the next section.

The climax of the political struggle was accentuated by certain new developments in the Chinese economy. The border states, particularly Ch'in, which had contact with the nomadic barbarians of the steppe, began to use cavalry instead of the traditional chariots. Also they learned to use iron. A money economy began to develop. The states further strengthened their economy by water control projects for irrigation and for communications. All these factors were particularly important in enhancing the power of Ch'in.

The ancient religion had depended upon the various princes maintaining the old cult. But as the principalities were destroyed the official ceremonies were continued only in about ten centers; there was less popular participation. Also some changes occurred in the religious practices of the Warring States period. There was an increase in the worship of the spirits of ancestors, with sacrifices in recognition of special merits not only by their immediate descendants but by others who may be called outsiders, a change that had already developed by the time of Confucius. Scholars were used as political advisers by the great lords of the Warring States period and their ideas importantly influenced the development of Chinese religion. In their minds religion and politics were closely associated, although they were less interested in fine ceremonies than they were in the moral perfection of those who officiated and participated in such rites. Hence among the scholars the gods were considered less as personal deities and more as impersonal forces. Two currents of thinking developed. One was in the direction of rationalization leading toward a scientific explanation of the universe, and the other was a philosophical movement towards personal religion.

Meanwhile there was a popular type of religion which we need to understand as a background for the philosophical Taoism which will be described in the next section. With sorcerers both male and female as religious intermediaries, the lower-class Chinese attempted to establish personal contact with the gods. They were concerned also with human destiny after death. The attainment of paradise had not been a consideration of the older official religion, but by the end of the Warring States period, there was interest in immortality. The first Ch'in emperor carried on great state sacrifices because of his own special interest in future life. Philosophically this interest was associated with the political unification of the country, which was thought to be a step in the direction of a utopia.

The greater importance of scholars was reflected not only in religion, but also in literary activities. Important for the scholars were the great books of antiquity, the so-called "Classics" of China which were written down and highly valued in the time from Confucius to the third century B.C. The actual texts of these writings were the subject of controversy in later times.

By the time of the Warring States several important works were already in existence. The *Book of Poetry* included poems which depicted social conditions and thus constituted historical documents for the life of the time before Confucius. In addition there was a collection of omen and divination texts (the *Book of Changes*), and histories of the royal house as well as of some of the states. The one dealing with the royal house is known as the *Book of Documents* (or *History*). The most important of the state histories was that of the state of Lu known as the *Spring and Autumn Annals*. In addition to these four there were a collection of rituals as practiced at the court (the *Book of Rites*). No exact dates are known for any of these. During the Warring States period itself other important books on politics and philosophy were compiled. Some of this writing together with the earlier *Analects* of Confucius later was included as part of the "Classics." This leads to a consideration of the various schools of philosophy which developed in the Warring States Period.

SCHOOLS OF PHILOSOPHY.   After Confucius and while the several feudal states were contending ever more bitterly against each other there was an increasing interest in man and his place in society and the universe. The followers of Confucius were only one of a number of rival schools who competed for the attention of thinking men during the fifth, fourth, and third centuries B.C. One might take notice of the fact that these same centuries saw intellectual ferment in the Greek and Indian worlds as well.

Of the several schools which developed during the Warring States period four important ones need to be mentioned. First, as noted above, there were the followers of Confucius. Among them the philosopher Mencius was particularly important. Next there were those who were interested in a quite different philosophy, that associated with the name Lao-tzu, and who are known to us as the Taoists. A third system of thinking was developed by the philosopher Mo-tzu; unlike the others it did not have a lasting effect on later centuries of Chinese development. A fourth group, very important in the Warring States period, were the Legalists.

In Wei, a successor state to Chin, lived the philosopher Meng, who is known in the West by his latinized name, Mencius. He was a follower of Confucius who added certain important ideas to the teachings of the master, especially the importance of the people in government and the concept that man was essentially good.

Among the Confucianists there was also one in the latter part of the period, about 300 B.C., who denied Mencius' ideas about the goodness of man and who said that man was essentially evil. This was the philosopher Hsün-tzu, who stressed the need for regulations and institutions. It should be noted that both were Confucian in that they believed in education.

The Confucianists engaged in teaching, debating, and writing, and took a common-sense attitude toward political and ethical problems. They assumed the existence of religion but they did not propagate it. They had an increasing influence during the period and especially in the periods which follow the Warring States.

Very different from the followers of Confucius were the Taoists, so-called because of their interest in the concept of "Tao" (the way). The originator of this school is a mythical character, whom the Chinese refer to as Lao-tzu, the "Old Philosopher." The ideas expressed in the classic book of Taoism are supposed to be his ideas. The main features of Taoism were a simple naturalism which would lead men to ignore the teaching of definite virtues and ethics and to believe in the Tao (the way, perhaps better translated as the eternal essence, the essence of heaven and earth in all things). This was then a mystical system, involved in metaphysics and not only concerned about the affairs of men.

> There was something formless yet complete,
> That existed before heaven and earth;
> Without sound, without substance,
> Dependent on nothing, unchanging,
> All pervading, unfailing,
> One may think of it as the mother of all things under heaven.
> Its true name we do not know;
> The Tao, the "Way" is the by-name that we give it.[1]

Concerning men, the Taoists believed that a ruler or a person in a position of power could best act by *not* asserting himself, not interfering with the affairs of other people (a form of laissez-faire). This was in contrast with the Confucian emphasis on proper relations, on proper government from above. The principle of nonassertion may be better understood from the following quotation:

> The best charioteers do not rush ahead;
> The best fighters do not make displays of wrath.
> The greatest conqueror wins without joining issue;
> The best user of men acts as though he were their inferior.
> This is called the power that comes of not contending,
> Is called the capacity to use men,
> The secret of being mated to heaven, to what was of old.[2]

Following the teachings of Lao-tzu as noted above and living in the period 350-250 B.C. was another in the school of Taoists known as Chuang-tzu, important because of his adding a feeling of romanticism to the mysticism of Lao-tzu. This romanticism may be glimpsed by reference to a poem which he is said to have written about himself.

---

[1] Arthur Waley, *The Way and Its Power* (London: George Allen & Unwin Ltd., 1934), p. 174.
[2] *Ibid.*, p. 227.

"Formerly, I, Chwang Chou, dreamt that I was a butterfly, a butterfly flying about, feeling that it was enjoying itself. I did not know that it was Chou. Suddenly I awoke and was myself again, the veritable Chou. I did not know whether it had formerly been Chou dreaming that he was a butterfly, or whether it was now a butterfly dreaming that it was Chou." [3]

The third school of importance during the time of the Warring States was the school of the philosopher Mo, Mo-tzu.

The philosopher Mo (479-c. 400 B.C.), like the Confucianists, believed in social organization, but he did not believe in regulated personal relationships. Instead he thought in terms of universal love without differentiation among people. He based this doctrine on a belief in heaven and taught that men had a duty to follow the will of heaven.

At this point we may note the comparison between these three philosophies in regard to their attitudes toward the individual. The followers of Mo-tzu believed that in respect to people there should be "no difference"; the followers of Confucius believed in an aristocratic ideal and that among men there was a "difference"; on the other hand, the followers of Lao-tzu, the Taoists, in regard to these relationships adopted an attitude of "indifference."

During the social and political disturbances of the fourth century B.C. there developed still another school of thought which was concerned with order both in the state and in society. The Legalists, or the School of Law, advocated a single law governing all men, quite different from the Confucian idea of rites for men of superior quality and punishments for the men of a lower class. This emphasis on law differed also from the concepts of the West. The law of the Legalists represented only the will of the ruler; that is to say, it was his personal dictate, his fiat, which was the law that had to be applied universally throughout the state, not a permanent code such as Roman law in the West. The Legalists believed in rewards and harsh punishments for the control of the populace. This Legalist philosophy was one of the strengthening characteristics of the state of Ch'in in its rise to power.

Two New Empires

CH'IN.   The Warring States period culminated in the rise of one state, Ch'in in northwest China. Following the Legalist authoritarian philosophy, the rulers of Ch'in consolidated their position in the Wei river valley and nearby territory. They ended feudalism in their own territory, proceeded to defeat their enemies, and brought all of China under one government. The first Ch'in emperor also took steps in the direction of cultural unification. Territorially China had never before been expanded to such a great extent, but the power of the Ch'in lasted only until 206 B.C.

[3] Daisetz Teitaro Suzuki, *A Brief History of Early Chinese Philosophy,* 2nd ed. (London: Arthur Probsthain, 1914), p. 163.

FIGURE 17.1. Bronze mirror with spiral pattern, probably Ch'in period.

The Ch'in created a centralized, well-organized empire comparable to that of Darius in Iran and to that of the Maurya in India. The rulers of Ch'in established a purposive disciplined regime, a government opposed to hereditary nobility and feudalism and operating under a system of universal law. Laws were harsh, with precise rewards and punishments for different types of conduct. The absolute rule of the Ch'in was established through a centralized bureaucracy. As part of the process the population was organized in groups, families in clusters responsible for the good behavior of their members. The old aristocracy was ended. Feudalism ceased to exist wherever the Ch'in extended their rule. Land ownership was placed in the hands of individual peasant proprietors and agriculture as such was encouraged. Ch'in itself was made self-sufficient, partly through development of an irrigation system which increased the grain yield and made central Shensi, the Wei river valley, a key economic area in the Chinese economy. On the other hand there was less interest in interstate commerce than there had been formerly.

Ch'in was organized for war with the creation of an effective military machine. The people of the northwest were accustomed to fighting against the nomadic barbarians of the northern steppe regions and from them had adopted the use of horses, cavalry, and foot soldiers in warfare instead of the chariots favored by their rivals in China. Also the Ch'in were favored by geography. The center of their power was in the "region within the passes," the Wei river valley, where mountains gave them a commanding position in which they were not easily overrun as were so many of the other states during the campaigns of the Warring States period.

In 256 B.C. the Ch'in put an end to the authority of the Chou at Lo-yang. The Ch'in took over the royal domain and other states acknowledged their supremacy. In the years that followed personal character also played its part in the rise of the Ch'in. The Ch'in king who reigned from 247 to 210 B.C. and who came to the throne at the age of twelve secured personal control of the government in 238 B.C.

The unification of China was brought about through the elimination, mainly from 230 to 221 B.C., of the other important states which had survived until the third century. After the conquest of central China there followed the destruction of Ch'u, and finally the surrender of Ch'i in 221, by which time all the independent states had been eliminated. At that point the Ch'in ruler took the significant new title of "Emperor" (*Huang-ti*), or "First Emperor" (*Shih Huang-ti*), rather than the Chou title of king (*wang*).

Military and political unification was accompanied by unification of culture. The official ideology was that of the Legalists. Teachers and scholars were put on government salaries, and those who opposed the Ch'in regime were executed. Many books were burned, although copies of important books were kept in the imperial collection. Language reform also took place. One written form was promulgated for practical needs, and a beginning was made toward unification of dialects within the country.

Territorial expansion went considerably beyond the area of the former contending states. To the north the Hsiung-nu were driven out of north China, and previous fortifications were united into one "Great Wall" as a military barrier against raids from the steppe. Parts of China that had hitherto been outside the political system were conquered for the first time, including the present province of Fukien on the southeast coast and Kwangtung and Kwangsi in southern China. Ch'in Shih Huang's forces went beyond this into Tongking, part of northern Vietnam.

After the First Emperor died in 210 B.C. the weaknesses within his system became apparent. In the first place the authoritarian rule of the Ch'in depended on the strength of character of the ruler. His son was not a strong type, so was not successful in holding the country together. He had to face the opposition of the scholars, whose ideas and connections with former feudal families created a core of dissatisfaction. In addition there were many unemployed, partly because of the economic changes put into effect. Some of the unemployed were used for great public works such as unification of the Great Wall and canal building, but this in turn caused popular discontent and risings against the Ch'in shortly after the death of the First Emperor. In a very few years the country was in a state of civil war. When the Ch'in authority was overthrown various leaders rose up to compete for power in China.

HSIUNG-NU. Before continuing with the internal history it is necessary to have some understanding of relations with the peoples of the northern border region, relations which were to have a profound effect throughout most of Chinese history. Here, non-Chinese people with a steppe culture formed a confederation of tribes and became a key factor in China's external relations until the end of the Han dynasty.

In the steppe area north of China extending both north and south of the Gobi desert peoples from early times had a nomadic culture dependent on the nature of the open country which reached from present Manchuria to southern Russia. This was a pastoral culture which was supported in a manner completely different from that of the irrigated agricultural regions of China. Nomads of various tribes and languages made periodic raids from this steppe area into Chinese territory. It was one of these groups which sacked and destroyed the west Chinese capital of the Chou in the Wei valley in the eighth century.

By the time of the Warring States period the dominant element among the tribes of present Mongolia were the Hsiung-nu. In the fourth and third centuries B.C. the Hsiung-nu became an important political factor. A true nomad pastoralism not dependent on agriculture made the tribesmen more mobile, capable of being organized and less concerned with marginal lands on which crops might be raised.

At the same time that the first emperor of the Ch'in was unifying China the Hsiung-nu were being combined into an effective confederation, the first such unification of the steppe people north of China. Their territory extended to the Chinese borders. Because of this new military and political threat to the north the first Ch'in emperor ordered the combining of border fortifications into the line of the Great Wall.

After the death of Ch'in Shih Huang-ti a great leader among the Hsiung-nu, Mao Tun, was successful in making his state even stronger, partly at the expense of the Chinese. From 210 to 174 B.C. Mao Tun was supreme ruler of a steppe empire consisting of all present Mongolia, the Liao valley in southwest Manchuria, the trade routes extending west of China in Chinese Turkistan, and the region of western Siberia, thus posing a threat to the weak Ch'in ruler who succeeded the First Emperor.

During the years after the fall of the Ch'in and when a new line of rulers, the Han dynasty, began to reign in China, the Hsiung-nu disputed the control of the trade routes to the west with the Chinese. The Yüeh-chi tribe which resisted Hsiung-nu domination northwest of China was forced to migrate early in the second century B.C. far to the west, to the upper Syr-darya valley in Fergana. Later the Yüeh-chi moved into the Amu-darya valley (about 140 B.C.), Sogdia, and Bactria with important consequences for the history of Central Asia (see Chapter 6.)

Thus the Hsiung-nu occupied the borderlands of China and controlled a vast territory from Tibet to the Yellow Sea while the Han were rising to power. Mao Tun intended ultimately to conquer China itself, and he had the satisfaction of making a peace treaty with the first Han emperor on his own terms. The Chinese were forced to send food, clothing materials, including silk, and a Chinese princess to those whom they thought of as "barbarians". This was only a temporary expedient, a matter of appeasement, and the Hsiung-nu continued to raid the Han frontiers.

This Hsiung-nu empire, which lasted for many years, finally disintegrated in the years 58 to 51 B.C. Later on the struggle was renewed between the Chinese and border barbarians. The usurper Wang Mang, whose history is told below, failed in his attempts to control the peoples of the northern borders. Only later, in the eighth to ninth decades of the first century A.D., were the restored Han rulers with the aid of the great general Pan Ch'ao able to gain successes and to secure control of the silk routes leading through Central Asia to the west.

The Han Dynasty

WESTERN HAN. The great Han empire, which endured from the third century B.C. until the third century A.D., started with two strong rulers, one of whom took advantage of the chaos at the end of the Ch'in period to establish himself as first emperor of a new dynasty, the Han, and to reunify China. The first emperor and the Emperor Wu, his successor fifty-five years later, established an imperial bureaucracy which maintained itself even when there was not a strong emperor on the throne. Thus they began the first enduring Chinese empire. The state was based on Confucian doctrine, which was important both in education and in politics. These rulers and their successors expanded commerce, extended Chinese control to border regions, and in the process faced new economic problems of taxation and administration. The Western Han ended about the beginning of the Christian era with a factional split and a usurpation of power at the Han court.

The man who first took the name of "King of Han" during the rebellions against the Ch'in at the end of the third century was a minor official named Liu Chi. Starting with control of the Wei river valley, Liu reunified China, made himself the first "Emperor" of the Han, and reigned from 202 to 195 B.C. This first emperor of the Han, known to history as Kao-tsu, established his family in power, rewarded his subordinates, and preserved some of the traditions of former times, but in establishing a new and strong government on the model of the Ch'in empire he realized it was necessary to have his advisors watch over the local princes in different parts of the country. Vassal kingdoms, created among those rebels against the Ch'in who now swore loyalty to the Han, were a weakness of the early Han regime. Only gradually was the state centralized. Towards the end of his reign Kao-tsu became very suspicious of even his closest intimates and ruthlessly suppressed rebellious subordinates.

The Han Emperor Wu (140–87 B.C.) was especially noted for his success in establishing centralized government over an empire which he also greatly expanded. A centralized bureaucratic system was created in which the ideas of Confucius played an important part. In accordance with such concepts the emperor called to his service men of ability wherever he found them. This meant a disregard for birth and a divergence from the emphasis on noble inheritance such as had prevailed in Chou times. Wu commanded local officials to recommend men of virtue and wisdom for the imperial government and thus began an organized method of selection which developed into an enduring educational and examination system. The emperor made use of scholars as officials, as interpreters of the governmental ideology, and as writers who produced works of history and political thought for the state. Along with scholarship went an official concern for cosmology and morality, and a belief in the connection between the elements of the universe and the conduct of men. The training of scholar officials was carried on through a study of the Confucian Classics.

The Han is noted for the interpretation of these Classics by such philosophers as Tung Chung-shu. Han Confucianism was an important element in the culture of this period and became the basis for the thinking of later centuries. The so-called Confucianism of the Han scholars was a philosophy in which contemporary superstitions and many ideas other than those of Confucius were incorporated. However, the main feature that gives it its name was the fact that among the Han scholars Confucius was the ideal person, the one whose ideas were revered. They termed those books concerned with Confucian teachings the "Classics" of literature and thereby placed them higher than any other writings.

The histories written in the Confucian tradition, by such men as Ssu-ma Ch'ien and the writers of the Eastern Han period, looked to Confucius and his way of interpreting events as an ideal. In the cycles of dynasties as portrayed by these historians the personal elements were emphasized.

Confucianism's importance in Han times was also shown in the fact that scholars in the Confucian tradition held high government posts. They ran the state even though the state itself was Legalist in operation. How the conflict between the ideas of Confucius and the emphasis on the law of the ruler worked out in actual practice will be mentioned further on.

Although Legalist theories and Taoist ideas predominated during the first few reigns of the Western Han period, the ideas of Confucian adherents grew in political importance starting with the time of the Emperor Wu. In addition to the interest in the Confucian Classics, the rise of the examination system also helped establish Confucianism as the philosophy of the new Han system of government. Since Emperor Wu wished to have officials chosen competitively on a basis of ability, selection became based on the results of examinations on the Classics. Schools were thus needed at the capital and in the provinces to train candidates for official position. A state-supported imperial academy was founded by Emperor Wu in 124 B.C. and this system was gradually extended to the provinces.

The new reverence for the Classics during the Han led naturally to an intense study of these writings by various scholars, and one significant feature was the development of scientific textual criticism and an interpretation of the Classics. The Han interpretation of the Classics was important for many centuries, actually until about the thirteenth century, the period of the Sung. In recent times the version of the understanding of the Classics by the Han school of scholars has been given precedence over the later version of the Sung scholars.

In developing the political theory of Han times based on the study of the Confucian Classics, the court minister and great scholar, Tung Chung-shu, 170–90 B.C., was particularly important. According to Tung, the imperial state was without territorial limits. "All under heaven," all countries and lands, constituted the "state." It was a state which was cosmic-universal in character.

Thus the people of the Chinese state included all mankind, over whom the emperor was supreme, directly under heaven. Heaven's intentions were made known only to the emperor who was referred to as the "Son of Heaven." The emperor received commands from heaven, and the lords of the empire would receive their commands from the Son of Heaven.

The relative peace within a large unified empire during Han times encouraged the development of internal trade and industry inside China. The government took an active part in the construction of canals, both for communications and irrigation purposes, and of roads, and in the regulation of commerce. As will be noted in the next section, the international expansion in the time of the Han required special financing on the part of the central government. To meet such needs the Han administration developed certain state monopolies and participated in the exploitation of salt and iron resources.

In the border relations of the Western Han period, expansion of the empire commenced in the time of Emperor Wu, south into Vietnam and northeast into Korea. Campaigns conducted by the emperor from 133 to 119 B.C. drove back the Hsiung-nu. He prevented their raids into China and safeguarded the caravan trade across Central Asia. After the reign of Emperor Wu hostilities continued. To keep their neighbors in check the Chinese incited other tribes against the Hsiung-nu, a method which they were to follow frequently in the future.

Chinese military expeditions into Central Asia were part of a process of gaining information and opening the trade routes across Turkistan. Emperor Wu's armies conducted successful campaigns in Central Asia from 121 to 102 B.C. and military colonies of Han soldiery were planted along the trade routes. Gradually all of Chinese Turkistan came under Chinese control. The Chinese obtained horses from Fergana and came into contact with the peoples of Sogdia and Bactria, and through them entered into commercial relations with the Parthians and Romans. Thus was established the famous silk trade, which was not only important for the Chinese but also very desirable for the Romans, particularly after the unification of the empire by Augustus in 31 B.C.

Wu was a dynamic type of emperor, often found at the beginning of a Chinese dynasty. In his career and in the years immediately following his reign we see the beginnings of a pattern of alternation of types of rule which became characteristic in Chinese development. The personal administration of a strong emperor using and supporting Confucianism would be followed by the rule of "high bureaucrats" who, although less decisive than the energetic ruler, actually might have a more flexible administration than that of the single strong ruler himself. The unified Chinese state of Han times assumed approximately the shape it was to have until very recent times.

Although there were financial difficulties due to military expenditures and the state tended to be weakened from time to time because of great tax-free estates outside central control, nevertheless the Han regime was successful in establishing an imperial government that was centralized, financially stable, administratively efficient, and militarily powerful. Thus immediately following the reign of Emperor Wu the system continued to work despite a succession of mediocre emperors. Another element of advantage to the continuity of the Han regime was the decline of the Hsiung-nu. Their empire collapsed in the years 58 to 51 B.C., and other tribes came to be as important as the Hsiung-nu in the years that followed.

The end of the Western Han resulted from the development of factionalism between influential court families, especially between the Liu family of the founding line and the Wang family connected with the empresses.

WANG MANG. The span of the Han dynasty is divided by the usurpation of Wang Mang, a Han official whose short reign is noted for his radical reform policies. Wang Mang was appointed commander-in-chief of the Han armies because of the influence of his aunt, the empress dowager mother of the reigning Han emperor in the year 8 B.C. Later he was regent for a boy emperor who reigned from A.D. 1 to 6. Thereafter he usurped complete control and in A.D. 9 had himself proclaimed emperor, superseding the Han dynasty and proclaiming the beginning of the Hsin ("New") dynasty. A vigorous ruler with original ideas, Wang Mang nevertheless claimed to base his policy on the teachings of Confucius, and sponsored a revival of interest in ancient Confucian texts.

Wang Mang attempted to strengthen the bureaucracy as well as to solve the financial crisis of the Chinese government. His method was to attempt to inaugurate a number of very radical policies, reforms which he hoped would solve the existing economic problems. The most important of these was his land policy, whereby all land was declared property of the state and was to be divided among the peasants, who then would pay taxes on this land. Other policies of Wang Mang were the institution of state monopolies, the establishment of government storehouses, and the use of the profits of the monopolies for making loans to farmers without interest. He also endeavored to fix prices and to manipulate the currency in the direction of currency debasement. His most important plans, those for nationalizing the land and dividing it among the peasants, could not be enforced, largely because his government had no power over the great estates. Thus he only antagonized wealthy people by his attempts at socialistic reforms.

In his foreign relations Wang Mang aroused the hostility of the Hsiung-nu without any effective action being taken against them. At home floods and dislocation of peasants due to a change in course of the Yellow river led to a popular uprising. When Wang Mang attempted to suppress the rebellion his army disintegrated. He was unable to counteract a real attempt at restoration of Han power and was put to death by his own troops.

EASTERN HAN. Taking advantage of the confusion in the country, a member of the Liu family led the opposition to Wang Mang and restored that family to the throne under the name of the Han dynasty. In this period, known as the

"Eastern Han" because the capital was transferred from Ch'ang-an to Lo-yang, scholars were employed again in important positions in the government and Confucianism became a religious cult as well as an official ideology. By the end of the first century A.D. Chinese power was extended once more along the trade routes and into the heart of Central Asia. Along the overland trails came Buddhism, one of the most important outside influences in Chinese history, from India by way of Central Asia. The Eastern Han was also a time of growth in popularity of religious Taoism. Taoism became associated with the secret societies, some of which engaged in revolts and constituted one of the reasons for the decline of the Han. Other reasons were the barbarian invasions from the steppe and a growth of factionalism at the court.

The founder of the Eastern Han was a prosperous landowner named Liu Hsiu. Known to history as Emporer Kuang-wu, he created a powerful government and reigned from 25 to 57 A.D. Thus the successors of the original Han line of rulers were re-established throughout China. On the other hand, Kuang-wu at the start was not successful in establishing Chinese power along the frontiers against the Hsiung-nu.

This first emperor of the Eastern Han carried on the tradition of relying on scholars as officials in his government. The scholars were trained in the Classics of Confucius, and Confucianism was now firmly established as "the Master" was actually deified in what became a religious cult. This aspect of Confucianism had already begun in the Western Han in the time of the first emperor, Kao-tsu, who made a sacrifice at the grave of Confucius at Ch'ü-fou. Regular ceremonies at temples to Confucius were carried on all over the empire. Emperor Kuang-wu commanded that a descendant of Confucius should perform sacrifices at the sage's burial place (A.D. 37), and from this time forward worship at the tomb of Confucius was a part of the state religion. In the schools, also starting with the reign of the second emperor of the Eastern Han, Confucius was regularly honored. Confucius became the patron saint of the scholars and religion was brought into what had previously been an ethical, political, and philosophic school of thought. In connection with Confucian ethics it should be noted that the Eastern Han period saw the development of the doctrine of filial piety supplementing the classic teachings of former times.

A good example of an important family of scholars at the Eastern Han court during the end of the first and beginning of the second century A.D. was a family named Pan. The father was the historian Pan Piao, who commenced the *History of the Former Han Dynasty*. He was followed by three famous children, including Pan Ku, who wrote most of the history, and his sister, the noted authoress Pan Chao, who took up her brother's work after his death and completed it.

Another son of Pan Piao, the general Pan Ch'ao (A.D. 30–102), re-established Chinese power in Turkistan. At the time when Pan Ch'ao led expeditions into Central Asia, the Yüeh-chi whom we have seen flee before the strength of the Hsiung-nu in an earlier time, were established in Bactria and in Gandhara, under the Kushan branch of their tribe. They controlled the passes leading towards China proper. Thus when the Han government sent out Pan Ch'ao to reassert Chinese authority in the west, he found himself confronting the power of the Kushan and succeeded in defeating them in battle. Chinese prestige was at a high point along the transcontinental trade routes.

The transport of silk from China to the Mediterranean world was more important than ever before. Fragments of Chinese silk, dating from this period, have been found in tombs at Palmyra in Syria, an indication of the extensive commerce which went by way of Parthia to the Roman empire.

Pan Ch'ao brought into submission more than fifty small principalities in Central Asia. Chinese authority lasted until the beginning of the second century, when Tibetans united with Hsiung-nu to break Chinese control of the trade route. Later the Chinese temporarily reasserted their influence. By the second century many Hsiung-nu were actually serving in Chinese armies, and other tribes were coming to prominence in the steppe area of what we now call Mongolia. Meanwhile, not only silk but paper (which had been invented in China about 100 B.C.) and even iron was taken in trade to the west. From the west in return the Chinese imported horses and such new plants as grapes and alfalfa.

RELIGION AND ART. Han cultural life preserved much of the older Chinese tradition and also absorbed new ideas which arrived over the transcontinental trade routes. Certain elements in Taoism such as the nature worship that expressed itself in ceremonies in honor of sacred mountains and rivers and which became part of the state cult, had been significant since very ancient times. The concept of "two in one" (Yin and Yang), the reciprocity of male and female, was a philosophical concept going back to the earliest historical times. Basic in Taoist teaching were the books attributed to philosophers of the Warring States period, the *Tao te ching* (*The Book of the Way and Its Virtue*) and the *Chuang-tzu* (*The Philosopher Chuang*).

Taoists were associated with the historian's office of the government from very early times. Later alchemists and magicians who were teachers of Taoism were influential at the court of the first Ch'in emperor, the first emperor of the Han, and Emperor Wu of the Western Han dynasty. These men combined mysticism and magic with scientific investigation and deceptive practices in their appeal to the superstitious minds of that age.

Some of the basic ideas of Taoism also influenced the state religion of Confucianism. The all-encompassing system of relationships between man, human institutions, events, and natural phenomena could be better explained by Taoism. The Taoists helped the Confucianists to rationalize the position of man in nature. In accordance with the teachings of Tung Chung-shu, the emperors made offerings not only to heaven but also to the mountains, to the rivers, and to the spirits of the ancestors. And in Han times the emperors continued the ancient worship of the spirit of the earth. In addition, by the second century of the Eastern Han the emperors were making sacrifices at the supposed birthplace of Lao-tzu and erected a temple there in his honor.

Along with this influence at court, Taoism, as a religion, became popular in Eastern Han times through the leadership of a man named Chang Tao-ling, who lived during the first and second centuries of the Christian era. He was an alchemist who claimed to have discovered the elixir of life and to have ascended as an immortal to the skies. He founded a sect in which the converts were taxed for his support, and he has sometimes been referred to as the "first Taoist pope." During the declining years of the Han dynasty at the end of the second century A.D. the Chang family supported by this sect created an independent state in western China and governed through a Taoist priesthood, under the leadership of the Chang family.

Another development connected with this was the rise of a Taoist sect known as the "Yellow Turbans." Maintaining Taoist beliefs and secret ritual, this group was the prototype of many pseudoreligious secret cults which played a part in subsequent centuries of Chinese history. A rebellion of this group was one of the factors contributing to the end of the Han dynasty, as will be noted further on, and was only crushed after enormous loss of life.

With the disintegration of the state at the end of the Han period the scholars were no longer sure of the intellectual synthesis which had provided the basis for their role in the state. As the provincial scholar gentry lost their power at the capital they were inclined to turn not only to the teachings of Confucius, but also to other schools of thought, particularly the ideas of Taoism. Meanwhile an entirely new element had been brought from outside China.

From Gandhara during the rule of Indo-Greek princes and spreading along the trade routes into Bactria and Chinese Central Asia had come the religion of Buddhism. We have noted previously that the Kushan turned to Buddhism of the Mahayana type, and that their king Kanishka in the second century of the Christian era was a devoted patron of Buddhism (see Chapter 9). Missionaries from the domains of the Kushan reached Khotan and other oases of Chinese Turkistan.

Buddhist missionaries came to China both by land and by sea, probably as early as the first century A.D. By the second century there are known to have been monastic communities of Indian and Central Asian Buddhists in north China at such places as Ch'ang-an and Lo-yang. There were numerous laymen in these Buddhist communities and Chinese as well as foreign monks. The first Chinese Buddhist monk whose name is definitely known was an officer of the Han court in the end of the second century who left the imperial service to become a Buddhist monk. By the end of the Han period there were Buddhists in south China as well as in the north.

At Lo-yang and other centers translations were made of the Buddhist classics (Sutras) into Chinese. Some 409 works are said to have been translated before the end of the Han. This was a very difficult process, not only because of the ideas which were new to the Chinese but because of the linguistic problems involved in rendering religious concepts from Indian languages into

Chinese. Actually, in spite of all this writing in China there was very little Buddhist influence among the community of Chinese scholars until after the Han period.

The archaeological remains of Han times reveal a continued high level of achievement in jade, stone, bronze (including mirrors), and lacquer-work. The designs represent great changes from the conventions of Shang and Chou times in the direction of simplicity and realism. Evidence of skillful painting is shown in stone bas-reliefs carved as decorations for the tombs in the Eastern Han period. From these we can gain further insight into the mythological and historical beliefs of the period as well as information concerning the architecture, clothing, and chariots of Han times. Especially important among the stone

FIGURE 17.2. House model in polychrome pottery to be placed in a tomb; a fine example of Han realism.

bas-reliefs are the tomb caves found in Szechuan and also the impressive tombs of the Wu family in Shantung.

END OF THE HAN. Noble families, such as those able to commission the beautiful carvings at their tombs in Shantung, were well entrenched by the end of the Han period in positions of power and constituted one of the important.

FIGURE 17.3.   Han jadework; head and shoulders of a horse.

factions in the politics of the time. They had to contend with a varied group of political elements at the court. The emperors themselves were weaklings and puppets in the hands of those who controlled court politics. Among the latter one highly important clique was formed by the court eunuchs attached to the imperial family who had a great deal of influence at the end of the Han. They persecuted the scholar class who had been so important earlier. Another faction was the newly-rich relatives of the empresses of the late Han emperors. Among these numerous factions, the scholar intelligentsia had little opportunity to continue to wield such power as they had known in earlier times.

FIGURE 17.4.   Rubbing from a tomb tile, Western Han period. Dark grey clay, stamped with warrior and dragon design. An example of contorted, fantastic Han motifs.

FIGURE 17.5. Detail from a rubbing of the stone bas-reliefs from the tomb of the Wu family in Shantung, Eastern Han period. The scene indicates the mythological beliefs of the times. It represents the unsuccessful attempt (the broken string) of the First Emperor of the Ch'in to recover the ancient cauldron of Yu and shows movement and grace throughout.

The Han government was also in difficulty economically, partly because of the military expenses necessary to maintain a vast empire, but also because the great landowning families did not pay taxes. Another factor in Han decline was the condition of the peasantry. During this late Eastern Han period the peasants were oppressed by the upper classes, there were more displaced persons and there was suffering due to drought and famine. The discontent among the peasantry, as has already been mentioned, came to be associated with popular uprisings led by religious men of the Taoist sect. These leaders of popular religious Taoism gained power over large areas. The most important resulted in the rebellions of the Yellow Turbans of A.D. 184 in the east and 189 in west China.

At the capital, opponents united temporarily to suppress the rebellions, not without considerable bloodshed and further suffering in the country. After this, the various factions mentioned before turned on each other, and the power of the central government was near collapse. The scholar class, together with the noble families, liquidated the eunuchs. Meanwhile the central government controlled only the capital districts, and power in the country generally passed into the hands of strong men, military adventurers, who had built up their own personal power in the wars against the Yellow Turbans.

Military men dominated the scene in China for the next thirty years. In the struggle between the generals in north China one man, Ts'ao Ts'ao, gradually gained control, first at the capital and then in the whole of north China. In many other areas the government was practically nonexistent and control was in the hands of local bandits. There were however two other important centers of political power by the end of the second century. In the Lower Yangtze region the Sun family were dominant and in the western province of Szechuan (Shu) the leader was Liu Pei, who with his famous friends (see Chapter 18) claimed to be carrying on the tradition of Han rule. They referred to themselves as the "Shu Han."

When Ts'ao Ts'ao, who controlled the capital, died in 220, his son, Ts'ao Pei, took the throne and established himself as the first emperor of the Wei dynasty (not to be confused with the term "Wei" as applied to one of the Warring States of an earlier time nor to be confused with the Wei of the Toba of the fifth and sixth centuries). This Wei dynasty ruled only in north China during the third century. The Shu Han, as noted above, were in control in Szechuan, and in the Lower Yangtze area Sun Ch'uan was proclaimed emperor of Wu.

Another important element had entered the political scene in China by the end of the Han period. Chinese generals during the fighting against the Yellow Turbans and against each other recruited barbarians from the northern frontier regions. Particularly important was the fact that Ts'ao Ts'ao brought in some nineteen tribes of Hsiung-nu, promising them pasturage in Shansi in return for their military service. These were not completely absorbed, however, into the Han body politic. Rather, there were too many of them to be completely controlled and they formed a small, separate political entity of their own under Hsiung-nu leaders. This in itself was not too important but is significant as the beginning of the migrations and invasions from the northern steppe which are characteristic of the period following the Han.

During the Han period, in the border areas the Chinese colonized both to the northeast in Korea and to the far south in Vietnam.

Han Colonies, North and South

KOREA IN CHOU AND HAN TIMES.   The tribes of the Korean peninsula until about the fourth century B.C. were still in a preagricultural, Neolithic, and tribal culture stage. Like other North Asian peoples they appear to have been ruled by aristocratic hereditary leaders. Their early religion was shamanistic demon worship. Into the land occupied by this primitive people came other tribes, Tungusic tribes from the area of Manchuria, migrating because of pressure from the Hsiung-nu power in Mongolia, much as the tribes of the Yüeh-chi, moved to the west into Central Asia because of Hsiung-nu expansion. These Tungusic tribes brought both iron and bronze, so that from this time on there was a gradual change in the culture of the peninsula. At the same time agriculture "began to seep in from China" and farming and the use of metals spread slowly through the peninsula.

Thus in contrast with the Chinese who for nearly a thousand years had been using writing and had a highly developed culture with groupings of states and the various aspects of civilization previously described, the tribes of Korea, only in about the third century B.C., began to develop relations with this more highly organized society to the west.

During the third century B.C. in northwest Korea there arose a political entity which may be called the first true state in Korea. It was known to the Koreans as Choson (commonly spelled Chosen). This political community or state was under the domination of the state of Yen in northeast China in the region of Peking. Into Choson and the other parts of the peninsula refugees from China came during the increasingly harsh wars of the third century which, as we have seen, led up to Ch'in control in the whole of China.

With the collapse of the Ch'in in 210–206 B.C. more refugees from China entered Korea, especially in the northern part near the Yalu river. With the coming of these new immigrants Choson increased in strength becoming a semi-Chinese Korean state, with its capital at Pyong-yang on the Taitong river. Choson exercised some control over much of the Korean peninsula and functioned from about 190 to 109 B.C.

It was not long before the expansionist Han government under Emperor Wu became interested in this Chinese colony and invaded the area by land and sea (109 to 108 B.C.). The purposes were to extend trade and to prevent the Hsiung-nu in the north from dominating this region on the Chinese eastern borders. The emperor Wu annexed north Korea as far as the Taitong river. There, at Pyong-yang, the Chinese established a capital for their regime in north Korea. The Han overextended themselves in north Korea by setting up a Chinese-style political organization with four commanderies at the beginning. Later, in a reduced area, Chinese rule continued and their colony, Lo-lang, flourished, with its capital at Pyong-yang, for several centuries. This Han colony has been compared with Roman colonies in Britain during a comparable period.

Into Lo-lang came Chinese cultural influences which gradually spread over the entire peninsula. At the capital city there are ruins of tombs which show much of the rich arts of the Han period in China itself. Such objects as bronze mirrors, very fine painted lacquer, jewelry, and gold filigree work are among the remains which have recently been discovered.

In the southern part of the peninsula tribal groups who acknowledged the authority of the Chinese officials at Lo-lang began to practice agriculture during this time and to work iron deposits which became important in trade within the peninsula and with China and Japan. Excavations in the south have shown that a culture similar to that in north Korea reached all over the peninsula by about 50 A.D.

In this period the first purely native state in Korea, Koguryo began. The forest and hunting tribes of the region asserted their independence in the first century B.C. and maintained their authority in South Manchuria as well as northeastern Korea in spite of Han attempts to control them. In Koguryo the society was an aristocratic tribal one. The early leaders were buried in large stone tombs and later ones in earthen mounds which constitute important archaeological evidence of the time. The princes of Koguryo extended their control over tribes on the east coast of Korea and into South Manchuria during the first century B.C.

VIETNAM, A CHINESE BORDERLAND.   The Red river basin, known to us to-day as Tongking, and the northern coastline of the Indo-Chinese peninsula in the early period of Chinese expansion were inhabited by Vietnamese, with a culture distinct from their neighbors to the north. Their way of life was a Mongol-Indonesian mixture, mentioned already in Chapter 14 as the famous Dongson culture.

The provinces of south China nearest to Vietnam, known in recent times as Kwangsi and Kwangtung, were only brought under control of the Chinese during the Ch'in. The armies of the first emperor of the Ch'in conquered these provinces and colonization began in 214 B.C. Chinese influence began to effect the neighboring Vietnamese, who, however, still remained outside the empire.

Before the end of the Ch'in a Chinese general brought Tongking and northern Annam (Vietnam) under the same government as that of Kwangsi and Kwangtung. The sphere of control of this Chinese general was known as "Nam-viet" and was to all intents a separate kingdom. When the Han came into power in China they recognized Nam-viet as an independent state under Chinese suzerainty.

It was nearly a century before the Chinese further extended their power in the area. This northern Vietnam region with its influence of Chinese culture on top of the old indigenous Dongson culture remained still very much apart until the time of the Emperor Wu. Then in 111 B.C. the Han armies were sent south and annexed Tongking and northern Annam. Emperor Wu brought the area formally under Chinese administration, somewhat as he had done in northern Korea. Three commanderies in the areas of Than-hoa, Tongking (which the Chinese called Chiao-chih), and northern Annam, were established under rather loose Chinese control.

Later, after a revolt against the Chinese authorities in A.D. 40, Chinese administration and institutions were imposed on the people of northern Vietnam and the area, like northern Korea, became a definite part of the Chinese empire. The actual degree of Chinese authority depended upon the strength of the central administration in China itself. Chinese culture in all its varied forms was superimposed on the local Vietnamese traditions. The latter continued to maintain themselves and give a different character to Vietnam and the Vietnamese, just as in Korea certain traditions continued and preserved Korean culture as a separate entity.

BASIC DATES

771-473 B.C.	Middle Chou period
551-479 B.C.	Confucius
473-256 B.C.	Late Chou period
5th century-221 B.C.	Warring States period
256 B.C.	Extinction of Chou state
3rd century-109 B.C.	Choson in Northwest Korea
221-207 B.C.	Ch'in dynasty
221-210 B.C.	Ch'in Shih Huang-ti
210-174 B.C.	Hsiung-nu Mao-tun
208 B.C.	Nam-viet kingdom established
202 B.C.-A.D. 9	Western Han
140-87 B.C.	Emperor Wu of Han
111 B.C.	Han annexation of North Vietnam
109-108 B.C.	Han conquest of Choson
A.D. 9-23	Wang Mang usurpation
A.D. 25-220	Eastern Han
A.D. 184 and 189	Yellow Turbans rebellions
2nd century A.D.	Buddhist monastic communities in North China

SUPPLEMENTARY READING

CHI, C. T. *Key Economic Areas in Chinese History as Revealed in the Development of Public Works for Water-Control*. London, 1936. An economic interpretation of history.

CREEL, H. G. *Chinese Thought from Confucius to Mao Tse-tung*. Chicago, 1953. Valuable and well-written study.

DE BARY, W. T., ED. *Sources of Chinese Tradition*. New York, 1960. Useful collection of source materials.

EBERHARD, W. *A History of China*. Berkeley, Cal., 1950. A sociological approach.

FAIRBANK, J. K. *The United States and China*. Cambridge, Mass., 1961.

FITZGERALD, C. P. *China: A Short Cultural History*. London, 1950.

GOODRICH, L. C. *A Short History of the Chinese People*, 3rd ed. New York, 1959.

GROUSSET, R. *The Civilizations of the East, Vol. III: China*. New York, 1935.

————The Rise and Splendor of the Chinese Empire. Berkeley, Cal., 1953.

HUDSON, G. F. *Europe and China*. London, 1931.

LATOURETTE, K. S. *The Chinese: Their History and Culture*. New York, 1946.

REISCHAUER, E. O. AND J. K. FAIRBANK. *East Asia: The Great Tradition*. Boston, 1958.

SICKMAN, L. AND A. SOPER. *The Art and Architecture of China*. Baltimore, 1956.

SULLIVAN, M. *An Introduction to Chinese Art*. Berkeley, Cal., 1961.

SUZUKI, D. T. *A Brief History of Early Chinese Philosophy*. London, 1914.

WALEY, A. *The Book of Songs*. London, 1937.

———— Translations from the Chinese. New York, 1941.

———— The Way and Its Power. London, 1934.

WRIGHT, A. F. *Buddhism in Chinese History*. Stanford, Cal., 1959.

ADVANCED READING

BIELENSTEIN, H. *The Restoration of the Han Dynasty.* Stockholm, 1953.

BODDE, D. *China's First Unifier: A Study of the Ch'in Dynasty as Seen in the Life of Li Ssu (280?–208 B.C.)* Leiden, 1938.

——————— "Feudalism in China," in R. Coulbourn, *Feudalism in History.* Princeton, N. J., 1956.

———————, TR. Fung Yu-lan, *A History of Chinese Philosophy,* 2nd ed. New York, 1945.

CREEL, H. G. *Confucius, the Man and the Myth.* New York, 1959. Interesting and controversial interpretation.

DUBS, H. H., TR. *The History of the Former Han Dynasty by Pan Ku.* Baltimore, 1938–1955.

HU SHIH. *Development of the Logical Method in Ancient China.* Shanghai, 1928.

LATTIMORE, O. *Inner Asian Frontiers of China.* Boston, 1940. A useful book on the "frontier" problem of China.

NEEDHAM, J. *Science and Civilisation in China.* Cambridge, 1956. An interesting, but much disputed study of the role of science in Chinese civilization.

SHRYOCK, J. K. *Origin and Development of the State Cult of Confucius.* New York, 1932.

SIREN, O. *A History of Early Chinese Art.* London, 1929.

SOOTHILL, W. E. *The Analects of Confucius.* New York, 1937.

STEIN, A. *On Ancient Central-Asian Tracks.* London, 1933. Account of discoveries illustrating Chinese role in Turkistan.

SWANN, N. L. *Pan Chao, the Foremost Woman Scholar of China.* New York, 1932.

TEGGART, F. J. *Rome and China: A Study of Correlations in Historical Events.* Berkeley, Cal., 1939. Tries rather unsuccessfully to establish correlations.

WALEY, A. *Anlects of Confucius.* New York, 1939.

WATSON, B. D., TR. *Records of the Grand Historian of China.* New York, 1961.

——————— *Ssu-ma Ch'ien, Grand Historian of China.* New York, 1958.

WRIGHT, A., ED. *The Confucian Persuasion.* Stanford, Cal., 1960. A collection of essays.

XVIII ✲✲✲

CHINA: DISUNION

AND REUNIFICATION, 220-618

FOLLOWING THE COLLAPSE OF THE HAN EMPIRE, China entered a period of division which lasted about 370 years, broken only by the short period of temporary unification at the end of the third and beginning of the fourth century. This division ended with the complete reunification under the Sui in 589. At the beginning of this period, China was divided into three rival states, and therefore it is known as the period of the Three Kingdoms. Later, from the early fourth century until nearly the end of the sixth, the country was divided north and south. In the north, during the latter period, the central development was migration to China of various nomadic tribes from the steppe area beyond the northern borders.

A second important element of this period in Chinese history was the spread of Buddhist ideas and practices from India. Meanwhile despite political chaos and disunion the tradition of Chinese political and cultural unity inherited from the great days of the Chou, the Ch'in, and the Han still continued. At the time of the Sui reunification in 589, there was a reassertion of the great tradition, enriched by the new political and religious ideas from outside, which had continued to develop in China during the centuries of division.

Also important in this period were the border regions which

were part of the Chinese world. The development of northern Vietnam in the
period of disunion in China is properly a part of the history of south China. On
the other hand, to the northeast the peninsula of Korea developed in its own
way and hence is accorded a separate section at the end of this chapter.

The Three Kingdoms and Chin

The "Three Kingdoms" period in Chinese history is a relatively short one
(A.D. 220–264). The balance of power between three fairly equal states, Wei,
Shu Han, and Wu, represented an uneasy stabilization following the chaos at
the end of the Eastern Han. The strongest of the Three Kingdoms was ruled
by a line which usurped the throne of the last of the Han and governed north
and north-central China as the Kingdom of Wei. The military leaders who
founded Wei had successfully competed for power at the end of the Han, but
still were not strong enough to control the western part of the country nor the
Yangtze valley and the regions further south.

The middle years of the third century saw an incessant struggle for supremacy between the Wei armies and those of the other two kingdoms. In this struggle
the rulers of the northern power, Wei, used barbarians from the steppe in their
forces and also opened communications with Central Asia.

In west China the province of Szechuan, sometimes known to the Chinese
as Shu, recognized the authority of a man named Liu Pei who claimed to be the
legitimate successor of the Han dynasty. His importance lies partly in his
association with two loyal companions who united with him under the "Peach
Garden Oath" and who waged warfare in support of him as the rightful heir
of the Han. One of the three hero companions was later deified as the "God of
War." The exploits of these men, the events connected with their lives and the
combat against their enemies were later popularized in the *Romance of the
Three Kingdoms,* one of the great literary tales of China. Because of the claim
that they were carrying on the dynasty of the Han this state is sometimes
referred to as Shu Han.

In the rich Yangtze valley, the most wealthy area of the Three Kingdoms,
was the state of Wu, governed by members of the Sun family. On China's
southern borders Wu entered into relations with parts of Indo-China. The Sun
rulers gained the submission of northern Vietnam (Tongking) in 226. Later
tributary relations were established between Wu as overlord and states further
south, particularly Champa and what is now southern Cambodia and Vietnam.

During the Wei ascendancy in north China an official whose family name
was Ssu-ma gained almost complete control within that state. He succeeded in
annexing Shu Han in 263. Two years later, the Ssu-ma family superseded the
rulers of Wei and became the Chin dynasty (although this name of Chin was
the same as that of the famous north China state of the early Warring States
period, it was, of course, not the same state). Ssu-ma later also annexed the

state of Wu in central and south China in 280 and thus temporarily unified the whole country.

During this period until 317, sometimes known as the "Western Chin," the capital was at Lo-yang. These were years of struggle for power within the Chin imperial family; the empire was ruined and the effectiveness of the government was much diminished.

In these years of internal conflict more and more barbarians from the north became involved in the civil wars. After 305, various groups of Hsiung-nu and other tribesmen entered the empire. The movement gradually became a landslide. Lo-yang itself was invaded and destroyed in 311, effete aristocratic ministers were taken prisoner by the barbarians, and by 317 all of north China was occupied. Meanwhile, partly because of the barbarian encroachment, communications with Central Asia, which had been important earlier, were now cut off.

The power of the Chin was weakened and fragmented in 317. One faction established a new capital further east and south at the site of present Nanking on the lower Yangtze, marking the real beginning of the North-South period, sometimes called the "Six Dynasties" period in Chinese history.

During the time of the Three Kingdoms, religious and philosophical trends which had commenced during the Han continued. Among these was the new importance of Taoism in China. As noted in Chapter 17, the teachings of Confucius had less influence during this time of political instability than they did during the great days of the Han empire. The tradition of Confucianism declined. At this time and into the fourth century there was much study of the Taoist classics, especially the *Lao-tzu* (or *Tao-te Ching*) and the *Chuang-tzu*. This "Neo-Taoism" found expression in metaphysics and aesthetics as well as in religion. There was a keen interest in Taoist magic, as evidenced by Liu Pei the King of Shu's reliance on a Taoist magician as his prime minister and military leader. We must also note the tradition of loyalty between military men in the case of the three heroes who supported each other as sworn brothers in their struggle to maintain the Shu Han against its enemies.

Steppe Powers and Invaders on the Northern Frontiers, 150–581

STEPPE POWERS TO ABOUT 550. While the old traditions within China were adapting themselves to invasions of peoples and ideas and the country remained politically divided, to the north in the steppe region of present Mongolia successors of the Hsiung-nu were a continuing source of direct concern to their neighbors in the south. The principal groups among these tribes to the north should be noted before continuing with the political events of China itself.

By the end of the Han period numbers of Hsiung-nu had already been employed in the armies contending for power, and there was actually a small

Hsiung-nu realm within north China when the Wei of the Three Kingdoms period succeeded the Han. However, there no longer existed the powerful Hsiung-nu confederation of Han times.

During the third century and into the period of Chin unification after 280 there were four groups of tribal peoples on China's northern frontiers. First, as we have noted, there were Hsiung-nu, who were probably Turkish-speaking; and some of whom had already entered China. Secondly there were the groups of tribes called Hsien-pi, sometimes referred to as proto-Mongol, who actually included some Hsiung-nu among their number. They were located mainly towards the east on the borders of Manchuria. Next were the T'o-pa, who included a nucleus of Turkish-speaking peoples. Finally, on the northwest borders of China proper there were Tibetans.

Among these tribes the Hsien-pi were of particular importance. Along with other tribes, they raided North China during the time of the Kingdom of Wei. The Hsien-pi formed no great confederation as did the Hsiung-nu in earlier times or the Jou-juan and Turks in the fifth and sixth centuries. The Hsien-pi it seems had no capacity to form an organized state and remained disunited in various tribal groups. After Chin unification at the end of the third century, many Chin troops were disbanded. Some of the soldiers moved north and settled on the borders of China. With them they took weapons, many of which fell into the hands of northern tribesman who later used the weapons against the Chinese.

At the end of the third century, one of the Hsien-pi groups invaded and established control in northeast China. Some of them also entered northwest China. The Hsiung-nu meanwhile attacked the Chinese in the north-central part of the country, the modern provinces of Shansi and Shensi. In addition there were attacks from Tibetans in the west. This was the beginning of what we have referred to as the landslide of steppe barbarians into north China during the early part of the fourth century.

By the end of the fourth century, that is less than a hundred years after the heavy stream of barbarians from Mongolia into China, a new group began to be prominent in the steppe region—the political confederacy of tribes known as the Jou-juan (or Juan-juan). Their empire included both Mongol and Turkish tribes and was the ruling group in Mongolia from 407 to 553. (The Jou-juan have sometimes been identified with the Avars who invaded Central Europe in the latter half of the sixth century.)

TURKS.   Among the border peoples on China's northern frontiers from the third to the end of the sixth century the Turks (in Chinese T'u-chüeh) were of special importance. Their rise and their significance in the history of Central Asia have already been recounted in Chapter 5.

During Jou-juan supremacy the Turks were only a subordinate tribe who gradually became more important than the Jou-juan. In alliance with the Chinese of northwest China the Turks overthrew the Jou-juan in 552. For a long period afterwards the Turks were the dominant element on China's frontiers, the real power in Turkistan and Mongolia.

The center of Turkish influence was in northern Chinese Turkistan. From there they extended their power to the west in alliance with the Sassanian Persians and destroyed the Hephthalites, or White Huns, during the 560's. They later seized Fergana and Sogdia and gained control of the Central Asian caravan routes. In 569 they sent an embassy to Constantinople.

Thus the Turks constituted a great steppe confederation all the way from Mongolia to Central Asia, with influence beyond that region. However, this tribal organization and power did not last. Encouraged by the first Sui emperor a leader of the Turks in Mongolia broke with the Turks of Turkistan in 582, resulting in a permanent split between the "Eastern" and "Western" Turks.

The Tarim basin south of the Heavenly mountains, T'ien Shan, became definitely part of "Turkistan" from this time on. More Turks came into the area than had Hsiung-nu or Hsien-pi in previous centuries. Some of them became farmers in the sixth and seventh centuries, gradually changing the language of the region from Indo-European to Turkish.

Western Turks raided the Chinese borders in 599. In attempting to expand they failed to regain authority among the Eastern Turks, but by the end of the Sui period the Khan of the Western Turks exercised control over the land trade routes between China and the West.

The Eastern Turks, those who controlled Mongolia, were in close relations with the Sui in north China. Periods of raiding and border warfare alternated with recognition by the Khan of the overlordship of the Chinese emperor. During the reign of the Emperor Yang the East Turkish Khan controlled a great empire in the steppe regions extending from Korea to the borders of the Western Turks in Central Asia. When the Chinese attempted to undermine his power the Eastern Turks became increasingly hostile and were a complicating factor in the politics of the last Sui reign.

North-South Period: "Six Dynasties," 317–589

NORTH CHINA. While the steppe forces to the north continued to be an element in Chinese politics, within China the essential fact was the North-South division. The term "Six Dynasties" may be mentioned as a traditional Chinese designation for the Western Chin, the Eastern Chin (after the split in 317), and the four dynasties of South China which followed the Eastern Chin. The term North-South period may be easier to understand if one remembers that a succession of Chinese dynasties reigned in the south and were thought of as the official inheritors of the earlier lines of dynasties.

In the north the situation was more complicated. That part of China, as we have noted, was completely overrun by the barbarians from the steppe during Chin times, and by the year 350 there was very little Chinese rule in north China. The chronology is roughly as follows: with the collapse of the Chin there were many states, mostly barbarian, in the north. Then about 370 there was a temporary unification under a Tibetan leader who took the dynastic title of Ch'in (not to be confused with the great Ch'in period preceding the Han in the third century B.C.). This unification of the north did not last, but was followed by division into about nine states, one of which became especially important. This was the Northern Wei, the T'o-pa (or Toba) state, which was the dominant power of north China from 386 to 534. Thus under the Northern Wei dynasty north China was unified for a hundred and fifty years. The Wei empire then split into two successor states in the east and west. North China stayed divided until one of the two successor states of Wei, that is the Northern "Chou" (note again the use of a historic name to designate a new dynasty), which ruled in northwest China, also gained control in the northeast. North China was thus unified under the Northern Chou from 577 to 581, when an official of the Chou usurped power and established the Sui as the controlling dynasty of north China. It was the Sui which again brought about unification of the whole of China in 589. Their line of two emperors ruled over a unified China until the collapse of the Sui power in 618.

In all these changes both north and south we see the assumption of names and titles which implied centralized power and unification under one imperial line. The political tradition of Han times remained a firm memory. Both Chinese and barbarian rulers hoped that by gaining control over a wider area than their own state, perhaps each or any one of them might become the successor to the greatness of the Han.

The main characteristics of the North-South period in the north were the invasion and infiltration of various tribes and the establishment of "barbarian" dynasties. They adopted Chinese culture and many of them settled in agricultural communities and were absorbed into the population. As they formed new Chinese states in north China they defended the borders against other peoples who controlled Mongolia and threatened China from the north. This process was far from peaceful. There were sharp differences between the steppe culture of the newcomer and that of the Chinese. There was racial antagonism not only between barbarians and Chinese but also between various tribal groups. The result was a period of violence, mass slaughter, endless wars, and rule by autocratic methods.

The most important state among the northern dynasties was the Wei, that dynasty established by the T'o-pa, also referred to as the Northern Wei.

NORTHERN WEI, T'O-PA (386–534). T'o-pa power in north China marks a new period in Chinese history. A barbarian people from the steppe area became an integral part of the Chinese political and cultural system. Its ruling classes were much concerned both with their own steppe culture and with Chinese culture. This tribal group from the north took over Chinese institutions, worked with the Chinese population, and established political power over a large part of the country.

The T'o-pa or Northern Wei dynasty may be dated from 386 to 534. The rulers actually took the title of emperor in A.D. 398. At first they made their capital at the present Ta-t'ung in northern Shansi province. In the beginning this was a tribal, not a military state, different from the older-style states based on settled agricultural populations and cities to the south. In country that was not very productive, the T'o-pa felt the need for fertile agricultural land and hence attacked their neighbors in northeast China; they conquered that region from the Hsien-pi in 409.

There were already Chinese at the T'o-pa court before this time, but now they found that in order to govern the area they must work closely with the Chinese officials. More and more, Chinese were used in the administration, and the T'o-pa tribal families were organized by their rulers into military formations, not always to the liking of these nomadic peoples. Thus there was a joint arrangement of two races working together in the government.

In addition to these tribal and the settled Chinese elements, another factor of great importance for future history was also present. This was Buddhism, which came to be the most popular religion among the T'o-pa. It was practically an official religion; the emperor himself was termed the "Protector of Buddhism." This Buddhist element at the court was important only until the transfer of the capital to Lo-yang, but the royal patronage was significant in the progress of Buddhism in later Chinese history.

The T'o-pa, now governing not only nomads but also agricultural Chinese, found themselves the defenders of civilization against other nomads to the north. In the early years of the Northern Wei dynasty the Jou-juan confederacy was formed in Mongolia. The Jou-juan raided north China, as their predecessors had done before them, in order to gain some of the riches of Chinese territory. This meant an extended struggle between Jou-juan and the T'o-pa in which the T'o-pa were eventually successful. There was no threat from the Jou-juan after 429.

The T'o-pa then conquered northwest China in campaigns in 431 and in 439. Meanwhile they also moved further south, conquering a large part of Honan province, including the city of Lo-yang (430–431). As a result of these wars the T'o-pa capital at Ta-t'ung was enriched by booty and wealth. By about 440, when they controlled all of north China, the Northern Wei of the T'o-pa was the most powerful state in the Far East. With their extension of power into the northwest they were also able to control the commerce between China and Turkistan, which, as we have seen in previous periods, was an important source of revenue to the controlling Chinese state.

After 440, the civil administration passed more and more into Chinese hands. Chinese families were the leading element at the court. They also had an important part in the military administration, since they knew the type of warfare (different from the military operations of the steppe) necessary in fighting against Chinese armies.

FIGURE 18.1   Dark grey pottery horse, a tomb figurine of the North-South period.

By the mid-fifth century the Northern Wei, the T'o-pa, had adopted the whole of Chinese culture. They used Chinese bureaucratic methods, were versed in Chinese literature, and adopted the Chinese written language as the official language of the court. It was the Chinese element at the court who persuaded the Emperor Wen to move his capital from Ta-t'ung, on the border of the steppe area, to Lo-yang in Honan in the years 493-494.

In ruling all of north China (see map, page 184), the T'o-pa Wei were also faced with typically Chinese problems of civil administration. In particular, there was the matter of controlling the rich, independent families, who had helped undermine the authority of the Han and who were still a power.

With the effective military power at their disposal the T'o-pa government of the Northern Wei were able to establish more centralized control than had been possible for the relatively weaker states which had ruled in north China since the time of the Han. In the first place, they kept as many peasants as possible in a tax-paying status as free farmers and aimed at preventing their absorption into the large estates of the great families. This tax-paying status meant that they were required to undertake forced labor for the state; corvée labor was the principal tax levied against the free peasants. The peasants were encouraged to maintain their free status through a policy called the "equal field" system, under which agricultural lands of specified dimensions were assigned to peasant families. The equal-field system was enforced through an arrangement of collective responsibility lodged in small local groups. In spite of these efforts to maintain a broad tax base, the Wei government did not deprive the great families of their holdings or of their influence in the country. The T'o-pa also further reinforced their centralized power by means of a militia recruited from able-bodied peasants. These militia were organized and trained in regular forces comparable to the tribal soldiery.

Even though the T'o-pa had some success in centralizing their government, the Wei empire split up after nearly one hundred fifty years of power in north China. The T'o-pa Wei failed in their attempt to perpetuate either the steppe tribal or military organization, both of which had been important at the beginning of their rule. As Chinese officials drawn from the scholar-gentry class tended to assume more and more importance and actually to control the government, the tribal nobles were not able to maintain their supremacy. Meanwhile many of the nomad tribesmen who had little part in the new organization became impoverished and the government was faced with a series of revolts.

The uprisings became more and more serious in the early 530's, especially in Shansi and the Ordos region south of the great bend of the Yellow river. A climax was reached when a T'o-pa group concerned with maintaining their tribal rights seized the capital and massacred the Chinese and those of their tribe who had been favorable to the Chinese. Eventually, out of this tumult, there arose a new ruling line, the Northern "Chou," but soon after they had succeeded in unifying north China in 577 they lost their throne in 581 to one of their own officials, Yang Chien, who established the Sui dynasty.[1]

SOUTH CHINA IN THE NORTH-SOUTH PERIOD.   While the northern sections of China were ruled by a number of barbarian dynasties, the central and southern sections were for the most part under one government, administered in the name of a succession of ruling Chinese families with their capital at Nanking. From the Eastern Chin to the Ch'en, there were five lines of politically feeble emperors between 317 and 589. In this period none of the dynasties survived long. The general characteristic of society under these southern Chinese dynasties was aristocratic as contrasted with the more autocratic regime in the north.

The Eastern Chin (317–420) began with one of the most extensive migrations in Chinese history. In the refugee movement of Chinese migrating south to escape the invaders it is said that one million northerners had fled south of the Yangtze by the end of the fourth century. This movement was accompanied by conflict and social change previously unknown in the southern part of China. The new refugee gentry was added to the older Chinese families who had been settled in south China for a long period, many of them since the time of the Three Kingdoms. These older Chinese families were settled on large estates or engaged in extensive commerce. Their typically Chinese pattern of life was reinforced by the influx of newcomers. As the population became more dense, the old families were able to profit from a boom in land development. The principal group in south Chinese society from this time on was the wealthy landed aristocracy, made up of both old and new members. The eleven Chin emperors during the fourth century themselves were not personally or politically important. With only limited power they reigned amid the luxuries and refinements of their capital at Nanking.

[1] For an account of the Sui dynasty see pp. 347–352.

Government under the southern dynasties followed in general the form of the Ch'in and Han bureaucracies with a tendency toward neo-Legalist political ideas. As more people settled on the land, new administrative subdivisions were established in conformity with older Chinese-type units of local government.

For positions in the central government the refugee gentry competed with the old landowning families. Both of these aristocratic groups tended to monopolize the chief offices in the government. Key figures in the administration of the Eastern Chin were a series of generals whose power was based on military strength together with the support of cliques and family connections.

After the Chin and before the reunification of China in 589 there were four dynasties on the throne at Nanking: the Liu-Sung, 420–479; the Southern Ch'i, 479–502; the Liang, 502–557; and the Ch'en, 557–589. But all of these were weak and subject to frequent attacks by the T'o-pa from the north, and the last of them was easily conquered by the new power of the Sui which unified all of China.

South China during this period, when the north was ruled by descendants of invading tribes, was the chief center of Chinese culture. Its patrons were the landed aristocracy, people interested not only in the Confucian tradition and the new developments of Taoism, but among whom were also to be found a growing number of Buddhists.

CULTURE OF NORTH-SOUTH PERIOD.   For a time of barbarian invasions it may be useful to compare events in China with a similar situation in Europe and the Mediterranean world at the time of the breakup of the Roman empire. In China there was much greater cultural continuity, from the Han through this time of disunion to the period of the T'ang greatness beginning in the seventh century (618–907), than there was between the Roman empire and medieval and Renaissance Europe. On the other hand, the new cultural developments in this time of political disunion were so significant as to lead some writers to characterize this as the first phase in "a new culture."

In the realm of ideas continuity may be observed in the preservation of the Confucianism of ancient times although it did give way in this period to other forms of philosophy and religion. In the North-South period there was a new interest in Taoism. The indigenous popular religion appeared in new cults. Most prominent, of course, was the spread of Buddhism, influencing the culture of the whole country, and in south China, where it was affected by Neo-Taoism, giving rise to new Chinese forms of Buddhism itself. At the courts of the rulers a diversity of influences was apparent in the state cult with its eclecticism of worship.

In literature, especially in the realm of poetry, there was a vigorous indigenous development. It was also a time of the flowering of many forms of art, especially those influenced by Buddhism.

The intellectual and artistic phases of the North-South period were paralleled by technological advances and new tastes, important not only in China but later on in other parts of the world. Merely to enumerate them is to reveal the diversity of Chinese activity in this time of political disunion. There were developments in medicine (partly through influences coming along the trade routes from India and elsewhere), the invention of gunpowder, the practice of tea-drinking, and the use of coal as a fuel.

The intellectual link with the past in the North-South period was shown especially in the continued interest in Confucian learning. Doctrines of government based on cosmological principles and dependent on the teachings of the Classics had their supporters, especially in south China, where they provided an ideology which gave legitimacy to the reigning dynasties and maintained cultural continuity with the past. The Confucianism of south China was associated with the aristocratic belief in hereditary right rather than talent as a qualification for office-holding, a natural reaction to the growing power of the northern barbarians who were ruling a large part of the country.

The study of early Confucian literature during the North-South period resulted in the production of special commentaries, often diverging one from another. Additions to this literature were made partly through the writing of spurious history and partly by various legends which came to be connected with the name of Confucius and which may have been influenced by Taoism as well as Buddhism.

The various forms of Taoism that were developing during the Han dynasty and in the third century continued to flourish during the North-South period, particularly in south China. As an organized religion Taoism continued to emphasize special exercises aiming at immortality and the search for an elixir of life. This search led to the development of alchemy. The theological doctrines of Taoism were elaborated between the fourth and sixth centuries, particularly in the fifth and sixth, and Taoist religious organization was further developed. Parallel with these developments was the important philosophical movement known as Neo-Taoism, previously mentioned. Refugees from the north in the fourth century brought Neo-Taoism to south China. There the intellectuals found in Taoism a philosophic basis for their escape from the disorders of the time. This individualistic Taoist attitude of escape is typified in the life and writings of the great poet T'ao Ch'ien, whose poetry is mentioned below in connection with the literature of the period.

As a result of the new importance of Taoism and Buddhism from the third to the fifth centuries the state cult of Confucianism lost much of its former prestige. The emperors sacrificed to various spirits, Taoist and Buddhist, as well as the spirit of Confucius. However, by the sixth century the state cult was revived. In south China in the early part of the sixth century Emperor Wu of the Liang dynasty is usually associated with his patronage of Buddhism. But he also took more interest in the worship of Confucius than had the rulers of the immediately preceding dynasties. In connection with the Liang emperor's encouragement of the work of Confucian scholars in south China he also erected public temples to Confucius in which sacrifices were offered every year. To the north in the middle of the century the short-lived Northern Ch'i dynasty emphasized Confucian education. Sacrifices were offered to Confucius at various seasons and students who did not attend these ceremonies were punished. This type of worship of the spirit of Confucius lasted well into the twentieth century, even after the state worship of Confucius was disestablished.

In the realm of literature the traditions of Han times were continued and vigorously developed. The great interest of writers in their own country, China, its geography, its people, and various aspects of its culture, is notable during this North-South period. Geographical compendiums giving information both descriptive and historical about one locality were started during this time. Histories continued to be written. Comments on the Classics have already been mentioned in connection with the Confucian literature. Biographies were written, including the lives of Buddhist monks, who were now an important part of Chinese society. Works on the language included such topics as the different tones and phonetics of Chinese. Literary criticism developed in the fifth and sixth centuries; and the history and principles of painting in China were described in literary works.

More important and certainly more generally known in the West was the creative writing, the *belles lettres* of this North-South period, a writing which was essentially an aristocratic art, using poetic forms from the past as well as carefully balanced prose style. Verse forms included lyrics in a five-syllable meter. Much of the lyric poetry was typically Taoist in sentiment, revealing the individual in conflict with society. In spite of their individualism the poets were much preoccupied with form, and they developed some rigidity of pattern.

Especially worthy of note among the greatest of Chinese poets was T'ao Ch'ien (365–427), also known as T'ao Yuan-ming, a minor official in the Yangtze valley in the time of the Chin and Liu-Sung dynasties. T'ao Ch'ien has been known ever since for his love of country living and his fondness for drink, both of which typified his individualism and revealed his Taoist attitude towards life. He refused to conform to the conventions of his time and retired from office rather than bear the responsibilities of government. In his thinking he was not affected by Buddhism nor was he much concerned with immortality or popular Taoism. His Taoist attitude, however, is shown by his keen interest in developing his own literary talents, as may be noted in the following prose poem:

> Renouncing my cap of office
>> I will return to my old home
> Never more entangled
>> with love for high position.
> I will nourish my REAL self
>> under my gates and thatch
> And by doing this
>> be all the better known.[2]

[2] William Acker, *T'ao the Hermit: Sixty Poems by T'ao Ch'ien, 365–427* (London: Thames and Hudson, 1952), p. 26.

During the North-South period the music of China was much influenced by the traditions of the barbarians who entered from the steppes to the north and west. With the re-establishment of trade along the routes to Turkistan and beyond during the time of the Northern Wei older musical traditions of China were mostly superseded by the music and instruments of the peoples of Central Asia.

In the field of painting the North-South period represented a climax in Chinese cultural history. It was the last phase of archaic Chinese culture according to some writers; others have seen the start of a period of revival which led into the cultural greatness of a reunified China. Unfortunately very little remains of the painting of that day, but from what examples we have and from the literature we know that painting of the North-South period was very highly developed. Particularly at the southern courts, painting flourished from the fifth to the middle of the sixth century. Most artists lived and worked in the Yangtze region of central China.

Both in Chinese painting and in handwriting the cursive lines of the brush-strokes have been greatly valued. Calligraphers or creators of fine writing with the brush, as well as painters, are honored by the Chinese. It is significant then that China's greatest calligrapher, Wang Hsi-chi, lived in the fourth century. The Chinese ever since have looked back to Wang as the great model of excellence in handwriting.

From the literature we know much about the artists and the subjects of their paintings during the North-South period. They were interested in portraiture, in pictures of birds and horses, court scenes, historic figures such as Confucius and dragons. Buddhist subjects were very important and will be discussed later on in connection with the history of Buddhism in this period. Very little remains of this art so there is little that can be said about the actual style.

Among the important remains of sculpture of the North-South period are fabulous beasts carved out of stone, intended to be placed near the tombs of emperors and of other important men. Notable among such monuments are the lions of Liang near Nanking. Also the art of molding pottery tomb figurines was more highly developed than in the Han period and foreshadowed the greatness of the statuettes of T'ang times. Today's museums house warriors, ladies, horses, and other figurines, rather stiff, rather formal, but typical of a popular and developing art.

The craftsmanship of this sculpture was of a lesser excellence compared with the artistic creations inspired by the Buddhism of the North-South period, discussed below.

BUDDHISM IN THE NORTH-SOUTH PERIOD.   Between the great dynasty of the Han and the T'ang period, which began in the seventh century, two important outside influences affected China. One we have already dealt with,—the barbarians of the steppe who established themselves in north China. The second was the great religion of India, Buddhism, which we have seen had already entered China and become established in small monastic communities during the time of the Eastern Han. In the period of political disunion the process which began then continued on a larger scale.

The Buddhism of north India which came by way of Central Asia was chiefly Mahayana Buddhism in its many forms (see Chapters 9 and 17). This popular religion of salvation was brought by missionaries, Indian and Central Asian. They and their Chinese converts translated the sacred writings into Chinese. The faith spread widely among all classes and included among its patrons members of the ruling families both in north and south China. Chinese were inspired to go to India to visit the holy places, and by Chin times, at the end of the third century, pilgrims already were making the long journey over-land or by sea. The results were apparent in the art of China as Buddhist paint-ing, sculpture, and architecture developed and had a profound influence in later periods. As older systems of philosophy were affected by Buddhist teaching there was some tendency to equate the ideas of one with those of another. Strong indigenous Chinese Buddhist sects began to develop, and the scene was further complicated by the entrance of still other religions from more remote parts of Asia into China.

By the time of the Chin dynasty (third century) there were already many translations from both Mahayana and Theravada scriptures, including rules for ordination and for monastic life. Temples were to be found in the middle Yangtze region as well as in north China.

Later, in the fourth century, when the barbarian invasions from the steppe began there were already in north China numbers of Indian, Sogdian, and Turkistani monks, and during the North-South period missionaries continued to come to China via Central Asia and directly from India, by land and by sea. As alien barbarian rulers gained power in north China they welcomed these monks, possibly because they also were non-Chinese. In any case, the foreign missionaries increased in number during the fourth and fifth centuries.

Among these one of the greatest was Kumarajiva (344–413), who arrived in China overland from India in about 383. He became celebrated as a trans-lator, and when he reached Ch'ang-an shortly after 400, many Chinese monks were assembled to work with him on translation projects. In their teaching he and other Mahayana monks emphasized spiritual other-worldly concepts in a time of political and military disorder. Some of these concepts as found in the famous "Diamond Sutra," whose translation is attributed to Kumarajiva, were the following: "All objective existences are unsubstantial and unreal. If a man can see clearly that they are so, then can he see the Buddha. . . . Every external phenomenon is like a dream, like a vision, like a bubble, like shadow, like dew, like lightning, and should be regarded as such." [3]

Buddhist teachings which reached China during this period included the famous meditation doctrines which were later highly developed by the Chinese

[3] H. A. Giles, *History of Chinese Literature* (New York: Appleton-Century-Crofts, 1937), pp. 114–115.

as Ch'an (or Zen) Buddhism. Among the missionaries who brought such concepts into China was the Indian Bodhidharma, who came either in the fifth or
the early sixth century. From him and others who preached the meditation
doctrines the Chinese were informed that true religion was not to be learned
from books and ceremonies, but was to be found by following the teachings of
the original Buddha and by depending upon their own inner qualities and intuition for salvation.

Buddhist preachers had an influence all over China during the North-
South period. The religion spread among people of various classes, and temples
became established institutions in Chinese society. Merchants used the monasteries as places of business, for banking, and for storing goods. Peasants came
to live on temple lands and had a tenant-landlord relationship with the monastic
establishments. The rulers of the various states found that monks who were
educated in Buddhist monasteries might be useful as advisors at their courts.

Buddhism had different effects on north and south China. In the north,
the barbarians were influenced by the fact that the monks seemed to be divinely
favored with spiritual power and believed that they themselves might find
spiritual consolation and hope in Buddhist doctrine. This religion moreover was
non-Chinese and hence provided an alternative for those who did not wish to
become wholly Chinese. In addition, Buddhism was a universal religion and
might embrace members of all strata of society. As such the rulers in north
China found it an aid in building a unified state.

In the political confusion of north China, especially after the mid-fourth
century, rulers, upper-class intellectuals with a background of Confucianism
and Neo-Taoism, and people of the lower classes all turned to Buddhism as a
religion of hope. Particularly important among the emperors of the northern
states who were patrons of Buddhism were the T'o-pa line. These rulers made
elaborate gifts, built temples, and showed an interest in the copying of texts, even
to the extent of sending monks to India to bring back the correct versions of
Buddhist writings. The thousands of monasteries of the Northern Wei were inhabited by hundreds of thousands of monks.

In the Northern Wei temples was to be found a wealth of painting,
statuary, and fine architecture. Especially important was the Buddhist center at
Yun-kang, near the capital Ta-t'ung. Cave-chapels were carved out of the side
of a cliff and decorated with rock-hewn statues and bas-reliefs. The sculpture
was created with a perfection of detail which reveals something of the spiritual
quality of Chinese Buddhism in this period.

The popularity of Buddhism, the power of its temple organizations, and
the abuses which sometimes resulted soon led to opposition from Taoist clergy
and Chinese gentry officials. In north China, attempts were made to control the
Buddhists through bureaucratic methods and by means of drastic restrictions
(in 446), but these were not very effective. During this North-South period
Buddhism flourished in north China, which became a key center for translation
of texts.

In south China some of the emperors also favored Buddhism, partly as a matter of personal salvation, partly because of the rituals through which they might invoke the help of Buddhist deities, and because they found in Buddhist writings models for kingship in the Indian tradition of a theocratic ruler. Most important among the southern patrons of Buddhism was the Emperor Wu of Liang, who actually took Buddhist vows for a time, ordered the destruction of Taoist temples, and followed the Buddhist model as an ideal of kingly behavior. There were Buddhists not only at court but among the landed gentry and the intellectuals. Temples were built, the wealthy displayed their interest through decoration and ornament, and those who wished to cultivate the mind and spirit found in the temples retreats where they might devote themselves to religion and scholarship.

FIGURE 18.2.   An altarpiece in gilt and bronze depicting the Buddha Maitreya and attendant divinities. In its upward sweep of form and intense religiosity the art of the Northern Wei has been aptly compared with the European Gothic.

An important sign of the keen interest in Buddhism during this period was the succession of pilgrimages made by Chinese monks taking the difficult journey to India overland or by sea. These pilgrims went to the holy places in north India which were sacred to the memory of Gautama Buddha and visited Buddhist communities along the way. Among the early pilgrims Fa Hsien became especially famous, largely because he left an account of his journey between 399 to 414 from the empire of the Northern Wei overland to the Gupta empire in India (see map in Chapter 10). Pilgrims' accounts of their travels have been helpful to modern scholars in reconstructing parts of Indian history (see Chapter 10).

One of the great contributions of Buddhism to Chinese culture during this period was in the realm of art. Painting, sculpture, and architectural traditions from India and Iran came by way of Central Asia to north China. Other art influences probably were brought by sea. Evidences of the art of Central Asian Buddhism are particularly apparent in the monuments from north China made in the time of the T'o-pa Wei.

FIGURE 18.3. A stone bas-relief of an empress as donor, with attendants. Northern Wei, from Lung-men. A superb combination of grace and elegance with spiritual expression.

In the painted interiors of the cave chapels at Tun-huang, where the roads through Chinese Turkistan met to enter China, Buddhist artists of the Northern Wei period depicted deities, paradise scenes, illustrations of sacred texts and legends—painting which was done for devotional contemplation as well as for instruction. The earlier paintings showed strong Central Asian (including Iranian) influence, and later the style was more purely Chinese. The early cave temples carved in India at such places as Ajanta and in Bamyan in modern Afghanistan were models for the cave temples at Tun-huang, Yun-kang, and later at Lung-men near Lo-yang.

FIGURE 18.4. Stone statues of a monk and two Bodhisattvas from south China, Northern Ch'i period. The spread of Buddhism was not limited to the north.

The temples of the Northern Wei period were characterized by the pagoda, which became one of the most important developments of Buddhist architecture in China. These wooden towers with curved roofs which rose up to seven and nine stories were originally inspired by earlier Buddhist buildings of the Kushan state. Most of the Buddhist architecture in this North-South period has disappeared, but the style of the time may be seen at Horyuji in Japan (see Chapter 24). In their rock-cut temples and in separate creations of stone and bronze Chinese devotees of Buddhism created some of the finest sculpture that has remained from the past.

While Buddhism was a foreign religion and while Buddhist art displayed many foreign characteristics, Chinese thought also soon began to be noticeable in the work of remodeling that faith in the form of a variety of Buddhist sects, which were later to be very important in China as well as in Japan. One of the earliest started under the leadership of a monk named Hui-yuan of a Confucian and Taoist background who secluded himself with his followers in mountain fastnesses to meditate on the values of Buddhism. Hui-yuan first taught salvation through faith in Amitabha (or Amida, a Buddhist deity), and thus founded a sect known as the "Pure Land" sect which became the most popular form of Buddhism in East Asia. The beginning of the "White Lotus Society," a secret organization with Buddhist connections, is also attributed to Hui-yuan.

FIGURE 18.5. Bronze gilt statue of Maitreya, probably of Northern Wei period, showing very clearly the influence of Indian Gupta art, especially in the transparency and flow of the drapery.

One of the most famous branches of Chinese Buddhism, particularly important in T'ang times, was the Meditative Sect, known as Ch'an (or Zen). The beginnings of Ch'an Buddhism are attributed to Bodhidharma, who, as previously noted, is believed to have come from India to China in the North-South period. Also in the latter part of that period, during the sixth century, the T'ien-t'ai sect had its beginnings. T'ien-t'ai Buddhism took its name from the mountain in southeast China where the founder, Chih-k'ai, had his headquarters. This important eclectic sect later gained many adherents in Japan.

The integration of this foreign religion into the Chinese environment during these centuries was to have a continuing effect in Chinese intellectual history. In this period many inclined towards a philosophical syncretism, leading them to identify Buddhism and its ideas with the older teachings of China. We have noted that some emperors favored both Confucian doctrine and Buddhism. The merging of these two systems of thought was one of the traditions handed down to the next period, which was ushered in by the reunification of the whole country under the leadership of a new and vigorous dynasty, the Sui.

Reunification Under the Sui

THE SUI EMPIRE. The period of Sui rule, which began in north China in 581 and extended to the whole of China in 589, marked a climax in the great tradition of Chinese political and cultural unity. The country was temporarily unified in the hands of two strong emperors, who inaugurated a vigorous government and a resurgence of culture. Their "dynasty," the Sui, was in many ways an opening phase of the great period of the T'ang. Beyond China's borders the Sui were generally successful—in their relations with the Turks, in reopening trade along the western routes leading to Central Asia, and finally, in maintaining Chinese prestige in Vietnam. On the other hand, they were unsuccessful against Koguryo, the strong northernmost of the Three Kingdoms in Korea. In spite of successive campaigns, military efforts which weakened the empire, the second Sui emperor failed to impose Chinese suzerainty on the Koreans. Later in his reign he was faced with rebellions, and finally with a general collapse of authority in 617 and 618.

The men who accomplished the establishment of the Sui empire and the reunification of China were Chinese, whose family name was Yang. The father of the first Sui emperor had assisted in the founding of the Northern Chou dynasty, and was honored by the title of the Duke of Sui. The son, Yang Chien, was married to a lady of noble Hsiung-nu ancestry, strongly Buddhist and domineering. Yang Chien himself was calculating and suspicious, anti-intellectual but nevertheless an able administrator. His daughter married the third Chou emperor and became empress in the year 578. For the next few years, until the end of the Chou dynasty, Yang Chien was the most powerful minister at court.

This third Chou emperor was "capricious and lascivious," a weakling who was only partly under the control of his father-in-law. He did order the killing of some of his most reliable relatives and officials. But when it seemed likely that the emperor would act against the Yang family, he was forced to abdicate in favor of his infant son (579). The Chou emperor himself died the next year at the age of twenty-seven.

After a regency of a few months, Yang Chien persuaded his grandson, the child sovereign, to resign the throne and had himself proclaimed the first emperor of the Sui dynasty. Ch'ang-an in the northwest was the seat of power of the Northern Chou, and this was where Yang Chien, known to history as Emperor Wen (581–604), established his own capital.

Because Yang Chien succeeded where others before him had failed in their attempts to unify the country, some of his characteristics and his methods of administration should be noted. Yang Chien was decisive and autocratic, an excellent administrator in spite of some of his own doubts of the legitimacy of his rule. He employed able ministers in establishing a rigorous centralized control. The government was definitely improved in the early years of the Sui by economy, moderation of existing laws, and a codification of the legal system. A regular tax structure based on the equal field system inaugurated in Northern Wei times was applied to all of China. Large landholdings of the great families were integrated into the system by assigning permanent grants of limited extent. However, when Emperor Wen undertook to check the profits of the gentry, he was met by dissatisfaction and opposition.

To ensure acceptance of Sui rule among the educated classes, Emperor Wen used Confucian scholars and enlisted the sanctions of Confucianism to legitimize and consolidate his empire. As an ardent Buddhist he also turned to Buddhist concepts for support. In addition to both of these the official ideology of the Sui used Taoism as a source of values.

After improving the internal administration of north China, Emperor Wen sent an army of some 518,000 men under the leadership of his son, Yang Kuang, and other generals to attack and overwhelm the unprepared Ch'en government of south China in 589. After annexing Ch'en territory Yang Chien employed many southern officials in the government of what now became a unified Chinese empire.

Another extension of Sui power was undertaken during the last years of Emperor Wen's reign. Vietnam had been part of the Chinese empire since Ch'in and Han times, although the region had been in more or less "permanent revolt" since 541. In 603 Tongking and part of the coast to the south were reconquered. South of this territory the Chinese forces later invaded Champa.

Yang Chien ended his remarkable career murdered at the instigation of his ambitious and unscrupulous son, Yang Kuang. The latter, known to history as Emperor Yang (reign, 604–618), showed his ability by large-scale public works and literary endeavors, while he vigorously continued national policies of defense and expansion. Yang weakened the power of the Turks, extended Chinese authority, visited the frontiers, and led expeditions against Korea, and also maintained an elaborate court at three capitals.

Notable among Emperor Yang's public works was the construction of an eastern capital at Lo-yang and a Yangtze capital at modern Yangchow. In order to transport grain tribute from the lower Yangtze region to the Yellow river valley and to his administrative headquarters, he connected a system of older canals to make one Grand Canal, completed in 611. Another project of vast dimensions which involved hundreds of thousands of men at forced labor and eventually led to economic distress was the reconstruction of the Great Wall along the frontiers, undertaken because of Emperor Yang's concern over the Eastern Turks' threat.

In the Sui regulation of the central government both emperors continued the great imperial tradition, separating civil and military administrations and centralizing control of the local authority. The Sui governmental system was a model for future T'ang administration.

Both Sui emperors used Confucian scholars in official capacities. They established schools at the capital, and arranged sacrifices to Confucius. Emperor Yang particularly promoted the classical Confucian education and began a system of civil service examinations, including that for the doctorate, the *chin-shih* degree, whose importance continued to the twentieth century.

Emperor Wen had not been personally interested in scholarship and literature, but his son was not only a patron of scholars but also a poet himself. Under Emperor Yang the Chinese commenced a resurgence of literature and art which was to continue for the next three hundred years, one of the reasons for speaking of the Sui-T'ang period as the "golden age of China." Libraries of books were assembled at the capital, scholars put to work editing and cataloguing, and fine calligraphy and painting were encouraged.

Emperor Yang was also interested in Buddhism; during his reign the "Pure Land" (*Ch'ing-t'u*) Amidist teaching and the "Lotus" (*T'ien-t'ai*) syncretic teaching came into favor. The emperor wrote Buddhist poetry and collected sutras. Buddhist art reached a climax of perfection in painting and the production of images. The latter remain as fine examples of bronze and stone sculpture. Cave statues and carving at Yün-kang and Lung-men continued the tradition of the Northern Wei.

China, reunified and reorganized with a culture revitalized under strong emperors, became again, as it had been in Han times, the center of civilization in the Far Eastern world. After the unification under Emperor Wen, tributary missions came to the Sui court from the Koguryo king of northern Korea acknowledging the suzerainty of the Chinese Sui emperor and from Japan, where the Soga leaders and later Shotoku Taishi sought methods whereby they might strengthen the Japanese state (see Chapter 24).

When Emperor Yang came to the throne he extended Sui authority south of Vietnam by invading territory disputed with the Chams. Their capital, Indrapura, was invaded in 605, and Champa was forced to pay tribute to the Sui government. Envoys continued to come from Japan to the Sui court during the reign of Emperor Yang, a process not very significant for the Chinese but with a lasting effect in Japan. Most important were the relations between China and her neighbors to the north and west. Emperor Yang sent envoys to and received tribute-bearing missions from the small states of the Tarim basin. The prestige of the Sui was enhanced by military operations and skillful diplomacy.

Early in the Sui dynasty the Chinese were faced with a great Turkish power, which was divided between Eastern and Western Turks in 582, partly due to Chinese encouragement of disunity. Both Sui emperors favored certain Turkish princes and attempted to weaken others. In spite of the split between East and West two great rulers among the Western Turks, She-kuei Khan and T'ung-she-hu Khan, held a commanding position in Central Asia and controlled the trade routes leading west from the borders of northwest China during the period 611–630.

Among the Eastern Turks, meanwhile, a khan who had broken with the Western Turks when Yang Chien rose to power in China, was for a time on very good terms with the Sui emperor and acknowledged the overlordship of the Sui in China. Tribute missions and commerce crossed the borders, sometimes alternating with frontier warfare. At the end of Emperor Wen's reign there was a struggle among the Eastern Turks, and in the early years of Emperor Yang's rule a tribal leader called Shih-pi Khan, hostile to the Chinese, strengthened his position. Chinese attempts to undermine his power by intrigue led to conflict. Relations with the Eastern Turks were complicated by the Turks' involvement also in the affairs of Koguryo. As a check on the power of Shih-pi Khan, Emperor Yang reinforced his northern defenses along the line of the Great Wall. The resistance of both the Eastern Turks and the rulers of Koguryo to Emperor Yang's authority contributed to the fall of the Sui.

THE FALL OF SUI. The strong position of Emperor Yang from 610 to 612 was weakened by a series of internal disasters as well as an overexpansion of activity outside China. Rebellions sprang up all over the country, starting in 613, and leading to a complete collapse of the Sui government in 616 and 617. By that time a new leader who had been an official of the Sui, Li Yuan, came into prominence. He and his followers took advantage of the weakness of the Sui to gain power in the north and eventually to found the T'ang dynasty.

Although Emperor Yang was in a position of power in 610 with a new and resplendent capital at Lo-yang, improved fortifications along the line of the Great Wall, new waterways linking north and central China for communications and commerce, and frontiers extending to the oases of Turkistan and the coast of Indo-China, nevertheless within the next few years this great empire collapsed.

Signs of disaffection were seen at the time of the Korean campaigns of 612 to 614, particularly in northeast China. In this area in spite of flood and drought in the years 611 and 612 the emperor recruited men for his expeditions against Koguryo. The campaign of 612 against that north Korean state led to resistance in what is now southern Manchuria and failure for the Sui forces. When the emperor decreed new taxes and further conscription, banditry commenced in northeast China.

During the campaign of 613 a serious rebellion broke out in the heart of the empire, and Emperor Yang had to withdraw his forces in Korea in order to suppress the uprising. The third campaign was more successful. The Sui forces marched deep into the Korean peninsula and threatened the Koguryo capital at P'yong-yang, but by that time there were other signs of disaffection. Both Chinese and Koreans were exhausted by the war, and the campaign was broken off without conclusive result.

The threat of the powerful Eastern Turks on his northern frontier led Emperor Yang to inspect fortifications himself in 614, but he was temporarily besieged by the Turks and had to withdraw, having lost prestige in this border area. In the next few years, rebels in the north of China allied themselves with the Turks. Emperor Yang himself moved to his capital on the Yangtze in 616, a date marking the end of his power. In the ensuing contest as to who would succeed to the Sui, Li Yuan gained control first in Shansi and then at Ch'ang-an, and soon thereafter mounted the throne as the founder of a new dynasty, the T'ang. Meanwhile Emperor Yang had been put to death by another rebel in the south.

During the Sui period new leadership in north China paved the way for political greatness to come. The Sui emperors improved the administrative and economic institutions for all China, codified the laws, and gave the nation a new concept of empire. Thus they laid the basis for the much more significant period of the T'ang which was to follow.

The T'ang also inherited from the Sui the problem of relations with Koguryo, to whose history in the period of the "Three Kingdoms" in Korea we return.

Three Kingdoms in Korea

THE FORMATIVE YEARS. During the period of anarchy at the end of the Han dynasty, in addition to Koguryo two other states rose to political importance in Korea: Paekche in the southwest, and Silla in the southeast parts of the peninsula. At a time when China itself was divided, these new small states began to participate extensively in Chinese civilization. This process included the entry and growing importance of Buddhism in the Korean states. During this period the Japanese also absorbed much of Chinese civilization from Korea. In a time of rivalry between the states, Koguryo became the most important; its political dominance was followed by the expansion of Silla in the sixth and seventh centuries. During the Sui dynasty after the Chinese had achieved reunification and a degree of imperial expansion the emperor unsuccessfully attempted to dominate Koguryo. Chinese control in north Korea was to wait until the next period, the T'ang.

Since the tribes of south Manchuria and northeastern Korea began to assert their independence of the Han as far back as the first century B.C., that time is sometimes considered the beginning of the "Three Kingdoms" period in Korea. However, Koguryo as a state was not very important until the very end of the Eastern Han period. The rulers of Koguryo then made war against the Chinese at their colonial base in Lo-lang, also learning about the writing and literature of China in the process. As Han power weakened in the second century, Koguryo and the other states to the south began to assert their independence of the Chinese colony. But Lo-lang continued as a Chinese colony and was reinforced by more people from China during the Chinese Three Kingdoms period and even later. Only in 313 did Koguryo completely end the separate existence of the Chinese colonists at Lo-lang and annex their territory, so that 313 is now customarily referred to as the commencement of the Three Kingdoms in Korea.

Silla began as a small tribal unit in southeast Korea, probably in the second or third centuries A.D. The first settlers had come there as refugees from China after the fall of the Ch'in. It was a small region with little arable land and poorer harbors than the other two kingdoms. In the Han river valley of west-central Korea about A.D. 250 a settlement of northern invaders began to be known as Paekche. By the fourth century Paekche had unified the southwest corner of the peninsula.

In the central part of the southern coast of Korea was a wedge-shaped area between Paekche and Silla. This region, known to the Koreans as "Kaya" (or Karak) and called by the Japanese "Mimana," was not included in either Silla or Paekche. During the early part of the Three Kingdoms period the people of Kaya had a special connection with the growing power to the southeast, the state of Yamato in Japan.

After the native states in Korea destroyed the last of the Chinese colonies early in the fourth century, the colonists and their culture scattered throughout the peninsula into all of the Three Kingdoms. Meanwhile even before 313 in the southeast part of the peninsula, where the kingdom of Silla was being formed, there was some connection with Yamato in Japan; gifts were exchanged between these neighboring kingdoms. In the centuries that followed, however, Silla was not as close politically to the Japanese as was the state of Paekche. The situation as it developed in the years from 313 down to the middle of the sixth century was this: Koguryo in the north was increasingly well organized and expanded toward the south; Paekche was weak, and friendly with Japan; Silla gradually developed a strong leadership and became the lasting power among the three. During this time the Chinese were not interested in Korean affairs.

KOREA AS A CULTURAL BRIDGE. In the Three Kingdoms period to the middle of the sixth century the Japanese state of Yamato (as described in Chapter 24) had not yet become an important power; in their relations with Korea the Japanese sought what the Koreans had already gained from China. What the Koreans learned from China concerning government, literature, Buddhism, and art was transmitted to Japan, with the active interest and intervention of the Japanese themselves.

Koguryo reached the height of its power during the first century after 313. The kings of Koguryo in the fourth and fifth centuries adopted various aspects of Chinese culture. In their government, taxation, and organization of the bureaucracy, they also copied the Chinese. Meanwhile, Koguryo received Buddhism from China, traditionally in 372. The law code of Koguryo was modeled on that of the Chinese, a "university" was established for the teaching of Confucianism, and a new capital was founded at P'yong-yang in 427. Some of the prosperity of Koguryo has been revealed from tombs which have been opened in modern times. Paintings in these tombs are full of life and energy, somewhat conventionalized but developing a variety of themes with great imagination.

However, Korean culture was not entirely derived from China. In Silla in the southeast tombs have revealed a culture quite different from either China or Japan. Much of the beadwork, jewelry, and particularly the magnificent gold crowns of Silla show features typically "Korean" in style. Gradually, however, as the regions to the north and west were more affected by Chinese culture, so also the Chinese influences came to Silla, where the rulers took Chinese titles, adopted the Chinese Confucian code, and finally in 528 also adopted Buddhism.

The dynamic culture of the Northern Wei in the North-South period in China and of other Chinese states had a lasting effect in Korea. Buddhism, both Mahayana and Hinayana, Chinese writing, philosophy, medicine, geography, and astronomy, were absorbed by the Koreans who showed themselves generally adept at participating in and continuing with vigor the civilization which they adopted.

As discussed in Chapter 24 the period of most intense Japanese interest in the Korean Three Kingdoms was late in the fourth century. Using Kaya (Mimana) as a base, the Japanese attacked and temporarily conquered both Paekche and Silla, and maintained some authority in south Korea until the sixth century. The Japanese came not only to acquire examples of the fine Chinese art found in Korea, but they also brought back to Japan from Korea superior craftsmen, both Chinese and Korean. Thus although the Japanese did not have direct relations with China, there was considerable Chinese migration from Korea into Japan. In the politics of the time Koguryo, the most powerful and aggressive of the Three Kingdoms, was somewhat removed from the Japanese influence. But Silla maintained constant hostility towards the Japanese, and Paekche, on the other hand, tended to side with and to seek aid from the Japanese in the rivalries between states.

Although during much of the fourth to sixth centuries the Japanese maintained a government outpost in Kaya (Mimana), a headquarters from which scholars, books, calendars, and objects of art might be sent to Japan, they were not so much interested in governing Korea as they were in obtaining the products of Chinese civilization. It is said that a Korean scholar brought the Chinese Classics and hence Chinese writing to the Japanese court in 405. In the sixth century, Paekche, which was especially friendly towards the Japanese, presented Buddhist gifts to the ruler of Yamato (about 552).

INTERSTATE POLITICS. Five states were involved in the international relations of Korea in the late sixth and early seventh centuries: China and Japan as well as the Three Kingdoms of Korea. The main developments were the expansion of Silla and the resistance of Koguryo against attack from Sui China.

During the second quarter of the sixth century Silla attacked Koguryo and seized part of that state. Expansionist Silla overran the eastern part of Kaya in 532, and gained an outlet to the East China Sea, thus bringing itself into closer communications with China.

The invasion of Kaya brought Silla into conflict with the Japanese. The latter sent armed forces to protect their Korean outpost, but they did not strongly resist the expansion of Silla. The Japanese had gained most of what was known in southern Korea about Chinese civilization, and hence they had less interest there. Kaya was in a ruined condition and now less valuable to them. In Yamato itself the Japanese clans were fighting against each other, resulting in concentration on internal politics.

The growth of Silla brought it into opposition also with Paekche, and Paekche in turn looked to the Japanese for assistance. In this connection the king of Paekche sent a statue of the Buddha and Buddhist sutras to the Japanese court in about 552, hoping thereby to gain assistance against Silla and Koguryo. In spite of this, Silla moved further to the west, conquering all of Kaya in 562. While the Japanese thus ceased to hold territory in Korea, they maintained contact with Paekche chiefly because of their interest in Buddhism.

The kings of Silla could rely on the defensive value of a mountainous region where they were safe from attack. Also by the latter part of the sixth century Silla entered into closer and more friendly relations with China, especially in the period after the founding of the Sui dynasty. In this latter period Silla expanded northward along the east coast at the expense of Koguryo.

Meanwhile, as previously mentioned, the Sui reunified all China in 589. After this, Emperor Wen began to take an active interest in Korea. However, when the Sui attempted to expand into the peninsula following the example of their great predecessors, the Han dynasty, they found that the Korean kingdoms had become much stronger. When Emperor Wen attacked Koguryo in 598 he was repulsed. Nevertheless, the people of Koguryo acknowledged the greatness of the Sui, and the king entered into tributary relations with the Sui court, accepting investiture from the Sui Emperor Wen and sending envoys to Ch'ang-an.

Emperor Yang, the second emperor of the Sui, failed in 612–614 in a series of attempts to enforce his power on the state of Koguryo. Only in 614 did he even succeed in entering the peninsula itself. The Koreans showed special defensive skill and the Sui suffered an expensive setback which was one of the causes for the downfall of the dynasty.

BASIC DATES

2nd and 3rd centuries	Korea. Start of "Three Kingdoms"
220–264	China. "Three Kingdoms" period
280–317	Chin unification of all China
311	Hsiung-nu destruction of Lo-yang
313	Koguryo seizure of Lo-lang
317–589	North-South period, "Six Dynasties" in South China
317–420	Eastern Chin
372	Buddhism to Koguryo
383	Kumarajiva to China
386–534	Northern Wei, T'o-pa
399–414	Fa Hsien's journey
407–551	Jou-juan in Mongolia
502–549	Emperor Wu of Liang in South China
552	Buddhism to Japan

SUPPLEMENTARY READING

ASHTON, L. AND B. GRAY. *Chinese Art*. London, 1937.

DE BARY, W. T., ED. *Sources of Chinese Tradition*. New York, 1960.

CAHILL, J. *Chinese Painting*. Cleveland, 1960. Excellent text, superb illustrations.

CHI, C. T. *Key Economic Areas in Chinese History as Revealed in the Development of Public Works for Water-Control*. London, 1936.

CREEL, H. G. *Chinese Thought from Confucius to Mao Tse-tung*. Chicago, 1953.

EBERHARD, W. *A History of China from Earliest Times to the Present Day*, 2nd ed., rev. Berkeley, Cal., 1960.

FITZGERALD, C. P. *China: A Short Cultural History*. London, 1950.

GOODRICH, L. C. *A Short History of the Chinese People*, 3rd ed. New York, 1959.

GROUSSET, R. *Civilizations of the East, Vol. III: China*. New York, 1935.

———————— *The Rise and Splendor of the Chinese Empire*. Berkeley, Cal., 1953.

HUDSON, G. F. *Europe and China: A Survey of Their Relations from the Earliest Times to 1800*. London, 1931.

LATOURETTE, K. S. *The Chinese: Their History and Culture*. New York, 1946.

REISCHAUER, E. O. AND J. K. FAIRBANK. *East Asia: The Great Tradition*. Boston, 1958.

SICKMAN, L. AND A. SOPER. *The Art and Architecture of China*. Baltimore, 1956.

SWANN, P. C. *Art of China, Korea, and Japan*. New York, 1963.

WALEY, A. *Translations from the Chinese*. New York, 1941.

WRIGHT, A. F. *Buddhism in Chinese History*. Stanford, Cal., 1959.

ADVANCED READING

ACKER, W. R. B. *T'ao the Hermit: Sixty Poems by T'ao Ch'ien (365–427)*. London, 1952.

BINGHAM, W. *Founding of the T'ang Dynasty, the Fall of Sui and Rise of T'ang: A Preliminary Survey*. Baltimore, 1941.

BODDE, D. "Feudalism in China," in R. Coulbourn, *Feudalism in History*. Princeton, N. J., 1956.

BREWITT-TAYLOR, C. H. *San Kuo, or Romance of the Three Kingdoms*. Shanghai, 1925. Translation of the famous novel.

CHEN, S. H. *Biography of Ku K'ai-chih*. Chinese Dynastic Histories Translations, No. 2. Berkeley, Cal., 1953.

EBERHARD, W. *Conquerors and Rulers: Social Forces in Medieval China*. Leiden, 1952.

ELIOT, C. *Hinduism and Buddhism*. London, 1954.

FUNG YU-LAN. *A Short History of Chinese Philosophy.* New York, 1948.

GILES, H. A. *History of Chinese Literature.* New York, 1937.

GRAY, B. AND J. B. VINCENT. *Buddhist Cave Paintings at Tun-huang.* London, 1959. Excellent illustrations.

GRIFFIS, W. E. *Corea, the Hermit Nation,* 9th ed. New York, 1911. A classic work.

LEE, M. P. H. *Economic History of China, with Special Reference to Agriculture.* New York, 1921.

MC CUNE, EVELYN. *The Arts of Korea: An Illustrated History.* Rutland, Vt., 1961.

NEEDHAM, J. *Science and Civilisation in China,* Vol. 1. Cambridge, 1956.

SHRYOCK, J. K. *The Origin and Development of the State Cult of Confucius.* New York, 1932.

SIREN, O. *Chinese Sculpture from the 5th to the 14th Century,* 3 vols. London, 1925.

STEIN, A. *On Ancient Central-Asian Tracks: Brief Narrative of Three Expeditions in Innermost Asia and Northwestern China.* London, 1933.

SULLIVAN, M. *An Introduction to Chinese Art.* Berkeley, Cal., 1961.

WALEY, A. *A Hundred and Seventy Chinese Poems.* London, 1918.

ZURCHER, E. *The Buddhist Conquest of China.* Leiden, 1959.

XIX ✷✷

T'ANG AND FIVE DYNASTIES

THE HISTORY OF CHINA in the great T'ang period and the time of the "Five Dynasties" may be considered in three main epochs: the first, a time of vigorous growth and colorful originality from 618 to 755 includes the flowering of the culture developed during the North-South period and the Sui, the reigns of great rulers, political expansion, and a crest in the development of Chinese religion, art and poetry; the second, from 755 to about 881, an era when the bureaucratic Confucian state survived internal convulsions and maintained along well-established lines a reigning dynasty and a society based on urban centers; finally from 881 to 960 a period of political disunity though cultural continuity remained. Accompanying these developments within China, were changing conditions among the peoples on China's frontiers, especially Turks, Tibetans, Koreans, and those in the lands to the southwest.

Strong Rulers Extend China's Influence

T'ANG T'AI-TSUNG.   Under strong leadership the T'ang dynasty was established as the ruling group in China. Li Shih-min, known to history as T'ang T'ai-tsung, co-operated with his father in bringing the family to power and then himself became one of China's greatest emperors. With the aid of Confucian scholars he strengthened the central administration; China in his time was unrivaled as the great empire of East Asia.

358

Li Shih-min's father, Li Yuan, Duke of T'ang, came of a family partly descended from the tribal invaders of the North-South period and related to the Yangs of the Sui dynasty. Li Yuan had served as a loyal official under both Sui emperors, but because of a popular ballad prophesying "the rise of Li" he was suspected by Emperor Yang. At the same time he showed his military ability by defeating rebels in Shansi province and also Turkish raiders from the north. Thousands flocked to his standard. When in 611 he decided to raise a "Righteous Army" and march on Ch'ang-an, which the Sui emperor Yang had abandoned, the East Turkish Khan also entered into alliance with him and supplied men and horses for the campaign.

With the able military assistance of Li Shih-min and others, Li Yuan was able to defeat Sui forces defending the route to the capital. Thus the Duke of T'ang gained control of Ch'ang-an and of the strategic Wei valley. At the capital Li Yuan set up a young prince of the Yang family as puppet emperor. In the south within the year that followed Emperor Yang was murdered by dissatisfied soldiers and officials. Meanwhile other military leaders were either remote from the capital or were engaged in exhausting struggles among themselves. The Lis, father and son, gained many adherents in the areas near the Wei river valley. Under their surveillance the puppet Sui emperor was "allowed" to resign and Li Yuan ascended the throne as first emperor of the T'ang on June 18, 618. He is known to history as T'ang Kao-tsu.

In coming to power at Ch'ang-an Li Yuan was fortunate in having the support of an able group, including military men and scholar-officials. He also sought and obtained the backing of the Taoists; the name Li was associated with Lao-tzu, the "founder" of Taoism. At the start of the reign the government was administered according to the pattern set up by the Sui. Changes began to be made after 624, by which time the position of the T'ang was assured.

During the first six years of the dynasty the emperor, T'ang Kao-tsu (Li Yuan), was overshadowed by the military successes of Li Shih-min. In a series of campaigns the latter gained supremacy for the T'ang against his rivals. Although a number of campaigns were necessary, the last serious opposition within China proper was suppressed by 624. These victorious campaigns against his rivals were celebrated by Li Shih-min in poetry and art. After he became emperor, bas-reliefs of his battle horses were carved to be placed at Li Shih-min's tomb.

The year 626 was a turning point in the fortunes of Li Shih-min. In that year he had to face the open opposition of two brothers, one of whom had been designated heir apparent. After the brothers had attempted to poison him, Li Shih-min, with the aid of his closest supporters, struck quickly and ambushed and killed his disloyal brothers. His father Li Yuan then abdicated and Li Shih-min became emperor, known to history as T'ang T'ai-tsung. Following the signing of a treaty with the Eastern Turks, Li Shih-min was then free to turn his attention to the administration of the empire.

The long and effective reign of T'ang T'ai-tsung (626–649) depended, as so often in Chinese history, upon the personality of the emperor and upon those whom he selected as his personal advisors. By the time Li Shih-min became

FIGURE 19.1.   Stone bas-relief from the tomb of T'ang T'ai-tsung. The sculpture shows an arrow being removed from the chestnut bay ridden by Li Shih-min at the capture of Lo-yang in 621. A fine example of T'ang animal realism conveying a feeling of power and vigorous action.

emperor he had already gained the personal loyalty not only of military men but also of some of the best scholar-officials in the country. Under his direction books were catalogued and comprehensive histories of the preceding dynasties compiled. A state university at the capital was founded to educate the youth of the upper classes in the Confucian literature primarily, but also in calligraphy, law, and mathematics. To this university came also noble youths from Korea and Central Asian states.

With the support of a loyal group of competent officials T'ang T'ai-tsung proceeded to restore the imperial government as an effective instrument of centralized administration and as a model for future Chinese rulers and for the administration of neighboring countries. The codification of the criminal law code was one of the important achievements of the time. In state economics the "equal field" system of the Northern Wei and Sui dynasties was elaborated and applied as a means of determining the amount of taxation. The centralized bureaucracy was recruited by examination mainly on the Confucian classics. The official ideology was further reinforced by the establishment of state-supported temples to Confucius in towns all over the country.

In the central government the emperor was supreme (in theory) and rendered judgments at imperial audiences. Actually the emperor selected and relied upon "Chief Ministers" who controlled the main departments and boards which con-

stituted the central government of the empire. The officials in the local governments of provinces, prefectures, and districts were appointed directly from the
national capital. The military organization of T'ang T'ai-tsung's time continued
the Northern Wei policy of conscripting peasants for a national militia to serve
in the imperial guards and on the frontiers. Effective organization and adequate
tax income were also characteristics of government during the reign of T'ang
T'ai-tsung. The period was one of prosperity, growth of population, and growing
interests outside China proper.

EXPANSION WEST AND EAST, 626–649.   In extending T'ang power north,
west, and east T'ang T'ai-tsung continued the tradition of previous great Chinese
dynasties by acting to secure China's borders and to develop overland trade.
From the west foreign peoples, styles, and religions came to his capital, Ch'ang-an.
At the same time the greatness of the T'ang drew Tibetans, Koreans, and Japanese
closer to China and involved the Chinese in warfare on their frontiers both west
and east.

In his relations with the Turks, T'ang T'ai-tsung took advantage of internal
dissension among the Eastern Turks, first to favor groups opposed to the Khan
and then to attack him within his own territory. In the year 630 the Khan was
defeated and taken prisoner.

The Khan of the Western Turks, whose power had impressed the pilgrim
Hsuan-tsang (see Chapter 5), died in this same year, 630, and the West Turkish
tribes split into two groups, east and west of Lake Issyk-kol. Consequently T'ai-
tsung was able to extend T'ang influence into one region after another. Within
a few years all the princes of the oasis states of Turfan and the Tarim basin
acknowledged T'ang suzerainty. The real establishment of Chinese authority
came only after a series of campaigns. Turfan was annexed in 640, Karashar
and Kucha in 644 and 648. Meanwhile a rising against T'ang authority among
the Eastern Turks was suppressed with the aid of Uighur Turks on whom the
T'ang came to depend more and more for support.

The prestige of the Chinese in the years immediately after 630 extended
beyond the Pamirs to the principalities of Sogdia and Afghanistan. Along the
trans-Asiatic routes to the west the princes of Bukhara and Samarkand acknowledged T'ang suzerainty and shared in the great expansion of trade that developed
between China and Western and Central Asia. Overland to the southwest T'ang
T'ai-tsung was in close relations with the powerful rulers of Tibet and north
India. From this time onward Chinese foreign commerce expanded to proportions previously unknown. Among the exports were such special products of
China as silk and pottery (and later, porcelain).

Luxury items were brought into China by traders and others from all across
Asia. Among these people were Central Asian Turks, Tocharians, Khotanese,
and Sogdians. From further west came Persians, Jews, and possibly Armenians.
Across the land routes ideas and fashions of Iran entered China; especially
notable were the Sassanian styles in armor, horse ornaments, clothing, fabrics,
cosmetics, and hair arrangements. The Persian game of polo reached China by
way of Tibet.

The reopening of the land routes and the development of trade by sea led to a greater influx of ideas from the west than ever before. By the reign of T'ai-tsung, Mazdaist (Zoroastrian) priests were worshipping at regularly established shrines in China. More important were the missionaries of the Syrian Nestorian church who came to Ch'ang-an in 635, the first Christians known to have settled in China. The cult spread to various towns probably among the traders from Southwest Asia.

The reopening of the trade routes led also to increased communications between China and India. Chinese Buddhist monks were encouraged to resume pilgrimages to the sacred places of their faith. Especially notable among them was the journey to India made by Hsuan-tsang from 629 to 645 (see also Chapter 5). On his return Hsuan-tsang translated Indian Buddhist scriptures into Chinese. T'ai-tsung's relations with Harsha and his successor have already been mentioned in Chapter 10.

The spread of Buddhism was further advanced by its introduction into Tibet during this same period (about 632) under the patronage of Srong-tsan Gam-po, king of Tibet from about 630 to 650. He exchanged embassies with T'ang T'ai-tsung. The Chinese however refused a request for an imperial princess in marriage; the Tibetans invaded China but were defeated. Later, in 641, however, T'ai-tsung did send a Chinese princess to the Tibetans. It was significant that she was a Buddhist. Harsha at Kanauj in India sent his daughter to be married to Sron-tsan Gam-po in this same year. She also aided in establishing Buddhism in Tibet. Thus the spread of the Indian religion and the border politics of China were closely connected in the time of T'ang T'ai-tsung, and again in later centuries.

Interest in Buddhism also was one of the reasons for the succession of Japanese missions which continued to arrive at the Chinese capital in the reign of T'ai-tsung and during the next two hundred years. In this period it was primarily the well-organized T'ang empire which was the object of study for the Japanese men of noble families who came to Ch'ang-an and other parts of China. Some students stayed for as long as thirty years and on their return had a great influence in Japanese governmental changes such as the Taika Reforms of 646. The whole range of culture from the law code compiled under T'ang T'ai-tsung to the art and architecture of T'ang China was copied and incorporated into the civilization of Japan (see Chapter 24).

Young Koreans also came to study at Ch'ang-an during the reign of T'ang T'ai-tsung. But after a generation of peaceful relations the Chinese were again involved in warfare on the peninsula. As the power and influence of Silla increased in this period that state was faced by a hostile coalition. When Koguryo forces supported by Paekche and Japan invaded Silla in 643 the latter called on the Chinese emperor for help. T'ang troops seized Koguryo territory west of the Yalu and unsuccessfully besieged Anji, north of the Koguryo capital at P'yong-yang, in 645. T'ang forces had relieved the pressure on Silla but this campaign and another in 647 failed to cause the submission of Koguryo.

KAO-TSUNG AND EMPRESS WU. During the later years of the reign of T'ang T'ai-tsung there occurred at the imperial court two events which were to have a profound effect on the history of the empire during the next fifty years. The first was the arrival in 637 of a beautiful thirteen-year-old girl named Wu Chao to serve in the emperor's palace. The second was the unsuccessful conspiracy of the eccentric heir apparent Li Ch'eng-ch'ien in 643, which resulted in Ch'eng-ch'ien's death in exile and in the promotion of another brother, Li Chih, to succeed his father. Li Chih ascended the throne in 649 and is known to history as the emperor T'ang Kao-tsung.

Kao-tsung inherited both an imperial tradition and an established position of undisputed power together with the services of elder statesmen, civil and military, who had helped his father T'ai-tsung build up an expanded empire. Under their guidance China continued to prosper. Important policies and projects of T'ai-tsung's reign were brought to successful conclusion. Military successes enlarged Kao-tsung's empire abroad and the patronage of monks, scholars, and artists heightened its prestige at home.

The emperor Kao-tsung was not a man of strong character and his reign is especially marked by the rise to power of his father's former concubine, Wu Chao. This lady had retired to a Buddhist nunnery and from there was brought back to court as Kao-tsung's favorite in 654. Clever and unscrupulous, she intrigued first against Kao-tsung's empress, whom she superseded as the empress Wu, and against Kao-tsung's older advisors, against whom charges were brought which resulted in their exile, suicide, or execution. Within ten years she had caused the suicide of the heir apparent and by 664 had secured from Kao-tsung the right to participate, from behind a screen, in all conferences between the emperor and his ministers. Questions of succession were decided by the empress Wu even against her own sons. When her eldest was made heir apparent he proved to be intractable and was poisoned at her command. Her second son after a few years was reduced from heir apparent to commoner. The third, known to history as the emperor Chung-tsung, succeeded to the throne at his father's death in 683. Chung-tsung attempted to rule independently; the empress Wu then used her influence to have him deposed and to have her fourth son made emperor. The latter, T'ang Jui-tsung, ruled in name only from 684 to 688.

The climax of Empress Wu's career came when she succeeded in suppressing two revolts of T'ang nobles and followed this by arranging in 690 to have herself proclaimed "Emperor" and to have the dynastic title changed to "Chou." Her success was based on unusual talent in politics and administration. With well-organized espionage, with the use of secret reports and sometimes with wholesale executions, the empress Wu governed ruthlessly yet with real efficiency. Order was maintained, the civil service strengthened, and the army kept under firm control. She secured a measure of popular approval through amnesties and she had the skill to keep the services of able advisors until the last years of her reign.

During the latter half of the seventh century the peaceful conditions within China were reflected in literary and artistic accomplishments. The writing of history, including works started during the reign of T'ai-tsung, was continued and that reign was itself brought under critical examination. Scholar-poets were employed by the government, but their office holding and their opportunities for writing poetry depended upon whether or not they were in favor at court.

The foreign relations of China during the latter half of the seventh century consisted of three principal phases. In the time of Kao-tsung T'ang territorial power reached its greatest extent. An attack by the Western Turkish Khan on Chinese garrisons in Turkistan led to a midwinter campaign in which the experienced general Su Ting-fang defeated and put him to flight (657), thus ending the West Turkish empire. The T'ang superseded the Western Turks as the great power of Central Asia, and the princes of Ferghana, Sogdia (Samarkand and Bukhara), and the borders of Iran acknowledged the Chinese emperor as their suzerain. In the domain of the Eastern Turks (present Outer Mongolia) rebellious tribes were suppressed and T'ang forces aided by Uighur Turkish allies established Chinese authority as far north as the Orkhon valley. In Korea meanwhile, Paekche and Koguryo, in alliance with the Japanese, had attacked Silla, the ally of T'ang. Chinese naval and land forces (the latter under Su Ting-fang) aided Silla in conquering Paekche in 660. After the Japanese had been decisively defeated in a naval battle (663), Silla and T'ang armies overran Koguryo and brought the power of that state to an end in 668. Korea south of the Taedong (Taitong) river was unified under the state of Silla. The territory north of the Taedong was annexed to the T'ang empire.

In order to maintain direct Chinese rule over these frontier territories the government of T'ang Kao-tsung and Empress Wu established administrative protectorates or "Governments-General" at strategic points to the west, north, and east: at Kucha in the Tarim basin, in Uighur territory (present Mongolia), and in what is now southern Manchuria.

The next phase in border relations was affected by the development of military power in Tibet. While the T'ang were engaged in operations in Korea, the Tibetans first occupied the region of Kokonor (663), and later gained control of the Tarim basin oases and the Ili valley in 670. With all Turkistan in the hands of the Tibetans the T'ang was forced into defensive warfare in which the Tibetans for some years had the upper hand.

At the same time to the west, beyond the range of the Chinese-Tibetan conflict, Umayyad Moslems were raiding Central Asia. Among the Iranians who fled before the Arab advance Prince Feruz (or Peroz), the last of the Sassanians, made his way overland to China and the court of T'ang Kao-tsung at Ch'ang-an in 674. Iranians who came to China in the seventh century included some who were followers of Mani. Their faith, Manichaeism, is believed to have been brought to China in 694 and later was an important influence among the Uighurs.

The third phase in the foreign relations of the period of the empress Wu was the reassertion of T'ang power in Turkistan. Under her direction Chinese armies defeated the Tibetans (692) and regained control of the Tarim oases and hence of the trade routes to the west.

Towards the end of her reign the Chinese were again on the defensive, faced with new leadership among the Eastern Turks. In the Orkhon river region the Khan Mo-ch'o (or Bakchor), who reigned from 691 to 716, established the Khanate of Orkhon. He declared his independence from the Chinese. Mo-ch'o raided the north China frontiers and trade routes from 698 to 716. Also a tribe called the Khitan, living in what is now southern Manchuria (the Liao river valley), rebelled against Chinese control. Mo-ch'o feared their possible rise and assisted in suppressing them, but by the middle of the eighth century the Khitan had become a force demanding serious military operations.

At eighty years of age, after controlling the Chinese government for forty years, the empress Wu's health failed and she tended to rely upon less capable favorites among her officials. A coalition against her was formed among members of the Li family, followers of the old ministers and families who had been less favored during her regime. Government officials conspired with this group and engineered a coup at the famous Hsuan-wu or North Gate of the Palace City in 705. The empress was forced to abdicate and the T'ang emperor Chung-tsung, who had been deposed in 684, was restored to the throne. Empress Wu died in retirement a few months after losing her power.

A Golden Age

RELIGION IN LATE SEVENTH AND EARLY EIGHTH CENTURY.   In this time of firm rule religion, especially Buddhism, flourished as never before. Although largely outside the mainstream of Chinese official and intellectual life, religious influences deepened the thinking of the Chinese and greatly enriched the whole culture of the T'ang and subsequent periods.

Both Kao-tsung and the empress Wu officially favored the performance of religious ceremonies. Kao-tsung continued to honor the "founder" of Taoism, Lao-tzu. Chief importance was given however to other rites, those of the state cult and of Mahayana Buddhism. Sacrifices to heaven and in honor of Confucius were undertaken at great expense to the imperial government but with heightened prestige for the monarchy. When the empress Wu was suppressing the Li nobles and preparing to set aside the T'ang dynasty she herself personally made sacrifices to heaven.

Religious influences from Persia continued to be reinforced in spite of political and military disturbances along the land trade routes. Early arrivals among the Mazdeans, Manichaeans, and Christians were officially encouraged in carrying on their worship in China. But this was of minor significance compared with the imperial patronage of Buddhism and the general interest in it evidenced by the travel of Buddhist monks.

The T'ang is sometimes called the "Buddhist period" of Chinese history. The spread of Buddhism, started in earlier times, continued under the special favor of T'ang Kao-tsung and the empress Wu. Small spiritual centers became well-organized monasteries. These centers of learning and culture were now an integral part of Chinese society. Monasteries endowed by wealthy patrons expanded their land-holdings. With their riches the Buddhist monks might support or undermine the power of the state.

FIGURE 19.2.   A view of the gigantic Buddhist sculpture of Lung-men, seventh century.

In this period Buddhist sects which had started earlier became even more important. These included the philosophical T'ien-t'ai and the Amidist Pure Land sect. Ch'an Buddhist doctrines were perfected in the time of the empress Wu by the monk Hui-neng who identified wisdom with intuition and established a patriarchate (a succession of Ch'an Buddhist leadership) at Lo-yang.

A new Chinese Buddhist sect was the Fa-hsiang sect which emphasized abstract philosophy. The concepts of pure idealism of this sect were developed from Mahayana scriptures brought from India and translated by the monk Hsuan-tsang. The purely Chinese Hua-yen sect, whose doctrines were based on syncretic metaphysics, was also a development of the seventh century.

Buddhist pilgrims who went to India from China during the latter half of the seventh century, and of whom we have a record, numbered more than fifty. Monks traveled also from Korea and Vietnam. However, during the period of Tibetan domination and later because of East Turkish raids overland travel was interrupted and the pilgrims preferred to go by sea. Especially famous was the Buddhist monk I-ching who traveled by sea and whose journeys and periods of study in India and Sumatra occupied him during the years 671 to 695.

Remains of this Chinese interest in Buddhism have come down to us in the great Buddhist art of Sui and T'ang times. Examples of Chinese temple and pagoda architecture of the seventh century are still to be seen at a few places, such as Horyuji near Nara in Japan and the Ta Yen T'a (Great Goose Pagoda) at Ch'ang-an (modern Sian). The most important sculpture of this period is the group of gigantic rounded stone figures and background bas-reliefs cut out of the solid rock at Lung-men a few miles from Lo-yang. The 35-foot high Vairo-

cana and attendant Bodhisattvas were carved during the reign of T'ang Kao-
tsung. Many small bronze Buddhist figures of great elegance were also cast
during this general period. The colorful Buddhist paintings of the time have
mostly disappeared, although the vigorous lines and symmetrical groupings of
figures may still be seen in such incised stone reliefs as those over the doorways
at the Ta Yen T'a and on the sides of the Buddhist stone shrine (dated 704) in
the Boston Museum of Fine Arts.

A religious practice connected with concern for the dead was greatly elaborated in T'ang times. This was the placing of clay or wooden figures of men and
animals in the tombs. Clay figurines of officials, horses, camels, and guardian
spirits (such as those in the set placed in a tomb of 693 now in the Royal Ontario
Museum of Archeology at Toronto) show the life and vigor of T'ang art. Other
figurines, which tell us much about the people and fashions of the time, represent
warriors, court ladies, dancers, musicians, women polo players, and foreigners
from Central Asia.

T'ANG HSUAN-TSUNG. T'ang greatness in administration and in artistic
achievement came to a climax during the next half century, a period which
both Chinese and foreigners later referred to as the "golden age" of Chinese
culture.

After seven years of weak emperors and two palace revolts, we come to
the reign of one of the great emperors of Chinese history, the third outstanding
ruler of the T'ang period. Li Lung-chi, a grandson of Empress Wu, re-established
his father Jui-tsung on the throne as emperor for a second short reign from 710
to 712 and then in the latter year he mounted the Dragon Throne himself. He
is known to history as T'ang Hsuan-tsung, or Ming-huang ("the brilliant emperor"). He started his rule with energy and ability. Administration, based
solidly on the examination system and Confucian ideology, was improved. With
more economy in government and a check on luxuries at court, China continued to prosper until the 740's.

Some administrative changes were made in Hsuan-tsung's reign which later
resulted in decentralization and a weakened system of government. Local officials
were given greater power than formerly, and for the administration of the fifteen
provinces of the country new imperial commissioners (or legates) were created.
These regional commanders became permanent officials who controlled civil
and military affairs in large border areas.

The emphasis on scholarship during the preceding hundred years, the
nation-wide system of schools in Hsuan-tsung's time, and the personal interest
of the emperor resulted in a peak of artistic and literary attainment. The creative
spirit of the times was manifest in the city-planning and the architecture of the
capital itself. The Chinese walled city of previous centuries was in T'ang times
at Ch'ang-an given a grandeur of form which made it a model for future city-
planning in China and also in neighboring countries, especially Japan. The
rectangular symmetrical design with an extensive Palace City in the northern
part was copied at Nara and Kyoto. Its magnificence was enhanced by great
temples and pagodas inside the walls and by additional imperial palaces outside.

The cultural center at the imperial court was an academy (Chi-hsien-tien) founded in 725 and later known as the Han-lin. Here the emperor indulged his love of aesthetic refinement and gathered poets and painters whose works were to be the models for later times. In an art tradition now greatly enriched by Buddhism and patronized by the emperor himself, the painters reached heights of artistic achievement unequalled in succeeding periods. Famous artists were numerous. Li Ssu-hsün was one of the first to use landscape in his pictures. Wang Wei and Wu Tao-tzu also were masters of landscape painting and Wu was noted for his portraiture and religious pictures. Han Kan is remembered for portraits and paintings of horses.

FIGURE 19.3.   Head of a Bodhisattva by an unidentified artist. A T'ang fresco.

The poets of the time were inspired by Buddhism and by Taoist mysticism. They felt an intimate association between man and nature and were tenderly romantic about mountains, the seasons, friendship, the transitoriness of life, and the court within which they found themselves. Among these Li Po (about 701–762) was perhaps the greatest. Tu Fu (about 712–770) has left us a record in poetry of the great days of Hsuan-tsung and the days of disaster which followed. Of Wang Wei it was said that his poems are pictures and his pictures poems.

The artisans of the T'ang employed various materials not only for magical purposes, but to meet the demand for fine crafted objects. Work in gold, silver, and bronze reached a high degree of refinement. The clay pottery of antiquity was now developed as true porcelain, "China-ware," which came into demand in remote regions, such as India and Egypt.

Foreigners trading in T'ang China introduced vegetables, fruits and medicines not known before. Games such as polo, and West Asian ideas in music, astronomy, and map-making also enriched the culture of China.

FIGURE 19.4. T'ang bronze mirror decorated with so-called sea animals. Vigor is the keynote of this art.

This rich culture in turn was transmitted by the Chinese to visitors from Silla in Korea and from Japan. We shall note further on the profound effect the religion, the arts, and the government of the period of T'ang greatness had outside China.

EXTENSION OF EMPIRE AND COLLAPSE AT THE CENTER. This cultural "Golden Age" was a period of political expansion and of great prestige and influence beyond the borders of T'ang authority, which lasted, however, only a few years. The weakening of the government within China was accompanied by defeats on the borders. The subsequent disintegration and collapse of the old imperial power in the mid-eighth century was a most significant turning point in Chinese history.

Early in his reign Hsuan-tsung was faced with Turkish strength to the north and to the west. As a check on Mo-ch'o Khan and the Eastern or Orkhon Turks, the Chinese during the early eighth century supported the Türgesh in Central Asia. This West Turkish tribe was the dominant power between the expanding Arabs and the T'ang Chinese from 716 to 733 (see Chapter 5).

When Mo-ch'o was conducting raids against the Chinese northern frontiers at the beginning of Hsuan-tsung's reign, Hsuan-tsung used other Turks to undermine his power. In addition to the Türgesh in Ili, he stirred up revolts among the Karluk, Uighurs and others. Mo-ch'o was killed by rival tribesmen and his successor came to terms with the T'ang. A few years later the eastern Turks inscribed on two stone monuments near the Orkhon a record of their relations with the Chinese.

The Chinese people, who give in abundance gold, silver, millet, and silk, have always used ingratiating words and have at their disposal enervating riches. While ensnaring them with their ingratiating talk and enervating riches, they have drawn the far-dwelling peoples nearer to themselves. . .
. . . Because of want of harmony between the princes and the people, and because of the Chinese people's cunning and craft and intrigues, and because the younger and the elder brothers chose to take counsel against one another and bring discord between princes and people, they brought the old realm of the Turkish people to dissolution, and brought destruction on its lawful khans. The sons of the nobles became the bondsmen of the Chinese people, their unsullied daughters became its slaves.[1]

The Orkhon khanate ended in 743–745 when Uighurs in Mongolia and a loose confederation of western Turks known as the Karluk, again supported by the Chinese, combined to defeat the last of the line of Mo-ch'o.

To the west, when the Türgesh turned ill-advisedly against the T'ang they were defeated by the Chinese in 739. Two years later a Korean in the service of the T'ang, General Kao Hsien-chih, was put in command of the Chinese forces in Turkistan. In 747 when the Tibetans expanded their influence into the Gilgit area (near the Hindu Kush Mountains), he checked an attempted junction between them and the Arabs by leading a force of several thousand men over the passes of the Pamirs to the upper valley of the Amu-darya, and defeated the Tibetans. In 747–749, Kao Hsien-chih defeated the Karluk, who were taking the place of the Türgesh as the dominant tribe among the western Turks. Thus the T'ang asserted their influence on the borders of the steppe in modern Kazakhstan and along the trade routes leading to Iran and India. With this manifestation of Chinese power princes of Central Asia whose frontiers were threatened by the expansion of the Arab caliphate continued to look to China for trade and possible military support. Embassies came from them and from Indian princes of the Indus valley all the way to Ch'ang-an.

The change which soon took place in T'ang foreign relations can only be understood in connection with the weakening of the Chinese government. This was a complicated process of disintegration which affected Chinese society as a whole and which some regard as the most important transition point between the post-Han culture of China and the new developments of Sung times. First, the tax system of the North-South and early T'ang periods was greatly altered. By the eighth century with an increase in population peasants inherited less land and were less able than formerly to pay taxes levied on a per capita basis. Also the total land available to the tax-paying peasants was decreased because of imperial grants and falsification of records. Taxes did not fall as heavily on the increasing number of wealthy landholders with large estates. The T'ang government during Hsuan-tsung's reign abandoned the old "equal field" system and shifted from taxation on a per capita basis to increased taxation on land. New taxes on land, commerce, and households were imposed.

[1] Adapted from E. D. Ross, "Orkhon Inscriptions," *Bulletin, School of Oriental Studies,* London, V, Part 4, 1930, pp. 862, 864–5.

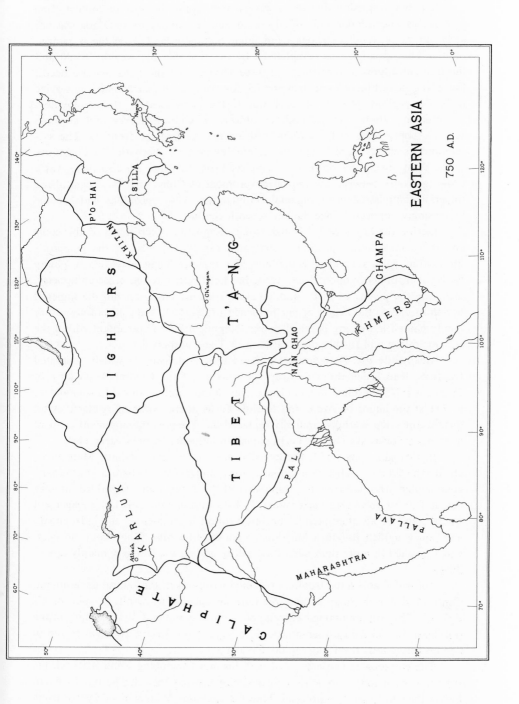

EASTERN ASIA

750 A.D.

UIGHURS

KHITAN

P'O-HAI

SILLA

T'A·N·G

o Ch'angan

TIBET

NAN CHAO

CHAMPA

KHMERS

PALA

KARLUK

o Atlach

CALIPHATE

PALLAVA

MAHARASHTRA

It is not surprising that there was an increase of popular discontent. One sign of this was in labor and military organization. Loyalty to the T'ang was not sufficient to prevent desertions from labor battalions and from the organized militia. This situation was complicated by the fact that the wealthy could and did hire substitutes to participate in these services. To meet the defense needs, the T'ang government used mercenaries for the palace guards and for service in border regions. Military defense was further weakened by the employment of foreigners (non-Chinese) both as officers in Chinese forces and as large separate contingents of troops who assisted in guarding the frontiers. The system and its effects were similar to the employment of "barbarian" mercenaries in the West during the late Roman empire. From this time on also there was a growing rivalry between the central government of China and the decentralized imperial commissioners or regional commanders whose positions had become increasingly important since the late seventh century.

During the last years of Hsuan-tsung's reign the effectiveness of the court and the central administration deteriorated rapidly, because of the emperor's infatuation with a favorite concubine, the famous Yang Kuei-fei. A plump beauty, her influence upon Hsuan-tsung has been celebrated in prose and poetry, including the poems of Li Po and Tu Fu. From her entrance into the imperial harem in 738 to the height of her influence (752–755), Yang Kuei-fei and her family gained increasing political power. Nepotism led to corruption within the administration and further disintegration of T'ang authority.

Meanwhile the T'ang armies suffered serious defeats on widely separated frontiers. Kao Hsien-chih's arbitrary destruction of the Central Asian king of Tashkent in 750 resulted in an alliance against the Chinese and a decisive defeat in 751 at the hands of Arabs and Karluk Turks at the battle of Athlach. After their victory, the Karluks gradually replaced the T'ang as the dominant element in western Turkistan. Uighur Turks gained in influence in the eastern part.

In this same year, 751, border tribesmen in present southern Manchuria, chiefly the Khitan, defeated a Chinese army under An Lu-shan, a "barbarian" commander, who had risen to prominence at the T'ang court. In a third military defeat T'ang forces were beaten near Ta-li-fu in Yunnan. This last engagement was a result of an attempted T'ang intervention in Nan-chao, the independent and newly unified Buddhist kingdom in southwest China. The Nan-chao campaign resulted in more than 60,000 casualties among the Chinese, mainly due to illness.

These defeats on the frontiers reflected weakness in the central government. Centralized power collapsed and An Lu-shan decided to revolt. In spite of his defeat in 751, An maintained a strong position in command of the armies in the northeast. In 755 An Lu-shan attacked Lo-yang in the Yellow river valley and in 756 his forces took the T'ang capital, Ch'ang-an.

The emperor Hsuan-tsung fled with his court including Yang Kuei-fei. On the road the troops who were escorting him insisted that she be put to death before the emperor might proceed. Thus the era came to an end and Hsuan-tsung went into semi-exile in Szechuan.

The emperor's son fled into northwest Shensi and there rallied supporters of the T'ang to resist the rebels. An Lu-shan meanwhile had proclaimed himself "emperor" at Lo-yang, but was murdered in 757 by his own son. The rebellion continued mainly under Turkish leadership until 763. To suppress this uprising the son of Hsuan-tsung brought back garrisons from Central Asia and used the fighting men of border peoples, especially Uighurs, men from Khotan and Ferghana, as well as Arab troops. After a decisive defeat of the rebels near Ch'ang-an in 757, T'ang forces re-entered the capital. Hsuan-tsung returned and then formally abdicated in favor of his son, known to history as the emperor Su-tsung. Father and son both died in 762.

In these years of rebellion China was in a state of confusion. Military governors acted independently and most of north China was devastated by the civil wars. The central government had little power. Much of its strength depended upon foreign allies, particularly the Khan of the Uighur Turks. When for a few years the Uighurs failed to support the T'ang the way lay open for an army of Tibetans to do more than raid the frontiers.

Tibet was at the zenith of her power under King Ti-song De-tsen (or Khri-sron Lde-bcan), about 755–797, noted for his strong leadership in the introduction of Tantric Buddhism as well as for his military successes. He exacted tribute from the court at Ch'ang-an, and when, after the death of Su-tsung, the Chinese failed to pay, he made an alliance with some of the Uighurs and marched on Ch'ang-an. The central government failed to offer any resistance and the Tibetans proceeded to capture and burn the city in 763. Shortly thereafter Chinese forces with Uighur assistance retook the capital; the emperor and his court returned.

The T'ang Continues

POLITICAL WEAKNESS AND CULTURAL CHANGE, 763–873. During the next hundred years T'ang administration survived strong Tibetan and Turkish influences at the court and a tendency toward decentralization. The followers of Confucius became conspicuously stronger and China extended relations with peoples overseas as never before. A society with new interests began to show characteristics which it maintained during the following periods of division and of reunification. Among these trends the most significant is the survival of T'ang authority; for a long period the empire remained relatively orderly in spite of the lack of outstanding men on the throne.

The emperors of this period were mostly incompetent men. At the court power was shared by three elements: palace eunuchs, some of whom served as generals in the capital guard armies; scholar-officials, chiefly recruited by the examination system and among whom were some able administrators; and army officers, who were influential because with their forces they kept the dynasty on the throne in the face of recurrent foreign invasion and serious rebellions. This was also a time of increasing independence of military leaders in the provinces, men whose actions were not crucial as long as they remained loyal to the T'ang dynasty.

The struggle for power at the court between eunuchs and scholar-statesmen (between "the within" and "the without") was an important factor in making the government less effective. But the choice of superior administrators by examination and the tax reforms which they instituted and which led to a wider tax support for the central government were sources of strength which kept the T'ang an effective regime until the latter part of the ninth century.

In the politics until 873 the conduct of certain individuals stands out even though the ten reigns of this 110-year period (reigns of the eighth to seventeenth T'ang emperors) need not for the most part concern us by name. The scholar-advisors at the T'ang court during the two reigns following the Tibetan invasion were responsible for important reforms. The forced labor (or corvée) previously relied upon was abolished. General consolidated taxes (on a money basis) were levied on land areas twice a year. This meant taxation on a more diversified basis than formerly. Transportation of grain from the Yangtze valley to Ch'ang-an was done by professional transport workers and the service generally improved. Meanwhile in northeast China, from 781 to 786, resistance to the central government took the form of open rebellion and required military action for its suppression.

The tenth T'ang emperor had been incapacitated by a stroke prior to his accession. He was forced to abdicate in favor of his son, known to history as Hsien-tsung, who reigned for fourteen years during the famous Yuan-ho period (806–820). In this time several ministers worked seriously for good administration in spite of opposition, including a constant struggle with court eunuchs. The noted scholar poet Po Chü-i openly expressed his sentiments in favor of social reform. For example, in one poem he told of the celebration of a feast for high officials at Ch'ang-an while nearby prisoners in jail were freezing to death. Among the able administrators of this reign was Li Chi-fu, twice Chief Minister and the author of important reference works on geography and administration. Scholars who served in the central government had to face political opposition, possible assassination, and civil war (as in cases of regional commanders asserting their own local authority). The fact that they did maintain T'ang supremacy in the face of rebellion, eunuch opposition, and the pressures of border peoples indicates the continued resiliency and basic strength of the T'ang government.

The twelfth T'ang emperor was noted for his enjoyment of hunting and theatricals. The thirteenth was only a boy of eighteen when he died in a drunken brawl. The fourteenth, also a boy when he came to the throne in 827, made a serious attempt to govern. He and his ministers twice failed in attempting to check the power of the court eunuchs. Instead three Chief Ministers themselves were put to death. Eunuchs controlled the succession in 840 and were responsible for the enthronement of the emperor Wu-tsung, who reigned until 846. During this reign Taoism was an important influence at court; on religious and economic grounds action was taken restricting Buddhists. The sixteenth T'ang emperor at first resisted Taoist influence and later succumbed to the fatal effects of a "drug of immortality." The seventeenth reign (859–873) was characterized by a Buddhist revival, court extravagance, and the beginning of a period of serious rebellions.

In spite of factionalism at court and revolts in the provinces (Honan in 815–819, Hopei in 839, 845, Chekiang in 860, and south and central China in 868–869), the China of this period was orderly and the T'ang regime was one which worked. From the accounts of the Japanese monk Ennin we know that China in the 830's and 840's was a safe place to travel, free from exactions of bandits or officials. Ennin's picture of the government in operation is significant.

> The remarkable degree of centralized control still existing, the meticulous attention to written instructions from higher authorities, and the tremendous amount of paper work involved in even the smallest matters of administration are all the more striking just because this was a period of dynastic decline.[2]

One element in the maintenance of the dynasty during this period between the 760's and the great rebellions of a century later was the alliance with the Uighur Turks. Ruling from their headquarters in the Orkhon valley until 840, they helped protect the northwest approaches to Ch'ang-an "on a basis of equality with the T'ang." They profited from the relationship by trade, obtaining silk in exchange for horses.

Having a position of importance among the Chinese the Uighurs shared in the cosmopolitanism of the T'ang court. It was in China in 762 that the Uighur Khan met a high priest of the Manichaeans, the melancholy faith which originated among the Sassanians in the third century. Manichaeism spread among the Uighurs and became the prevailing religion among them. Uighur patronage led to an increase of converts among the Chinese, until its proscription in 843.

Uighur power in Outer Mongolia was threatened by Kirghiz tribesmen on the upper Yenisei river to the north. After some twenty years of hostilities the Kirghiz in 840 combined with the Karluk Turks to defeat the Uighurs and to drive them away from the Orkhon. Some Uighurs raided the Chinese borders, some went west beyond the Altai and others, the more important group, settled near the eastern T'ien-shan mountains, especially at Turfan.

The capital of the Uighur Turks, Karakhoja, became a crossroads for commerce and cultural influences along the trade routes in both directions. Their Sogdian form of writing was adopted by other Turks and later became the written language of the Mongols. Buddhists flourished under Uighur rule and left behind paintings and writings in many languages.

For some years after their seizure of Ch'ang-an the Tibetans continued to be a menace to the T'ang capital. For a while they held a large section of northwest China. The T'ang dynasty's Uighur allies defeated the Tibetans in 789, 791, and 808; in the 790's the Tibetans became involved with the state of Nan-chao in

---

[2] E. O. Reischauer, *Ennin's Travels in T'ang China* (New York, 1955), p. 7. Copyright 1955 by the Ronald Press Company.

southwest China. Meanwhile the Chinese sought support against Tibet from the Abbasid caliphate and a treaty of alliance was concluded in 798 (see below). After 808 the Tibetans reached an agreement with the T'ang.

Among the Tibetans in the eighth century, as has been mentioned above, Tantric Buddhism of the Red Sect became influential. This may have been a factor in leading them to adopt a more peaceful policy toward the Chinese. In any case, a prime minister who was a Buddhist monk concluded a peace treaty with the T'ang in 822, an important turning point in Tibetan history. A struggle against the growing powers of Lamaist monasteries within Tibet led to civil war in 840 followed by dissolution of the monarchy. The monks predominated and from the tenth century onwards Tibet was ruled as a theocracy with a division of power among the clergy of various semi-independent lamaseries.

As has already been noted the Chinese had no authority in Turkistan during this period. To the west of the friendly Uighurs at Karakhoja (Turfan) and separating them from the Arabs in Bactria and Sogdia, the Karluk Turks were the ruling power (see Chapter 5). The Karluk transmitted Iranian influences along the trade routes to the east and they later, under the Qarakhanids, were converted to Islam. A large part of the population of Chinese Turkistan has been Moslem since their time.

During later T'ang times, after the end of Uighur power on the Orkhon, there was no strong power among the tribes in Mongolia and Manchuria. In southeastern Manchuria, beyond the territory of the Khitan, the Tungusic kingdom of P'o-hai bordered on Silla. Like Silla, this state was tributary to China until its conquest by the Khitan in 926 (see p. 383).

The continued prestige of T'ang authority manifested itself in Chinese relations with peoples to the southwest. T'ang forces cooperated with the king of Nan-chao in driving the Tibetans out of west China in 791. Later, in 863, T'ang territory in northern Annam (present Vietnam) was invaded from Nan-chao. The Chinese governor Kao P'ien repelled their attack. When China was disrupted by rebellion in 875 the king of Nan-chao took advantage of the situation to invade Szechuan. Again Kao led the resistance and in 877 Nan-chao asked for peace.

Despite general political weakness, there were during the last century of T'ang rule many factors which contributed to the development of a more sophisticated, more urban life for the gentry class: a cosmopolitan society at the capital, with traders, priests, and envoys coming from all directions; a highly-developed interest in scholarship, literature, art, and music; an increasing quantity of artistic production; and a change in basic cultural values. All of these elements foreshadowed and commenced the still more pronounced growth of a transformed Chinese culture characteristic of Sung times in the tenth to thirteenth centuries.

As we shall note further on, the great period of Chinese Buddhism lasted until the restrictive measures of the 840's. Poets of this time were influenced by Buddhist as well as Confucian idealism. Among them Po Chü-i was imbued also with Taoist concepts. He romantically felt himself one with the essence of life. At the same time he believed: "The duty of literature is to be of service to the writer's generation; that of poetry to influence public affairs." [3] He gained popularity with such poems as the "Lute Song" in which he featured autumn, moonlight, a neglected wife, and an exiled genius. Another poet much influenced by Buddhism, Liu Tsung-yuan, also attacked social abuses and satirized the exactions of officials.

Taoist concepts which influenced poets were something different from the organized Taoist magicians engaged in political competition with Buddhist interests at court. From the time of the emperor Hsuan-tsung Taoist studies and writings were given official recognition. "Longevity pills" recommended by Taoists were the cause of the death of two T'ang emperors, the eleventh, Hsien-tsung, and also the sixteenth. Wu-tsung's edict against the Buddhists in 845 was partly due to the persuasion of a Taoist.

In comparison with Buddhism, Confucianism might have seemed to be at a low ebb. But it remained the accepted official philosophy. In temples across the land scholars and government officials offered sacrifices to the Sage. The Classics and the writings of Confucian historians were necessary topics of study for passing the civil service examinations. Although an artificial literary style was highly prized, by the late T'ang period the best minds and artistic talents of China were turning away from Buddhism and Taoism and back to the Confucian tradition.

A leader who was actively opposed to Buddhism was the scholar statesman Han Yü, 768–824. He attacked Buddhism as a foreign faith and in 819 courageously wrote a famous protest against the celebration at the capital of a popular festival including a "Procession of the Bones" in honor of a relic of the Buddha. He argued that imperial patronage of such an event, which had the backing of court eunuchs, would bring on disaster. The result was that he himself was temporarily banished to a remote area. This incident during the reign of the emperor Hsien-tsung exemplifies the opposition to eunuch influence by scholar-officials. The writing of Han Yü became famous also as the beginning of a new direct prose style which was to serve as a model for the essays of later authors into our own time. The new literary forms of the ninth century including vernacular fiction, especially short stories, are considered one of the great achievements of T'ang times.

Important for the study of the institutions of the T'ang are the works of description and compilation. This literature of administration contains an encyclopedia of political science, a work on administrative geography composed by Li Chi-fu during the reign of Hsien-tsung, and the systematic compilation of documents pertaining to the central government.

The many contacts with peoples from Central and South Asia at the T'ang court during the eighth and ninth centuries had another influence on Chinese culture. The music which was popular everywhere in T'ang China reflected ideas brought in from outside. New instruments became fashionable; there were new trends in transposition and the creation of scales. The conservative Po Chü-i decried the distracting influences of foreign music at court.

[3] A. Waley, *The Life and Times of Po Chü-i* (New York: The Macmillan Company, 1949), p. 110.

The painting of this period continued the traditions of the reign of Hsuan-tsung. Court circles included painters, such as Chou Fang, who depicted scenes from a life of refinement in restrained, decorative scroll paintings. We know that portraits were painted, but few have survived. Much art work was done by craft specialists. Some of the best examples of painting are to be found among Buddhist materials. To understand this art history and to complete the survey of the main features of T'ang culture some knowledge of Buddhist development of the eighth and ninth centuries is necessary.

BUDDHISM, 700–907.   Until the middle of the ninth century, Chinese Buddhism remained creative and independent. Even though in the end the Indian religion was forced to yield precedence to the native Chinese Confucianism, Buddhism had become by this time an essential part of Chinese life and thought and up to the reign of Wu-tsung (840–846) it held a strong position all over the T'ang empire. Then came a time of restriction, of secularization, the end of pilgrimages to India, and a decline in artistic inspiration. Meanwhile, however, the Buddhism of T'ang China attracted leading monks from Japan who transmitted the religion to their own country with lasting effects.

Sects which have been mentioned earlier were enriched in this period by the teachings and translations of travelers to the Buddhist holy land. The last great Chinese pilgrim, Wu-k'ung, returned from Gandhara and the Ganges valley in 790. Ch'an Buddhism continued as an amalgam of Buddhist and Taoist ideas. In the eighth century a split developed in Ch'an between those who believed in sudden illumination and those who felt the necessity for discipline through Indian yoga practices and meditation. In either case the stress on individual enlightenment and intuition found in Ch'an gave it a special appeal for Chinese artists and writers both during the late T'ang and in the subsequent Sung period.

Much of the great influence of Buddhism among the Chinese was the fact that this religion, unlike anything in their older culture, provided a saving faith. There was a strong appeal to the Chinese in the saving power of Buddhas and Bodhisattvas. A new manifestation of this appeal developed with the arrival in China during the eighth century of two great Indian Buddhist missionaries, Vajrabodhi and Amoghavadjra, who preached the doctrines of Indian Tantric Buddhism. This doctrine, as we have seen, included worship of Maha-Vairocana (the universal soul) and emphasis on symbolism and magic formulae as a short cut to salvation. It was known in China as the "True Word," or *Chen-yen*.

Buddhism continued to inspire Chinese artists during the late T'ang period. There were for example the portraits of five patriarchs of the "True Word" sect executed by Li Chen, a contemporary of the court painter Chou Fang, and which were taken to Japan by the Japanese priest Kobo Daishi in 804 after his trip to China. Greater in number although perhaps more provincial in quality are the murals, scrolls, and statuary found in the cave temples at Tun-huang, in far northwest China. Bodhisattvas, scenes from paradise, and Buddhist tales were depicted with the vivid colors and the clear precise designs of a great religious art. The style of painting reflects influences from Iran and India as well as China.

The decline of Buddhism was partly due to opposition from Confucianists and Taoists as already noted. From the point of view of the central government there was danger because of the independent political and financial position of the Buddhist temples. As early as 714 restrictions were imposed; some priests and nuns were secularized and an attempt made to check the growth of Buddhism in China. By the 840's the temples were more powerful and wealthy than before. Their lands were exempt from taxes and their gold and copper were coveted by the state.

The moves against the Buddhists were made largely on economic and social grounds during 842–845 in the reign of Wu-tsung. Large numbers of monks and nuns were forced to return to lay life. Temples were destroyed and bronze images melted down for coins. Many restrictions were withdrawn in 846 and Buddhism continued as a part of Chinese life, but it never regained its former position of importance.[4]

During the period of Buddhist greatness Chinese learning had been enriched, not only with the knowledge of Sanskrit but also with Indian medicine, astronomy, and mathematics.

Buddhist influence was also important in the development of wood-block printing used for the duplication of charms, probably beginning in the eighth century. By the ninth century this process came to be used for making books. The oldest known printed book is a *Diamond Sutra* of 868 found at Tun-huang.

The Buddhism of T'ang China was studied by Korean and Japanese monks who spent years in Chinese monasteries. The proximity of Silla to the centers of T'ang culture made this relatively easy for the Koreans. But to reach China from Japan meant undertaking hazardous sea voyages. The long pilgrimages of Japanese Buddhist monks to China provide evidence of great religious zeal.

During the Nara period (710–794) in Japan, as we shall see in Chapter 25, Buddhism was the established court religion. The greatest temple of the time, the Todaiji, was dedicated to the worship of Vairocana (in Japanese, Roshana) and owed its inspiration to the efforts of travelers, both Chinese and Japanese, who brought texts and ideas from eighth-century China. T'ang Buddhist art has been preserved in the temple storehouse, the Shosoin, ever since. During this time Buddhist charm leaflets began to be printed with wood blocks in Japan. Charms ordered in 764 in Japan are the world's earliest remaining printed documents.

Japanese pilgrims were especially active during the ninth century, in going directly from Japan to China. Saicho (Dengyo Daishi) visited China and went back to introduce T'ien-t'ai Buddhism into his own country. Kukai (Kobo Daishi), who arrived in China in 805, was attracted by the "True Word" sect and returned to found a Japanese counterpart, "Shingon" (see Chapter 25).

The most famous and last of the twelve embassies from the Japanese to T'ang China included the scholar monk Ennin, a disciple of Saicho. Ennin traveled in

----

[4] The ninth century was a period of general opposition to foreign faiths. Manichaeism was proscribed in 843. Mazdeans and Nestorian Christians were also suppressed.

many parts of China from 838 to 847. His mission was important mainly because of the new ideas and religious practices which he and his fellow monks brought back to Japan. Ennin is also known for the detailed diary on his travels which is one of our best sources of information about ninth-century China.

SEA TRADE IN T'ANG TIMES.   Voyages of travelers between China and the countries to the east were part of China's general sea connections, interrelations which reached significant proportions in T'ang times and which included Chinese sharing in the culture of Southwest Asia.

Chinese, Japanese, and Koreans were engaged in the commercial and religious interchange that has already been mentioned as a means of spreading of new ideas from China to Japan. The close relations between T'ang China and Korea under Silla domination will be mentioned more fully later in this chapter.

The striking new development in T'ang China's commercial relations was the growth of sea trade to the south and west. Canton, the chief port up to the ninth century, was visited by large sailing vessels from places as far away as the Persian Gulf, manned by Persians, Arabs, and Indians. To register the ships and to regulate exports and customs duties the T'ang government established a special control office at Canton.

By the ninth century the T'ang government had gained a reputation among the Arab merchants from the caliphate for fair dealing and efficient, orderly management of the Canton trade. Gold, silver, pearls, and especially silk from China were exchanged for copper ingots and such luxury imports as ivory, incense, camphor, and tortoise shell. The number of persons of Arab or Persian ancestry who resided regularly on the China coast increased to such an extent that the T'ang government arranged for a Moslem to administer Islamic law among his own people.[5] This system was a form of extraterritoriality but it differed from the modern arrangements in that the superintendent was chosen by the Chinese government and had no connection with any foreign authorities.

The ships that visited T'ang China after 750 came from ports controlled by the vigorous Abbasid caliphate at Baghdad. Whether they were from Basra in Mesopotamia or the thriving Iranian port of Siraf on the eastern shore of the Persian Gulf, these mariners and merchants represented one of the great powers of the eighth and ninth centuries. To this power the T'ang government looked also for diplomatic and possible military support during the time of Tibetan encroachment at the end of the eighth century. In 787 the emperor applied to the authorities at Baghdad as well as to nearer friendly states. The Tibetans, however, were still a menace ten years later. At that time the great caliph Harun-al-Rashid sent forces to attack the Tibetans. The next year (798) the caliph sent ambassadors to the Chinese court to reaffirm their common concern with affairs in Central Asia. After the Tibetans adopted a more peaceful policy and especially after the friendly Uighurs established themselves at Turfan, the Chinese were less con-

---

[5] During the ninth century Ch'uan-chou in Fukien and Yang-chou near the mouth of the Yangtze also had their foreign colonies.

cerned with influence along the land routes and it may be that the later T'ang relations with the caliphate were only by sea.

The sea trade and the land trade were both important in bringing new influences from western Asia into T'ang culture. Such foods as grape wine, cane sugar, spinach, and peas came from the west to China in this period. Knowledge of optical lenses reached the Chinese from further west. On the other hand Chinese prisoners captured by the Arabs at the battle of Athlach brought to the caliphate information about the manufacture of paper.

Disintegration and Division

REBELLION, COURT FACTIONS, AND SEPARATISM (873–907).   The sophisticated life of the T'ang upper class and the traditional system of bureaucracy were weakened by incompetence at court, poor social conditions, government abuses, decentralization, and drought. The result was a popular rebellion, followed by rivalry between military commanders, continued civil war, fragmentation of the country, and the killing of the last members of the T'ang dynasty. Following that one of the rebels replaced the T'ang in north China and the whole country was divided for many years.

The crisis came in the reign of the boy emperor, Hsi-tsung, who sat on the throne from the age of eleven (873) until 888. The administrative disintegration of earlier periods had progressed so that there was increasing independence of the military "Imperial Commissioners," or legates. Less efficiency in the government resulted in social dissatisfaction. These conditions were aggravated by a severe drought in 873 when the government was incapable of providing relief; and within the next two years an important rebellion began in the northeastern part of the country, the region of modern Hopei and Shantung. The outstanding leader of this popular revolt from 878 to 884 was Huang Ch'ao. The rebellion had started in the northeast, but Huang Ch'ao campaigned south to Canton, which was sacked in 879. Huang Ch'ao also captured various imperial officials and attempted to win them over to his side. Although a discontented member of the bureaucracy himself, his methods antagonized the gentry scholar class and he was unable to secure the support of any important imperial officials.

The rebellion became most serious for the dynasty when the eastern capital, Lo-yang, was pillaged in 880. Early in 881, Huang Ch'ao's forces entered the principal capital, Ch'ang-an. The court fled and Huang Ch'ao proclaimed himself emperor. But civil war continued, and China was torn by factions. Eventually, a former subordinate of Huang Ch'ao, Chu Wen seized power and in 904 he took the T'ang emperor as his puppet to Lo-yang. Soon after that the emperor was murdered.

Chu placed another boy on the throne and then proceeded to kill the ruler's brothers and other officials. He finally forced the "emperor's" abdication and had him assassinated, after which Chu Wen was enthroned as the first emperor of the Later Liang, thus ending the great T'ang dynasty.

FIVE DYNASTIES. 907–960. During the last two reigns of the T'ang period the country was fragmented into some ten principalities. This condition persisted during what is known as the time of the "Five Dynasties." Actually, the five ruling houses which followed the T'ang reigned only in north China. In general this was a period of very hard social conditions, of warfare and bloodshed, tyrannical government of petty rulers, and regimes characterized by corruption and severe levies of men and horses. Organized banditry was widespread; many suffered death or the destruction of property. Transportation facilities deteriorated and anarchy prevailed in a great part of the country. However, despite disturbed conditions, comparable to those in Europe during some of the most chaotic parts of the Middle Ages, there was economic and cultural growth.

The five dynasties from which this period takes its name based their power in the regions of the Wei and lower Yellow river valleys. Their capitals were at Lo-yang and at Pien-chou (modern K'ai-feng). Although generally they controlled most of north China, their territory did not extend beyond the Yangtze basin to the south.

The first of these so-called dynasties was the Later Liang (907–923). Chu Wen ruled with the support of the peasantry in central north China. Chu was murdered by his own son in the year 914, and the family was superseded by another in 923. Meanwhile their position in the north had been weakened by the rise of the Khitan, whose ruler took the title of "emperor" in 916.

A Turkish general seized the throne from the descendant of Chu Wen in 923 and reigned as an emperor of the Later T'ang. After only thirteen years the Later T'ang was overthrown by another Turkish general, aided by the Khitan to whom he subsequently was forced to pay tribute. When his son attempted to assert his independence, the Khitan turned against him and took him prisoner. The Later Chin, as this brief dynasty is known, ruled only from 936 to 947.

There followed the rule of yet another Turkish general who, because his name was Liu, took the title for his dynasty of the "Later Han" (947–950). His young successor lost his position due to the rebellion of a court clique, and a Chinese general whose family name was Kuo took the place of the Later Han. The new dynasty, which reigned from 951 to 960, was known as the "Later Chou." The scholar gentry class supported these rulers. The second Later Chou ruler is noted for his destruction of Buddhist monasteries and confiscation of their property, as well as his attempts to enlarge the power of this north China state. In 960, with a small child on the throne, another usurper entered the scene, a man more fortunate than his predecessors in being able to found a dynasty, the "Sung," which lasted for a long period.

Meanwhile, south China was split up into six or seven parts. There were some ten dynasties of military governors, none of which was of lasting significance except the one which was established in 937 in the long-independent southwest China state of Nan-chao, where a Chinese general whose ancestors had served in this region for generations seized power and established the first dynasty of Ta-li.

Along the northern borders of China in this period arose a new power, that of the Khitan. By the end of the T'ang this tribe, who originated in the Liao valley, had become the leading people in Manchuria and Mongolia. Their chief from 872 to 926 was Yeh-lü A-pao-chi, who was faced with the opposition of Sha-t'o Turks in north China and the Tungusic state of P'o-hai in northern Korea. By 916 the Khitan ruler was strong enough to proclaim himself emperor. Some eleven years later, in 926, the Khitan destroyed the state of P'o-hai.

By about 936 or 937 the Khitan dominated all north China. They encroached on the territory of the Later T'ang and actually established a capital in what is now Peking. They also took the dynastic title of "Liao," and are known to history as the Liao Dynasty. The Liao Khitan were a constant threat to the Northern Dynasties in China and invaded as far south as K'ai-feng in 946. Within their sphere of control the Khitan developed a dual form of government, a tribal organization for their own people and a Chinese-style bureaucratic administration for the Chinese whom they had conquered. Further west along the trade routes to Turkistan the old Uighur power had diminished so that these people only controlled the oasis area of Turfan. During the tenth century the Uighurs became the vassals of the Khitan.

Culturally the tenth century saw the beginning of many features which were characteristic of modern China for centuries to come, such as the large-scale tea trade and porcelain production, especially in southeast China. Another feature which was one of the amazing social customs of the country, the binding of women's feet, also began in the Five Dynasties period and lasted until the twentieth century.

Interest in learning was shown by the engraving of the Confucian classics on stone in the western province of Szechuan and the development of the new invention of wood-block printing, a process used to print the whole of the Confucian classics. Printing spread from China to the states to the north and to the east.

Although restrictions were imposed on Buddhists in part of China, elsewhere Buddhists were using the printing process for the reproduction of the *Tripitaka*. Traditions of Chinese are continued during the Five Dynasties period, especially at the oasis of Tun-huang, on the route leading from northwest China towards Turkistan. The wonderful cave chapels with their carving and wall paintings, together with the marvelous rolls of painting, literary documents, early printed material, and textiles which have been recovered from a walled-up chapel are largely of the tenth century and form an important part of our knowledge of the period. This time then may be considered not a real break but a period of continuous development from the preceding T'ang into the Sung dynastic period which followed.

Korea

SILLA (670–935). Contemporary with the T'ang and Five Dynasties periods in China, Korea continued to be influenced by the strong culture of her great neighbor. Politically this period saw the end of the division into Three Kingdoms, the end of Japanese influence, the rise of a strong Silla as a unified Korean state, and the beginnings of a new dynasty under the Wang, known to history as the period of "Koryo."

As we have noted before, Silla aided the T'ang in destroying Paekche in 660 and Koguryo in 668. With a strong Silla controlling most of the peninsula, the T'ang were unable to hold territory as far south as they had in the Han period and withdrew to north of the Taedong river. However, the forces of the T'ang prevented Silla from further expansion beyond that boundary.

Silla had been reorganized and strengthened along Chinese lines in the sixth century. Now, with the political unification of the country, we find a wholesale borrowing of Chinese culture and institutions. The first hundred years of a unified Silla were a golden age of cultural activity. The capital of Silla at Kyongju was a brilliant center of Far Eastern civilization. As the political ally and vassal of the T'ang, Silla and its people had close relations with China during this period. Embassies went from the capital of Silla to Ch'ang-an; tribute bearers, Buddhist monks, and merchants went from Korea to T'ang China. Koreans played the leading part in the trade between China, Japan, and their own country. Many Korean traders lived in the northeastern coastal areas of China, facing Korea across the Yellow Sea.

Koreans not only went to the capital of T'ang China to study at the Imperial University but some stayed in China to take service with the T'ang government. Most famous among these is the great general, Kao Hsien-chih, who, we have noted, was successful in extending T'ang power across the Pamirs.

Chinese influence included the organization of the Silla government on T'ang lines although the aristocratic nature of Silla society persisted and most high government posts were monopolized by the top hereditary classes. Then came Buddhism, perhaps the most important single Chinese contribution. The optimistic philosophy of Mahayana and the magical strength which might be obtained through participating in Buddhist ceremonies appealed to them. During the Silla period Buddhist arts and architecture flourished as never before. Finally, among the other Chinese influences which the Koreans brought in was the use of Chinese writing. In the late seventh century Chinese characters were used in a new way, that is phonetically, so as to transcribe the sounds of Korean words.

We have mentioned that the great period of Silla was the hundred years after the unification. By the late eighth century various factors contributed to a disintegration of Silla society. At the court there was rivalry over succession. In various parts of the country there were rebellions. Men rose to power through a succession of coups d'état. Many of the discontented peasantry turned to banditry. And another feature of the times was that some lower-class groups turned to commerce; this we have noticed was important for the trade of the Far East.

In the ninth century several revolutionary movements began and extended into a long period of civil wars. Really serious rebellions started in 889 and the years following, and resulted in two new rival states. One in the southeast was known as "Later Paekche." The other, known as "Later Koguryo," was established in north-central Korea in 901 and lasted until about 918.

To the northeast in what is now eastern Manchuria another state, P'o-hai, had historical importance for a period of over two hundred years. It was begun partly by some of the Korean opponents of the T'ang and those who fled from the unification of Korea by Silla. Among the founders were also Tungusic tribes. P'o-hai was important as an autonomous state from its founding in 713 to 926. Like Silla, P'o-hai was tributary to the T'ang empire. It also had a Chinese-type administration. Buddhist monasteries were built in T'ang style during this period, and literature was written in the Chinese language. Trade was carried on with Japan as well as China. After the end of the T'ang dynasty the power of P'o-hai was finally ended by the Khitan, as already mentioned above. This was in the year 926, following which refugees from the P'o-hai area went south into Korea.

Out of the political confusion at the end of the ninth and beginning of the tenth centuries in Korea, more or less simultaneous with but not necessarily connected to the fall of the T'ang, we find a new strong state originating in Korea. In the northern part of the peninsula in "Later Koguryo" a man named Wang Kon seized power and founded the state of Koryo (an abbreviation of Koguryo). This was in 918, and the center of Wang Kon's power was at Kaesong, in west-central Korea. In 935 the last Silla king, who no longer had any power in his own territory, turned to Wang Kon for protection. The latter accepted the submission of the Silla king. After he had destroyed "Later Paekche" Wang Kon ruled over a reunited Korea.

The Wang dynasty, which started with Wang Kon, lasted until 1392; this era is also known as the "Koryo period." It had a government closely patterned after the T'ang. But its social and economic system differed very much from the contemporary society of Sung China. The Koryo period in Korea will be taken up in Chapter 20 in connection with the history of the Sung. The end of the T'ang and "Five Dynasties" periods in China found Korea reunited under the Wang kings and China reunited under the strong Sung dynasty.

BASIC DATES

618–626	T'ang Kao-tsu
626–649	T'ang T'ai-tsung
629–645	Hsuan-tsang's travels
630	T'ang defeat of Eastern Turks
c. 630–650	Srong-tsan Gam-po in Tibet
635	Syrian Christianity reaches China
654–705	Period of influence of Empress Wu

SUPPLEMENTARY READING

ASHTON, L. AND B. GRAY. *Chinese Art*. London, 1937.

DE BARY, W. T., ED. *Sources of Chinese Tradition*. New York, 1960.

CAHILL, J. *Chinese Painting*. Cleveland, 1960.

CHI, C. T. *Key Economic Areas in Chinese History*. London, 1936.

CRANMER-BYNG, L. *A Lute of Jade: Being Selections from the Classical Poets of China*. London, 1911.

————— *The Vision of Asia: An Interpretation of Chinese Art and Culture*. London, 1932. Interesting essay dealing with aesthetic values.

EBERHARD, W. *A History of China*. Berkeley, Cal., 1950.

FITZGERALD, C. P. *China: A Short Cultural History*. London, 1950.

GOODRICH, L. C. *A Short History of the Chinese People*, 3rd ed. New York, 1959.

GROUSSET, R. *The Civilizations of the East, Vol. III: China*. New York, 1935.

————— *In the Footsteps of the Buddha*. London, 1932.

————— *The Rise and Splendor of the Chinese Empire*. Berkeley, Cal., 1953.

LATOURETTE, K. S. *The Chinese: Their History and Culture*. New York, 1946.

REISCHAUER, E. O. AND J. K. FAIRBANK. *East Asia: The Great Tradition*. Boston, 1958.

WRIGHT, A. F. *Buddhism in Chinese History*. Stanford, Cal., 1959.

ADVANCED READING

BINGHAM, W. *Founding of the T'ang Dynasty, the Fall of Sui and Rise of T'ang: A Preliminary Survey.* Baltimore, 1941.

CARTER, T. F. *The Invention of Printing in China and Its Spread Westward.* New York, 1955.

EBERHARD, W. *Conquerors and Rulers: Social Forces in Medieval China.* Leiden, 1952.

FITZGERALD, C. P. *The Empress Wu.* Melbourne, 1956.

——————— *Son of Heaven, a Biography of Li Shih-min, Founder of the T'ang Dynasty.* Cambridge, 1933.

GILES, H. A. *A History of Chinese Literature.* New York, 1927.

GRIFFIS, W. E. *Corea, the Hermit Nation.* New York, 1911.

HUNG, W. *Tu Fu: China's Greatest Poet.* Cambridge, Mass., 1952.

LATOURETTE, K. S. *A History of Christian Missions in China.* New York, 1929.

LEE, M. P. H. *Economic History of China with Special Reference to Agriculture.* New York, 1921.

LEVY, HOWARD S. *Biography of An Lu-shan.* Berkeley, Cal., 1961.

——————— *Biography of Huang Ch'ao.* Berkeley, Cal., 1955.

MAHLER, J. G. *The Westerners among the Figurines of the T'ang Dynasty of China,* Rome, 1959.

MC CUNE, E. *The Arts of Korea.* Rutland, Vt., 1961.

PULLEYBLANK, E. G. *The Background of the Rebellion of An Lu-shan.* Oxford, 1955.

REISCHAUER, E. O. *Ennin's Travels in T'ang China.* New York, 1955.

SCHAFER, E. H. *The Empire of Min.* Rutland, Vt., 1954. A careful study of one of the states of the Five Dynasties period.

SHRYOCK, J. K. *The Origin and Development of the State Cult of Confucius.* New York, 1932.

SICKMAN, L. AND A. SOPER. *The Art and Architecture of China.* Baltimore, 1956.

STEIN, A. *On Ancient Central-Asian Tracks.* London, 1933.

WALEY, A. *A Hundred and Seventy Chinese Poems.* London, 1918.

——————— *An Introduction to the Study of Chinese Painting.* New York, 1923.

——————— *The Life and Times of Po Chü-i.* New York, 1949.

——————— *The Poetry and Career of Li Po, 701–762 A.D.* New York, 1950.

——————— *The Real Tripitaka and Other Pieces.* London, 1952.

——————— *Translations from the Chinese.* New York, 1941.

XX

THE SUNG PERIOD IN CHINA

AND THE BORDERLANDS

THE RISE AND FALL OF DYNASTIES is a recurrent theme in Chinese history. Yet the principle which is the basic concept of Chinese politics, the idea of national unity, survived. The Sung rulers reaffirmed this principle by reuniting China and renewing the dynastic cycle.

The Sung began after no such break with the past as had occurred when the Sui and the T'ang reunited China after the disunion of the North-South period. The disintegration and division at the end of the T'ang was not comparable with the centuries of political fragmentation after the close of the Han dynasty. Following less than a hundred years of division after 907, a Chinese dynasty carried on again the traditions of T'ang times, traditions which were not seriously interrupted by the political division of the country during the Five Dynasties period.

A new element in the Sung was the control exercised by strong northern peoples over parts of north China as well as the steppe areas beyond. These peoples developed a mixed society of Chinese and steppe traditions. During the Sung period each of these northern powers seized successively more Chinese territory.

Meanwhile in the area controlled by the Sung, principally in south China, there were new developments. South China progressed, both economically and culturally. Within this Chinese state, threatened by northern invaders, a reinterpretation and crystallization of the culture of former periods took place. Also here, facing the southern seas, the Chinese developed transoceanic commerce beyond past levels.

Steppe Powers

LIAO AND CHIN.   Five important peoples became powerful in the steppe areas just beyond the borders of China proper. We have already noted the Khitan as a factor in Chinese foreign relations during the last century and a half of T'ang rule. Using the dynastic title of Liao (after 947) they ruled in Manchuria, Mongolia, and north China until 1125. They controlled only the northern tier of Chinese provinces, but the warfare against these provinces and the diplomatic relations between the Liao and the Chinese after 1005 were important elements in the history of the early Northern Sung. In northwest China from the tenth century until their defeat by the Mongols in the thirteenth, a Tangut power known as the Hsi-hsia or Western Hsia was a factor in Chinese politics. The Khitan Liao were superseded in northeastern China and in Manchuria by a people known as Jurchen, who took the Chinese dynastic title of "Chin," meaning "gold." The Chin eliminated the Liao, seized the Sung capital, K'ai-feng, forced the Chinese to accept their suzerainty and to move the center of government south of the Yangtze. The Chin held more of China and adopted Chinese culture more completely than had the Khitan. A few Khitan fled to Chinese Turkistan, where one of the Liao princes founded what is known as the Kara-khitai dynasty (1130–1211). The fifth among these peoples along China's northern borders during the Sung period were the Mongols themselves. They became powerful at the end of the twelfth century but did not have important relations with the Sung until after the overthrow of the Chin in north China.

The Khitan, we have already seen, began creating an empire shortly after the fall of the T'ang. Unlike the Chinese, the Khitan society was tribal, based on extended kin groups. They were originally breeders of horses and oxen in the Liao river valley northeast of modern Peking. In extending their power they used fortified border cities to control the nomadic peoples of other areas. Although they had ruthlessly suppressed the people of P'o-hai northeast of the Korean peninsula and controlled this area to the Sea of Japan, nevertheless they faced recurring rebellions on the part of that subject people.

The Chinese under Liao control were divided by their rulers and resettled. The Liao also assigned Chinese officials to what has been termed "a junior administrative partnership" to help them rule their subjects.

When the Sung came into power they faced the Khitan on the north and a series of wars resulted which were not concluded until a definite peace was established in 1005. For the next 110 years the Liao held military supremacy in north China, Manchuria, and Mongolia.

During some two hundred years of Liao rule the Khitan retained their own culture. They did borrow, of course, from the Chinese, and there was a peaceful evolution of existing institutions. But the important feature was a dual structure of society. The tribal organization was maintained alongside a bureaucratic rule over the Chinese in settled farming communities and towns.

In the eleventh century a period of decline set in, marked by large-scale land ownership, decreasing tax revenue, and a gradual decline of military power. Finally in the beginning of the twelfth century there was serious rebellion and the Liao empire collapsed.

The second of these steppe powers were the Tangut people in northwest China, who had a language related to that of the tribal peoples on the Sino-Tibetan border today (the Lo-lo and Mo-so). Although the Tanguts were usually independent over a long period, from about 882 until 1227, they were not yet an important state at the time of the founding of the Sung. In 986 they acknowledged Liao overlordship. By 990, a Tangut leader had consolidated his state as the kingdom of Hsi-hsia and was powerful enough to invade Sung China. The Sung were forced to pay tribute to Hsi-hsia as they paid to the Liao. In 1040 and 1041 the Sung again were faced with an attack by the Hsi-hsia. The existence of this hostile power along the trade routes to Central Asia effectively prevented communication across the continent which had been characteristic of T'ang times, when the Chinese government for long periods controlled these routes. The Sung Chinese were cut off from trade relations by land with Turkistan and the West.

The Jurchen (sometimes spelled Jurched) were a tribal people in central and eastern Manchuria who came to prominence under one king, Wan-yen A-ku-ta, who reigned from about 1113 to 1123, broke with the Khitan, his overlords, defeated them, and then commenced the conquest of the Liao empire. The Sung to the south, noting that their ancient enemies, the Liao, were being attacked, welcomed the rise of the Jurchen. While the Jurchen were conquering northern Shansi in the 1120's, the Sung profited by the weakness of the Liao to regain northern Hopei for a short time. The brother and successor of Wan-yen A-ku-ta took the dynastic title of Chin, meaning "gold."[1] The Sung conducted diplomatic relations with the new king of Chin, but found themselves in a position in which they had to pay tribute and where they themselves were attacked as soon as the Chin had completed the conquest of Liao. Under this second king of the Chin the Jurchen forces approached the Sung capital at K'ai-feng. The Sung emperor was forced to flee; and abdicated in favor of his son. The son bought off the Chin armies by a huge indemnity, and the two emperors returned to their capital, although not for long. It was in the beginning of the next year, 1127, that the Chin attacked again and made a permanent seizure of K'ai-feng. They captured both emperors and took them off to Manchuria. The emperor who thus ended his life in captivity was the famous ruler Hui-tsung, discussed later.

[1] Hence sometimes these people have been referred to as the Golden Tatars.

The Chin rulers made their capital at the site of modern Peking, then called Yenching. For over a hundred years they were the ruling power of north China and Manchuria and the overlord of many of the peoples of modern Mongolia. The Chin may be thought of as a Chinese dynasty since they ruled a large part of China down to the basin of the Yangtze. Under their rule the culture and the population of north China were little affected, unlike the changes which came about during the North-South period after the Han when, as we have noted, hordes of people from the steppe made a big change in the life of north China. There is no appreciable break in the cultural or economic patterns.

At the beginning of Chin rule in north China a prince of the Liao dynasty fled westward in 1130 and established himself in Turkistan. This prince found some of the peoples of Central Asia who had formerly been vassals of the Liao still faithful in their allegiance. He proved himself to be an able military leader, and proclaimed himself Gurkhan or "Universal Sovereign." His state, known as Kara-khitai, controlled Turkistan from Turfan to the Amu-darya. The Kara-khitai controlled Sogdia and forced the ruler of Kharism to pay tribute. Their dynasty lasted almost until the coming of the Mongols in 1211.

MONGOLS.   During the time when the Jurchen, (Chin dynasty), were the overlords of the Chinese frontiers there was a people on the north among the tribes who acknowledged their suzerainty in the areas of the Gobi desert and beyond who were to become more famous than any of these. The story of the Mongols' rise to power under Temuchin (Chingis Khan) is told in the next chapter. Here let us note only that as the Khitan Liao were superseded by the Jurchen Chin, so the latter gave way to a new, better-organized people coming from further north—the Mongols under Chingis Khan and his successors.

Northern Sung

REUNIFICATION AND REORGANIZATION.   The early years of the new Sung dynasty were marked by the skillful leadership of the first two emperors in both civil and military affairs. The first emperor, T'ai-tsu (Chao K'uang-yin), and his brother reunified the country and created what was to be the greatest extent of the Sung domain. The third ruler was also a scholar and a man of ability. During his reign a peace was signed with the Khitan Liao.

The founder of the Sung, Chao K'uang-yin, had been a trusted official of the Later Chao, the last of the Five Dynasties in north China in the tenth century. As a careful student of government and military affairs and thus more than merely another usurping general, he was able to establish a long-enduring dynasty, the Sung. As founder Chao K'uang-yin has been given the title "T'ai-tsu." The new emperor had the support of civilian and military officials from the start.

Sung T'ai-tsu faced the difficult task of gaining effective control over the area of north China in which he came to power, because of the almost unrestricted power in the hands of local military commanders. However, he accomplished the centralization of the military forces and induced old military leaders to resign.

New administrative machinery was created and was brought more directly under the personal control of the emperor than had been the case during even the strongest periods of T'ang rule. His counselors served as an informal cabinet and did not exercise the powers wielded by the great ministers of the T'ang. Government finances were reorganized so as to control directly the taxes of the empire. During the next century, under the new financial administration, government income increased very greatly. Sung T'ai-tsu gave his personal attention to the central administration and saw to it that officials were educated men. Even the highest ranking scholars who had been serving in the government prior to the beginning of the Sung were re-examined. Officials were allowed long tenure of office. To recruit new members of the civil service the old examination system which had begun in Han times and developed during the T'ang was now still further elaborated. It was so well perfected that the bureaucracy which came up through this system was able to maintain itself for a period of over three hundred years in spite of invasions and decrease in territory. Most officials rose through the examination system. Among them were fewer men of independent wealth and status than there had been in previous times. Thus the potential challenge to the ruler's power was reduced.

At the start of the Sung the Chao brothers controlled only the region around the capital at K'ai-feng, in modern Honan. They expanded their power east and west and through a series of campaigns brought a large number of the separate states into which the country had been divided during the tenth century under their control, starting with the central Yangtze valley, moving west into Szechuan, south into the Canton area, and east down the Yangtze to Nanking. The latter was brought under the control of the Sung government during the last years of the reign of the first emperor.

The second emperor completed the work of his brother and as a helper in founding the dynasty he received the posthumous title "Tai-tsung," which it will be noted was that of the second emperor largely responsible for the founding of the T'ang dynasty. In his campaigns to extend the domain controlled by the Sung the second emperor also was aided by able generals who had served in his brother's reign. The southeast coast, the area of modern Chekiang province, was brought under Sung control in 978 and in the next year a successful campaign was directed against a strong kingdom in modern Shansi, where the local ruler had the support of the Khitan Liao to the north. However, the Sung never controlled the whole of what we term China proper today. There was a strip along the northern border held by the Liao which was never conquered. In the southwest the state of Nan-chao was independent, as was the northern part of Indo-China, called Annam by the Chinese. Annam had been controlled by the Chinese during Han and T'ang times.

Before his death in 997, Sung T'ai-tsung had chosen as his successor his third son, a man of some ability but who was faced at the very start by a plot by the empress and a eunuch who had been employed as a general. After T'ai-tsung's death, a trusted minister, Lü Tuan, fortunately prevented the plotters from setting aside the heir apparent and instead arranged for his investiture as emperor. This third Sung ruler afterwards raised Lü Tuan to high rank in his government. With the succession well established after the reign of two rulers and the accession of the third, the government was able to expand its activities. In connection with the emperor's interest in education, which he continued to promote, he saw to it that Confucius was especially honored by temples built in all the district cities of the empire. He also was interested in Taoism and spent money on costly sacrifices. During his reign peace was arranged between Sung China and the Liao empire to the north.

BORDER RELATIONS.   After the Sung reunification, a period of border warfare began which was to last for over twenty years. Having successfully eliminated most of their rivals in the greater part of China proper, the Sung turned their attention to their strong neighbors to the north, the Khitan Liao. In fighting from 979 to 981 the Sung armies were twice defeated. Some five years later the Sung forces attacked and took some Liao territory. However, they were repulsed in the campaigns of 986 to 987. By the end of the reign of Sung T'ai-tsung the Chinese hoped to make peaceful arrangements with the Liao. Negotiations were conducted in 994, but Sung offers were rejected. Five years later the Liao themselves attacked and successfully campaigned against the Sung.

The Khitan Liao invaded again in 1004; the result was disastrous. Over half of the Chinese army were killed or taken prisoner. However, soon the leader of the Khitan Liao, himself, was shot and both sides were ready to negotiate a peace. The treaty of 1005 settled the borders between the two states. The Liao held some territory south of the Great Wall, in northern Hopei and northern Shansi. The two states regarded one another on a basis of equality but the Sung agreed to pay an annual tribute of 100,000 ounces of silver and 200,000 bolts of silk. Relations between the Liao and the Sung continued peacefully for the next 110 years, until invaders from the north, the Jurchen, conquered the Liao.

POLITICS AND COURT.   From the reign of the third Sung emperor to that of Emperor Hui-tsung in the beginning of the twelfth century, China was at peace with the peoples to the north and was able to devote herself to politics and art. During this period of peace the scholar-statesmen at the Sung court were predominant. It was they who maintained the government in this time of weak emperors. The latter half of the eleventh century is characterized by an important reform movement which became the main issue of political factionalism for years to come. Several of the most important scholar-officials in Chinese history lived in the latter part of the eleventh century. They also influenced the new young emperor who came to the throne in 1101, Hui-tsung, in his interest in the art and the great cultural heritage of China.

The most important feature of this period was the great reform movement of Wang An-shih. Wang rose to power through the regular official system, having been a local official, a prefect in three locations, and an assistant in the central revenue office where he showed extraordinary ability and gained a reputation for his scholarly discussion of governmental affairs. He entered the emperor's confidence and was named to the emperor's council in 1069 at a time when the emperor was concerned with expensive military operations and wanted more revenue.

Wang had been trained as a Confucian scholar; he himself claimed to follow ancient precedents in spirit if not in fact. In his statements of policy Wang aimed at the material prosperity of the people; he emphasized the practical and pressing needs of the government. He was opposed to the selection of officials by the literary examinations as then constituted, because of the excess of recitation and memorization of an enormous amount of literature. Hence, he was strongly in favor of educational reforms. Under his direction the number of government schools was increased and government examinations were directed more toward the practical problems of policy and administration and used less as literary tests. The government also undertook some economic reforms, including savings made for the government through an improved budget commission. Wang also promoted a state monopoly of trade and production for revenue purposes, a fixed market, and agricultural loans. Another reform was a more equitable distribution of the land tax. There was also a reorganization of the militia with a system of draft whereby every home would provide one militiaman.

These reform schemes had defects which prevented their complete adoption or lasting operation. Some were too complicated and others too difficult to operate. In any case most of them, especially the economic reforms, stirred up the opposition of the wealthy classes. Wang An-shih nevertheless had strong adherents and, as we will see, these reforms provided a platform for political factionalism in subsequent years. By 1076, seven years after he had been appointed to power, Wang An-shih retired from the Ministry. He kept the confidence of the emperor, but he did not attempt to carry out the reforms or take part in the central government after that time.

During the period of emperor Shen-tsung when the reforms of Wang An-shih were being tried out, some famous intellectuals among the scholar-officials were also active. One of the great Chinese historians, Ssu-ma Kuang, was a principal opponent of the reforms of Wang An-shih and a leader of the traditional and conservative group among the Confucian scholars. Because the emperor favored Wang's ideas, Ssu-ma Kuang retired and compiled the great history, translated as *The Comprehensive Mirror for Aid in Government,* which he completed in 1084. This was a large work covering the period from 403 B.C. to the end of the Five Dynasties.

The reign of the following emperor, commencing in 1085, was a time of conservatism, factionalism, and of decline in the effectiveness of the Sung administration. At the start of the reign conservative men were called to office. First, Ssu-ma Kuang was recalled and brought into the administration. After his death the equally conservative Su Shih (Su Tung-p'o) was made a high official. Then, later on, it was the turn of the reformers. Su Shih was exiled to southernmost China, and members of Wang An-Shih's party were back in power.

The reformist leader of the time was Ts'ai Ching, a brother of Wang's son-in-law, who, however, lacked genuine interest in the reforms of Wang An-shih and who used the reformist policies to further his own ambitions.

This was the situation when an emperor ascended the throne who is known to history chiefly for his artistic talents. The emperor Hui-tsung, the eighth and last emperor of the Northern Sung, reigned from 1100 to 1125. In his earlier years he had associated chiefly with literary men and painters. He knew little about politics and favored first the reformists and then the conservatives without any definite convictions about their political programs. The empress dowager was regent for a year and she tended to favor the conservatives, but in 1101 when Hui-tsung ended the regency he recalled Ts'ai Ching. The latter controlled the administration with an experienced hand as a harsh official who favored his own partisans and bitterly persecuted the conservatives. After five years the emperor turned to the conservatives whose views actually were more to his liking. During the next few years, factional alignments shifted in relative power while the emperor was primarily concerned with painting, poetry, and superstitious Taoism.

Hui-tsung's interest in the artistic and the unusual led him to seek rare and costly objects of "tribute." An official and friend of Ts'ai Ching gained influence through such gifts. As head of the tribute office this man was noted for his extortions, his cruel oppression and his great wealth. Thus a period of aesthetic refinement and love of the fine arts, coincided with misgovernment and corruption.

As may be imagined, the emperor was no military leader. The army in his time was controlled by a eunuch who used the military organization for his personal power. When the Khitan Liao were attacked and the Jurchen then proceeded to conquer north China it is not surprising that the Sung were unable to resist their further advance. In 1125 Hui-tsung abdicated and was later captured by the Jurchen. He died in captivity in 1135.

Southern Sung

DYNASTIC POLITICS AND RELATIONS WITH NORTHERN INVADERS. The next century in Chinese history is known as that of the "Southern Sung." The Chao family continued on the throne but having lost north China to the Jurchen Chin, they ruled themselves only in the Yangtze valley and further south. In general, political control was maintained to the northern limit of the region where water transport (rather than carts) was the principal means of communication. There was no prospect of regaining the north from the invaders. Scholar-officials were recruited through the elaborate civil service examination system and gave loyal support to the Sung dynasty until the Mongols overran the country and the last of the Sung lost control in any part of China in 1279.

The younger brother of Hui-tsung fled to Nanking in the Yangtze valley and there was proclaimed emperor in 1127. He is known as Kao-tsung and reigned until 1162. He was not interested in politics or war but preferred the peace and comfort of his southern capital, which was permanently moved to Hangchow in 1138. Political control was held by scholar-officials, who were divided on the advisability of war against the Jurchen. The war party had some success in the field, especially when General Yo Fei held military command. He recovered much territory taken by the Chin and forced them to retire as far back as Honan in the Yellow river valley. Opponents of his effective military policy then gained the upper hand, and Yo Fei was degraded and executed at the behest of the "peace" party. Peace was then arranged in 1141, between the Southern Sung and the Jurchen. According to the terms of this treaty, the Chinese regained the territory covered by water communications; that is, up to and including the Huai river valley just north of the Yangtze, which was an effective boundary for some years to come. The Sung also effectively became the vassal of the Chin and were required to pay an annual tribute of silver and silk. After renewed fighting another peace was arranged in 1162–1163.

Kao-tsung abdicated in favor of his adopted son in 1163. The latter, known as the Sung emperor Hsiao-tsung, desired to recover the ancestral possessions, but the country was impoverished and he was forced to accept the peace arranged in 1163. This emperor himself attended carefully to the education of his third son, in whose favor he abdicated in 1189. This third emperor of the Southern Sung was a firm and effective ruler at the start, but he gradually fell under the complete domination of his wife. At length he was forced to abdicate in favor of his son. These and later rulers were hardly more than puppets, controlled partly by the court and partly by the strong officials of the time.

Ever since 1141 the Chin were more or less assured of a peaceful Sung in the south, but their own eventual destruction was certain when they were faced with a Mongol attack in the north as well as attacks from other enemies. Chingis Khan had organized the Mongols in 1206, and in the next few years he won over to his side tribes that had formerly been loyal to the Chin in Inner Mongolia and southern Manchuria. Then in 1211 the Mongols struck. They invaded Hopei and Shansi, and within a few years the Chin gained a truce only by sending tribute to Chingis and by moving their capital south to K'ai-feng in Honan.

The war reopened in 1215 when the Mongols attacked, seizing most of north China in the next seven years until the Chin held only a small area around K'ai-feng. Meanwhile they were also attacked from the rear by the Sung, who thought this was an opportunity to get even with their northern enemies.

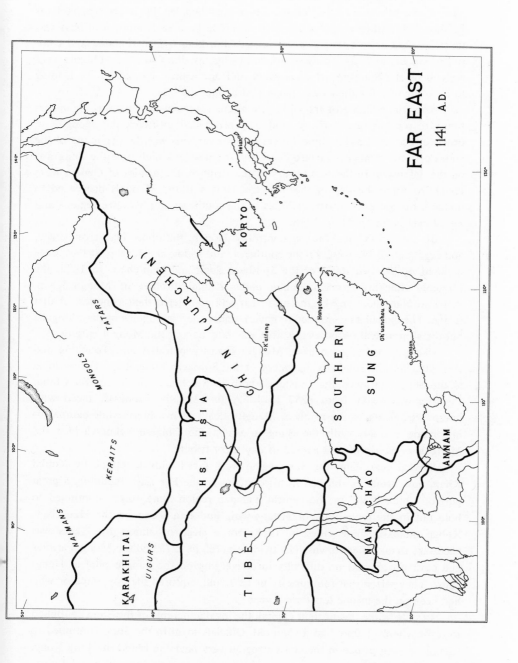

FAR EAST

1141 A.D.

The Chin continued resistance for several years and it was only in the 1230's, after the death of Chingis Khan, that Ogodai, his successor, and his brother Tului attacked the Chin in their home base in Honan. K'ai-feng was taken in 1233 after a long siege. The last Chin king was surrounded and committed suicide in 1234. In these operations against the Chin the Mongols were assisted by the Sung government which did not realize that they were helping to pave the way for their own defeat and conquest.

After the collapse of the Chin, Sung officials believed there was an opportunity to recover lost territory, and they proceeded to attack the Mongols in order to recover K'ai-feng and Lo-yang. However, this was the beginning of the end. Forty-five years of warfare began during most of which time the Sung was on the defensive. In the early years of the struggle, the armies of Ogodai were unable to force the line of the Yangtze. However, the Mongols proceeded to outflank the Sung state with its bases in the southeast and Yangtze regions and seized part of Szechuan in 1236.

By the 1250's the Mongols controlled Honan, the upper Han river valley, and Szechuan to the west. To the southeast, and south, and southwest they were opposed by the two states of the Southern Sung and Nan-chao. In 1252, the Mongols attacking from Szechuan under Kublai, brother of Mangu Khan, struck at Nan-chao, and by the next year had completed their conquest of that region. The old rulers continued to govern under the surveillance of the Mongols, but for all practical purposes this area was now part of the Mongol empire.

Using Nan-chao as a base, Mongol forces penetrated into Tongking and then attacked the southern provinces of the Southern Sung state. Forces loyal to the Sung continued the resistance both in Szechuan and in central China. Fighting was heavy from 1257 to 1259. In 1259 the Mongols, faced with internal problems, as the result of Mangu's death of dysentery while campaigning, made a treaty with the Sung in which the Chinese acknowledged the Mongols as overlords and agreed to pay them tribute.

Several years later the Sung again were faced with an attack by Kublai Khan, now firmly established in his domains in the Far East, including a great part of China itself. In the central Yangtze region Sung forces continued to hold out in the twin cities of Hsiang-yang and Fan-cheng on the Han river. Kublai attacked these cities in 1268, but a siege of almost five years was necessary to take these towns. The twin cities fell in 1273 and the Mongol armies and naval forces had no difficulty in converging on the Sung capital at Hangchow. They seized that famous city in 1276 and captured the boy emperor who had been on the throne less than a year.

In spite of the loss of their capital, the loyal adherents of the Sung continued to resist wherever they had a foothold. Officials loyal to the Sung continued to support a Sung prince in the coastal region very near the island of Hong Kong. This remnant of Sung greatness was finally overcome by Mongol naval forces, and the last ruler of the Sung dynasty died in a sea battle off the coast in 1279.

Culture, Trade, and Foreign Relations

SUNG CULTURE AND SOCIETY. In Sung times intellectuals were able to build upon the great cultural progress of the T'ang period. The systems of thought, art, and politics which had been developed, were altered during the Sung and reached a new degree of maturity. In the Sung philosophy gained precedence over religion as the most profound influence on men and society. Literature and scholarship were expanded, partly because of the more prevalent use of printing. In spite of the fact that much of the north had fallen to conquerors from the steppe, in south China flourished the culture of the past and there were new refinements in arts and crafts. In this peaceful, well-ordered society technical advances were possible and contributed to a great economic expansion which was shown in the growth of trade, both domestic and foreign. During the Sung, Chinese society and culture as a whole crystallized into forms which were to last to modern times.

In the realm of ideas and the arts several new elements had a profound influence and certain factors which had been operating since T'ang times became even more important. Ch'an Buddhism permeated Chinese thinking and affected the whole culture. One important aspect of this influence was the development of the Sung school of Confucian philosophy. The perfection of wood-block printing meant ease of reproduction and hence the wider transmission of literature.

The culture of Sung China reached a peak at the end of the eleventh and the beginning of the twelfth century in the reign of the emperor Hui-tsung, which is noted for its aesthetic refinement. The emperor had a special fondness for the great cultural achievements of the past and gathered at his court men of similar tastes. He collected books, bronzes, and *objets d'art,* and was himself a painter of great ability. Immediately after Hui-tsung's reign north China was lost to the invaders, the Jurchen Chin, but political loss did not mean cultural decline. At the new Southern Sung capital of Hangchow the old traditions were preserved and perfected in a setting which itself was an inspiration to the lovers of fine landscapes. In the surroundings of Hangchow and the West Lake scholar-officials such as Su-shih used their artistic talents to develop the natural beauties of the place and to enhance the quality of an environment in which people might enjoy and develop the fine arts. The use of tea increased and at the same time the finding and use of fine clays for exquisite porcelain gave tea drinking a quality of aesthetic pleasure.

The climate of south China was conducive to the retirement of scholars and artists into beautiful mountain retreats where they might develop philosophic concepts without the struggle for material existence required in the more rigorous north. A renewed interest in Buddhism was part of this revival of philosophy. Although Buddhism was not as vital a force in China in Sung times as it had been in the T'ang, it still had a lasting influence as the chief religion of the people. Especially notable during the Sung is the fact that Ch'an Buddhism or

Zen (as the Japanese call it) was perfected and became much more important in Sung times than it had been during its early stages in the T'ang period. The emphasis on meditation in Ch'an Buddhism combined well with the new custom of tea drinking, and an elaborate ritual was formulated which was partly stimulated by religious ideas. This whole concept and ceremony became even more important in Japan later on.

Printing with wooden blocks had been developed partly as the result of religious interest in preserving Buddhist sacred texts during the T'ang dynasty; in the Sung it had its effect in popularizing Buddhism. The whole Buddhist canon, consisting of more than fifteen hundred separate works, was printed early in Sung times and reprinted many times afterwards. A copy of this canon or *Tripitaka* was taken to Japan in 987 and to Korea in 995. The printing of Buddhist sutras in those countries followed soon afterwards.

Among those who retired for meditation and study in the twelfth century, that is in Southern Sung times, was the Confucian scholar Chu Hsi, who lived from 1130 to 1200. In his youth he was influenced both by his study for the Confucian civil service examinations, the highest of which he passed at the age of nineteen, and also by Buddhism. Soon after attaining the doctorate Chu Hsi became a magistrate in the government service. Chu Hsi is especially noted for his study of Confucian doctrines and as the most important philosopher in the creation of a Sung school of Confucianism, which was to remain a powerful influence in China in succeeding centuries.

Chu Hsi delighted in synthesis. He is noted for his clarity of thought, his fine literary style, his consistency in interpretation and in integrating all traditions of Chinese thought. Ch'an Buddhism stressed sudden enlightenment; Chu Hsi reacted against purely subjective processes of this sort. He believed and taught that men should study thoroughly all phenomena and stressed the idea of "investigation of things." However, these things were things of the mind mainly intellectual in nature—the ethics of the Confucian classics—and hence his philosophy is largely subjective.

We have noted the interest of Wang An-shih and other scholars during the eleventh century in social and ethical problems. They were opposed to the other-worldliness and the antisocial values associated with Buddhism. But Chu Hsi in the twelfth century gave the Confucian tradition a form acceptable to the intellectual class, then already strongly influenced by Buddhism (including Ch'an) and Taoism. In facing the philosophical problems introduced by Buddhism in China, Chu Hsi and his school developed a cosmology comparable to that developed by the Buddhists. They also attempted to explain the world and the Confucian ethics metaphysically, which had not seemed necessary to Confucian scholars in earlier centuries. In meeting the competition of Buddhism, these Sung Confucianists of the school of Chu Hsi justified social and political activity and vindicated man's right to find happiness in the ordinary pursuits of normal life. In all of this there is an attempt to meet the ideas of Buddhism while at the same time there is continued emphasis on the need for a social philosophy, as originally stated by Confucius himself.

Interest in man's nature led these Sung philosophers to further analysis. According to them, part of man's nature is pure and good and results in such virtues as love, uprightness, propriety, knowledge, and reliability. But because of the physical aspects of human nature there is a second side which must be improved by education, especially through self-cultivation. In order to achieve this improvement, Chu Hsi and the others stressed the five human relationships of Confucian origin. They taught the value of benevolent paternalism in politics and the influence of good example. For the actual administration of government the Sung philosophers had great confidence in the bureaucracy of which they were a part and in the examination system. Chu Hsi brought to perfection a balance in the political, social, and intellectual systems of the times. The system of ideas which Chu Hsi and his school worked out became the established orthodox cult for the whole nation, a way of thinking which was to last for some seven hundred years.

In addition to their great contributions to political and social philosophy, the great scholar-officials of Sung times were also poets. They all enjoyed writing about their appreciation of nature. Their sentiments included Chu Hsi's romanticizing about a rural atmosphere, Ou-yang Hsiu's song about autumn and death, and the mellow humor of Su Shih (Su Tung-p'o).

However, Sung literature is more notable for prose writing than for lyric poetry. We have noted the philosophic writings of the Sung school of Confucianism, the interest in political science of Wang An-shih, and accomplishments of Sung historians. Sung scholars not only interpreted the classics, as we have seen in the case of Chu Hsi and his school, but they also wrote critical essays on history, government, literature, ritual, archaeology, art.

We have noted that the new techniques of printing enabled the wider spread of Buddhism throughout China and beyond her borders. The quality of printing in Sung China was exceptionally high. Projects were undertaken by the government which commissioned the publication of the classics and part of the dynastic histories. Private printing also spread throughout the empire and some of the hereditary printing houses which were to be famous for centuries were established. Thus this technical development was stimulated by and was also an impetus to the literary and intellectual activity of the Sung. Paper money was also printed beginning in the tenth century, and this process led to periods of terrific inflation, especially after the reforms of Wang An-shih and the need for paying war indemnities in the twelfth century. Thus it contributed to the decline of the Sung and the inability to resist the invaders from the north.

The Sung was one of the great periods of Chinese art. The fine arts, as one might expect, expressed the aesthetic ideals and the philosophical concerns of the time. The creative artists were first of all the scholars, who considered fine handwriting and painting among the necessary talents of the Confucian gentleman. On the other hand, catering to the scholar-official class and the growing number of wealthy people in prosperous south China were the craftsmen, especially the makers of fine porcelain, who have made the name of Sung particularly famous.

FIGURE 20.1.   Seated figure of the goddess Kuan-yin in painted wood. Although sculpture was far less significant than painting in Sung times, nevertheless it continued to show some of the skill and delight in realism characteristic of previous periods.

In T'ang times there was a variety of painting including much religious art. By Sung times, emphasis on Buddhist painting had given way to a more purely secular art, an art practiced for its own sake by the scholar-officials. While there was an interest in depicting human figures and events, their main emphasis was more and more on landscape and nature painting.

FIGURE 20.2.   Detail from the "Hundred Geese Scroll," Sung period. Flight, take-off, and landing are perfectly executed.

The scholar-painters of Sung times delighted in contemplating nature and also in interpreting their own personalities as individuals. Although in their painting they used certain subjects as their models repeatedly, this scholar's art of the Sung was individualistic. In landscape painting they tried to express their own philosophy, their own idealistic conceptions of the world. This attempt was influenced somewhat by Ch'an (or Zen) Buddhism.

Specially noted for his patronage of the Sung painters was the emperor Hui-tsung who, we have seen, was a great painter himself. He is famous for his bird and flower pictures which set a style followed long after. Hui-tsung promoted an academy of painting at the court and examinations in painting as well as literature were given to officials. The Southern Sung is especially famous for its landscapists, some of whom painted in monochrome with a minimum of color or detail, a style characteristic of that period. The names of Ma Yuan and Hsia Kuei are associated with this style of painting. In their works we note the loveliness of country scenes in which mountains are only partially visible through the mist and in which a great deal is left to the viewer's imagination. In their technique this Sung black and white painting was similar to calligraphy, the fine brushwork of Chinese handwriting.

Associated with the interest in landscapes executed on paper or silk was the creation of actual miniature landscapes in gardens. These gardens, which expressed current philosophic ideas, were introduced into Japan. In Japan also artists such as Sesshu carried on and developed the Sung tradition of landscape painting.

FIGURE 20.3.   Clearing autumn skies over mountains and valleys. In monochrome attributed to Kuo Hsi. The mountains are distant, only partially visible. It is the whole universe we behold in this idealist conception influenced by Ch'an Buddhism.

FIGURE 20.4.   The Four Sages of Shang-san; monochrome by Ma Yuan. Three
of the sages play chess in silent absorption. The landscape features are characteristic of Southern Sung monochrome painting. On the scroll is a colophon of
the famous Ch'ien-lung emperor of the later Ch'ing dynasty with his imperial
seal to the left. At the extreme left is the artist's signature.

The manufacture of true porcelain, which had just commenced in T'ang
times, became important in the Sung dynasty. The characteristic wares are
the exquisite bowls and vases, very thin, with a stone-like quality and single
colors (especially blue and grey greens) which have been the prized possessions
of collectors ever since.

The Sung was a period of intellectual originality and sophistication, characteristics which set off the Sung from the periods both before and after. Unlike
T'ang thinkers, the scholar-officials of the Sung period were interested in questions of philosophy rather than religion. Art and scholarship were the interests
of laymen as well as of Buddhists and other religious men. In both literature
and in art there was a continuity of tradition and new developments as well,
for example the emphasis on prose writing instead of lyric poetry. The Sung
reached a ripe maturity in culture, as contrasted with the enthusiasm and the
religious faith of earlier periods.

Internal economic development was marked by the expansion of population and technical advances in many lines such as porcelain, lacquer-making,
fine silk, and explosive projectiles. In the agricultural field rice crops were
improved so as to double the yield. Tea and cotton were new and important
crops. Private trade and trade guilds expanded in what has been referred to as
a Sung "commercial revolution."

A great part of this development took place in the Yangtze valley and in
areas further south. The great rice-growing region of the Yangtze basin with
its easy water communications became the center of production and business
activity for the country, especially the regions south of the Yangtze. These
provinces received many migrant families who formerly lived in the north. New
population centers and more important centers of administration resulted in
the construction of more walled cities south of the Yangtze. Thus for the south

this was a time of rapid economic expansion, a time when the people from this area were the leaders in business, in the intellectual world, and in cultural activities.

Greater commercial activity and greater wealth increased the temptation for businessmen to engage in speculation, especially with paper money. This was a time characterized by extravagance and of wealthy landowners. State activity and controls increased in order to secure revenue from the new business which had developed. Taxes on restaurants and public houses were increased. The government also took an interest in institutions for the aged, hospitals, orphanages, and other social welfare activities. In connection with the great economic development, a much more numerous landholding class, the class of the "scholar-gentry officials," became present in Sung society. Urbanization was accompanied by refinement in arts and letters, the economic developments mentioned, and a greater degree of sophistication and a more varied life. In the cities life was freer, more luxurious. There was also increased poverty, and we may note that this is a time when women's position in society declined and when foot-binding increased. Emphasis was on civilian accomplishment, unlike the greater respect paid to the military in T'ang and earlier times. There was also a growth in pacificism, as we have seen in the reactions to the invaders from the north.

FOREIGN TRADE AND NEIGHBORS.   The prosperity of China during much of T'ang and Sung times attracted foreign traders. During the Sung when there were no open hostilities along the northern and northwestern borders the Mongolian peoples, the Tungus, Turks, and Tibetans exchanged horses for Chinese commodities. This border trade was valuable but was far exceeded in importance by maritime trade. Early in the Sung sea trade was especially encouraged. Foreign merchants were invited to come to China and granted special licenses. Special officials were designated to control commerce and shipping, and the government exercised a monopoly over trade in certain commodities. Goods had to be obtained at state warehouses.

China's overseas trade was carried on with Koryo, Late Heian and Kamakura Japan, the Philippines, and Champa. The eleventh century was also a period of great maritime powers along the southern coasts of Asia. Srivijaya in Indonesia, Chola on the southeast coast of India and, still more important, the ports of the Abbasid caliphate on the Persian Gulf both attracted the Chinese and sent their own merchants to southern China.

We have noted that Arab traders came to the coast of China in T'ang times; they continued to arrive at Canton and other ports further east. By the end of the Northern Sung and the start of the Southern Sung period Ch'uan-chou on the Straits of Formosa was the most frequently visited port. This city rivaled Canton and was still a great port in the days of Marco Polo at the end of the thirteenth century.

The most important commodities were those of small bulk and great value. For example, from southern Asia came incense and scented woods, drugs, ivory, rhinoceros horn, and precious stones. Exports included silk, porcelain, and gold, silver and copper cash. The significance of the metal exports resulted in an adverse balance of trade for the Chinese.

The Arabs (who took about two years for the voyage to China and return) used mostly their own ships, although Chinese ships were also in use. These were large vessels with four decks and were armed to meet possible pirate attacks and might have five or six hundred men in the crew. Of particular importance during the Sung was the improvement of navigation, particularly by the use of the magnetic needle. Probably used first in T'ang times for geomancy (the determination of the auspicious magical properties of certain sites), in Sung times the compass began to be used in navigation and facilitated long voyages to remote places across open stretches of water. The Chinese went as far as the Malabar coast in southwest India.

Tributary trade relations continued between Korea and China in the Sung period. From the middle of the tenth century to about 1170 Koryo power and culture was at its height. Although the kings of Koryo under the Wang dynasty looked to the Chinese emperor as their suzerain, no effective control over Korea was exercised by the Sung. In the latter part of the tenth century Koryo was forced to recognize the Khitan Liao as overlords. The Khitan invaded Korea in 1011. The Koryo government later built a wall across north Korea as a defense against invasion from Manchuria and became allied with the Jurchen Chin against the Khitan Liao. They carried on tributary relations with the Chin from 1123 until the thirteenth century, until the Mongol conquest of both Chin and of Koryo. Koryo under the Wang dynasty up to the thirteenth century was governed by a closed hereditary aristocracy. Political and economic influence was concentrated at the capital, Kaesong. Here the aristocratic bureaucrats made their homes and here most of the wealth of the country was to be found. Buddhism was an important element in Koryo culture, the monasteries were major centers of learning, and the Buddhist clergy had their hand in politics.

Twelfth-century Koryo was torn by civil wars, resulting finally in the dominance of one aristocratic family, the Ch'oe. Ch'oe power was based on a private army, with which they dominated Korea from 1196 until the Mongols asserted complete control of the country in 1258. Because of the invasions of China from the north this was not a time of close association between the Sung and Koryo.

The Sung dynasty in China corresponds to Late Heian and the early Kamakura times in Japan. Although some Japanese monks and students visited Sung China, there had been no official exchange of missions since the end of the ninth century. Trade was carried on intermittently, mostly by the Chinese. Most significant in the relations between China and Japan at this time were the ideas taken to their own country by the Japanese Buddhist monks. Ch'an Buddhism, known to the Japanese as Zen, became particularly important and practically an official religion in Japan in the fourteenth century and after. Painting, porcelain making, and the rest of the fine arts of China in Sung times had a profound effect on Japanese culture.

Although the Abbasid caliph was still the nominal ruler at Baghdad and its great culture continued in the period corresponding to the Sung, the actual rulers of Iran and Mesopotamia were first a line of Persian Buwayhids and then in the eleventh century the Seljuks, as was mentioned in Chapter 6. Thus the Chinese of the Sung were in contact with lands enjoying a great period of Arabic and Persian literature, scholarship, and science. The Chinese noted that some twenty embassies came with "tribute" from the caliphs during the Sung period.

Trade with the caliphate was chiefly in the hands of Moslem Persians and Arabs who came to China. Arabs were especially active in the commercial world of the Far East from the beginning of the eighth century to the end of the fifteenth. They established themselves in fixed quarters in the open ports of the China coast and there were permitted to regulate their own affairs.[1]

These relations of the Sung Chinese with distant peoples increased geographical knowledge among Chinese scholars. The ocean trade along the eastern and southern coasts resulted in those regions gaining economic and cultural dominance within China. However, the Chinese were not close enough to Europe and Southwest Asia or even to India to feel themselves part of a world in which great civilizations of comparable importance existed alongside of their own. On the contrary, the ideas formulated in Sung times, the greatness of the art, the system of philosophy, the social order which resisted for long years the attacks from the north and was to revive and continue after the fall of the Mongols provided the Chinese with a well-established and self-sufficient pattern of life. Our knowledge of this pattern is basic to an understanding of modern China. In fact, some scholars regard the Sung as the beginning period of modern history in China.

BASIC DATES

935–1392	Wang dynasty in Korea
947–1125	Liao (Khitan)
960–1127	Northern Sung
1005	Sung-Liao Treaty
1069–1076	Wang An-shih's reforms
1101–1125	Emperor Hui-tsung
1114–1123	Chin (Jurchen) conquer Liao
1127	Chin seize K'ai-feng
1127–1279	Southern Sung
1128–1141	Wars against Chin
1130–1200	Chu Hsi
1130–1211	Kara-khitai
1211–1223	Mongol campaigns against Chin
1233	Mongols seize K'ai-feng
1234	End of Chin
1234–1279	Sung wars against Mongols

[1] This arrangement was different from modern extraterritoriality in that the government of the caliphs or the Seljuk sultans took no part in regulating the lives of their subjects who resided in China.

SUPPLEMENTARY READING

DE BARY, W. T., ED. *Sources of Chinese Tradition.* New York, 1960.

CAHILL, J. *Chinese Painting.* Cleveland, 1960.

CRANMER-BYNG, L. *The Vision of Asia: An Interpretation of Chinese Art and Culture.* London, 1932.

CREEL, H. G. *Chinese Thought from Confucius to Mao Tse-tung.* Chicago, 1953.

EBERHARD, W. *A History of China.* Berkeley, Cal., 1950.

FITZGERALD, C. P. *China: A Short Cultural History.* London, 1950.

GOODRICH, L. C. *A Short History of the Chinese People,* 3rd ed. New York, 1959.

GROUSSET, R. *The Civilizations of the East, Vol. III: China.* New York, 1935.

——————— *The Rise and Splendor of the Chinese Empire.* Berkeley, Cal., 1953.

LATOURETTE, K. S. *The Chinese: Their History and Culture.* New York, 1946.

REISCHAUER, E. O. AND J. K. FAIRBANK. *East Asia: The Great Tradition.* Boston, 1958.

SICKMAN, L. AND A. SOPER. *The Art and Architecture of China.* Baltimore, 1956.

WRIGHT, A. F. *Buddhism in Chinese History.* Stanford, Cal., 1959.

ADVANCED READING

BRUCE, J. P. *Chu Hsi and His Masters.* London, 1923.

CARTER, T. F. *The Invention of Printing in China and Its Spread Westward.* New York, 1955.

CHI, C. T. *Key Economic Areas in Chinese History.* London, 1936.

FUNG, YU-LAN. *A Short History of Chinese Philosophy.* New York, 1948.

GILES, H. A. *History of Chinese Literature.* New York, 1927.

HIRTH, F. AND W. W. ROCKHILL. *Chau Ju-kua: His Work on the Chinese and Arab Trade in the 12th and 13th Centuries, entitled Chu-fan-chi.* St. Petersburg, 1911.

KRACKE, E. A. *Civil Service in Early Sung China.* Cambridge, 1953.

LIN, Y. T. *The Gay Genius: The Life and Times of Su Tung Po.* New York, 1947.

MARTIN, H. D. *The Rise of Chingis Khan and His Conquest of North China.* Baltimore, 1950.

MC CUNE, E. *The Arts of Korea.* Rutland, Vt., 1961.

SHRYOCK, J. K. *The Origin and Development of the State Cult of Confucius.* New York, 1932.

WALEY, A. *An Introduction to the Study of Chinese Painting.* London, 1958.

WITTFOGEL, K. A. and FENG CHIA-SHENG. *History of Chinese Society: Liao (907–1125).* New York, 1949.

XXI

THE CREATION OF

THE MONGOL EMPIRE

Chingis Khan

In the history of Asia there had been formidable invasions of nomads from the steppes of Central Asia, such as those of the Hsiung-nu (see Chapter 17) and those of the Khitan and Jurchen (see Chapters 19 and 20), but none of these produced empires comparable with the empire of the Mongols, the latest in the series of invaders. The Mongols created their empire at the end of the twelfth century, when new national states and new military powers were rising in various parts of Europe and Asia. In the West strong monarchs controlled Germany, England and France, and the papacy was increasing in power; while in the Near East the Seljuk Turks were reinvigorating Islam with new energy and successfully warding off the Crusaders. The strong Turkish sultanate of Delhi controlled India while the Southern Sung and Chin dynasties shared rule over China.

The empire which the Mongols created represents a unique development in Asian history. It was an empire of nomads, utterly different from those empires of the settled civilizations of India and China. Its rise was meteoric, somewhat like the rise of the Arabs, but its irresistible power was based not on a religious driving idea, but rather almost solely on the genius of the Mongol military leaders.

It was the greatest and the largest empire in all Asian history. However, despite the fact that it was the most enormous military empire the world has ever seen, its effects upon posterity were neither lasting nor profound.

EARLY MONGOLS.   The Mongols made their appearance in history as one clan among a number of nomad tribes in Central Asia. They occupied the area to the south and east of Lake Baikal along the banks of the Orkhon, Onon, and Kerulen rivers. The Mongols ethnologically and linguistically were related to the Turks and the Manchus, speaking an Altaic language. In the eleventh century they were a minor clan among the far more prominent tribes of the Tatars and of the Keraits who had been converted to Nestorian Christianity and who were more culturally advanced than the other tribes. The name Mongol was later applied to all of these named tribes, but the name Tatar, or the European corruption thereof, Tartar (deriving from a pun wherein one wished to see the Tatars go to the river of hell, Tartarus), was also frequently used to describe the Mongol people.

Originally poor, disunited, and subject to the control of Turkish tribes, the Mongols lived a typical nomadic existence. Ignorant of town life, agriculture, and writing, their economic life consisted of seasonal migrations in search of pasture for their flocks, their sole wealth. Pasturing and hunting, they moved north in the summer, south in the winter in constant search of grazing grounds. As all Central Asiatic nomads, the Mongols were horsemen: they lived in felt tents, ate horsemeat, and drank *kumiss,* a drink made from fermented mare's milk. Their original religion was shamanism, with the eternal blue sky worshipped as the chief deity.

During the mid-twelfth century the Mongol clan managed to unify several other clans and achieve a more important position. They were aided in their rise by an alliance they formed with the tribe of the Keraits, and by the leadership of Yesugai, a valorous and renowned fighter. Fighting with the Keraits against the Tatars and their overlords, the Chin, the Mongols profited by gaining greater self-confidence, developing increasing ambitions, and also by utilizing new elements of culture, ease of assimilation being a Mongol trait. This unification of tribes, led by Yesugai and the Mongols, proved merely temporary. Yesugai was poisoned and the power of the Mongols subsequently was destroyed by another rival tribe, the Taidshuts, leaving Yesugai's widow as regent of the Mongol clan.

THE YOUNG TEMUCHIN.   In 1162 this widow gave birth to a son, Temuchin, born as the legend has it with a clot of blood in his right hand to be the future conqueror of the world. Both mother and the orphan sons of Yesugai faced very difficult years, deserted as they soon were by their relatives and the majority of the clan. Temuchin and his brothers spent a wretched existence in their early youth. The traditional aristocratic occupations of grazing herds of horses and supervising shepherds had to give way to menial work such as fishing and hunting for small game, and collecting wild onions, garlic and other roots necessary for their bare subsistence. Despite these hardships, Temuchin's mother instilled in her sons the ideals of a pastoral aristocracy. Temuchin, himself, a tall, red-haired, green-eyed youth, with an excellent physique, soon had to prove his mettle. Attacked by the enemies of his father, the Taidshuts, Temuchin was made their prisoner, but he escaped by hiding in a cart full of wool. During his early years, his wife was abducted, and held prisoner by yet another enemy of the Mongols, the Merkits. Gradually, however, Temuchin was able to follow his father's example and unite a number of clans. In this project he was greatly helped by being the vassal of the shrewd Kerait Khan Tughrul, who, although cruel and treacherous, aided Temuchin in uniting a number of Mongol, Merkit, and Tatar tribes. Tughrul Khan, or as he is better known by his later title, Wang Khan (as a Nestorian Christian he became one of the incarnations of the legendary Prester John), aided Temuchin in bringing together his kinsmen and the vassals who had seceded, and also contributed materially when Temuchin avenged the abduction of his wife and seizure of his mother by the Merkits by attacking and defeating them. Temuchin's prestige grew rapidly after the defeat of the Merkits. The number of his followers began to increase, as men of aristocratic nomad families, attracted by his personality, talents, self-discipline, and of course, his successes, came to follow his banners. The really important step in the process of unifying the various nomad tribes came when Temuchin and the Kerait Wang Khan jointly attacked the Tatars. By 1201 Temuchin had defeated and totally destroyed the power of the Tatars, and established firm discipline among his own adherents.

Wang Khan had grown jealous and suspicious of the young Mongol, and tried to kill him by treachery. In 1203 Temuchin finally surprised, defeated, and killed the leader of the Keraits, and brought the tribe under his own control. In the same year he attacked the Naimans to the west in the upper Orkhon valley, perhaps the most civilized of the Mongol peoples, since among them there was much Uighur influence, many Nestorian Christians and Moslem merchants as well. This campaign was a great success, the Naiman Khan losing his life and his son Guchluk fleeing first into the Altai mountains, and then, after a further defeat, seeking refuge in the west in the state known as Karakhitai. Most of the Naimans submitted to Temuchin. Clearly, Temuchin by 1203 had won the lordship of the steppes and his great white standard with nine yak tails appeared to enjoy the unlimited protection of the "Everlasting Blue Sky."

TEMUCHIN'S PERSONALITY. Temuchin's success owed much to his personality. He was shrewd, cautious, patient, steady, and talented. Essentially he was the very ideal of a steppe warrior, possessed with an unquenchable thirst for power. His talents and his self-discipline were the qualities which attracted his followers. He was known for his liberality and thought nothing of giving his horse to one of his subordinates if the latter's action warranted a reward. Personally brave, he valued highly courage and loyalty in others. Another important trait of Temuchin's was his willingness to permit his generals a certain amount of freedom, yet he never made the cardinal mistake of overreaching himself. Whatever plan he formulated he adhered to with unbreakable determination and tenacity.

FIGURE 21.1.   Portrait of Chingis Khan from the collection of the Imperial Palace, Peking.

MONGOL MILITARY ORGANIZATION.   By 1203 Temuchin had not only fused the Mongols together into a formidable power, but had also endowed them with a superb military organization. Every male Mongol between 15 and 70 years of age served as a soldier so that the Mongols were truly a people in arms, a purely military state. The mounted archer was its basic unit. The Mongol pony, which the Mongol soldier rode firmly seated on a high saddle, was an animal of amazing energy and stamina; it could cover 130 miles in two days in the high and rough countryside of Afghanistan. With relatively small numbers (the total number of soldiers in 1203 was estimated at 138,000), and with experienced leaders in charge, the Mongols conducted warfare with consummate skill, all battles being won by cavalry alone, unlike those fought by Alexander who relied upon the decisive impact of the infantry phalanx.

The Mongols were controlled from the tent headquarters of Temuchin, where a retinue of archers and swordbearers was constantly in attendance and swarms of messengers scurried back and forth to carry the Khan's orders. Iron discipline governed every Mongol; absolute submission to the Khan was unquestioningly given. Each officer was responsible for the training of his troops; flight and desertion of soldiers in his command resulted in the death penalty for the commander. This severe discipline resulted in a morale of troops unsurpassed by any army. All felt the urge to conquer. None apparently experienced fear. Loyalty and courage were the two virtues constantly inculcated, but a Mongol soldier could also expect liberal returns for his services.

The organization of army units was based on the decimal system. Ten thousand men formed a division of ten regiments of ten squadrons of 100 men each; ten men were grouped together in each of the ten basic units of the squadron. Once a man was enrolled into his basic unit, no transfer was permitted. There were three main forces: the army of the left wing, the army of the right wing, and the army of the center; each of these being in charge of an army commander whose sign of authority was a great drum. In addition, there existed a crack force, the guard division of 1,000 men. This elite bodyguard was carefully selected, and served as a nursery for future field commanders. In peace it was in constant attendance on the Khan; in war it always stood in the front line of battle. Here too, of course, the most rigid discipline prevailed and the death penalty was meted out to any soldier, whether guard or otherwise, who did not aid the injured comrade, failed to pick up equipment, or turned back in action. The guards enjoyed the greatest privileges of all Mongol soldiers, but all were well cared for, and Temuchin made it a point to know as many of his soldiers personally as he could. It is said that he knew by name every soldier in his guard division.

Temuchin devoted much energy to the training of his army. He organized hunts which served as exercises for his soldiers. A vast area would be cordoned off, and the animals would be driven together and hunted; sometimes these hunts would be conducted in the roughest terrain possible and would last as long as a month. The Mongol cavalryman was equipped with a compound large bow, a light saber, and sometimes also with a lance with a hook and a mace. Thirty arrows were issued per man. For defense, the Mongol mounted archer wore a steel helmet, and a light serviceable body-armor of hide lacquered to keep the dampness out. In battle the Mongols also often wore a silk shirt which could easily be pulled out of a wound inflicted by an arrow together with the hostile arrowhead. Each soldier's kit also included a needle and thread, and a file with which to sharpen arrowheads.

MONGOL STRATEGY AND TACTICS. As far as strategy and tactics were concerned, Temuchin was one of the unsurpassed geniuses of war. In the application of the basic principles of economy of force, concentration, mobility, and surprise, no one, not even Napoleon, rivaled the great Mongol Khan. He practiced with excellent results the principle of marching units separately to the scene of battle where they fought in unison; and this most difficult feat of liaison work was perfected by him. The ability to concentrate widely separated columns upon short notice gave superior mobility to the Mongol armies, while a mobile screen of scouts operating in advance of each unit made it impossible for the enemy to spring a surprise attack. In tactics, the Mongols relied not only upon the devastating effect of their superior archery, but also developed to perfection a number of tactical skills of which the feigned flight was perhaps

Figure 21.2.   Mongol soldier with horse and camel; Yuan painting.

the most famous and most successful. For days the enemy might pursue the
precipitately fleeing Mongols only to be lured to certain ambush and doom
in isolated areas. Other tactical manoeuvres included the use of branches tied
to the tails of horses in order to stir up dust so as to give the impression of
large forces on the march, and dummies mounted on spare horses for the
same purpose. No trick, but fact, was the incredible speed by which Mongol
units could retire or advance.

A special place in Mongol warfare was reserved for military intelligence.
Each campaign was carefully worked out in advance at a great assembly of
the Mongols, the *kuriltai*. No campaign was ever set in motion until all possible
intelligence regarding the enemy's roads, passes, rivers, fords, fortifications,
towns, political and economic situation had been fully collected and evaluated.
The Mongols, in this connection, made excellent use of spies and fifth column
agents sent out ahead to prepare the way for Mongol forces. Spies, scouts,
and regular couriers were employed for this purpose. Once the plan for a
campaign had been approved, military intelligence made the best possible use
of dissension in the enemy's camp by sending forged letters to the opponent,
sowing distrust and suspicion among his own generals, as well as spreading
rumors. For instance, agents would ceaselessly spread stories about the size
of the Mongol armies, instilling fear everywhere and thereby neutralizing the

will to resist. When the last detail regarding the number of men, horses (two or three per man), and necessary supplies had been decided upon, the campaign began and was never terminated until the final extinction of the enemy; tireless pursuit and the bodily removal of the hostile ruler was another of Temuchin's basic principles.

In the campaigns themselves full use was consciously made of a policy of terror to break any resistance. Prisoners of war were forced to dig ditches against fortresses held by their own people and they were then made to lead the assault and scale the walls of these fortresses. This had the double value of protecting valuable Mongol lives and causing hesitation among the defenders. After a campaign was won, or a city taken, these prisoners would be massacred and this was followed by a more selective massacre of the general population of the captured towns. Little wonder that the world trembled before the man who had declared man's greatest pleasure to be:

> to defeat enemies, to drive them before one, to take from them that which they possessed, to see those whom they cherished in tears, to ride their horses, to hold their wives and daughters in one's arms.[1]

LAWS AND CULTURE. At the same time Temuchin, while perfecting an incredible machine of war, was conscious of the value of culture and of learning for the Mongols. To provide a firm foundation for a Mongol empire he promulgated the *yasa* or "Institutions," a body of law, unalterable and unchangeable for all times, which was based on the ancient traditions, usages, and ideas of his clan. This imperial code, setting forth eternal norms good for all times, was aristocratic in conception; it was severe and demanded absolute obedience, but it was most effective in securing peace and order. The government was conducted from a fairly permanent tent camp at the site of Karakorum in the Orkhon river valley. Here Temuchin supervised the military, civil, and religious activities of his people.

Temuchin was especially aware of the Mongol need to adopt a higher culture. This civilization he found among the Uighurs (see Chapters 19 and 20) and he systematically proceeded to adopt the Uighur language and legal system. Uighur civilization was taken over *in toto* by the Khan, the Uighurs set down the Mongol language in writing, and Uighurs were employed as tutors to the sons of Temuchin. The adoption of the civilization of the highly cultured Buddhist and Nestorian Uighurs who flourished in the oasis city-states of the Tarim basin, particularly around Turfan, resulted also in their voluntary submission to the Mongols, so that eastern Turkistan fell under the military control of the Mongols.

In 1206 a great assembly was held, attended by all the Mongols and their subject tribes. In this assembly, or *kuriltai*, Temuchin, now the master of all the vast area between the Altai mountains and the Great Khingan range, was proclaimed Chingis Khan, or "Illustrious Khan." World conquest was now

[1] Prawdin, M. *The Mongol Empire: Its Rise and Legacy* (London: Allen and Urwin, 1952), p. 60.

the goal of Temuchin, and after preliminary campaigns in 1207 against some forest tribes, the Oirats and the Kirghiz, Chingis Khan surveyed the political situation confronting him, and decided to start the first of his great campaigns in 1209, to be launched against the Tanguts and their state of Hsi-Hsia.

Empire in the Far East

What was the political situation which confronted the Mongols after 1206? In south China the Sung ruled, with their capital at Hangchow, while in the north the Chin dynasty held sway from Yenching. Both were formidable powers. Northwest China, the area containing the great Ordos bend of the Yellow river and Kansu, was controlled by the Tibetan people known as Tanguts who had established the kingdom of Hsi-hsia. In the west the Mongols were faced by the state of Kara-khitai, founded by refugees of the Liao dynasty in Chinese Turkistan north of the T'ien-shan and by the powerful Turkish Moslem state of Kharism on the lower Amu-darya (see map on p. 397). After careful appraisal of this situation Chingis chose the Tanguts on the first step on the road to Mongol conquest of the world.

Conquest of Hsi-hsia.   The Tanguts of Hsi-hsia, a sedentary and sinified people, had two virtues in the eyes of Chingis Khan which made them the logical choice as first victims in his career of expansion. They were the weakest of the three neighbors to the east, and they were also a nuisance to both the Sung and Chin empires because they interfered with the trade routes between China and the Tarim basin and often engaged in brigandage. A successful attack by the Mongols against Hsi-hsia thus would be a popular move. At the same time it would result in the Mongols obtaining a western frontier with the Chin state as well as bringing Mongol territory in touch with the Sung domains, foreshadowing a possible alliance for the future. It would also ensure Chingis that the Mongols would have exclusive control of the western trade routes and, finally, it would bring in large quantities of booty. War preparations were meticulous. The Tangut country was systematically ravaged, while its cities were invested. The Tangut army was defeated by the employment of surprise marches and successful flank attacks. By the end of 1209 Tangut resistance had been decisively crushed, and the state of Hsi-hsia reduced to tributary status. This Mongol attack was the more remarkable since Guchluk, the defeated leader of the Naimans, chose the same year to invade Mongolia, only to be defeated again.

The Tanguts as subjects of Chingis Khan nursed their resentment and hostility for some years, and in 1225 their king thought he saw an opportunity to shake off the detested Mongol yoke. Chingis was fully occupied to the west, while other Mongol armies were in north China. This was a futile hope, however, and Chingis Khan himself led a renewed invasion of the Tangut kingdom and defeated and deposed the unfortunate king. The final reduction came two years later when a successor revolted, only to be quickly defeated and put to death, so that the state of Hsi-hsia was finally and permanently annexed to the Mongol empire in 1227.

CONQUEST OF CHIN EMPIRE.   An attack against the formidable Chin empire in northern China was begun as early as 1211 as another step in Chingis Khan's career of conquest. The Chin were old enemies of the Mongols. They were a most powerful state which had defeated the Sung to the south in repeated attacks, and Chingis' decision to attack the Chin resulted in his most difficult and remarkable campaigns. Here, too, very careful preparations and extensive gathering of espionage paved the way. One military weakness of the Chin, heavy reliance upon infantry, seemed to promise Chingis some hope of success, despite the fact that he would have to face troops led by the same generals of the Chin who had so ably dealt with the armies of the Sung empire (see Chapter 20).

The open break between Temuchin and the Chin came in 1210, when the Mongol leader refused homage and in a gesture of defiance spat on the ground before the envoy of the new Chin monarch, Wei Shao-wang, and rode away. In no sense was this a sudden and impulsive gesture. Rather, it came after the Mongols had effectively gathered detailed information and were aware of the dissaffection of the Chin border regions. Even so, the attack against the Chin was a hazardous undertaking. The Chin empire in 1211 was still a most powerful state of great fortified cities and an army which was numerically far superior to that of the Mongols. Against these handicaps Chingis pitted his superior mobility, and, above all, his unsurpassed leadership. The Mongol army which began the attack in 1211 consisted of 200,000 men, led by the four sons of Chingis Khan: Juchi, Chagatai, Ogodai, and Tului. For 450 miles the Mongols marched across the Gobi desert without losing a single man, a singular achievement. They made maximum use of climatic conditions, crossing in spring during a time when melted snow water could be used. There was also the added precaution of each soldier having a spare horse, and supply was facilitated by driving along a herd of cattle. The goal was the Chin capital city of Yenching (on the site of modern Peking). In accordance with Mongol strategic thinking, a feint attack was made from the north, while the bulk of the Mongol armies moved in from the west.

The Chin found themselves in a most difficult position, having to face not only the fierce Mongols, but also simultaneous attacks in the south from their old enemies, the Sung, and local rebellions. But the Chin were saved in the first campaign by their excellent fortifications. The Mongols encountered at Yenching huge, well-fortified walls, supported by outside forts which were connected by subterranean tunnels, all of them amply supplied. Although the Mongols were forced to retire, taking with them the brood-mares of the Chin but with little of the Chin territory permanently annexed to their dominion, the first Chin campaign still represents the greatest feat of arms of Chingis.

He had met very powerful armies, and had inflicted three crushing defeats upon them, and the Chin had suffered very heavy losses.

The next year, 1212, saw a new Mongol attack upon the Chin, carried out on a smaller scale with relatively little success. The next major effort came in 1213 when the Mongols operated in Shansi province, where they laid siege to the fortified city of Ta-t'ung, and where Chingis himself suffered an arrow wound. During this year, three Mongol armies ravaged the open country, murdering, burning, and pillaging everywhere they went, and this led to a general devastation of the whole Chin countryside. Never resting until full victory had been achieved, Chingis in 1214 again attacked Yenching, and in the face of this threat the Chin emperor made peace on abject terms. The Chin also abandoned their capital, Yenching, for a new capital in the south at K'ai-feng.

The peace lasted less than a year. In fact, intermittent war with the Chin continued after Chingis' lifetime. Not until 1234 did the Mongols finally subdue the Chin empire. The length of time needed to conquer north China does not detract from the Mongol achievement. The struggle was against a formidable power; it was the greatest of Chingis' undertakings and perhaps also the most brilliant of all of his military conquests.

CONQUEST OF MANCHURIA AND KOREA. The ultimately successful conquest of the Chin gave great prestige to Chingis Khan. The Mongols were now a world power with an empire in the Far East. In 1216 Mongol control had also been extended into Manchuria, where the seminomadic Khitan submitted without the necessity of many campaigns. Two years later, in 1218, the Mongols invaded the Korean peninsula. The king of the Wang dynasty fled in terror to an island, while no effective resistance was organized against the invaders. Mongol governors ruled, levying heavy tribute, and Korea suffered horribly from the iron rule of the conquerors.

MONGOL GOVERNMENT. In the conquered territory of Chin in north China, Chingis Khan, after some reflection, came to the far-reaching conclusion that the importance and benefit of Chinese culture outweighed the alternative solution of complete annihilation and devastation, making China fit only for nomads to graze their horses in. Consequently, Chingis decided with great wisdom to make use of Chinese officials and scholars in order to govern the country, and to benefit from the positive values of an alien culture. Of cardinal importance in this policy was the advice of a very noble figure in Chinese history, that of Ye-lü Ch'u-ts'ai. He was a Khitan who had been captured by the Chin, but had served them loyally until their downfall. His loyalty to the fallen regime impressed Chingis, as he was always struck by faithfulness, and he employed him after the fall of Yenching first as astrologer and soon as his Grand Chancellor. Ye-lü Ch'u-ts'ai proved to be a most able administrator. Having been trained as a Confucian scholar he persuaded the Mongol ruler to adopt for his dominions in the Far East an orderly administration, with regular taxation collected at periodic intervals, and a Confucian system of order and etiquette.

Chinese political, legal, and social systems were continued by the Mongols for their Chinese subjects, while the employment of Chinese officials marked the ever-growing Chinese influence upon the structure of the Mongol state. A dual system of government operated, containing all the problems which had already faced other dynasties of conquest in Chinese history. As had the Liao and the Jurchen, the Mongols also had to cope with the problem of simultaneously ruling both nomad steppe and settled agricultural lands. Since the Mongols were more truly nomadic than either of their two predecessors, this problem was even more difficult for them.

While engaged in the great attack against the Chin and the setting-up of a Chinese style of administration in the east, Chingis had been troubled once more in the west in Central Asia by Guchluk the Naiman prince, who had found refuge in Kara-khitai, had there married a princess and had become the ruler of that country. His reign was very harsh, and he had taken drastic measures against the Moslems, closing their mosques and confiscating their property. As a result, Chingis had no trouble in posing as a "protector of Islam," when his armies invaded the domain of Kara-khitai in 1218 and in routing their army in a decisive battle the following year. Kara-khitai submitted to the authority of the great Mongol Khan. The rest of the learned and literate Uighur people, who had been subject to Kara-khitai, also were brought at this time under Mongol control. The operations in 1216 and 1217 in the west by the Mongols were all the more remarkable since they took place at a moment when the Mongols exercised maximum effort in the critical campaigns in far-off China.

Later Campaigns

CONQUEST OF KHARISM. Another major step in the Mongol plan of conquest was the attack and destruction of the empire of Kharism, a Turkish Moslem state, originally dependent upon the Seljuk Turks and independent since the middle of the twelfth century (see Chapter 6). Its capital was Samarkand in the Amu-darya river valley, and it was ruled by Muhammad of Kharism, the offspring of a Turkish slave who had created a powerful state reaching from the Syr-darya river to the Persian Gulf and from the Indus to the Caspian Sea. Muhammad Shah had even been able to displace the Seljuks as the rulers of Persia. The empire of Kharism was, however, a recent acquisition of Muhammad's, and there was much dissension and dissatisfaction among his subjects. Although Muhammad was an able military leader, his troops, being for the most part mercenary levies, were none too reliable in battle.

The first relations between the Mongols and Kharism had been friendly. Muhammad had been interested in the career of the Mongols, particularly after he heard of their great feat in conquering the Chin empire, and he sent an embassy to the Mongol Khan to gather news and information. Chingis, on his side, received the embassy extremely well, since he was interested in trade and eager for the superior goods from the Moslem world, and a mutually satisfactory treaty of reciprocal friendship and trade was concluded between the two heads of state. The Moslem embassy returned to Samarkand, laden with gifts of silver, jade, and furs. This most promising beginning was rudely interrupted by the independent and arbitrary action of the governor of the frontier fortress at Otrar, who captured some Mongol merchants, robbed them, and then had them executed. Chingis Khan quite naturally complained about this outrage and sent a mission to Muhammad at Samarkand. The latter showed a singular lack of judgment, for he put to death the chief envoy, singed the beards of the other members of the embassy, and then sent them back to the ruler of the Mongols.

Chingis fell into a terrible fury at the news and vowed that he would not cease until he had exterminated Muhammad and his kingdom. Consequently, a great assembly of the Mongols, a *kuriltai,* was held in 1218, at which 200,000 Mongols met, and great preparations for the coming war were initiated.

The Mongols launched their attack in 1218. While Muhammad went on the defensive and refused battle, the main Mongol armies with great success completely outflanked his position, and fell into his unprotected rear. One of the first victims of Chingis' wrath was the unfortunate governor of Otrar. Fighting heroically to the last, he was captured and then executed by having molten silver poured into his eyes and ears as retribution for the injury he had inflicted. The first major city which fell to the Mongols was Bukhara. Here the Turkish mercenaries chose to surrender rather than to fight, but they were massacred after their betrayal, since Chingis abhorred disloyalty. Next came the turn of the magnificent capital city of Samarkand. It escaped the general massacre which Bukhara had suffered, but it was systematically and thoroughly plundered and pillaged. By this time the very effective policy of terror which the Mongols employed inspired dread everywhere. The city of Herat, next on the Mongol's list, offered stout resistance, but Chingis had its river diverted, and the unfortunate town had to capitulate. There followed one week of killing, burning, and destruction. About one million people were slaughtered in cold blood. The city was entirely depopulated and was left a smoking ruin. Everywhere the Mongols went their dreadful massacres went on. People who survived initially, fleeing into the wilderness, were tricked into returning to their old abodes when the Mongols forced a Moslem *imam* to call for prayers, whereupon the few survivors who responded were also put to the sword.

The stricken ruler of Kharism, Muhammad Shah, could only flee, but wherever he went, he soon found relentless Mongol detachments in pursuit. He finally ended up an utterly broken man on a small island in the Caspian where he died in desperate poverty in 1220, and was buried in the same ragged clothes he had worn during the exhausting chase. Muhammad's son, Jalal-ud-din, somewhat retrieved the ill luck of his house by showing heroic courage in the face of the Mongol onslaught. A very brave fighter, so much so that his courage elicited admiration from Chingis Khan himself, he attempted to organize resistance against the terrible invaders. He was soon defeated, however, and fled to India, where in 1221 he fought another battle with Chingis' troops on the upper Indus. It was a splendid fight, but he lost and saved himself only by a hair's breadth by plunging into the raging river and swimming across the swollen stream. He sought refuge in India, where the Delhi sultanate, aghast at the coming of the Mongols, granted his request in Delhi. This drew the Mongols into India also, and in pursuit of Jalal-ud-din they ravaged the lands of the Punjab.

MONGOL ADVANCE INTO EUROPE.   Not only did the Mongols enter India as the result of their conquest of Kharism, but they also turned further to the west. Twenty-five thousand Mongols, led by Subotai and Jebe, who had originally been dispatched to kill Muhammad Shah, continued their operations to the west after their prey had been snatched from them by death. Subotai conducted campaigns in Persia in 1220, and the next year his army went into the Caucasus, where the Mongols defeated the Georgians and the inhabitants of Azerbaijan. Moving to the northwest across the east end of the Caucasus mountains, they then encountered and attacked the Kipchaks, or Cumans, a Turkish people who had settled on the Volga and Don steppes. Subotai had first prepared the way by propaganda. Pleading the fraternity between Mongol and Turkish blood, and handing out lavish gifts, he had lulled the Kipchaks into a state of false security, from which they were rudely awakened when the Mongols suddenly turned against them, destroyed them, and retrieved their presents.

In the meantime the Kipchaks had appealed to the Russian princes in Europe. Subotai promptly dispatched a Mongol envoy to warn the Russian nobles against extending aid to the Kipchaks, but the envoy was killed on the Dnieper by the Russians, who decided to aid the sorely beset Kipchaks. The Russian armies, led by their various princes, met the Mongol forces on the banks of the Khalka river in 1223. Eighty thousand Russians, fighting well, were unable to match the numerically much inferior Mongol troops, and the Russians suffered a terrible defeat. Their leaders were made prisoners, and then killed by being smothered in blankets, so as to avoid the shedding of blood. Afterwards the Mongols held a victory banquet on planks laid upon their bodies.

DEATH OF CHINGIS KHAN.   Having swept away organized resistance in Eastern Europe, Subotai and his men were then free to roam the Russian plains and to ravage the Don and Dnieper steppes at will. Chingis himself, in the meanwhile, stayed in Central Asia, while the Mongol armies continued the war against the fierce resistance of the Chin. In 1220 the Mongol armies also began their first attack against the Sung, ravaged their lands, and seized extensive territory. The Sung quickly sued for peace, but were at first rejected. Chingis Khan decided to return to the east when he heard of the rebellion of the Hsi-hsia kingdom which had been in secret negotiations with the Chin.

He personally led the final attack against the Tanguts who were decisively defeated and then annexed. This was the last feat of Mongol arms which Chingis lived to see, for he died in 1227. In accordance with his expressed wish he was secretly buried in his homeland, Mongolia, beneath a huge tree which he had selected himself. The escort which brought the corpse to this site, and those unfortunate travelers who met the cortège enroute, were all killed so that the exact location of the grave should remain a secret.

Chingis created the largest military empire the world has ever seen, extending from China to Eastern Europe. This he had achieved by his genius for military organization and by his extraordinary knowledge of men. His empire he built upon the foundations of iron discipline and of careful organization. He was, it is true, a genius of destruction, and he never hesitated to use treachery and brutality in war and conquest. Chingis Khan had a definite aim— world conquest. He himself had stated: "the sky has ordered me to rule all nations." Yet he was always conscious of the advantages of civilization and employed many educated men. His armies usually conducted selective massacres. Artisans, skilled craftsmen, and young women were carefully spared. Many foreigners—Uighurs, Arabs, Chinese, Persians, and Armenians—were in the employ of Chingis Khan and rather than eradicate foreign culture, it was a cardinal point of his policy to make use of it to further his purpose of world conquest and to raise the level of civilization among his own people.

This aspect of the thought of Chingis Khan is strikingly illustrated by his policy of religious toleration adopted for political reasons, to enhance the prestige of the ruler as protector of religion, and to conciliate the conquered people. Although the Grand Khan himself did not display any religious interest, he made it a point to tolerate all religions and to honor their clergy by freeing them from taxes, paying them substantial salaries, and giving them positions of dignity at his court. A famous incident illustrates this policy. Chingis Khan invited the famed Taoist sage Ch'ang Ch'un, then a man of seventy-two years, to travel all the way from Shantung to the Hindu Kush mountains and to converse with the Mongol chief. The conversation did nothing to make Chingis Khan a Chinese sage. He was primarily interested in obtaining the elixir of immortality from the great teacher, but the incident shows the concern displayed by the Mongols toward the religions of their subject people.

Immediate Successors of Chingis Khan

At the time of the death of Chingis Khan in 1227 the Mongol empire stretched from the Caspian Sea to the Pacific Ocean. In this empire, peace was enforced everywhere. This "Pax Tatarica" allowed uninterrupted cultural interchange; and as long as only one man ruled the whole structure, travel was open to all. The empire was considered to be the property of the whole imperial family, but the necessity of a single successor to be Grand Khan in order to preserve unchanged the nomad outlook had been obvious to Chingis

Khan. His choice was his son Ogodai, who after the brief regency of Tului (1227–1229) became the Grand Khan in 1229.

OGODAI. Ogodai was a typical Mongol, shrewd and intelligent, generous, jovial, but also simple, brutish, and frequently drunk. Although Ogodai was Grand Khan, the vastness of the empire resulted in the effective division of the empire into four parts among the three surviving sons of Chingis and his grandson. Each of these considered the part which he governed as his own property, although at first it had been clearly understood by the Mongols that the Grand Khan had sovereign rights over all of them.

The first division of the empire was that of the Kipchak empire, or the Khanate of the Golden Horde, established by Batu, the grandson of Chingis Khan in Western Asia, and ruled by his "golden family." Its nucleus was the steppe around the Caspian Sea and the Aral Sea, and its headquarters were to be found at Sarai. Next came the Khanate of Chagatai, a son of Chingis Khan, in Central Asia, with its center at Almalik. It included Afghanistan, the region between the Amu-darya and Syr-darya rivers, and the Tarim basin. To the youngest son, Tului, was given eastern Mongolia, as well as Manchuria and Korea. Finally, Ogodai ruled directly over Outer Mongolia, north China and Chinese Turkistan north of the T'ien-shan, with his center at Karakorum. In this way was the Mongol empire divided into appanages.

Ogodai was elected Grand Khan by plenary kuriltai on the Kerulen in 1229 and ruled until 1241. In his reign the influence of Chinese ideas became constantly stronger, with Ye-lü Ch'u-ts'ai being appointed chancellor in north China in 1231. He introduced the Chinese system of taxation, together with customhouses to collect tolls, public granaries to serve the food needs of the population, and a courier service for rapid communication. The Mongol government in China thus became increasingly Chinese. The resulting complexity of government required literate personnel. Educated Chinese were used in large numbers, and colleges for their training were established in 1236. Complex government also required a permanent center, and Karakorum in the Orkhon valley was chosen as the site of a walled city.

END OF THE CHIN. At the same time that Chinese influence increased, the Mongols persisted in the goal of world conquest with no slackening of their aggressive foreign policy. Quite the contrary, with the rule of Ogodai foreign wars continued on a large scale. Most important was the renewed attack against the remnants of the Chin empire. The final phase of this struggle began in 1231. After a tough fight, the Chin armies were annihilated; but, even so, some Chin cities held out against terrible odds. Conditions were so bad during the Mongol siege, that people were reduced to eating saddle leather, green weeds, and human bones in their soup. In 1233, K'ai-feng, the last Chin capital fell, but it was spared at the recommendation of Ye-lü Ch'u-t'sai. The last Chin emperor committed suicide, and by 1234 the Chin state ceased to exist. The most difficult of all the Mongol campaigns had been won.

FIGURE 21.3.   Enthronement of Ogodai from a Persian miniature.

WAR AGAINST THE SUNG.   Between 1222 and 1224 the Sung had been foolish enough to aid the Mongols against the Chin in order to inflict damage upon their northern rival, but beginning in 1225 they were in opposition to the Mongols. After desultory fighting and a brief peace, the Mongols attacked in earnest, beginning in 1234. The Sung resisted stoutly, but the war, which lasted forty-five years, ended in their complete destruction. In 1236, Mongol armies seized territory in Szechuan, in the southwest, which gave them an excellent strategic base for flanking operations, always dear to the heart of Mongol generals. Other developments in eastern Asia during Ogodai's Grand Khanate included the re-invasion of Korea in 1231 as the result of the murder of a Mongol envoy and general discontent with Korea's role as vassal to the Mongols. The Korean king fled for his life to Kanghwa island, while his unfortunate country was first thoroughly ravaged, and then annexed as an integral part of the Mongol dominions.

INVASION OF EUROPE.   In the west, too, great conquests were in the making. With Central Asia firmly in their grip, the Mongols looked abroad for further conquests, and the kuritai of 1235 decided upon a great raid and an invasion of Europe. Batu and Subotai were appointed as leaders in charge of some 150,000 men to conduct a major operation against whatever resistance they might encounter in the European west. As always, the invasion was characterized by great strategic skill. In 1238 the Mongols established their control over the steppes of south and central Russia and turned north against the Russian princes. The Russian princes refused harsh Mongol terms. Invariably, this brought down upon the luckless Russian rulers the concentrated wrath of the Mongols, who proceeded systematically to sack the Russian towns and to massacre their inhabitants. In December 1237 they took Ryazan, and then invaded the principality of Vladimir, where Moscow at that time was but a little, insignificant town. The Mongol attack was particularly successful since it was carried out unexpectedly in mid-winter, the Mongol cavalry making good use of frozen rivers, and achieving once again the element of surprise against their opponents. Novgorod the Great, the wealthy trading republic in the north, was saved only by rain and thaw which forced the Mongol cavalry to suspend operations.

After having swept through the north with terrible effect, it was the turn of the south of Russia to feel the full fury of the Mongol horsemen. In 1240, the Mongol envoys to Kiev having been thrown from that city's walls, the place was taken and so thoroughly sacked that Kiev for many years had not a single inhabitant, while the surrounding steppe was strewn with skulls. In 1241 the Mongols turned further to the west against Hungary and Poland.

The Hungarian king, Bela II, had granted asylum to some of the horror-struck Kipchak refugees, and this served as an excuse for the Mongols to send an envoy, an Englishman no less this time, to demand from Bela the surrender of the fugitives, and his own submission to the all-powerful Ogodai. When this was refused, military operations began. As usual, the Mongols displayed the greatest of strategic skills by executing a pincer movement. One army, led by Kaidu, moved to the north into Poland, where it had no special troubles in defeating Boleslav the Chaste, and capturing and burning Cracow. Continuing, the Mongols then moved into Silesia, where a strong German army of 30,000 men under the command of Duke Henry the Pious of Silesia waited to give them battle at Liegnitz in April of 1241. The Mongols resorted to the time-honored ruse of a pretended rout, luring the eager Germans after them into ambush, where they were exterminated. After devastating territory in Poland and Silesia, the Mongols turned into Moravia, ravaging wherever they went, and joined forces in Hungary with the main Mongol forces which had attacked Hungary directly across the Carpathians from the east. King Bela, thus caught from both sides, did the best he could in a difficult situation by selecting a site on the plain of the Sajo river, and there entrenching himself with some 100,000 troops composed of his Magyars, some Germans, Croats, and some French Templars who had come to his assistance in response to the frantic pleas by the Hungarians. But here, too, the superior tactics of the Mongols carried the day.

The victory was accompanied by terrible massacres of enemy military and civilian personnel, the capture of the cities of Gran and Pest, and the thorough ravaging of the Danubian plains. Their policy of terror was more

refined than ever, as they now made it a practice to wait for the peasants to
return to their fields, complete the sowing and raising of the crop, and to cut
them down only after the harvest had been completed, thus assuring for themselves needed supplies. From this wholesale carnage the luckless king managed
to escape, fleeing for his life, and finding safety only on an island in the
Adriatic, since the Mongols, true to their maxims, hunted Bela down just
as relentlessly as they had hunted Muhammad Shah of Kharism and the king
of the Koreans. In pursuit Mongol cavalry even reached the shores of the
Mediterranean in Dalmatia; thus Mongol armies had covered the whole continent from the Sea of Japan to the Adriatic. Salt water seemed to be the only
effective barrier to their ambitions, and a significant limit to their power it
prophesied.

The impression of the Mongol advance upon Europe was one of utter con-
sternation and abject terror. The chronicler Matthew of Paris wrote that the
fishermen of Gothland and Friesland refused to go out and fish for herring,
while the Emperor Frederick II looked upon the coming of the "Tartars" as
a punishment of God visited upon Christendom for its sins. St. Louis of France,
that noble figure, when asked by his mother if there might be any rescue from
these dreadful enemies, answered: "We have the heavenly consolation that,
should these Tartars come, we shall either be able to send them back to
Tartarus, whence they have emerged, or else, shall ourselves enter heaven to
enjoy the rapture that awaits the elect."

The year 1241 saw the zenith of the expansion of the Mongol armies,
and when the news of the death of Ogodai in that year reached his troops in
Europe, they retired, making no attempt to hold their conquests in Poland
and Hungary beyond plundering them thoroughly. Mongol operations in the
west remained always subsidiary to those on the Chinese front, and the
Mongols themselves knew the limits of their capacity due to the burden which
operations in Europe placed on their immensely long lines of communication.
The death of Ogodai was the signal that Europe was to be saved, while it was
the death knell for the Sung in China.

BASIC DATES

1162–1227	Temuchin
1206	Elected Chingis Khan
1209	Campaign against Hsi-hsia
1211–1215	Defeat of Chin
1217–1218	Campaign against Kara-khitai
1218–1219	Campaign against Korea
1217–1222	Campaign against Chin
1219–1220	Campaign against Kharism
1220	Campaign in Persia
1221–1228	Campaign in Russia

1221	Campaign in India
1227	Final defeat of Hsi-hsia
1227–1229	Tului Regent
1229–1241	Ogodai as Grand Khan
1231	Ye-lü Ch'u-ts'ai appointed chancellor
1231–1234	Campaign against Chin
1234	End of Chin
1234	Start of war against Sung
1236–1238	Capture of Szechuan
1236–1240	Capture of South and Central Russia
1241	Invasion of Poland and Hungary
1241	Death of Ogodai

SUPPLEMENTARY READING

HUDSON, G. F. *Europe and China*. London, 1931. An excellent chapter on the Mongols.

LAMB, H. *Genghis Khan*. New York, 1930. A popular account.

——— *The March of the Barbarians*. New York, 1940.

MARTIN, H. D. *The Rise of Chingis-Khan*. Baltimore, 1950. A good account, particularly of Mongol military organization and warfare against the Chin.

PRAWDIN, M. *The Mongol Empire: Its Rise and Legacy*. London, 1952.

ADVANCED READING

HOWORTH, H. *History of the Mongols*. London, 1880. A classic work.

JUVAINI, A., TR. J. A. BOYLE. *The History of the World-Conqueror*. 2 Vols. Cambridge, Mass., 1958. Persian biography of Chingis-Khan written 1252–1260.

LATTIMORE, O. *Inner Asian Frontiers of China*, 2nd ed. New York, 1951.

VERNADSKY, G. *The Mongols and Russia*. New Haven, 1953.

VLADIMIRTSOV, B. Y. *The Life of Chingis-Khan*. Boston, 1930. A scholarly biography by a great expert on the Mongols.

XXII ✵

MONGOLS IN EASTERN

ASIA, 1241-1368

Lords of Eurasia

The year of the death of the Grand Khan Ogodai in some ways may
be said to represent the high point in the destiny of the Mongols.
In 1241 they controlled an empire in Eurasia which reached from
Korea to Hungary. But Ogodai's death was followed by disorganization of the Mongol government, by the beginning of decline of
Mongol power, and perhaps most importantly, by the process of
cultural assimilation by which the Mongols became fused with the
people and cultures whom they had conquered.

KUYUK.   For five years after the death of Ogodai there was an
interregnum. Not until 1246 did the Mongol nobles agree to the
choice of Kuyuk, the son of Ogodai Khan, as their next Grand Khan.
Kuyuk was generous, good-natured, fond of wrestling, but a drunk-
ard who suffered from the gout, and his reign lasted only two years
until 1248. To the court of Kuyuk came the first European diplomatic emissary, the Franciscan friar John Plano Carpini, who, sent
by pope Innocent IV, traveled from 1245 to 1247. The reason for
this embassy was simple enough—fear of the Mongols had gripped
Europe. The purpose of Carpini's trip was to gather all possible
information about the Mongols. He was instructed by the papal curia

to find out whether the Mongols would return to Europe, and against whom they would fight; when and where attack might occur; what could be done in the way of defense against them; whether there was any truth in the assertion that they were Christians, ruled by the mythical Prester John (this illusion was based on the fact that some Keraits had been Christians) and if so, if they could be used in the fight against the Moslems. Finally, Carpini's instructions directed him to convert the Mongols to Christendom, if possible.

With this rather lengthy list of commands Carpini set off and travelled via Bohemia, Cracow, and Kiev to the Mongols on the Dnieper and the Volga, where he was received by Batu. Thence the heavy Franciscan friar was strapped on a horse, by command of Batu, and dispatched on a formidable voyage of four months to a point near Karakorum and Kuyuk's headquarters.

After his return to Europe in 1247 Carpini wrote a distinguished account based on his careful and detailed observations. His *History of the Mongols* is a remarkable book, orderly, minute, and shows keen diplomatic awareness. To the chief question which agitated Europe, whether the Mongols would return, Carpini gave an unqualified affirmative: their intent and purpose was to subdue the whole world. On the issue of Europe's defense against this terrible threat Carpini pleaded the necessity of a united Europe and the adoption of new military tactics moulded after those of the Mongols themselves. European armies needed to employ scouts and to choose their own field of battle; the individual soldiers needed strong crossbows, good arrows, and fine armor. He particularly warned against the danger of pursuit of the Mongols, since this invariably lured their confident pursuers into a well-prepared ambush, and he pointed out the possibility of lifting the Mongol horseman out of his saddle by an accurate lance thrust.

Carpini was well received at Kuyuk's camp and witnessed the election of the Grand Khan of the Mongols. He was one of a great number of foreign witnesses, Chinese, Korean, Turk, Persian, Russian, who assembled to pay tribute to Mongol greatness and power. After the ceremony Carpini was given a return letter from Kuyuk to the pope of Rome, which commanded the pope to appear in person to do homage:

> . . . you in person must come to tender us service, pay us homage, then only will we recognize your submission. But if you do not obey the commands of heaven and run counter to our orders, we shall know that you are our foe. This is what we have to tell you. If you fail to act in accordance therewith, how can we foresee what will happen to you? Heaven alone knows.[1]

These ominous and arrogant words Carpini carried back with him to the papal court, but he refused to serve as a guide to Mongol envoys to Europe, since he feared that they would observe the dissension and wars in Christendom. He also cautioned European monarchs against receiving such persons since they came as spies and he urged them to put to death all Mongol ambassadors.

[1] M. Prawdin, *The Mongol Empire: Its Rise and Legacy* (London: Allen and Unwin 1952), p. 281.

Carpini returned to a Europe which remained menaced by this great threat from the steppes of Central Asia, but Kuyuk had not sufficient time to deal with the West as he might have wished. He was involved in a new war against the Sung and in war against Persia. Besides he drank heavily, and within two years he died.

MANGU. Kuyuk's death in 1248 was followed by a three-year factional struggle and much indecision among the Mongols. Not until 1251 was a grandson of Chingis Khan, Mangu, a hard, energetic, and intelligent politician, and a first-rate soldier, elected Grand Khan. It seemed that the fate of the Mongol armies was held once more in a strong hand, able to wield them into one unified striking force, but the process of disruption of the Mongol Empire had begun. Mangu himself was opposed by Kaidu, the leader of the Mongols in the territory of Chagatai in Turkistan, who revolted against him.

WAR AGAINST THE SUNG RENEWED. Even though the first signs of decline seemed to have appeared, Mangu as Grand Khan followed the policy of world conquest cherished by his great ancestor. His reign was distinguished by two major new wars, against the Sung in China and against Persia and the Abbasid caliphate of Baghdad. Operations against China were entrusted to Mangu's brother, Kublai, who was in charge of the province of Honan. The campaign against the Sung again demonstrated the consummate strategic skill of the Mongols, who used a great strategic envelopment movement, designed to conquer the Sung territories from the south. For this purpose it was first necessary to establish Mongol bases in southwest China, especially in Yunnan and Szechuan provinces, and Kublai marched his Mongol armies into that area. Southwest China at that time was ruled by the Tai kingdom of Nan-chao, whose king bore the title of Maharaja. Although the Mongols exercised but slight control over the kingdom of Nan-chao and permitted the old rulers to continue to govern, the Mongol move into Nan-chao in 1253 was to have far-reaching consequences for the history of Southeast Asia, since it set in motion a stream of Tai emigrants to the south and east (see chapter 15). By 1257 Mongol armies had been sent into Annam and the Tongking area as well, which recognized Mongol suzerainty, so that Mongol armies were then deployed west, southwest and south of the Sung in an excellent position which threatened the Sung empire from three directions simultaneously. The Mongols then renewed the war against the Sung. Mangu himself led the armies from Szechuan against the Chinese, but his death in 1259, the result apparently of dysentery, caused the temporary suspension of operations.

While the Mongols were thus engaged in ending Chinese independence, they also took the occasion to complete the conquest of Korea which was achieved in 1257 when the Korean king of the Wang dynasty submitted to the Mongols at last. Korea then became an integral part of the Mongol empire.

CONQUEST OF PERSIA AND MESOPOTAMIA. In the west Mangu dispatched the brother of Kublai, Hulagu, as the chief commander of the Mongol armies to reduce Persia (see Chapter 6). The campaign began in 1256 when Hulagu ended the formidable religious and political power of the Assassins by destroying their great fortress in Persia. These devoted followers of the Old Man of the Mountain, who obeyed his orders implicitly, found their match in the Mongols. Since they refused to submit to Hulagu they were ruthlessly destroyed and Persia, Georgia, Armenia, and parts of Asia Minor were added to the Mongol territories. Next Hulagu moved his forces against the Abbasid caliph in Baghdad. The Mongol siege of that great capital of Islam began in 1257, and the city fell in January 1258. The last caliph of the Abbasids was made a prisoner, and when

FIGURE 22.1 Hulagu's capture of Baghdad; from a sixteenth-century Indian painting.

he asked for bread he was given gold with the reply he should have known better and paid the gold earlier to the Mongols and acknowledged their suzerainty. Then, in order not to offend heaven by shedding the blood of princes, the Mongols put him in a sack and had him trampled to death by horses. Baghdad itself was cruelly plundered, and the population suffered the usual selective massacre. After Hulagu had established Mongol control over Mesopotamia, he made a systematic attempt to destroy the irrigation system of the Tigris and Euphrates basin, so as to render the country permanently unfit for agriculture and fit only for nomads. This interesting attempt to eliminate agriculture completely resulted in lasting damage to Mesopotamia. Having conquered Persia and then Mesopotamia, Hulagu sent his troops west into Syria where they took Aleppo and Damascus, but in 1260 the Mongols suffered their first check at the hands of Bibars, the excellent general of the Egyptian Mamluks, who wrested Damascus from them. The armies of Hulagu had reached their furthest point, and Egypt was saved from Mongol invasion. Checked by Egypt, Hulagu settled down to create for himself a powerful state in Persia, the Ilkhanate, with his capital at Tabriz.

WILLIAM OF RUBRUCK.   It was also at Mangu's court at Karakorum that a new envoy from the West appeared, again a Franciscan, who had been whisked across the Mongol world in hard travel atop a Mongol pony. He was a Fleming, William of Rubruck, chosen by the great French king, St. Louis, to seek the conversion of the Mongols to Christendom, as well as determine the possibilities of gaining the Mongols as allies against the common foe, the Moslems. Entrusted with this task Rubruck set out in 1252 traveling via Acre, Constantinople, and the Crimea into the Mongol steppes and thence to Karakorum. As had his illustrious predecessor, John Plano Carpini, so also Rubruck gives us excellent information with vivid detail on all phases of Mongol life. Rubruck agreed with Carpini's earlier description of the Mongols:

> Toward other people they are exceedingly proud and overbearing, looking upon all other men, however noble, with contempt. For we saw in the Emperor's court the great duke of Russia, the son of the king of Georgia, and many other sultans and other great men who had no honor and respect. Indeed, even the Tatars appointed to attend them, however low their condition, always went before these high-born captives and took the upper places. They are irritable and disdainful to other men and beyond belief deceitful. Whatever mischief they intend they carefully conceal, that no one may provide against it. And the slaughter of other people they consider as nothing.[2]

While at Karakorum Rubruck met many Europeans, including not only Hungarians, Russians, Greeks, and Germans, but also the nephew of a Norman bishop and a Parisian jeweller who had been made captive at Belgrade. In the truly cosmopolitan atmosphere of the Mongol headquarters Rubruck also encountered and admired Chinese craftsmen, and he carried back with him to Europe first hand information on China.

Of particular interest to the friar were the various religious personages he encountered at Mangu's capital. Since the Mongols made it a practice to tolerate all religions for political purposes, there were to be found in Karakorum not only shamans, the Mongol religious leaders, but also Moslems, Nestorian Christians, Manicheans, Taoists, and Buddhists of the Lamaist church. To Mangu and the Mongols this religious aggregation served as a useful tool in governing

[2] Harold Lamb, *Genghis Khan* (New York: Doubleday & Co., 1960), p. 72.

subject peoples, and, as Mangu in person announced to the Franciscan friar, everyone at his court worshipped the same God, one and eternal.

As a whole Rubruck's mission was a failure, since the Mongols were neither converted to Christianity, nor seemed they eager to coordinate their attacks against Islam with that of the crusading West, yet Rubruck upon his return to Europe in 1255 brought with him a great deal of most valuable information about the Mongols and about China.

Kublai Khan

BEGINNING OF POLITICAL DISUNITY. After Mangu's death in 1259 the tensions and conflicts which had grown among the Mongol princes became more apparent. While the forty-three year old Kublai was elected by one assembly and his army as the new Grand Khan of the Mongols, his brother Arikboga was chosen by another assembly in Karakorum and was supported by Hulagu and the Golden Horde. Only after four years of hostilities did Karakorum finally recognize the authority of Kublai. The cousin of Kublai and grandson of Ogodai, Kaidu, who controlled Turkistan, also revolted against him. A long and terrible contest between Kublai and Kaidu led to stalemate. Kublai was unable to conquer his relative, while Kaidu at one time in 1271 invaded Mongolia. Kaidu, who had inherited the possessions of Chagatai in Central Asia, which included the Tarim basin, the region north of the T'ien-shan mountains, and Bukhara, completely severed his relations with Kublai, and for forty years fought his supposed overlord. Another Mongol prince, Nayan, also joined Kaidu in his rebellion against Kublai Khan when he rebelled in Manchuria and Korea in 1287, but he was defeated and killed, and the revolt in Manchuria was successfully suppressed. These developments clearly indicated the dissensions, splits and growing disruption of the Mongol empire. At the very height of its political power the great empire began to disintegrate as Central Asia became the scene of open and irrepressible rebellion. At the same time, while Mongol opposition to Kublai Khan produced splits in the political structure, the process of cultural assimilation also began, whereby the Mongols everywhere tended to adopt more and more part of the culture of the area which they governed. This process was never complete, but it did cause the Mongols of the Golden Horde to come under Russian influence, while those of the Ilkhanate in Persia fell under the cultural influence of Islam and Iran. The Mongols in China too shared the same fate by becoming partially sinicized, so that the only pure Mongols remaining were those of the ancestral home of Mongolia. Thus not only political disunity, but also a cultural gap effectively separated the eastern parts of the empire from those of the west.

FIGURE 22.2. Portrait of Kublai Khan from the Imperial Palace Museum, Peking.

THE FOUNDING OF THE YUAN DYNASTY. Kublai was a fine military leader, a born statesman, a shrewd politician, and without question the most remarkable of Chingis Khan's successors. His reign began with a necessary suspension of the war against the Sung. Kublai offered to make peace, but only on harsh terms. The Sung were forced to accept the Mongols as their overlords, and to pay tribute. Faced with the opposition and open hostility of his relatives, Kublai decided to concentrate on the consolidation of his power in China. Since his effective rule did not go beyond China and Mongolia despite the fact that he was Grand Khan, Kublai deliberately adopted Chinese culture, founded a new Chinese dynasty, the Yuan, and considered himself to be a Chinese emperor. In 1263 Kublai established an ancestral hall on the Confucian model. A few years later he built on the site of present Peking a new city, the city of the Khan or Khanbalig. Khanbalig at a strategic location close to the Mongolian homeland, which by now had become merely a military district, was built upon a grand scale based on a Chinese plan and with Chinese architecture.

FINAL CONQUEST OF CHINA. In 1267 the war against the Sung dynasty in south China was resumed. The struggle was still a long one, since the Sung fought with great tenacity and determination, as evidenced by the five-year siege of the cities of Hsiang-yang and Fan-ch'eng. In 1276 the Sung capital of Hang-chow fell to the Mongol armies led by Bayan and the empress dowager surrendered the city on condition that the boy emperor would be spared. How changed the habits of the Mongols had become since the days of Temuchin may be seen by the fact that Hangchow was not looted, but rather that all precautions were taken to preserve artistic treasures and the fine libraries. The child emperor himself was received by Kublai Khan, and performed the kowtow in front of him, upon instructions from his mother to do so since the new "son of heaven" had granted him his life, and he was then sent into a monastery to become a Buddhist priest. In the next year, Canton, the great port in the south, also fell to the Mongols, but remnants of Sung forces continued the fight until 1279 when they also were defeated in a naval battle off Hainan island, and the last Sung prince, the brother of the child emperor, was drowned. Thus, by 1279 all China was in the hands of a foreign conqueror; it was the first time in the history of China that a dynasty of conquest had achieved its ultimate goal, the complete possession of the country. As Marco Polo wrote, there was no question of Kublai Khan's having become "the most puisant of men, in subjects, lands and treasure, that there is on earth or ever was, from the time of our first father Adam to this day".[3]

After the conquest of China by Kublai Khan the Mongols continued their warfare, true to the original idea of world conquest formulated by Chingis Khan. Unless the rulers of other areas submitted completely by personally appearing at Khanbalig and doing homage to Kublai Khan, the Mongols pursued their aggressive wars. This demand for abject submission stood in contrast to the previous Chinese diplomatic relationships with surrounding areas when tributary acknowledgment sufficed without personal appearance of the ruling prince. In accordance with their goal of world conquest, the Mongols launched a series of vast campaigns on land against Indo-China and Burma, and overseas against Java, the Liu-ch'iu islands, and Japan.

INVASIONS OF SOUTHEAST ASIA.   Warfare against Annam, Champa, and Burma produced victories for the Mongols of Kublai Khan, but did not result in lasting successes. Sung remnants had found refuge in Annam and although the king of Annam was willing to admit Mongol suzerainty, he did not appear in person at the Mongol court. In Champa the ruler also refused to appear before Kublai Khan. Annam made its submission, in the face of Mongol forces, but the ruler of the Chams fled into the jungle after the Mongols captured his major fortress. Subsequently other Mongol attacks were launched in 1285 and 1287, but the Mongols, unused to jungle warfare, were severely weakened by tropical fever and disease. In Burma events were very much the same; there too their expeditions were able to defeat the Burmese troops, but the Mongols could not gain a lasting foothold and they soon withdrew. All three, Annam, Champa, and Burma, did finally recognize the Yuan dynasty, but their rulers could not be coerced to appear in person before the Mongol Grand Khan. Tropical climate and the jungle had set limits to Mongol military prowess.

[3] René Grousset, *The Rise and Splendor of the Chinese Empire* (Berkeley, Cal.: Univ. of California Press, 1953), p. 236. Published in Great Britain by Geoffrey Bles Ltd.

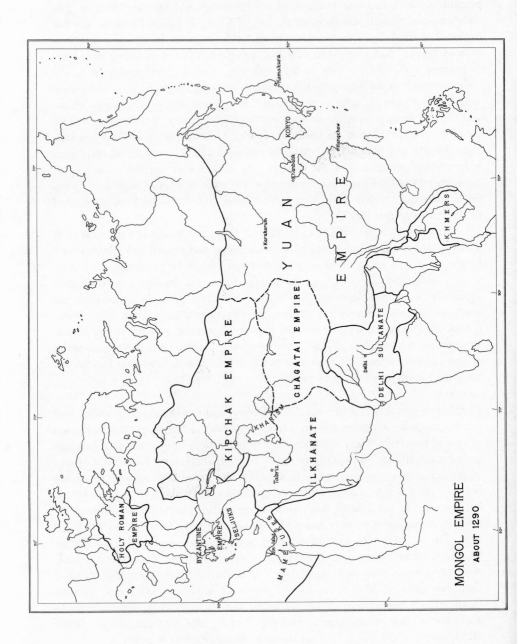

MONGOL EMPIRE
ABOUT 1290

KHMERS

YUAN EMPIRE

oKarakorum

KORYO

oKhanbalik

oHangchow

Kamakura

KIPCHAK EMPIRE

CHAGATAI EMPIRE

KHARISM

ILKHANATE

DELHI SULTANATE

Delhi o

Tabriz o

SELJUKS

BYZANTINE
EMPIRE

HOLY ROMAN
EMPIRE

MAMELUKES

The five invasions of Burma completely ruined the dynasty of Pagan, and the country became the prey of the Shan and Tai who followed in the wake of the Mongols. The greatest effect of the Mongols' land operations in Southeast Asia was the impetus given to new people, particularly the Tai, who built a new powerful state, Siam, upon the ruins of the older culture of Cambodia.

NAVAL EXPEDITIONS OVERSEAS. As the jungle and tropical climate was an effective barrier to Mongol land operations in Southeast Asia, so also the sea set definite limits to their power. The fate of Mongol naval expeditions, conceived on a vast scale and executed with great determination showed to a most reluctant Kublai Khan that Mongol conquest of the world, his cherished ideal, was a phantom that could not be realized.

These Mongol overseas expeditions were directed against the Liuch'iu islands, against Java, and, most importantly, against Japan. The Liuch'iu attempt in 1291 was a complete failure, since the Mongol vessels could not even find the islands. The expedition of 1293 which was directed against Java was of a more serious nature. King Kertanagara of Singosari, the principal ruler on the island, had been ordered to pay homage to Kublai, but he had refused to do so, and his refusal had been tattooed on the face of the Mongol envoy. This terrible insult meant, of course, war and a Mongol expeditionary force sailed in 1,000 ships in 1293 for Java. As related in Chapter 14 Kertanagara himself in the meantime had been overthrown and killed by his vassal of the state of Kadiri. Kertanagara's son-in-law had set up a rival kingdom, Madjapahit, destined to become the last of the great native empires of the Indonesian archipelago, and it was he who received on their arrival the Mongol fleet and troops, informing them unblushingly that it had been the ruler of Kadiri who was responsible for the insult perpetrated against the dignity of the Grand Khan. Thereupon the Mongol army proceeded to destroy Kadiri, only to fall victim to the treachery of Madjapahit. When Kadiri had been successfully defeated and the Mongol troops had been dispersed, they were ambushed by the forces of Madjapahit. The Mongols suffered heavy losses and evacuated the area.

But the greatest and most tenacious efforts at conquest overseas were reserved for Japan. The island kingdom of Japan was reported to be fabulously wealthy (Marco Polo was greatly impressed by the stories of its gold), and true to their ideas of international relations the Mongols here too demanded direct recognition of Kublai Khan as overlord and the personal appearance of the Japanese ruler at Khanbalig. In 1268 a letter from Kublai was sent with a Chinese envoy via Korea to Japan, and this procedure was repeated in the next year. When these overtures were rejected Kublai sent as his ambassador Chao Liang-pi in 1270, and again in 1273. Again the Japanese refused to acknowledge Mongol suzerainty, and Kublai decided upon an overseas expedition, despite his ambassador's warning against such an invasion attempt which he depicted as a most difficult and dangerous enterprise.

The expedition was launched against Japan in 1274. About 900 Korean ships manned by about 25,000 Mongols and some Korean soldiers, set forth from Korean ports with Korean crews. Mongol equipment was first rate, as they possessed not only their famous bow, superior to any of their enemy's, but also employed catapults and rockets. The Mongol amphibious force first took and sacked Tsushima, between Korea and Japan, and finally it was disembarked on Kyushu at Hakozaki Bay in November 1274. The Mongols had some tactical advantages, in their superb discipline, tight fighting formations, and superior weapons, but the Japanese resistance was very determined. The result of battle was not decisive but it served as a demonstration to the Japanese, and in Kublai Khan's thinking it had accomplished its purpose. Consequently he dispatched further envoys in 1275, and in the next years until 1279, reiterating the Mongol demand for complete submission. The Japanese refused unequivocally, and beheaded all of these unfortunate ambassadors.

Since Japan refused to yield, Kublai in great anger ordered the preparation of a second and more powerful maritime expedition. Kublai assembled a vast force, estimated at 100,000 Mongols, 20,000 Koreans, and 50,000 Chinese embarked in two fleets, of perhaps 4,500 ships in all.

These two fleets, one sailing from China and one from Korea, effected a junction off the coast of Japan, and in June 1281 the vast armada landed once more on Japanese soil, again at Hakozaki bay in Kyushu. The landing spot chosen was a mistake, because the Japanese had built there a strong defensive wall.

The battle in 1281 between the Mongols, Chinese, and Koreans, and the Japanese was desperate, and raged for nearly eight weeks. The Japanese fought with great bravery and were able to hold their own against the formidable force. A southwest typhoon on 1 August, 1281 drove many of the Mongol vessels upon sandbars and beaches and reduced the Mongols to helplessness, permitting the Japanese to fall upon them. Many other ships were driven out to sea where they capsized, and many Mongols perished by drowning. The Japanese victory, thanks to this "divine wind," or *kamikaze,* was decisive, and the whole nation offered up prayers in gratitude to the gods.

Kublai Khan, on hearing the news, was furious, and insisted on yet another expedition, which was planned for 1288. Again new preparations were begun, and heavy requisitions of men, money, and ships were levied upon Chinese and Koreans alike. But the burden proved too heavy. Korea had been exhausted from previous attempts, and could aid little, and in China there was spreading unrest and even rebellion among the subjects of the Mongols. The expedition had to be postponed and the whole plan was finally abandoned, but only with the greatest of reluctance by the Mongols. As late as 1299 there were still serious proposals, and a special "department for the invasion of Japan" could be found in the Mongol government. The Mongol empire was a military land power. The sea, as had the jungle, set natural limits to its expansion.

China Under the Yuan

The Mongols ruled China separately from the rest of the Mongol empire. Nominally, of course, Kublai Khan, the founder of the Chinese Yuan dynasty was also the Grand Khan of the Mongols, and suzerain over the Mongol Khanates; in fact by this time these had become more or less independent, and the Yuan ruled simply as a Chinese dynasty, and Kublai Khan as a Chinese emperor. The internal administration of the empire was carried on from the capital in north China, Khanbalig, on the present site of Peking, where Kublai had built for himself a splendid palace.

MONGOL ADMINISTRATION IN CHINA. The Yuan controlled both nomad and settled farmer, and special nationality legislation was enacted to keep the Mongols apart from the Chinese. In the hierarchical society which the Khan created the Mongols were of course the privileged class, and they occupied the chief positions in the state without having to go through the civil service examination system. The army was composed mainly of Mongols, and garrisons of Mongol troops were placed at the strategic centers of the empire. Beneath the Mongols came their Central Asiatic and other alien auxiliaries, who were used extensively by the Yuan. The employment of foreigners in high administrative posts was a characteristic of the Mongol empire in China. Kublai's bodyguard consisted of Christian Alans from the Caucasus; two Germans served him as his chief huntsmen, and a German siege engineer rose to great heights in Mongol military service. The most famous European serving the Grand Khan was Marco Polo. Another alien who rose to great power was a Moslem, Ahmed, who controlled the finances of the kingdom for a time. Beneath the foreigners came the Chinese, first those of the north and then those of the south. Both categories were forbidden to carry arms. Thus every effort was made by Kublai Khan to prevent the Mongols from being too close to the Chinese and from becoming assimilated into Chinese society.

Although the political center of the power of the Yuan was in the North China Plain, its economic center was the Yangtze basin from which grain shipments on a large scale were transported north to the capital city. This reliance upon the Yangtze basin for food supplies caused the reconstruction of the Grand Canal which connected Khanbalig with the Yellow river and the southern producing areas. Other public works of Kublai's reign included the building and restoration of roads over which an official Mongol courier service tied together Khanbalig and the most remote provinces. Kublai Khan was fully aware of the need for a contented subject population and such measures as the establishment of public granaries, the expansion of existing colleges, and the encouragement of education were designed with this purpose in mind, as was public welfare for the aged, blind, and orphans, and the institution of traveling inspectors who were to report periodically on the economic situation of the empire. An edict which forbade Mongol horsemen to ride over planted crops also shows the concern Kublai had to govern China peacefully.

ECONOMIC CONDITIONS UNDER THE YUAN.   Despite these efforts the economic picture of the Mongol rule in China was not a happy one. There were
steadily increasing taxes, many of which went to support the unsuccessful
overseas expeditions, much forced labor, and, above all, inflation, caused by the
extensive use of paper currency. Kublai used paper money on a large scale, to
the great amazement of Marco Polo who exclaimed that: "One may well say
that the great Khan is a perfect alchemist." Inflation caused a flow of specie
abroad and it intensified the distress and discontent of the Chinese subjects of
the Grand Khan. Other economic weaknesses were connected with the lavish
spending for the building of great temples as the Mongols increased their interest
in the Buddhist religion, and the corruption at court, particularly under the
financial official, Ahmed. The fact that he was finally exposed, killed, and his
body thrown to the dogs did nothing to stop the rapid depreciation of China's
finances. The Yuan regime led to a continual and rapid impoverishment of China.

RELIGION.   Kublai Khan continued the old Mongol policy of religious toleration of all faiths; for political reasons he did give new honors to Confucianism,
and for the same reason he occasionally took strong measures against the Taoists
who were a distracting element in the state with their violent attacks against the
Buddhist priesthood. Although officially all religions enjoyed imperial bounty
and were exempt from taxation, Kublai himself inclined towards Tibetan Buddhism, or Lamaism. The personal leanings of Kublai and his successors cost the
Yuan dynasty the support of the Confucian scholar class, and were but another
sign of how unacceptable the Mongols were to the Chinese, and how alien they
remained while ruling China.

CULTURE UNDER THE YUAN.   The culture of the Yuan was cosmopolitan as
might be expected from the contact with many foreign civilizations which Mongol rule over Asia afforded. Yet the period provided no stimulation for China,
and there were few new religious and intellectual movements, quite unlike the
earlier T'ang period in which China had also been open to foreign influences.
Rather the Yuan cultural developments were backward-looking to the golden
age and to the brilliance of the Sung. China tended to idealize the past, was
more tradition-conscious than before, and was concerned primarily with the
restoration and conservation of its national heritage. The Yuan then was a
period characterized, with some important exceptions, by a lack of creativity
and originality, a decline in art, literature, and scholarship, and finally by an
antiforeign and anti-Mongol reaction. The major exceptions to these trends
were in the fields of applied science, the drama, and the novel.

In material achievement, however, the Mongol period was one of great
progress. Kublai sponsored the building of new astronomical observatories and
in military science gunpowder became widely employed. Of particular interest
were developments in printing, since it appears that it was during Mongol times
that this great invention was carried from eastern Asia into Europe. Printing

production was extensive during the Yuan, and the output of medical works, almanacs, and plays rapidly increased. There was a government printing office in Khanbalig, and a similar office in Mongolia. Certainly it does not seem to be a coincidence that the first primitive block prints made their appearance in Europe at the end of the Mongol period. Although there is no clear documentary evidence for the fact that the invention of printing was brought to Europe via the Mongols, there no longer exists any doubt about the possibility of printed playing cards making their way across Central Asia, perhaps to the great trading city of Novgorod, and that the idea of the printed page traveled westward, where Gutenberg and others made full use of it.

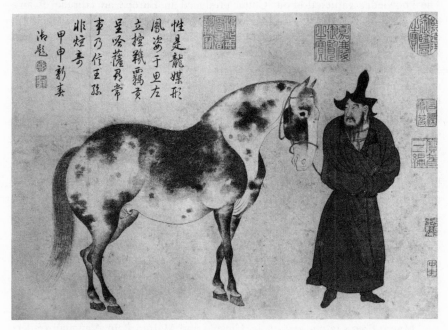

FIGURE 22.3.   Horse and trainer. Mongol period painting.

There is little to be said of the fine arts. There was some Persian influence in ceramics, and the process of cloisonné seems to have been introduced from Byzantium. In painting the Yuan artists were primarily concerned with carrying on the Sung tradition, although the Mongols did stimulate interest in animals and military subjects. Chao Meng-fu, an artist of Kublai Khan's court, was especially famous for his vigorous, strong horses, and his animal realism in general. The really major developments however belong to the drama and the novel. Yuan drama is the first Chinese drama. Non-realistic and based upon Confucian themes, its plays have survived to the present time. The Chinese novel, although perhaps it too shows signs of Persian influence, was the greatest creation of the period. Such a work as the *Romance of the Three Kingdoms,* a historical novel based on the wars of the Three Kingdoms of the third century

A.D. (see Chapter 18), has remained one of the most popular novels in China
to the present day. Its style is easy, and it deals with fascinating scenes of
warfare, cunning plans of military leaders, and the great deeds of courageous
warriors.

MARCO POLO AND THE VISION OF CHINA.   Perhaps the greatest cultural
effect of the Mongols was that their empire, with its open trade routes, permitted for a short time between the mid-thirteenth and fourteenth centuries
close contact between Europe and Asia. China during this period came to be
better known to Europeans than it was to be again until the nineteenth century.
The knowledge gathered about China produced in Europe an attitude of awe
and wonder. China was a land of marvels, of wealth, of intellectual culture,
exceeding Europe in population, splendour, luxury, and scope of activities.
When thirteenth-century Europeans looked at China, they did so with an outlook
entirely different from that of the Westerner who was to arrive in China in the
nineteenth century. One Franciscan described Canton as a city three times as
large as Venice, and yet another spoke of Hangchow as "the most marvelous
city that now exists or perhaps ever did exist." The size and splendor of China
impressed all visitors, but none of them came to be so well known as the con-
veyor of Asia's greatness to the West as Marco Polo. No other European compared with this outstanding Venetian in exactness and sincerity of description,
breadth of experience, and vast compass of journeys. It was from his book that
the attitude of Europe was derived for centuries; Asia was a superior, wealthier,
and a more powerful part of the world. The *Travels* went through many editions,
and the effect produced on European thought and geographical conceptions
was revolutionary. Marco Polo's eyewitness accounts are a very great contribution, because he discovered the East for medieval Europe, and also because of
him many details of the Yuan empire are known to us, whether they concerned
the fabulous city of Hangchow, conditions in west China, or the campaigns of
Mongol armies against Burma.

     Marco Polo's father and uncle, Niccolo and Maffeo Polo, Venetian traders
and jewelers, had reached the court of Kublai Khan between the years 1263
and 1264, and had been given a warm and cordial reception by Kublai himself,
who questioned both about European affairs. Upon their return Kublai sent a
message to the pope with them, requesting him to send to China a number of
learned men. The Mongol khan was interested in obtaining European craftsmen
and in learning of Western scientific achievement. The two elder Polos returned
in 1271 once more to the Far East, accompanied not by learned friars, but by
Marco, Niccolo's son, then a twenty-one year old youth. They traveled via
Persia and Afghanistan, then across the Pamirs and through the Tarim basin into
Kansu and north China, where they arrived in 1275. Marco Polo made a fine
impression upon Kublai Khan and he remained in China for seventeen years,
serving his master in a variety of occupations and remaining in his high favor.
His duties included a post as salt tax administrator in Yangchow and a number
of special missions and inspection tours which permitted him to observe a great

FIGURE 22.4.   Niccolo and Maffeo Polo en route to China; from a fourteenth-century Catalan map.

number of astonishing things throughout the Yuan empire, such as coal which he described as "a kind of black stone, which is dug out of the mountains like any other kind of stone and burns like wood." In 1292 Marco Polo was sent west as escort to a Mongol princess who was to be the bride of the Ilkhan in Persia. His return voyage was by way of a south China port and then by sea to Sumatra, thence to India and Persia, and on to Venice. After his return to his native city he was captured in a battle, and he dictated his account of his travels to a fellow prisoner of war.

After the publication of the *Travels,* China captured the imagination of many Europeans. Cartography was greatly enriched and the journeys stimulated European expansion in the fifteenth century, since it was Columbus' intention to sail west to Polo's fabled, wealthy, and populous "Cathay." From the book of Marco Polo Europeans came to look upon the East with awe, not with the superiority which Westerners of the nineteenth century cultivated. Any country with cities containing 12,000 bridges, and which was ruled by a man like Kublai who surpassed, in Marco Polo's estimate, every sovereign, including all those of the past, evoked profound respect. Venice was but a pale reflection of such cities as Hangchow.

TRAVEL AND TRADE DURING THE "PAX TATARICA."   Marco Polo was only the most outstanding of European travelers to find their way during the Mongol period in China. There were many others, particularly Italians, both from Venice and Genoa who made the long trip across the Asian continent in quest of silk. This can be inferred from travel and trade guides such as

Pegolotti's handbook, an excellent manual compiled by a Florentine, which gives detailed instructions as to the best routes of travel, chief import and export commodities, and information on currency, taxes, and duties. Two chapters of the book deal exclusively with China, and according to the author travel there was perfectly safe by day or by night. The flow of Western travelers to the East was matched by a current in the other direction, and many Eastern travelers could be found in the West, benefiting from the security of travel the Mongols had established. The most famous of these counterparts of Marco Polo was a Nestorian Christian, Rabban Sauma, who was born near Peking, and who after traveling in the Near East came to Europe and was received at the courts of Philip IV of France and Edward I of England. He was also granted an audience by the pope, and received communion from the pontiff himself, as it was in the interest of both the European secular rulers and the papacy to explore the possibility of an alliance with the Mongols against the Moslems in general, and the Mamluks in Egypt in particular. Chinese merchants also went abroad, and we know of the existence of Chinese trading colonies in Moscow, Tabriz, and Novgorod during this period, while Chinese engineers were employed on irrigation projects in Mesopotamia.

This widespread travel reflected the peace, the "Pax Tatarica," which Mongol rule had given to most of the continent, and the importance of the trade which flowed between East and West, both overland and by sea. Trade was prospering, bringing to China such items as spices, pearls, fine cloths, and precious stones in exchange for Chinese silk and porcelain. Silk was the most important commodity. Unlike the silk trade between Rome and China which handled plain white silk stuffs and raw silk, finished and dyed in Syria, Yuan trade dealt in patterned silk. The silk trade gave new stimulus to the caravan routes across Central Asia, and also accounted for the great activity of the south China ports in trade with South and West Asia, notably that of Ch'uan-chou (known to Marco Polo as "Zayton") near modern Amoy. Here and in other ports trade was in the hands of Arabs and Persians who were permitted a certain measure of self-government.

FOREIGN RELIGIONS IN THE YUAN EMPIRE.   Another aspect of this freedom of travel and the exchange of goods and ideas was the introduction or reintroduction of a number of foreign religions to China, especially Catholic and Nestorian Christianity and Islam.

Catholic Christianity in Far East. The arrival of the Catholic church in the Far East was due to the missionary zeal of the Franciscans in the thirteenth century. The most important and noble figure among them was John of Montecorvino, who left Europe in 1294 with the sanction of pope Clement V, and who reached China after traveling by way of Tabriz, Hormuz, and the sea route via India and Malacca. Montecorvino made an excellent impression upon the Yuan Emperor Timur, the direct successor of Kublai Khan, and worked with some success in China between 1294 and 1328.

During this time, after acquainting himself with the Mongol language, Montecorvino had the New Testament and Psalter translated, and he was also able to establish other missionary establishments not only at Khanbalig but also at the great trade center and port of Ch'uan-chou in south China. Montecorvino was in high favor at the Yuan court, was received in audience by the emperor himself, and was given liberal allowances for food and clothing. His missionary work brought about the conversion of some 5,000 Mongols and Central Asian auxiliaries, notably the people of the Alani, who originally had belonged to the Greek church, but had been uprooted by the Mongols and forcibly transplanted to the Far East. But the success of the Franciscans always remained limited to conversion from among the Mongols or other Central Asian peoples; no Chinese became adherents of the Church of Rome. The papacy, recognizing the great labors of Montecorvino, appointed him archbishop of Peking in 1307, and Rome sent out many other Franciscan friars to north China and Fukien, where mission centers had been established.

One of these friars was Oderic of Pordenone, who went to China in 1324 and returned to Europe four years later. Oderic's account of his travels again points out the wealth of the Far East and the density of its population. In 1342 a papal legate, John of Marignolli, was sent out to investigate conditions in the archbishopric of Peking. He returned in 1368 and prepared a report, the last one describing a flourishing Roman Catholic community in China. Since the friars had made conversions only among the foreign elements which governed China, they were unpopular among the Chinese and the collapse of the Mongol empire was accompanied by the decline of those foreign religions who had ministered to non-Chinese.

Nestorian Christianity in the Far East. The fate of Nestorian Christianity in China was similar. Nestorianism, also motivated by a strong missionary zeal (see Chapter 4), had been active ever since the eleventh century in Central Asia, where the Keraits and the Onguts, as well as some Uighurs, had been won to the Christian faith as early as 1007. Nestorianism flourished in the Mongol empire, and in China, at Khanbalig, there were to be found many high state officials who were adherents of this faith. There was a Nestorian astronomer, many Nestorian physicians, and even a Nestorian archbishop. A special office in charge of the supervision of Nestorians was established by the government, and many of the foreigners at the capital and the great trading ports belonged to this variety of Christianity. The Nestorian Christians, as well as the Armenian Christians who also had communities in China during the Yuan period, became extinct with the fall of the Mongol empire in China, victims of the antiforeign reaction of the Chinese.

Islam. Islam, although not new to China, made great strides during the Mongol period. Many Moslem traders came to China, and established Moslem merchant communities in Kansu, while the province of Yunnan actually was governed by Moslem officials. The Moslems survived the downfall of the Mongols since their numbers were much greater and their contact with Islam in Central Asia was not broken.

Confucianism. The flourishing of foreign religions showed the tolerant attitude of the Mongols. In a way, this policy was a mistaken one in China, since equal support to all religions deprived the dynasty of the essential support of the Confucian scholars and gentry. Despite the fact that the Yuan emperors went out of their way to give official sanction to Confucianism by restoring the civil examinations and the Hanlin academy, by erecting new temples to Confucius, by decreeing new honors for the sage and his disciples, and by conducting elaborate Confucian ceremonies, the Chinese Confucian gentry was alienated by the Mongol regime, particularly when that regime showed an increasing tendency to favor the Tibetan variety of Buddhism, Lamaism. Detailed acts of sacrifice and the most elaborate Confucian ritual ever conducted in Chinese annals were no substitute for the personal inclination of the later Yuan rulers towards a faith which was abhorred by Chinese scholars and officials. This loss of support played a major role in the decline of Mongol power.

Decline of Yuan

Kublai Khan died in 1294 at the age of 80 and was succeeded by his grandson Timur, an able and courageous man. But Timur died when he was only 31 years old, leaving no able successor. The later rulers of the Yuan dynasty were weak; the descendants of Chingis Khan had become soft in the luxury of secluded palace life, and the decline of the Yuan was rapid. Although the rulers still bore the title of Mongol Grand Khans, the Mongol structure had fallen apart. Distances and cultural differences had ended unity and cohesion among the Mongols themselves.

With their power steadily declining and with loss of energy and vigor, the Yuan dynasty soon faced Chinese opposition. Rebellious secret societies, of whom the most formidable one was the White Lotus, fomented revolt in the country. Frequent floods of the Yellow river and famine in the north further contributed to discontent and rebellion among the Chinese subjects of the Mongols, who had additional grievances in the heavy taxes and the financial difficulties created by the use of inflationary paper money. The deteriorating economic situation was accompanied and aggravated by renewed ravages of Japanese pirates after 1356. What maintained the Yuan in power in China, unlike Korea where their control was overthrown in 1356, was not their strength, but rather the fact that the rebels could not agree among themselves, and the fact that most of the Chinese gentry still preferred the rule of the Mongols to the feared consequences of a successful peasant uprising. This prolonged struggle was finally concluded with the emergence of Chu Yuan-chang, the able leader of the Chinese opposition. Born of poor stock in Anhui in 1328, he had been a Buddhist monk, but then joined a military band, where his ability in operations against the Mongols in the Yangtze valley soon won him adherents. Landlords and officials also began to give him support once he transformed a disorganized peasant rebellion directed against the rich into a movement aimed primarily at expelling the hated Mongols and their foreign auxiliaries. Chu Yuan-chang succeeded in giving popular sentiment a definite direction, and when this had been accomplished, he enjoyed rapid successes.

The rebellion soon became a nation-wide movement, and Chu Yuan-chang's energy and discretion won him easy victories. By 1364 the whole Lower Yangtze valley was in his hands, and in 1368 the capital city of Khanbalig fell to him. The remnants of the Mongols fled back to their homeland, Mongolia, but they were disunited and broken up in splinter groups, and their military prowess had been tamed by the pacifying influence of Tibetan Lamaïsm.

The Mongols had been dominant in Asian history from 1203 to 1368. Their genius in war and astounding victories had created a great military empire, stretching from Japan to Austria. Yet their disintegration was rapid, they had shown little cohesion and had consequently been quickly assimilated by other cultures. Theirs had been primarily a destructive force, but it had also been one of integration, permitting cultural intercourse across the whole Asiatic continent. Both China and Europe had benefited from their rule. China, despite misgovernment and destruction, had seen its political unity restored for the first time since the T'ang. Europe benefited by the development of a new outlook towards a more open world and by the stimulus engendered towards new discoveries and the explorations of the Renaissance, a result of the view of Asia as an enormously wealthy and culturally superior civilization.

BASIC DATES

1241	Death of Ogodai
1246–1248	Kuyuk Grand Khan
1246	Carpini at Karakorum
1251–1259	Mangu Grand Khan
1252–1253	Annexation of Nan-chao
1260–1294	Kublai Grand Khan
1260–1264	Opposition of Arikboga
1275–1292	Marco Polo in China
1267	Khanbalig built
1277, 1287–1288	Opposition of Kaidu
1276	Fall of Hangchow
1277–1301	Expeditions against Burma
1277	Fall of Canton
1279	End of Sung
1274, 1281	Expeditions against Japan
1283–1288	Expeditions against Champa and Annam
1292–1293	Expeditions against Java
1356	Koreans overthrow Mongols
1364	Loss of Yangtze valley
1368	Loss of Khanbalig, end of Yuan

SUPPLEMENTARY READING

GROUSSET, R. *The Rise and Splendor of the Chinese Empire*. Berkeley, Cal., 1953. Two good chapters on Kublai Khan and Marco Polo.

HUDSON, G. F. *Europe and China*. London, 1931.

LAMB, H. *The March of the Barbarians*. New York, 1940.

PRAWDIN, M. *The Mongol Empire: Its Rise and Legacy*. London, 1952.

REISCHAUER, E. O. AND J. K. FAIRBANK. *East Asia: The Great Traditions*. Boston, 1958.

SYKES, P. *The Quest for Cathay*. London, 1932.

ADVANCED READING

BUDGE, E. A. W. *The Monks of Kublai Khan*. London, 1928. The story of Nestorian travelers from China to Europe.

CARTER, T. F. *The Invention of Printing in China and Its Spread Westward*. New York, 1955.

HOWORTH, H. *History of the Mongols*. London, 1880.

KOMROFF, M. *Contemporaries of Marco Polo*. New York, 1937. Contains the accounts of Carpini, Rubruck, and Oderic of Pordenone.

MOULE, A. C. AND P. PELLIOT. *Marco Polo*. London, 1938.

OLSCHKI, L. *Guillaume Boucher, a French Artist at the Court of the Khans*. Baltimore, 1956. Interesting story of conditions at Karakorum.

——————— *Marco Polo's Asia: An Introduction to His "Description of the World" called "Il Milione."* Berkeley, Cal., 1961.

——————— *Marco Polo's Precursors*. Baltimore, 1943.

SCHURMANN, H. F. *Economic Structure of the Yüan Dynasty*. Cambridge, Mass., 1956.

YULE, H. *The Book of Ser Marco Polo*. New York, 1903. A classic edition.

XXIII

CHINA IN THE

MING PERIOD

Establishment of the Dynasty

The decline of Mongol overlordship in China was characterized by frequent anti-Mongol riots and rebellions, particularly in south and central China. In these, individual bandits as well as certain secret societies, notably the White Lotus which preached the advent of Maitreya and of the millenium, all played a role in reducing China by the middle of the fourteenth century to a state of universal and appalling anarchy. Some of the rebel movements were peasant revolutions directed primarily against the rich landlord-gentry class, and were more concerned with slaughtering the wealthy than in recovering all of China from the Mongols. However, from this state of general chaos there eventually emerged a leader of acknowledged ability and power, the founder of the Ming dynasty, Chu Yuan-chang.

THE HUNG-WU EMPEROR.   Chu Yuan-chang was born in 1327 in Anhui province of very poor peasant stock, and his parents later perished in a famine which devastated central China. An orphan at 17, be became a Buddhist monk for seven years, but life in monastic surroundings did not appeal to him, and after being defrocked, this young man of grotesque appearance with a snout-like face which later earned him the sobriquet "pig-emperor," turned to his true avocation—military leadership. As a soldier he was able, ruthless, and an excellent organizer. He rose rapidly in the world and the very ease of his success instilled in him a feeling of superiority. Although he had been nothing but another bandit leader at the beginning of his rise, he perceived clearly that what was necessary above all was to change the nature of the revolt from one of peasant revolution against the rich into a national revolt against the hated Mongols, a change that was soon effected. In arousing national feeling among the Chinese and hatred of foreigners, Chu was aided by the Mongols themselves who chose unwisely this time to introduce tightened racial laws discriminatory against their Chinese subjects. After 1352 Chu led a national revolt against the Mongols, repressed pillaging, and repealed laws against the rich. Success came quickly and by 1356 he was able to establish a regular government in the lower Yangtze valley, with Nanking as its center. A few years later his troops moved north into Honan and Shantung provinces, while in 1368 one of his generals captured Peking, or Khanbalig, the capital of the Yuan dynasty. The northern expedition of his forces was almost a triumphal march, and the rest of China was conquered easily. Szechuan fell to him in 1371 and Yunnan in 1382, so that the whole of China, including the southwestern region, was once more united under one government. After the expulsion of the Mongols from Peking in 1368 Chu established in that year a new dynasty, the Ming or "brilliant dynasty," and he also adopted in that year as his reign name or *nien hao* the title Hung-wu or "Vastly Martial." As Hung-wu emperor Chu ruled until 1398 from his capital of Nanking in the south. Nanking was chosen because north China had been under alien countrol for some three hundred years, the city was situated in the wealthiest and most populous portion of the Chinese empire, and the south was more familiar to Chu Yuan-chang. The south also had the added advantage of being more remote from the dangers of the northern frontier.

Chu Yuan-chang's role in Chinese history is an important one since he restored a purely Chinese dynasty which ruled a unified nation. Although the Ming never possessed as extensive dominions as did the Han and T'ang, nevertheless the Ming is a period of triumph for the Chinese spirit, and one which also saw an active foreign policy of cultural imperialism. The thirty-year reign of the Hung-wu emperor was one of vigor and expansion, as well as of peace and prosperity in the later years (although after the death of his wife, Empress Ma, who was a capable and levelheaded person, his reign became considerably harsher and his suspicions sometimes resulted in repressive measures, as in Nanking where 15,000 perished when a plot had been disclosed against him). When the Hung-wu emperor died in 1398 at the age of 70, the Ming dynasty had become firmly established, indeed so solidly that it could survive a four-year succession struggle for the throne.

THE YUNG-LO EMPEROR.   The Hung-wu emperor had designated his sixteen-year-old grandson, Chu Yün-wen, as his successor to the Dragon Throne, but this was a poor choice. The youth was not very capable and he soon antagonized his powerful uncle, Chu Ti, who governed the northeast. Chu Ti rebelled and successfully seized power by 1402. Chu Yün-wen disappeared from history, either perishing in a palace fire, or, as rumor had it, surviving secretly as a Buddhist monk. Chu Ti in 1403 adopted for himself the reign name of Yung-lo or "Eternal Happiness." During the Yung-lo reign which lasted from 1403 to 1424 the Ming reached its zenith. The Yung-lo emperor, although harsh and severe, was very able. He maintained Ming power within China, while expanding Chinese prestige abroad. In 1421 he moved the capital to the north, to Peking, for easier surveillance of the northern frontier regions and the Mongols beyond. Peking was completely rebuilt, and the migration of settlers to the north from south China was encouraged and facilitated by improvements along the Grand Canal connecting north and south. The reigns of the Hung-wu and of the Yung-lo emperors are the only two of importance in the history of the Ming dynasty until 1500. Later emperors proved weak and less capable, and the accomplishments of the Ming, both externally and internally, rested upon the foundations of Chu Yuan-chang's and Chu Ti's achievements. Both were strong rulers who suppressed any signs of subversive movements within China, such as the activities of the White Lotus society, and both also shared in bringing to full fruition a most vigorous Chinese foreign policy which found its expression in the creation of the unique tributary system.

Foreign Policy

THE TRIBUTARY SYSTEM.   The tributary system was a system of cultural imperialism designed to stabilize foreign relations in the Far Eastern world order, and it found a theoretical basis in Confucian ideology. The theory was simple; it argued that Chinese culture being supreme, it was hence attractive to all the "barbarians" who surrounded China, and it thus implied the voluntary submission of the culturally inferior to the culturally superior. Its basic aim was to secure peace and order for China along her vast boundaries, and in practice the policy worked well. By abstaining from any interference in the internal affairs of the tributary nations, and by making the tributary status economically attractive to the "barbarian" (since more in value was given to the tributary in return for tribute), China's foreign relations were peaceful and orderly over an enormous expanse. At the height of the development of the tributary system the government office in charge of foreign relations, the *li pu* or Board of Ceremonies, had listed some 38 "tributaries," including Korea, Japan, the Liuch'iu islands, Tibet, Annam, Cambodia, Siam, Champa, Java, Borneo, Palembang, Malacca, Ceylon, the Philippines, the Maldives, Bengal, Aden, Mogadiscio, Turfan, Samarkand, Isfahan, and Khorasan. The Board of Ceremonies carefully regulated all communications between the tributary nations and China, either by land across Central Asia via Hami, or through designated ports such as Canton and Ningpo, and it was also in charge of the reception and entertainment of tributary missions at the capital in Peking where they were received in a special guest house and entertained according to status with ritual feasting. The tributary system worked largely because it was profitable for such countries as Korea, Annam, the Liuch'iu islands, and for the nomads of Mongolia and Manchuria. By voluntarily submitting to it they gained thereby economic benefits, and cultural advantages and prestige. Presents sent to foreign rulers in return for tributary demands were always greater in value than those received in China. They might even include the highly prized dragon robes, magnificently woven silk garments, embroidered with handsome patterns which gave immense prestige to the recipient. The highest in grade were robes upon which were embroidered five-clawed dragons, these were sent regularly to Korea and the king of the Liuch'iu islands, and on special occasions to such rulers as the Sultan of Malacca. a ruler of Java, and the Sherif of Mecca.

This tributary system embraced both China's land frontiers and her maritime borders, and it was begun almost immediately after the accession of the Hung-wu emperor in 1368. In that year both Korea and the Liuch'iu islands recognized the Ming as their overlords, while formal diplomatic relations were also established between China and Burma and Nepal. In 1384 a Buddhist monk was sent from Nanking to Nepal. He returned three years later with a Nepalese mission which acknowledged China's suzerainty. In 1385 an embassy from the Burmese capital of Ava to the Hung-wu emperor also brought that country into the tributary system.

MONGOLIA AND CENTRAL ASIA. More important in the reign of the Hung-wu emperor were relations with the nomads of Mongolia and Manchuria. After the expulsion of the Mongols from China in 1368 the Ming consolidated their success by a vigorous foreign policy including a series of military campaigns against the Mongols in their own home land. In 1378, and again ten years later, Chinese armies reached and burned Karakorum, and after defeating the Mongols were instrumental in splitting them up into the Eastern and Western Mongols. Chinese power under the "Vastly Martial" emperor now also began to reach into eastern Turkistan, where Chinese armies took Hami and used it as an outpost against the Mongols and as a base for control of the western trade route across the Tarim basin, while some other oases in Sinkiang, such as Turfan and Ili, also submitted to Chinese overlordship. Beyond that, Ming envoys were even sent to Samarkand to the great Timur, but he had them imprisoned and planned a great expedition to conquer China, which was prevented only by his death in 1405. Among the nomads and seminomads of south Manchuria, Ming power was also felt during the first years of the dynasty, and here too the tributary system was extended to some Manchu tribes in the north. They were showered with honors, ranks, and decorations and trade was made attractive to them. Although this trade with Manchuria was uneconomical to China, this really did not matter as long as the tributary relationship secured for China peace and security along her borders.

The aggressive foreign policy which had been initiated by the Hung-wu emperor was continued by his successor, the Yung-lo emperor, who also interfered militarily in Mongolia. The Mongols remained still a formidable threat to later Ming rulers. In 1449 they managed to defeat a Ming army which had been grossly mismanaged in its campaign. They captured the Ming emperor Cheng-t'ung, as he sat serenely, showing no emotion whatsoever among some 100,000 Chinese corpses and his slaughtered bodyguard. He was eventually released, and in 1453 the Ming made a new peace with the Mongols. From that time on Chinese policy toward Central Asia became a defensive one, and the Ming maintained their forces behind the shelter of the Great Wall, without, however, abandoning their policy of tributary relations. The result of this defeat was that Central Asia fell under the control of the Chagatai sultans, who gained control of the important trade routes and thus virtually closed them.

VIETNAM. In Vietnam the vigor of the Yung-lo reign was especially notable. In 1406, due to internal strife, the emperor dispatched an armed expedition into that country, occupied, and then annexed it. Until 1428 Vietnam was governed by a Chinese administration supported by Ming troops. Vietnamese government was completely reorganized after the Chinese system, and even after nationalist feeling in Vietnam had resulted in a successful revolt, led by Le Loi, the new state of Vietnam whose independence was recognized by the Ming in 1431 continued to recognize China and to send tribute.

KOREA. One country that occupied a very special position in China's tributary system along her land frontiers was Korea. Korea expelled the Mongols also shortly after they had been ousted from China by the Hung-wu emperor. The leading role in this expulsion was played by a Korean general, Yi Syeng-kyei, who had distinguished himself in the suppression of Japanese pirates, and who, as head of the army and with the support of most of the Korean bureaucracy, in 1392 deposed the last king of the Wang dynasty. He assumed the title of Yi T'aejo, the first ruler of the Yi dynasty, which lasted until 1910. The very first act of Yi T'aejo, after installing himself on the throne of Korea, was voluntarily to recognize the suzerainty of the Ming dynasty by sending envoys and tribute to Nanking, by adopting Chinese culture, and by conducting the relations between Korea and the Dragon Throne according to the Confucian principles of *li*, or proper conduct. Yi T'aejo himself bowed to the Chinese envoy, and Korean princes were sent to Nanking to be educated, while Korea in many ways became a cultural extension of China, adopting the Chinese calendar, the Ming legal and penal code, and a Chinese system of centralized administration.

Yi T'aejo reigned until 1398, and was a very able monarch who gave to his new state, called Chosen with its capital at Seoul, an excellent government based upon the Chinese pattern. Buddhism ceased to be the official religion of Korea and many monastic privileges were ended; instead Korea became a Confucian state, with a reorganized government, where official examinations based on the

Confucian Classics rather than reliance on Buddhist liturgy opened the way to bureaucratic advancement, and where misgovernment and corruption, which had flourished during the Wang dynasty was at least temporarily curbed. Fifteenth-century Korea was a prosperous and peaceful country, and although it presents the classic case of the success of the policy of Chinese cultural imperialism, it also demonstrates the fact that noninterference by China in Korean internal affairs gave sufficient leeway to Korean inventive genius so that Korea was able not merely voluntarily to adopt Chinese culture, but also to make significant cultural contributions of her own, such as the invention of a true alphabet, the *on-mun*, and the development of printing by the use of moveable copper types.

TIBET.   Yet another region on the land frontiers of Ming China was also brought successfully within the Ming system of tributary relations, and that was Tibet.

The history of Tibet in T'ang times is covered in Chapter 19, and it was not until the eleventh century that major new developments took place in Tibet. Then there began a movement of monastic reform, beginning with a great reform council held at Lhasa in 1050, which condemned some practices of Tantric Buddhism, and attempted to re-establish some measure of monastic discipline. These, and further reforms, were however, only partially successful, and the Red Bonnets continued to be the most powerful force in Tibetan political and religious life, their hereditary abbots being in fact the absolute rulers of the country.

A major break with the past came with the appearance of a great Tibetan reformer and theologian, Tsongkapa. Tsongkapa was born in 1357 in the Amdo district of eastern Tibet, and at an early age embraced a life of study and asceticism. As a monk and saintly man he soon attracted followers, and 1409 he founded a new monastery, the Galdan monastery in Lhasa, which became the headquarters of a new sect, the Gelugpa, or Yellow Bonnets, the "Virtuous Sect." As the title indicates, Tsongkapa was concerned primarily with monastic reform, but he also added a major theological contribution to Tibetan Buddhism whose chief feature was the emphasis on the doctrine of transmigration. Tsongkapa taught that each abbot of each Buddhist monastery was the incarnation of an *arhat*, or Buddhist saint, of the region, while Tsongkapa believed himself to be the incarnation of the Amitabha Buddha, the mystical Buddha of Infinite Light. Upon his death his reincarnation was to be found in a baby, who was then to become the leader of the Gelugpa and of Tibet's spiritual life. This new doctrine resulted, as one might expect, in a spirited theological controversy, but Tsongkapa's learning and his spirituality carried the day for the Yellow Bonnets who held preponderant power in Tibetan affairs until very recent years. The theory of reincarnation in the body of a child also meant the necessity of a regency with all its attendant evils. Yet even so, Tsongkapa's teachings and the political power of the Yellow Bonnets were solidly established.

Of particular importance to China was the influence of Tibetan Buddhism among the Mongols, who had favored Tantrism ever since the days of Kublai

Khan and the Yuan dynasty. The Ming in China, in order to keep both the Mongols and Tibet in a state of peace and quiescence, did their best to support Tibetan Lamaism as a religious force designed to insure against renewed Mongol invasions.

RELATIONS WITH JAPAN. The Ming tributary system of foreign relations, which had as its primary aim the securing of peace and order along the borders of the Ming empire, was conducted not only along the land frontiers of China, but an effort was also made to bring overseas countries into that system and to apply it to the sea frontiers as well.

One of the chief problems of the Hung-wu emperor and his successor as far as the seacoasts of China were concerned, were the relations with Japan. But here too, after much effort, the Ming were able, at least temporarily, to secure acknowledgement of Chinese suzerainty by the *shogun* of Japan, Ashikaga Yoshimitsu. Japanese pirates had made it a habit to raid the Chinese coast for plunder in revenge against Kublai's attempts to conquer Japan, and these Japanese raids had become a serious danger, as they increased to large-scale operations, inflicting great losses on the Chinese coastal population, with much plundering and pillaging. As early as 1369, the very year after the foundation of the Ming, the Hung-wu emperor dispatched an envoy to Japan, who was instructed to complain bitterly about the brutal and destructive acts of the Japanese pirates or *wako,* and who was charged to threaten Japan with war, if necessary, in order to restore peace and security along China's coasts. This embassy proved unsuccessful, as the envoy was imprisoned by the Japanese and later returned home. In 1370 Japanese raids covered the whole of the coastline from Shantung in the north to Fukien in the south, and again the emperor sent an envoy. Chao Yi, the ambassador, was told to complain to the Japanese that they offended heaven by their misdeeds, and he was instructed to tell the Japanese that it behooved their king to "be a humble subject of Our Empire." The result of this mission was, as one might expect, not very different from the first one. Chao Yi too suffered imprisonment, and a rather humiliating return home. The relations between Japan and China did not prosper precisely because, although the Japanese evinced interest in the possibility of trade, they would not admit an inferior status and had no wish to enter into the tributary system based on such a concept. Since the Ming, in their effort to restrain Japanese piracy and reduce Japan voluntarily to an inferior position in international relations, used strong language in their letters to Japan, not hesitating to refer to the Japanese as "stupid Eastern barbarians—haughty and disloyal" and since the Hung-wu emperor did not hesitate to threaten force against the Japanese ruler ("You permit your subjects to do evil. Will this not bring inevitable disaster upon you?"), attempts at negotiations failed and relations were broken off. The Hung-wu emperor then proceeded to build extensive defensive works along the entire Chinese coast, with a complex of fortresses connected to each other by a system of fire signals and heavily garrisoned with troops. Matters remained in this unsatisfactory state until after the death of the emperor in 1398.

With the accession of the Yung-lo emperor and the simultaneous victory of the forces of the Ashikaga shoguns in Japan, a new period of Sino-Japanese relations began. On the one hand, the Ming emperor continued to desire peaceful and secure frontiers, both interior and coastal, while the Ashikaga shoguns in Japan, who required revenue, began to consider seriously the potential advantages of lucrative trade with China, and consequently displayed an interest in commercial expansion. This attitude was particularly true of the shogun Ashikaga Yoshimitsu, who, in addition to perceiving the possibility of monetary gain, was also himself a great admirer of Chinese civilization, and was strongly supported in these views by the monks of Zen Buddhism in Japan, who for their own spiritual needs pressed him towards a closer relationship with the homeland of their sect. All these factors—desire for commercial profit, the great influence of Zen Buddhism in Japan, and true appreciation of Chinese art and literature— led to a different attitude in Japan. The Ming, on the other hand, in order to stamp out piracy were willing to make economic concessions to Japan if necessary, true to the principle that peace and order was always more important than trade. Both sides seeing mutual benefit in resuming relations, a Japanese mission arrived in China in 1401 to conclude a treaty of peace and friendship. This mission brought tribute, and was willing to accept the relationship which the Ming court demanded. In 1402 the Ming reply indicated great satisfaction with this Japanese attitude. Yoshimitsu was given the title king, together with a golden seal and the usual Dragon Robe, and the Chinese calendar was sent to Japan as a symbol of the adoption of China's culture by that country. In return the Ashikaga suppressed Japanese piracy, and as a token of faith sent some of the captured pirates to China. These were put into large boilers and steamed to death, and although this was perhaps a more wasteful method than strangling, it did produce a good show, and the Ming were greatly pleased. From this moment on, the Ming were successful in bringing Japan into the tributary system, and a Ming document of 1436 clearly states this view:

Since our Empire owns the world, there is no country on this or yonder side of the seas which does not submit to us. The sage Emperors who followed one another had had the same regard and uniform benevolence for all countries far and near. You, Japan, are our Eastern frontier, and for generations you have performed tributary duties. The longer the time, the more respectful you have become.

However, it must, of course, be noted that although the Ming were able to employ the Confucian system of international relations to Japan, this system was successful only as long as one side was willing to submit to it for purposes of trade.

MING MARITIME EXPANSION. The Ming period in Chinese history is unique, because for the first time in her past China turned to the sea and towards maritime expansion. Indeed, the sea frontier for a time played the most important role in China's foreign relations. This was a development in addition to the normalization of relations across the waters between China and Japan, and it was concerned with Chinese maritime expansion to the *Nan-yang,* or South Seas. Between 1405 and 1431 China launched seven naval expeditions on a very large scale to the countries of the south and beyond—Indo-China, Java, Sumatra, Cambodia, Siam, India, Ceylon, the Philippines, the Persian Gulf, the coast of Somaliland in Africa, and to Mogadiscio in East Africa. These expeditions were entrusted by the Yung-lo emperor to Cheng Ho, a Moslem eunuch from Yunnan, who was probably chosen for his faith, and who sailed from the Yangtze estuary in large fleets which numbered as many as 62 ships. The first expedition (1405–07) brought Cheng Ho to Champa, Java, the island of Ceylon, and the port of Calicut; the one in 1413 saw Chinese vessels in the roadstead of Hormuz in the Persian Gulf and in the ports of the gulf of Bengal, while in 1421–22 Chinese ships reached the coasts of Somaliland of Africa, the furthest point reached. Other voyages occurred in 1407–09, 1409–11, 1417–19, and the last one, 1431–33, during which generally the same ports of call were included as in the earlier voyages, ranging all the way from Indonesia to the Persian Gulf.

What were the reasons behind this unprecedented, spectacular and sudden Chinese concern with naval matters and the attention paid to the sea frontier of the Chinese empire? Were they economic and commercial? One authority, the distinguished Dutch scholar, Duyvendak, argues that China had real need for overseas products during this period since the trade routes through Central Asia were closing and since the court (including the eunuch clique of which Cheng Ho was a member) was anxious for foreign luxuries such as spices and exotic woods.[1] This seems to explain the employment of huge ships, with many decks loaded with Chinese export merchandise such as silk, gold, porcelain, silver, and cotton cloth, ships which were not naval vessels at all, but fitted out with numerous private cabins used by merchants. Another authority, Fairbank, sees in these expeditions primarily a political motivation.[2] They were designed to renew Chinese prestige in foreign eyes and to bring the sources of Chinese maritime trade into the formal structure of the tributary system. This view is supported by the fact that the vessels carried as many as 37,000 soldiers, and that Cheng Ho was able to receive tribute from at least fifty states, who became members of the Chinese tributary system. This view is also reinforced by the fact that the Chinese naval expeditions did not hesitate to interfere, when necessary, in affairs abroad which threatened Chinese interest. In 1407, for example, a Chinese pirate chief in Palembang on Sumatra who plotted against Cheng Ho was seized and sent to Peking, while in 1408 the ruler of Ceylon, who had treated a Chinese envoy rather badly, was arrested together with his family and his officials and also sent to China, where the Yung-lo emperor himself then deigned to appoint a new king of Ceylon who had to pay tribute to China. In a battle in Java, too, where some Chinese had been killed, the local ruler was fined heavily by Cheng Ho and forced to acknowledge Chinese suzerainty. Chinese suzerainty over Malacca was successfully disputed by the Chinese against the claims of Siam.

[1] J. Duyvendak, *China's Discovery of Africa* (London, 1949).
[2] J. K. Fairbank, *Trade and Diplomacy on the China Coast* (Cambridge, Mass., 1953), p. 33 *et seq.*

Whether or not these voyages were economic or political in motivation cannot be clearly determined. As a matter of fact, neither can the question of what led to the sudden abandonment of Chinese maritime expansion, when Cheng Ho's naval expeditions came to a precipitate stop after 1431, be answered. Was it because they were too expensive? Was it because of palace politics? Or was it because the tribute system did not seem to work well on the seas, but only on land? Perhaps, as Fairbank argues, the latter question provides the key, since it was one thing if the tributary system worked passively, that is if the barbarian voluntarily came to China, but quite another when the tributary system was being actively extended overseas by the Chinese.

In either case, the fact remains that during the early Ming Chinese authority for a brief time had expanded overseas as never before. But the results of this maritime expansion were meager. It is true that, in their time, they produced a great sensation, and it is also true that the expeditions of Cheng Ho may have contributed to the undermining of the power of the empire of Madjapahit in Indonesia, but in the final analysis China gained little. The first giraffe, together with ostriches and zebras, made their appearance at the Ming court and were greeted with amazement, but concretely there was little beyond the enrichment of China's knowledge of the world's fauna. After 1431, and the end of maritime expansion, the Ming more and more began to withdraw within China herself, and isolation succeeded a policy of active overseas interest. The sea was abandoned to the Arabs and later to the Portuguese, and on the northern land frontier the Ming increasingly stayed behind the shelter of the Great Wall. When Japanese piracy recurred later in the century, the Ming appealed to Japan by sending money, copper coins in particular, in order to buy off their ravages. By 1500 Ming vigor in foreign relations, embodied in the tributary system both on land as well as on the sea, had disappeared.

Internal Policy

The Ming rulers after 1430 were neither impressive nor important, but the system which had been set up by the first two great Ming rulers continued in force until the fall of the dynasty itself. Ming internal policy essentially was the product of China's antiforeign reaction after centuries of alien rule, it thus meant a return to tradition and to the Confucian scholar officialdom. Ming policy, once the Mongols had been ousted, meant the uninterrupted triumph and the dominance of the conservative scholar class.

Ming Administration.   The Hung-wu emperor illustrates this tendency very well indeed. Anticosmopolitan in his outlook, he displayed little originality in government, and was perfectly satisfied to restore the ancient Confucian system of administration. He employed and honored the scholars of the great Hanlin Confucian Academy in the reorganization of government and in state religious observances, he accepted the traditional Confucian bureaucratic organization, and he adopted the T'ang legal code. All this was done to ensure the creation of a Confucian self-perpetuating bureaucracy.

However, a major innovation in central government was initiated by the Hung-wu emperor. The office of Prime Minister was abolished and replaced by a cabinet, the Grand Secretariat or *nei-ko*. The reason seems to have been the desire of the emperor for greater direct power. It was he, of course, who stood at the top of the administrative system of the country, which had been divided into 15 provinces, and he was aided by the Grand Secretariat, his cabinet, which in turn relied upon the work of the six ministries. These, too, were reorganized, so that instead of the four ministries of the Mongol period (finance, justice, war, and rites), China was now administered by six boards (revenue, war, justice, rites, public works, civil office). Incidentally, as will be noticed, in the Ming administrative system there was no special office to deal with foreign affairs. These were under the Board of Ceremonies (Rites). In addition to his ministers, the emperor relied upon the reports of the Censors, who were responsible directly to him.

Below the level of the central government was the provincial government, responsible for the country's fifteen provinces. Here the Ming insisted that all governors and magistrates always serve outside their native provinces; and they furthermore instituted a system of rotation designed to prevent the evils of nepotism. The key to the entire system of Ming internal administration, however, could be found in the district government below the provincial level. It was the district magistrate, both an administrative and judicial officer, who represented government to the vast majority of the Chinese, and who kept the central government in touch with the masses. One of his many duties was to avoid concealment of unpleasant truths, and he was ordered to report all disasters, such as floods, or drought, to his superiors. To aid him in his task of ruling a district the Ming instituted a system of mutual responsibility among the village elders and representatives of family groups designed to maintain law and order. This was a system known as the *li-chia* in which certain elders were appointed to supervise village communities, and neighborhood units were created to impose collective responsibility.

Simplicity was characteristic of Ming internal administration. The Hung-wu emperor described himself, in a letter to a Byzantine merchant, as a simple peasant addicted to the idea of saving his people, and there was considerable truth in this assertion. He managed greatly to strengthen the Ming government, not only by the simplicity of his own reign, but also by the simplicity of his internal measures, and the direct appeal to the Chinese people made in the pious injunctions and maxims which he promulgated to his subjects, one of which merely stated: "Do no evil." Although most Chinese, as always, were primarily concerned with having as little as possible in the way of government, the restoration of a simple, traditional Confucian system of government no doubt contributed to the strength of the dynasty.

As already indicated, the Ming adopted most of their internal administration from past dynasties, the T'ang and the Sung, but, if anything, this adoption of past ways was marked by increasing emphasis upon tradition. Civil service examinations were restored, but they became increasingly inflexible, based exclusively on the five Classics and four books of the Confucian canon. Learning was revived, but it too became more conservative than ever. As a reaction against foreign influence this revived and newly strengthened Confucianism, with its new schools, its important ceremonies, and its rigid teachings of the Classics, had orthodoxy as its final aim, with precious little room or desire for any kind of novel interpretation. Despite the fact, however, that the Ming system of internal administration became increasingly traditional as time went on, which eventually resulted in a serious weakness to the state, it must be remembered that it did its work for a long period, and that it gave great prestige to government officials. In Ming China it was true, as it is not true in many modern countries and value schemes, that the best minds were in government, and the class of scholars commanded respect for its achievements.

ECONOMIC CONDITIONS. The early Ming period up to 1500 was one of considerable prosperity. Internal and external peace, of course, were major factors in this. Prosperity was evidenced by the presence of many gold and silver coins, the downward revision of taxation, and rapidly increasing trade, both domestic as well as foreign in the coastal provinces. Particular attention was paid by the government to improvements in communications, resulting in the construction of paved highways, the dredging of river channels, and the creation of imperial commissions to inspect and improve waterways. Many reservoirs and irrigation canals were constructed to maintain adequate supplies of water for times of drought, dikes to prevent floods were built, and public granaries were established in many parts of the country to provide for needs in time of poor harvest. The Ming period also saw the opening of much waste land to agricultural production, the large-scale planting of mulberry trees for sericulture, and the large-scale production of cotton fiber and manufacture of cotton cloth by the middle of the fifteenth century. The Ming government was interested in the economic welfare of its subjects. It paid attention to a reform movement which attempted to combine tax and labor payments ("single-whip" system), while the army was employed in transporting tribute rice to Peking in the north, thereby reducing the burden of taxation. As a whole, Ming China up to 1500 presents a picture of considerable economic well-being, in striking contrast to the declining years of Mongol rule in the preceding century.

Ming Culture

As might be expected of a society which looked toward the past and the glories of the T'ang and Sung period, the Ming was essentially not an age of creativity

FIGURE 23.1. The Temple of Heaven, Peking. Three times a year the emperor would carry out the ceremonial sacrifices—at winter solstice, the first moon, and at the beginning of spring. The use of the number three is reflected in the architecture itself. The temple was completed by the Yung-lo emperor.

or originality; rather it was an age of tradition and refinement, in which a society of Confucian scholars, recently returned to power, was primarily concerned with imitating, interpreting, and standardizing traditional styles, whether in thought, art, or literature.

PHILOSOPHY. In no field was this more true than in philosophy. Ming philosophy was Sung Neo-Confucianism, in which the teachings of Chu Hsi were triumphant. His works were accepted by the thinkers of the Ming dogmatically, and what little interpretation there was, was of the most conservative kind. Chinese philosophy entered a period of considerable sterility, characterized by distrust of any kind of speculation and dislike of any kind of novelty. The supremacy of a conservative class of scholars brought with it orthodoxy and conventionality, in which there was no inquiry, but rather the rigid acceptance of stereotyped learning. Hand in hand with this went emphasis on form and perfect style, and although this encouraged mental discipline, it mitigated against original thinking. Distrust of speculation, dogmatism, and orthodoxy were the aims of Ming intellectual life, and in this, a moral machine in which conformity was deified, lay, of course, a great danger.

Some minor reorganization of the Confucian cult took place during the Yung-lo period when tablets were substituted for images in honor of Confucius. As part of the state cult of Confucianism the Yung-lo emperor in 1420 built in Peking a splendid hall for the joint sacrifice to heaven and earth. During his reign the teachings of Chu Hsi, the great Sung metaphysician, also were condensed to become the basis of all education in the form of the "great philosophy." This became the sole source for the examination system, and all questions were rigidly based upon classical themes. Here again, in the grading of test papers, the examiners looked above all for a traditional treatment of the theme, for elegance of style, and perfection of form, but they discriminated against any original interpretation of the question by any candidate. As one Ming writer put it: "Ever since the time of the philosopher Chu, the truth has been made manifest to the world. No more writing is needed: What is left to us is practice."

Nevertheless, in this picture of conventionality and tradition, there was one major exception, and a major independent thinker—Wang Yang-ming. Born in 1472 in Chekiang, he had become an important Confucian official. However, as the result of a quarrel with a powerful eunuch at the court, Wang Yang-ming was transferred into exile to southwest China. There he lost most of the books in his library and concluded, quite sensibly given his circumstances, that books were not really necessary for a thinker. Instead he argued for a return to the subjective study of the mind, stating that it was not reason, ideology, nor style, that was important, but rather intuition. Greatly influenced by the teachings of Zen Buddhism and Taoism, Wang Yang-ming thus stood in opposition to Chu Hsi by declaring that man's nature was intuitively good and that "our share in the cosmic order, in universal law, lies in the heart rather than in reason." He believed in sudden illumination and the finding of truth within one's self, since it was in one's intuition that moral law could be encountered. "Throughout time and space the intuitive knowledge in the human heart never varies." Thus Wang Yang-ming taught a monistic idealism, opposing abstract speculation, and he stood for self-discipline and ethical living which alone could save society. "In the heart of each and every man there lives a Confucius." It will be noted that the philosophy of Wang Yang-ming was, in a sense, as practical as that of classical Neo-Confucianism; it too was concerned with the problem of society. Thus, though in Chinese thought during the Ming answers might differ, there was no breaking out of a cycle which had begun during the golden age of Chinese philosophy, the late Chou. In this sense Wang Yang-ming too lacked originality, and what he did was to fall back and invoke the known replies to orthodoxy, those of the Taoist creed and Buddhist intuitive philosophy.

The teachings of Wang Yang-ming, who died in 1528, were not much esteemed in China during his lifetime, and he was held unorthodox, but his ideas later on were to have great vogue in Japan where the philosophy of Wang Yang-ming became known as that of O-yo-mei and became most influential. Apart from him, Chinese philosophy did not offer much else during the Ming, being primarily interested in the question of ethical living, and even orthodox Neo-Confucian standards declined after the middle of the fifteenth century.

As far as Buddhism and Taoism were concerned, these remained as a whole rather popular, despite official neglect and occasional official restrictions. The Hung-wu emperor, for instance, had a retinue of Buddhist monks some of whom were appointed tutors to his sons, but he did not hesitate to restrict the number of Buddhist monasteries in China, and to execute some unfortunate officials who had dared to protest this move. The Yung-lo emperor also was much interested in Buddhism, personally favoring the Buddhism of Tibet. In 1403 he invited Tsongkapa in person to come to Peking, although the great reformer politely declined. On the other hand, the emperor showed no hesitation whatever in curbing the growth of the religion, and he at one time commanded that 1,800 young men who wanted to be monks be enrolled in the army instead.

LITERATURE. In a sense, literature mirrored as much the prevailing intellectual climate of the Ming period as did philosophy. Again, it was a period of little originality, but one of much activity and large output, and again there were some exceptions to that rule so that in some branches there were produced works of inspiration and great brilliance. The Ming period is first of all characterized by the creation of great compilation and great library collections, made possible by the vast amount of printing which was done both by the government and privately. Among these sober and somewhat unimaginitive works of compilation the first place must go to the *Yung-lo ta-tien,* a huge encyclopedia and thesaurus, containing all knowledge of the Chinese up to 1400. This enormous work, which the emperor ordered in 1403, took some five years for completion, was the work of some 3,000 scholars, and since its 11,000 volumes of 22,877 chapters were far too expensive to be printed it remained only as a manuscript. Perhaps, as has been argued, the Yung-lo emperor saw the usefulness of such work in keeping the scholars continually busy and winning their support for his usurpation of the throne. There were also compiled, in addition to the *Yung-lo ta-tien,* similar works in the field of history, geography, botany, ethics, medicine, and pharmacology. All of these reference works were characterized by a passionate regard for detail and exact information, and they all shared more or less the same quality of diligence coupled with mediocrity. Among these many treatises on agriculture, law, and medicine, perhaps the most interesting one was a great medical encyclopedia, published in 1578, which listed some 2,000 known drugs and gave 8160 prescriptions. It knew inoculation to prevent smallpox, and already listed a treatment for syphilis, a new disease to China, which had been introduced apparently by the Portuguese. The quality of printing of these reference works, and dictionaries which were also published, was uniformly excellent, and their color woodcut illustrations were of an equally high standard.

The exceptions that break the prevailing rule of mediocrity of Ming literature took place in the fields of the novel and the play, where originality and freshness were encountered. Ming plays employed more characters, more singing parts, and as a rule were much longer than were the plays of the Mongol period, and through the Ming Chinese theater continued to flourish and to improve. But it was particularly in the field of the prose novel, employing the actual speech of the people or *pai hua,* that Ming writing attained real excellence. The novel was considered outside the Confucian realm, never quite proper, and at the most an entertainment for moments of relaxation, and thus it was free to develop along fresh and new, unfettered lines. The Ming period produced some fine travel diaries, such as the one written by Hsü Hsia-k'o, who wrote detailed descriptions of his travels throughout the empire and added to the geographical knowledge of the country, particularly of the southwest where he determined the source of the West river, and showed that the Mekong and Salween were separate streams. Above all the Ming novel glories in historical tales and romances, stories of adventure and of love affairs. Among the masterpieces of the novel produced during the Ming was a very popular novel called *Shui-hu-chuan* or *All Men Are Brothers* as translated by the American writer Pearl Buck, the theme of which dealt with an outlaw band and whose heroes are bandits. A kind of harbinger of social revolution, the *Shui-hu-chuan* portrays these men as honorable, courageous, and loyal, and their opponents, the Confucian officials, as unjust, vile, and greedy creatures. However, whereas the Ming novel excelled, Ming poetry was dismal. A great amount was produced, all of it inferior and academic in the worst meaning of the term.

PAINTING.   In moving from literature to a discussion of Ming art, again the same pattern exists. Here, too, the Ming by and large was mostly inferior in its quality to what the Sung had produced, but again an exception must be made in the field of architecture and of applied arts. As far as painting is concerned, the Ming period definitely was inferior to the glorious epoch of the Sung painters. Ming painters mostly imitated Sung tradition, and were unoriginal. Ming painters were perfect masters of technique, but their products suffered from academic artificiality, ornateness, the search for the pretty, and general conventionality. Occasionally there were new techniques in painting in watercolors, where greater use was made of landscapes and figures. Occasionally, too, there was great refinement, elegance, and grace, and many of the bird and flower paintings possess great decorative qualities, but there is little that is absolutely first rate. Instead, in painting, just as in literature, there was a great deal of interest in criticism, and there was the same tendency to compile encyclopedias which would contain all that was known by looking back towards past masters. This interest in theory of painting and the codification of rules of the art led to the writing of the most famous of these encyclopedias, the *Mustard Seed Garden,* which attempted, by studying the qualities of the Sung, to establish permanent rules of painting. Sculpture, one might add, shared the fate of painting. Here too there was much production, but most of it of an inferior quality, particularly in religious sculpture where there was little genuine religious sentiment. On the other hand, some pieces of secular sculpture were of much better quality.

FIGURE 23.2. Landscape by Ch'en Shih. New techniques are effectively employed in the painting of this fantastic mountain and the clumps of trees that lead the eye into the distance.

FIGURE 23.3. Mountain landscape by Chiu-ying, late Ming period. Unsurpassed craftsmanship has been substituted for the idealism of Sung painting. The power of seeing in details the whole of the cosmos has declined greatly.

ARCHITECTURE. Turning now to the fields of art in which the Ming period did excel, architecture and the applied arts, one encounters very high standards and excellence of production. The Ming period was one of great building and the city of Peking is virtually a Ming creation. The Ming emperors used the old site of Kublai Khan's Khanbalig and, indirectly, adopted the rectangular city lay-out

FIGURE 23.4. "Judge of Hell," a Ming statue.

of Ch'ang-an to produce a capital of huge size, traditional monumentality, and, due to its absolute symmetry, of great appeal to the eye. Within the rectangular enclosure, the city contained a harmonious grouping of gates, grand courtyards, bridges, temples, shrines, and memorial arches. Three gates, one each to the south, east and west opened into those courtyards which contained official buildings, such as the halls of audience, accessible to ministers and officials and in which were conducted official ceremonies and functions. The fourth gate, that to the north, led into the private part of the palace, the "Purple Forbidden City," essentially the palace of the Yung-lo emperor, which was composed of a maze of courtyards, gardens, and alleyways for domestic convenience, and which gave a more intimate feeling than did the grandiose and symmetrical official halls and gateways. The whole magnificent succession of palaces, marble terraces, throne rooms, gardens, lakes, and artificial hills, all surrounded and defended by a crenellated wall and a wide moat, was designed to impress the visitor with the power and the splendor of the Son of Heaven. The Temple of Heaven, completed in 1420, the Temple of Agriculture finished four years later, and the Forbidden City itself, were all built during the reign of the Yung-lo emperor, and they were oriented along astronomical principles in order to reflect his splendor just as the pole star reflects the center of the world. The grace and strength of the architectural lines, and the lavish use of colored porcelain tiles make Peking today one of the most distinctive and beautiful cities in the world. Architecture of a similar high quality was also in various independent buildings, such as Buddhist pagodas.

FIGURE 23.5. A Ming Buddhist pagoda on the outskirts of Peking.

APPLIED ARTS. In the field of applied arts the Ming period produced excellent work in cloisonné and damascene (introduced into China from the west during the Yuan), fine rugs and carpets, magnificent woven silk, both plain and brocaded, and it also saw the manufacture of exquisite articles in jade, bronze, and lacquer, the last indicating Persian influence. The outstanding art form of the period, however, was porcelain. Ceramics were not new to China, and they had become a great art during the Sung period, but the Ming introduced polychrome, which, superseding monochrome, produced effects of great richness, delicate shading, and subtle harmonies. The use of many glazes and enamels, and the combination of colors permitted a variety of pictorial design adding to the subtle simplicity and spiritualization of matter which had already been attained in Sung monochrome ceramics. Blues in particular, both cobalt and the so-called Muhammadan blue, were strikingly employed. The combination of blue scenes and white background are the outstanding combination among Ming polychromes, but to these two colors soon came to be added porcelain in three colors, green-yellow-aubergine, and finally even five colors by the addition of red and another blue. These colors were employed in bold juxtaposition, with glowing tones, and they contributed to a ceramic art which excelled not only by the beauty of its painted decorations, but also by its texture, its lustre, the resonance of its thin shell, which gave forth a musical ring, and its brilliance. The chief center of Ming ceramic production was Ching-te-chen in Kiangsi province, where a white clay was present, kaolin, which could resist high temperatures, thus permitting the addition of a number of glazes. From the kilns of Ching-te-chen came forth a great variety of forms, vases, ewers, and figurines, and the ceramic art of the Ming period soon became a major export article, reaching Korea, Japan, Annam, and Europe. The spread of Ming art abroad was especially important in Europe, where Chinese porcelain was copied, and in Korea, where most of that country's architecture, and even costume, was based on Ming styles.

In summarizing the Ming period in Chinese history up to 1500 one can describe its essential features as those of efficiency and practicality. It was a period politically inferior to either Han or T'ang, and culturally to either T'ang or Sung, but it nevertheless gave unity and internal peace to China. The Ming rulers were masters of China proper. They successfully interfered only temporarily among the Mongols and in the time of the Yung-lo emperor were forced to acknowledge the independent status of Vietnam. To the south, Ceylon was temporarily subdued. Korea and Japan voluntarily acknowledged Chinese suzerainty, but the later Ming had to cope with the serious menace of Japanese piracy. Ming government was a well-balanced structure, and its culture produced masterpieces of architecture and of applied arts. Wealthy, peaceful, prosperous, populous, and elegant are adjectives sometimes applied to the Ming, and with reason, but against these achievements there must be balanced the increasingly traditional and conservative nature of its times, frowning upon originality and creativity in thought, literature, and many art forms. Distrust of any form of innovation or experimentation, and the increasing sterility of the intellectual climate of the Ming period were serious danger signs by 1500, indicating essential weaknesses of the structure. By 1450 the zenith of the Ming period had clearly been passed.

China in the Sixteenth Century

COURT AND ADMINISTRATION. The Ming state in the sixteenth century was very weak. The strong rulers of the Chu family of the late fourteenth and early fifteenth centuries had given way to a line of weak emperors secluded in their palaces at Peking. During most of the sixteenth century, the tenth, eleventh, and twelfth rulers of the Ming line (1506–1572) were on the throne. In 1573 began the famous Wan-li reign period. The government was actually in the hands of a bureaucracy of scholar-officials recruited by literary examinations. This bureaucracy worked well as long as the system was honestly conducted. However, court factions, especially a powerful group of eunuchs, gained excessive power during this century. By the end of the century, as we shall see, local rebellious forces were a menace to the authority of the Ming, secret societies became powerful, and the coasts were harassed by Chinese and Japanese pirates.

THE LAND FRONTIERS

Aggressive Mongol Power. In the fifteenth, sixteenth, and early seventeenth centuries, the Ming faced the aggressive power of the Mongols of the Mongolian homeland. There was constant threat of invasion in the fifteenth century, and the period ended with the temporary unity of the Mongols under a leader named Dayan (about 1470-1543). This Mongol leader of the line of Chingis Khan conquered the Oirats, who had been powerful earlier. At the end of his reign he divided his territory among his sons and grandsons, and the Mongols soon split up principally among the Chahar to the south and a group of five khanates of Khalkha Mongols in the north.

Among the most important leaders of the Mongols in the early sixteenth century was Altan Khan in Inner Mongolia and northern Shansi. He was the ruler of the Ordos Tümed Mongols and resided north of Shansi province. From his base there he waged continual warfare against China from 1529 to 1550. He invaded Shansi as far as the center of the province, he came down and burned the suburbs of Peking, and there was no peace until 1571. Meanwhile Altan Khan and other Mongol leaders had been influenced by the Buddhism of the Tibetan Yellow Sect.

Mongols Turn to Yellow Sect of Tibetan Buddhism. Altan Khan was only one of the more prominent who turned to Tibetan Buddhism at this time (see Chapter 23 for earlier developments in Tibet). The Mongols, first in Inner Mongolia and later in Outer Mongolia, formed a close alliance with the Tibetan Buddhist leaders. Altan Khan was especially active in these relations. He called the third Grand Lama of the Yellow Sect to preside at a diet, a great meeting at Kokonor, and proclaimed this Grand Lama to be the Dalai-lama (universal lama) among those who looked to the Yellow Sect as the true form of Buddhism. Altan Khan had previously proclaimed the teaching of the Yellow Sect to be the official religion of his people.

Later when the first Dalai-lama died, his successor was found among the descendants of Altan Khan. At the same time, among the Khalkhas of Outer Mongolia the Mongols were organized into religious groups whose principal Buddhist leader was at Urga. He was regarded as the incarnation of Maitreya and was given the title of "Hutuktu," translated as "Living Buddha." The Hutuktu at Urga exercised powers similar to his Tibetan prototype. During the early years of the seventeenth century the Kalmuk Mongols of the west were also converted to the Yellow Sect and later were engaged in active intervention in Tibetan affairs (1639 and later).

The Manchus to 1618. On the Ming northeastern frontier the Manchus rose to pre-eminence in what is now known as Manchuria. This tribe was a Tungusic people related to the old Jurchen, who had ruled as the Chin dynasty in China in the twelfth and thirteenth centuries. The center of their authority was in the basin of the upper Sungari river. They were forest dwellers both at the edge of Chinese culture and also at the edge of the steppe region. In the fifteenth century they began to harry the borders of China and Korea. After 1450, the Koreans established a no-man's-land northwest of the Yalu river, an uninhabited strip which served as a defense for more than a century.

By the middle of the sixteenth century a strong leader named Nurhachu controlled the Manchus (1559-1626) from Kirin, in the basin of the upper Sungari. Nurhachu's success was due partly to the weakness of the Ming and of the Mongols during this period; it was also due to his personal position. He was a minor aristocrat, who understood the tribal social and political peculiarities not only of the forest and steppe people nearby but of the Chinese of southern Manchuria, near his own home.

Nurhachu started as a small-scale raider in 1583. In the years following he gained control of some of all the three parts of Manchuria: the Chinese-inhabited territory, the land of the forest tribes, and the steppe-fringe tribes. He united successfully a number of tribes in one khanate by about 1606. Some of the East Mongol tribes allied themselves to the Manchus, partly as a means of protecting themselves against the Chahar Mongols further west. Nurhachu took the title of "Khan" in 1616 and declared himself completely independent of the Ming in 1618. Thus while his rise to power falls within the sixteenth century, the effect of his new position in Manchuria is part of the story of the seventeenth century, and will be recounted in Volume II.

Korea, Sixteenth Century.   Korea during this period was a loyal vassal of the Ming. The start of the sixteenth century included a reign, that of the eleventh ruler of the Yi dynasty, which has come to be known as the "Golden Age" of Korean morals. The king, who reigned from 1507 to 1544, was an active reformer, who turned to Confucianist ideals and attempted to increase the prosperity of the common people. The army was reorganized, although this was a period of peace. Buddhism declined to its lowest degree of influence in Korean history. In 1512 a great copper Buddha was broken up to be used for new arms for the soldiers. The king was greatly influenced by Confucian scholars. Buddhism and sorcery were considered useless.

China had definitely ended any policy of intervention in Mongol affairs. Instead the Chinese had to deal with aggressive forces from the steppe. A symbol of the defensive action taken by the Ming government was the reconstruction of the Great Wall of China, a line of defense against possible attackers from the north. In spite of being on the defensive, the Ming had great prestige and the peoples of Korea and Vietnam looked to Ming China as their suzerain. In this role the Ming government sent armed forces to aid the Koreans against the Japanese in the last decade of the sixteenth century. This brings us to consideration of China's sea frontier during the late Ming period.

THE SEA FRONTIER.   In Chinese history the sea frontier was relatively unimportant until about the sixteenth century. In spite of pirate raids there never
was any serious threat of invasion, and consequently a rather weak, conservative attitude prevailed in the central government which was reflected in the
conditions along the coast. There had been exceptions as we have seen, in
the early Ming times in the beginning of the fifteenth century. But after the
1430's the Ming government abandoned its interest in the South China Sea,
and the Arabs held a dominant position in the important spice trade of Southeast Asia. Pirates along the Chinese coast took advantage of this situation.
Dissatisfied Chinese as well as Japanese were among the pirates who harassed
the towns and ports of the southeast China coast. They raided Chekiang province
in about 1523 and 1552; they were at the mouth of the Yangtze river in 1555;
they raided Fukien in 1563, and even as far south as Hainan island in the
following years. The imperial forces of the Ming did not aid the local authorities except as a last resort. According to their policy of timid conservatism
a law was passed forbidding Chinese subjects to go abroad under pain of
death. Actually this law was not enforced and there was trade between the
Chinese along the coast and the peoples nearby, with Chinese merchants going
in their own ships to Manila and to Indo-China.

Ming Relations with Japan.   After the Japanese military dictator Hideyoshi
had unified Japan in 1590 he found many pirates and other Japanese who
were used to going to sea available to him in assembling a force large enough
to make an attack on China. Hideyoshi asked permission of the Yi government to cross Korea in 1591. Permission was refused and the Japanese attacked in 1592. They overran Korea until the arrival of the Ming army, which
forced the Japanese to retreat to the southern end of the peninsula at Pusan.
A second expedition was launched by Hideyoshi in 1597 to 1598 ending in a
siege of the Japanese forces at Yolsan in southern Korea and the death of
Hideyoshi in 1598. Thus Ming forces had come to the aid of the Koreans in
repulsing Japanese invasion. Actually, the Japanese called off the invasion
attempt after the second campaign and the death of Hideyoshi, and Tokugawa
Ieyasu renounced his claim to Korea and made peace with the Ming in 1607.

Portuguese and the China Trade.   There was a new factor in Ming international relations in the sixteenth century due to European expansion. The
Portuguese were the first Europeans to reach China by sea. The Chinese already were trading at that time with Siam, Cambodia, and Sumatra, in spite
of the Ming restriction against going overseas, but the Portuguese were newcomers in the situation when they took Malacca in 1511. As previously mentioned in Chapter 15, there was a Chinese vassal, a Moslem sultan, at Malacca
at that time. The first Portuguese ships came to Canton in 1514 and 1516,
and returned in the following years. A Portuguese embassy went from the coast
to the Chinese court at Peking in 1517. The man who led this embassy was

tactful, but two years later another Portuguese succeeded in thoroughly
antagonizing the Chinese. He built a fort on the south China coast, restricted
trade, robbed other ships, and kidnapped Chinese children. His arrogance and
improper language to the Chinese court gained the hostility of the Chinese
officials. The Portuguese were expelled from the vicinity of Canton after a fierce
battle in 1523, and Canton was closed to all foreign traders. Some smuggling
continued, however.

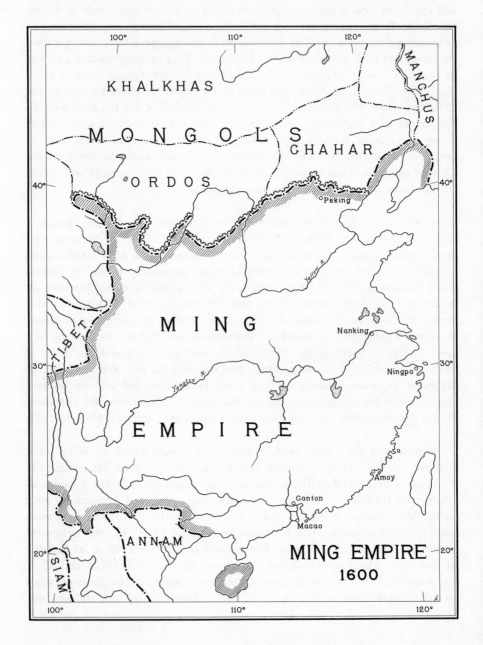

Canton was reopened in 1530, although the Portuguese were not allowed to trade at this time. It was not until 1557, after the Portuguese had assisted the Ming government against pirates along the coast, that they were permitted to build at Macao a little settlement on a tiny peninsula in the southern part of the Canton delta, where they lived under careful supervision and were allowed to manage their own affairs. This arrangement had very little effect among the Chinese at that time; however, it was important for the Portuguese and for all who would trade with that part of the world.

The Portuguese monopolized the trade with China, controlling the sea routes to Japan, Southeast Asia, India, and Europe. The Chinese were somewhat apprehensive about this, but due to the weakness of their government they did nothing to check the Portuguese monopoly. The most flourishing period of Portuguese trade was the last twenty years of the sixteenth century. As noted in an earlier chapter, the Portuguese greatness declined towards the end of the sixteenth century.

Jesuits in China. As noted in connection with the Portuguese advance elsewhere, the Roman Catholic Jesuit order came with the Portuguese at the time of their expansion into South and Southeast Asia and on to China and Japan. One of the original group of Jesuits, Francis Xavier, came to Japan in 1549 and to China in 1552. The Italian, Matteo Ricci, came to Macao in 1582 and was in China from that time until 1610. He gained the intellectual respect of the Chinese upper class and made many converts by the end of the century. Relations with Europe by sea had commenced.

MING GOVERNMENT IN THE WAN-LI PERIOD (reign, 1573–1620). The Wan-li emperor was educated under the influence of women and eunuchs of the palace, and all government during his time was in the hands of eunuchs. In spite of this, an outstanding Chinese scholar, Chang Chu-cheng, who became Grand Secretary at the court in 1567, gained extraordinary power and managed the Ming government in such a way that it continued for several decades longer. Chang emphasized economy and a balanced budget, chose able subordinates, and remeasured the arable land and thus increased the land tax receipts. The emperor at the start of his reign was a mere boy and Chang impressed on him a love of the people, fair treatment of his ministers, as well as a spirit of economy. Thus for many years in the 1570's and 1580's there was peace and prosperity in China. Chang Chu-cheng raised the position of the emperor and centralized the government. He would not allow criticism by the censors and was said to have "harried his opponents remorselessly."

After the death of Chang in 1582, the emperor was more experienced in ruling but at the same time he was surrounded by eunuchs who encouraged him to indulge in extravagance and sensualism. Those who criticized the changes in government policy, including a famous judge who accused the emperor of excesses in 1590, were punished as a result of their temerity. By the end of the century extravagance and corruption characterized the government of the Ming. Special taxes were collected by the eunuchs. Half the government offices were left vacant, memorials were not answered, and scholars who protested were executed.

At the beginning of the seventeenth century all government business was handled through the eunuchs. Dissatisfaction increased in the empire, and an attempt was made on the life of the heir apparent in 1615. By this time secret societies with a politico-religious ideology were among the groups stirring up rebellion against the government.

In spite of its weaknesses, Ming China in the sixteenth century was still a great power and the center of the Far Eastern world. Men in the surrounding countries looked to the Chinese because of the traditions and prestige of the past and also because of the high degree of culture which continued in a time of political deterioration.

BASIC DATES

1328–1398	Chu Yuan-chang
1356	Chu's rule established in lower Yangtze valley
1357–1419	Tsongkapa
1368	Seizure of Khanbalig, proclamation of Ming dynasty
1368–1398	Hung-wu emperor
1388	Ming suzerainty extended into Mongolia
1392	Yi Syeng-kyei established Yi dynasty in Korea
1392	Ming suzerainty extended into Korea
1398–1403	Civil war
1403–1424	Yung-lo emperor
1403–1431	Voyages of Cheng Ho
1406–1428	Occupation of Vietnam
1449	Mongols capture Ming emperor
1472–1528	Wang Yang-ming
1539–1626	Nurhachu in Manchuria
1557	Portuguese establish settlement of Macao
1573–1620	Wan Li emperor

SUPPLEMENTARY READING

FUNG YU-LAN. *A Short History of Chinese Philosophy*. New York, 1948.
GROUSSET, R. *The Rise and Splendor of the Chinese Empire*. Berkeley, Cal., 1953.
HUDSON, G. F. *Europe and China*. London, 1931. Excellent chapter on the Ming period.
LATOURETTE, K. S. *The Chinese: Their History and Culture*. New York, 1946.
REISCHAUER, E. O. AND J. K. FAIRBANK. *East Asia: The Great Tradition*. Boston, 1958.
WANG, Y. T. *Official Relations between China and Japan, 1368–1549*. Cambridge, Mass., 1953.

ADVANCED READING

BACKHOUSE, E. AND J. O. P. BLAND. *Annals and Memoirs of the Court of Peking.* Boston, 1914.

BOXER, C. R., ED. *South China in the Sixteenth Century. Being the Narratives of Galeote Pereira, Fr. Gaspar da Cruz, O.P., and Fr. Martin de Rada, O.E.S.A.* London, 1953.

BUCK, P., TR. *All Men Are Brothers.* New York, 1957. Translation of a famous Ming novel.

CHANG T'IEN-TSE. *Sino-Portuguese Trade from 1514 to 1644: A Synthesis of Portuguese and Chinese Sources.* Leiden, 1935.

GALLAGHER, L. J., TR. *China in the Sixteenth Century: The Journals of Matthew Ricci, 1583–1610.* New York, 1953.

GRIFFIS, W. E. *Corea, the Hermit Nation.* New York, 1911.

HOBSON, R. L. *The Wares of the Ming.* London, 1923. Authoritative account of Ming ceramic art.

HUCKER, C. O. *The Traditional Chinese State in Ming Times.* Tucson, 1961.

LATOURETTE, K. S. *A History of Christian Missions in China.* New York, 1929.

LATTIMORE, O. *Inner Asian Frontiers of China.* New York, 1951.

XXIV ✸✸✸

EARLY JAPAN

Geography

The geography of a country is something its people must live with throughout their history. It is particularly influential in the case of a country like Japan which has been confined by geography to certain narrow limits. Japan, except for a relatively brief period in the late nineteenth and early twentieth century, has been entirely, as the Japanese say, an "island country" (*shimaguni*). The Japanese use this term frequently even today to describe their homeland and to explain not only physical and economic problems of Japan, but even social and cultural attitudes as well. Certainly the fact that Japan has been an island country has been of overwhelming importance in Japanese history. It has allowed Japan to develop in comparative safety and at times isolation from outside influences. Probably the fact that Japan had never until 1945 been conquered by outsiders is attributable to its island situation off the coast of East Asia. It was, of course, close enough to the mainland of East Asia and to the vast and complex Chinese civilization which held sway there to be much influenced by China, but at the same time it remained separate enough never to be overwhelmed, and the Japanese were therefore able to work out cultural importations in their own way. The island situation also meant a certain degree of cultural retardation. The spread of ideas and techniques from the continent was slower than if there had been a land connection and Chinese inventions often reached Japan only after a time lag of several centuries. Thus the relatively isolated location may be said to have left the Japanese with a sense of being in charge of their own destiny, to have given them feelings of uniqueness and solidarity, and perhaps to have contributed to the persistence of early beliefs that they were different in kind from other peoples, set apart by the gods for some special mission.

Japan may be described as a "natural region," one in which the people are forced by nature and the geographical facts of life to participate in the same kind of economic activities, leading to a general homogeneity, to common practices and customs of all kinds, not only in the economic but in religious, social, political, and even literary and artistic facets of life. It is a "natural region" despite the fact that the country is divided into four main islands, and, of course, numerous smaller ones, and despite the fact that those islands are rugged and mountainous to an extent that would seem likely to foster a high degree of localism. However, plains along the coast are easily reached by sea and the construction of relatively short roads made possible easy contact between these plains. This was particularly true of the southern islands, namely Honshu, the largest of the Japanese islands, Kyushu, the southernmost, and Shikoku, the smallest of the three main islands, where in fact over 95 per cent of the population has lived up to recent times. Hokkaido, while an integral part of the Japanese island chain, was for centuries merely a frontier area, little populated and not integrated with the political and economic structure of the rest of the country. Even in 1940 it supported only 3.3 million of a total population of 73 million Japanese. However, the people of the populous three southern islands have been from very early times bound together by ties which developed out of similar economic activities. The climate, due to the famous Black Current which follows the eastern coast of Japan, has been relatively warm and most of the country has enjoyed heavy summer rainfall. This has led to the development of rice growing as the principal occupation of an agricultural people, and to the use of rice as the principal food staple. Hardly less important than rice growing as an economic activity has been fishing. Japan, though comparable only to California in area, has a coast line almost as long as the entire United States, and the Japanese from very early times have used the sea as a major source of food supply. Thus despite the fact that Japan is broken into numerous small areas by her mountains, the occupations of the valleys, rice growing, and of the seashore, fishing, have contributed to the solidarity of the Japanese people.

The mineral resources of Japan are meager. Even assuming maximum estimates on probable reserves her coal supply if mined at the American rate of coal mining would be used up in no more than fifteen years. Coal reserves, most of which are located in Hokkaido and in Kyushu, may approximate six billion metric tons. Also Japan has little oil and iron ore. Her largest mineral deposits are in gold, copper, and sulphur. There is also a fair supply of silver, lead, and tin. In general, however, vast quantities of minerals necessary to an industrialized nation must be imported. Probably Japan's greatest resource for power lies in her heavy rains and mountain streams which enabled her to develop hydroelectric power output second only to the United States and Canada in the pre-World War II period. Even in World War II when the Japanese made intensive efforts to develop their electric power system to the utmost they fell considerably short of realizing its full potential. Japan is also rich in forests. These vary from the tropical growth of southern Japan, which includes such valuable trees as the camphor tree, to the cold temperate forests of northern Hokkaido, mainly coniferous. There are many varieties of pine, oak, chestnut, and maple trees in Japan. Also, large numbers of mulberry trees are grown for the raising of silk worms.

Japan is mountainous from one end to the other, and one is rarely out of sight of mountains on the horizon. There is not a clear-cut arrangement of mountain chains although there is a high range paralleling the east coast and another paralleling the west coast. Many of the mountains are volcanic, the most famous of these being Mount Fuji, which is over 12,000 feet high and can be seen from Tokyo on a clear day. The mountains cut the country up in such a way that aside from the coastal plain there are no large plains areas except the famous Kanto plain which surrounds Tokyo and the Kansai plain of the Kyoto-Nagoya-Osaka area. These two plains have always supported a very large segment of the population of Japan. On these and the other smaller plains in the country are raised not only rice, the chief crop, but also wheat, tea, vegetables of all kinds, and a few other agricultural products. There is some grazing land, but the cattle supply is small.

Although the geography of Japan has in general been a limiting factor in Japanese life and development, one aspect of it, which may be described as a broadening aspect, should not be overlooked. There is breathtaking scenery in Japan, in every part of the country. The mountains may not be quite so high as the mountains in some parts of the world but arranged as they are, in limited space, with the sharp contrasts between mountain and valley, cliffs and sea shore, they are very beautiful. Furthermore, the change of seasons in Japan brings remarkable color contrasts. Perhaps this is not more so than in other parts of the world, but the Japanese people are extremely conscious of the beauties of nature, and extremely proud of them. The beauties of the season are a constant topic of conversation in Japan and their important place in the old language and literature attests that this has always been the case.

Creation Legends

The Japanese, like other peoples when they achieved a degree of civilization high enough to contemplate cosmic forces, devised their legends of the creation of the world, or more particularly of their own land. And like others they blended legend into history without clearly distinguishing between the two. The Japanese have been unusual perhaps in the tenacity with which they later refused to separate myth from fact and gods from emperors. Even in the last century, as searchlights of historical criticism and rational analysis relentlessly exposed what had passed for early "history" everywhere, and relegated much of it to the category of myth, the Japanese persisted in their blending of the two. There were political reasons for this in our era, indeed just as there were political reasons for the compilation in the eighth century A.D. of Japan's oldest written histories, the *Kojiki* (*Records of Ancient Matters*) and the *Nihongi* (*Chronicles of Japan*), which effectively combined legend and early fact. In both cases the cause of centralization of political power was served, the imperial throne exalted, and the people led to accept, for emotional and irrational reasons, whatever dictum came forth from the emperor, or from those who contrived to speak in his behalf. It is perhaps symbolic of the terrible price the Japanese have paid for this reverence to myth-history that it was a defeated, shattered, and occupied Japan, wherein, on New Year's Day, 1946, the Japanese emperor finally disclaimed the legends by denying that he was descended from the gods.

Although the legends of the creation of Japan and the founding of the Japanese state have served the cause of authoritarian government and imperialist expansion in our time, they are probably in themselves no better and no worse than the myths of origin of other peoples. To us they may seem poorer and cruder than those of Western Asia, impressed as we are with the development of the concept of one god and of a concern with the problem of good versus evil. But we should perhaps let their legends like ours speak for themselves.

The Japanese creation legend begins with Chaos, a mass like a raw egg, from which the purer, cleaner part is drawn out to become Heaven, the heavier, grosser element settling eventually to become earth. Meanwhile several generations of Heavenly Deities were "born alone" (spontaneously) and "hid their persons" (disappear) until finally there appeared two all-important deities, the August-Male-Who-Invites, Izanagi, and the August-Female-Who-Invites, Izanami. These two were commanded by all the existing Heavenly Deities to "make, consolidate and give birth to this drifting land" (Japan), and they were given a jeweled spear to help in the process. Standing on the "bridge of Heaven" the pair thrust the spear down into the "brine" (unsolidified earth) and stirred up a tiny islet, one of the Japanese group. They descended to this islet and there they set about producing the rest of the Japanese islands, one by one, and also numerous deities. The reproductive process by this time was no longer spontaneous, but the result of sexual relations between Izanagi and Izanami.

In all Izanagi and Izanami produced some fourteen islands and thirty-five deities, including sea deities, earth deities, wind deities, and at last the Fire God, whose birth cost Izanami her life. In giving birth to this Fire God she was burned so severely that she died, and went to the nether world. Izanagi, at once heartsick and furious, wept and sorrowed and brandished his sword unrestrainedly. He killed his offspring, the offending Fire God, but from the drops of blood, as well as from his own tears, tens of new deities were born. He then undertook a trip to the nether world to bring Izanami back, but horrified and sickened at the putrefaction he found there, he fled back to earth to purify his august person by bathing in water. More deities were born from every item of clothing he discarded, and even from the filth he washed from his body. Of these new deities Izanagi designated the Sun Goddess, who ascended immediately to Heaven, as the principal ruler of the universe.

Thereafter other deities played principal roles in a great number of stories of the doings of the gods, but in the end it was the Sun Goddess who resolved to settle affairs on the earth islands and who after some experimentation sent her grandson, Jimmu Tenno, the first emperor, to rule them, a god on earth. Some eight hundred myriad "other deities" were sent along to inhabit the land and become the ancestors of the Japanese people.

Having thus provided the background of Jimmu Tenno's accession to emperorship (660 B.C.), these earliest Japanese histories, compiled as we have seen in the eighth century A.D., then proceed to trace the imperial succession almost to their own time, sometimes embellishing the succession lists of emperors with stories about their reigns. Deities continued to mingle with princes, little distinction being made, and supernatural occurrences continued, but gradually reign periods became shorter, more like the lifetime of an average man, happenings became more believable and even began to tally more or less with contemporary records from China and Korea, and by perhaps the fourth or fifth century A.D. true historic times begin. But very important is the fact that there is no clear place at which myth ends and history begins. Rather the one merges with the other just as gods merge with men, so that in the twentieth century, as in the eighth, it was possible for Japan to claim unique origins and destiny, a country created by the gods and ruled over by one of their number in one line of succession from ages eternal.

For all their mixing of fact and legend, these early Japanese histories, when used critically and checked against archaeological evidence and notices of Japan in contemporary Chinese and Korean records, can help us to piece together the story of the beginnings of Japanese civilization.

Early Japanese History

Divested of deities and superstitions the story is something of the following. The Japanese islands seem to have been populated by several waves of immigrants, some from southern and some from northern Asia, all of whom may have been fleeing from technically more advanced peoples pressing upon them from further west. In the islands, a cul-de-sac of immigration, a mixing of strains occurred very early, although some members of one group, the Caucasoid Ainu, retained a separate identity, banded together, and in fact have never been completely assimilated. Century after century they were pushed farther to the north, until today they live as government wards on reservations in Hokkaido, though technically the Occupation freed them of any bondage.

Most of the immigrants, however, whether of Northern Mongoloid, Southern Mongoloid, or Malaysian stock, were amalgamated too early to trace them as distinct groups. In one obvious sense the southern strain predominated, for certainly the Japanese living and eating habits are south rather than north Asian.

The prehistoric inhabitants of Japan are better divided culturally than racially, and this division has been made most effectively on the basis of pottery patterns. The earliest pottery type, the Jomon or rope cord pattern, reveals a people already in the neolithic age. (Not much is known about the paleolithic age in Japan, for the first paleolithic finds were unearthed as recently as 1949 and few conclusions about them can as yet be made.) The neolithic Jomon period probably began as early as 7,500 B.C. and lasted until about the third century B.C. (see Chapter 2.)

When we remember that Jimmu Tenno, according to the earliest Japanese histories, by 660 B.C. was slaying his enemies, whether earth spiders or men, with *swords*, we see that indeed he must have got his weapons from heaven if he had them at all, for the Jomon culture could not produce them, and had he lived in 660 B.C., he would have been a part of that culture.

Metal implements came to Japan only after the development of a new type pottery, the Yayoi, named for a street in Tokyo where the type was first discovered. The Yayoi period begins about 100 B.C. and extends perhaps to A.D. 250. The pottery itself is characterized by kneading and plaiting of the clay rather than the rope-like twisting of Jomon. The earlier Yayoi sites yield, along with the pottery pieces, such items as stone tools, arrows, axes, spoons, doll-like statuettes, and bone needles, and the later ones all of these plus metal implements, especially iron. There seems to have been been no true bronze age in Japan, perhaps because the knowledge of metals was imported from continental Asia and the Japanese themselves did not have to proceed so slowly through copper and bronze into the iron stage as did, for instance, the people of Mesopotamia.

At any rate it is far more likely, both from an analysis of the chronological sequence as well as the state of the technology of his age, that Jimmu Tenno founded his empire in about 40 B.C. than in 660 B.C. Recent evidence also discredits the idea that Jimmu did more than weld together some of the tribes of Kyushu, where he and his successors seem to have remained until the fourth century A.D.

The year A.D. 391 is an important one, for it gives us the first precise date in Japanese history. That year ties together information from Chinese historical records, a north Korean monument, and the Japanese histories, with corrected chronology, to show that Korea had been subject to Japanese invasion or expansion from Kyushu, led by a Japanese empress, Jingo, in the fourth century. Thereafter, it seems, the conquest of Korea having failed, the Japanese from Kyushu expanded northward into the Japanese main island, Honshu, and established a center of government in the region known as the Yamato plain (Nara-Kyoto-Osaka area), where the headquarters of the imperial family remained, though at several different capitals, until 1867.

The warrior emperor who completed the establishment of this "greater Japan," Ojin, son of Jingo, has been deified as the war god Hachiman in the Japanese religious (Shinto) pantheon. And this constitutes religion with the logic of history in it, for the events of the fourth century, climaxed by the career of Ojin, brought to fruition the forging by conquest of an "imperial state," a process begun by Jimmu perhaps four centuries before.

THE NATURE OF EARLY JAPANESE SOCIETY.   This would seem a logical point, therefore, at which to discuss briefly the nature of this early Japanese "imperial state," before it was colored almost beyond recognition by the impact of a far more advanced Chinese civilization. The basic unit of political, social, and even religious organization was the clan (*uji*), whose members were linked by blood ties, used the clan name, obeyed the clan chieftain, appeased the clan god, and controlled the clan lands. The imperial clan had to exercise its authority indirectly through other clans. Indeed the imperial clan had at first been merely one clan among many, but it was the achievement of the early emperors that by the fifth century A.D. they could claim a certain ascendancy over the other clans and thus over the whole country, an ascendancy based on conquest, power, and superior ancestry. Religion helped them, for out of the chaos of innumerable nature deities and clan deities (anything that inspired awe was a deity to the early Japanese) the imperial clan was forging a certain order, associating itself with the supremacy of the Sun Goddess and possessing the imperial regalia, jewel, mirror, and sword, which tradition said had been handed down to it by that goddess.

Associated with and attached to the clans were guild-like institutions (*be* or *tomo*), bound together, not by blood ties, but by occupation or profession, which might range from teller of stories or performer of purification rituals to goldsmith or livery man or rice cultivator. The last profession seems to have been the most numerous be of all. The emperor appears to have been a principal creator of these specialized nonconsanguinous groups, and this fact worked to the advantage of the imperial over other clans. However, it is by no means clear or to be assumed that all the be or tomo were directly controlled by the imperial family, for many of them seem to have been of other clan or of private (nonclan) origin. Some, of course, were esteemed more than others, depending on the prestige of the occupation. Below these status groups were slaves. Membership in clan and guild alike was hereditary.

Within these larger groupings the family was the basic unit, though its conventions were much less definite than those we meet in later Japanese history. Generally the family was presided over in patriarchal fashion by the eldest male member, yet there still remained evidences of a once matriarchal society, where mother and brood even lived apart from a wandering spouse. Again generally, though by no means universally, a man had one wife, with perhaps many concubines if he were rich enough. Here too was much indefiniteness, and even in the imperial family there was great irregularity in matters of family priority, as evidenced by the accession to emperorship of other than first sons of empresses, and by the retirement before death of emperors themselves.

EARLY JAPANESE RELIGION. Religion, the native Shinto, involved the worship of multitudes of deities (*kami*), many of them nature deities, of a sort which indicates more a love and appreciation of nature's beauties than fear of its destructive powers. There is no flood story in Japanese mythology, nor is there any overpowering sense of sin or evil for which such a calamity should be punishment. The worst mythological calamity was the Sun Goddess' retirement into a cave in Heaven, due to anger at a brother god, which darkened the universe. Religious ceremonies, conducted by members of priest guilds (the most powerful being the Nakatomi, who had supposedly recited a liturgy to urge the Sun Goddess forth from her cave), were chiefly purification rituals which, as with Izanagi's bathing, were concerned with purification from uncleanness rather than sin. Such things as illness, menstruation, the birth process, and death were considered unclean. Indeed earlier tradition held that these events should not occur in the house, or if they did, that the house should be moved afterwards from the place of pollution. This sort of thinking helps to explain the frequent movings of the seat of the central government, for Japan had no permanent capital until A.D. 710. And, of course, the persistence with which the Japanese have clung to the tradition of the daily hot bath even in the most trying conditions is testimony to the Japanese determination to maintain personal cleanliness.

In addition to beauties of nature and purification early Shinto was concerned with fertility, especially as it affected rice production. Somehow the fox, perhaps as a frequent though mysterious visitor to rice fields, and rice itself became combined in the popular mind so that fox shrines as magical protectors of rice fields became one of the most commonplace religious manifestations of early Japan. And more generally, to the common people prayers for the harvest were surely as important a part of the Shinto priest's duties as the rituals of purification.

Such was the "imperial .ate" of Japan before the advent of Chinese civilization: a not so supreme emperor, whose power, however, was growing; clans, guilds, slaves, hereditary classes; proud, though disjointed creation myths; purification, nature worship, concern for fertility; a primitive agricultural economy with metal implements. But there was no money, no higher religion, no coherent philosophy, and perhaps most important of all no writing—thus nothing to give form and permanence to any of these institutions and beliefs.

Impact of Chinese Civilization and Taika Reform

Though all of these pre-Chinese elements worked to modify, and sometimes to distort it, Chinese civilization nevertheless greatly influenced historic Japan. The Korean peninsula, pointing, as Japanese nationalists said later, like a dagger toward southern Honshu and Kyushu, served as the natural bridge across which Chinese civilization invaded Japan. It was not a military invasion, for no Chinese soldiers touched the Japanese islands; it was an invasion of ideas and techniques, so far superior to anything known in Japan at the time that the Japanese, upon tasting the wonders of Chinese civilization, were soon not merely enthusiastically receiving what was brought to them but were sending emissaries to China to seek out the wonders at their source.

The vehicle of expression, the Chinese written language, was vitally important to the transmission of Chinese culture. Korean tutors were teaching Japanese students to write Chinese characters by the early fifth century A.D., and by the eighth century, in court circles at least, the measure of a man's worth was his ability in Chinese. Knowledge of the Chinese language, of course, was important in itself, but through it vistas undreamed of were opened to the Japanese, for in Chinese writings were expressed the vast experience and thought of China in matters political, historical, philosophical, and religious. The vast literature of Confucianism and Buddhism became known in Japan. For the emerging Japanese imperial clan, struggling to maintain and extend its political authority, the situation was pregnant with opportunity, yet also with disaster, for as the new enlightenment entered Japan the question of whose interests it should serve and whose it would endanger was a moot one.

In A.D. 552 the king of the Korean kingdom of Paekche posed the question of sponsorship of Chinese civilization in an acute form when he sent to the Japanese court gifts of Buddhist statuary and Buddhist scriptures. This gave rise to a great debate among the imperial advisors, the great clan leaders. Those clans which had a particular vested interest in the status quo, notably the Nakatomi, hereditary liturgists, and the Mononobe, hereditary guardsmen, were opposed to reverencing these alien importations, but the Soga, a less powerful, but increasingly influential clan, urged their acceptance upon the emperor.

Finally the emperor said: "Let it be given to Soga no Iname, who has shown his willingness to take it, and as an experiment, make him worship it."

The experiment was almost fatal for the imperial line, for in the years that followed the Soga clan prospered as the sponsors of Chinese civilization, won leading positions at court, intermarried with the imperial clan, overawed emperors, and very nearly, in the mid-seventh century, took over the throne of Japan.

Meanwhile, as court politics grew increasingly tense, Chinese civilization flowed in. This was especially true during the regency of the imperial prince, Shotoku Taishi, whose mother was a Soga, and who exercised the imperial authority through most of the reign of his aunt, Empress Suiko (593–628). Prince Shotoku, who was himself a master of Chinese studies, together with his Soga relatives and adherents were ardent champions of things Chinese. During his rule embassies were dispatched to China, both to open relations with the Sui court at Lo-yang and to study the Chinese governmental structure, as well as to bring back books and information on all phases of Chinese life. Shotoku was a devout Buddhist, but like the Sui rulers of China, he was quick to see the possibilities afforded by Confucian social and political ideals in stabilizing society and in bringing order and centralization to the political structure. Indeed his famous "Seventeen Injunctions" of 604 mix Buddhist and Confucian ideas in a remarkable way, exhorting officials to respect Buddhist law and Confucian filial piety, thus—and this of vital political importance—to revere the imperial command: "for in a country there are not two lords; the people have not two masters."

It is clear enough that Shotoku's principal political object was to bring the great prestige of Chinese civilization to the task of strengthening the imperial position in Japan, a position at the time controlled by himself and his Soga relatives. Unquestionably he had considerable success in this and certainly his efforts guaranteed the continued and accelerated importation of the trappings of Chinese civilization. However, Shotoku's death in 621 left still unsettled the question of supremacy at the Japanese court. The Soga family continued to dominate the scene, utilizing and setting aside puppet emperors, and by the early 640's it became clear that they were preparing themselves to assume the role of "imperial" family. In more and more obvious ways they took to themselves imperial prerogatives.

However, as would seem natural, resentment in some quarters crystallized against the Soga, and in a young and vigorous leader of the Nakatomi clan, Nakatomi (or Fujiwara) no Kamatari, the forces of the opposition found their leader. Nakatomi sought out the various imperial princes, one by one, until he discovered one Naka no Oye, and the two together plotted the undoing of the arrogant Soga. The plot came to a climax in 645 with a coup d'état in which Soga Iruka, leader of the Soga clan, was killed, and after which Kamatari and the young prince took over the government, though the prince himself did not become emperor for a number of years (668). These men initiated a remarkable series of reform measures, called the *Taika,* or Great Reform, by which they undertook to establish the imperial authority, through a centralization of administration, over the entire country. One might expect them to have led a reaction against the Chinese "enlightenment," since their Soga enemies had sponsored it, but they did not. In fact they took upon themselves the sponsorship of Chinese civilization, and the government structure which they sought to establish was clearly modeled after the great T'ang bureaucracy even down to the tassels on the caps of the officials. The Great Reform was not confined to the year 645. It began then with the appointment of two "National Doctors" (students lately returned from China) as consultants, and with certain measures aimed at undermining the independent authority of the clan chieftains; and it continued step by step until about A.D. 710 when with the establishment of the first permanent Japanese capital at Nara—a copy of T'ang China's greatest city, Ch'ang-an—there arose a Chinese-style imperial government of Japan in full bloom.

By that time a sophisticated and complex governmental structure had been fastened upon the country by the architects of Taika and their successors. How well it would work remained to be seen. And the Nara period, roughly the eighth century, may be regarded as a century of experimentation, during which the effort of Japanese court and capital to operate these Chinese forms was tested in the entire country, and by the end of which there were first indications that indigenous conditions and developments would eventually overturn the political structure, though the cultural, religious, and philosophic imprints would last even to the twentieth century.

Nara Japan

GOVERNMENT AND SOCIETY. The political framework of eighth-century Japan is best revealed in law codes of the ninth and tenth centuries. These were developed from a sort of parent code of the eighth century, the famous Taiho code of 702, which is no longer extant. This Taiho code was revised in 718 as the Yoro code, which, of course, is revealing also of the contents of the parent code. The Yoro code indicates clearly that, whereas the Japanese were following T'ang models to a large extent, they were also making modifications which seemed appropriate to conditions in Japan, and for these they relied sometimes on pre-T'ang, chiefly Han, models as well as on improvisations of their own.

The following description of the organization and operation of the Japanese government has been gleaned from this eighth-century law code and subsequent modifications made during the next three centuries while the Japanese were still seriously attempting to operate the central bureaucracy established by the Great Reform of 645.

Under the emperor the chief organ of government was the Dajokan, a Supreme Council of State, which consisted of a Dajo daijin or Chancellor, ministers of the Left and Right, and which directed the activities of eight executive departments. These included the Chinese-style Boards of Ceremonies (Rites), Civil Office, Treasury, Punishments, War, Home Affairs, and two peculiarly Japanese boards, Nakatsukasa-sho (Imperial Household) and Kunai-sho (Treasury of the Imperial Household). The addition of these last two boards serves to underscore the importance of the emperor, who continued to be regarded as a god on earth rather than, as with the Chinese emperor, a temporary adjudicator of Heaven's will, holding office on good behavior. There were two other important deviations from T'ang models in the central administration. These concerned the place of religion and education for office. The old presinification religious cults, now reordered about emperor worship and dignified in Chinese terminology as Shinto, the Way of the Gods, were represented at the highest level in the Jingikan (Council of Religion), a body theoretically standing on the same lofty level as the Dajokan. There was no comparable body in T'ang China.

On the matter of educating for office the Chinese placed great stress, and selection for position in the T'ang bureaucracy depended in great measure upon the candidate's success in examinations which tested his learning in the philosophy, the history, and the language of the empire. The Japanese paid lip service to this, and the Taika reformers even established a university to train bright young men for government service. But instead of developing a country-wide examination system to uncover talent wherever it might be found in Japanese society, the university and such provincial schools as developed became increasingly strongholds of the aristocracy. Thus family, not intellect, remained the key to office in Japan.

The provincial administration of Nara Japan was conducted under the authority of a provincial governor who was appointed by the emperor. He had a multitude of responsibilities. The provincial governor, by the eighth century, was almost certainly a man of high rank who would likely be a prince or the head of a lesser branch of a great court family. And, perhaps more often than not, as an elegant person, he was not seriously interested in provincial affairs. Pleased to receive the substantial income which came with his rank (24 acres), his office (perhaps five acres), and his "opportunities" for legal or extra legal shares of taxes collected, he nevertheless would be willing or anxious to leave the duties of administration to subordinates, chiefly the district governors, and himself spend as much time as possible at the capital.

The office of district governor thus became important in the Nara structure. This official, though an imperial appointee, would normally be a ranking member of a local clan, recommended by the governor as one competent to handle the problems of the area. Undoubtedly he could do this, for his district would include great numbers of his clansmen. He could also gather in the taxes, which as far as the central government was concerned became more and more the principal objective of the whole provincial administration. But efficient and locally influential as he was, there were signs, even in Nara times, that a district governor had opportunity to build an imperium of his own, especially as the appointments were often for life and tended to become hereditary.

The officialdom of the empire was in effect a closed hereditary aristocracy, inaccessible from below and, though in later Japanese history upstarts sometimes held political power, the families who comprised the Nara aristocracy have maintained their social position, together with accompanying wealth and influence, even into modern times. So tight indeed was the class structure that adoption by a family of higher rank became standard practice in those cases in which a man from below, whether through wealth or genius, pushed his way up in the hierarchy.

Beneath the carefully graded aristocracy were the common people. These also were divided into classes, the chief distinction being between "free" and "unfree," but there were further subdivisions within those two large categories;

for example, the "unfree" ranged from "serf" custodians of the imperial tombs, who by tradition had the job for life, to "private slaves" who could be bought and sold like chattel by their owners, except that "persons reaching the age of 76 shall be released and become free men."

The free commoners were mainly farmers. They were, temporarily at least, the beneficiaries of the redistribution of land which followed the emperor's claim to it all under the Taika reform edicts. Under the Taika system a free man received two tan (or 0.58 acres) of land, a woman two-thirds as much. Thus an entire family might possess as much as two or three acres. The basic unit of social organization was the household, or family, presided over by the head of the household, who might be an old man with several adult sons or, at the other extreme, a minor son, eldest of a deceased father, and this son would be chief of the household, even though there were adult uncles about.

The farmer, in return for his land allotment, of course undertook the burdens of tax—a tax on the land itself, a labor tax (road work, or other special service to the government for a specified number of days per year), and various produce taxes. The labor conscription, for that is what the labor tax amounted to, was always a curse to the farmer, for it took the able-bodied from the fields at critical times and the conscript himself often suffered intense hardship away from home, with insufficient rations even to starvation. The produce taxes were considerable, but whenever a man could escape the labor conscription by paying extra in produce or by paying a substitute, he seems to have done so. The land tax as such was not especially heavy, being generally under five per cent of the total yield.

GROWTH OF THE TAX-FREE ESTATE.   However, the tendency of the Nara period, in terms of land and tax, was toward the development of many large estates, which by one means or another became tax free. (*Shō* or *shōen* is the special Japanese term to describe "tax-free estate.") This came about as a result of the failure of the allotment, or rather reallotment system, because of the exercise of remarkable influence by certain individuals and institutions at court, and because of the frontier development policies of the government. These developments now require some explanation.

Originally the Taika land reform schedule called for reallotting the land after each five-year period in order to keep it in the hands of free farmers operating as individual or small family economic units. But, unfortunately for the system, these reallotments were not carried out. Thus successful land ac-quisitions by a family were piled up as a family domain generation after genera-tion, and those who lost land in the process became increasingly worse off. Furthermore, the larger the acquisitions of a family, and those who began the race with the benefit of high rank were naturally in a favored position, the more pressure it could bring at court to render those lands tax free. This was accomplished through a variety of means but they all amounted to special rewards or dispensations to court favorites.

Then, too, the government was anxious to push the area of cultivated land even farther toward the frontier, and it rewarded those who would undertake such reclamation with tax-free privileges for a period of years, but these tended to become permanent. Unfortunately this condition seems not to have resulted in a free, small farmer type of the frontier area, for the problem of security, particularly the security of the tax-free privilege, was dependent either upon connections at court or sufficient power and prestige to defy the government, either of which required the presence of a rich and powerful man as overlord for the area. The small man was only too willing to surrender his land rights, and even personal rights if necessary, in exchange for the privilege of protection.

Lastly the Nara period saw the flowering of Buddhism in Japan. We shall reserve for later discussion its significance for Japan in religious, cultural, and political matters; but here it should be mentioned that Buddhism had an enormous economic effect in Japan, and not the least aspect of this may be described as the Buddhist contribution to the development of the tax-free estate. Buddhism made a strong beginning in Japan because of the court sponsorship it received from the time of Prince Shotoku onward. By Nara times it not only remained much favored at court but was well enough organized institutionally to make full use of this favored position to receive economic benefits, such as tax-free lands. The least and easiest thing a grateful emperor could do for the priests, who kept the Heavens working in his behalf, was to bestow upon them the tax-free privilege. Thus temple lands began to loom large in the tax-free Shō of the empire.

The overall effect of the development of tax-free estates was twofold: it intensified the tax burden on those unfortunate nonprivileged common people who had found no way to escape payment, and it caused the government to lose interest in those estates from which it collected no taxes, leaving them also less and less subject to its political control. Thus, beneath the highly centralized political structure, an economic pull toward decentralization was working.

MONEY ECONOMY. Passing to another economic matter we again see the working in Nara times of Chinese-style centralization with an undercurrent pulling in the opposite direction. This concerns the introduction of a system of monetary exchange. As in so many other areas, Japan learned about money from China, and though a barter system had been sufficient for the primitive economy of earlier days, by the seventh century Chinese coins were well known in Japan and with the Nara period the Japanese government for the first time minted coins and promoted a money-based system of exchange. This was made possible by the discovery and development of deposits of precious metals, and it is interesting that in 708 the Nara period was heralded with copper discoveries so noteworthy that the reigning empress changed her era name to Wado (soft copper).

People in general, as might be expected, only slowly responded to government urgings to accept coins for their goods, especially in view of the fact that counterfeiters got into the minting business almost simultaneously with the government. But gradually the immense convenience of using coins brought about their widespread use in the Nara area and in major markets, although barter was still preferred in distant rural areas.

The extension of a money economy, however gradual, constituted a clear step forward in the direction of political centralization and stability in Japan, but even before the end of the Nara era (784) there was a countertendency at work. As the demand for coins became greater the government found itself unable to produce enough to meet the demand. In fact, the money problem as it developed came to the simple question of how much precious metal was available for coinage, in comparison with how much was required to hold together the Nara economic structure. Unfortunately the answer was more complex than the question, for it was not just a matter of precious metal output of the mines, although it is clear that even their output was insufficient. But in addition there was, just as with the tax-free estates, a deep involvement with Buddhism, especially in its cultural manifestations. For the flowering of Buddhism in Nara Japan was due not alone, perhaps not even primarily, to the stimulus of its religious and philosophic ideas, which impressed the thinkers, but which were too complicated for the uneducated. Perhaps the most marvelous thing about Buddhism to the broader Japanese community of the time was its aesthetic appeal rather than its ideas. The magnificence of its statuary particularly surpassed anything heretofore dreamed of by the Japanese. And as Korean and Chinese artists produced Buddhist images in Nara and taught Japanese artisans the secrets of their technique, there developed a marked tendency on the part of the Japanese, official and private persons alike, to pour a larger and larger percentage of the output of the precious metal mines into Buddhist statuary and bells. The Daibutsu (Great Buddha) of Todai-ji (Eastern Temple) is the colossal example. It was successfully cast in 749 after years of effort and scouring the country for contributions, and it removed from circulation over 900,000 pounds of copper.

Murdoch, relying on inventories dated A.D. 747, tells us that two of the large temples of Nara themselves held no less than 46 estates (tax free, of course), embracing some 5,000 acres of the most fertile land in Japan, alongside "immense treasures of various kinds." [1] The economic position of Buddhism in Nara Japan was strong enough to suggest that the end result of the Taika reforms might be a Buddhist theocratic state.

BUDDHISM AS A POLITICAL POWER.   And indeed a consideration of political developments of the period reveals that this almost came about. We recall that the centralized political structure had been the result of the combined efforts of the imperial prince Naka no Oe and his erstwhile mentor Kamatari, the founder of a family tradition of emperor promotion, protection, and guid-

[1] J. Murdoch, *A History of Japan,* I (London, 1925), p. 195.

ance. His family, known from the seventh century as the Fujiwara, became as much a court institution as the emperor himself, and into modern times they have remained the arbiters of court politics in Japan. But the eighth century, and Nara Buddhism, provided an acid test for them. It was their triumph which prevented the triumph of Buddhist theocracy in Japan.

Naka no Oe and Kamatari had defeated the Soga, Japan's original sponsors of Buddhism, in the coup of 645, but in their own subsequent riding of the crest of the Chinese wave as they sought to secure their position atop a centralized political structure, they invited a situation in which their less wary descendants were all but engulfed in a Buddhist sea.

Endless problems from smallpox epidemics to avenging spirits of dead (murdered?) political rivals required the propitiation of supernatural forces. The Buddhist priesthood not only could point to a veritable galaxy of gods and goddesses who could hear appeals, but were themselves the only ones possessed of a vocabulary learned enough and furnishings artistic enough for their invocation. The rising influence of Buddhism in politics is clearly evident in the time of Emperor Shomu, builder of the Nara Daibutsu. He officially proclaimed himself the servant of Buddhism at the time of the completion of the great image, and perhaps it was in the natural course of events that a scant twenty years later a Buddhist priest was in a position to seize the imperial power in Japan. This was during the reign of Shomu's daughter, and the priest in question was one Dokyo, who, it has been suggested, shared that lady's bed as well as directed her conscience, and who through her was able to control government affairs at will. He was not satisfied even with this, however, for he wished to become emperor himself. He almost succeeded, but at the last moment the empress demurred. Meanwhile the Fujiwara family, naturally aghast at what was happening, made a mighty effort to thwart his advent to the throne and, finally, were able to muster an opposition strong enough to oust him from the court and send him into banishment (but only after the death of the empress).

After this episode, which reached its climax in 769–770, the political power of Buddhism waned somewhat at the Nara court. But it was still strong enough to be a principal reason for a subsequent strong-minded emperor, Kammu, who became emperor with strong Fujiwara backing in 782, to decide to move court and capital almost immediately after his accession. The move, undertaken in 782, was first to Nagaoka, but after ten years there was a subsequent move to Heian (Kyoto), a few miles farther north. Kyoto was destined to remain the abode of Japanese emperors from the end of the eighth century until the middle of the nineteenth, when with the Meiji Restoration in 1868 the emperor came to Tokyo.

Nara Culture

Before discussing the Heian period it is necessary to say something more of the cultural life of eighth-century Japan, of Nara art and literature. For, although Chinese-inspired political and economic innovations seemed destined for failure even by the close of the epoch, the cultural impact of Chinese civilization was by no means abating. And if conquest can be understood in cultural terms, certainly Chinese culture conquered Japan in the Nara period.

NARA ART.   Entering Nara it is well to remind oneself of a small village passed a few miles north of Nara City. This village is called Korai-mura (Korean Village) and though the date and circumstances of its origin are obscure it seems likely that it served even in Nara times to house Koreans, artists and artisans whose skill in Chinese and Korean arts and artifacts gave them a vital role in Nara culture. For the Japanese had not yet, even at the end of the Nara epoch, begun to deviate seriously in some Japanese direction from the Chinese models they sought to reproduce. Rather, where Nara art deviates from Chinese models of the Northern Wei, Sui, and T'ang, it tends to do so in the direction of the Korean intermediary, who, even before Japan had direct contact with China, was teaching the subject to his Japanese employers.

    Seven miles southwest of Nara are the pre-Nara foundations of Nara art, including the three oldest wooden structures in the world and restored replicas of numerous other buildings, housing art treasures dating to the time of that first ardent importer of Chinese civilization, Regent Prince Shotoku (593–621). This is Horyuji, the temple area whose middle gate, pagoda, and

FIGURE 24.1.   *Kondo* or main hall of Horyuji, near Nara. It is the world's oldest wooden structure and the nucleus from which Chinese influence began to make its impact upon Japanese architecture.

main hall have stood for fourteen centuries to become the world's oldest wooden structures. A short distance away stands the reconstructed replica (done in the thirteenth century) of Shotoku's study, a strange looking eight-sided affair with

FIGURE 24.2. A thirteenth-century reconstruction of Prince Shotoku's study, the octagonal "Hall of Dreams" at Horyuji, near Nara.

a small veranda-like extension, no doubt for outdoor contemplation. And a little distance farther stands a series of buildings comprising the Chuguji nunnery.

All of the buildings, with the exception of the three oldest wooden structures, are reconstructed models of this pre-Nara period. Even so it is clear that they followed the sixth-century Chinese design. But the treasures housed within them go back to the period itself. Especially noteworthy is sculpture.

FIGURE 24.3. Statue of a guardian deity at Horyuji. A fine example of the realism characteristic of Nara sculpture.

Perhaps the most fascinating of all the statuary of the Horyuji area and period is the man-sized camphor wood statue called Nyoirin Kannon which now sits beneath a sort of canopy in a semi-darkened, though beautifully polished, room at Chuguji nunnery. The image is seated with one leg thrown

Figure 24.4.   Nyoirin Kannon, Chuguji.

at right angles across the other knee and with the folds of a skirt draped about. The upper torso is bare with the left hand resting easily on the crossed leg, and the right elbow on the knee. The right arm and hand are directed upwards, as if in motion toward the face, and the fingers seem to be about to stroke the chin. The eyes are half closed and about the mouth there plays a haunting half smile. Some scholars think the figure represents the Buddha as a young man, before he achieved enlightenment, perhaps while he was seeking it. It is a lean youthful figure, warm, human, and gracious. Obviously it has inspired the most scrupulous care from its attendants over the centuries, and though the wood has darkened with age to an almost metallic look, it remains in almost perfect condition.

The many images housed in these buildings, of course, could have been made elsewhere, in Korea, or even in China and imported. Some of them are so fine that one would presume a tradition of workmanship longer than Japan had at this time, even considering the presence of Korean and Chinese artists. But doubtless some of them were produced in Japan.

That there was large-scale artistic production at Horyuji itself is amply illustrated in the famous mural paintings of the main hall, which took as subjects numerous figures of the Buddhist pantheon and scenes from Nirvana. Unfortunately these murals, preserved for centuries, were largely destroyed by fire in 1950 even as artists sought to copy them. But good photographic reproductions are available, which reveal, even through centuries of deterioration, skillful drawing of Buddhas in human form, and animals. The colors must have been brilliant, especially the blending of shades of red and brown, which show clearly even in color photo reproductions. Some of these paintings display even the Indian (the Ajanta cave) influence behind the Chinese and can be traced for their inspiration to the art treasures unearthed in Chinese Turkistan along the great silk route.

In Nara itself is the Todaiji, the Great Eastern Temple, where stands the mammoth Buddha, Roshana, the supreme manifestation of the universal Buddha. This was completed in 749, as we have seen, at tremendous cost in materials and labor, by order of Emperor Shomu, to adorn his "permanent" capital. It is much too big to be artistic, and is housed in the largest single wooden building in the world. But if not exactly beautiful it is certainly majestic, a Buddha 53 feet high sitting on a lotus throne 68 feet in diameter. It is surrounded by lesser figures in profusion, like worlds about a great sun, which indeed is the basic idea of the Kegon sutra and sect to which it belongs.

Other art treasures dating back to the eighth century include pottery pieces and vessels, made for use in temple ceremonies, and utensils of various kinds. They display fine workmanship, reproducing and even improving upon Chinese models. Certainly by the latter part of the eighth century we may say that Japan had absorbed the best in the Sui-T'ang art tradition and was now prepared to modify it or depart from it.

NARA LITERATURE.   The Japanese, without a written language of their own, adopted Chinese characters. The process began, as we have seen, with the introduction of Chinese character writing in Japan in the early fifth century, apparently by a Korean teacher Wani in A.D. 405. At first the efforts of Japanese scholars were directed mainly at the mastery of the written Chinese itself, that they might better copy and understand the texts and scriptures which came to them in that language. But by Nara times they were embarking on large-scale literary projects of their own, particularly the compilation of the national histories, of which we have discussed the *Kojiki* and *Nihongi* as the earliest extant examples. This project ripened into a series of histories of the reigns of emperors which were carried on without interruption until 888. These histories, or chronicles, which begin with the *Nihongi*, are written in Chinese and they follow generally the pattern of the Chinese dynastic histories. In addition, various government documents from Prince Shotoku's "Injunctions" to the aforementioned law codes were compiled in Chinese. In all of these effort was directed toward perfecting the Chinese language employed. However, in the course of solving some of the problems of compilation certain compromises had to be made. For example, how to render Japanese proper names? Here reproducing the sound of the Japanese name was all important, for the name of a person is not so much an idea as a sound, and in this it is not surprising to find the Japanese doing what the Chinese had done earlier with Indian names. They simply chose a character or several characters which were pronounced in Chinese somewhat like the sound they wished to reproduce. Thus in the early texts many characters appear which must be read phonetically, for sound not for meaning. Furthermore there were Japanese expressions and words, necessary to meaning, which had to be incorporated in the Chinese text, and the same method of phonetic usage of characters recommended itself. In fact, in the *Kojiki* itself so many such usages appear that the author thought it necessary to apologize for the fact that it was not good Chinese and explain that he was taking down the words of an old Japanese storyteller who did not know Chinese.

Although in the early eighth century it was felt necessary to apologize for such corrupted use of Chinese, this tended to become less true. In fact about midway through the period the first great compilation of Japanese poems was made, the *Manyoshu,* in which this phonetic use of Chinese characters is employed throughout as the medium of expression. There is as yet no standardization of forms, and a Japanese sound such as *ri* may be expressed by any one of a number of Chinese characters. But the process of change from a timid and self-conscious effort to write in Chinese to a bold and confident use of the Chinese script to write down the Japanese language and to express Japanese thoughts is evident, and the post-Nara epoch carries these tendencies further.

In summary how can we describe the state of Japanese civilization at the end of the Nara period; what was the result of the wholesale borrowing from China which had characterized the seventh and eighth centuries? Clearly it was in the cultural area, art and literature, that the borrowing had been fullest, most complete, most understanding—so much so that Japanese artists and writers now stood prepared to modify and experiment with that heritage.

Similarly in political and economic fields changes were in the making. But here the base was not so secure, for the Japanese had never fully accepted or even understood certain essential underlying concepts of Chinese political and economic life. The vital role of the scholar officialdom, dynastic changes, barriers to localism and feudalism, a functioning money economy in insuring the continuance of the centralized political structure was either not apparent or not congenial to the ruling circles in Japan. For this reason the succeeding Heian era, although culturally brilliant, was also to reveal fundamental political and economic weaknesses.

BASIC DATES

660 B.C.	Jimmu Tenno, traditional date
C. 40 B.C.	Jimmu Tenno, probable historical date

C. 100 B.C.–	
A.D. 250	Yayoi (metal) period
A.D. 391	Monument in Korea records Japanese invasion (of Empress Jingo?)
A.D. 405	Traditional date for introduction of Chinese characters into Japan
A.D. 552	Traditional date for introduction of Buddhism into Japan
593–628	Reign of Empress Suiko (regent Prince Shotoku)
604	Prince Shotoku's "constitution"
646	Taika Reform
710–784	Nara Period; influence from T'ang China
712	*Kojiki (Record of Ancient Matters)*
720	*Nihongi (Chronicles of Japan)*
759	*Manyoshu (Poetry Anthology)*

SUPPLEMENTARY READING

DE BARY, W. T., ED. *Sources of the Japanese Tradition.* New York, 1958.

MUNSTERBERG, H. *The Arts of Japan.* Tokyo, 1957. Illustrated discussion of early Japanese art.

REISCHAUER, E. O. *Japan: Past and Present.* New York, 1953. Good brief discussion.

REISCHAUER, E. O. AND J. K. FAIRBANK. *East Asia: The Great Tradition.* Boston, 1958. Excellent discussion of this period.

SANSOM, G. B. *Japan: A Short Cultural History.* New York, 1943. Well written cultural history.

TERRY, C. *Masterworks of Japanese Art.* Rutland, Vt., 1956. Good text; outstanding illustrations.

ADVANCED READING

ASTON, W. G., TR. *Nihongi: Chronicles of Japan.* London, 1956.

BROWN, D. M. *Nationalism in Japan.* Berkeley, Cal., 1955. Contains material on "national consciousness" in early Japan.

CHAMBERLAIN, B. H., TR. *Kojiki or Records of Ancient Matters.* Kobe and Tokyo, 1932.

ELIOT, C. N. E. *Japanese Buddhism.* London, 1935. Somewhat dated, but fullest treatment.

KIDDER, J. E. *Japan Before Buddhism.* London, 1959. Excellent recent study of Japanese prehistory.

MURDOCH, J. *A History of Japan.* London, 1925. Classic history; somewhat outdated but still valuable for wealth of detail. Vol. I from prehistory to 1542.

PAINE, R. T. AND A. SOPER. *The Art and Architecture of Japan.* Baltimore, 1955.

REISCHAUER, R. K. *Early Japanese History.* Princeton, N. J., 1937.

SANSOM, G. B. *A History of Japan to 1334.* Stanford, Cal., 1958. Thorough study, beautifully written, authoritative.

SAUNDERS, E. D. "Japanese Mythology," in S. N. Kramer, ed., *Mythologies of the Ancient World.* New York, 1961.

TREWARTHA, G. *Japan: A Physical, Cultural and Regional Geography.* Madison, Wis., 1945.

YOUNG, J. *The Problem of Yamatai in Japanese Historiography.* Baltimore, 1956.

XXV

THE HEIAN PERIOD,

784-1156

Beginnings of the Heian Era

In 782 a powerful and gifted man became emperor of Japan. This was Kammu, eldest son of Emperor Konin by a lesser wife, who being possessed of a rather low court rank (fifth class) would seem to have had no chance to be emperor at all. He was, in fact, merely a professor in the imperial university. But a powerful Fujiwara championed him and finally Konin designated him as his successor.

It took Kammu less than two years to decide that changes were necessary in the Nara political and religious structure if he were to exercise power as he wished, and he decided upon the drastic measure of moving the "permanent" capital. It is clear from the circumstances that his principal motive was to escape the powerful influence of Nara Buddhism, which had become, in fact, the state religion. Temmu Tenno (682–687) had begun the process by ordering every household in Japan to have a Buddhist altar, and Shomu, in dedicating himself to the service of Buddhism, had brought about a condition wherein the Buddhist clergy could overawe emperors and subjects alike. Todaiji, with its mammoth Roshana Buddha, its exclusive right to ordain members of the priesthood, and the universal claims of its Kegon Sutra was the supreme manifestation of rising strength. But fortunately for the purposes of Kammu, Todaiji and the mammoth Buddha within were too big to move. In 784 the Emperor moved his government a few miles north in a preliminary move and in 794 he established a new permanent capital at Heian (Kyoto) some thirty miles from Nara. The site was a picturesque valley, protected by mountains from debilitating outside influences.

SAICHO AND THE TENDAI SECT. Kammu was also fortunate enough, or sufficiently clever, to find a remarkable Buddhist monk, Saicho, as dissatisfied as himself with Nara, and capable of founding a powerful new order of Buddhism, under the imperial favor. This Saicho in 788 had rejected what he considered the narrowness and worldliness of Nara Buddhism to seek some higher morality in the mountain fastnesses to the north, and on Mt. Hiei, just northeast of the Kyoto plain he had founded a tiny monastery as his mountain retreat. At first he had little following and less standing in Buddhist circles in Japan, but with the emperor's support his establishment began to prosper, and in 804 Kammu sent him to China. When he returned a year later, he came as the apostle of a new type of Buddhism then prospering in China, the T'ien-t'ai, or Tendai as it came to be called in Japan. With it Saicho attacked Nara Buddhism at certain weak points in its doctrine. For example, he argued that though Nara claimed to be Mahayanist in character, many of its tenets were in fact Hinayanist in inspiration, and further he proclaimed with considerable truth that Nara Buddhism was built upon derivative texts, not the original sutras, and even when, as with the Kegon sect, the original Lotus Sutra was used, it was interpreted incorrectly. The true Lotus (Tendai brand), Saicho said, "will rise above the mire and foul water of the Hinayana and Quasi-Mahayana . . . to open in full glory." [1] Saicho held his neophytes to rigid moral discipline, requiring them to spend 12 years in rigorous training on their monastery mountain, a marked contrast to luxurious Nara, but he held that all who persevered could find enlightenment.

Also the orientation of Tendai was outward toward the world, seeking to influence it rather than to withdraw. Stern moralist though he was Saicho was able to capitalize on the theme of service to the state. The northeast was regarded as the direction from which unseen evil influences might descend on the capital. The stalwart priests of Mt. Hiei would keep them off. Saicho described his disciples and their knowledge as "treasures of the nation." His monastery operated under an imperial license, and he identified the "true" Mahayanism of his sect as something that would serve Japan beneficently. Also he made the most of his year in China, taking pains to call himself even years later "Saicho, the monk who formerly sought the Law in China."

The Nara Buddhists, of course, became his bitter enemies, and denounced Saicho at every turn, but he and Tendai prospered anyway, though Nara did

[1] Wm. T. De Bary, ed. *Sources of the Japanese Tradition* (New York: Columbia Univ. Press, 1958), p. 118.

succeed in preventing during his lifetime the accomplishment of one of his most cherished desires, the erection of a *kaidan,* or ordination platform, on Mt. Hiei. His petition for *kaidan* privileges was not granted until 827, five years after his death. But posthumously anyway, the victory was his, and Saicho received more honors than any priest before him in Japan. He has been known to posterity as Dengyo Daishi, the Great Teacher, and his temple on Mt. Hiei, Enryakuji, came to encompass 3000 buildings before it was burned in the civil wars of the sixteenth century.

KUKAI AND THE SHINGON SECT.   In his struggle against Nara Buddhism Saicho was aided by another dissident sect, which eventually became a competitor of Tendai, but which in Saicho's time served as an ally against Nara. This was the Shingon (or True Word) sect, founded by a younger contemporary and friend of Saicho, another dissatisfied Nara monk, Kukai. Kukai, as an individual, was even more brilliant than Saicho, though his organizational abilities were not so great and the orientation of Shingon was more introspective and monastic than social and worldly as was Tendai. Kukai's genius spread to many fields, including not only religion and philosophy but also poetry, painting, sculpture, and he is credited with the final formulation of the concept of the *kana* syllabary (Japanese phonetic signs made by abbreviating Chinese characters). This latter, of course, was a logical step growing out of the Manyoshu's rather helter-skelter use of Chinese characters to identify Japanese sounds.

Kukai went to China in the same year as Saicho (804) but he stayed longer and perhaps studied more intensely. At any rate he much impressed even the renowned Saicho upon his return, though Saicho lost a good deal of his enthusiasm when some of his own disciples deserted to Kukai. Kukai erected a monastery on Mt. Koya, near present Osaka, in 816, and after Saicho's death in 822 he became Buddhism's "Great Teacher" in Japan. He is known to posterity as Kobo Daishi.

Kukai's brand of Buddhism is best described as esoteric. It was Tantric in origin, full of mysteries, formulas, incantations, and oral transmissions. Secrets were the essence of Shingon, and the master would traditionally keep to himself certain final, ultimate secrets until just before his death, when he would impart all to one particularly favored disciple. This had been the case with Kukai, who had learned the final secrets in China from his great teacher at Ch'ang-an, Hui-kuo.

Though the greatest secrets of Shingon were withheld for oral transmission and not committed to writing, Kukai wrote a great deal, and brilliantly. He did not quarrel with other types of Buddhism, or even with Confucianism, Taoism, or animism, all of which he regarded as lower stages in the development of the ultimate truth, Shingon, the True Word. Hinayana, the Nara sects, and Tendai, all had their place in the scale, but Shingon was the last and the highest truth. This truth could not really be expressed in words, so written explanation was useless beyond a certain point, and Kukai turned to art, at which he was very gifted, to express many of his ideas.

Kukai in the years after the death of Saicho acceded to the position of chief Buddhist of the state, and he, like Saicho, proclaimed that Buddhism helped and protected the imperial rule. Further he laid a foundation for what has been called Ryobu Shinto (or Dual Shinto), in which the Sun Goddess and lesser figures of the native Shinto pantheon were given places in the hierarchy of Buddhism; for example, Hachiman, the Shinto god of war, became a Bodhisattva. This was obviously congenial to the Shinto clergy and the imperial court alike.

In the generation after the two "great teachers" a disciple of Saicho, Ennin by name, produced a remarkable combination of Tendai philosophy and the esoteric mysteries first associated with Kukai's Shingon. He journeyed to China in 838 and spent the next eight years in intimate association with Buddhism and Buddhist leaders there, returning to Japan in 847 and leaving to posterity a remarkable diary of his trip. During his stay the great persecution of Buddhism by the T'ang emperor Wu-tsung took place (843–845; see Chapter 19) and Ennin himself was finally defrocked and deported, but although greatly distressed at the sufferings of his Chinese Buddhist friends, he never wavered in his determination to learn all he could about the Buddhist faith and practice in China in order to transmit the knowledge to Japan. He was especially impressed by the esoteric practices, symbolic acts of faith, and mysteries which were very popular in China at the time, and certain minor miracles which he observed (e.g. five beams of light shining into the hall and then suddenly disappearing) no doubt helped to convince him of their validity. At any rate upon his return to Japan he sought to inject an aura of inner mystery into the hitherto extroverted and exoteric Tendai philosophy. Curiously this did not decrease its influence by turning it inward or setting up internal conflict, for the dynamic Tendai organization, with its many connections at the capital, embraced the new ideas as its own. And Ennin and Tendai together, combining the two main strains of Heian Buddhism, brought new heights of acclaim for Mt. Hiei and more discomfort to the Nara sects.

The acclaim was great and the triumph of Tendai was real, but it should not be assumed that Tendai teachings or even Buddhism in general had yet permeated Japan. The sects of Heian times argued and competed amongst themselves on a lofty philosophic plane and their arguments were too academic to have much effect on the life of the average person, however much they were the talk of the capital. True, Japan was officially a Buddhist land, with a Buddhist temple by imperial order in every district and an altar in every household, but it remained for later, less complicated types of Buddhism to touch the hearts and feelings of the mass of the Japanese people. Perhaps the chief effect of the great religious controversies of early Heian Buddhism was to divide religious leaders and thus make impossible the construction of a Buddhist theocratic government. This was precisely what Kammu had wanted, and although no strong emperors succeeded Kammu, political power was to remain in secular hands thereafter.

With the passing of Buddhism as a major political problem, the principal theme of Heian politics becomes the rise of the Fujiwara family to undisputed mastery of the central government, including the methods which brought triumph over rivals, their technique of control, and their ultimate loss of real power to military men. But before proceeding to this principal theme it may be well to deal briefly with another problem brought to solution in Kammu's reign, one which had come down from prehistoric times. This was the frontier or Ainu problem.

THE FRONTIER PROBLEM.   As has been said earlier, the Ainu belong to the Caucasian race; they are tall, their skins are white, their eyes often blue, their faces and bodies hairy, all of which distinguishes them from the Mongoloid-Malayasian mixture which are the people we know historically as the Japanese. Most of the Ainu have by now been assimilated by the Japanese and have left almost no trace, the assimilated Ainu characteristics appearing only occasionally in an unusually tall or unusually hairy Japanese. But they were absorbed gradually and unwillingly, so that even today a few of them remain, unassimilated, on reservations in Hokkaido, where they persist in customs entirely foreign to their Japanese compatriots.

In Kammu's time the assimilation process was already underway. Many Ainu had even settled within the boundaries of the Japanese frontier, begun to intermarry with their Japanese neighbors, taken up a Japanese way of agriculture and of life, and begun to lose their identity. But at that time many of them remained still unconquered and unsettled, and determined to resist Japanese control. They held out principally in northern Honshu, and though their general tendency was to retreat northward, they had by no means lost their striking power. They often ventured south, especially into the eastern Kanto districts, to raid and raze and to challenge the penetration of that area by Japanese settlers. This rough and tumble situation in the frontier areas had an important long-range effect on the development of military feudalism in Japan, for it kept the frontier Japanese armed and alert, and helped develop a military class in eastern Japan. We should remember this as important to future developments in Japan, but here we are more specifically concerned with the "Ainu problem" as such, and with the "solution" to it wrought in Kammu's time.

Before Kammu Japanese emperors had raised imperial troops to protect and advance the frontier, but just before Kammu's becoming emperor, the situation, from the Japanese point of view, had deteriorated, and the Ainu had not only increased the tempo of their attacks on Japanese frontier settlements, but had openly challenged and defeated the imperial troops themselves. Kammu therefore hastened to take the offensive. He levied thousands of troops from various parts of his empire and set them under the command of the first significant military leader in Japanese history, one Sakanoue Tamuramaro. Tamuramaro received the title of Sei-i-tai-shogun (Great Barbarian Subduing

General), a title which was to have much more than military significance later in the feudal period, but which in Tamuramaro's time meant a temporary military commission for dealing with some specific problem. Tamuramaro marched in command of the forces of emperor Kammu, and after a carefully planned and executed campaign, he returned triumphant, having dealt the Ainu blows from which they never fully recovered. After Kammu's reign there was sporadic trouble from them for about 50 years, but they no longer constituted a serious military problem. They were gradually settled in small agricultural communities under Japanese control or they were dispersed about the empire and attached to already established Japanese communities.

The Fujiwara

The ascent of the Fujiwara family to almost complete dominion over political affairs at Heian was facilitated by the unwillingness of Kammu's successors to attend to their imperial duties. After Kammu's death in 806 three of his sons succeeded to the throne in succession. They were brilliant men in their way, particularly the second, the emperor Saga who was a really substantial scholar, but they were more attracted to Chinese letters and art, which they helped make into a vogue at the capital, than to the business of government. The three ruled a total of only seventeen years, each abdicating when he had the chance, to earn the historical appellation "Learned Emperor" (perhaps better "Learned ex-Emperor") and to establish a tradition of imperial abdication which left the political field wide open for Fujiwara in-laws.

The secret of Fujiwara power was marriage manipulation and knowledge of court ceremonies. The family had an old and aristocratic lineage running back through the famous Kamatari of Taika reform days to the Nakatomi clan, whose members had for generations specialized in traditional (pre-Buddhist) religious recitations and who claimed descent from a principal advisor of the first god-emperor Jimmu. Thus they were close to emperors from earliest times, but their maximum opportunity came only after Kammu had broken the Buddhist stranglehold on the court and then in turn left heirs who were unfit or unwilling to rule. Into this opening the Fujiwara stepped or perhaps one could say glided, so smoothly did their seizure of power occur; for there was no coup d'état, no obvious force applied, only gentle stratagems which unfailingly involved the weaker sex.

Fujiwara Yoshifusa, aged 22 in 826 when he succeeded to the leadership of the Fujiwara house, laid the foundations for complete Fujiwara dominance of the Heian court and government. He himself married a daughter of the emperor Saga and contrived to have his sister made consort (one of several) to Saga's learned successor. It was on her son, his nephew, that Yoshifusa concentrated all his efforts, finally seeing him crowned in 850 as Emperor Montoku. To cap his efforts Yoshifusa promptly had his own daughter marry his emperor nephew. And when fortunately (for Yoshifusa) this nephew died a few years later, the son of his Fujiwara consort, Yoshifusa's grandson, became emperor (at the age of 9). Yoshifusa immediately took over the reigns of government as regent, a role which he did not relinquish when the young emperor came of age.

This established a precedent of government by Fujiwara regency. The presumption of regency is, of course, that for some reason the sovereign is incapable of exercising his powers adequately or properly. Fujiwara grandfathers after Yoshifusa took care that this was, in fact, usually the case, seeing to the abdication of their emperor grandsons whenever the boy emperor might become of age and have produced a son by his Fujiwara consort. Of the next fifteen emperors (to 1059) seven ruled only as children and during this whole period the head of the Fujiwara house was de facto ruler of Japan, with Fujiwara consorts as mothers of emperors, and Fujiwara courtiers occupying the most influential positions at court, where only they could correctly guide the court in the "traditional" ceremonies. Indeed for over three centuries, from Yoshifusa's success in securing the throne for his nephew in 850 to the seizure of power at Kyoto by Taira Kiyomori in 1160, the Fujiwara successfully resisted all challenges to their authority. Perhaps the most spectacular such challenge came in the last decade of the ninth century, before Fujiwara control of the court had become firmly established. This involved the rise of a non-Fujiwara court official and man of letters, Sugawara Michizane, to astonishing heights of power and influence before the Fujiwara arranged to dispose of him, as was their habit with political adversaries, by sending him to a post far from the capital.

Michizane found his opportunity in the interval between the death of a Fujiwara regent-chancellor in 891 and the consolidation of power by his successor. He enjoyed a splendid reputation, largely for his scholarship in the field of Chinese studies, in which he was apparently without peer at the capital at a time when the prestige of Chinese studies was such that no one, not even a Fujiwara, could go far at court without some claim to ability in them. Michizane, much sought after as a tutor, turned his contacts to political advantage. Ironically, to do this he had to betray himself as a scholar, when in 894 he was entrusted to head a mission to China, where, of course, he might have immensely improved his competence in the field. But he begged off, knowing that his absence from Kyoto for one or perhaps several years would probably eliminate him as a political influence at the Japanese court. In fact so energetic was his argument against sending this embassy that it was decided to send no more embassies to China at all.

Despite his avoidance of the China mission Michizane's political ambitions were thwarted. His Fujiwara rivals contrived to have him appointed as viceroy of Kyushu whence he was speedily dispatched, and where he remained the rest of his life, though he resorted to every persuasion he could muster, even putting his pleas into poetry, to negotiate a return to the capital. He was, however, posthumously showered with honors and offices, acts by which the Fujiwara assured themselves he would not haunt them.

The Fujiwara, in order to reach a position of nearly complete dominion over the Heian government, undermined the Chinese-style bureaucratic system which the Taika reform had introduced. Not only did heredity and family connections come to outweigh education and ability in the securing of governmental positions, but the positions themselves became merely empty titles to anyone without Fujiwara backing. T'ang-type tassles, caps, and ranks became merely social plumes while the real operations of government were handled by Fujiwara dominated "minor" agencies which had been nonexistent or unimportant in earlier days. For example, the Bureau of Archivists, simply a depository for palace documents at first, under Fujiwara headship began to draft the actual edicts for the emperor to sign and to issue on its own authority other decrees and instructions which had the force of imperial command. Some palace guards, designated as a "police commission" with very minor functions, began to draft and enforce penal codes quite without reference to the Chinese-inspired official legal structure; and minor "audit officers" took over principal revenue functions.

The failure of Sugawara Michizane and others to break Fujiwara political supremacy does not mean that there were no vulnerable points in the Fujiwara system. Rather it indicates that such a rival as Michizane tried to build his political stature on relatively superficial grounds, without utilizing fundamental contradictions in the existing structure.

Occasionally we do catch a glimmer of realization by politicians of the day of the basic problems of Heian Japan. One Miyoshi Kiyotsura was particularly acute, pointing out in memorials to the emperor that certain groups of Buddhist priests were operating in a very independent way, even to coining money and arming themselves, and that certain "guardsmen," who called themselves *bushi* (warrior gentlemen), with arms and horses of their own, were failing to take their monthly turns of duty at the capital, and instead were roaming the countryside preying on travelers and farmers. Others took notice of pirates operating in the Inland Sea with bases in Kyushu and Shikoku, who were in collaboration with local noblemen.

One could say that Sugawara Michizane as viceroy of Kyushu little realized his opportunities in this regard, for from such a position he might have impressed the capital far more at the head of organized bands of pirates and *bushi*, than with his poetic entreaties.

Eventually others would do this, but much later, for in the tenth century these were merely small dark clouds on the horizon, far from the brilliance of the Heian court. There Fujiwara glory reigned supreme and would continue to do so for another two hundred years.

TAX-FREE ESTATES. Yet we should be aware, even if the Fujiwara were not, that the dark clouds, bushi, pirates, and such were not likely to vanish. They had a territorial base out in the provinces far from the view of the capital. The great failing of the Fujiwara was that they paid too little attention to the provinces. The Fujiwara policy of banishing dissenters generally to the outer areas, as far as possible from the capital, was to prove their undoing.

The real base of Fujiwara weakness was the shō, tax-free estates, mentioned in the last chapter. Their development began in the Nara period, but it was accelerated rather than curtailed in the Heian. Governors of the provinces were still appointed by the court and presumably they and their subordinates controlled, under orders from the capital, the entire area under their jurisdiction. But in practice they did not. By the tenth century a large proportion of the agricultural land in Japan was in fact divided up into shō, which, since they enjoyed partial or complete tax exemption, were of little concern to the central government and tended to become completely independent of it. Furthermore, tax-free status being most attractive, landholders would seek ways of securing it for themselves. Many were so bold as simply to claim it on the basis of some fictitious previous arrangement or to obtain by bribery some kind of official paper attesting the privilege. An imperial decree of the year 902 forbade such false claims but this decree seems to have been ineffective. The government then tried to control matters by issuing charters to all the tax-free estates which could provide proof of their status, and in 1069 the emperor decreed that all shō without such definite charters were abolished. However, though this may have proved a temporary discouragement to the development for a while, it provided large numbers of estates with definite proof that they had the tax-free privilege and rendered them all the more independent. It also tended to consolidate into larger estates many smaller agricultural sections, for a man who might not be sure of his influence at court or of his ability to maintain the tax-free privilege would commend his small estate to the care of a more influential man or institution which could assure it. Commender and commendee would then share the income of the estate.

SHIKI. The matter of the division of income on these tax-free estates constitutes a second important feature of the system which was developing into something best described as approaching feudalism. *Shiki* was the special Japanese term for income or "rights" from such land and the division of shiki was systemized in late Heian times. The shiki was divided, unequally of course, among those who worked, protected, and managed the estate, and the person or institution responsible for the tax-free privilege. At the top of the hierarchy was the patron, who was the equivalent of the seigneur of a European feudal estate. The patron might be a very powerful individual at court, or a noble family, or an institution such as a Buddhist monastery. He or they were almost always absent from the estate, being resident at the capital or, in the case of Buddhist overlordship, at one of the great monasteries, perhaps Koyasan or Enryakuji. Eventually the patron lost his importance but during Heian times he played a vital role in providing and maintaining the tax-free privilege, for which he received a large share of the shiki.

The estate itself was under the overlordship of a proprietor, who stood at the head of a group of administrators and managed the affairs of the estate on the spot. He and his assistants naturally also received a large share of the shiki. Third in rank stood the protectors of the estate, warriors, called in Japanese bushi, professional soldiers who saw that there were no encroachments upon the estate by others, and who in fact "protected it" even from the inspections of the provincial officials. There was a noticeable tendency in the late Heian period for the protector to become identical with the proprietor, thus combining the functions of management and protection into one. Next lowest in the scale were cultivators, who organized and carried out the work in the field. These might be former owners of land who, fearful lest their small holding be left without protection, had commended them to the more powerful patron of a larger estate. These, as with their European counterparts, tended to become identified with specific pieces of land. Below the cultivators were laborers who were not, at least in the beginning, tied to the land but who were hired to work at its cultivation for wages. They tended also to become associated with a specific piece of land. The various shiki were not, however, clearly fixed in Heian times; they might be subdivided among several sons and also daughters or consolidated, or even transferred from one family to another. And class and rank lines on the estates were not so definitely set as they were in court ranks at the capital. Mobility depended on ability and especially military prowess, so that these estates naturally attracted adventurous people who wanted to get ahead.

THE RISE OF THE MILITARY CLASS. While shō and shiki provided the economic bases for the tendency toward feudalism, the newly rising military class was the force which eventually broke the political power of the imperial court and paved the way for the establishment of a military feudal structure throughout the whole of Japan. Signs that the military men, who were indispensable to the protection of the nearly autonomous shō, were gaining power sufficient to overawe the Heian government itself appeared in the tenth century and accelerated thereafter. The Chinese-style bureaucracy had never been

FIGURE 25.1. Wooden figure of a Japanese soldier, pre-tenth century.

militarily oriented or dominated. Under it a few military men had obtained some prominence fighting in the Ainu wars but such civilian virtues as family connections, social prestige, and learning, not martial prowess, had been the determinants of prominence and power during Nara and early Heian times. In fact, by the tenth century provincial governors and their staff members, as civil officers, were forbidden to carry weapons.

The year 940, however, produced something of a shock at court when an obstreperous member of the Taira family, one Masakado, created military disturbances of alarming proportions in eastern Japan. Several decades before, members of the Taira family, whose court rank was low, had settled in eastern Japan, risen to prominence in local administration there, and built up large property holdings. Masakado's uncle was a court appointee as vice-governor of Hitachi. But neither this nor kinship deterred young Masakado from becoming involved in a bitter dispute with him, arranging his assassination, and then stirring up a general revolt against the administration of the province. Military adventurers from far and wide flocked to the area to take service under him, public offices were burned, official seals carried off, and matters brought to so serious a point that court officials at Kyoto, who preferred not to be bothered with provincial matters, had to take a stand. They raised an army to send against him under the leadership of a Fujiwara, who was utterly without military experience and would surely have been defeated had he joined battle with Masakado's vigorous *bushi*. But fortunately for the court a family dispute broke out in the east in which another Taira relative proved the rebel's undoing. Masakado's head was sent to the capital where court officials congratulated themselves on putting down the revolt, though they must have known that it had really been taken out of their hands. After this for a time some of the prohibitions against wearing swords by civil officials were removed and an air of vigilance was assumed, but gradually the court and its representatives in the provinces resumed their unmilitary ways.

MILITARY CHALLENGE TO FUJIWARA SUPREMACY. The military men were not strictly the product of the shō, nor were they content in the last analysis to be merely agents of the patron, protecting his estate. Their loyalties and operations were deeply involved in family and clan connections which transcended the boundaries of the individual estates and which gradually coalesced in the twelfth century into two great military organizations, one built around the Taira clan and the other around the Minamoto. During the eleventh century and increasingly in the twelfth there were numerous conflicts between various factions of the military, which were concerned much more with military rivalries than with the interests of the patrons of the various shō. When one group won they would confiscate the shō which the other group was presumably defending, with the result that more and more shō passed under exclusively military domination without reference to their original patronage. The military were tied together by oaths and alliances, which they broke when it seemed convenient or advantageous to change sides. But no matter how a quarrel ended one military group or another reaped the main profit. Gradually they intruded into the squabbles of various factions at the capital itself. At first court cliques would employ military men merely to help them win an advantage, but by the middle of the twelfth century the military were no longer being used; rather they were using the factions at court to advance their own interests.

The military intrusion into affairs at the capital was particularly abetted by a rift between Fujiwara regents and ex-emperors which developed late in the eleventh century, and was still unhealed when a military man took over the government in 1160. The Fujiwara had long been able to obtain the abdication of emperors at their pleasure to make way for Fujiwara regents, but beginning with an emperor called Shirakawa (reign, 1072–1086; died 1129) they lost control over ex-emperors. Shirakawa became a priest after his abdication in 1086, and although in the past such taking orders had ended the political activities of emperors, Shirakawa did not relinquish them. Instead he established another court organization which soon began to overshadow the one which his son and then his grandson ruled as legitimate emperors under Fujiwara domination. Thus there developed an emperor (Fujiwara) party and ex-emperor (anti-Fujiwara) party. Shirakawa was sufficiently astute to be able to undermine the position of the Fujiwara, although not to displace them. His system, which was practiced by several ex-emperors after him also, was called *insei,* government by retired sovereigns. It resulted in such a bitter cleavage in court circles that both sides began to call in military support. The Fujiwaras mainly relied on Minamoto warriors, whom they called their "nails and teeth," and who had land holdings and a reservoir of power close to the capital. The retired but active ex-emperors found especially useful members of the Taira clan, whose principal holdings, as we have seen, were in eastern Japan. When one military faction lined up with a particular court group, the other could readily find employment with its rival. Perhaps the essential difference from previous court politics was that whereas in earlier times banishment or at most imprisonment had been the penalty for losing to a rival group at court, heads now began to roll in the capital. By 1156 the rivalry had gone beyond the stage of plots, counterplots, and assassinations, and the old court parties had become obsolete. What had emerged was wholesale and bloody conflict between Taira and Minamoto for control of the capital. The first victory went to the Taira, whose heavy-handed leader, Kiyomori, emerged in 1160 as dictator of Kyoto and its environs, his Minamoto rivals temporarily dispersed and all court factions thoroughly cowed. The end of the Heian era was at hand.

Heian Culture

While the Heian era must be judged a period of political degeneration and failure, its cultural attainments are impressive, especially in the realm of literature. Society at the capital was luxurious and effete and certainly it neglected its political duties, but with the business of government not taken very seriously, there was much leisure, time for study, reflection, gaiety, and gossip, resulting in the production of a truly great literature.

LANGUAGE DEVELOPMENT.   Other arts, such as sculpture and painting, had been more advanced than literature in the Nara period but now, although there continued to be development in these, literature forged ahead. It may be asked

FIGURE 25.2.   A famous Heian scroll of caricatures by a Buddhist abbot, Toba Sojo. Rabbits and frogs in human attitudes are delineated in skillful brushstrokes.

why this was so; why did literature develop later than the others? The answer is probably that it took the Japanese longer to adjust the Chinese written language to their own modes of oral expression than it did to learn to wield the painter's brush and the sculptor's knife. And it is probably fair to say that Japanese literature had to await a decrease in dependence on China before it could escape the straitjacket of classical Chinese. This occurred in the ninth century as the T'ang declined and Japanese visitors found China less stimulating, official missions entirely ceasing with the decision to cancel the embassy of Sugawara Michizane in 894. The fact that there was less regard for China is clearly revealed in language developments of the period. More and more Japanese writers came to use Chinese characters freely, phonetically, and in fact a whole syllabary system of 48 kana signs or separate "letters," 20 of which could be modified by adding diacritical marks, was developed. This is the Japanese equivalent of our alphabet, though its "letters" combine a consonant and a vowel in most cases.

The Japanese did not in the long run overturn the whole ideographic basis of the Chinese script. They were actually working in the direction of a compromise whereby nouns and uninflected idea words generally, together with the roots of inflected words, would be represented by a complete Chinese ideograph or a pair of them, and inflections, verb tenses, adjectival endings, connecting words and the like would be sounded out in kana. The result has been a complex of irreconcilables which is neither the one nor the other, neither consistently ideographic nor consistently phonetic, a condition which language students have found most distressing.

Nevertheless, kana literature did develop during the Heian period. Japanese court ladies, and a few men, were responsible for building kana to a respectable literary position. Perhaps some of them, the ladies especially, were too lazy or too inept to learn real Chinese, but whatever the cause, they found it more pleasing to write about the little, the unofficial, the human and interesting things of life in their own language. Of course, the prestige of the Chinese language remained great. Official documents continued to be written in painfully good Chinese.

HISTORY.   The greatest literary project of the first Heian century was the official history series, of which the great Nara compilation, the *Nihongi,* had been the first. Although these were histories of reigns, rather than dynasties— there being only one dynasty in Japan—they clearly followed the inspiration of the Chinese dynastic histories. But the national history project did not long outlast the period of official relations with China. Shortly after the cancellation of the embassy of Sugawara the regular compilation of these official histories came to an end.

POETRY.   For the main course of Japanese literature throughout the rest of the Heian period one must look back to the inspiration of, not the *Nihongi,* but the Nara period's famous verse collection, the aforementioned *Manyoshu,* wherein for the first time Chinese characters were used phonetically. Indeed, shortly after the national history project was abandoned a new anthology of Japanese poems was begun, which was finished in 922. This was called *Kokinshu* (*Old-New Collection*). Its chief editor was Ki no Tsurayuki, a Chinese scholar and head of the Imperial Library, who, however, also loved poetry and the lighter forms of writing. Not only was he the editor of this great collection of verse but he also wrote, entirely in kana, the so-called *Tosa Diary* (935). This is a simple, matter of fact, and often amusing diary of a trip home to Kyoto from Tosa where he had been governor. He explains in his preface that this being a very undignified sort of thing to write, he is putting it in the language of a woman. His poetry anthology is likewise rather lightly done although, since apparently this had the imperial sanction behind it, he made no apologies for it. He comments rather playfully on the authors whose works are included therein; for example, he calls one writer "profound but the connection between the beginning and end is indistinct." Another poet "overflows with sentiment but his language is deficient." Another is "skillful in the use of words, but they

ill match with his matter, as if a shopkeeper were to dress himself in fine silks."
The poems of the *Kokinshu* are almost all short poems, some eleven hundred
of them, mostly of the tanka (thirty-one-syllable) style. They are arranged
under various headings, from spring to five classifications of love. While the
themes of Heian poetry were frivolous, whether the poems were gay or senti-
mental, poetry writing itself was taken quite seriously at the capital. Poetry
competitions were very important to social success and the refrain, "I'll die of
grief, if I fail in the poetry contest" was a frequent one emitted by the young
ladies and poets at court.

The short poem itself is too constricted a medium to allow the reader to
obtain a very clear view of the attitudes and standards of the court, but "sketch
books" such as the famous *Pillow Book* of the court lady, Sei Shonagon, ram-
bling collections of notes on affairs at the capital, give some very sharp insights.
In the *Pillow Book* it is interesting, and amusing, to see the ease with which the
authoress shifts from poetry contests to political contests, seeming to regard
them with about equivalent seriousness. To her "there is nothing in the world
so painful as feeling that one is not liked." As regards appearance,
"it is most essential of all that the boys who feed the carriage-oxen should be
presentable. If one's other servants are not fit to be seen, they can be stowed
away behind the carriage. But outriders or the like, who are bound to catch
the eye, make a painful impression if they are not perfectly trim."

Shonagon found religious practices rather amusing. For example, she speaks
of a priest called to read at the bedside of a sick gentlewoman, whose friends
were also present in the room: "At this exposed bevy of young women the
priest constantly glances while he reads, for which he will certainly suffer in the
life to come."

While Shonagon's knowledge of the court was both intimate and winsome,
when she came in contact with the lower classes she found them either un-
attractive or somewhat mystifying. She found that "the things that workmen eat
are most extraordinary. When the roof of the eastern wing was being mended,
there were a whole lot of workmen sitting in a row having dinner . . . they gulped
down the gravy . . . they all ate in the same way . . . I can't say I think that
it is a very attractive one." [2]

One need not begrudge Shonagon and her set the pleasures and frivolities
which they enjoyed at court; but clearly they were very narrow and reflected
an almost total unconcern for affairs beyond the precincts of the capital.

THE NOVEL.   The most astonishing literary development of Heian times was
in the genre of the novel, which after a few halting attempts in the tenth
century reached truly magnificent proportions in the eleventh with the production of the famous *Tale of Genji*. Two tenth-century prototypes of the novel
form are the *Bamboo Gathering Stories* and the *Tales of Ise*. These are fanciful

---

[2] Waley, Arthur, tr. *The Pillow Book of Sei Shonagon* (Boston: Houghton Mifflin,
1929), pp. 90–93, 135.

stories which, however, have a certain coherence. The former tells of a three-inch maiden found in a bamboo stem, her growth into a beautiful woman, and her love affairs which revolve around adventurous expeditions by her various suitors to find treasures which would win her affection; the latter, a bit more realistic, revolves around the love affairs of a young court nobleman.

The *Tale of Genji* (*Genji Monogatari*) was written by a court lady, Murasaki Shikibu of the Fujiwara family, about the first decade of the eleventh century. The Lady Murasaki was the daughter of a scholar, was herself well versed in scholarship, including the Chinese Classics, and she was intimately acquainted with all aspects of life at court and in the capital. It is a very long story. The translation by Arthur Waley, which itself is a literary masterpiece, fills six volumes. The principal character in the story is Prince Genji, son of the emperor by a concubine, who in his appearance and personality is a sort of composite of all of the best characteristics of a court gentleman of that period. He is incredibly handsome and at the same time intelligent, witty, friendly, and delightful, an entirely engaging person. Although gifted in the fine arts of society, he is not effeminate, but rather is manly in a gentle and attractive way. He is very skilled at fencing and riding, as well as the gentler pursuits of dancing, poetry and calligraphy.

For those who regard the Japanese as a stony people, lacking in romance and sentiment, the *Tale of Genji* is a good corrective. It describes the amorous adventures of the gentlemen and ladies of the court in episodic form. The reader follows Prince Genji through one set of romantic adventures after another, adventures which so nearly become repetitious that but for the delightful language in which they are told one might become bored. But the cumulative effect of the book is one of gentle pathos, a sense of the fleetingness of life, of the impermanence of human relationships, and indeed of all things. Beauty fades, love grows cold, lovers die, friendships are broken, and again and again only memories tempered with remorse remain. Awareness that this is the case even with the highest ranking and presumably the most attractive people heightens the pathos. The priests who are called in to assuage grief, the prayers they offer, and the ceremonies they perform seem curiously inadequate, and the explanations which credit misfortune to various evil spirits or mysterious ghosts seem somehow unsatisfying not only to the reader but even to the characters in the story. They go through the ceremonial motions of doing what seems proper but without much real belief in their efficacy. Deeper questions such as why are we here, what does life mean, lie unanswered beneath the surface of the continuing search for happiness in little things and give the tale a meaning and a universality beyond the episodes which it recounts.

There is considerable realism as well as romance in the *Tale of Genji*, although it cannot be classed as a true historical novel. However, several genuine, if not very elegant, historical novels were produced during the later Heian period. One describes the life and times of Fujiwara Michinaga, whose death in 1027 climaxed the most flourishing period of Fujiwara rule. Also there were several *Mirror* (*Kagami*) stories, which are particularly interesting for their

FIGURE 25.3.   View of the Phoenix Hall of the Byodo-in at Uji near Kyoto. It was built in 1053 and is a superb example of Heian architecture. Its elegance, refinement, and grace are characteristics of the setting in which the hero of the *Genji Monogatari* moved.

strong Buddhist overtones and the idea of decline and anxiety for the future. This was the Buddhist idea of *mappō* ("later law"), which held that the time of writing represented a rather late stage of decline from earlier better days when the "law" of the Buddha was more strictly adhered to. Other novels are probably not deserving of mention, but in addition from the late Heian period there have come down to us a number of short stories, perhaps the oldest short stories in the world, and some of these are fascinating. Like the *Tale of Genji* they reveal an aristocratic and aesthetic society emphasizing manners but not morals. Love is again a central theme and there are many tales of excursions, eavesdropping, disguises, seductions, and much attention to such fine arts as painting, calligraphy, poetry, dancing, and even perfume contests. Some of the stories reveal, however, interesting touches of irony which seem to indicate that the unknown authors were quite aware of the superficiality of the values of the society which they were describing. For example "The Lesser Commanders Who Passed the Night in Unexpected Places" is an amusing story of mistaken identities wherein each of these worthies, though "devotedly" in love with his special court girl, through a mixup of carriages, finds himself with the wrong young lady. Making the best of a bad situation the "lesser commanders" find the switch rather to their liking, but the girls realizing this in discussing the matter the next day are "sorely pained." How intriguing, says the author.

Another story, entitled "The Lady Who Loved Worms," shows even stronger signs of amusement with and questioning of the values of the Heian court. Where the ideal woman of the time was supposed to be perfectly feminine, a lover and practitioner of fine cursive calligraphy and gentle poetry, and possessed of perfect taste from court apparel to betel-blackened teeth, the leading character of this story is a young lady who seemed to have none of the finer graces. Her language was rather rough, she wrote in the printed type of *kana* on rough paper, and she preferred caterpillars to butterflies. She refused to pluck her eyebrows, which made her look something like a caterpillar, and she even refused to blacken her teeth, which gave her a "ghastly white smile." Yet despite the fact that she flouted the conventions of the society she somehow seems attractive and interesting; the author, in making her so, is clearly chiding the society, not her.

In Heian times the government was failing, political matters were unattended, life at court became more and more a life of gaiety and ease quite divorced from the needs of the rest of the country. Brinkley, the British author of a multivolumed, early twentieth-century appraisal of Japanese history, sums up the Heian period as "sensual excesses without limit." Perhaps this is an overly moralistic indictment of people who were merely trying to enjoy life, but certainly Heian Japan, and the system and standards it represented, were too narrowly based, too self-centered at the capital and the court to provide valid, long-range answers to the political, social, and economic needs of the entire country. Beyond the court, feudal barons were rising to minister to these needs. Their unblushing militarism brutalized the society, but, perhaps as the crude embodiment of an insistence that "outside" people could not be forgotten, feudalism was a sign of progress.

BASIC DATES

781–806	Reign of emperor Kammu
794	Capital established at Heian (Kyoto)
805	Saicho returns from China, founds Tendai sect in Japan
816	Kukai founds Mt. Koya monastery for Shingon sect
827	Buddhist ordination privileges allowed outside of Nara
838–847	Ennin's travels in China
850–1160	Fujiwara power
891–903	Challenge of Sugawara Michizane
894	End of official relations with T'ang China
922	Kokinshu poetry anthology completed
940	Revolt of Taira Masakado
1008–1020	*Tale of Genji*
1086–1160	Retired sovereigns challenge Fujiwara; chaos in provinces; military factions at court
1160	Taira Kiyomori dictator of Kyoto

SUPPLEMENTARY READING

DE BARY, W. T., ED. *Sources of the Japanese Tradition.* New York, 1958.

KEENE, D., ED. *Anthology of Japanese Literature.* New York, 1955. An excellent selection of translations.

MUNSTERBERG, H. *The Arts of Japan.* Tokyo, 1957.

REISCHAUER, E. O. *Japan: Past and Present.* New York, 1953.

REISCHAUER, E. O. AND J. K. FAIRBANK. *East Asia: The Great Tradition.* Boston, 1958.

SANSOM, G. B. *Japan: A Short Cultural History.* New York, 1943.

TERRY, C. *Masterworks of Japanese Art.* Rutland, Vt., 1956.

ADVANCED READING

COULBORN, R., ED. *Feudalism in History.* Princeton, N.J., 1956. Includes an article on Japan by E. O. Reischauer.

ELIOT, C. N. E. *Japanese Buddhism.* London, 1935.

MURDOCH, J. *A History of Japan.* London, 1925. Vol. I.

PAINE, R. T. AND A. SOPER. *The Art and Architecture of Japan.* Baltimore, 1955.

REISCHAUER, E. O. *Ennin's Travels in T'ang China; Ennin's Diary.* New York, 1955.

REISCHAUER, E. O. AND J. K. YAMAGIWA. *Translations from Early Japanese Literature.* Cambridge, Mass., 1951.

REISCHAUER, R. K. *Early Japanese History*. Princeton, N.J., 1937.
SANSOM, G. B. *A History of Japan to 1334*. Stanford, Cal., 1958.
WALEY, A., TR. *The Pillow Book of Sei Shonagon*. Boston, 1929.
————*The Tale of Genji*. London, 1935.

XXVI ✻✻✻

KAMAKURA JAPAN

Rise of the Military

Kamakura today is a sleepy little resort town on Sagami Bay about ninety minutes south of Tokyo. But its many historic landmarks, the shrine to Hachiman, God of War, and the tombs of military dictators Minamoto Yoritomo and Hojo Tokimune, provide testimony to the violence of the age of Kamakura. For Kamakura was the age which first brought the warrior to the top of Japanese society and exalted the profession of arms above all others, the age which valued swords even above Chinese poetry.

The Kamakura period began with the investiture of Minamoto Yoritomo as Great Barbarian Subduing General (*Sei-i-tai-shogun*) at his "camp capital" (*bakufu*) in Kamakura in 1192, but actually this event represented more a climax than a beginning. It put a capstone on a political-social system of military feudalism, which had been growing slowly but steadily beneath and outside the brilliant Heian court. Its growth was at the expense of the Taika-Nara centralized political structure. As has been shown, undermining forces were at work even in the late Nara period, and though there was an apparent rally in early Heian, in the rise of the Fujiwara family, later Heian times saw a rapid acceleration in the process of political disintegration. Through the twelfth century, as court officials played and squabbled, military feudalism grew, and during the intense succession struggles of 1156–1160, it spilled over into the capital at Kyoto (Heian). At first the military men participated at the invitation of competing court factions, but soon they were competing among themselves without serious reference to civilian rivalries, and with the seizure of de facto political power by the military warlord, Taira Kiyomori, in 1160, we may say the prologue to Kamakura had begun.

The conflict at Kyoto (1156–1160) brought to the center of the political stage two military families, the Taira and the Minamoto. The first victory went to the Taira, headed by the aforementioned Kiyomori, but his coup of 1160 merely gave him Kyoto and bent the civilian population to his will. Beyond that it inaugurated a twenty-five-year struggle with his Minamoto rivals, a struggle fought in various parts of Japan largely outside the capital. The fortunes of war went increasingly against the Taira and in the great sea battle of Dan-no-ura off northern Kyushu (1185) they went down in final defeat. Kiyomori, just before his death in 1185, after twenty years as master of Kyoto, could only lament that he was dying without yet having seen the head of Minamoto Yoritomo. "After my death," he urged, "read no sacred books for me, only cut off the head of Yoritomo and hang it on my tomb."

By that time Kyoto was only an honorary possession for a military victor, and Yoritomo, secure in the eastern Kanto district, was busily erecting the foundations of what later became the Kamakura Shogunate. Actually the outcome of the Taira-Minamoto struggle represented not merely a triumph of the Minamoto clan over the Taira, for Yoritomo had a number of Taira leaders on his side, and, as will be shown, through his wife's family lesser Taira clansmen came to dominate the Kamakura administration after Yoritomo's death. More correctly it represented the victory of military over civilian government in Japan, and secondly, a victory for Kanto over Kansai, for boorish frontier-like eastern Japan over cultured, traditional western Japan.

The meaning of these changes in concrete terms may be illustrated by the following points. In preceding centuries, perhaps as a reflection of Buddhist influence, there was considerable respect for human life in Japan. Even political rivalries, although they were numerous and bitter, had rarely resulted in the execution of members of the losing faction. Banishment to distant parts of the empire was common, but generally this was the supreme penalty until the mid-twelfth century when such inhibitions were ignored. Beheadings, knifings, and bloody vengeance of every kind became not only acceptable in dealing with rivals or potential rivals, but were even glorified in a code of "honor," later, in the seventeenth century, called *bushido,* the way of the warrior. Indeed disrespect for human life became so prevalent in succeeding centuries that some four centuries later it was a legal privilege for a member of the sword-bearing class to exercise *kirisute* (to kill and leave without further ado) on any common person he might find offensive. This change in attitudes is not mentioned as a comparison unfavorable for Japan with European countries, whose record is as bad or worse, but is meant as a significant point of contrast to Japan's own less violent Nara and Heian eras.

The transfer of political power from Kansai to Kanto also had widespread cultural effects. Where Heian writers had produced a remarkable literature, Kamakura writing was extremely clumsy, and in place of the subtle prose and sensitive poetry of Heian, the Kamakura literary output consisted of terse feudal contracts and matter-of-fact accounts of journeys or battles. It was as if even the written language were half forgotten, and indeed the warrior of Kamakura cared little for brilliance of phrasing, so long as the wording at hand settled the issue.

Of course, Kyoto was not dead, even though it was temporarily impotent politically, and although the Kamakura leaders enforced strict measures to insure its political sterility, the Heian cultural influence eventually began to appear even in the camp capital. But for the time being the reaction against the culture of Kyoto was strong.

What Kamakura lacked in refinement, it partly made up for in what could be called efficiency—if this can be understood as a basically *in*efficient system of government efficiently operated. The feudal system had grown up haphazardly. As centralized government deteriorated individuals and localities increasingly made their own arrangements for solving social and economic problems. The most pressing of these was local security, for law and order had broken down, and the sword was becoming more and more the decisive factor in disputes over land, trade, and even religion. Every institution, including the monasteries, armed heavily for defense. The best defense being a good offense, the more powerful and successful at arms were able to attract or force into their fold numerous weaker individuals or groups. Gradually a system of protectors and protected emerged—the protectors, with swords, and armor, by right of strength becoming the superior class. They were now called *samurai,* a shortened single character form of the early *bushi* (military gentlemen). The great mass of nonmilitary common people, with no recourse but to accept such protection as the swordsmen provided, went on tilling the fields, hoping for the best.

The great protector of an area might be the holder of large tax-free estates, if he had taken the precaution of building a local military organization to protect his privileges and peasants. Perhaps he would be a former district official, who had done the same thing or a military upstart who ousted his own patron. At any rate the great protector would have a private army of sword-bearing "protectors" who owed allegiance to him, and who were awarded income from a certain portion of the land for their services. As explained earlier (Chapter 25) the right to income from land (shiki), although it was often confused with the land itself, was divided up among the various participants in the feudal milieu: those who worked the land, various foremen cultivators, the samurai protectors, who would also be the administrators of the estates, and the great protector, or patron.

Kamakura Shogunate

Though at first the great protector, or patron, of an area might recognize no higher authority (save perhaps a ceremonial bow towards Kyoto occasionally), it was the achievement of Minamoto Yoritomo to raise himself, his family, and his personal followers to first rank within the system. His victory over the Taira made him the most powerful military man in Japan, and having secured that position, he worked to organize and centralize the feudal structure. In this task he and his successors were remarkably successful, combining power and diplomacy to accomplish their ends.

FIGURE 26.1. Portrait of Minamoto Yoritomo. A fine contemporary psychological study of the founder of the Kamakura shogunate, using powerful black and white contrasts.

INSTITUTIONAL FOUNDATIONS. Yoritomo was suspicious and ruthless, killing many relatives and friends, including his colorful brother, Yoshitsune, in his rise to power. However, he could also play the diplomat when occasion demanded and in his relations with the Heian court he tempered power with generosity. He seems not to have harbored any idea of abolishing the court or of making himself emperor. After he had forced imperial compliance to his appointment as shogun he dealt rather gently with court circles, working through a Fujiwara family leader, Kanezane, whose career he aided, to secure Kyoto's cooperation on necessary matters. He did not destroy the Chinese-inspired court institutions, but merely bypassed them, while at Kamakura he erected simple, direct non-Chinese government organs. These consisted chiefly of a War Department (Samurai Dokoro), which regulated the affairs of his warrior vassals and set codes of conduct for them, an Administrative Department (Man Dokoro) which handled business and financial matters and in which a number of former Kyoto officials were given high posts, and a Judicial Department (Monchujo) which settled disputes and questions of land titles.

Provincial governorships and district offices filled by Heian court appointments were likewise not abolished. Rather they were rendered innocuous and real power was put into the hands of two sets of feudal officials whose loyalties tended toward Kamakura. These were constables (*shugo*), whom Yoritomo first appointed as military governors for his estates in eastern Japan and then, as he was able, to other areas, and land stewards (*jitō*), whom he appointed to manage estates. Of course, in the case of both constables and stewards, these "appointments" were frequently merely confirmations. A great protector, who was actively resident in an area would likely be named Yoritomo's constable (the basis of the later daimyo, great feudal names), and the stewards, more often than not, would have been superintending for absent landlords the lands to which Kamakura now gave them title. It was to the advantage of both to have Yoritomo's backing against possible claims by absentee protectors or owners, who had in all probability been enjoying life at Kyoto for several generations and lost all direct touch with their estates.

HOJO REGENCY. Although Minamoto Yoritomo established the Kamakura system and intended to pass the shogunal power on to his descendants, his family, in fact, did not continue to rule. Rather it was his in-laws, the Hojo family, who took over the reins of authority at Kamakura. His father-in-law, Hojo Tokimasa was his active assistant in establishing the regime, and when after Yoritomo's death at the relatively youthful age of 52 in 1199 his son and successor proved inept, Hojo took over as regent for the shogun. Thereafter a Hojo regency remained the real key to power until 1333, the end of the Kamakura era. Thus the Hojo ruled behind a triple façade of emperors and Fujiwara regents at Kyoto and the shogun at Kamakura, but it is quite clear that this family held the real authority, and the Kamakura era is thus often called rightly the Hojo period.

SHOKYU STRUGGLE. The only serious challenge to Hojo authority between 1199 and 1333 was a plot engineered at Kyoto by an ex-Emperor, Toba II or Go-Toba, which ended in the brief but exciting Shokyu (Jokyu) Struggle of 1221. Go-Toba, who had dutifully abdicated the throne "to enter religion" in 1198 at age 18 after having produced a son, failed to appreciate retirement at such an early age and tried to utilize his social connections and genuine charm to influence political appointments and economic decisions. Since Sanetomo, Yoritomo's second son, liked him, he was allowed considerable freedom by the dour Hojo regency which watched over Sanetomo during the latter's

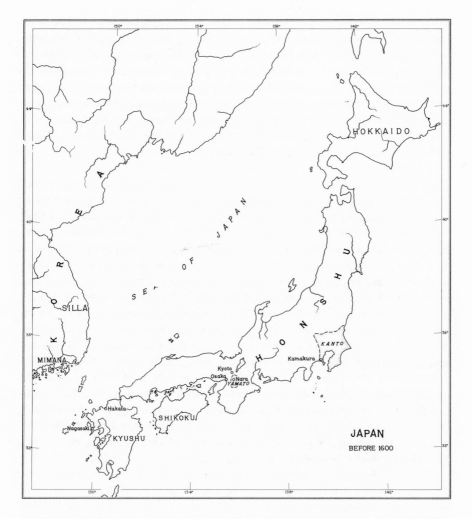

JAPAN

BEFORE 1600

shogunal reign, but finally Go-Toba went too far. He tried to maneuver a change of land title for a favorite dancing girl in preference to certain loyal vassals of Kamakura. When rebuked he began to plot at Kyoto with formerly militant religious leaders, both Buddhist and Shinto, who had been cowed by the shogunate and relieved of some of their land holdings, court nobles, and a few dissident warriors. In June 1221 Go-Toba declared the Hojo regent a rebel and issued a call to arms against him. Some rallied to the ex-emperor, but Kamakura was far better organized than Go-Toba perhaps had realized. Within a month shogunal troops were pouring into Kyoto and Go-Toba was exiled, while his principal supporters faced execution. Since many of these were large landholders, the Hojo took advantage of the opportunity to redistribute some three thousand parcels of land to loyal supporters. At this time many managerial stewards became enfeoffed stewards. Also a change of emperors was effected, a new baby being substituted for the "reigning" one. After this Kamakura reaffirmed its "loyalty" to the imperial house and announced its gratification that evil counsels had been removed from the scene. To guard against future trouble a military inspector was appointed from among Hojo clansmen to reside at Kyoto and oversee the keeping of law and order there, and the appointment of an ex-emperor to the position of chief retired cloistered emperor, was made referrable to Kamakura.

KAMAKURA LAW.   After order was restored in Kyoto the Hojo regents devoted the next few years to the adjudication, as fairly as possible, of arguments over land and income rights, in which they frequently trimmed the claims of their own adherents when these became excessively greedy. As Kamakura's reputation for practical and fair handling of cases grew, the country stood in need of and was willing to accept a formulation of the basic principles on which their *ad hoc* judgments rested. In 1232 this was accomplished by the Joei Code, a new set of rules for judges to follow, which became the supreme law of the land, replacing the now hopelessly outmoded eighth-century Taiho parent code and its several offshoots. The Joei Code was short, direct and so simple that "even the most illiterate fellows can understand its meaning." It avoided abstract philosophizing, Chinese ideas, and other matters remote from everyday life and concentrated on the duties of feudal officials, land titles, and specific personal crimes and punishments. It was harsh, but clear, leaving little room for technical arguments and legal niceties. In certain ways it contained a broader sense of humanity than earlier codes, notably in giving specific consideration to the legal rights of women and in placing emphasis on the impartiality of justice irrespective of social position.

Along with these regulations important for the whole of Japan there developed various feudal house laws and sets of maxims of conduct. Pride of family and ancestry was intense among the warriors and conduct which soiled the family honor was severely penalized. Injunctions to fight bravely and well, preferring death to surrender, to honor one's oaths of loyalty, to carry out duties faithfully, to preserve dignity, to maintain discipline, to judge the character of subordinates astutely, never to act in anger or in haste are the sort of precepts that characterize these house laws. We see in these the "moral" underpinnings of the Warriors' Code, whose bloodier side we have already noted.

ECONOMIC LIFE.   As explained previously the onset of feudalism was in part due to the breakdown of economic institutions, including a system of money exchange, which were necessary to the smooth functioning of a centralized governmental structure. For a time in the eleventh and twelfth centuries the economy fell into chaos; barter became the only means of exchange, as money disappeared from circulation, and land remained the only reliable form of wealth. However, as feudal controls were fastened on the country and a semblance of order returned, economic life began to revive. This was occasioned in part by the need to manufacture the implements of war, which gave a spurt to metalworking, sword and armor manufacture, and mining. Incidental to this, but central to economic revival, was the discovery of new deposits of gold in the province of Mutsu about 1175, which in the succeeding century gave Japan the means of reviving trade with China and importing Chinese copper coins. These reassumed their former position of the pre-Nara period as an important medium of exchange in Japan. At first the shogunate was suspicious of this development and for a time prohibited the use of Chinese coins, but the prohibition was ineffective. In 1226 Chinese coins were made legal tender and later the Hojo regency sent envoys to China with gold to be used in purchasing copper coins there. Records of thirteenth-century Japan show that payments for taxes, loans, and tolls more and more tended to be made in copper coins, and that even land values came to be expressed in copper money. This reinstitution of a monetary medium encouraged various aspects of trade, and although on a scale small in comparison with commerce of later times, the foundations were laid for such institutions as wholesalers of surplus grain from a fief or a number of fiefs. The institution of the pawnshop, often in combination with a saké shop, where money could be borrowed for pledges, not only obtained a start, but flourished to the point of becoming a national problem.

The trade with China, which was quite lively, brought to Japan, in addition to copper coins, such goods as silk, porcelain ware, and sandalwood in exchange for swords, lacquer ware, fans, and timber, along with gold. However, there was a rude interruption of the trade in the 1270's when the Mongol dynasty, in control of the Chinese mainland, made the first of two attempts to invade Japan. The invasion attempts were successfully resisted by the Japanese, but their economic and political effects on the Kamakura regime were so deleterious as to constitute a principal cause for its downfall.

Mongol Invasions and the End of Kamakura

The Mongols were determined to control not only China but all the countries and peoples of Eastern Asia which, having been in the Chinese cultural orbit, had been counted by the Chinese as tributary states (see Chapter 22). However, they were too crude to understand the politics of attraction, which the Chinese had practiced so artfully that they had been able to exercise tremendous influence on the historical course, not only of adjacent countries like Korea and Vietnam where they could apply military pressure if need be, but of Japan, where no Chinese soldier had set foot. The Japanese had never admitted precisely that they were tributaries, although from the time of Prince

Shotoku to the Heian era there can be no doubt that they followed China in philosophy, religion, art, literature, and even in politics and economics. They had sent many missions to China, which had been classed there as tribute bearing missions. But the Chinese court had not made an issue of forcing extreme humility, having become aware very early of Japanese sensitiveness. Indeed one of the earliest missions, in 607, had borne a message from Japan which designated the Japanese empress Suiko as the ruler of the land of the rising sun and addressed the Chinese emperor as the ruler of the land of the setting sun. The Chinese had denounced this arrogance, but allowed subsequent Japanese embassies to maintain an unusual degree of ceremonial self-respect.

One can imagine then the irritation felt by the proud warriors of Kama-kura, who were inclined to be contemptuous of Chinese civilization anyway, when they received a message from Kublai Khan in 1268 demanding that they submit to his authority or suffer invasion. Of course, they realized that they were not dealing with traditional China, having received information from Korea on the might of Mongol armies and of the subjection of that kingdom. Their answer was to turn back this and two subsequent invitations to submit without the slightest indication of compromise, and to hasten to prepare Japanese defenses. They ordered all available men to Kyushu where the attack was to be expected and put the fiefs of western Japan on full war footing. At the same time the court of Kyoto invoked divine protection with a great assort-ment of prayers and ceremonies. The Mongols, on ships built and manned for them by Koreans under duress, appeared off Kyushu in November, 1274.

INVASION OF 1274.   The Mongol force consisted of approximately 15,000 fighting men, plus perhaps half as many unwilling Koreans. The Mongols were far superior to the Japanese in long range weaponry, their stone and flame throwers being especially terrifying, and in battle strategy, for the Japanese were overly attached to single combat in which men of equal ranking ancestry battled each other. However the Mongols were not skilled in launching sea-borne invasions. They were able to get ashore and to push back the Japanese to an inland defense line, but shortly thereafter met with a serious setback. Heavy winds blew up, threatening their entire fleet, and rather than risk being cut off on shore, they tried to re-embark their main body of troops and wait out the storm at sea. But the winds became worse and many of the ships in trying to put out to sea were wrecked and thousands of soldiers were drowned. The Mongol commanders could not reorganize the attack and sailed with what remained of their fleet back to Korea.

The Japanese were jubilant, and thanked the gods for the storm that had contributed so much to their salvation. However, Kublai was not ready to give up the conquest of Japan. He sent another message of warning, that if the "King of Japan" did not appear immediately at Peking to submit, a greater invasion would be launched. This time the Kamakura government in June, 1275 executed the Mongol envoys who brought the message.

FIGURE 26.2.   Ink sketches of Japanese samurai during the period of the Mongol invasions.

The Mongols did not launch another attack immediately, having learned from their first failure that a larger and more carefully planned expedition would be necessary to subdue Japan and having to complete the conquest of the Sung in south China, which was not finally done until 1279. In addition the Korean king, puppet though he was, pleaded the impossibility of equipping another fleet immediately.

INVASION OF 1281.   However, by 1280 Kublai was ready to focus attention on Japan again, and he sent another embassy to demand capitulation. Again Kamakura executed the envoys and the Mongols began invasion preparations on a huge scale. This time about 50,000 Mongols and 20,000 Koreans were to embark from Korea and 100,000 Chinese from south China. This mighty armada reached the shores of Kyushu in late June, 1281. Meanwhile the Japanese had been making feverish preparations. They constructed a stone wall running many miles in either direction from the town of Hakata, so as almost to encompass Hakata Bay, where the Mongols had landed on their previous invasion attempt and which was most accessible from the staging area on Iki Island the Mongols had used before and were to use again. Of course, that wall could be flanked, and in fact the south China contingent seems to have landed farther south near Takashima. Thus the Japanese also prepared mobile units to hurl against flank attacks. From late June until the middle of August the fighting raged fiercely at the wall. The Japanese, were still holding, although not without severe losses, when once again the elements came to their aid.

On August 14-16 a great typhoon swept in from the sea and the Mongol ships made a dash to gain the comparative safety of open water, but were largely unsuccessful. Hundreds of vessels and thousands of men were victims of the storm. Especially decimated was the south China contingent which had arrived later than the Korean one and had only partially unloaded its forces and supplies. The back of the invasion was completely broken, and the Japanese left their fortifications to wipe out the scattered remaining units of invaders. For a second time Japan had been saved by the intercession of the elements and the concept of *kamikaze*, the idea that a Divine Wind protected the Japanese islands, was born. Regarding this, it might be said that the first wind-storm, that of 1274, which came in November, was the more unusual, being later than the normal typhoon season. Typhoons come in August and September almost every year, so the one of 1281 can hardly be considered a miracle.

DECLINE OF HOJO REGENCY.   Paradoxically, successful as the defense against the Mongols had been, it ruined the Kamakura system. There was no immediate collapse of the shogunate, but subsequent events and trends reveal that Kublai's efforts to destroy this defiant Japanese government were more successful than he ever knew. The Great Khan himself seems to have given up the idea of subjugating Japan by 1286 and, after his death in 1294, his successor abandoned it. But Kamakura could not be sure. Every sign of ship-building in Korea was cause for alarm in Japan, and the country was kept on a war basis until 1294 and only gradually relaxed. This meant vast expenditures and a continuous drain of manpower from productive occupations. Not the least of the economic demands came from religious establishments which claimed, without widespread contradiction, that their invocation of the Divine Winds had been the decisive factor in saving the country.

Moreover the expenses of the defense establishment were borne unequally. The feudal houses of the southwestern area, where the greatest burden had fallen, were especially disgruntled that they were not handsomely rewarded. Actually Kamakura did the best it could for them, but its own treasury was depleted and since this victory had resulted in no new conquests of land or seizure of booty, it had no new rewards to offer. The shogunate was besieged with law suits and complaints, the latter coming especially from warriors who, finding that they could not get a "bonus" from the government, began to borrow their "celebration" money from pawnshops, and continued to pawn their possessions and even feudal income due them in the future to meet current expenses. This practice, which unfortunately became widespread, had serious repercussions. As the "war veterans" (and others) found themselves pinched by pawnbrokers (which included not only saké shops, but merchants and Buddhist temples), they began to petition the government for debt postpone-ments and cancellations. The government could not refuse its loyal supporters and in 1297 issued the first of a long line of *tokusei* (Acts of Benevolent Government) which cancelled many outstanding obligations. This gave tem-porary relief, but led to higher interest rates, the inclusion of anti-tokusei clauses in loans, and the employment of hired warriors, or ruffians, by lending agencies to protect their collateral holdings from debtors. The confidence that their judgments would be impartial and their economics solvent, so assiduously built up by Kamakura in the early thirteenth century, was gradually destroyed in the early fourteenth, and retainers and institutions alike began to handle their own disputes.

While the national spirit that had supported Kamakura for a hundred years and turned back the Mongols was being disturbed by economic dislocations, a new court squabble at Kyoto invited dissatisfied elements around the country to begin choosing sides. The difficulty was occasioned by an argument over the proper meaning of the will of the "retired-cloistered" emperor Go-Saga, who had died in 1272. A firm supporter of the shogunate, he had intended to make political life easier for its Hojo directorship by "solving" a problem of rivalry between his two sons, not so much for the throne as for the vast estates which a senior ex-emperor controlled. He divided the estates and though it remained for Kamakura to decide matters of succession to emperorhood, there seems to have been an implication that the two branches would take the throne alternately. At least Kamakura tried to arrange matters that way.

GO-DAIGO AND THE DESTRUCTION OF KAMAKURA. These arrangements did not satisfy the families and followers of either of his sons. Factions formed and after 1300 there was a crisis at Kyoto each time a new emperor was chosen, which was frequently, since to abdicate was the avenue to enjoyment of the revenues and prestige of ex-emperorhood. Ten-year "terms" as emperor became the custom. However, in 1326 a serious crisis was reached. One of the ten-year emperors, Go-Daigo, who accidentally, and unfortunately for the system, had been a grown man when his term started, had an opportunity to demand that his own son be designated heir apparent when the heir apparent from the alternating line died. Kamakura refused to approve and designated a boy from the other branch, whereupon Daigo avoided abdication and began to plot the undoing of the shogunate. He arranged for his "disappointed" son to become the chief abbot of the Mt. Hiei temple complex, which, in fact, gave Daigo command of thousands of warrior monks, and he began to collect other allies via pilgrimages around the Kansai area "to ward off pestilence." The shogunate, beset by other problems and more accustomed to trouble from ex-emperors than from emperors, did not become seriously alarmed until 1331, when it demanded Daigo's abdication. He resisted, but was taken by force, and exiled to the island of Oki. However, his adherents continued to defy the shogunate and when Daigo escaped from his captors and returned to the western shore of Honshu in the spring of 1333, they flocked to his support.

During the earlier uproar Kamakura had, of course, dispatched a large expeditionary force to Kyoto. Its command had been shared by a Hojo and one Ashikaga Takauji, a man of Minamoto stock through one of its junior lines. But the Hojo commander had fallen in battle, and Ashikaga was in charge of this force when Daigo's "return" was effected, though, of course, the inspectorate appointed by Kamakura to maintain order in Kyoto, under the direction of a Hojo, was outside and superior to his authority. In early June, 1333, Ashikaga was ordered to proceed westward to crush Daigo and his supporters. But it seems that Ashikaga's Minamoto spirit rebelled at excessive orders from his Hojo masters. At any rate outside hearing distance of Kyoto he made an exciting proposition to his army: change flags, support Daigo, oust the Hojo, and redistribute their land holdings. The army accepted the invitation and returned to take Kyoto from the Hojo adherents. Almost immediately revolt broke out in eastern Japan and within a month the rebels, their forces swelled by defections from the Hojo army, took Kamakura and burned it. In late July Go-Daigo was "restored" to imperial rule in Kyoto. The question of whether there would be another shogunate was left unanswered for the moment.

Religious and Cultural Trends

The Kamakura was a violent age, an age in which life was cheap, an age in which young men died before fathers, in which ordinary people sold themselves for security and still did not find it. With instability and uncertainty as prevailing conditions, people needed some release, especially away from the battlefield, when they could reflect and when the sense of futility or revulsion seized them. Something to look forward to, to hope for, perhaps to give some point to violence, or at least to calm nerves and relax tensions was necessary. Not art forms and philosophic arguments, but intense personal religion filled that need and gave rise to Japan's Buddhist "Reformation." This reformation followed three lines of development which conformed to the three varieties of need set forth above—for hope, for justification, for peace and calm. These three varieties can conveniently be identified with the three principal sects of Buddhism which emerged in Kamakura times: Shin, Nichiren, Zen.

SHIN BUDDHISM.   Shin Buddhism (full name Jodo Shinshu, and otherwise known as Pure Land or Amidist Buddhism) may be characterized as hope emerging from black despair through faith. This world, according to Jodo Shinshu, is an evil and hopeless place. In the latter days (*mappō*) of the Buddhist Law (i.e., Kamakura times), the great teachings are no longer heeded and decline and degradation are so complete that rectification is impossible. Man can do nothing by his own power, good works are useless, study and strict monastic life are in vain. Man can only appeal to the merciful Buddha (Amida is the God of Boundless Light, one of the many Buddhas of Mahayana Buddhism, and one of many reincarnations of Gautama, the historical Buddha) and have faith that he may be saved. By such faith and faith alone he will be saved. The alternatives are horrible to contemplate, not only in this world, which is unspeakably evil, but after death yawning, cavernous, fiery hells await.

FIGURE 26.3.   An illustration from a Buddhist scroll of the Kamakura period, showing diverse evils of life on earth. Depicted are the agonies of bad teeth.

Faith alone can lead to paradise. Faith in the power and the mercy of Amida Buddha is the one way to salvation, to rebirth in a land of bliss, the Pure Land. Salvation is universal, open to low and high, to peasant and priest alike, to anyone who has faith.

Similar to earlier forms of Japanese Buddhism, Shin had its counterpart in China (the "Pure Land" sects of the T'ang period), but in Japan it began, without a name, in the practices of certain Tendai monks of the tenth century. During that century one Kuya of Mt. Hiei came down from the mountain to sing and dance in the streets of Kyoto, and called upon the multitude to invoke the name of Amida Buddha and sing prayers for salvation. He and others who followed urged the continuous recitation of a phrase glorifying Amida Buddha, a prayerful invocation *"Namu Amida Butsu,"* (Praise be to Amida Buddha) the *nembutsu,* as that formula came to be called. This was simple; it was clear. Anyone could do it and thousands did. Then one Genshin (942–1017), also a Tendai monk, who was both artist and writer, set forth the power of the *nembutsu* in a vividly illustrated, simply written tract called *The Essentials of Salvation.* This book, written in *kana* for mass consumption, presented horrible pictures of the hells awaiting the unfaithful contrasted with blissful, happy scenes of paradise which, he said, awaited the faithful who invoked in true belief and all sincerity the name of Amida. As the Heian era drew to its close and Kamakura began tens of thousands took up the chant. A despairing emperor is credited with seven million repetitions of the prayer to Amida.

In the twelfth century a monk called Honen (1133–1212) took a decisive step. He declared the Amidist way the only way to salvation, and pronounced the good works and monastic practices still indulged in by the more conservative Buddhist community as nonsense, even a hindrance to salvation. To make manifest his rejection of other forms of Buddhism he proclaimed the new Pure Land (Jodo) sect in 1175. His life was stormy after that. His conservative enemies banded together and forced him into exile; some of his followers were even executed. But he died firm in his faith, proclaiming as death approached that he could already see the paradise that awaited him. After Honen his follower Shinran (1173–1262) carried the simple call to faith to its logical conclusion. Honen had traded temples and ceremony for repetition of nembutsu, but he was still a monk, living a life of monkish self-denial. However, Shinran shocked the religious community by abandoning celibacy. He had a wife and a brood of children, and proclaimed the home a better place for religion than the monastery. Furthermore he argued that a man, having found his faith, had no further need of prayers and recitations. One sincere *Namu Amida Butsu* spoken in true faith was enough. Then a person might best lead a normal life, secure in his faith in the power of Amida to bring him to paradise. This was too extreme even for followers of Honen's Jodo, but Shinran, although attacked, worked especially among the lower classes and began to build a sect called Jodo Shinshu, or simply Shin, which was destined to have more followers than all the others combined.

In the Kamakura period Amidist Buddhism became the religion of both the masses and of many important people. Placing on its followers no burden of good works, tedious study, or unnatural disciplined life, it promised paradise in return for simple faith and represented hope in chaotic times.

Perhaps ironically, in the course of its subsequent development Jodo Shinshu, which began as a revolt against priests and temples, came to embrace the most far flung institutional organization of them all. It radiated from a simple Shinran memorial building to become the mammoth Honganji organization of today, with its thousands of temples and priests. It has spread wherever Japanese people have gone, even to Hawaii and America. Without the bond of celibacy on its leadership, it developed a hereditary hierarchical organization, with descendants of Shinran as "popes" of the church. Its financial resources have become so great that it is accounted one of the *zaibatsu* (great financial combines) of modern Japan.

NICHIREN. The other great popular sect which emerged in the Kamakura period was Nichiren whose followers have come to stand in number second only to Shin. Its founder, the priest Nichiren (1222–1282), styled himself the "Bodhisattva of Superb Action." He was a fiery person, violent in language, bold, challenging, and defiant in attitude and action. Where the faith of Shin was passive, its nembutsu to Amida quiet and sincere, the faith of Nichiren was shouted boldly. Nichiren found his inspiration not in Amida, but in the Lotus Sutra, in which, of course, Tendai monks had found the highest truth for centuries. But Nichiren reduced it to a slogan, "Praise be to the Lotus Scripture of Truth" (*Namu Myoho-renge-kyo*), and he and his inspired followers roared it out like a battle cry.

Until Nichiren, Buddhism had been relatively gentle. Some of its rivalries had been bitter, but they were fought on a high, impersonal plane, rather in the nature of scholarly debate. But Nichiren began by consigning all disbelievers to flaming hell, and he proclaimed threats and warnings of the direst nature for country and people if his words were not heeded. He addressed the leaders of other sects by name and called them fiends, devils, liars, and traitors. Nichiren was a product of rough and militant eastern Japan. His principal base was Kamakura itself, and his exhortations although extreme enough to worry the military government, nevertheless attracted many rugged spirits to his band. By Nichiren's time the Hojo government, which had worked tolerably well, had passed its height. The political situation was deteriorating, and Japan was threatened for the first time by foreign invasion. Mongol threats arrived at Kamakura even as Nichiren shouted his predictions of disaster. His criticisms of those in authority became so pointed and vehement that he was once sentenced to death, but a bolt of lightning on the execution ground saved him. Then with typical audacity he proclaimed himself reborn, and continued to harass the officialdom of Kamakura until they sent him into exile.

Nichiren has long been associated with nationalism in Japan, probably in exaggeration of the facts. But it is true that he utilized the theme of danger to the state to reinforce his demands that his brand of Buddhism be accepted to the exclusion of all others. He was not really a nationalist, for his fierce devotion was to his Lotus Sutra and not the state. Like Muhammad he thought he had a vision of truth and on such points as the equal right of men and women of all classes to be saved he was certainly advanced for his time, but his idea of brotherhood too was limited to believers and his choice of words and line of argument gave inspiration to nationalists in later times. Nichiren himself seems to have regarded the Mongol invasions, which he had predicted, with a sort of fierce satisfaction as Heaven-sent punishment of the Hojo government for their continued support of "hellish" sects of Buddhism. The title of his greatest tract, *On Establishing Righteousness and the Safety of the Country (Rissho Ankoku Ron)* and the name he took, Nichiren (*nichi* - sun; *ren* - lotus) testify to his curious mixing of country and religion.

ZEN BUDDHISM. Of all the religious developments of Kamakura times Zen is the most difficult to explain, although it was perhaps the most important. Zen as a religious sect never achieved the numerical following of Shin or Nichiren, yet its influence has pervaded Japan not only in religion, but in other fields as well—in art, architecture, philosophy, and in that indefinable area called attitudes toward life, aspirations, ideals. Zen is an element in many aspects of Japanese life, even in the twentieth century, but its influence is not obvious, or easy to trace.

Zen is contemplative Buddhism. It was brought to Japan from China (where it was known as Ch'an) by a Tendai monk named Eisai in the late twelfth century, but in the military atmosphere of feudal Japan it came to mean much more than mere contemplation. In Japan Zen became a part of the cult of military feudalism. It proved peculiarly attractive to the warrior class, giving them release and occupation in their hours away from the battle field. At the same time it strengthened their mental stamina for future combat and rein- forced their presumption of superiority, the basis of their claim to rule Japan. Zen scorned books, and the warriors, many of whom could not read, and who associated book learning with the Kyoto courtiers, also scorned books.

Zen held that no amount of reading or study would bring enlightenment, that enlightenment could come only as a sudden flash of insight, like a sudden bolt of lightning. It was highly individual and very personal; it could not be taught. To hope to experience it a man must first be master of himself and his surroundings. He must be calm when others are excited, unafraid in a situation where terror would be natural; he must be able to sip tea and talk casually about the tea cup while his enemy stalked him. He must be able to eat a strawberry and enjoy its delicious flavor while clinging to a cliff with a yawning cavern below and a man-eating tiger above (a Zen parable). He must be prepared to die at any moment without a murmur, or live deliciously with- out caring. He would be scornful of intelligence, knowing it to be only of limited influence. What does the intelligence say is the sound of clapping one hand? When asked to explain the meaning of a paradoxical expression he had just used, the Zen master might answer, "There is deep meaning," or he might say nothing at all, just sigh at the stupidity of the inquirer, and smile that the fool thought the explanation could be expressed in words.

Anyone who has studied a geometric diagram, drawn to illustrate a theorem, and seen at first only a jumble of lines, then suddenly, "in a flash of insight," become aware of the interrelationships which prove the theorem, knows the meaning of Zen in a small, particularized way. It is certainly true that Zen, in its efforts to penetrate the area between particular knowledge and generalized perception, was on the track of still unanswered psychological questions, and Zen contributions to the arts were to be immense. However, in medieval Japan, the warrior class, by adopting the stern, superior countenance of Zen practitioners and turning aside common people's timid inquiries with haughty parables, could fortify their rule. So they appreciated Zen, whether they really sought enlightenment or not.

The foregoing discussion of religion is entirely concerned with Buddhism, which should not be taken to imply that Shinto was dead, although it was certainly of secondary importance. Nature worship involving Shinto spirits was still practiced, especially by peasants, but at the higher levels Shinto

FIGURE 26.4. A Buddhist monk of the Kamakura period. A masterpiece of quiet realism.

deities were largely amalgamated into the Buddhist pantheon. One Shinto god, Hachiman, god of war, remained, as might be expected, something of a favorite with Kamakura warriors. A fuller consideration of the progress of Shinto is best postponed until discussion of the Ashikaga era, when a significant Shintoist interpretation of Japanese history and politics appeared.

KAMAKURA LITERATURE. In nonreligious literature the Kamakura period is not nearly so rich, qualitatively, as Heian, but there was considerable writing. Its chief original contribution, in addition to the legal documents already discussed, was the war romance. A number of these were written on scrolls with appropriate illustrations and with the Taira-Minamoto struggle as the central theme. They are replete with heroic deeds, of course, but occasionally catch the futility of it all, as illustrated by the following lines from the most famous of these stories, the *Heike Monogatari,* a fictionalized tale of the House of Taira from 1131 to its fall in 1185: "The proud ones do not last long, but vanish like a spring night's dream. And the mighty ones too will perish in the end, like dust before the wind."

There was also a semiofficial history of the Kamakura Shogunate (to 1266), called the Mirror of the East (*Azuma Kagami*) largely chronological, and a strange but interesting attempt at intepretative history, the *Gukansho.* This work, whose title defies translation, was apparently done by a Buddhist monk, who was also a Fujiwara, and it was written under a strong sense of *mappō,* the accelerating degeneration of the world after the time of the Buddha.

Kyoto literary circles did not die in the Kamakura period. In fact some of their influence reached Kamakura, where there was at times rather more poetry composing than pleased the Hojo, but the idea that poetry or literary or artistic activity of any kind could be a sufficient end in itself was lost amidst military strife. Of all the arts perhaps swordmaking was the most valued. A fine sword was an object of veneration.

BASIC DATES

1160–1181	Taira Kiyomori dictator at Kyoto
1180	Minamoto Yoritomo starts revolt
1185	Minamoto destroy Taira forces at Dan-no-ura
1192–1199	Minamoto Yoritomo shogun at Kamakura
1199–1333	Hojo regency
1221	Shokyu struggle
1222–1282	Nichiren
1274 and 1281	Mongol Invasions
1297	First "Act of Benevolent Government" (*tokusei*)
1331	Emperor Go-Daigo challenges Kamakura shogunate
1333	Ashikaga Takauji destroys Kamakura

SUPPLEMENTARY READING

BROWN, D. M. *Nationalism in Japan*. Berkeley, Cal., 1955.

DE BARY, W. T., ED. *Sources of the Japanese Tradition*. New York, 1958.

KEENE, D., ED. *Anthology of Japanese Literature*. New York, 1955.

MUNSTERBERG, H. *The Arts of Japan*. Tokyo, 1957.

REISCHAUER, E. O. *Japan Past and Present*. New York, 1953.

REISCHAUER, E. O. AND J. K. FAIRBANK. *East Asia: The Great Tradition*. Boston, 1958.

SANSOM, G. B. *Japan: A Short Cultural History*. New York, 1943.

TERRY, C. *Masterworks of Japanese Art*. Rutland, Vt., 1956.

ADVANCED READING

ANESAKI, M. *History of Japanese Religion*. London, 1930.

ASAKAWA, K. *Documents of Iriki*. New Haven, 1929. An intensive study of a single estate.

COULBORN, R., ED. *Feudalism in History*. Princeton, N.J., 1956.

ELIOT, C. N. E. *Japanese Buddhism*. London, 1935.

MC CULLOUGH, H. C., TR. *The Taiheiki: A Chronicle of Medieval Japan.* New York, 1959.

MURDOCH, J. *A History of Japan.* London, 1925. Vol. I.

ELIOT, C. N. E. *Japanese Buddhism,* 2nd ed. New York, 1959.

PAINE, R. T. AND A. SOPER. *The Art and Architecture of Japan.* Baltimore, 1955.

REISCHAUER, E. O. AND J. K. YAMAGIWA. *Translations from Early Japanese Literature.* Cambridge, Mass., 1951.

SANSOM, G. B. *A History of Japan to 1334.* Stanford, Cal., 1958.

SHINODA, M. *The Founding of the Kamakura Shogunate.* New York, 1960.

XXVII ❀❀❀

ASHIKAGA, CIVIL WAR,

AND THE UNIFICATION

OF JAPAN, 1333-1600

The Kemmu Restoration

Although he owed his return to the throne to Ashikaga Takauji and
other military men who had revolted against Kamakura, the emperor
Go-Daigo was inclined to take his restoration seriously. He attempted
to revive the prestige and power enjoyed by the imperial court in the
tenth century, before the advent of feudalism. For a two-year period,
1334–1336, called the Kemmu era after the title of a treatise on
the revival of old ceremonies written by the emperor himself, he
tried to eradicate certain aspects of the feudal system with boldness,
but perhaps not with wisdom, for he was forced to flee again.

Go-Daigo began his rule by "neglecting" to designate a new
shogun, and he undertook to enlarge and strengthen the holdings
of some of the Buddhist monasteries to the detriment of secular
warrior chieftains. To enhance the emperor's prestige a tremendous
palace building program was inaugurated, and it was assumed that
the warriors who had helped restore the emperor would accept delay
in the redistribution of the spoils taken from the supporters of

defeated Kamakura. However, this was not to be the case. Soon Kyoto was swarming with military men who demanded the lands of defeated Hojo supporters, and they were irritated beyond measure at having to stand in line at a Court of Awards manned by palace courtiers.

Ashikaga Takauji was potentially the most dangerous of the warrior claimants and though he was rewarded handsomely with lands and ranks, it was done in such a way as to avoid any implication that he might become a new shogun. Imperial princes, even though mere children, were given the most important governorships and word circulated that one of them might become shogun, perhaps with an Ashikaga regent. Meanwhile Go-Daigo and his chief advisor Kitabatake Chikafusa placed their greatest reliance on the emperor's eldest son, Prince Morinaga, who had formerly been chief abbot of Hieizan and who was now groomed to challenge Ashikaga Takauji if there should be a struggle. Prince Morinaga was able and active, and apparently devoted to the imperial cause, but his undoing was promoted in part from within the palace itself where Go-Daigo's current favorite lady resented so much power held by imperial offspring not her own. She intrigued with Takauji and contrived to have the prince sent to Kamakura where he was murdered by order of Takauji's brother, who was charged with maintaining order there. The excuse was that there was turbulence in the area created by a rising of former Hojo partisans who for a time retook the city.

This turbulence in eastern Japan also provided Takauji with the opportunity to demand from the emperor a commission as shogun to subdue in the east. The emperor refused, but Takauji marched eastward anyway in overt defiance of the court. By November, 1335, he was in control of the Kamakura area and was systematically ousting pro-imperial elements from eastern Japan, who fled back to Kyoto to stand with the Emperor. Between December, 1335, and February, 1336, the Ashikaga forces defeated the imperial armies blocking the way to Kyoto and Takauji re-entered the city in triumph on February 25. Once again Go-Daigo had to flee to the monastery complex on Mt. Hiei.

The struggle was by no means over, for strong imperial support arrived from northern provinces, led by Kitabatake Akiiye, son of Chikafusa, but during the next two years, after obtaining reinforcements from Kyushu, the Ashikaga prevailed. Akiiye was killed in 1338. Meanwhile Ashikaga Takauji had obtained his commission as shogun, not from Go-Daigo, but from a retired ex-emperor of the alternating "senior" line, whose younger brother he placed on the throne at Kyoto as a puppet emperor. Takauji was willing to let Go-Daigo live in peace as a retired emperor, and he approved the nomination of one of Daigo's younger sons as crown prince, thus indicating his intention to resume the alternating line principle. Go-Daigo feigned acceptance, but when he saw his opportunity in January, 1337, he fled the environs of Kyoto for the last time and took refuge in a remote mountain district to the south, at Yoshino. There, with the aid of Kitabatake Chikafusa, he established a rival "southern" court, which Chikafusa "proved" was the legitimate court with his brilliant, if somewhat tendentious

history of Japan, the *Jinno Shotoki*. This work was an ambitious study of
Japanese history built around the theme of the centrality of the imperial court,
and the need to preserve the legitimacy of its sovereigns:

> Only in our country has the succession remained inviolate, from the
> beginning of heaven and earth to the present. It has been maintained
> within a single lineage, and even when, as inevitably has happened, the
> succession has been transmitted collaterally, it has returned to the true
> line. This is due to the ever-renewed Divine Oath, and makes Japan un-
> like all other countries.[1]

Northern and Southern Courts

Go-Daigo died in 1339, but the Southern Court he had established at Yoshino
remained to plague the Ashikaga-sponsored Northern Court at Kyoto until 1392.
For about a decade after the former emperor's death Yoshino was not able to
mount a serious offensive, but the feudal lords of the country who had grievances
against the Ashikaga or special interests of their own gradually rallied around
Go-Daigo's successor, his son Go-Murakami. Kitabatake Chikafusa continued
to work ardently and persistently for the "legitimate" line and Go-Daigo's sixteenth son, Prince Kanenaga, who had been sent to Kyushu in 1336 at the age
of seven, grew up to be a vigorous and able organizer of support for the Yoshino
cause. By the 1350's they were seriously threatening Shogun Takauji again.

The Ashikaga position was made even more precarious by division within
their own ranks. Takauji's younger brother, who had been a great source of
strength to his regime in the early years, developed ambitions which promised
conflict with the interests of Takauji's favorite son, Yoshiakira, who was being
groomed as the next shogun. Takauji effected the defeat and death of his
brother, but in the process found his support so weakened that he made overtures
to the Southern Court, which gave it a chance to regain a foothold in Kyoto.
In fact Kitabatake Chikafusa, after years of defeats, had his moment of joy
near the end of his life, when, during the fight between the Ashikaga brothers,
the emperor of the Southern line was able to re-enter Kyoto and receive back
the imperial regalia Go-Daigo had been forced to surrender. The Southerners
were in control of Kyoto when Chikafusa died in 1354.

However, in April 1355, Ashikaga Takauji returned to Kyoto and although
the civil war that had become endemic made his control tenuous, he was able
to hold the capital until his death in 1358. Takauji had held the title of shogun
for two decades and had campaigned throughout Japan with great vigor, but
having destroyed the delicate balances of the Kamakura era, he had been unable
to resurrect a substitute balance. His only lasting political contribution was a
new law code, the Kemmu Shikimoku, which he had issued in 1336 as part

---

[1] W. T. De Bary, ed., *Sources of the Japanese Tradition*. (New York: Columbia
Univ. Press, 1958), pp. 279–280.

of his effort to stabilize his rule. It was more a statement of lofty principles than a code, setting down seventeen of these, in emulation of Prince Shotoku's famous "Seventeen-Article Constitution." They enjoined economy, reconstruction, meritorious service, and justice, while condemning drinking, gambling, indiscriminate punishments, and disorder. Clearly these had been honored more in the breach than in the practice during his career as shogun.

The death of Takauji was followed by years of deepening chaos. His son, Yoshiakira, became shogun, but his position was dependent on shifting alliances. Prince Kanenaga continued to be the strongest power in Kyushu until his death in 1383. However, after that the third Ashikaga, Yoshimitsu, who had become shogun at Kyoto in 1368, gained the offensive, after which he undertook serious negotiations with the Southern Court to end the schism. Finally, in 1392, amidst general war weariness, he succeeded in negotiating an agreement by which the alternating succession between the two imperial lines should be resumed, the Ashikaga should guard and rule as shoguns, and the civil war should be ended.

Relations with China

One of the factors that contributed to the settling of the civil war in Japan was concern about relations with China. Ashikaga Takauji as shogun had wished to lay to rest the longstanding bitterness between Mongol China and Japan and to gain some pecuniary profit therefrom. He had therefore authorized the great Tenryu (Zen) temple in Kyoto to open trade relations with China, ostensibly for the purpose of obtaining funds and materials for the construction of a building to honor ex-Emperor Go-Daigo. The result had been the development of a lively exchange whereby the Japanese regime received quantities of Chinese copper coins in exchange for various commodities. However, the question of official relations was left aside and the matter was complicated by the entrance into the trade of nonlicensed rivals of the Ashikaga, who began to prey on Chinese coastal towns in the era of revolt that preceded the overthrow of the Mongol (Yuan) dynasty in China.

When the Ming came into power in China in 1368 they were determined to regularize relations with Japan according to the time-honored tributary system and to bring an end to the illegal piratical activities that had developed. As related above (Chapter 23) the Hung-wu emperor dispatched edicts to Japan announcing his enthronement, inviting the tributary envoys, and demanding that coastal piracy be suppressed. It is noteworthy also that the existence of two rival governments in Japan complicated matters. Some of these communications reached the Ashikaga in Kyoto, but some of them were cut off by Prince Kanenaga in Kyushu. The Japanese replies were not subservient enough to please Hung-wu, and one in particular, from Kanenaga, dispatched in 1382 or somewhat before, was openly defiant.

The world is the world's world; it does not belong to a single person . . .
I have heard that the Celestial Court is making plans for war. This small
country too has a plan for meeting the enemy . . . . When your generals
come we shall meet them with troops . . . . May Your Majesty think
this matter over.[2]

After this the Hung-wu emperor broke off all relations with Japan and
began military preparations along the China coast, though he seems not to have
thought seriously of invading Japan. However, after making the settlement with
the Southern Court in 1392 and gaining, temporarily, at least, a large measure
of hegemony in Japan, Shogun Yoshimitsu himself took up the Chinese question
with a view to improving relations. He remembered the financial advantages his
grandfather had reaped and he was desirous of bringing under control the
troublesome pirates, or wakō, who defied his authority along the coast of
Kyushu and in small nearby islands. In 1395 and again in 1397 he sent conciliatory messages to China, and then in 1401 he sent gold, horses, paper, fans,
screens, armor, and swords as humble gifts to the Chinese court. The Chinese
court pronounced itself "well pleased" and sent congratulations and gifts to the
"King of Japan." Thereafter, until Yoshimitsu's death in 1408, relations were
cordial.

Yoshimitsu's acceptance of the Ming seal investing him as "King of Japan,"
which acknowledged Japan to be a dependent, tributary state of China, was a
new departure. In Nara and early Heian times Japan had certainly been a
cultural tributary, but the Japanese had resisted Chinese attempts to register
this in political terms. The estrangement from China that had occurred in the
later Heian and Kamakura periods makes Yoshimitsu's action seem even more
peculiar. He has been roundly condemned by national-minded Japanese historians. However, it should be noted that Yoshimitsu was playing a sort of
diplomatic game for money and that the Ming court was motivated by anxiety
rather than strength. In fact both sides were relying on elaborate pretences to
gloss over existing facts.

One Japanese historian has used the Japanese word *kamen* in discussing
the relationship between Yoshimitsu and the later Ashikaga shoguns and the
Ming court. Literally kamen means "temporary face" or, more freely, "false
face, mask." It is an apt description, for the relationship, if studied closely,
betrays several "false faces," each seeking a special advantage. Yoshimitsu,
anxious to strengthen his position *vis-à-vis* other powerful feudal lords in Japan,
wanted financial support from China as well as the added prestige a ceremonial
relationship with the Chinese emperor might bring him. The Ming emperor
was quite willing to buy the shogun's "loyalty" with gifts, if the latter would
use honorifics in addressing him and would undertake to stop Japanese piracy
along the mainland coasts. The pirates were definitely a problem to the Ashikaga
as well for they represented defiance of shogunal authority, but stopping them

    [2] Wang Yi-t'ung, *Official Relations Between China and Japan, 1368–1549* (Cam-
bridge: Harvard Univ. Press, 1953), p. 19.

was difficult because they operated with the connivance of certain feudal lords in southwestern Japan.

The pirates wore many false faces. They might pose as legitimate envoys of the "King of Japan" bearing humble tribute to the Ming court; after giving these gifts they would demand rich rewards. Sometimes they would be "honest merchants" who wished to enjoy the prerogatives of trade a "tributary" state of China should have. But whenever the opportunity presented itself, they would turn into marauders, who, in league with Chinese confederates, would sack coastal towns.

In return for Chinese coins, other gifts, and trading privileges Ashikaga Yoshimitsu did make strenuous efforts to control the pirates. A tally system, devised in 1404, worked tolerably well for a number of years. The shogunate would give out special tallies, whose stubs were held by the Ming court, to approved missions. Japanese missions which arrived in China without a proper tally were subject to arrest. Approved Chinese missions to Japan likewise carried tallies, the stubs of which were kept by the shogun. In addition Yoshimitsu several times rounded up Japanese "pirates" and sent them to China for punishment.

Though Yoshimitsu's son, who succeeded him as shogun in 1408, at first promised to carry on his father's policies toward China, he did not in fact do so. In 1411 he refused to entertain an official Chinese mission and thereafter he let both his official missions to China and efforts to control the pirates lapse. The Chinese emperor admonished him repeatedly, but to no avail, and it was only after his death that relations with China resumed the course designed by Yoshimitsu.

Between 1432 and 1549 some eleven official Japanese missions carrying tallies went to China. How many pirates went is not known, but there were increasingly spectacular raids along the Chinese coast during this period. Also the pirates seem to have stolen or reproduced tallies and even to have infiltrated official embassies. There were numerous admonitions from Peking and many arguments. For example, an official Japanese embassy which arrived at Peking in 1453 brought with it a large entourage and quantities of merchandise for sale or trade, and its members had heated arguments with the Chinese Board of Rites over prices at which merchandise was to be sold and the amount of gifts the embassy was to receive. This was very irregular for the tributary system, but the Chinese tried to smooth matters over.

The fact was that the position of the Ashikaga shoguns was becoming increasingly unstable, so whatever promises they gave to control pirates or other obstreperous Japanese subjects were of no value except insofar as they might induce the Ming court to send financial aid to bolster the rapidly weakening shogunate. Ashikaga Yoshimasa could offer nothing except a piteous plea when he addressed the Ming emperor in 1475, as follows:

Just as Heaven looks down with affection and just as the sun shines with great brilliancy, the Ming rules myriads of nations and makes them revere the throne . . . . As for my humble state, it suffers continually from military disturbances . . . . Because of the long continued warfare in my humble state, all the copper coins have been scattered and lost. The state coffers are empty. The land is laid waste . . . . As the records show, in the Yung-lo era the Imperial (Chinese) throne made abundant gifts of copper coins to our state. Recently no gifts of this sort have been sent . . . . This state of affairs is hereby urgently laid before the throne with urgent hope for Imperial consideration and grants.[3]

On this occasion the Chinese emperor responded with a grant of 50,000 strings of copper coins. After Yoshimasa, who died in 1490, the management of the missions to China and the tallies which made them legal fell more and more into the hands of the powerful feudal lords who were beyond the control of the Ashikaga. In 1523 rival missions from the Ouchi and Hosokawa clans arrived at the Chinese port of Ningpo only ten days apart and literally fought each other for the privilege of going to Peking. Needless to say the Ming court reprimanded Japan, and the shogun, who had no control over either party, could only apologize abjectly. There is evidence that in the 1540's one of the most powerful pirate chiefs was invited by a leading feudal lord in northern Kyushu to live at his principal port city, Hirado, from whence he directed operations all over the China Sea. Japanese piracy reached its height in 1555, with 34 raids on the Chinese coast being recorded by the Ming government for that year. In the next decade there was a sharp decrease, however. A principal reason for this may have been that civil war, which had become endemic in Japan, was approaching a climax and, with the overthrow of the Ashikaga imminent, adventurous eyes turned inward to watch for chances to participate in the power struggle at home.

Cultural Brilliance Amidst Incessant Warfare

The last century of the Ashikaga period, from about 1460 to 1560, displays a remarkable paradox: complete political breakdown into incessant civil war, accompanied by a remarkable cultural flowering.

ONIN WAR. Politically the times were decidedly unpropitious. The temporary stability that Ashikaga Yoshimitsu had fashioned deteriorated under his successors to the point where all the coins in China probably could not have saved the Ashikaga shogunate by Yoshimasa's time. In 1467 an era of chaos was inaugurated by the outbreak of the so-called Onin war, which itself lasted for a decade and which unleashed such turmoil that the country was not restored to order until a peasant-born general, Hideyoshi, made himself its dictator in the late sixteenth century. Basically the Onin war was caused by a decline

[3] Yoshi S. Kuno, *Japanese Expansion on the Asiatic Continent,* Vol. I (Berkeley: Univ. of California Press, 1937), p. 287.

in feudal discipline and the development of open, warlike competition for power, not only among leading feudal families, but at all levels of society. Peasants warred against landlords, warriors against each other, almost every powerful family had violent succession disputes, and no one, seemingly, hesitated to defy the authority of the shogun or his deputies. One Yamana, called the Red Monk, and his son-in-law, Hosokawa, were the principal adversaries in the first stage of the war, with their forces in turn ravaging and occupying Kyoto itself, under the very nose of the shogun. Then uprisings in their respective provinces took these two principal warlords home, where they both died, but their successors fought for generations until the Hosokawa family collapsed completely in 1558.

Meanwhile the central stage at Kyoto was taken by other warlords, such as the Ouchi family, who eventually were attacked by one set of vassals, then avenged by another, the Mori. These Mori, having punished the treachery, took over Ouchi lands themselves and lived on into modern times as controllers of the vast Choshu domain on the western part of the main island. In eastern Japan, a powerful family called Uyesugi held sway during much of the fifteenth century, dominating Kamakura and becoming so arrogant that it paved the way for its own downfall. Within its ranks there was succession rivalry among three branches that allowed an outside clan to challenge successfully Uyesugi hegemony. Another family which fought its way through the Onin war era and emerged as a strong contender in the final elimination contest of the mid-sixteenth century was the Takeda, of the province of Kai. Among them Takeda Shingen seemed for a time to be the most likely to come out on top in that contest of warlords. Actually it was Oda Nobunaga, a minor lord, who controlled a small area east of Kyoto, near Lake Biwa, whose forces were to triumph in the bloody civil war. But before telling the story of Nobunaga and his associates a brief description of the arts in this chaotic period will be given.

It has been observed that war stories and swordmaking were prominent among the arts of the earlier Kamakura era. However, amidst the deepening chaos of Ashikaga times, enthusiasm for these pursuits waned, as in their more sober moments people sought relief from war, not its further celebration. Millions found some solace in the new popular Buddhist sects, Jodo, Shin, and Nichiren, which promised salvation by faith, and when not engaged in fighting or fleeing war, they intoned countless prayers and paid vast sums of money to those temples which, through spirited defense by armed monks or sagacious military politics by their abbots, avoided destruction.

However, some were too proud or intelligent merely to pray. They found not salvation, but a certain amount of relief, and even pleasure, in self-disciplined meditation on the remarkable paradox of life in which man, the most intelligent being in a beautiful world, had succeeded in making it into a living hell. From this meditation they discovered that by conscious and deliberate self-control they could detach themselves from the chaos about them, and create, within a limited spatial and temporal setting, a world of exquisite if transient beauty.

Their inspiration for this way of thinking was Zen, which means meditation. However, to interpret it as *merely* a type or sect of Buddhism is to confuse an organizational structure with both a principle of philosophy or a rule of art, which perhaps had been discovered by men called Zen priests, but which remained to be rediscovered by anyone who could discipline himself sufficiently and which came to be applied in a thousand different ways. The applications which were devised and perfected in Ashikaga times were principally in five areas: in tea ceremony, architecture and landscape gardening (all of which are interrelated), in painting, and in a theatrical dance, the Nō.

TEA CEREMONY. The tea ceremony is at once the simplest aspect of Ashikaga art and the heart of it. Perhaps it began with a monk in meditation pausing to make himself a cup of tea. He may have been joined by a warrior lately come from the battlefield, who, seeking relief from the bloody scenes he had witnessed, put down his sword and squatted close by in silence. Nothing extraordinary occurs. While the water boils in the teapot, there may be a slight whistling of the wind outside, or the sound of an animal or bird. The tea master may apologize for the bitterness of the tea he is preparing (a bitter variety is in fact preferred). The guest may comment on the flower arrangement

FIGURE 27.1.   View of the Ryuanji rock garden, Kyoto. Sand and rock replace grass and trees, creating the impression of vast space.

or hanging scroll which decorates the otherwise bare room, or he may remark on the shape or beauty of the teacup. The tea master will respond that it is made of common clay. The guest, accepting it, will encircle it with both hands and lift it up, enjoying at once the warmth and the odor of the tea, and he may speak of the perfect suitability of the cup's simple beauty. He may say nothing at all, only handle the cup of tea as though it were a great treasure, and end by drinking it slowly and deliberately as though savoring the whole world. Indeed that is the principal idea, to savor the whole world and sense eternity in a fleeting few moments at tea.

ARCHITECTURE.   The architecture of the tea house heightens the effect. It is unpretentious, but perfect, being set harmoniously in a small garden whose landscaping is such that tea house and natural surroundings blend together in unobtrusive elegance. The art of *bonsai* (dwarf trees) may be employed so skillfully that even a tiny garden will give the impression of vast space, or sand and rock may replace grass and trees if the effect of islets in the sea is desired. The most famous examples of Ashikaga era blending of buildings and gardens into an artistic whole are the Golden Pavilion (Kinkakuji) and the Silver Pavilion (Ginkakuji), which were constructed for Yoshimitsu and

FIGURE 27.2.   Kinkakuji, or the Golden Pavilion, in Kyoto. The walls and transoms are lined with gold leaf. The pavilion was built for the shogun Ashikaga Yoshimitsu, was burned down after World War II, and has recently been reconstructed.

Yoshimasa, respectively in Kyoto. The Golden Pavilion certainly is more elaborate than a Zen master might have desired, but considering that it was for the use of the shogun, even it, as well as the Silver Pavilion, are remarkably unpretentious structures and convey that delicacy of understatement which pervades Zen inspired art.

FIGURE 27.3.　　Ginkakuji, or the Silver Pavilion, in Kyoto. Built by Ashikaga Yoshimasa, the pavilion is an unpretentious structure along Chinese lines, but it conveys the understatement which is so typically part of Zen-inspired art.

PAINTING.　In painting the black ink brush work of Sesshu (1420–1506) is the greatest that has survived, although he was only one of a group of Ashikaga artists whose application of Zen aesthetics to the visual arts was brilliant. Again the secret lies in simplicity, in understatement, in leaving something to the imagination of the viewer, and in conveying a sense of eternity in an ordinary scene. Sung landscapes provided a principal element in the inspiration of these Ashikaga painters, but they were able somehow to convey more, while using less, even than the Sung masters. This they accomplished through the highly skilled use of "unskilfullness," wherein the artist creates his desired effect with a few rapid and seemingly casual brush strokes delivered in a way that obscures the long practice and precise technique that lies behind his ability. The observer is misled into feeling that he could easily draw the picture himself, until he tries to visualize how he would do it. Then he stands back in awe.

FIGURE 27.4. A winter landscape by Sesshu in black ink. One of the great masterpieces of Japanese art.

Nō. The Nō dance, or drama, is the last and in some ways the most subtle of all the Zen-inspired arts perfected in the Ashikaga era. To call it a dance seems almost absurd to anyone who has seen a performance, for almost no physical movement takes place. Every step is so measured and precise, even as the No actor moves onto the stage, that it seems an eternity before he is even ready to begin. And in the dance proper such a violent passion as jealousy or lust will be indicated merely by a thrust of the head or the motion of an eye, which the inattentive observer will miss entirely. The Nō performer operates in a state of controlled tension wherein every movement, from the half-step to the raising of an eyebrow, is so meaningfully performed that every random motion is eliminated, and the audience must almost match his state of tension to catch the meaning of his performance. It is an exercise in concentration so powerful that both performer and audience may be exhausted at its conclusion, without, physically speaking, the audience's having moved a muscle and with the performer having moved one muscle at a time.

In summary it may be said that Ashikaga artists sought escape from the chaos of their time, but not in usual and unsophisticated forms of escapism, like dreaming, fantasy, and romance. Instead they fashioned an art of self-control and concentration, through which the artist and those who could follow him were able to shut out the world of fools and folly, suspend time, and momentarily glimpse perfection.

Economic Developments and the Arrival of Europeans

Despite the feudal strife and political chaos of Ashikaga times there was, in addition to progress in the arts, considerable economic growth. The activities of the *tonya,* agents of the fief who marketed its surplus commodities outside its boundaries, increased. Also trade and mercantile guilds developed. These were known as *za,* a term meaning seat or perhaps place in the market. There swordmakers or metal smiths or tradesmen of any sort, even professional painters, writers, or actors, would gather together to market their wares. Their common interests led to the development of formal associations, and these began to form connections with similar groups in distant towns or market areas. Sometimes merchants who merely marketed goods which they did not produce themselves formed associations, also called za. Many of the street names in the towns of medieval Japan were named for the za which were most active on them.

Technological competence also increased, especially in the field of mining. Experimentation with shaft, as distinct from surface, mining began in the 1520's and as a result the supply of copper, silver, and gold increased markedly. In addition, later in the century techniques of separating the precious metals from each other and from lead were vastly improved. Probably ideas obtained from the Portuguese, who first landed in Japan in 1542, were very helpful in this. In addition the technique of making hand guns was learned from the Portuguese, as attested by the fact that Japanese muskets of the later sixteenth century were called *tanegashima,* the name of the small island on which the Portuguese first landed. Gunmaking became an important industry, quite aside from its military and political implications.

The Portuguese, once they had established active trading connections with Japan, also brought increased volume and dependability to her mainland trade, particularly with China. The China trade had been so much involved with coastal piracy that the Chinese had tried to curtail rather than encourage it, but with the Portuguese established at Macao in the 1550's, it began to flourish in Portuguese ships. The huge, well-armed Portuguese carracks swept pirates aside and became the carriers in a connected trade extending through all southern Asia and back to Europe. Foreign goods flowed into Japan, including gold from China, which the contending Japanese feudal lords valued highly as the most easily protected and transported type of wealth, suitable for taking on campaigns and buying allies. Silver, in high demand in China and somewhat in surplus in Japan, was exported. Nobunaga outlawed the use of rice as a medium of exchange and proclaimed gold and silver to be legal tender in his area of control in 1569.

The active Portuguese trade also stimulated the growth of port cities in southwestern Japan, like Nagasaki, Hirado, and Sakai. They became so commercially active and politically assertive that they seemed for a time like nascent Italian city-states, capable of defying feudal overlords. This rise of free cities, however, was cut short by the triumph of the Nobunaga-Hideyoshi faction and the emergence of centralized political authority in Japan.

Nobunaga, Hideyoshi, and National Unification

THE CAREER OF ODA NOBUNAGA. The spread of Portuguese guns, trade, and ideas in Japan coincided with and aided the rise of Nobunaga to power in the environs of Kyoto. Oda Nobunaga (1534–1582), like his chief lieutenant and successor, Toyotomi Hideyoshi (1537–1598) is so famous in Japanese history that he is known by his given rather than his family name. In 1551, he inherited control of his father's estates in Owari province, where the latter had been Deputy Constable. The area in question was located east of Lake Biwa and it was so situated that to move into Kyoto from an east or north-easterly direction an invading army would first have to cross that area. Nobunaga, after fighting off a succession challenge from some of his relatives, made himself master of the whole province and then began to engage in politics at Kyoto, where he ingratiated himself with the Ashikaga shogun, Yoshiteru. While the more powerful lords of the north and east, Uyesugi, Takeda, and others were fighting among themselves, a lesser lord, Imagawa, who controlled the area around present day Shizuoka, tried to force his way through Nobunaga's territory to Kyoto in 1560. Nobunaga, with a force much inferior in numbers, surprised, defeated, and killed him, and then took into his service one of Imagawa's subordinates, Tokugawa Ieyasu, who later became a most important figure. However, for the time being Tokugawa was assigned to guard Nobunaga's rear in eastern Japan.

Nobunaga spent the next several years gaining control of the province of Mino, adjacent to Owari, and in establishing himself in the castle town of Gifu. Meanwhile Ashikaga Yoshiteru, the shogun, was murdered in Kyoto and his younger brother, Yoshiaki, sought Nobunaga's aid in securing his place as successor. Nobunaga entered Kyoto in the fall of 1568, saw to the installation of Yoshiaki, and undertook to restore the dignity of both the shogun and the emperor by building new palaces for them. However, he made it clear with a series of edicts issued in 1569 that they would not concern themselves with politics or military affairs, which he himself would handle. In 1573 he ousted Yoshiaki, without nominating another shogun, thus ending the Ashikaga era.

Meanwhile the principal challenge to Nobunaga's control of the capital came not from distant feudal lords, who, although powerful, were occupied with problems and rivalries in their own areas, but from militant Buddhist monasteries which regarded themselves as guardians of the capital. These included Enryakuji, the Tendai stronghold on Mount Hiei to the north, which had "guarded" Kyoto since the days of Emperor Kammu, and the more recently risen Honganji (Shin sect), whose principal stronghold was at Osaka

to the south. Nobunaga smashed Enryakuji in 1571, destroying some 3000
buildings and slaughtering thousands of monks. The Shin sect, forewarned,
was not so easily crushed. Calling in adherents from all parts of the country,
it offered tenacious resistance to Nobunaga and even inflicted temporary defeats on him. It was 1580 before he finally took their great Osaka fortress
monastery. Meanwhile he undermined Buddhism in every possible way, which
included befriending Jesuits who first contacted him in Kyoto in 1569. He
encouraged their proselytizing and had many intimate conversations with them
in which they mutually denounced the hypocrisy of the Buddhist warrior-
monks. He allowed them to establish a school at Azuchi, the great castle town
he constructed on Lake Biwa between 1576–1579 as his permanent headquarters, and took the Jesuit General in Japan, Valignano, on a tour of his
inner fortress in 1581.

One of Nobunaga's important lieutenants, Takayama Dario, who was
the first important figure in the Kyoto area to adopt Christianity and who had
arranged the introduction of the Jesuits to Nobunaga, led some 8000 of his
followers to Christianity and began a sort of vogue for the new faith among
highly placed men and women in Nobunaga's faction. These included Nobunaga's son, Nobutada, who though not a Christian became a great friend of the
Jesuits. Takayama's Christian son Ukon, also called Justo, continued to promote Christianity after Nobunaga's death in 1582, and he and another Christian became members of Hideyoshi's inner circle.

It should not be implied that Christianity offered a serious challenge to
Buddhism as a popular faith in the provinces around Kyoto. That was hardly
the case even in the main centers of Jesuit activity in Kyushu, where there
were ten times a many as the Kyoto area's 15,000 converts. However, the
favor shown to the Christians by important Japanese helped to emphasize the
point which Nobunaga and subsequently Hideyoshi were determined to emphasize, namely that the era of feudal politicking and warfare was over for
the Buddhist monasteries, as surely as it was drawing to a close for the great
feudal houses beyond the capital precincts.

If Christianity was useful to Nobunaga, so were the new style *tanegashima*
guns which the Japanese copied from Portuguese models. Nobunaga was quick
to see the possibilities of their use by organized armies of well-drilled, armed
foot soldiers. He closely controlled their manufacture and distribution, seeing
that the gun makers in his territories were well supplied with the needs of
their trade, including temple bells, for metal.

Nobunaga's military tactics were ruthless in the extreme. Once he had
broken an enemy's power he was wont to pursue the most ferocious mopping-
up operations, including the burning of captives and the slaughter of their
noncombatant associates. Even the Jesuits, who basked in his favors, were dis-
gusted at his cruelty.

At his death Nobunaga controlled only 32 of the 68 provinces of Japan,
but these comprised the heartland around Kyoto, and his power was growing

in more distant areas. His greatest rivals in the east and north, Takeda and Uyesugi, after being held at bay by Tokugawa Ieyasu through the crucial years of his consolidation of power at Kyoto, had both died suddenly as they were mounting campaigns against him, Takeda in 1573 and Uyesugi in 1577. It remained only a matter of time before their lands could be taken over. Also Hideyoshi, his most skillful general, was rapidly bringing the great Mori (successor to Ouchi) in far western Honshu to his knees. Perhaps it was because the auguries were so good that Nobunaga became a bit careless one day in June, 1582 in Kyoto. He had received word from Hideyoshi that if he could come with more men he might accomplish the final subjugation of Mori, most of whose forces were trapped. Accordingly Nobunaga ordered his various troop commanders in the Kyoto area to head west with their troops, while he waited in Kyoto with only a handful of men to put matters in order before joining them. Tokugawa Ieyasu, having just completed a victorious campaign in the east, was vacationing at Sakai.

On June 21 Akechi Mitsuhide, one of his commanders who, unknown to Nobunaga, had been plotting a coup, wheeled back into Kyoto with a large force of men from his own feudatory, which was adjacent to the capital, attacked Nobunaga, and killed him. Akechi's triumph was short-lived, however, for Hideyoshi, upon hearing the news, quickly concluded a truce with Mori, returned to the capital and within two weeks struck down Akechi.

RISE OF HIDEYOSHI. Toyotomi Hideyoshi seems to have been born a peasant, but for a man of his ingenuity and daring the transition to samurai status would not have been difficult in the confused conditions of mid-sixteenth-century Japan. He is said to have deliberately sought service with Nobunaga after a careful analysis had brought him to the conclusion that Nobunaga was the man of the future. In 1560 he apparently contributed much to Nobunaga's victory over Imagawa, and after that he became Nobunaga's chief strategist.

After his victory over Akechi, Hideyoshi moved rapidly to consolidate his position as Nobunaga's successor. His most dangerous potential opponent in southern Honshu was Tokugawa Ieyasu, who after the events of 1582 retired to his castle. But Ieyasu accepted service under Hideyoshi in 1585 after prolonged negotiations, in which family hostages were exchanged. Then after helping Hideyoshi reduce in 1590 the castle of Odawara, the last great outpost in eastern Japan, he accepted several provinces in far eastern Japan, with Edo (later Tokyo) as his castle town, in exchange for the former Imagawa fief (Shizuoka area) he had held. This gave Ieyasu a chance to develop into a "great name" (daimyo), a term which had been gradually applied to those feudal lords to whom numerous lesser lords owed allegiance and who themselves were responsible only to the central authority. However, Ieyasu's remote location rendered his potential threat to Hideyoshi slight. During the late 1580's and early 1590's the lords of Kyushu, Shikoku and northern Honshu submitted to Hideyoshi, making his de facto supremacy complete. He ruled as *kampaku,* civil dictator, an old Fujiwara title which he received from the emperor in 1585.

Hideyoshi did not wait to complete his conquests to begin organizing the most far reaching and efficient administration Japan had known since the early days of Kamakura. He made it clear to the feudal lords who submitted to him that his rule was not merely nominal by ordering them immediately to begin surveys of their lands and registers of their population, which were to be the basis for taxes and administration, and he decreed the severest penalties for falsification or evasion. Also in 1588 he instituted his famous Sword Hunt, which was designed to disarm all non-samurai and to fix the class distinctions between them and their samurai rulers (hence no more peasants like himself could organize armies).

In 1587 Hideyoshi inaugurated the official minting of gold, silver, and copper coins by his central government, an act which Nobunaga had anticipated with his legal tender law of 1569 but which he had not been able to put into practice. Having a uniform coinage both stimulated commerce and made easier political-financial relationships among the feudal lords. Regarding the latter, it should be said that Hideyoshi used gold coins very effectively to reward faithfulness among his subordinates and to operate a political structure which was built more on personal relationships than on impersonal institutional arrangements. Unlike Nobunaga, Hideyoshi was always ready to salve a defeated rival's

FIGURE 27.5.   The castle at Himeji, the best surviving example of the feudal strongholds of Japan, dating from the period of Nobunaga and Hideyoshi.

wounds with a generous financial settlement, and so make it unprofitable, as well as physically dangerous, for a follower to fall out of favor. This genius for personal finance helps to explain Hideyoshi's secure hold on the country during his lifetime, but his general failure to institutionalize his governmental structure militated against its being transferred intact to his heirs.

Hideyoshi ruled from Osaka, where in 1590 he completed construction of the greatest castle Japan had ever seen. As far as Kyoto and the emperor were concerned, he treated them with generosity, often giving lavish entertainments for the emperor and his court noblemen. However, he allowed them no political role. He was "serving the emperor" by ruling Japan and scorned the title of shogun, which had become much abased in the later Ashikaga period. In 1592 he gave his own title, *kampaku,* but not his power, to his nephew Hidetsugu, whom he thought for a time of grooming to succeed him. But in 1595, after the birth of a son, Hideyori, to his favorite consort, he killed Hidetsugu, his children and wives, lest perhaps the latter be pregnant. By this time a sort of madness seems to have been coming over the formerly shrewd and calculating dictator. The last great project of his life, his brutal Korean war, may be further evidence that madness, or overweening ambition, gained the better of his senses.

INVASIONS OF KOREA.   It has been argued by some writers that Hideyoshi's first purpose in invading Korea was to keep his army occupied and to draw attention from the unrest in Japan that his interference in the affairs of various formerly independent feudal domains had occasioned. This is probably a partial explanation, although there was an element of megalomania present also. Hideyoshi sent messages to Korea and the Liuch'iu islands in 1588 and 1589 respectively demanding tribute. The replies were evasive, and in 1591 he informed them both that he would expect not only submission, but military assistance from them, for he intended to conquer China. He also sent letters to the Spanish authorities in the Philippines and the Portuguese viceroy at Goa telling of the "miracle" of his birth, when the "sun had entered his mother's bosom" and of his destiny to rule nations.

In 1592 he ordered the invasion of Korea by a huge army of about 150,000 men, probably the most powerful military force Asia had seen since the days of Chingis Khan. The forces of Korea and later Ming China, which answered a Korean appeal for help, were certainly no match for it. However, Hideyoshi, who did not go to Korea, allowed his field commanders to be careless about Japanese supply lines, and the Koreans, in their hour of need, produced a genius at naval warfare. Their admiral, Yi Sun-sin, using ingenious "turtle back" ships and employing ramming tactics, played havoc with Japanese supply vessels. Also the Japanese field commanders, General Konishi Yukinaga (a Christian) and General Kato Kiyomasa (a Buddhist), engaged in some personal rivalry. Nevertheless the Japanese forces advanced up the peninsula, taking Seoul, P'yongyang, and nearly reaching the Yalu river before they were halted. Then they became bogged down, lost ground, and entered into peace negotiations with a Ming envoy.

Hideyoshi gave Konishi authority to negotiate, assuming that the Ming were anxious for peace, and set minimum terms to be recognition of Japanese overlordship of the southern half of Korea, a daughter of the Ming emperor to be sent to Japan as a consort for the Japanese emperor, Korean hostages to be sent to Japan, and Sino-Japanese trade to be resumed on terms favorable to Japan. The negotiations were long and tedious, but in 1596, when the Ming agreed to send their envoy to Japan to make the final settlement, Hideyoshi thought his hour of triumph had come and prepared a grand celebration. He was shortly chagrined and infuriated, however, when the Ming documents delivered to him were translated. They were in the usual haughty tone which the Chinese court used in communications to dependent states. They proclaimed investiture of Hideyoshi as "King of Japan," ordered him to withdraw all Japanese troops from Korean soil, enjoined him never again to invade Korea, and even refused the trade arrangements he had sought.

It is said that Hideyoshi had already donned some elaborate robes delivered to him by the Ming ambassadors before he knew what the documents said. Upon understanding that the robes were for a tributary king he became so angry that he tore them off on the spot, redeclared war, and ordered the ambassadors out of the country. He was persuaded by his advisors not to insult or injure the ambassadors further, but he shortly ordered a new mobilization and dispatched another expeditionary force to Korea. The Japanese won several more victories there, but no decisive outcome was in sight when, after a brief illness, Hideyoshi died in September, 1598. His generals, who had been anxious to end the war for a long time, quickly arranged a truce in Korea.

Some of Hideyoshi's anger about the Korean war may also have adversely affected Christians in Japan in the last two years of his life. After treating them with easy tolerance for many years, despite a growing rivalry between the Jesuits and their followers and newly arriving Franciscans, Hideyoshi suddenly ordered the arrest, torture, and execution of 26 Christians, including six foreign priests, in January 1597. He seems to have been offended at something associated with Christians—whether Konishi's failures as a negotiator in Korea, or the alleged boastings of a Spanish sea captain, or a general sense of irritation at the growing number of Christian converts—although the reason is not clear. It is curious too that, although the 26 were killed with great brutality, others were not seriously persecuted. Perhaps it was a momentary flash of the dictator's anger.

Hideyoshi intended that his infant son, Hideyori, should succeed him. He had the boy officially named kampaku in 1595, following Hidetsugu's death, when he was only a year old. And in the last days before his own death Hideyoshi tried to arrange a regency to protect the boy's position. He appointed a board of five to govern the empire and insure Hideyori's subsequent succession. These were Tokugawa Ieyasu, Maeda Toshiie of Kaga, and three other great feudatories, Mori, Uyesugi, heir to Nobunaga's powerful rival, and one Ukida.

Tokugawa was to supervise the general administration of the empire, not from Osaka castle, but from Fushimi, a much less impregnable palace near Kyoto, which Hideyoshi had used for more pleasurable quarters. Maeda was to be the special guardian of the young Hideyori, controlling the ramparts of Osaka castle, where the boy was to live. Unfortunately for this arrangement, Maeda died in May, 1599, and his death left the position of Hideyori very insecure indeed.

TOKUGAWA IEYASU AND THE BATTLE OF SEKIGAHARA. Tokugawa Ieyasu soon gave evidence that he intended to take over the control of Osaka castle, and the strength of his position, based on vast holdings in eastern Japan, was such that only a coalition of the others could hope to stop him. One Ishida Mitsunari, a former favorite of Hideyoshi whose position in the hierarchy, however, was of the second order, below that of the regents, took the lead in arranging an anti-Tokugawa coalition. Uyesugi was to make the first move from his northeastern stronghold, which would presumably draw Ieyasu from the Osaka area to defend his home possessions around Edo. This was partially successful, for Ieyasu moved to meet the threat. However, he did not commit his full forces against Uyesugi, but merely neutralized him, and then turned his forces back westward to meet the main onslaught of the allies, coming up on his rear from the west.

The decisive battle was fought on the plain at Sekigahara, east of Lake Biwa, in Nobunaga's old home domain, which was now controlled by Ishida. There on October 20, 1600, some 70,000 men under Ieyasu decisively defeated about 80,000 soldiers under the allied commanders. Not all of these forces were actively engaged, and a number of minor skirmishes fought in fog and rain before the main engagement helped to predetermine the outcome. After Konishi Yukinaga's troops were defeated, Ishida panicked and fled, and the other allies extricated their troops as best they could. The whole coalition collapsed; Ishida and Konishi were captured and executed, and Mori, who had been left in command of Osaka castle, surrendered it to Ieyasu. By the end of 1600 Tokugawa Ieyasu was in a position to reorganize the whole empire.

MOMOYAMA ART. This chapter may properly close with mention of new styles in art which developed in the latter part of the sixteenth century, with the rise of Nobunaga and Hideyoshi. The egotism of these powerful conquerors was much too great to be satisfied with the restrained Zen-inspired art of the earlier Ashikaga period. Their tastes, on the contrary, were lavish in the extreme, and more than a little vulgar. In the great castles and palaces which they erected, beginning with Nobunaga's Azuchi castle, completed in 1579, gold was not only stored in the vaults, but it was used extensively in decoration. Profusely illustrated screens, gold-leafed walls, and flamboyant designs set a new mode in art, which is usually called the Momoyama style. The name is taken from the name of a suburb of Kyoto where Hideyoshi built one of his palaces.

Momoyama art is too ostentatious to convey the subtleness of meaning that the Zen masters captured, but that is not to say that it was not well executed. Some very great artists, utilizing techniques and materials unknown to the earlier schools, produced some remarkable pieces, and the two Kanos, Eitoku and Sanraku, who were the leaders of this school, rank among Japan's best painters. And it is a further measure of the rugged genius of Japan's unifiers that they overturned art as well as political canons.

The Ashikaga was the true feudal period in Japanese history, in the sense that it most clearly matched the European conditions to which the term "feudalism" first applied. As in Europe it was characterized by political decentralization and frequent warfare. In the economic sphere the self-sufficiency of the manors was punctured by a money economy to a greater degree than in Europe and there was no "universal," catholic church authority. However, attitudes, institutions and practices were surprisingly similar.

The rapid unification and centralization that occurred in the latter half of the sixteenth century was likewise similar to the development of nation states in Europe. Late sixteenth-century Japan, with its commercialism and expansionism, was in some ways more like Elizabethan England than like the other Asian states of the period. However, Japan was not to continue on this path. Tokugawa policy was to close the doors of Japan and leave Western countries to direct the new forces of commercialism, expansionism, and colonialism toward the Asian continent and its southern periphery.

BASIC DATES

1333	Emperor Go-Daigo (Daigo II) challenges Kamakura shogunate
1335	Revolt of Ashikaga Takauji
1336–1392	Southern court at Yoshino
1338–1358	Ashikaga Takauji shogun
1368	Yoshimitsu becomes third Ashikaga shogun
1392	Consolidation of northern and southern courts
1395	Yoshimitsu retires, governs as "retired shogun"
1401	Yoshimitsu accepts tributary status to China as "King of Japan"
1408	Death of Yoshimitsu
1449–1490	Ashikaga Yoshimasa shogun
1467–1477	Onin War
1420–1506	Sesshu
C. 1450–1550	Wako (Japanese pirates)
1542	Portuguese reach Japan
1549	Francis Xavier begins Christian activity in Japan
1568	Oda Nobunaga seizes Kyoto
1570–1580	Power of Buddhist monasteries broken
1573	End of Ashikaga shogunate
1582	Death of Nobunaga
1590	Toyotomi Hideyoshi master of Japan
1592–1598	Korean campaigns

1597	First martyrdom of Christians
1598	Death of Hideyoshi
1600	Triumph of Tokugawa Ieyasu at Sekigahara

SUPPLEMENTARY READING

DE BARY, W. T., ED. *Sources of the Japanese Tradition*. New York, 1958.

KEENE, D., ED. *Anthology of Japanese Literature*. New York, 1955.

REISCHAUER, E. O. *Japan Past and Present*. New York, 1953.

REISCHAUER, E. O. AND J. K. FAIRBANK. *East Asia: The Great Tradition*. Boston, 1958.

SANSOM, G. B. *Japan: A Short Cultural History*. New York, 1943.

TERRY, C. *Masterworks of Japanese Art*. Rutland, Vt., 1956.

ADVANCED READING

BOXER, C. R. *The Christian Century in Japan, 1549–1650*. Berkeley, Cal., 1951.

——*Fidalgos in the Far East, 1550–1770*. The Hague, 1948.

BROWN, D. M. "The Impact of Firearms on Japanese Feudal Warfare, 1543–1598," *Far Eastern Quarterly*, VII, No. 3 (May, 1948), pp. 236-253.

——"The Importation of Gold into Japan by the Portuguese During the Sixteenth Century," *Pacific Historical Review*, XVI, No. 2 (May, 1947), pp. 125-133.

——*Money Economy in Medieval Japan*. New Haven, 1951. Close view of economic trends, especially coins and coinage.

MURDOCH, J. *A History of Japan*. London, 1925. Vols. I and II.

ELIOT, C. N. E. *Japanese Buddhism*, 2nd ed. New York, 1959.

SANSOM, G. B. *A History of Japan, 1334–1615*. Stanford, Cal., 1961. Detailed analysis of political, social, and economic trends.

——*The Western World and Japan*. New York, 1950. Material dealing with the expansion of Portugal and other European powers in East Asia. Chapter 6 covers Christianity in Japan.

WANG YI-T'UNG. *Official Relations Between China and Japan, 1368–1549*. Cambridge, Mass., 1953.

INDEX

563